# THE SELECTED WRITINGS OF EQBAL AHMAD

# THE SELECTED WRITINGS OF
# EQBAL AHMAD

Foreword by Noam Chomsky

Edited by Carollee Bengelsdorf, Margaret Cerullo, and Yogesh Chandrani

COLUMBIA UNIVERSITY PRESS    New York

Columbia University Press
Publishers Since 1893
New York, Chichester, West Sussex
Copyright © 2006 Columbia University Press
All rights Reserved

Library of Congress Cataloging-in-Publication Data

Ahmad, Eqbal.
[Selections. 2006]
The selected writings of Eqbal Ahmad / edited by Carollee Bengelsdorf, Margaret Cerullo, and
Yogesh Chandrani ; foreword by Noam Chomsky.
p. cm.
Includes bibliographical references and index.
ISBN 0-231-12710-3 (cloth : alk. paper) — ISBN 0-231-12711-1 (pbk. : alk. paper)
1. World politics—20th century. 2. Eastern question. I. Bengelsdorf, Carollee. II. Cerullo,
Margaret. III. Chandrani, Yogesh. IV. Title.
D443.A28 2006
909.82—dc22
2005033839

Columbia University Press books are printed on permanent and durable acid-free paper
Printed in the United States of America

c 10 9 8 7 6 5 4 3 2

*for future generations, and in memory of Edward Said*

# CONTENTS

PAKISTAN: THE RETURN OF THE GENERALS

# FOREWORD

Noam Chomsky

It is a fascinating experience to view major events of the past half century through Eqbal Ahmad's discerning eye. His rendition of these events, and the tendencies in world affairs in which they find their proper place, benefits not only from his keen analytic faculties, broad knowledge, and many years of direct engagement but also from his ability, rarely even approached, to observe these developments from a perspective that integrates his deep immersion in the culture, history, and life experience of both North and South.

The conventional North-South metaphor brings to the fore what Ahmad regarded—rightly, I think—as the most fundamental divide of the post–World War II era, reflecting centuries of brutal conquest and oppression and later transmuted into new forms. From this perspective, enriched with the reservoirs of knowledge and insight from which he could draw, Ahmad was able to identify currents of modern history that few perceived. To mention only one distressingly timely illustration, he recognized at once that Washington and its allies were creating a terrorist monster when they exploited Afghan resistance to Soviet invasion by organizing and training Islamic fundamentalist extremists for their own cynical purposes. He warned that these initiatives were reviving a form of violent jihadism that had disappeared from the Muslim world centuries earlier and were also helping to implant similar forces in Pakistan under the brutal Zia ul-Haq dictatorship, with a devastating impact on Pakistani society, Afghanistan, and beyond.

Years later, still well ahead of his time, Ahmad recognized that "the United States has sowed in the Middle East and in South Asia very poisonous seeds," as Clinton bombed Afghanistan and Sudan in 1998. "These seeds are growing now," he observed. "Some have ripened, and others are ripening. An examination of why they were sown, what has grown, and how they should be reaped is needed. Missiles won't solve the problem." As is now widely and belatedly understood, missiles not only did not solve the problem but actually greatly intensified it. Clinton's bombing put al-Qaeda on the map, virtually created bin Laden as a charismatic leader and symbol of the new jihadism, forged close relations between him and the Taliban, and led to a sharp increase in recruitment, financing, and general sympathy and support for networks of the al-Qaeda variety. As is the norm, the conscious destruction of the major source of pharmaceutical supplies in the Sudan, leading to several tens of thousands of deaths (according to the few estimates from credible sources), scarcely raises an eyebrow among privileged circles in the West, let alone a twitter of protest. But the traditional victims tend to see the world rather differently. "Every use of force is another small victory for bin Laden," Jason Burke writes in the most penetrating analysis of the "networks of networks" loosely termed al-Qaeda, reviewing Clinton's contribution to their growth as well as later ones and reiterating Ahmad's insistence that those who are seriously concerned with these forms of terror and their consequences must seek to understand and address the "myriad grievances," many quite legitimate, that are "the root causes of modern Islamic militancy" (Burke, *Al-Qaeda*). The preferred approach, denial and violence, is a welcome gift to the jihadis, fertilizing these "very poisonous seeds."

One consequence that Ahmad did not live to see, though it would probably not have surprised him, is the global struggle between two fundamentalist extremists, both assuring us that they have a direct line to the Lord of Hosts, the War God, who instructs them to drive evil from the world in the manner of ancient epics and children's fairy tales, with loyal followers and awesome forces of destruction at their command and the world at their mercy.

From the same perspective, deeply rooted in both North and South, Ahmad was able to depart sharply from mainstream commentary, once again, and to predict with considerable accuracy the long-term continuities of policy that persisted after the Cold War came to an end. As he recognized immediately, the collapse of the Soviet Union was not likely to have a far-reaching impact on guiding policy choices of the world-dominant power, though tactical and rhetorical changes would take place in the light of new conditions: the return of the former Soviet Union to something like its traditional place in the world system, reduction of the space for limited independence for the South, and virtual elimination of the deterrent to the resort to force by the superpower that, after World War II, "assumed, out of self-interest, responsibility for the welfare of the world capitalist system," in the words of the senior historian of the CIA, diplomatic historian Gerald Haines.

Pursuing the matter in a way that I think is consistent with Ahmad's worldview, we can usefully interpret the Cold War itself as in large measure a North-South conflict, which took on a quality of its own because of enormous differences of scale. Eastern Europe was the original "Third World," diverging from the West even before the Columbian era, the West beginning to develop, the East becoming its service area. By the early twentieth century, much of the region was a quasi-colonial dependency of the West. The Bolshevik takeover in 1917 elicited much the same reactions as Third World liberation movements in later years. The new rulers of Russia sought to pursue a course of independent development that would extricate the society from the world capitalist system of which Britain and France were then the primary guardians. Furthermore, the Bolsheviks were perceived at once to be a "virus" that might "infect others" by providing a model they might seek to follow, to borrow the terminology of US planners once they had taken over "responsibility for the welfare of the world capitalist system." Worse still, the virus was infecting even Britain and France, David Lloyd George and Woodrow Wilson lamented.

In the eyes of Western commentators, the 1918 Western invasion of the Soviet Union was therefore justified in defense against "the Revolution's challenge . . . to the very survival of the capitalist order," as the prominent Cold War historian John Lewis Gaddis describes the origins of the Cold War confrontation. The challenge is similar to what Adlai Stevenson later called "internal aggression" in the case of Vietnam, where internal events also threatened to open the way to a form of independent development that is an intolerable challenge in itself, even more so if it threatens to be a "virus" (the real content of the domino theory and the reason it has persisted from the 1940s, when it was first clearly formulated, even after the regular collapse of the versions fed to the public for disciplinary purposes). The challenge in 1918 consisted of internal reforms that others might seek to follow, justifying violence in self-defense, a refrain throughout the Cold War years, as Ahmad vividly records.

Other influential and highly regarded Western analysts also trace the origins of the Cold War to the Bolshevik takeover, invoking different grounds.

The leading post–World War II planner, George Kennan, was also a distinguished historian of Soviet-American relations. In his scholarly study of the topic, he writes that the Bolsheviks established the Cold War divide with "an element of finality" in January 1918. Hence the Western invasion immediately after was justified in reaction, along with everything that followed, including the paramilitary operations inside the USSR organized and directed by Kennan's office in the State Department into the early 1950s. Kennan adopts the familiar stance for justifying the resort to force and violence—in fact, close to a historical universal—that Ahmad reviews for the post–World War II phase of the Cold War. Motives are always humanitarian, though sometimes benign intentions go astray because of innocence and naïveté or perhaps because of the evil nature of the target of benevolence. In Kennan's view, what initiated the Cold War with an "element of finality" in January 1918 was Lenin's dissolution of the Constituent Assembly, which "deeply shocked" Britain and particularly the idealistic Woodrow Wilson, who shared the "strong attachment to constitutionality" of the American public and was therefore unwilling to tolerate a government that had dismantled parliament and thus had no mandate beyond "the bayonets of the Red Guard."

It will surprise no one who has learned the lessons that Eqbal Ahmad patiently taught for many years that the reaction was slightly different a few months later, when Wilson's invading army dissolved Haiti's National Assembly "by genuinely Marine Corps methods," in the words of the Marine officer in command, Smedley Butler, who later offended right-thinking souls by exposing unacceptable truths about humanitarian intervention, which in this case killed thousands of peasants, reinstituted virtual slavery, and after nineteen years of Marine occupation left the country in the grips of a brutal national guard and corrupt and vicious indigenous elites from which it has yet to escape and whose rule US intervention regularly fortifies. The Haitian parliament had lost any legitimacy when it refused Wilson's orders to ratify a constitution that gave US investors the right to buy up Haiti's land and turn the country into a virtual US plantation. Once a government was installed with no mandate beyond the "bayonets of the Marines," the US-designed constitution was ratified by a 99.9 percent majority (with 5 percent of the population participating). There was thus nothing to offend the "strong attachment to constitutionality" of Wilson, Kennan, and others, no need to invade the United States to punish the crime, and certainly no need to contain the great power in charge, either then or after it had taken over global responsibility for the welfare of the world capitalist system and acted in just the manner one would expect as it fulfilled that task.

It made good sense, then, to anticipate the continuities of policy that Ahmad predicted, accurately, as Russia returned to its proper place, poised precariously on the North–South divide.

Ahmad's life was not confined to study and the academy; far from it. He was directly engaged in popular struggle in both South and North, in both arenas facing considerable risk with equanimity and fortitude. The lesson he drew, and taught, for revolutionary struggle was clear and explicit: it is necessary to "outadminister the enemy" before fighting it. Revolutionary wars must be primarily political. In two prototypical examples, Algeria and Vietnam, the revolutionaries won "the war of ideas," outadministered the foreign invader, and in this way were able to counter its overwhelming military power. The same has been true in other North–South confrontations that were successful in that military power was overcome and a form of independence gained. But, as Ahmad described with painful and searing honesty, the victories commonly became defeats for the population, as corrupt and brutal elements gained power.

The process is very natural, in some ways almost inevitable, given the nature of North–South conflict. And though there are often internal factors that contribute to these consequences, the dynamics have deep roots in the very nature of this confrontation. The Indochina wars, the most murderous and long-lasting of the post–World War II era, illustrate a pattern that is quite general and the reasons for it. In their own terms, the aggressors, at least those more free from dogma and fanaticism, understand the truths that Ahmad discussed. In Vietnam, it was clearly recognized by both Vietnamese and Americans that the Vietnamese nationalist movement was relying on its dominant political power to resist US military power. The leading US government scholar of Vietnamese Communism, Douglas Pike, lamented that the National Liberation Front (Viet Cong) was the only "truly mass-based political party in South Vietnam," and the US client regimes could not consider entering into a coalition with it, "fearing that if they did the whale would swallow the minnow"; the enemy "maintained that its contest with the GVN and the United States should be fought out at the political level and that the use of massed military might was in itself illegitimate," until US massed military might forced it "to use counterforce to survive." This recognition was common among counterinsurgency specialists and scholars, though the propaganda version for the public was different. The invading forces drew the logical conclusion: the society in which the resistance was based had to be demolished by military might. And it was. By 1967 prominent Vietnam specialist and military analyst Bernard Fall warned that "Viet-Nam as a cultural and historic entity" is "threatened with extinction," while in the South, "the countryside literally dies under the blows of the largest military machine ever unleashed on an area of this size." That was long before the mass murder operations of the post-Tet pacification campaigns.

In their own fashion, the ideological institutions perceive their own vicious savagery, though cloaking it in the standard virtuous garb. The editors of the *Washington Post* mused in 1992 over the "abiding irony that the United States lost the war in a military sense but ended up imposing a victor's terms for normalization." It was able to do so, they explained, "because it remained a country representing dominant global values, powerfully influencing the regional balance and the international economy. This is how all the concessions came to be made by Vietnam." The editors could not have been unaware that the "global values" included brutal economic warfare from the first moment, backing for a Chinese invasion to punish Vietnam for driving the Khmer Rouge from Cambodia just as their atrocities were peaking, and then direct support for the Khmer Rouge and enhanced economic warfare while Washington exploited its control over the international economy to intimidate anyone, including allies, who might venture to break the stranglehold. When they began to do so anyway, and US business interests began to fear that they might lose out on potential profits, the "global values" allowed Washington to release its murderous grip enough for them to gain a piece of the action, but not without onerous conditions to ensure that the crime of victory by political means would not go unpunished and that others who might be tempted to take their fate into their own hands would be duly warned. No novelties here, and a closer look reveals further depths of cowardice and dishonor.

When political power confronts military might, it will almost inevitably be seriously damaged or destroyed in one or another way. Vietnam's invasion of Cambodia, terminating Khmer Rouge terror, offered a convenient pretext, but there are always others. If military power is finally withdrawn from a ruined country, it is highly likely that only the more harsh, brutal, and corrupt will survive and take charge, constructive achievements and the popular forces behind them having been scattered or demolished. These predictable consequences of massive terror can be exploited by the aggressors as a pretext for terror and economic warfare to punish those who have dared to liberate themselves and by elements of the educated classes to offer a retrospective justification for the atrocities and crimes they supported: just look at how awful the consequences were after we withdrew. The dual pattern of vengeful punishment and cynical retrospective justification is illustrated dramatically in the case of Vietnam and many others. And since history is written by the privileged and powerful, that is the picture that commonly prevails.

In short, there is a close relation between political-versus-military war and the profound disappointment that regularly follows. Whatever weight one gives to these factors, they can only be regarded as another shameful chapter in the chronicles of crimes of state and treachery of intellectuals.

Among Ahmad's most remarkable qualities were his resources of empathy and understanding, even in the face of horrifying atrocities. After Bengali nationalists killed or wounded thousands of his fellow Biharis in the 1971 uprising that led finally to the independence of Bangladesh—a revolt for which he had little sympathy—Ahmad courageously criticized the vicious reaction of the Pakistani army and responded to official condemnation with an eloquent open letter to a Pakistani diplomat, reprinted in this book, explaining the stand he took with the simple integrity characteristic of his life. Few analysts exposed more vividly the criminal atrocities of the US wars of aggression in Indochina, but Ahmad nonetheless qualified his critique. He preferred the term "maternalism" for American policy, he explained, with a grim analogy to a kind mother elephant who benignly crushes infant birds she has orphaned by crushing their mother. Such honesty and generosity are also rare qualities, and they suffuse his work, lending it a special layer of significance.

Ahmad was an inspiring figure, in his work and his life. There could hardly be a better model to try to follow, as best we can.

July 2004

# EQBAL AHMAD

(CA. 1933-1999)

Eqbal Ahmad was born in the village of Irki in Bihar, India, in 1933 or 1934. During the partition of India in 1947, he and his elder brothers migrated to Pakistan. Ahmad lost contact with his family in New Delhi and trekked north to Lahore carrying a gun. John Berger's short story "Two Recumbent Male Figures Wrestling on a Sidewalk," from *Photocopies-Encounters* (Vintage, 1996), treats of that trek.

Ahmad's first degree, in 1951, from Foreman Christian College in Lahore, Pakistan, was in economics. He received an M.A. in modern history in 1953 from Punjab University in Lahore, went on to study American history at Occidental College in California as a Rotary fellow in 1957 and political science and Middle East history at Princeton. From 1960 to 1964, Ahmad lived in North Africa, mainly in Tunisia, where he conducted his thesis research on trade unions and became a close student and active supporter of the Algerian Revolution. In 1967, he earned his Ph.D. from Princeton.

Upon his return to the United States from North Africa, Ahmad taught at the University of Illinois at Carbondale (1964–1965) and in the School of Labor Relations at Cornell University (1965–1968). During these years, he became one of the earliest and most eloquent analysts and opponents of the US war in Vietnam. Following the 1967 Arab-Israeli war, he became a public advocate of Palestinian rights, a position that cost him isolation within the academy. From 1968 to 1972, he was a fellow at the Adlai Stevenson Institute in Chicago. In 1969, he married teacher and writer Julie Diamond. Their daughter, Dohra, was born in 1971.

In November 1970, J. Edgar Hoover, director of the FBI, informed Congress of an incipient plot on the part of an "anarchist group, the so-called East Coast Conspiracy to Save Lives," a "militant group of Catholic priests and nuns, teachers, students, and former students" aimed at ending the bombing in Southeast Asia and securing the release of all political prisoners as ransom. Just two months later, in January 1971, Ahmad was indicted with the antiwar Catholic priest Philip Berrigan and six other Catholic pacifists on federal charges of conspiracy to kidnap Henry Kissinger and to blow up the heating systems of several federal buildings in Washington, D.C. (Daniel Berrigan was an "unindicted coconspirator" in the case). The group became known as the Harrisburg 8; two thousand people protested at the Justice Department in Washington, D.C., the day the indictments were handed down in a demonstration organized by the Harrisburg Defense Committee together with other defense groups representing victims of political repression. The case with its spectacular charges received considerable attention in the year between the arrests and the trial. After fifty-nine hours of deliberations, the jury declared a mistrial in April 1972.

From 1972 to 1982, Ahmad was senior fellow at the Institute for Policy Studies in Washington, D.C. From 1973 to 1975, he served as the first director of its overseas affiliate, the Transnational Institute in Amsterdam. Between 1975 and 1982, he held visiting professorships at Rutgers in Newark, Sarah Lawrence, and the Institute of Third World Studies in the Hague.

In 1982, Ahmad joined the faculty at Hampshire College in Amherst, Massachusetts, where he was professor of politics and Middle East studies for fifteen years, until his retirement in 1997. In 1990, he began dividing his time between Islamabad and Amherst, a pattern that continued until his death. During this period, he began to write weekly columns for *Dawn*, Pakistan's oldest English-language newspaper. His columns also regularly appeared in *Al-Ahram* in Egypt.

In the early 1990s, Prime Minister Nawaz Sharif's government granted Ahmad a parcel of land in Pakistan on which to build an independent, secular, alternative university, Khaldunia, named for the fourteenth-century Arab historian and sociologist Ibn Khaldun. Khaldunia remained Ahmad's living dream and the focus of his considerable energies for the rest of his life.

A prolific writer and activist, Ahmad was widely consulted by revolutionaries, journalists, policy makers, activists, and students around the world. He was an editor of the journal *Race and Class*, contributing editor of *Middle*

*East Report* and *L'Economiste du Tiers Monde*, cofounder of *Pakistan Forum*, founding member and editor (1968–1983) of *Afrique-Asie*, and an editorial board member of *Arab Studies Quarterly*.

Eqbal Ahmad died in Islamabad on May 11, 1999, of heart failure, following surgery for colon cancer diagnosed just one week before. His last column for *Dawn*, on the war in Kosovo, was dated in April 25, 1999.

## ACKNOWLEDGMENTS

We received generous support, friendship, and encouragement from many individuals and foundations in preparing this manuscript. In particular, we acknowledge the support of Cora and Peter Weiss, the Samuel Rubin Foundation (New York), and Hampshire College summer faculty research grants
supported by the Joukowsky Family Foundation, the National Endowment
for the Humanities, and the Hewlett and Mellon foundations. The late Edward Said inspired the project when he encouraged Ahmad to gather his writings for future generations. He saw this project through from its inception
until his death. Julie Diamond, executor of the Eqbal Ahmad estate, accompanied us throughout the process and provided continual encouragement.
She, along with Stuart Schaar and Dohra Ahmad, clarified biographical details. Nubar Hovsepian contributed the introduction to part 4 (on the Middle East). Radha Kumar was central to the organizational conception of the
book, as well as coauthoring the introduction to part 5 (on South Asia). Noam
Chomsky generously found time in his unrelenting schedule of writing and
speaking to write the foreword to the volume. Many other friends helped us
select from the large and wide-ranging body of Ahmad's writings or responded to our introductory essays. Our gratitude is enormous to Jenine
Aboushi, David Barsamian, Michael Burawoy, Dan Clawson, Ahmad Dalal,
Marla Erlien, Tess Ewing, Nadia Guessous, the late Carmen Gonzalez, Frank
Holmquist, Ali Mirsepassi, Syed Nauman Naqvi, Fred Weaver, and Gloria
Weinberg. We were blessed with research assistants who themselves became
committed to the project: Karen Graubart, Christine Ingraham, Shannon

McKay Cook, Jay Rosenberg, and Tim Clifford. Susan Dayall, who so ably organized the Eqbal Ahmad Archives at the Hampshire College library, and Dan Schnurr, social science research librarian, provided assistance at every step of the process of assembling the materials for this book. Peter Dimock and Anne Routon of Columbia University Press have been unwavering in their support. In the final preparation of the manuscript, we had the great good fortune to have the extraordinary Sarah St. Onge as our copy editor and immensely diligent Leslie Bialler as our production editor.

THE SELECTED WRITINGS OF **EQBAL AHMAD**

# PART I
# REVOLUTIONARY WARFARE
# AND COUNTERINSURGENCY

# INTRODUCTION

Carollee Bengelsdorf and Margaret Cerullo

Eqbal Ahmad's articles in this section span three decades, multiple anticolonial struggles and revolutionary uprisings in the Third World, and Western imperial powers' aggressive and violent reactions to them. As will become clear later in this volume,[1] he argues that the post–World War II world cannot be understood in terms of the dominant Western paradigm: a confrontation between the forces of freedom and democracy, represented by the United States, and the forces of totalitarianism, represented by the Soviet Union. According to this paradigm, military conflict was avoided through the accumulation of nuclear weapons and the threat of mutual assured destruction (MAD). One fallacy of this framework at least should be obvious: for the majority of the peoples of the Third World—that is, for the majority of the world's people—this was hardly a period of "cold" war. In later articles, Ahmad makes the implications of this argument for today's world explicit: the epoch did not end with the conclusion of the Cold War. Cold War counterinsurgency was replaced by "limited" or "low-intensity" wars, first practiced as the strategy of Vietnamization and limited only in their consequences for the intervening power. In the essays in this section, he displaces the Cold War framework by positing national liberation struggles, revolutionary warfare, and counterinsurgency as the defining features of post–World War II world politics and sets about exploring their roots and dynamics.

Ahmad's analysis and critique are drawn from his intimate association with the wide range of revolutionary movements and situations about which he writes—Algeria, Vietnam, Iran, the PLO—as well as from his encyclopedic reading of the literatures of revolution and counterrevolution. Somewhat ironically, however, since he never published a fully fleshed-out study of it, it was the eight-year Algerian Revolution, which began in 1954, the year of France's defeat in Indochina, that provided the source of the principles and the arguments to which he would return, again and again in analyzing revolution and its aftermath and the strategies and logic of counterrevolution. It is no coincidence that every article in this section refers to Algeria. As a young man, Ahmad was an eyewitness to the Algerian Revolution, an intimate of members of its leadership. It is unclear whether he ever met Franz Fanon during this period, but they knew of each other, and Fanon was an abiding influence on his thought. Ahmad even worked on the reproduction of the Algerian Revolution, that is, he helped to research the script for what remains the classic movie on revolution, Gillo Pontecorvo's 1966 *The Battle of Algiers*. As Ahmad relates in a lecture on the film printed for the first time in this book, it remains a classic at least in part because its narrative and drama communicate the principles of revolutionary strategy so clearly.

The first and most critical of these principles is the primacy of politics in revolutionary warfare. The political task is to drain the enemy of legitimacy and begin to construct parallel counterinstitutions of a different, more humane, and more just society that transfer legitimacy to the revolution and anticipate the transfer of power. It is only then that the military phase of guerrilla war can begin in earnest, reliant wholly on popular support, both because this will help offset dramatic military imbalances and because the goal is to effect a popular transformation of society. (General Maxwell Taylor told President Lyndon Johnson in 1964 that the military rule of thumb in antiguerrilla operations is to outnumber guerrillas by at least ten to one. Ahmad reports that in Algeria the figure was more like twenty-three to one.) Ahmad develops this theme in the first article in this section, his famous, popularly written, and widely distributed "Revolutionary Warfare: How to Tell When the Rebels Have Won." The enemy must, in his classic prescription, be outadministered before he is outfought, morally isolated, drained of legitimacy, "that crucial and ubiquitous factor in politics that invests power with authority" (legitimacy will recur as one of his key analytical and political concepts).[2] While Ahmad is certainly not the first theorist of revolution to emphasize the primacy of politics, his distinctive contribution is to give detail and clarity to the process of the transfer of legitimacy and to illustrate its workings in an enormous range of contexts.

How, then, to tell when the rebels have won? At what point does the moral isolation of the existing regime become irreversible? This is precisely the question on which Ahmad's analyses of the revolutionary movements he addresses in this section will turn. He identifies the gap between counterinsurgency strategists (from Colonel Bigeard and General Massu in Algeria to US Vietnam specialists) and theorists and practitioners of revolutionary warfare: the former understand guerrilla warfare as a technical and military problem; the latter, as a moral and political one. This gap between revolution and counterrevolution, between the "coercive military capabilities of the rulers and the determined resistance of the ruled,"[3] he argues, contains both the possibility of revolutionaries' outadministering the enemy and the logic of counterinsurgency, a logic of military escalation, even genocide. His 1965 framework, stark in its conceptualization, anticipates the subsequent course of the Vietnam War and challenges its still-dominant contemporary interpretation in US culture as a series of blunders and mistakes, with no underlying logic.

Ahmad's command of the process of revolution in both Algeria and Vietnam allows him to critique both revolutionary and counterrevolutionary theorists. In "Radical but Wrong," despite disclaimers concerning his lack of knowledge about Latin America, he provides one of the earliest and still most clear-sighted and damning critiques of Regis Debray's *foco* theory, the theoretical backdrop for Ernesto "Che" Guevara's disastrous final guerrilla operation in Bolivia.[4] According to the *foco* theory, revolution can be detonated when an apparently unassailable power is revealed to be vulnerable through a surprise, carefully targeted attack by an armed mobile guerrilla serving as the single spark it takes to start a prairie fire. Ahmad argues that Debray, in completely denigrating the primacy of the political and inverting the revolutionary process, putting first military action by a small band of guerrillas who are to remain, in the initial stages, aloof and wary of the native population, reduces revolution to a set of tactics born of despair. Missing is the crucial condition for revolution: that the existing government has lost its legitimacy, its moral right, not simply its coercive capacity, to rule. Reducing the population to "spectators who will join the winning side" together with conceiving revolution as a military not a political challenge reveals unexpected affinities between Debray and US theorists (and practitioners) of counterrevolution. The remarkable coincidence of Debray's theory at almost every point with the views of the counterinsurgency experts, Ahmad implies, was exactly why Che was such an easy target for the Bolivian Special Forces, trained by those very

CIA counterinsurgency experts, who tracked him down and executed him in October 1967.

Throughout the 1960s and 1970s, Ahmad proved himself to be perhaps the most trenchant and perceptive critic of the counterinsurgency establishment. Using their own words and deeds, which he knew so well, he took them apart, from their fundamental value commitments, to their bureaucratic and managerial understanding of the world, to the logic of escalation these commitments entailed. His detailed and searing analyses of US policy, of the logic of counterrevolution, made him one of the most effective antiwar spokespersons in this country and in the world.

"Revolutionary Warfare: How to Tell When the Rebels Have Won" was published in August 1965, when Lyndon Johnson had just introduced into Vietnam the first twenty-five thousand of what would escalate to more than five hundred thousand US ground troops. Ahmad is writing to an American audience for whom Vietnam had not yet become a nightly TV spot, at a time when there was not yet a significant antiwar movement. The overwhelming majority of Americans supported the president's foreign policy initiatives, and the Senate had recently given Johnson carte blanche in carrying the war to the North.[5] Ahmad chooses his imagery carefully but cuts straight to the heart of the misconceptions and false assumptions, laying them out with a simplicity and clarity that belies the power of his assertions.

"Counterinsurgency" (1971) and "Epilogue: The Lessons of Vietnam" (1968) show how the logic of counterinsurgency had become apparent in the massive destruction being wrought on the Vietnamese people. It is a logic of escalation in the face of the continual failure of its techniques to produce results (dramatized by the Tet Offensive of January 1968) coupled with the inability of its colonial and bureaucratic mentality to understand that failure. Ahmad is writing for a very different audience from the one at which he aimed "Revolutionary Warfare," at a different moment and with a different objective politically. His argument, however, remains firmly rooted in the principles and strategies he has consistently identified at the core of revolution and counterrevolution. He distinguishes among multiple approaches to counterinsurgency but focuses on the "liberal reformist" variant,[6] because these were the people planning and enacting US policy toward Vietnam during the 1960s. Ahmad demonstrates how, for the US liberal establishment, the defeat of the Vietnamese revolution at any cost (that is, to the Vietnamese people) came to violate (as it had for a similar group in France during the Algerian War) both the principles of international warfare laid down at Nuremberg and the principles of liberalism and democracy. For the people who are their targets, these multiple approaches are combined and indistinguishable, but distinguishing among them is important because the policies actually devised and pursued are the result of a compromise that provides a later alibi for the failure of the entire enterprise and lays the groundwork for the so-called Vietnam experts' subsequent elaboration what they term the lessons of Vietnam.

Ahmad's previous gentler phrasing of faulty assumptions has disappeared, but his points remain the same: Since counterinsurgency theorists, and even the few US "experts" on Vietnam, refused to consider in their models either the political legitimacy of the NLF within Vietnam or the historical sources of that legitimacy, they were led inevitably to focus on the outside: outside conspiracies (Soviet or Chinese Communists) or infiltration from North Vietnam that explained the revolution's origins;[7] outside sources that provided its funding; outside sanctuaries that accounted for its supply. Such thinking justified the bombing of the North (on which more tonnage was dropped than in all of World War II) and, in 1970, the invasion of Cambodia and all that was to follow in that country. Above all, since counterinsurgency experts do not (he suggests, cannot) understand the conditions, the grievances, the suffering, or the commitments that propel revolutionary movements—the primacy of the political in revolutionary warfare—they define their task consistently as tactical: guerrilla warfare could be defeated by copying the guerrillas' model and executing it better than they did. Thus the formation of the Green Berets, the US Army Special Forces' counterguerrilla guerrillas, and even the attempts, using the infamous army acronym of the 1960s, to WHAM—Win the Hearts and Minds of—the Vietnamese people. But first these people had to be pacified and removed from their native villages to live in barbed wire–enclosed "strategic hamlets" (the intended opposites of the revolutionaries' popular base areas). Drawing on Mao's famous dictum that "the populace is for revolutionaries what water is for the fish," Sir Robert Thompson (the inventor of strategic hamlets) explained, "With the ocean walled off, the fish would surely die."[8] Liberal "reform" became inevitably genocidal.

Critical to Ahmad's analysis of the logic of escalation is the observation that, with the failure of counterinsurgency efforts to win hearts and minds in order to establish the legitimacy of the South Vietnamese regime, coercion, terror, and escalating and indiscriminate violence were the only alternatives to withdrawal. Before long, the preoccupation with hearts and minds was gone, and the liberals sought "control more than consent of the governed, obedience more than title to authority, stability more than change" (from "Counterinsurgency"). Samuel Huntington, professor of politics at Harvard University, to whom Ahmad responds in "Epilogue: The Lesson of Vietnam," was one of those liberal militarists or, as he names them here, proponents of "technocratic evangelism." The relentless bureaucratic and technical cast of mind that Huntington exemplifies is unable, in its quest for stability, to distinguish institutions built on a foundation of popular legitimacy from well-run, professional institutions of coercion and control; or at the extreme, in the judgment of one of his colleagues, "to distinguish urbanization from genocide."[9] Ahmad identifies both Huntington and Sir Robert Thompson, architect of Vietnamization, as exemplary counterinsurgents, whose will to mastery, a bound complex of knowledge and power, orders the world according to fixed, increasingly mathematized models that impose insistent and reassuring conceptual order on a reality increasingly beyond their understanding or control. Thus, even as the NLF was establishing its legitimacy over more than 80 percent of the territory of South Vietnam, he notes, the US State Department was producing optimistic reports from its HES (Hamlet Evaluation System) computer programs. The world had become a giant self-reflecting mirror so that Huntington could discern in Vietnam not failure but success: a gain in precision for those order-performing models. Yet, while Huntington and other architects of Vietnam policy insist on its aberrant and "unique" character, Ahmad argues that the uniqueness of Vietnam lies not in the character of US policy, which is all too familiar, but in the effectiveness of Vietnamese resistance.

Although it was published in 1971, Ahmad wrote "Revolutionary Warfare and Counterinsurgency" (from which "Counterinsurgency," in this volume, is drawn) before the Nixon-Kissinger invasion of Cambodia and the massive protests that followed that invasion, protests that would prove the climax of the antiwar movement in the United States. He is once more prophetic. At the end of the article, he points to ominous portents that would indeed come to pass. Above all, he warns that its experience in Vietnam—from the training of personnel to the mechanization of counterinsurgency, what he calls a technologic of extermination, to the institutionalization of Vietnamization, to the pacification and strategic hamlet programs—provided the United States with fertile tools for a policy of counterrevolution in its most virulent form. This is exactly what would come to pass, in the countries of Central America, for instance, in the late 1970s and 1980s. Moreover, Ahmad underlines the implications of counterinsurgency in eroding democratic institutions at home, as the "counterrevolutionary chickens . . . return home to roost," employing their techniques on domestic dissenters. Finally, he emphasizes that reducing the domestic costs of foreign intervention requires the active fostering of ignorance and forgetting in the home population. President Bush I, in his inaugural address, understood the point, "The final lesson of Vietnam is that no great nation can long afford to be sundered by a memory." As several insightful commentators have detailed, post-Vietnam US popular and academic culture have been actively dedicated to rewriting its history,[10] perhaps none so tendentiously as Robert McNamara (within the Kennedy administration, Vietnam was seen as McNamara's war). In *In Retrospect,* he is still puzzling over how he and his associates in the Kennedy and Johnson administrations, "an exceptional group: young, vigorous, intelligent, well-meaning, patriotic servants of the United States, the 'best and the brightest' . . . got it wrong on Vietnam."[11] Ahmad's Vietnam essays are valuable today not only because they strip bare the question of how the United States got it wrong in Vietnam but also because Vietnam was a laboratory, whose lessons and logic resound in multiple situations, as the rest of this book bears out.

In the short article "ANC and PLO: Painful Contrasts," written on the occasion of Nelson Mandela's ascendance to the presidency of South Africa, Ahmad uses the success of the ANC to highlight the failure of the PLO as a liberation movement, in terms that resonate with his criticism of Debray. While he was a vocal and unrelenting advocate of the cause of the Palestinian people for more than thirty years—and indeed because of his commitment to that cause—he argues that the PLO reduced politics to the negotiations among states, failing to understand the need for a multifaceted approach to addressing people in the civil societies in the enemy's strongholds. In "ANC and PLO," he highlights by contrast the ANC's success in keeping apartheid in the forefront of the consciousness of the world, generating a movement of international solidarity, a critical source of the pressure, and the moral isolation that eventually brought down the apartheid regime. We include it here because it underscores once again his insistent belief in the primacy of politics in any liberation movement.

Ahmad's discussion of the shortsightedness of PLO strategy was further elaborated in an interview he gave to the Middle East Research and Information Project (MERIP) in the aftermath of the 1982 Israeli invasion of Lebanon, as well as in articles collected in part 4 of this volume. In "Yasser Arafat's Nightmare," which space limitations prevent our including here,[12] Ahmad brought his study and observation of revolutionary warfare to an analysis and critique of the PLO. His discussion illuminates ongoing realities in the Middle East: both the strategy and goals of the Israelis and the continuing strategic weaknesses of the PLO. First, Ahmad analyzes Israeli counterinsurgency strategy in terms of the Maoist dictum "draining the water": the long-term and detailed strategy was not to subjugate the Palestinian population but to eliminate it. While physical elimination of the Palestinians—their removal to Jordan, for example—was clearly contemplated, the Israelis, in Ahmad's analysis, have since Camp David pursued the goal of systematically assaulting not only the material bases of Palestinian existence, land and water, but "two other key elements to communal life—leadership and culture. . . . From arrests, expulsion and intimidation of local leaders to closing schools and publications, the Israelis have gone at the sustaining elements of Palestinian life very systematically, with attention to detail."[13] The Palestinian/Arab strategy by contrast inverted the principles of revolutionary warfare, as Ahmad understands them, "the only liberation movement which fought a war of position, while the incumbent fought a war of movement, both militarily and politically."[14] That is, instead of building a nonviolent movement in the Occupied Territories and refugee camps, the PLO established fixed and indefensible military camps in Lebanon and Jordan. Instead of developing guerrilla war tactics of surprise and mobility in diplomacy and politics, it adopted inflexible, rejectionist negotiating positions that resulted in its isolation rather than its enemy's. (That the leadership's ambivalent support for suicide bombers continues this tradition of ceding moral legitimacy to Israel hardly needs underlining.) Ahmad consistently elaborated strategies that dramatized the justice of the Palestinian cause and the profound moral and historical contradictions that haunt Israeli policy, indeed that haunt Israelis and Jewish communities in the diaspora. He suggested, for example, funeral processions from the refugee camps across the borders of Israel that "reverse the symbols of exodus,"[15] only one of innumerable symbolic nonviolent action ideas he proposed to the PLO leadership over twenty years that were never taken seriously. Perhaps most interesting, in his interview with MERIP, Ahmad suggested why the PLO chose the strategies it did, pointing to the fact that its understanding of revolution imitated "Mao and Giap and Ho Chi Minh," but crucially "as these great revolutionaries were interpreted by the Western media and [counter]insurgency experts," that is, as practitioners of armed struggle not politics.[16]

"Iran's Landmark Revolution: Fifteen Years Later" is representative of Ahmad's writing on the Iranian Revolution,[17] which he likened in world historical importance to the French Revolution, although not, as he writes, in terms of its results for Iran itself. In his view, the importance of the Iranian Revolution (and its analogy to the French) lay in "the trends . . . it announced and the fears it aroused" among neighboring ruling elites and in the United States. For the Third World, the Iranian Revolution represented a break with the dominant model of revolution, which involved a lengthy, largely rural struggle. Here was an eminently urban revolution, which took power on the shoulders of a general strike, overthrowing an autocrat whose position depended on the United States. Again, Ahmad challenges commonly held images: the Iranian Revolution, he argues, was not made by fundamentalist, antimodern elements; to the contrary, it was "the most modern and objectively advanced revolution in the Third World," led by progressive Islamic forces against the despotism and "westomania" represented by the shah. The emergence of Khomeini as its most powerful figure came only after the revolution took power.

We conclude this introduction by returning to the beginning: Algeria. As we indicated, *The Battle of Algiers* was both an embodiment of Ahmad's theory of revolution and a tribute to its critical source. In discussing the film and the revolution thirty-five years later, he underlines the significance of the battle of Algiers for the subsequent course of the victorious revolution. Forced out of the city of Algiers following the French victory, the leadership of the revolution retired to Tunis, where the provisional government created the ALN (Armée de Libération Nationale), a well-trained, well-equipped, traditional, conventional military force that eventually took power under Boumedienne and Ben Bella. In his pained reflections on the disastrous course of Algerian politics culminating in the suppression of the Islamic Front in the 1990s, Ahmad traces its roots to this moment, concluding that "Algeria began badly." He highlights the substitution of a military for political forces in the power scramble after the revolution, along with Boumedienne's and Ben Bella's abandonment of collective leadership (and thereby institutional accountability) and substitution of an authoritarian and bureaucratic (Stalinist) political and economic development model. With neither an ideology nor institutions to ensure accountability, he emphasizes, even a people's army can degenerate into a self-perpetuating junta. Sketched only briefly in his articles on Algeria, in his interview on the PLO, and in the margins of "Radical but

Wrong," these ideas are developed into a full-blown interpretation of the "pathologies of power" in the postcolonial world, presented in the essays included in part 2. For now, we have his summary verdict on the Algerian Revolution:"After seven years of a very costly struggle Algerians had achieved liberation from the colonial politics of repression. Now they were to experience a nearly total repression of politics."[18]

# 1 / REVOLUTIONARY WARFARE

How to Tell When the Rebels Have Won

America's interest in revolutionary warfare began from a defensive posture as a result of reverses in China, Korea, Cuba, and Laos and of protracted involvement in Vietnam. It was natural for its officials to be attracted more to the myths and methods of those who have had to defend themselves against guerrillas than to an understanding of the causes and characteristics of such a war. Americans are therefore unable to avoid the psychological and political pitfalls of colonial powers and feudal regimes like France and Nationalist China. A symptom of this negative posture is that while recognizing "a bold new form" of warfare, government publications, including the course books of Fort Bragg, reject the term "revolutionary war" in favor of old terms which do not suggest the vital distinction between revolutionary and other types of guerrilla conflict.

Vice President [Hubert] Humphrey [1965–1969] expressed the national concern over guerrilla warfare recently when he spoke of this "bold new form of aggression which could rank with the discovery of gunpowder" as constituting the "major challenge to our security." It is viewed as the latest weapon in the Communist arsenal with Vietnam as its testing ground.[1] "If guerrilla techniques succeed in Vietnam," wrote James Reston in the *New York Times*, "nobody in Washington dare assume that the same techniques will not be applied in all Communist rimlands from Korea to Iran." This view is based on two assumptions and at least one serious misconception. It assumes that the Vietnamese situation is typical, historically and politically, of other underdeveloped countries and that American policy toward other nations would be comparable to the one pursued in Vietnam. The misconception concerns the nature of revolutionary warfare.

The official American interpretation of revolutionary war can be summarized as follows: (1) It is essentially a technical problem, i.e., a problem of plotting and subversion on the one hand and of intelligence and suppression on the other. As the chief conspiratorial group, the Communists are believed to be the most likely initiators and beneficiaries of revolution. It was this attitude which led to the recent attempt to nip in the bud what was construed as the Dominican Communist conspiracy.[2] A logical extension of this theory is the belief that any revolutionary movement is inspired, directed, and controlled from abroad. (2) The active sanctuary—from which guerrillas can smuggle supplies and train their troops—is considered the primary factor in their success. (3) The guerrilla movement is believed to enjoy considerable advantage because, in the words of W. W. Rostow, "its task is merely to destroy while the government must build and protect what it is building." (4) The civilian population is considered important for providing information and protection to the guerrillas; it is believed that civilian-guerrilla cooperation is enforced by terror. (Dean Rusk, while complaining of the "gullibility of educated men and their stubborn disregard of plain facts," asserted that the Vietcong "has no significant popular following . . . it relies heavily on terror.") Serious inquiry into other bases of guerrilla support and mass mobilization is therefore deemed of no great importance.

*false*

Judging from the failure of Washington's prophecies in Vietnam and from the policies followed to date, it would seem that these assumptions represent the actual official view and cannot be dismissed as myths consciously constructed for public consumption. Wrong premises do not usually produce right policies, and these assumptions are, at best, half truths—credible and misleading. (Oliver Wendell Holmes once remarked that a half truth is like half a brick: it can be thrown a considerable distance.) Studies in the field of revolutionary wars and my personal observation of the Algerian struggle lead to very different conclusions which may be summarized as follows: (1) Revolutionaries consider mass support the primary condition for their success; winning and maintaining popular support remain their central objective throughout the struggle. (2) The requirements of guerrilla war, as well as the history of its failures and successes, confirm the primacy of political factors in such a conflict. (3) Popular support for the guerrillas is predicated upon the moral alienation of the masses from the existing government. The revolutionaries' chief aim is to activate and perpetuate the moral isolation of the enemy regime until such isolation has become total and irreversible. (4) The conditions leading to revolutionary wars are not created by conspiracy. They are partly inherent in a situation of rapid social change, but the outbreak normally results mainly from the failure of a ruling elite to respond to the challenge of modernization. (5) A revolutionary guerrilla movement concentrates on "out-administering" not on "outfighting" the enemy. This is a constructive and not simply a destructive undertaking. (6) The use of terror by guerrillas is highly selective; it does not constitute the main reason for the favorable reaction of the masses to their cause. (7) The external sanctuary has greater psychological and diplomatic than military or political value to the guerrillas. A discussion of these points follows.

Organizers of guerrilla warfare give prime attention, in practice no less than in theory, to the human factor. T. E. Lawrence (of Arabia) spoke of guerrilla war in terms of "the algebraic element of things, the biological element of life, and the psychological element of ideas." In other words, although Lawrence's goals were essentially military, military considerations constituted, for him, only one-third of the problem of organizing and sustaining guerrilla troops. When Tito was told of the exceptionally unfavorable terrain in the region of Srem ("the area is level as the palm of your hand . . . and with little forests"), he remarked, "What a first-class example it is of the relative unimportance of geographical factors in the development of a rising. The basic factor is studious political work, the attitude of the mass of people and the fighting leadership—if these are present the population would fight to the last man." Mao Tse-tung states, "Because guerrilla warfare basically derives from the masses and is supported by them, it can neither exist nor flourish if it separates itself from their sympathies and cooperation." This belief in the need to command popular support governs the movement through all stages of its development.

History confirms the sovereignty of the human factor in revolutionary warfare. While shying away from the wars that were "lost," American military analysts are prone to cite cases of successful antiguerrilla operations. A heavy favorite—the British "counterinsurgency" in Malaya—is faithfully imitated in Vietnam. (Sometimes too faithfully, as in the case of the strategic hamlets program launched in April 1962.) But comparisons with Malaya are fallacious, because there the guerrillas were at a severe disadvantage. Their support was limited to a minority of 423,000 Chinese squatters, who were ethnically distinct from and distrusted by the majority of Malays, and popular grievances were not acute enough to make the guerrillas look like liberators to the Malay peasants. Furthermore, the British acted quickly to remove the grievances on which the rebellion was based. Even then it took thirteen years and a total of 260,000 soldiers and police (80,000 British, 180,000 Malays) to put down 8,000 guerrillas (a ratio of thirty to one). Another success story, the joint US-Philippine victory over the Huks, is less frequently cited because of its embarrassing aspects. The Huk movement collapsed dramatically when [President Ramon] Magsaysay [1953–1957] convinced the peasants of his will and capacity to introduce reforms. However, the promises made to them were not kept, and the Garcia administration witnessed a resurgence of guerrillas.[3] In April 1962, [Diosdado] Macapagal [1961–1965] swallowed his embarrassment and ordered a mop-up operation in Central Luzon. According to the latest reports, guerrilla strength in the Philippines is increasing.

The Algerian Revolution, the least studied in this country though it comes closest to the Vietnamese situation, had actually been crushed militarily but had won politically when de Gaulle negotiated independence. By 1961, the guerrillas had been reduced to some five thousand and their ability to engage the French at will had markedly declined. But France faced a sullen Algerian population that it had conquered but could not rule. The FLN was defeated in the field, but it continued to outadminister and "illegitimize" the French.

Why did the Algerian peasants risk, for seven remorseless years, their lives, the honor of their women, and the security of their paltry belongings? Nationalism alone could not explain their violent and resolute rejection of French rule. In no other colony, except Indochina, did the movement for independence take so violent a turn. And why did not the peasants respond earlier to the militants' calls to arms? The answer comes from one of the historic chiefs of the Algerian Revolution. The time was not "ripe," he said. "These events occur where foreign rule is resented, where acute grievances exist and institutional channels for ventilating and satisfying them are ineffective."

Peasant rebellions had occurred in past years of famine and high taxation, but these spontaneous and periodic disturbances, as expressions of frustration over social and economic conditions, are not a sufficient condition for guerrilla revolution. "Revolutionary warfare does not require simply discontent among the masses but a sense of desperation and a grim determination to end injustice and humiliation. It demands patience with prolonged suffering, and a determined conspiracy of silence, and militancy."

A people can summon up that resolution only if they feel morally alienated from their rulers. "The success of a revolutionary war is predicated upon the continual and increasing moral isolation of the enemy. When it becomes total the war has been won, for the population will then fight to the last man." Later, other Algerian leaders told me they had spent more effort fighting the French promises of eventual independence and reforms than fighting the military. The Algerians became increasingly alienated from the French as the latter increased their military effort, which in revolutionary warfare means large-scale killing of civilians (if for no other reason than because the guerrilla is undistinguishable from other peasants), and the FLN became more confident of winning not the military battles but the revolutionary war.

The conditions leading to revolutionary warfare are not created by conspiracy. They are inherent in the dislocations and demands produced by rapid social change and are predicated on the failure of ruling elites to respond to the challenge of modernization. The pressures for change in the political, economic, and social relationships of the past inevitably lead to a confrontation with those whose interests lie in the maintenance of the status quo. In countries and colonies whose rulers are willing to abdicate their monopoly of power and privileges, where genuine reforms are introduced and new institutions begin to provide for a sharing of power and responsibility, the change is effected in an orderly (if not entirely peaceful) and democratic manner. But when a ruling class resists reforms (which invariably mean reduction in its power and privileges), its confrontation with the new political forces becomes increasingly violent. A regime unwilling to satisfy popular aspirations begins to lose legitimacy; revolutionary forces deliberately accelerate this process, by weakening the efficacy and cohesion of the ruling elite and by giving form to the amorphous revolutionary conflagration. In the competition for leadership which often takes place in this volatile situation, non–Communist revolutionary groups are handicapped by several factors, the most important of which are the attitudes and policies of Western powers. By supporting the defenders of the old order, a great nation like the United States weakens the fighting power of the democratic forces, drives the Cold War neutralists to seek the help of the Communists, and gives the latter new heroes and martyrs.

Once a revolutionary movement enters the guerrilla phase its central objective is to confirm, perpetuate, and institutionalize the moral isolation of the enemy by providing an alternative to the discredited regime through the creation of "parallel hierarchies." The major task of the movement is not to outfight but to outadminister the government. The main target in this bid is the village, where the majority of the population lives and where the government's presence is often exploitative (the collection of taxes, for example). Here the chief and his council are the main link between the people and the government. Breaking this link demands careful planning, organization, and hard work. The government is systematically eliminated from the countryside by the conversion or killing of village officials, who are then controlled or replaced by the political arm of the movement. The rebels must then build an administrative structure to collect taxes, to provide some education and social welfare, and to maintain a modicum of economic activity. A revolutionary guerrilla movement which does not have these administrative concerns and structures to fulfill its obligations to the populace would degenerate into banditry. The official American view that the guerrillas' tasks are easier because they only destroy contradicts the findings of those who have studied and observed these movements. During this phase, military confrontation is normally avoided, and the government also treats assassinations as a police problem and ascribes nonpayment of taxes to administrative lags, bad harvests, etc. The Vietcong are known to have gained control over 70 percent of rural Vietnam during 1957–1960—a period when Americans were presenting Uncle Diem as a rival of Uncle Ho and were going around saying: "Look, no Vietnamese army units are attacked. Therefore, there is no guerrilla threat."

Most compelling, but also most self-defeating, is the myth that terror is the basis of civilian support for the guerrillas. Guerrilla warfare requires a highly committed but covert civilian support which cannot be obtained at gun point. Only degenerate and defeated guerrillas are known to have risked the loss of mass support by terrorizing civilians (some Huk and Malayan diehards were reduced to it). An outstanding feature of guerrilla training is the stress on scrupulously "correct and just" behavior toward civilians. Political work, believes General Giap, is "the soul of the army," and a Chinese guerrilla expert explains that "army indoctrination is primarily aimed at training the troops to act in such a way that they will gain this total support [of the people]." Guerrilla use of terror therefore is sociologically and psychologically selective. It strikes those who are popularly identified as the "enemy of the people"—officials, landlords, and the like.

Killing a village chief, however, is often a more complicated affair. Since most chiefs are local farmers who command legitimacy and loyalty through tradition and kinship, the militants ideally want to persuade them into the movement. When that fails, it takes painstaking political work to engineer their assassination and to prepare the villagers to accept it. In the early years of the Algerian Revolution, it took the FLN from two months to a year to kill a village chief without incurring the liability of public hostility, and that was an anticolonial war. I was therefore amazed to learn that in Vietnam about thirteen thousand local officials were killed between 1957 and 1961. Professor Bernard Fall gives a simple explanation: These chiefs, as appointees of Diem, had little legitimacy compared with the Vietminh cadres who had liberated the country from France. Furthermore, the local officials became involved, along with the American-equipped and -trained army, in the sordid business of restoring the landlords who had fled the country during the war. (A de facto land reform was achieved under the Vietminh.) These absentee aristocrats even demanded eight years' worth of back rent, covering the period from 1945 to 1954. Before the war, the rent had been 50 percent of the yield; the peasants were thus required to pay 400 percent of their produce and to surrender their rights to the land! The Vietcong had no problem preparing them to accept the killing of officials engaged in such work.

Terror is also used to ensure survival of the militants and of the movement. Robert Kleiman of the *New York Times* (May 3, 1965) informs us that in Vietnam's "contested areas, with 40 percent of the population, Saigon usually gets cooperation by day and the Vietcong by night—because that is when their troops and officials are present. It is an old Asian custom." I was amused by the last sentence, for I know it is not our custom but a universal practice of guerrilla warfare. The population must seem at least neutral if it hopes to escape full enemy treatment from government troops. Rebel troops and officials do not arrive at night from "somewhere in the mountains"; they are present during the day, too, and often lead the show of obedience to the government. At night, the loyal peasant turns into a guerrilla, and all know him as such. To ensure that the popular conspiracy of silence develops no seams, exemplary punishments are given to those suspected of having informed.

Second-degree terror, which normally does not result in killing, is used to sabotage the government's belated effort to gain popular support. Government schoolteachers and health workers are favorite targets of kidnapping and indoctrination. In June 1962, a South Vietnamese UN observer informed UNESCO that the Vietcong had kidnapped more than twelve hundred teachers; the government's malaria-eradication campaign collapsed after twenty-two health officers had been killed and sixty kidnapped. Guerrilla sabotage normally guards against causing too much hardship on the population and long-range damages to the economy. Industry and even foreign-owned plantations are spared if they pay their "taxes" to the liberation front. And they normally do so when the government is unable to protect them. (In Vietnam, the large European rubber plantations, Michelin, SIPH, Terres Rouges, resisted for a while but started paying taxes to the Vietcong after their French supervisors were kidnapped.)

It is difficult to say at what point the moral isolation of a government becomes total and irreversible, so that no amount of promises and reforms would restore the lost confidence and reduce the people's resistance. In Algeria, at least, the point seems to have been reached when the French were reduced to torturing and killing civilians and to "regrouping" the population. Many Algerian leaders believe that their revolution became irreversible at the moment of France's greatest military victory—General Bigeard's conquest of the Casbah (the Muslim section of Algiers was reduced to rubble during 1957–1958). France could no longer expect the confidence, much less the loyalty, of a people it was destroying indiscriminately, albeit unwillingly and despite itself.

The desertion of the intellectuals and moderates often signals not so much the irreversibility of a revolutionary war but its takeoff. Intellectuals, especially the Asian variety, are a democratic, liberal group, who view organized violence with distaste. Somewhat alienated from their culture, Westernized, and city-centered, they distrust the peasants but desire an improvement of their condition. When an armed revolution breaks out, they are likely to play in the middle ground, hoping to get some reforms under way by using the armed threat as a counter for bargaining. They begin to go into exile or to defect to the rebels after the failure of the regime and the success of the revolution become imminent.

The defending army's pressure for conventional attack on an external sanctuary is yet another sign that a revolutionary war has been lost on home grounds. In revolutionary warfare, armies trained for conventional combat follow a vicious logic of escalation, which derives from acute frustration over an elusive war that puts in question not only their effectiveness but the very validity of their training and organization. Moreover, the morale of professional soldiers cannot be maintained if they know they are fighting a popular rebellion. Hence the compulsion to believe that behind the popular behavior lies the terror of an army trained, equipped, and directed by a foreign power and the wish to draw the enemy into open battles. Since reprisals against the population fail to produce the desired result, carrying the war to a sovereign nation becomes the only road to a conventional showdown. In Algeria, this demand led to French participation in the invasion of Suez, then to the bombing of the Tunisian border town of Sakiet Sidi Youssef, and produced a succession of army revolts, the last of which destroyed the Fourth Republic. Had the French government succumbed to these pressures, France would have been the first power to violate the international practice of respecting the rights of sanctuary—a principle that was observed in Korea, Greece, Cyprus, and Malaya.

The importance of an active sanctuary should not be underestimated, although it is not essential to guerrilla success. In Cuba, Yugoslavia, and China, the revolutionaries did not have active sanctuaries. In Burma and to a lesser extent in Greece, sanctuaries proved of limited value. Politically and militarily, revolutionary guerrillas are, by and large, a self-sustaining group that can go on fighting indefinitely even if infiltration from across the border stops. External help, however, has great psychological and diplomatic value. In a war of attrition, there can be no decisive victory over a strong foreign enemy. At best, one hopes to inflict on it heavy losses, tire it out, and, through international pressure, force it to negotiate withdrawal. External help is important in internationalizing guerrilla demands and keeps alive the hope of liberation. When a revolutionary army loses an ally, it loses not so much military support; it loses hope. When the world is not watching, when the fear of diplomatic sanctions and the threat of a widened war are absent, a foreign power trapped in counterguerrilla operations is likely to make the final and the only move that may "win"—it starts to commit genocide.

Finally, the assumption that a guerrilla outfit, like a conventional army, can be controlled and commanded by a foreign or externally based government ignores the organizational, psychological, and political facts of revolutionary warfare. The distrust of the "home-based" guerrillas, even for their own government in exile, cannot be overstated. The resourceful and tough "interior" leaders and cadres who face the enemy daily, collect taxes, administer, make promises, and give hopes to the population are not easily controlled from abroad and make suspicious, exacting, and hard-to-please allies. Therefore, zone commanders and political commissars are, for the most part, monarchs of what they survey. As a group, they are joined together by shared experiences, by a common mood which is defiant and insular, by a shared suspicion of "politicians and diplomats over there" selling them out, and by a collective will to defy a settlement that is not of their making.

In Vietnam, the signs are clear. The South Vietnamese regime has no legitimacy, and no government backed by a Western power can hope for popular support in a country where the Communists have capitalized on the nationalist appeal of restoring independence and unity, and where the pro-Western leaders have been Bao-Dai, Diem, and the musical-chair generals.[4] The massacre of civilians began as early as 1960 (not counting the earlier repressive measures of the Diem regime), as attested by reputable scholars and even a former chief US military adviser (Lt. Gen. Samuel T. Williams; see *U.S. News and World Report*, November 9, 1964). It has since escalated. The intellectuals and moderates have deserted or defected. And North Vietnam is subjected to daily bombings. America and its South Vietnamese allies have lost the revolutionary war because they could not win the support of the Vietnamese people, and now their moral isolation is total.

As an Asian, I am aware of the appeals and threat of communism, and I would support policies likely to prevent its expansion. But I do not believe that communism is the wave of the future, and therefore I am neither panicked nor paralyzed. I believe that Vietnam is a unique case—culturally, historically, and politically. I hope that the United States will not repeat its Vietnam blunders elsewhere. I do not subscribe to the domino theory, and I am anguished by Americans who call Vietnam a test case. Vietnam is the only country in the world where the nationalist movement for independence was led by the Communists during its most crucial and heroic decades. In new countries where institutional loyalties are still weak, the legitimacy and popularity of a regime derives from its nationalist heroes and martyrs. Unfortunately for the free world, the George Washington of Vietnam, its Gandhi, was a Communist nationalist. Ho Chi Minh and his associates (including General Giap of Dien Bien Phu fame) are understandably considered the founding fathers of modern Vietnam. It was morbid optimism to expect an absentee aristocrat to supplant a leader who had devoted a lifetime to the liberation of his country and to defeat a leadership and cadres whose organic ties with the peasants were cemented by the bitter struggle for independence. It is not fair to blame Diem for driving the Vietnamese to desperation. He had no choice. Given his circumstances, his only possible weapons were a power apparatus to regiment the population, all-out support of minorities, and widespread terror. These were not aberrations of a program but the program itself.

Vietnam is also the only country in which the United States gave substantial support to a colonial power in a war of independence. This could not have endeared America to the Vietnamese people. Then in the "Southern zone" America replaced France and supported the ex–French puppet Bao-Dai; next it put up Diem as "the democratic alternative to [the] Vietcong" and also failed to honor its pledge to hold elections for the unification of the country. To most Vietnamese, the present war therefore is a continuation of the struggle for independence. I know how Asians feel about America's action. They call it neocolonialism; some think it is imperialism. I know this is very wrong because Americans are naturally sympathetic to peoples' struggles for freedom and justice, and they would like to help if they could. I prefer the term "maternalism" for American policy in countries like Vietnam, because it reminds me of the story of an elephant who, as she strolled benignly in the jungle, stepped on a mother partridge and killed her. When she noticed the orphaned siblings, tears filled the kind elephant's eyes. "Ah, I, too, have maternal instincts," she said, turning to the orphans, and sat on them.

[1965]

# 2 / RADICAL BUT WRONG

For someone who lacks firsthand knowledge of Latin America, it appears at first difficult, if not hazardous, to comment on Régis Debray's *Revolution in the Revolution?* The basic framework within which the book moves concerns the uniqueness of the "tactical content" of the Cuban among modern revolutions and its importance as a model for Latin America. Debray believes that the Russian, Chinese, and Vietnamese revolutions are poor examples for South American countries because each revolution must respond to its regional and national peculiarities. Learning from foreign examples can cost dearly through the adoption of tactics unsuited to local conditions. The Latin American revolutionary war, according to Debray, "possesses highly special and profoundly distinct conditions of development which can only be discovered through a particular experience. In that sense all the theoretical works on peoples' war do as much harm as good."[1] Hence "one may well consider it a stroke of good luck that Fidel had not read the military writings of Mao Tse-tung before disembarking on the coast of the Oriente" (p. 20). Since historical examples as well as the writings of the non-Latin theorists and practitioners of revolutionary warfare are rejected as irrelevant to South America, the validity of the assumptions on which Debray's theory is based may best be questioned by those who claim expertise on that region. Insofar as this theory claims to be rooted in the experience of one successful (Cuba) and several ongoing Latin revolutions, it would seem to follow that its usefulness can ultimately be judged only by those who have been and will be actively engaged in the struggle.

In undertaking to comment on his work, I am implicitly rejecting Debray's contention that specific conditions in any country or region are so unique as to transcend history and thus render irrelevant past revolutionary theory no less than practice. This does not mean, however, that I deny the importance of the congruence between tactics/strategy and local realities without which no revolutionary movement can succeed. Secondly, insofar as Debray's justification for his theory is based on the argument of the uniqueness of Latin America, his thesis is convincing only to the extent that he brings out, meaningfully, those distinctive characteristics of the region which bear on his theory.

Debray's own writings do not help in understanding the "highly special and profoundly distinct conditions" which distinguish South America from the other regions of the Third World. In an earlier, and empirically meatier, article outlining the *foco* theory, he had stated: "It remains to be demonstrated how the Castroist tactics of insurrection and take-over of power conform to the system of contradictions peculiar to each Latin American country; and how they are undoubtedly founded on the Marxist-Leninist theory."[2] If there is a promise implicit in *Revolution in the Revolution?* we have a right to disappointment. Insofar as Debray refers to some specific conditions in Latin America, they are so general as to apply to most Western-dominated underdeveloped countries under oligarchic rule and infested by parties and politicians whose reflexes are traditional, when not outright reactionary.

It is noteworthy that to the extent that *Revolution in the Revolution?* differs from Debray's earlier formulation of the *foco* theory, it is in the direction of greater rigidity, greater denigration of the primacy of politics, and less attention to the environment in which the *foco* may succeed. It is incorrect, I believe, to consider, as Robin Blackburn and Perry Anderson do, the two earlier essays as constituting the "indispensable complement, the theoretical-political premises of the call to arms in *Revolution in the Revolution?*"[3] They undoubtedly foreshadow the model drawn in the book, but the *foco* theory of *Revolution in the Revolution?* differs in a fundamental manner from the one he had advocated in "Latin America: The Long March." In *Revolution in the Revolution?* the revolutionary process is inverted; in the *foco* theory published in early 1965, it was not.

In "Latin America: The Long March" (pp. 30–31), Debray stated: (a) The *foco*, installed as a "detonator at the least guarded position and at the moment most favorable to the explosion, . . . can have no active function unless it finds a point of insertion within maturing conditions. . . . Chronologically, it cannot be born in the trough of the wave, but must be the culmination of a political crisis." (b) It must be in existence as a political organization when the appropriate moment comes. "For the prairie to catch fire, it is necessary that the spark should be there, present, waiting. The very lengthy work of building a *foco* can only be done on the spot, and only a center that is politically rooted in an agrarian zone can seize the offensive at the appropriate moment." (c) "The *foco*, at the beginning, can only survive to the extent to which it obtains the support of the peasantry: the center is welded to the milieu, congenitally." In *Revolution in the Revolution?* Debray ignores or denies these principles.

His discussion in "Latin America: The Long March" of the causes of the failures of important guerrilla centers in Latin America (he lists eleven between 1959 and 1964) as well as his description of the "gains" (Bolivia, Colombia, Venezuela) tended to reinforce his belief in the primacy of politics at all stages of revolution. He listed four causes of failure: (1) treachery by enemy infiltrators; (2) absence or deficiency of political education of cadres; (3) lack of political apparatus to coordinate with the urban workers, to provide political support, and to diffuse a program of action and basic demands; and (4) lack of adequate preparation on the spot.

Elaborating on the last point, Debray contrasts the successful case of Venezuela, where the district of Bachiller ("one hour by road from Caracas") had seen the "installation of a social, economic, and political infrastructure on the basis of existing political structure long in advance of the launching of the guerrilla center properly speaking. Further, this guerrilla action did not break out haphazardly but at the exact moment (July 1964) when the Leoni regime had demonstrated by its actions that the 'broadly based government' was betraying its promises and that repression was acquiring a new lease of life in the country" ("Latin America," p. 33). In *Revolution in the Revolution?* Debray denies to the *foco* in its formative period precisely these aspects of revolutionary preparation.

Similarly, Castro's and Guevara's well-known opinion on the impossibility of exporting revolutions is ignored. To the contrary, Debray argues that the fact that peasants may regard the *foco* as a foreign element among them requires that guerrillas remain, at first, aloof from the population. There is no discussion of Che Guevara's earlier contention that guerrilla insurgency cannot succeed against a government which is able to maintain some legitimacy through the pretense of democracy. Yet Debray's tactical model is in accord with Che Guevara's effort in Bolivia. Hence his shift deserves attention, and explanation. There is a note of urgency, a sense of immediacy in his book. Perhaps it results from a concern to divide United States strength and thus help the Vietnamese people. After Vietnam, the United States might turn to Cuba out of frustration or intoxicated by a Pyrrhic victory; hence the need to find allies on the continent. Above all, the setbacks suffered by the revolutionary sectors in Colombia and Bolivia and the losses in Venezuela may have been the most crucial factors in hardening Debray's convictions on behalf of an armed, mobile *foco* independent of party and population.

In 1965, as Debray surveyed a succession of guerrilla movements, only three out of fourteen main centers appeared promising. Of these, one (Bolivia) seemed to him to be closer to the Bolshevik model. Bolivia, he noted, is "the country where the subjective and objective conditions are best combined . . . the only country in South America where a socialist revolution is on the agenda . . . where the revolution might take a Bolshevik form. . . . The theory of the *foco* is thus in Bolivia, for reasons of historical formation which are unique in America, if not inadequate at any rate secondary" ("Latin America," pp. 26–27). Another (Colombia) appeared comparable to Vietnam ("where civil war has given the guerrilla its Vietnamese character . . . peasants are at the same time cultivators of their land and guerrilleros") (ibid., p. 27). "Only Venezuela," he wrote, "provides an example of the *foco* as Guevara conceives it." Very little in contrast with the failures! The high mortality rate, Debray explained, was "due to a too hasty imitation of the Cuban model, and did not combine all the necessary conditions for success" (ibid.).

The collapse of the Bolivian miners' resistance and the defeat of the autonomous zone of Marquetalia in Colombia give Debray his strongest arguments against the imitation of extra–Latin American models and in favor of the *foco* derived from the Cuban model. "This double defeat," he says, "signifies the end of an epoch and attests to the death of a certain ideology" (*Revolution in the Revolution?* p. 27). He makes out a convincing case against armed self-defense and points out that in Colombia and Bolivia armed zones of peasants' and workers' self-defense were defeated with substantial losses to the population. He writes poignantly of the tragic isolation of Bolivian miners in revolt: in a hostile, cold, arid milieu, the scattered miners were starved, surrounded, and subjugated, one isolated community after another. Unless it results from guerrilla victory and is protected by a mobile front, a self-defense zone will be isolated and destroyed or, left to itself, will be institutionalized and atrophied. "The failure of armed self-defense of the masses," says Debray, "corresponds on the military level to the failure of reformism on the political level" (ibid., pp. 27–28). No one should argue that the creation of base areas is a viable strategy until a situation of substantial mass mobilization and the possibility of creating multiple points of pressure has been developed. However, Debray misses an important point when he concludes that these failures leave only one alternative, the military *foco*. Their defeat was due to the fact that both zones were isolated pockets lacking nationwide popular and organizational (including armed) support. A *foco* is as vulnerable to destruction in isolation as rural or industrial base areas. Hence detonation of a *foco*, too, must occur, as Debray had earlier acknowledged, with reference to a dialectical analysis of its revolutionary possibilities. More importantly, the residual effects of the defeat of a *foco* are likely to be less favorable to accelerating the revolutionary processes than the failures of organized mass resistance, even when they are isolated.

Cuba under Batista is assumed to represent conditions analogous to the rest of Latin America with the exception, perhaps, of Uruguay, the only country Debray identifies as one where "conditions for armed struggle do not exist at present" (*Revolution in the Revolution?* p. 124).[4] He does not, however, tell us what these "conditions" are or why Uruguay constitutes an exception. He speaks of but does not discuss the "objective and subjective" conditions of revolution. The existence of objective conditions is assumed, as is the commonality of political, social, and economic configurations in Latin America (though, from his examples, it appears that he is concerned mainly with the Andean region). The formation of subjective conditions, he presumes, will be hastened by the creation of guerrilla *focos*.

More disappointing is Debray's admitted inability to come to grips with the Cuban Revolution. In the introduction to *Revolution in the Revolution?* (pp. 15–16), he decries the current clichés, the "flagrant oversights," the "conjuring trick" of "reducing" Cuba to a "golden legend"; and he makes a passionate plea against overlooking "the essential, the complex reality of the Cuban insurrectional process," its "inner working," its " 'how' . . . rather than its surface glitter." But, he adds with characteristic integrity, the "continuing lack of a detailed history of the Cuban insurrectional process . . . constrains us to reduce our references to allusions whereas what is needed is a systematic investigation."

On the basis of these allusions and in the absence of any systematic comparisons between Cuba and other Latin American nations, we are given a certain prescription for revolution which inverts the usual process of revolutionary warfare, flies in the face of past theory no less than practice, and even contradicts the earlier views of America's most articulate theorist of revolutionary war, Che Guevara.

The core of Debray's tactical model is his stress on the primacy of the military *foco* (a word used to describe the unitary focus of guerrilla operation) in the formative stages of an armed revolution. He believes that only a mobile, flexible, aggressive *foco* can create the conditions for gaining mass support and for political organizing. By inflicting losses on government forces, it will subvert the legitimacy of the system, end the peasants' habit of obedience to it, and eventually provide the protective shield necessary for organizing the mass. Successful military action "catalyzes the people's energy and transforms the *foco* into a pole of attraction" (*Revolution in the Revolution?* p. 45). The best form of political work is armed attack on the enemy. Debray states: "The destruction of a troop transport truck or the public execution of a police torturer is more effective propaganda than a hundred speeches. . . . The agitational and propagandists' impact resides in this very concentration of effects. A significant detail: *during two years of warfare, Fidel did not hold a single political rally in his zone of operations*" (ibid., pp. 53–54, italics added).

He draws a contrast with Vietnam: "Whereas in Vietnam the military pyramid of the liberation forces is built from the base up, in Latin America . . . it tends to be built from the apex down—the permanent forces first (the *foco*), then the semi-regular forces in the vicinity of the *foco*, and lastly or after victory (Cuba) the militia" (*Revolution in the Revolution?* p. 51). This, Debray rightly claims, is a radical departure from the insurrectional process observable in China, Vietnam, and Algeria; it also inverts the theories of such men as Mao, Giap, and even Lenin. This view leads to the reversal of the stages of development not only in the military but also in the political and organizational aspects of revolutionary warfare. The incumbent government is outfought before it is outadministered. The military factor takes precedence over the political. Tactical considerations must precede questions of overall strategy. Political parties cannot initiate the guerrilla movement; rather, the guerrillas later galvanize into a party and establish a socialist state. The guerrilla (operational) and political leadership must be combined in the same man.

Debray argues cogently against guerrilla base areas, whose establishment demands a combination of favorable circumstances—extensive territory without modern roads and rails, high population density, common border with a friendly country, weak enemy air power, numerical weakness of government forces—none of which is present in Latin America. Hence, during "the initial stage, the base support is in the guerrilla fighter's knapsack" (*Revolution in the Revolution?* p. 65).

> The only viable alternative, in his view, is the mobile *foco*—independent of the civilian population, in action as well as in military organization; consequently it need not assume the direct defense of the peasant population. The protection of the population depends on the progressive destruction of the enemy's military potential; . . . if the principal objective of a revolutionary guerrilla force is the destruction of the enemy's potential, it cannot wait for the enemy to approach before taking the initiative. . . . In every case this objective requires that the guerrilla *foco* be independent of the families residing within the zone of operations.
>
> (ibid., pp. 41–42)

Debray's *foco* theory does not reject organic ties with the civilians simply for fear of exposing them to governmental repression, although this is undoubtedly the most attractive aspect of his position. Nor is it only a matter of concern with achieving maximum mobility and initiative. One senses something deeper and disturbing—an awareness of distance from if not exactly a distrust of the rural population, an unadmitted estimation that the objective conditions for revolution do not exist in Latin America, total disbelief in the political processes and existing political parties as possible instruments for independence and social revolution, and above all a desperate drive to create the revolutionary environment through armed action and thus to defeat the increasing involvement of the United States.

The *foco* is not only organically distinct but also isolated from the population. Says Debray: "Various considerations of common sense necessitate wariness toward the civilian population and the maintenance of a certain aloofness" (*Revolution in the Revolution?* p. 42) (he explains, however, that "this vigilance does not necessarily mean mistrust"). This feeling of isolation, as well as his estimation of the revolutionary environment, are most clearly expressed in the chapter on "Armed Propaganda." The *foco* begins in sparsely populated, highly dispersed regions because, he says, "no new arrival goes unnoticed in an Andean village. . . . Above all else, a stranger inspires distrust. The Quechua or Cakchiquel (Mayan) peasants have good reason to distrust the 'outsider,' the 'white man'" (ibid., p. 51).

While arguing against involvement in political work among peasants, Debray indicates that the local governments enjoy legitimacy (he does not use this word—I am using it in the passive sense of legitimacy by tradition or by default) in the rural areas, while peasants regard the revolutionaries as alien. These passages are crucial to understanding his theory and deserve to be discussed at length: "The poor peasant believes, first of all, in anyone who has a certain power, beginning with the power to do what he says. The system of oppression is subtle: it has existed from time immemorial, fixed, entrenched, and solid. The army, the guardia rural, the latifundistas' private police, or nowadays the Green Berets and Rangers, enjoy a prestige all the greater for being subconscious. This prestige constitutes the principal form of oppression. . . . The neo-colonial ideal is still to show force in order not to have to use it, but to show it is in effect to use it" (*Revolution in the Revolution?* p. 51).

The guerrillas are not dealing in Latin America "with a foreign expeditionary force, with limited manpower, but with a well established system of local domination. *They themselves are the foreigners, lacking status, who at the beginning offer the populace nothing but bloodshed and pain*" (*Revolution in the Revolution?* p. 52, italics added). Also, incumbent regimes have been greatly improving their control, facilities, instruments of repression, and even their adjustive mechanisms. Highways have greatly expanded, skirting the jungle and linking up countries and capitals; airstrips spot the formerly impenetrable tropical zones. North American sociologists and economists have been mapping out man and his milieu in detail, making available to their governmental employers hitherto unknown information. "Thousands of Peace Corpsmen have succeeded in integrating themselves in rural areas—some of them by dint of hard work, patience, and at times real sacrifice—where they profit by the lack of political work by left-wing organizations. Even the most remote regions are today teeming with Catholic, Evangelical, Methodist, and Seventh-Day Adventist missionaries. In a word, all these close-knit networks of control strengthen the national machinery of domination" (ibid., p. 53). And, of course, there are the special forces trained and equipped for counterinsurgency.

Three interdependent points emerge from these quotations: (1) Debray's high estimation of the entrenched nature and increasing effectiveness of government control in rural areas; (2) his stress on power rather than on the revolutionary process and the concomitant belief that the peasants' acceptance of government is based mainly on fear of its coercive apparatus; (3) his view that the revolutionary elite is considered alien by the peasantry and that there is between them no commonality of interest on the basis of which a political tie-up could occur. I do not know much about Latin America. Therefore I cannot judge the validity of these assumptions. Yet it seems to me that so pessimistic a perspective of the environment drastically reduces one's political options to a choice between co-optation and a tactic born of despair. Those not inexorably committed to seizure of power for the sake of transforming society would probably seek different routes to sharing it. On the other hand, given the above estimation of the revolutionary environment, the *foco* is the only logical alternative for those who are unwilling to be compromised with the existing order.

The belief that peasant cooperation with the government results from the fear of its coercive power leads logically to the primacy of the military *foco* as a means for subverting the government's legitimacy. As Debray says, "Unassailability cannot be challenged by words. In order to destroy the idea of unassailability—that age old accumulation of fear and humility vis-à-vis the patrón [boss], the policeman, the guardia rural [paramilitaries in service of the landowners]—there is nothing better than combat" (*Revolution in the Revolution?* p. 52). The feeling of isolation, of being considered alien by the peasantry, must necessarily mean that guerrillas, for their own survival, must avoid the populace until they believe they have proved their armed superiority over incumbent forces. Hence Debray's initial rejection of political work, including "armed propaganda," in villages; hence, too, the deep fear of betrayal, suspicion of every liaison man (peasant or guerrilla) as a potential traitor, and the three "golden rules"—constant vigilance, constant mistrust, constant mobility. (Contrast these with the famous Three Tasks of the Army, the Three Main Rules of Discipline, and Eight Points of Attention.)[5] A combination of the three views understandably produces a theory of revolutionary despair which relegates politics to a secondary position; says Debray: "The main point is that under present conditions the most important form of propaganda is military action. . . . Given the social, ideological, and psychological conditions of the peasantry in the majority of Latin American countries, given the diverse intelligence agencies at the enemy's disposal (strongly reinforced since the Cuban Revolution), an agitational group, whether armed or not, will be watched, uncovered and liquidated; in embryo if necessary" (ibid., p. 56).

Debray's arguments regarding the relationship between parties and the guerrillas are predictable. All forms of reformism have failed in South America, and any political line which "is not susceptible to expression as a precise and consistent military line cannot be considered revolutionary" (*Revolution in the Revolution?* p. 24). "Who will make the revolution in South America? Who?" asks Castro and replies: "The people, the revolutionaries, with or without a party" (ibid., p. 98). Debray charges that Communist parties in Latin America lack the tradition, courage, and leadership to think about a seizure of power. Like other legal organizations, they suffer from bureaucratization, obsessive pursuit of alliances and political bargaining, electoral maneuvers, old-style leadership, and traditional ideological reflexes. As they are constituted today, they are unfit for the "New Dialectic of Tasks."

The setting up of military, not political, *focos* is seen as decisive for the future, and this task cannot be entrusted, Debray argues at length, to a party or front which, being urban based, is neither politically nor organizationally nor morally equipped to direct the guerrillas. "In most countries where conditions for armed struggle exist it is possible to move from a military *foco* to a political *foco* but to move in the opposite direction is virtually impossible" (*Revolution in the Revolution?* p. 120). The party, then, cannot create or lead the guerrilla force. Rather, the guerrilla force under a centralized command will beget an eventual party: "The vanguard party can exist in the form of the guerrilla *foco* itself. The guerrilla force is the party in embryo" (ibid., p. 106). Debray seems very confident that the *foco* forms the natural nucleus for the development of party; his arguments are sadly reminiscent of the earnest, confident assertions and promises one heard in Ghardimou [Tunisia] and Oujda [Morocco] from officers and men of the Algerian Liberation Army.

Debray's rhapsodizing about the virtues of life in the mountain, its liberating, resuscitating effects on man—"class egoism does not long endure"; "petty-bourgeois psychology melts like snow under the summer sun"; "bureaucratic faintheartedness becomes irrelevant"; "where better than in the guerrilla army could this shedding of skin and this resurrection take place?" (*Revolution in the Revolution?* pp. 110 and passim)—is familiar; his sense of wonderment at the courage and self-sacrifice of the guerrillas is understandable. But personal virtues and even group experiences do not easily transfer to national and public institutions. And it is too sweeping to say: "When the guerrilla army assumes the prerogatives of political leadership, it is responding to its class content and anticipating tomorrow's dangers. It alone can guarantee that the people's power will not be perverted after victory" (ibid., p. 109).

A thousand or so guerrillas did not make possible Cuba's transition from liberation to socialism; the postliberation alliance with the Communists probably did. Today the specter of a stagnant, bureaucratizing Algeria under the Liberation Army haunts us. Without an operative commitment to a functioning and consistent ideology, and without institutions that would ensure a degree of adherence to the principle of accountability, even guerrilla leaders can degenerate into self-seeking politicians, or the people's army can become a self-perpetuating junta.

As a theory, *Revolution in the Revolution?* is radical but wrong. It corresponds closely to the theory of revolutionary warfare favored in Washington. It views revolutionary war, "in its formative stages," essentially in military terms. The civilian population is ignored until after a certain success has been achieved. Government's legitimacy is viewed in terms of coercion; hence military action becomes the chief instrument of subversion. The revolutionaries, considered "outsiders" by the population, tend to view the civilians as spectators who will join the winning side.

In places, the coincidence of official American opinions with Debray's formulations is startling. When W. W. Rostow made his famous statement that the guerrilla force enjoyed considerable advantage over the government because "its task is merely to destroy while the government must build and protect what it is building," those who knew something about revolutionary warfare laughed at him. Debray, to my knowledge, is the first revolutionary writer to agree with Rostow, albeit inadvertently: "The government must, since it is the government, protect everywhere the interests of the property owners; the *guerrilleros* do not have to protect anything anywhere" (*Revolution in the Revolution?* p. 75).

These similarities between a revolutionary and counterrevolutionary theory are not coincidental. They stem from the fact that both start with the same basic assumptions about the nature of guerrilla warfare. Debray's *foco*, I am afraid, is a tailor's fit for the American counterinsurgency program. Che Guevara's Bolivian campaign was an example of the pitfalls of the *foco* theory; it also proved how successful counterinsurgency can be against this kind of adventure. I should quote Debray with strong agreement: "When the list of martyrs grows long, when every act of courage is converted into martyrdom, it is because something is wrong. And it is just as much a moral duty to seek out the causes as it is to pay homage to the murdered, imprisoned comrades" (*Revolution in the Revolution?* p. 86).

When all criticisms have been made, the many virtues of *Revolution in the Revolution?* ought to be underlined. Despite its faults as a theory of revolution, it is an important book, and not only as the latest formulation of Castroism. Its most remarkable qualities—deep commitment, stirring romanticism, concern with the transformation of men into humane, poetic, heroic figures—will have a timeless appeal. As an expression of the thirst for freedom from United States domination, the search for sovereignty and social justice, it is a touchstone of Latin aspirations. Its rejection of traditional leftist parties as instruments of self-seeking politicians will appeal to the youth alienated by the sad performance of their elders, for Latin America had its share of co-optable rebels. (One is reminded that such prominent figures as Victor Haya de la Torre, A. Alberto Lleras Camargo, and Romulo Betancourt were active members of Communist and Socialist cells formed in the 1920s.) Above all, the tactical model which Debray eloquently outlines undoubtedly has a certain congruence with the psychological makeup and political culture of Latin America. One is reminded of the sacrificial heroisms of the Spanish Civil War, of bullfights and matadors. There is the stress on individuals as units of action, the passion for living heightening the fascination with death, a profound sense of loneliness, enormous courage, and unrelenting heroism. In this cultural symmetry lies perhaps the strength and popularity of *Revolution in the Revolution?* Therein, too, lies the assurance that the legend of Che Guevara will grow among the people of Latin America and take its place second only to Bolivar's.

[1967]

# 3 / COUNTERINSURGENCY

*The Nature of Counterinsurgency*

The proponents of counterinsurgency have been the chief commentators and sources of information on the theory and practice of revolutionary warfare. As a result, the biases and prejudices of incumbents are built into the structure, images, and language of contemporary Western, especially American, literature on this subject. We have come to accept ideologically contrived concepts and words as objective terms descriptive of reality. One could take innumerable examples—terrorism, subversion, pacification, urbanization, protective reaction, defensive interdiction, etc.—and analyze the realities behind these words and phrases. The term "counterinsurgency" is itself an excellent example. Like all counterrevolutionary coinages it is value-laden and misleading. In fact, counterinsurgency is not at all directed against insurgency, which is defined as "a revolt against a government, not reaching the proportions of an organized revolution; and not recognized as belligerency."[1] It would be inappropriate to describe the Vietnamese and Laotian revolutions as insurgencies or the fateful American invasion of Indochina as an exercise in counterinsurgency. In fact, the Congress and the country would be in an uproar if the government claimed that US counterinsurgency capabilities were available to its clients for putting down revolts "not reaching the proportions of an organized revolution." The opposite is true: counterinsurgency involves a multifaceted assault against organized revolutions. This euphemism for counterrevolution is a product neither of accident nor of ignorance. It serves to conceal the reality of a foreign policy dedicated to combating revolutions abroad and helps to relegate revolutionaries to the status of outlaws. The reduction of a revolution to mere insurgency also constitutes an a priori denial of its legitimacy. In this article, counterinsurgency and counterrevolution are therefore used interchangeably.

Analytically, counterinsurgency may be discussed in terms of two primary approaches—the conventional-establishment and the liberal-reformist—and two ancillary approaches—the punitive-militarist and the technological-attritive. These latter are termed ancillary because they develop logically from involvement in counterrevolution and from the interplay between conventional and liberal institutions and the individuals involved in them. These approaches, though identifiable in terms of the intensity and scope of their application at given times and in terms of the agencies and individuals who favor them, are operationally integrated in the "field."

It must be stressed that the theory and the practice of counterinsurgency, although monolithic in their goal of suppressing revolutions, reflect the pluralism of the Western societies to which most of their practitioners and all of their theoreticians belong. For example, prominent among the partisans of pacification in its purest form have been CIA, AID, State Department, and some White House officials. The chiefs of staff and senior army officers generally favor conventional deployments. The air force also wants its share of action and does offer the "mobility" so highly prized by the counterinsurgency experts and the "air support" so craved by the embattled soldiers. The navy can hardly be left out; it must perfect its amphibious capabilities and also deserves a role in "softening" the coastal areas. Furthermore, experts differ passionately on specific details ("fix" and destroy or "search" and destroy) concerning targets, areas of pacification, methods of encirclement and interdiction, techniques of cadre training, etc.

In a pluralistic, bargaining political culture there is an institutionalized compulsion for compromise. There is something for everyone within a defined boundary, and, given a consensus on broad objectives, there is bound to be give and take. The actual strategy and tactics thus reflect a compromise such that no one blueprint is applied in its original, unadulterated form. This contributes to the most fateful phenomenon of counterrevolutionary involvement. Groups and individuals continue to feel that their particular prescriptions were never administered in full dosage and at the right intervals. They evince a tendency toward self-justification, a craving for continuing and improving their blueprints of success. As severe critics of specific "mistakes," "blunders," or "miscalculations," they seldom cease to see "light at the end of the tunnel."

We might view the conventional-establishment approach as constituting the common denominator of the assumptions and objectives shared by all incumbents, viz. a negative posture toward revolutions, a conspiratorial view of their origins, managerial attitudes toward them as a problem, and a technocratic-military approach to their suppression. In strategy and tactics, the conventional-establishment approach denotes a preference for conventional ground and air operations requiring large deployments of troops, search-and-destroy "missions" (also called "mop-up operations"), the tactics of "encirclement" and "attrition," which involve, on the one hand, the establishment of large military fortifications (bases, enclaves) connected by "mobile" battalions (which in Vietnam have come to mean helicopter-borne troops and air cavalries) and, on the other hand, the massive displacement of a civilian population and the creation of free-fire zones.[2] The conventionalists also evince deep longings for set-piece battles and help multiply the political and institutional pressures toward forcing, surprising, or luring the guerrillas into conventional showdowns. The results are massive and sustained aerial bombardment (e.g., North Vietnam) or invasion of enemy "sanctuaries" across the frontiers of conflict (e.g., Cambodia and Laos) and the tactic of offering an occasional bait in the hope of luring the enemy to a concentrated attack (e.g., Dien Bien Phu, Khe Sanh).

The strength of the conventional-establishment's strategy and tactics derives from the fact that it has an enormous attraction for senior officers of conventional armed forces. This approach was first associated in Algeria with General Cherrière and in Vietnam with General Westmoreland. Being rich in tradition, it yields to multiple variations, and every strong general gets the opportunity to introduce his preferred variant in a protracted intervention. While of considerable interest to competing commanders and their cliques, these variations have little theoretical importance and no significance whatsoever for the people and culture under assault.

If the conventional-establishment attitudes constitute the lowest common denominator of counterrevolution, the liberal-reformists comprise the chief exponents of its doctrine and the most sophisticated programmers of its practice. They provide the core of the policies associated with counterinsurgency: the creation of counterguerrilla guerrillas (special forces) and the stress on irregular tactics, the unity of civilian and military roles, maximum use of mercenaries, psychological warfare, counterterror, and, above all, pacification. The term liberal-reformist reflects the expressed goals as well as the political background of individuals involved in articulating and practicing this form of counterrevolution. The rhetoric which defines its goals is reformist and liberal. Freedom, progress, development, democracy, reforms, participation, and self-determination are its favorite working words. Generally, its theorists, of whom a majority come from France and the USA, have been men of impeccable liberal credentials.

In the US, among its most prominent exponents are many of [President John F.] Kennedy's New Frontiersmen and well-known liberal university professors. In France, the liberal-reformists include such eminent politicians as Jacques Soustelle and Robert Lacoste. In the army, its exponents were reputedly the most progressive commanders who had fought in the Resistance against Nazi occupation or with the Free French Army. Humiliated by defeat in Indochina, they proceeded with determination to practice *pacification* in Algeria. Frustrated by failures there, these soldier-reformers increasingly meddled in politics. They helped destroy the Fourth Republic, rebelled against the Fifth, became accomplices of the European Ultras, whom they had once openly detested and from whom they had been promising to deliver the Algerians, founded the fascistic OAS [Organization of the Secret Army], and ended up mercilessly massacring the natives whose freedom they had claimed to protect.

The punitive-militarist style is a product of the liberal-reformist doctrine of counterinsurgency, but it invariably acquires a life of its own. It entails irregular tactics, small-unit deployment, efficiently and relentlessly executed punitive measures against civilians suspected of aiding guerrillas, systematic use of torture, murder of prisoners, and the institution of total control over the population. At the same time, the rhetoric of pacification demands that the soldiers treat the friendly and neutral population with kindness and consideration. In practice, however, distinguishing between friendly and hostile villagers is impossible. Wary soldiers in an alien environment strewn with booby traps can only perceive all civilians as being hostile, admit the fact, act accordingly, and meet their ordered or understood quota of body counts. (It should be recalled that after the massacre of My Lai [on March 16, 1968, soldiers of Charlie Company, under the command of Lieutenant William Calley, entered My Lai village in South Vietnam on a "search and destroy" mission and massacred three hundred unarmed civilians, including women, children, and old people], General Westmoreland communicated his congratulations to

Company C for its body count of 129.)[3] They make few pretenses about winning hearts and minds, although in deference to the principles of pacification, candy is sometimes distributed, music is played, and food and first aid are provided to the survivors, especially after a hard strike.

In Algeria, the punitive-militarist style was known as *style-para* in reference to the paratroopers of General Massu whose exploits included the "winning" of the hair-raising Battle of Algiers. In Vietnam, it is more generalized although it appears particularly popular with the US Special Forces and the mercenaries recruited by them, the Koreans, and the ARVN [Army of the Republic of Vietnam—the South Vietnamese regular army] ranger battalions. The main virtue of this style lies in the fact that, unlike the massive "mop-ups" and clinically impersonal bombings entailed in conventional operations, it produces somewhat personalized massacres like that of My Lai which at least give the victims no less than the killers a sense of human contact. It also produces some public understanding of the war crimes which counterrevolutionary interventions often entail.[4]

Increasing reliance on technological-attritive methods marks the shift of counterrevolutionary foreign intervention in a genocidal direction. When a revolutionary war has been definitively lost—when the moral isolation and illegitimacy of the client regime become total and perceptibly irreversible, when even a prolonged and massive foreign intervention fails to break the "enemy's" will to resist but produces widespread antiwar sentiments at home, when draftees become restive and resistant, when the protracted war becomes bad for business and begins to contribute to the dual pressures of inflation and recession—then a great power caught in counterrevolutionary operations is left with only two alternatives. One is to negotiate withdrawal as [French president Charles] de Gaulle [1945–1946; 1958–1969] did in Algeria. The other is to continue the war and subsequently to create a quasi-permanent occupation of the belligerent country, at a cost acceptable to the people at home but costly to the "insurgents" abroad. That is the choice which defines President Nixon's policy of Vietnamization. A "semantic hoax," as Senator Harold E. Hughes [Democrat, Iowa, 1969–1975] described it, Vietnamization is a euphemism for the further mechanization of the war, for the application of the doctrine of permanent counterinsurgency. It is also, as Senator [George] McGovern [Democrat, South Dakota, 1963–1981] has stated, a manipulative move to "tranquilize the conscience of America while our government wages a war by proxy" and "perpetuates a corrupt and unrepresentative government."[5]

Sir Robert Thompson, a trusted adviser of Mr. Nixon's and a renowned expert on counterinsurgency, is one of the architects of Vietnamization, which he describes as a "long-haul, low-cost" strategy. His optimistic evaluation of Vietnamization was cited in the president's policy statement as proof of its success.[6] It is worth noting a few of the considerations which went into the making of the Vietnamization policy. First, Sir Robert warns that "a greater impact is made in a democratic society by the coffins coming home, and by higher taxes"; second, that it "will certainly take ten to fifteen years" to achieve the desired goal, i.e., a politically stable, noncommunist, independent state of South Vietnam. Hence he advises that in order to maintain public acceptance of a protracted involvement, one must show some progress: "As soon as progress is visible, even though success may still be many years away, time ceases to be such an important factor. There will be few indeed who are not then prepared to take the extra time required for victory." Third, Sir Robert thinks that "there is nothing new about the horror and tragedy of the Vietnam war except that it has been exposed to the camera and brought into the sitting room." He notes that " running insurgency sores in some Latin American countries . . . have made very little impact outside the area of conflict."[7]

Making the war domestically acceptable thus involves turning it into a "forgotten war" (Laos as the model) by relegating it to the back pages of the newspapers and by keeping it a maximum distance from television cameras. It entails stimulating false illusions of progress. Above all, it demands lowering the monetary costs and American casualties. The one requires reduction in the size of the expensive American manpower deployment; the other dictates avoidance of active fighting by US ground forces. Both help to maintain the illusion of progress and to keep the public quiet. As Sir Robert says, "In this way the whole cost of the war, in every sense, could be reduced to a level which would be acceptable to the majority in the US, without proving to be an excessive drain on her manpower, money or emotions."[8]

At the same time, victory requires that the war remain costly to the enemy. Their strength must be sapped, political "infrastructure" destroyed, morale undermined, and resources and bases depleted. It should be underscored that the latter is identified by Sir Robert as being "not outside the country" and not in "jungles and swamps" but in "populated areas . . . under insurgent control" and even those "areas still ostensibly under government control."[9] He recommends a return to the techniques of counterinsurgency which he successfully practiced in Malaya and which he has been prescribing as an adviser on Vietnam for more than a decade, with the conviction, of course, that they were never fully implemented. These include: inducing the Saigon regime to act in accordance with the law, without, however, preventing it from passing emergency laws; improving civil and military administration; defining the central government's and villages' responsibilities and obligations; selecting priority areas for pacification; and mounting fix-and-destroy ("fix," not "search," insists Sir Robert) operations in the areas outside the selected "ring." Finally: "Offensive operations into contested and enemy-held areas will still be necessary, for which reason the securely held areas should be limited to allow for an adequate reserve of forces for such operations."[10] Obviously, if the policy of defeating the NLF while minimizing American costs and casualties is to succeed, then the Saigon government must progressively take over the task of governing and fighting. If the Saigon regime does not or cannot do so, then the US, if unwilling to negotiate withdrawal, has only one course of action: maximum replacement of men with machines and cost-effective offensive operations in the areas Sir Robert defines as enemy bases.

Sir Robert's and others' administrative prescriptions are irrelevant, for in a country which has been fighting a long and bitter war of national liberation, no amount of managerial manipulation by foreign forces can equip *their* native "elite" with even a semblance of legitimacy, i.e., with the title to govern. This is especially true when that elite carries the stigma of having been the historic traitor to the nation, of having actively collaborated with colonial France, and, now, of sanctioning the systematic destruction, by the succeeding foreign power, of a people and a country it claims to govern.[11] Hence, notwithstanding the counterinsurgents' recommendations and their deep faith in the power of borrowed, bureaucratic, "cost-effective innovations," Vietnamization cannot mean that the Saigon government will take over the war and become viable even in "ten to fifteen years," as Sir Robert optimistically surmised.[12]

Under the impact of the massive American military presence and bomb-induced "urbanization" (in Laos, the "strategic movement of the people"), the Saigon regime is now in a worse predicament, although a "residual" American force equipped with the will and capacity to protect it can keep the regime in power indefinitely. A third of South Vietnam's people are estimated to be refugees (so are 25 percent of the Laotians and more than a million Cambodians) due almost entirely to the "air support" provided by the US. The Senate Judiciary Subcommittee on Refugees headed by Senator Edward Kennedy [Democrat, Massachusetts, 1962–present] has reported on how the pacification agencies and the Saigon government collaborate to keep the figures down and "solve" the refugee problem by "reclassifying the refugees out of existence." The report shows how "under the banner of 'Vietnamization' a plethora of new terms and slogans have been created to describe, and hide, old problems and unchanged programs" and how the "accelerated pacification" machinery (including the computerized HES) works to create illusions of "successes" in refugee resettlement while "new refugees continue to be generated daily, and old refugees remain where they have been for the past several years."[13]

I have mentioned the refugees rather than the dead because this "urbanized" mass, though classified out of existence, is still a reality; it makes the cities as hopeless for the incumbent regime as the rural areas. Students, workers, and Buddhists have recently risked severe repression to raise their voices in opposition. Don Luce, one of the few Americans who knows the Vietnamese language and culture and who led a group of congressmen to the tiger cages of Con Son, reported in a television interview (recorded on November 12, 1970) that in the previous two months nearly 150,000 persons had been arrested and that torture is widespread. Early in December 1970, the city of Qui Nhon had an unprecedented anti-US riot and massive demonstrations which then spread to Saigon in the form of widespread sabotage. Informed sources in Paris indicate that Saigon's shrewdest politicians are quietly currying favor with the Provisional Revolutionary Government; some *attentiste* conservatives like Deputy Ngo Cong Due openly favor a provisional, coalition government of reconciliation, which was proposed in Paris by the PRG as a move toward peace.

According to the *New York Times* (July 27, 1970), the ARVN's rate of desertion was "up nearly 50 percent during the summer months of 1970" despite what officials termed the "morale building effects of recent operations in Cambodia." In Cambodia itself, two paratrooper battalions of the expeditionary force "were operating with only 65 percent of their man-power—the rest having deserted." General Do Cao Tri, commander of the III Corps area which includes Saigon and leader of the Cambodian expedition, is reported to have been less conservative with his estimates. He told newsmen in Dalat [Vietnam] that 75 percent of his soldiers desert; of the remaining 25 percent, only 10 percent wish to fight, and for every ARVN soldier killed in battle, nine desert.[14]

Meanwhile, the *New York Times* (October 19, 1970) disclosed a top-secret CIA report revealing that in response to Vietnamization the NLF [National Liberation Front of Vietnam, formed in 1960 in opposition to the South Vietnamese government] had infiltrated some thirty thousand cadres, reaching the highest levels of the Saigon government (including its secret services); that the "VC [or "Viet Cong," short for Vietnam Cong San, or Vietnamese Communist, the name by which the US and the South Vietnamese government referred to the NLF] infrastructure" remained impenetrable; and that both conditions are predicated upon the complicity of the majority of the government's civilian and defense employees. The "disclosure" may have been meant to prepare the public for more repression and purges by the Saigon regime. But its significance is clear: its foreign trustees know that the regime, isolated from the people, is also hollow and eroding from within.

Even Sir Robert is reported to have returned gloomy from his recent mission to "Macedonia," as he unblushingly calls Vietnam. ("Come with me to Macedonia," he invites his readers in the preface to *No Exit From Vietnam,* fancying his relationship to Mr. Nixon as the modern equivalent of the expert-advisers to Roman emperors.) The Phoenix *(Phung Hoang)* program has an actual score of zero: not one ranking member of the NLF is known to have been killed or captured, although this notorious "counterterror" program is believed to have terrorized, tortured, and killed several thousand "suspects." No important defector has been received by the Chieu Hoi (Open Arms) program. In effect, it is the only decent refugee resettlement program in Vietnam, for refugees with official connections generally get registered as defectors to get favorable treatment. Even the French had done better than that in Vietnam and more so in Algeria. Yet in both places they had the wisdom and decency to negotiate withdrawal.

Such being the realities of Vietnamization, the US government, intent on winning, could only mechanize the war. GIs are being replaced by airplanes, electronic devices, helicopter gunships, long-range artillery, a variety of antipersonnel weapons, massive defoliation, crop destruction, and depopulation.[15] The details of these daily crimes and the extent of the damage they do are not and may never be completely known, especially since the US government remains the primary source of information on these matters. A reading of the highly censored hearings (1969–1970) of Senator [Stuart] Symington's [Democrat, Missouri, 1953–1971] Foreign Relations Subcommittee on United States Security Agreements and Commitments Abroad gives a picture of the devastation caused by bombings in Indochina which are being carried out from American sanctuaries in Thailand, Okinawa, the Pacific Fleet, Guam, and Vietnam itself. By early 1970, there were some 3.5 million B-52 bomb craters scarring the landscape of Vietnam alone, the breeders and repositories now of germs and diseases. Occasionally, bombing statistics released by authorities and "authoritative sources" give a glimpse of its magnitude. The "mission" of bombings is not only to interdict supplies but also to destroy "personnel" (i.e., people) as [Defense Secretary Melvin] Laird admitted early in August, even in the case of Cambodia.[16] The bombing of Indochina has exceeded several times the total tonnage dropped in all of World War II. As the *New York Times* editorially commented, "the headlines gradually faded, but the air-war did not"; nor did the chemical war, nor helicopter hunting, nor the gruesome antipersonnel weapons which maim so indiscriminately and leave so many disabled to care for.

If the population is to the guerrillas what water is to fish, the ultimate weapon of degenerate but powerful incumbents is to drain the water. That is the course that Mr. Johnson embarked on; Mr. Nixon is continuing the technological-attritive approach more skillfully and perhaps more consciously than did his predecessor. The policy may not be genocidal in intent; its goal appears to be attrition. And depending on how technically the word "genocide" is interpreted, it may not be in effect if it succeeds, but it will at least yield to the US the beaten and sunken remainder of a once proud and brave people—a sort of twentieth-century Indian reservation in the heart of Asia.

In counterinsurgency, then, democratic "pluralism" is experienced by the targeted population in its corrupt, morally inverted form. In the "field," the different styles blend. The guerrillas and the masses experience all four: they are swept and bombed conventional style; punished and tortured *style-para*; quartered and controlled pacification style; and, finally, face the prospects of a "long-haul, low-cost" technological extermination. In the lexicon of counterrevolutionaries, these wars are limited only in their consequences for the intervening power. For the people and country under assault, they are total.

The attitudes and assumptions which are shared by all believers in counterinsurgency may be summarized as follows:

1. There is a negative view of revolutionary warfare as a threat. Roger Hilsman (a well-known liberal scholar, associate of President Kennedy, and past director of intelligence and research at the State Department) recalls that President Kennedy "let us all know of his interest in the subject and started us thinking about it. From the beginning of his administration the President was convinced that the *techniques* of 'revolutionary warfare' constituted a special kind of threat."[17] In an address to the National War College, Vice-President Humphrey spoke of this "bold, new form of aggression which could rank with

the discovery of gunpowder" as constituting "the major challenge to our security."[18] If guerrilla warfare is viewed as the latest enemy weapon, Vietnam is its testing ground. "If guerrilla techniques succeed in Vietnam," wrote James Reston, "nobody in Washington dare assume that the same techniques will not be applied in all communist rimlands from Korea to Iran."[19] It is this view of revolutionary warfare as a menacing technique, a weapon lethal to the interests of the US, that led counterrevolutionary scholars like W. W. Rostow to portray the invasion of Vietnam as a war to end wars. He told a University of Leeds audience that: "If we have the common will to hold together and get on with the job—the struggle in Vietnam might be the last great confrontation of the post-war era. . . . If the Cuban missile crisis was the Gettysburg of the Cold War, Vietnam could be the Wilderness; for indeed the Cold War has been a kind of global civil conflict. Vietnam could be made the closing of one chapter in modern history and the opening of another."[20]

Since American interest in revolutionary warfare began with a counterrevolutionary posture, it is natural for its politicians and establishment academicians to be attracted more to the myths and methods of those who have had to defend themselves against guerrillas than to an understanding of the causes and characteristics of such a war. Americans are therefore unable to avoid the psychological and political pitfalls of colonial powers and feudal regimes. A symptom of this negativism is that, while describing it as a "bold new form of aggression," scholarly, no less than government, publications, including the course books at Fort Bragg, generally avoid the term "revolutionary war" (except occasionally in single quotes) in favor of old terms which do not express the vital distinction between revolutionary and other types of guerrilla conflict.

For example, the term "jungle warfare" is geographically limited, while "revolutionary wars" can be fought from the Sahara to the streets of Paris. "Guerrilla war" denotes some common features of such a conflict but does not emphasize the peculiarities of its modern, revolutionary variety. For example, like revolutionary wars, partisan movements known to us from the Napoleonic wars and World War II were armed struggles led by guerrillas against a vastly superior enemy in which the overtly neutral but covertly engaged civilians provided the demographic "sea" to the guerrilla "fish." Yet the differences between these two types of warfare are significant. The partisans operated in support of conventional forces in open conflicts and expected liberation by the Allies; they operated mostly as local bands which lacked nationwide structure and centralized direction; their aims were politically and socially limited to liberation. A revolutionary guerrilla movement, on the other hand, seeks not simply to inflict military losses on the enemy but to destroy the legitimacy of its government and to establish its own legitimacy through the creation of "parallel hierarchies" and a participatory, popular movement. The Chinese, Cuban, Algerian, and Indochinese conflicts are cases in point. Tito's partisan movement acquired many characteristics of a revolutionary war, but perhaps the earliest Western example is the Irish rebellion of 1916–1922.

The negative posture precludes a correct understanding of the processes which explain, in the Third World today, the unprecedented popularity of armed revolutions and the capacity of some to expand and sustain their struggles against incredibly heavy odds. Their purpose being counterrevolutionary, the theorists and practitioners of counterinsurgency are unable to grasp or unwilling to acknowledge the illegitimacy of incumbents, the finality of broken political and social links, and the forging of new ones. Recognition of the revolutionary process, its causes, creative thrust, inherent justice, and the achievement of legitimacy by a revolutionary movement must cost the counterinsurgents their raison d'être. Understandably then, counterinsurgents concentrate on studying and imitating the "techniques" and "tactics" of organizing and conducting revolutionary warfare and betray a defective comprehension of the essence, the inner logic of revolutions. I. F. Stone has accurately described a peculiarity of the literature on counterinsurgency:

> In reading the military literature on guerrilla warfare now so fashionable at the Pentagon, one feels that these writers are like men watching a dance from outside through heavy plate glass windows. They see the motions but they can't hear the music. They put the mechanical gestures down on paper with pedantic fidelity. But what rarely come through to them are the injured racial feelings, the misery, the rankling slights, the hatred, the devotion, the inspiration and the desperation. So they do not really understand what leads men to abandon wife, children, home, career, friends; to take to the bush and live gun in hand like a hunted animal; to challenge overwhelming military odds rather than acquiesce any longer in humiliation, injustice or poverty.[21]

2. Counterinsurgents share a conspiratorial theory which views revolutionary warfare as being primarily a technical problem, i.e., a problem of plotting and subversion, on the one hand, and of intelligence and suppression, on

the other. As the chief conspiratorial group, the "Communists" are alleged to be the most likely initiators and beneficiaries of such revolutions. "Technique" is a key word in counterinsurgency. "We have a long way to go," Defense Secretary [Robert] McNamara told a congressional committee in 1963, "in devising and implementing effective counter-measures against the communist techniques. But this is a challenge we must meet if we are to defeat the communists in this kind of war. It is quite possible that in the decade of the 1960's the decisive struggle will take place in this area."[22]

Given the preoccupation with technique, conduct of counterinsurgency is viewed as largely an exercise in the strategy and tactics of pacification and warfare, i.e., in managerial and military experimentations which come to be viewed as two facets of "one war." The military advantages of guerrillas— mobility, freedom from logistical anchors, good intelligence, surprise, etc.— are studied, and countermeasures and devices are developed. Irregular terrain is considered a primary condition for guerrilla warfare, as is the complicity of a coerced population. Therefore, counterinsurgent troops are trained in jungle warfare and are taught and motivated to WHAM (Win Hearts and Minds).

This preoccupation has provided US officials their only credible (in terms of facts), though less frequently expressed, justification for the invasion of Vietnam. In 1963, General Maxwell Taylor explained to a congressional committee:

> Here we have a going laboratory where we see subversive insurgency, the Ho Chi Minh doctrine, being applied in all its forms. This has been a challenge not just for the armed services, but for several of the agencies of Government, as many of them are involved in one way or another in South Vietnam. On the military side, however, we have recognized the importance of the area as a laboratory. We have had teams out there looking at the equipment requirements of this kind of guerrilla warfare. We have rotated senior officers through there, spending several weeks just to talk to people and get the feel of the operation, so even though not regularly assigned to Vietnam, they are carrying their experience back to their own organizations.[23]

It is amazing that, in a democracy, there was no serious public or parliamentary questioning of the consequences of an army considering another country a laboratory and making a collective, psychic investment in it by rotating its senior officers. It is even more amazing that six years and at least four million casualties later, General Westmoreland could publicly declare in a civilized country that Vietnam had in fact been a valuable laboratory for testing new weapons and techniques; that the "lessons" and "devices" coming out of there are "revolutionizing" the techniques of warfare; that having inflicted in Vietnam "over two-thirds of enemy casualties," long-range artillery and air power had proved their capacity to "rain destruction anywhere on the battlefield within minutes . . . , whether friendly troops are present or not"; that with new electronic devices the enemy could be mechanically located, tracked, and targeted; and that technology would permit a "tremendous economy of man-power." The general is technically accurate; he may even be right in believing that "no more than ten years" separate us from the "automated battlefield."[24] If that is a correct prediction, American troop withdrawal may meet Sir Robert's timetable.

The trouble with the tracking, targeting, and locating devices, however, is that they are even less capable of distinguishing between civilians and combatants than are the GIs, for they cannot even distinguish between humans and animals. Such, for example, is the defect with the most favorite recent devices of counterinsurgency—the people sniffers. A *New York Times* article (May 28, 1967) notes: "that degree of exactitude would be welcome, but that is not the way the war is fought today. War Zone C and large areas of South Vietnam have been designated as free bombing zones. Anything that moves there is regarded as fair game. Previous high readings on the 'people sniffers' have brought B-52 raids from Guam." Some pacification purists disapprove of such weapons and their use. By so doing they only absolve themselves of responsibility in crimes of war, for the technological-attritive approach is the logical outgrowth of the interaction between counterinsurgency and technology. When a technologically superior country becomes committed to developing techniques against a people's war, it must end up producing and using weapons of mass murder. Given the frustrations of a protracted war, given also the imperative of avoiding American casualties and the unwillingness of conscripted soldiers to fight for an unpopular regime, the distance between the Marine CAPS (Combined Action Platoons) and people sniffers was bound to be bridged by B-52s and free-fire zones.

The conspiratorial theory provides the needed rationale and justification for counterinsurgency and foreign interventions. The French theorists were notorious for ascribing all "insurgencies" to Communism. In their view, Algeria's FLN was a puppet alternately of Moscow, Peking, and Cairo, just as their

American colleagues view the NLF as a puppet of North Vietnam and/or China. Even Sir Robert Thompson, the shrewdest and by popular acclaim the most cogent exponent of counterinsurgency, begins his first book with a discussion of Communism, which, according to him, "was no real threat to *the security of the colonial governments or the well-being of the peoples of Southeast Asia*" until after World War II.[25] It is worth noting that in pairing the security of a foreign presence with the welfare of the natives, Sir Robert is not unique; his French and American counterparts share this propensity. Nor is the habit of viewing anticolonial and radical nationalist movements as facets, or at least the dupes, of the international communist conspiracy uncommon, even among certified "anticolonialist" American liberals.[26] The association of guerrilla warfare and radical nationalism with Communism helps justify US involvement in a wide range of counterrevolutionary operations from Ethiopia to Uruguay (the former against non-Marxist Eritrean nationalists, the latter against the Tupamaros, a group of anti–Communist Party, unorthodox radicals).

The insistence upon viewing revolutions in conspiratorial terms also permits a grossly distorted interpretation of the revolutionary process. For example, Sir Robert Thompson believes that the start and timing of an insurgency depends on an "order from Moscow." He notes that in liberated areas insurgents are "careful to reduce taxes on land and crops well below the government level or even to remit them for a period." "This," he explains, "they can afford to do, having no overhead, and still not lack for money."[27] The absence of overheads is not explained, and his suggestion that the Malayan Races Liberation Army and the NLF (Vietnam) are financially better off than their British and American opponents would be hilarious if it were not so cruel.

3. A logical extension of the conspiratorial theory is the belief, held with particular tenacity by counterrevolutionary army officers, that any revolutionary movement is inspired, directed, and controlled from abroad. The sanctuary—from which guerrillas can smuggle supplies and in which they can train their troops—is considered the primary factor in their success. In a widely acclaimed speech in 1961, W. W. Rostow, special assistant to President Kennedy, stated that "we are determined to help destroy this international disease, that is, guerrilla war designed, initiated, supplied, and led from outside an independent nation."[28] Indeed, so strong was the belief in the external origins of guerrillas that Washington promoted plans for the "offensive use of guerrillas" against undesirable regimes. Their performance in the Bay of Pigs and inside North Vietnam does not appear to have discouraged the enthusiasts.[29]

The importance of an active sanctuary should not be underestimated, particularly in cases when a great power intervenes with its full might. However, it is not essential to success. In Cuba, Yugoslavia, and China, the revolutionaries did not have active sanctuaries. In Burma, and to a lesser extent in Greece, sanctuaries proved of limited value. Neither the extremely effective Morice Line in Algeria, nor the Lattre Line around the Red River Delta, nor the armored Ping-Han Japanese railroad in North China had much effect on the outcome of each war. Politically and militarily, revolutionary guerrillas are a self-sustaining group who make a fetish of self-reliance and can go on fighting indefinitely even if infiltration from across the border stops. There is overwhelming evidence that prior to massive US escalation of the war, which necessitated the augmentation of Northern aid, the NLF was entirely self-sufficient in South Vietnam and that the bulk of its arms were captured or bought from Saigon. John Mecklin, a former US senior diplomat in Saigon, put it quite succinctly when he stated that the interdiction of Northern supplies to South Vietnam would weaken the Vietcong "probably not much more than the efficiency of the Pentagon would be reduced if the air-conditioning were shut off."[30]

The incumbent or occupying army's pressure for conventional attack on an external sanctuary, however, is a good indicator that the war has been lost on home grounds. In revolutionary warfare, professional armies trained for conventional combat follow a vicious logic of escalation which derives from acute frustration over an elusive war that puts in question not only their effectiveness but the very validity of their training and organization as well. Moreover, the morale of professional soldiers cannot be maintained if they know they are fighting a popular revolution; hence the compulsion to believe that behind the popular behavior lies the terror of an army trained, equipped, and directed by a foreign power and the wish to draw the enemy into open battles. (Military officers often attest that they subject civilians to artillery fire and air raids in the hope that, deprived of civilian cover, the guerrillas would be forced into open battles.) Since reprisals against the population fail to produce the desired result, carrying the war to a sovereign nation becomes the most compelling and indeed the only road to a conventional showdown with the enemy. In Algeria, this demand led to French participation in the invasion of Suez, then to a single bombing raid of the Tunisian border town of Sakiet Sidi Youssef, which produced considerable international protest, including that of John F. Kennedy. Had the French government succumbed to the pressures of its army, France would have been the first power to violate the international practice of respecting the rights of sanctuary—a principle that was observed in Korea, Greece, Cyprus, and Malaya. We know what the US might do if the Vietnamese were to bomb its sanctuaries in Thailand or the Pacific Ocean. But I wonder what position it will take as a major power when Portugal, Rhodesia, and South Africa follow its example and invade the African "sanctuaries" of their opponents? When practiced by a superpower, counterinsurgency involves the progressive breaking of the few rules which help keep potentially conflagrating conflicts within national boundaries.

4. The revolutionary movement is believed to enjoy considerable advantage because, in the words of W. W. Rostow, "its task is merely to destroy while the government must build and protect what it is building."[31] Whether seriously held or consciously contrived, this view contradicts the findings of those who have studied and observed these movements. Given the inevitable, and generally vast, disparity of military strength between the guerrillas and the government, the success of a revolutionary movement depends on the covert and sustained support of a substantial portion of the population.

A revolutionary movement capable of eliciting such support must bring an ideological thrust, organizational form, and programmatic content into the amorphous revolutionary situation. It must demonstrate, in practice, that there are alternative structures and arrangements which approximate the popular yearning for a just, communal, and participatory system. A revolutionary guerrilla movement whose organization, leaders, and policies do not reflect the promises of the revolution (particularly in the base areas) is not likely to receive the sustained mass support necessary for protracted struggle. Achieving moral isolation of the enemy and legitimacy for the revolution requires not only the severance of the old but also the forging of new political and social links.

Once a revolutionary movement enters the guerrilla phase, its central objective is not simply to achieve the moral isolation of the enemy but also to confirm, perpetuate, and institutionalize it by providing an alternative to the discredited regime through the creation of "parallel hierarchies." The major task of the movement, then, is not to outfight but to outlegitimize and outadminister the government. It must institute a measure of land reforms, reduce rents, equalize wages, and build an administrative structure to collect taxes, provide some education and social welfare, and maintain a modicum of economic activity. A revolutionary guerrilla movement which does not have these constructive concerns and structures to fulfill its obligations to the populace would degenerate into banditry. Even in clandestineness, the parallel government must prove its efficacy and maintain a measure of accountability to the population. These are not easy tasks. It would be a rare revolutionary war indeed in which the government's destruction of civilian population and property does not surpass, by a wide margin, the losses caused by the guerrillas' selective terror and sabotage.

5. The liberal-reformist theorists of pacification bring to the doctrine of counterinsurgency a certain comprehension of the interdependence of political, military, and psychological factors in revolutionary warfare. They postulate that, although guerrilla wars result from conspiracy and are waged by remote control, the cooperation or at least the neutrality of a passive population is essential to their survival and effectiveness. They recognize that politics play the dominant role in such conflicts and that, for revolutionaries, civilians are the first and remain the primary object of attention. They admit the central importance of "ideology" and the existence of a "cause" around which the masses could be mobilized and allow that the presence of acute economic and social grievances is causally linked with popular support for revolutionaries.

These theorists draw heavily on what they construe to be the revolutionary model. They search for a cause to match the enemy's. A counterideology is sought to compete with the revolutionary one. Strategic hamlets are the intended equals of popular base areas. Psychological warfare counters revolutionary political work. Pacification teams duplicate the revolutionary cadres. Reeducation centers seek to reverse the guerrillas' commitment. The doctrine suffers from serious flaws, however. These result from its colonial antecedents, bureaucratic bias, and operational preoccupations. Their limited insight into the revolutionary process is dissipated by their obsession with mechanisms of control and by their continued focus on coercion as a means of obtaining popular support.

Since classical liberalism provides little justification for counterrevolutionary involvements abroad, pacification theorists seek it in related Western traditions. This invariably entails a revival of the colonial and conservative ethos of the nation. They derive inspiration from colonial history and learn from its example. The French theorists, much like their American colleagues, emphasize that "pacification" is part of the Western tradition, that conventional warfare gained ascendancy only during the two world wars, and that it was again being superseded by "limited," unconventional conflicts. In their search for Western models and cultural continuity, the French theorists of *La*

*Guerre Revolutionnaire* invoked the memories of pacification in the heyday of colonialism. They frequently cited examples and works of the colonizers of North Africa—General [Thomas Robert] Bugeaud [1784–1849], Marshal [Louis Hubert] Lyautey [1854–1934], and Galiani. The latter's doctrine on the identity of civilian and military authority, the role of *officier-administrateur* and *officier-educateur* was extolled; their methods were emulated.[32]

In the US, the experiences with the Indians and other colonial exploits provide the source of inspiration. "It is ironic that we Americans have to learn this military lesson again in the twentieth century," wrote Roger Hilsman. After reminding his audience of American experiences in irregular warfare, in "Indian fighting," he invokes the memory of "one of the most successful counter-guerrilla campaigns in history," during the US colonization of the Philippines. Mr. Hilsman goes on to give some gory details and to draw some "fundamental lessons" from defeating the "extremists" and "bands of religious fanatics" who were vile enough to resist foreign occupation. The lessons include: (a) maximum use of native mercenaries as demonstrated by the "fabulous exploits" of the "famed Philippine constabulary"; (b) leadership role for Americans—"over each group [of native recruits] we put a trained American officer—a bold and determined leader" (the official euphemism is "advisory role"); (c) adoption of "Indian fighting" tactics of surprise and nighttime attacks—"the solution is to adopt the same weapons to fight him."[33] Mr. Hilsman does not mention that the "successful" Philippine campaign was "the bloodiest colonial war (in proportion to population) ever fought by a white power in Asia; it cost the lives of 300,000 Filipinos."[34]

Despite their rhetoric, which stresses the primacy of politics and calls peaceful revolution their goal, the liberal-reformists treat counterinsurgency essentially as an administrative problem subject to managerial and technical solutions. A vulgar symptom of this phenomenon is that, among the less sophisticated, second-rate counterinsurgency experts, managerial "innovations" become a fetish. Even changes in the size and appellation of platoons and pacification teams are viewed as innovations and improvements. Periodic changes in the abbreviations of essentially unchanged, artificial bureaucratic creations (RD, RF, PSDF, APT, APC, and so on) give the "pacifiers" a sense of motion, which they equate with progress.[35] Ambassador Bunker has announced that CORDS (previously OCO and USOM) is now to be called CD and LDP (Community Defense and Local Development Plan).[36]

Even Sir Robert Thompson, who evinces a keen understanding of some aspects of revolutionary warfare, has a fundamentally bureaucratic view of the problem. "The bias of this book," he says in the introduction of his highly acclaimed first work, "is heavily weighted on the administrative and other aspects of an insurgency."[37] The promise is kept. He offers a detailed and technically impeccable critique of the weaknesses and failings of counterinsurgency in Vietnam—cabinet-style government is lacking, the country is divided into too many provinces, hamlets are too small to be viable administrative units, the army has become larger than the police, security forces are fragmented, and strategic hamlets are not carefully planned and executed. Sir Robert's criticism is correct, but it is irrelevant, for no amount of bureaucratic wisdom could win the war in Vietnam. The relevant analysis would be concerned with the actual or potential legitimacy of the local as well as national authority represented by the Saigon regime and with an honest appraisal of the causes and character of the linkages between the revolutionary movement and the Vietnamese masses. But the posture of counterinsurgency as well as the colonial and bureaucratic mentality precludes objectivity as well as the full perception of reality on these questions.

As noted earlier, revolutionary warfare demands the development of new styles and institutions before the attainment of power. In order to elicit voluntary and maximum participation by the people under conditions of extreme stress, the revolutionary leaders and cadres must form organic ties with them. Revolutionary style and institutions are most successful when they are qualitatively different from the existing ones and, at the same time, appeal to the deepest and most natural yearnings of the masses. Revolutionary behavior therefore defies conventional styles and expectations. In revolutions, life begins to manifest itself in forms which are incomprehensible to bureaucrats and social engineers. Wolin and Schaar's analysis of the "educational bureaucracy" applies admirably to the counterinsurgency experts: "The bureaucratic search for 'understanding' does not begin in wonder, but in the reduction of the world to the ordinary and manageable. In order to deal with the world in the cognitive mode, the world must first be approached as an exercise in 'problem-solving.'" Finding the solution implies devising the right techniques, hence "reality is parsed into an ensemble of discrete though related parts, and each part is assigned to the expert specially assigned to deal with that part."[38]

Examples of the "reduction of the world to the ordinary and manageable" abound in the literature of counterrevolution. Only one should suffice: Professor Ithiel de Sola Pool rules out as "not acceptable . . . the inclusion of the Vietcong in a coalition government or even the persistence of the Vietcong as a legal organization in South Vietnam." This yields him a problem: "the Vietcong is too strong to be simply beaten or suppressed." Whereupon cognitive dissonance theory suggests the solution: "discontented leadership" has "the potential for making a total break when the going gets too rough." The latter having been achieved by American firepower, the Vietcong need "a political rationalization for changing sides." Pacification must address itself to this task. The Vietcong's "image of reality" and "naive ideology" which regard the Saigon government as consisting of America's puppets and the peasants' exploiters must be replaced by a more realistic view. Toward this end, reforms should be introduced, and the deserting Vietcong cadres should be given the opportunity to serve the government.[39] Professor Pool assumes that being bureaucrats on the "make," they will accept the opportunity to join the government. Dr. Pool is not a novice in political analysis; he is chairman of the political science department at MIT. Nor is he a stranger to Vietnam; over the years, he has been conducting research there for the Pentagon. Yet this is how he understands the dedication and motivation of the men who have successfully resisted, for more than two bloody decades, the fully employed might of one great power and one superpower. In counterrevolution, political analysis surrenders to the pathology of bureaucratic perception.

Students of French counterinsurgency have noted that the vast bibliography of *La Guerre Revolutionnaire* theorists contained no work on the ideology of the Algerian FLN. This observation is equally true of Vietnam, although Douglas Pike has seemingly devoted his attention to the organization and ideology of the NLF.[40] In fact, so pervasive has been the counterrevolutionary ethos of contemporary social science in the US that the lack of attention to revolutionary ideology is generally true of contemporary liberal scholarship, i.e., if one understands ideology as the value commitment of a people, rather than as an administrative weapon. Richard Pfeffer has pointed out in connection with China studies "the tendency to comprehend revolutions largely in terms of techniques of manipulation and control; and its corollary, the tendency to ignore, devalue, or treat primarily as a component of administration the force of revolutionary spirit, class struggle, and commitment. Missing in liberal scholarship's examination of revolution (and counterrevolution) has been the appreciation of the intense value commitment to radical change in a particular direction—just any direction will not do—held by those in revolt."[41]

Similarly, while the counterrevolutionaries display deep interest in revolutionary programs and organization, they perceive these as being motivated opportunistically and instrumentally. For example, land reform by revolutionaries is viewed as an opportunistic instrument for establishing control in the countryside, not as the positive outcome of the complex interaction between the revolutionary movement and the masses, nor the result of strongly held convictions or deeply felt needs. The US government's most renowned expert on Vietnam writes of the NLF land reform: "In many cases this amounted to a virtual bribe; the rural Vietnamese was offered the thing he wanted above all else: Land."[42] He does not inform us why the GVN [Government of the Republic of Vietnam], or South Vietnam-US has been unwilling or unable to offer a similar "bribe," nor what happens to the peasant's land when government control is reestablished in a village. He also does not tell us why the US, with its enormous resources, has failed in competing with the VC to buy off the peasants.

It is only natural that their own opportunism and preoccupation with stability and control should lead these theorists to at first *qualify*, then *distort*, and finally *abandon* their central, albeit only, positive theme—that revolutionary warfare has its basis in the existence of acute grievances and that the achievement of social, economic, and political progress will reduce the chances of its outbreak and/or success. The qualification begins with the argument that although "modernization" is essential in the "long run," social and economic inequities and injustices pose no real threat to stability until they are exploited by conspirators. The essential requirements of stability are therefore efficient administration and the policing of the population. Hence reforms are seen only as useful auxiliaries to "pacification." Roger Hilsman concludes: "To summarize my feeling on popularity [of government], reform, and modernization: (1) they are important ingredients but are not the determinants of events; (2) their role must be measured more in terms of their contribution to physical security than we generally realize."[43]

As the dialectic of pacification approaches its denouement, these qualifications provide the bases for the emergence of a counterrevolutionary "revisionism"—totalitarian in precept, genocidal in effect. It postulates that the population's behavior, not its attitude, the revolutionary infrastructure's destruction, not the establishment of a government's popularity, are the operative factors in defeating "insurgency."[44]

The distortion develops, among other reasons, from continued focus on "coercion" and "terror" as the basis of mass support for guerrillas. At their best, counterinsurgency experts display an obvious contradiction between their rhetoric and their perception of reality. Sir Robert informs us that the "Communists are normally careful, however, not to murder a popular person before he has been discredited . . . are careful not to undertake general terror against the population as a whole. . . . Terror is more effective when selective. This allows the Communist behavior toward the people as a whole to be good and strict discipline is used to enforce it." Yet he describes this behavior as a "policy of wholesale murder . . . designed to keep the local population completely cowed."[45]

At their worst, some experts, among whom military men predominate, ascribe all the advantages of guerrillas to a "reign of terror." But the most pathetic are those who appear incapable of relating their facts to their interpretation. For example, Mr. Pike presents an impressive amount of evidence which illustrates that, except in the rarest instances, the NLF's use of sabotage and assassination is sociologically selective, politically judicious, and psychologically liberating. Yet his conclusions stand out in glaring opposition to his facts. One is struck by the schizophrenic quality of his study.

It is probably impossible for counterrevolutionaries to perceive the truth, for doing so entails admitting a revolution's legitimacy and their own side's lack of it. Even Sir Robert's statement contains more than mere rhetorical exaggeration. He views effective coercion of the people as the main purpose of "selective terror." These attitudes provide the justification for a government's "counterterror" which begins with "selective" reprisals only to escalate into massive and indiscriminate violence.

The complex reality behind "terror" is contrary to these views. By reason of its clandestineness and dependence on the masses for secrecy and information, the guerrilla movement cannot compete with the coercive ability of the legal government or the occupying power. Highly committed but covert civilian support cannot be obtained at gunpoint.

Given their low estimate of the masses, incumbents belatedly discover that their "counterterror" produces results quite opposite of those expected or desired. This realization increases their frustration and feeling of moral isolation.

Instead of providing a basis for correction, this belated and hazy perception of reality only augments their desperation and leads to incredible acts of inversion. Thus the bombing and burning of villages are often justified on the ground that the affected villagers will blame the Vietcong for "exposing" them to government reprisals; it is believed that the enemy thus loses popular support.

Since they are interested only in operational payoffs, the counterinsurgents' investigation into revolutionary theory and practice tends to be selective, superficial, and systems-oriented. For example, the military writings of Mao Tse-tung are reproduced and cited out of their political context, their specific, local character is ignored, and Mao is presented as a system builder rather than the leader of a historical revolution.[46] The "systems" orientation, as well as the conspiratorial view, produces a bias in favor of seeking similarities among revolutions. Hence the fact that, despite many similarities, the Chinese, Vietnamese, Algerians, and Cubans fought very different wars and owed little to Mao's "doctrine" is often ignored. Yet the same theorists rarely acknowledge the fact that the similarities among those revolutions result more from common conditions (e.g., Japanese, French, and American occupation) than a common doctrine or source of conspiracy.

The counterrevolutionary theorists are ultimately concerned with order more than participation, control more than consent of the governed, obedience more than title to authority, stability more than change. To them, the people are objects of policy, a means rather than an end, a manipulable, malleable mass whose behavior toward the government is ultimately more important than are their feelings and attitudes. It is only natural that counterrevolutionary theorists should dissipate their limited insight into revolutionary warfare as they focus on the links between the people and the revolutionary cadres. They conclude that the effectiveness and strength of revolutionaries rest in their ability to manipulate ("techniques of mass deception") and coerce the masses ("terror") and in their ruthless organizational skills ("infrastructure"). As a result, their prescriptions reveal considerable technical expertise, an obsession with controlling and manipulating the masses (strategic hamlets, Psy-Warfare), and an oblique if not altogether distorted view of the needs and demands of the people. Their indebtedness to what they construe to be the insurgent model is unmistakable, but their understanding of it remains crooked. The "reflection in the mirror is sharp," wrote Peter Paret of the French counterrevolutionary doctrine in Algeria, "while the thing reflected remains shadowy."[47] And so we return to Stone's classic description of these men "watching a dance from outside through heavy plate glass windows. They see the motions but they can't hear the music."

In practice the liberal-reformists seek to wage counterrevolutionary campaigns by adopting the organizing principles, "attitudes," and "behavior" of the revolutionaries. Sir Robert calls it the "Same Element Theory of Guerrilla Warfare." He advises engaging guerrillas "in their own element" by inserting government forces "into the same element as the insurgent forces to which they are opposed." A fierce dog cannot beat a tomcat in an alley, for the latter will "climb up the tree and leave the dog to chase female cats." The answer, says Sir Robert, is to use instead a fiercer tomcat; "the two cannot fail to meet because they are both in exactly the same element and have exactly the same purpose in life. The weaker will be eliminated."[48]

Sir Robert presupposes the incumbent government's legitimacy, justice, and willingness to accomplish the transformation of society. Without such an assumption, it would surely be impossible to assign to counterinsurgent forces "exactly the same purpose in life" as that of the revolutionaries or to expect that the population at large will provide the demographic sea to the counter-guerrilla fish. Yet barring a negotiated or unilateral abdication and withdrawal (the latter in the case of a foreign power), incumbents are by definition incapable of seriously seeking the removal of the causes upon which a successful revolution may be based. France, the USA, and their local collaborators could not credibly claim national liberation to be their goals in Algeria and Vietnam. Algerian *colons* and Vietnamese landlords who formed the backbone of incumbency could not be serious about instituting meaningful land reforms.

Lacking genuine revolutionary, even reformist, commitment, unable or unwilling to acknowledge the real aspirations of the people, the counterrevolutionary effort misses the heart of the matter. Hence they progressively give up on winning the hearts and concentrate instead on conquering the minds ("it's the minds that matter," says Sir Robert) and destroying bodies. Even Sir Robert, now retired from a relatively civilized colonial civil service and only a part-time missionary to "Macedonia," has been unable in his most recent book to escape the vicious logic of protracted counterinsurgency. Others, being less civil and more service-minded, may be even less fortunate, for, unlike Sir Robert, they do not feebly condemn or even acknowledge the GVN-US practices of "torture and the shooting of prisoners" and of using weapons of "mass destruction . . . in inhabited areas."[49] It is a nemesis of the liberal-reformist approach that it breeds among its believers and practitioners a contempt for the very liberal values and democratic institutions which they claim to represent. A closer look at the paradigm of counterrevolutionary practice in Algeria and Vietnam would lead us to the conclusion that the failure to transform the "fierce dog" into a "tomcat" produces a frustrated animal endowed with neofascist attributes and genocidal tendencies.

In Vietnam, more than in Algeria, the doctrine of counterinsurgency has had its full play. In both countries, its inner logic and corrupt and destructive nature was fully exposed to the world, stripped of the liberal, reformist pretenses of its practitioners. Yet there might be a fateful difference between Algeria and Vietnam. The former marked the end of France's involvement in counterinsurgency; its exponents ended up in prison or oblivion. The latter appears to have been a testing ground and training area rather than the terminal point for American counterrevolution. Its practitioners attend conferences and join public forums to discuss the "lessons" of Vietnam. There is little reason to hope that the US will soon end its policy of military support and interventions in behalf of the status quo in Asia and Latin America. Its officials are known to count among the benefits of the Vietnam war the unusual opportunity to develop and test new weapons for "irregular" warfare; a new generation of officers and men has gained combat experience in guerrilla warfare in unfamiliar terrain; lessons learned in Vietnam have led to improved techniques of pacification in the client states of Asia and Latin America. Developments in Indonesia, Thailand, Guatemala, and, above all, in Laos and Cambodia, are indications that the "lessons" of Vietnam have reinforced the most barbaric and destructive components of counterinsurgency. The technological-attritive approach is now likely to be practiced in its latest, revised form, which stresses the establishment of totalitarian controls over the population, massive displacement and dispossession of the peasants, and rapid and ruthless reprisals with maximum reliance on technology—bombings, napalm, and defoliation—rather than troops.

At a conference on violence and social change, organized by the Adlai Stevenson Institute in the summer of 1969, Robert W. Komer, former ambassador in charge of the American Pacification Program in Vietnam, explained that Vietnam had proved the inefficacy of "gradual escalation" which permitted the "guerrillas to make adjustments" and withstand allied pressure. Hence the "lesson" was to escalate ruthlessly and rapidly; "snow them under," he said. It is a measure of the helplessness of humanity rather than of freedom in

America that in my concern for the survival of the Indochinese people and culture I should have to share public platforms with men who, in the opinion of qualified persons, are at least deserving of trial as criminals of war.

*Conclusion.* There are many ways in which the practice of counterinsurgency erodes the democratic processes and institutions of metropolitan countries. The fall of the Fourth [French] Republic, the French army officers' involvement in the clandestine OAS, and their open rebellion in 1962 are examples for Americans to ponder. The pursuit of a counterrevolutionary foreign policy undermines a democracy in many ways. It enhances the power of the secret services of government over which parliamentary institutions can exercise little or no control and whose activities public organs (press, political parties, etc.) are normally unable to report and censure. The expanded roles of the CIA and of the armed forces' special branches are examples. As their activities and influence increase, such agencies not only circumvent representative institutions but even begin to infiltrate and corrupt civilian life. The CIA's clandestine use of the National Students Association and of several universities is a case in point.

In order to overcome the checks of parliamentary institutions and public opinion, a government involved in counterinsurgency seeks ways to reduce its accountability to representative bodies and to bypass pressures of public opinion. Expansion of the role of the secret services is only one of many ways in which this is done. Another favorite ploy is to employ puppet armies and experts to subvert foreign governments and fight wars by proxy. This is how Mr. E. L. Katzenbach stated the proposition in an anthology which received the approbation of President Kennedy: "We need not only troops which can strike on the peripheries of the free world, but also troops which can be sent not merely to fight but also to maintain order. *We need not only useful troops but usable troops—that is to say, troops which are politically expendable,* the kind of troops who can do the job as it is needed without too great a political outcry in a nation like our own which so abhors war."[50]

The emphasis on "usable troops" led the French to rely heavily not only on special units of enlisted men (e.g., the parachutists) and on African regiments but also, and increasingly, on the mercenary Foreign Legion units, which were largely composed of Germans. The US, in addition to providing armaments, training, and "advisers" to counterrevolutionary clients, raises private armies like that of the Cuban exiles who invaded Cuba or the Guatemalan rightists who have in recent years terrorized the peasants. In their Special Warfare units, they have also been recruiting Central and Eastern European exiles. A counterrevolutionary policy abroad can only reinforce reactionary trends within a society. It cuts a foreign power off from progressive forces and influences abroad, locks it in rigid alliances with reactionary elements, and encourages the rise and recruitment in the government of ultra-conservative and fascist elements.

Failure to defeat revolutionaries in protracted war alienates participants in counterinsurgency against the democratic values and institutions of their own country. The war is eventually seen as being lost at home rather than in the field; dissent and divisions at home contrast with the enviable solidarity and dedication of the enemy; and democratic institutions increasingly appear as unworkable in revolutionary settings. The "powerlessness" of the "democratic ideology" was the common complaint among the supporters of counterinsurgency in France. In America, too, it is becoming a familiar theme, in scholarly analyses no less than political pronouncements. One frequently sees statements similar to the following by Professor Ithiel de Sola Pool: "The agonizing political lesson that racks this country is that there has been a failure of our own political system. The intensity of dissent, the lack of public understanding of our national policy, and the divisions that rack American society today have thrown into some question the stability of government in the United States, the capacity of our system to govern effectively, the basic commitment of the American people to the payment of costs of our national goals. These are failings of which we usually accuse the Vietnamese, but the criticism is more fairly addressed against ourselves."[51]

Disaffection from the existing system occurs also among the opponents of counterrevolutionary war since their protests produce no result and new elections, while producing new promises, fail to yield a new policy. The divisions and disillusionments that follow involvement in counterrevolution ultimately reduce the legitimacy of existing institutions, inspire opposition to or contempt for them, and weaken the will to resist their corruption or destruction.

Above all, involvement in counterinsurgency politicizes the military and encourages its intrusion into civilian life. In France, it produced, at first, deep extraconstitutional involvement by the military in the political affairs of the country and finally a rebellion. Training and participation in counterinsurgency necessarily involve emphasis on the identity and interrelatedness of civilian and military tasks and authority. It is not realistic to expect military men who are trained to be "soldiers–political workers" to remain apolitical at home. The maintenance of a double standard for the army's role abroad and at home becomes especially difficult when the war is seen as being lost at home. The determination to equip the natives with the "will to fight" transfers eventually to the metropolitan country when the "will" of the people "at home" appears to be sagging. The crusade abroad may find expressions at home when the society is viewed as needing moral or political regeneration.

The counterrevolutionary chickens, therefore, have a tendency to return home to roost. Whether the "homecoming" is complete or partial depends on the strains and stresses of involvements abroad and a government's ability to extricate itself from the war in good time. The Fourth Republic survived the first Indochinese war but collapsed during the Algerian. It is impossible to tell how many more Vietnams the American republic can sustain. There is, however, considerable evidence that the forces of law and order, including the army and several local police departments, are applying the theories of pacification and counterguerrilla warfare to the problems at home. In recent years, the army and Marine Corps have been engaged in research (and presumably training) in "urban-guerrilla warfare." In 1968, a Directorate of Civil Disturbances was established in the Department of the Army, and the Pentagon now houses a Situation Room for domestic disturbances.

Less easy to identify but more pervasive are the influences which the climate created by involvement in counterinsurgency has on the attitudes toward, and styles of dealing with, political problems at home. The treatment, in recent years, of dissenters in America is probably not unrelated to the war in Vietnam. Official violence against demonstrators in Chicago during the 1968 Democratic Party convention is one example. Most recently, during the demonstrations for Peoples' Park in Berkeley, helicopters were used to spray the demonstrators with a variety of gas (CS) which is widely used in Vietnam but which is outlawed by the Geneva Conventions. The commander is reported to have regretted the "discomfort and inconvenience to innocent bystanders," adding that "it is an inescapable by-product of combating terrorists, anarchists, and hard core militants on the streets and on the campus."[52] Alameda County's Sheriff Madigan explained that "we have a bunch of young deputies back from Vietnam who tend to treat prisoners like Vietcong."[53] One can only hope that this does not constitute a preview of things to come.

[1971]

# 4 / EPILOGUE
The Lessons of Vietnam

Professor Huntington's presentations are a mixed bag of welfare imperialism and relentless optimism.[1] They reflect that strange compound of assumptions and attitudes which characterizes American policy in the Third World and which invokes among those of us from the Third World feelings of bewilderment and fear. The policy makers in Washington will be pleased by his earlier assertion that Vietnam may not after all be regarded as a failure when there is a "reckoning of the benefits of the intervention." The worried doubters, however, are assured that the uniqueness of Vietnam makes unlikely a duplication of the Vietnamese situation. The acknowledgment of the risks of historical analogies should please the modernistic social scientists who object to this form of analysis. Yet the more traditional among us should have no great cause for complaint after the prescience of a prophetic cycle theorist has been praised. The invocation of the Klingberg cycle must gratify the isolationists and the pacifists with the knowledge that America has reached the end of its twenty-seven-year period of "extroversion." But the Cold War liberals ought to be soothed by the intimation that while America may have to eschew military involvements of Vietnamese proportions, it cannot disengage from its responsibilities to the underdeveloped. The hawks, of course, can look forward to the next cycle of extroversion, sometime after 1984. Finally, those most vociferous of all Americans—the sociologists and political scientists—must rejoice over the promise of their promotion to an unquestionably lucrative and highly challenging role as engineers and architects of political ideologies, parties, and participation—modern-day philosopher-kings engaged and anointed by a super CIA. Only the New Left radicals may find it difficult going, unless, of course, they derive a vicarious satisfaction from the speculation that in the event of a fourth major military involvement (the earlier three being World War II, Korea, and Vietnam) the "constitutional structure of the Republic could well be shaken."

Professor Huntington's remarks, in an abstract sense, are an excellent product of the American pluralistic, bargaining political culture. There is something for everyone within a defined boundary, and there is room for orderly settlement of differences provided there is a consensus on broad goals. Yet precisely for the reasons of its cultural symmetry, it fails as an analysis for underdeveloped countries which are still torn by cleavages on goals and where antagonistic interests and values dominate social, political, and economic realities.

The phased modernization of West European countries, the United States, and even Japan enjoyed the luxuries of time, superior psychological, economic, and cultural resources, plus the opportunity of channeling to the colonies and the expanding frontier the tensions and ambitions produced by technology and social change. Yet they had their share of excesses, civil wars, revolutions, disorders, and ideological aberration. Today, the Third World countries must undergo a triple transformation—social, economic, and political—simultaneously, in telescoped time and under the multiple pressures of colonial heritage and growing population. In the circumstances, our relative calm should surprise observers. We may hope to avoid the extremes of excesses—regression into colonial, racist, fascist, or Stalinist aberrations. Yet we shall inevitably experience conflicts and disorders in the process of reformulating our values and reconstructing our societies. If a superpower enters our world committed obsessively to orderly change and with an interest in maintaining stable clients, it will necessarily distort our development, sharpen our conflicts, and will also render itself vulnerable to the perpetual temptation of intervening militarily on behalf of its losing protégés.

Our formal independence has given us, at best, an unenviable position as pawns in the game of high politics. That is why we react in fear when one superpower serves notice on a country, as America has done in Vietnam, that it will cajole, coerce, and finally conquer a people that would not conform to its inverted image of freedom and democracy and another great power insists, in the name of justice, on subverting a people driven by want and search for dignity, so that the attainment of justice becomes an excuse for the strangling of human freedom. Vietnam is important to us only because it has dramatized our agony and exacerbated our fears. And it leads me to conclude that unless there is a drastic change in Western attitudes toward a transforming world, the underdeveloped countries which stand in agony today at the threshold of the twentieth-first century could become the greatest suckers in history. But then who knows what price we may exact from the world for the destruction of our dignity, not to mention our lives and property, and our right to formulate our destiny without gross foreign interference?

The jealous nationalism of the underdeveloped countries is not simply a question of mood. It is a matter of survival. To the extent that even communist states like Cuba, North Vietnam, and North Korea, not to mention China, assert their independence from the dictates of the protecting power despite their acute dependence (on Russia) and their encirclement (by the United States), it is a measure of their responsiveness to this national need. It is curious indeed that in a discussion focused in great part on political development in underdeveloped countries, Professor Huntington has made no reference to this primary fact in our political life. I suspect that this omission, though unintentional, is not accidental. It reflects the antinationalist thrust of the United States, which, as suggested earlier, is related to certain aspects of the American political culture.

When a nationalist movement acquires a radical content, when it threatens to nationalize property and socialize national resources, when it becomes diplomatically assertive and neutralist, it initially elicits an unfavorable response from the United States. Its programs threaten potential or actual American investments; its diplomatic posture involves the loss of a potential or actual ally in the Cold War; its revolutionary doctrine appears dangerously congruent with the Communist enemy's. If a country threatened by such a nationalism happens to be a client state, then a United States–mounted coup d'état or sharp, swift military intervention seeks to restore the status quo. Interventions of this type include Guatemala, the Dominican Republic, and Iran. In nonclient underdeveloped states such a radical nationalist movement is tolerated by the United States if it comes to power unexpectedly or turns radical gradually and without serious challenge under a legitimate and popular leader—although relations with such regimes remain intermittently reserved if not restrained. Egypt is an example of the first type, Tanzania of the second.

American tolerance toward these countries appeared to be increasing in the Kennedy administration; neutralists were not regarded invariably as allies of Communism. There was even a tendency actively to encourage their radical posture, especially in the zones of French influence (Tunisia became an AID showpiece during this period and has since shown unabashed loyalty to the United States). The unusual popularity in the Third World of the Kennedy administration was due not so much to actual change in United States policy but largely to the feeling among us that America was beginning to understand the nature of our nationalism, that the puppeteer view of the world was giving way to a more sophisticated understanding of our drive toward sovereignty. But only among the East European clients of the USSR has American policy consistently welcomed and, where possible, encouraged reactive nationalism.

Professor Huntington gives us a very keen analysis of how, in the American alliance with conservative nationalism, the interaction between United States economic aid and desire for reform promotes the expansion of American presence and finally ends in intervention. Military assistance produces much the same, if more dangerous, symbiosis between the United States and the recipient indigenous elites. The more a foreign power involves itself in native problems, the greater become its economic and psychic investments. As the relationship gets more institutionalized, it becomes harder to extricate itself from the commitment. The tendency then is to blame individuals and not the system, which inherently lacks the capacity to maintain and enhance its legitimacy. Hence one gets rid of a dictator only to inherit a worse one. United States–supported Latin American coups provide innumerable examples of this vicious cycle.

The case of Vietnam is also illustrative. There is now a general tendency in America to blame Diem, who had once been billed as a democratic alternative to Ho Chi Minh. Yet it is not fair to blame him for failing to introduce meaningful reforms and thus driving the Vietnamese to desperation. It was morbid optimism to expect an absentee aristocrat to substitute for a heroic leader who had devoted a lifetime to the liberation of his country and to bypass a leadership and cadres whose organic ties with the peasants were cemented by the bitter struggle for independence. Given his situation, Diem had no choice; his only possible weapons were a power apparatus to regiment the population, fall-out support of minorities and the privileged, and widespread terror. These were not the aberrations of a program but the program itself. And his assassination left the United States at the mercy of the musical-chair generals, who had earlier collaborated with France and who further degenerated into sanctioning the systematic destruction of a country they claimed to govern.

Professor Huntington ignores the important problem of legitimacy when he makes his recommendation on behalf of political development. I do not question his central positive theme, that the achievement of consolidation of power by a regime followed by advances in the area of social reforms and political institutionalization will reduce the chances of United States military intervention. Yet his belief that the United States should actively engage in fostering political development is fraught with risks and is likely, at best, to be self-defeating.

No foreign power has the ability to equip a native government with legitimacy (the essential quality of rulership) or with the will and capacity to open channels for peaceful change—unless it is the case of a military occupation which for some historical or psychological reasons is accepted by the population.[2] In fact, the reverse is truer: identification with a foreign power erodes the legitimacy of a regime. And the correlation between growing legitimacy and willingness to open new domestic channels for participation is known to be positive. Even if I were to accept the questionable premise that the United States has not been involved in aiding and influencing political and administrative development in Vietnam, I should at least question the efficacy of such involvement. Given the absence of legitimacy and the reactionary character of the Diem regime, I doubt that a timely and firm American involvement in political development would have led to the creation of legitimate and popular institutions in Vietnam, thus preventing, as Professor Huntington appears to believe, the insurrection from spreading.

Professor Huntington seems to take an essentially technical view of political development. But the primary factor in promoting political institutions is not improved professionalism, as is largely true of the army, navy, hospitals, etc. Rather, it involves a vision of society, the choice of values and goals. These are not exportable goods or skills that can form part of foreign aid programs. It is incorrect, therefore, to put political parties in the same category as hospitals and armies. Political institutions unsupported by operative values become mere formalities or else turn into bureaucratic instruments of control rather than of participation. Professor Huntington does not discuss the question of prerequisites for an institution-building effort. He somehow assumes the pliability of recipient regimes to American pressures for and advice on how to build institutions. The error typical of American policy is repeated. The dramatic failure of the American mission in Vietnam should at least have laid to rest this kind of technocratic evangelism and culture-centered optimism.

Legitimate rulers who have a value commitment to maintaining a measure of accountability to the populace and to creatively confronting the crises of participation, development, and distribution are unlikely to need foreign help in creating and running political institutions. The recent history of underdeveloped countries provides ample evidence that their leaders do not lack organizing skills; nor are they in need of advice on institution building. If they do not promote political participation, it is because they do not wish to do so. The Algerians, many of whom are in power today, created one of the most powerful and, under assault, indestructible political institutions of this century. Yet the FLN, unlike the Neo-Destour party of Tunisia or the Istiqlal of Morocco, did not really survive independence, and not for lack of foreign advice or pressure. Potentially, it is still a revivable institution, for many of the old cadres and an eager populace are longing to be active participants again. What is lacking is the incentive on the part of Algeria's military leaders, who perhaps perceive in the development of popular institutions a threat to the power of the army.

Similarly, Pakistan's Muslim League degenerated into factions and Ghana's Convention Party turned into a bureaucratic behemoth not for lack of organizing skill or because of ignorance on the part of politicians about the meaning and importance of political institutions. They weakened as popular institutions because the leaders perceived them as threats or at least as useless for wielding power after independence had been achieved. These leaders lacked the radical commitment to social and economic transformation, on the basis of which they could continually communicate with the majority a consistent and functioning ideology which could provide guidelines against which political behavior could be tested and upon which political institutions could be based. They lacked an operative commitment to accountability which could ensure their adherence to institutionalized norms and practices.

These commitments are seldom acquired through pressures from allies. They result from social conflict or social movements, in response to continual, often violent pressures from below, or as a consequence of revolutionary upheaval. Unless an elite is already committed deeply and operatively to a set of political values, it is not likely to become so under foreign pressure. In fact, protective foreign involvement may only harden its unwillingness to distribute its privileges and power.[3]

Professor Huntington, in his discussion of political involvement, presents an excellent analysis of how the interaction between economic aid and United States pressures for social reforms produces the expansion of American presence as well as its frustration; the combination leads eventually to intervention. But he does not explain satisfactorily why similar involvement in political development will not produce the same result. In fact, the very forces which lead to a positive relationship between economic reform and intervention are likely to have a stronger correlation between political involvement and intervention. Political participation is even more difficult to sell to an entrenched ruling class than economic reforms, because it involves the sharing of power as well as resources. It is bound to produce greater resentment and truculence on the part of native allies: more frustration, greater psychic and material involvement, and more intervention on the part of the United States. Politics and power, more than economics, command the passions of men—especially well-fed men.

Professor Huntington's suggestion that the escalation of political involvement into military intervention can be avoided by keeping political commitments "conditional and/or covert" suffers from bad history no less than poor principles. Commitments, even conditional ones, have a vicious logic of proliferation. History is replete with examples of conditional commitments giving birth to unconditional ones. Vietnam itself is a case in point; need one recall that American boys were never committed to fighting the battle of Asian boys? As for covertness, how does one keep political activities of this magnitude covert in a democracy—or in a dictatorship, for that matter? And how does the professed commitment to the principles of participation and democracy square with the systematic denial to people of information on the nature of institutions to which they belong and to which they contribute?

Then there are the operational questions, far too many to merit detailed examination, but they all lead to the same thing—increasing military aid and "advisers" to incumbent regimes and possible military intervention. Who will the United States aid in building political parties and organization? Professor Huntington does not exactly answer. But his assumptions are clearly drawn from the American culture of management. He mentions groups "within the political system" as against a "group of urban intellectuals" whose organization of the peasantry "results in revolution." He implies that United States political involvement will be on behalf of the groups within the system and, since they exist practically everywhere, in competition with the revolutionary intellectuals. I wonder whose definition of groups within and outside the system is to be taken—America's? the native government's? the military's? I wonder, too, how this concept differs from United States–aided counterinsurgency being practiced in Thailand, the Philippines, or the more tragic Guatemala? And what would happen if the revolutionaries somehow do succeed in mobilizing the peasants and do seriously challenge the American-sponsored party or system?

If my earlier analysis of American political culture has any validity, it points out the danger of continued United States interventionism, especially in the client states. By way of summary, it seems (I) that the United States is not yet able to tolerate, much less encourage, radical nationalism in client states; the tendency to accept and encourage nationalism as a vehicle for social transformation has been proportionately greater in the countries where the United States does not command direct influence; (2) that the United States expects of the underdeveloped countries a style and norms of politics which are unlikely to be fulfilled at this stage of their development; (3) that in countries where its involvement is significant, failure to conform to American expectations produces a vicious cycle of expanding the American role in domestic affairs, erosion of the legitimacy of United States–supported elites, radicalization and enlargement of civil conflict, and military intervention in behalf of the status quo; while seeking order and stability, in fact the United States contributes to more disorder; (4) that the deeper its involvement in a country, the less flexible it becomes in dealing with diverse political groupings and the more it develops a vested interest in defending friendly governments against revolutionary forces; (5) that a colonial style, perhaps acquired in Latin America and reinforced by evangelism as well as incipient racism, persists and produces a relationship of dependence and protectiveness between native elites and the United States.

From these conclusions it should follow that if the dialectic of intervention is to be broken, scholars and policy makers have to give attention to the manner in which the United States must disengage from direct involvement in underdeveloped countries. Such a disengagement need not be the result of isolationist sentiments. It must envisage a new role for the United States and new styles of relationships which will take into account the interest of America as well as of the underdeveloped. Yet such a change in policy must necessarily be preceded by not only an examination of America's assumptions but also a redefinition of its goals.

Professor Huntington implicitly endorses the assumptions and goals of United States policy. He does not identify either, although a few may be inferred from his discussion. There is a preoccupation with success; we are given a "useful reminder that consequences are all that count." The criteria of success, however, are left unclear. Restoration of order, successful arbitration between conflicting native factions, organizing "honest elections" which the "right man" wins, and promoting reforms are cited as achievements of the Dominican intervention. He also argues that the "judgment that United States policy in the Vietnamese crisis was ultimately unsuccessful tends to be based upon an incomplete, perhaps misleading reckoning of the benefits of the intervention." Hence he defers a discussion of whether or not it was a salutary case of intervention.

One is led to ask, "benefits" for whom? For the United States? For the Thai and Filipino clients of the United States? For the men in Saigon who once collaborated with France and are now collaborating with America? Or for the people of Vietnam and Southeast Asia? If one judges from the point of view of the Pentagon or the White House, many benefits are already perceptible and more can be discerned for the future. For example, military officials are reportedly happy over the unusual opportunity to test and develop new weapons both for conventional and irregular warfare; a new generation of officers and men has gained combat experience in unfamiliar terrain; lessons learned in Vietnam have led to improved techniques of counterinsurgency and pacification in the other client states of Southeast Asia and Latin America. Domestically, the war may have served as a safety valve for absorbing thousands of young blacks, the most aggressive of whom opt to extend their service in the military. And insofar as the intentions of the United States are still unclear, it is possible that, unwilling to negotiate withdrawal (the status quo being the *casus belli* is nonnegotiable), it will eventually acquire a piece of strategic real estate near China, inhabited by the beaten and sunk remainder of a once brave and proud people—a sort of modern Indian reservation in the heart of Asia. The ruling elites of Thailand and the Philippines (and elsewhere) and other war profiteers may also have reasons to extol the benefits of the intervention, especially if the United States can demonstrate its willingness to commit a genocide in order to save its clients.

To the Vietnamese people, however, the American invasion has brought few benefits. Professor Huntington's earlier contention regarding the "relatively limited and undestructive" character of this war notwithstanding, their losses have been staggering, and many of them are statistically immeasurable. No one seems to have counted the dead in this computerized war, but if one were to accept even the lowest estimated ratio of civilian losses to claimed enemy casualties, more than a million Vietnamese may already be presumed to have died. A quarter of the Southern population has been displaced; the social and cultural fabric of the society has been badly torn. Even the ecological balance has been affected by defoliation and bombing, although only in the future shall we know the extent and permanence of this damage. And the end is not yet in sight.

The earlier argument that the right lesson of Vietnam may be an "unlesson" is based on a factually correct yet irrelevant observation. I can only agree with Professor Huntington on the uniqueness of the Vietnamese situation. But, as others have said, the uniqueness rests with Vietnam, not with American policy. It refers to the historical and political configurations which permitted the Vietnamese people to organize a successful resistance against American intervention. It does not refer to the assumptions, attitudes, and the pattern of relationships with indigenous elites which have frequently caused the United States to intervene militarily on behalf of a threatened status quo. The postwar interventions generally succeeded in obtaining their immediate goal of defeating a radical coalition and maintaining a friendly and manageable, preferably reformed status quo. The Philippines, Guatemala, Iran, and the Dominican Republic are frequently cited as examples of success. In Lebanon, it was a standoff; in Cuba, a fiasco; in Laos, a suspended failure. Only in Vietnam has the dialectic of intervention resolved into a seeming disaster; mistakes led to blunders, and blunders have been escalating into a crescendo of crimes. An effective style of protecting clients, which admitted American involvement in internal conflicts either by proxy (through advisers, training "special forces," and military aid) or by swift and discreet police action of short duration, has been stymied by the Vietnamese quagmire. Professor Huntington believes that the duplication of such a situation is unlikely, although he himself points out that Thailand and the Philippines, among others, are potential scenes for future United States military involvement in internal war.

Should we regard Vietnam as largely an accident for a policy which has a good record of "success"? Or does it put into question the basic attitudes and goals which define this policy for the Third World? Is Vietnam an "unlesson," better forgotten? Or is it a lesson calling for a fundamental change in a policy which, even if it were relevant in the earlier decades, may now have lost its relevance, which even when "successful" by American definition may have been essentially self-defeating? The answers depend on one's perspectives and priorities. And they are shaped by our environment, our social, intellectual, and moral location. The dialogue between many of my American colleagues, some of them critics of the present administration, and myself has been breaking down because I am progressively unable to share their phantoms and their fantasies.

In underdeveloped countries, the quiescence which followed independence is giving way to new disappointments and new demands which are unlikely to be satisfied by a politics of boundary management and selective co-optation—a fact which the United States, much like our ruling elites, is yet unable or unwilling to perceive. There is an increasingly perceptible gap between our need for social transformation and America's insistence on stability, between our impatience for change and America's obsession with order, our move toward revolution and America's belief in the plausibility of achieving reforms under the robber barons of the Third World, our longing for absolute national sovereignty and America's preference for pliable allies, our desire to see our national soil freed of foreign occupation and America's alleged need for military bases (at least in the rimlands surrounding China and the USSR). As the gap widens between our sorrow and America's contentment, so will, perhaps, these dichotomies of our perspectives and our priorities. Unless there is a fundamental redefinition of American interests and goals, our confrontations with the United States will be increasingly antagonistic. In the client states of Asia and Latin America, it may even be tragic. In this sense, Vietnam may not be so unique. It may be a warning of things to come.

[1965]

## 5 / PLO AND ANC

Painful Contrasts

Palestinian leaders were quite pleased in the 1970s with their equations of Zionism = racism and Israel = South Africa. The first formula became enshrined in a United Nations General Assembly Resolution; the second was a subject of many symposiums and anthologies.

They were logical formulae and carried large grains of truth. The Zionist vision of Jewish statehood is exclusionary: it denies non-Jews equal rights. Like white South Africa, Israel is a settler state where indigenous interests and rights are subordinated to those of the settler population. Such comparisons served for a while as a powerful propaganda tool. But as formulations of this sort tend to do, these equations pleased their creators more than enlightened them. Had PLO leaders examined their differences with the ANC, they might have been better off than they are today, running the world's most publicized municipalities.

The contrasts between the two liberation movements are striking. The PLO, which effectively began as an autonomous organization in the fall of 1967, was the Middle East's youngest political formation in 1970. The ANC, founded in 1912, was Africa's oldest. The difference in age matters. The ANC has deep institutional roots, an ideological anchor, a tradition of collective decision making, and a rationally structured, cadre-based organization. The PLO was a coalition of disparate parties dominated by an individual, Yasser Arafat, who led its largest component. In each of the PLO's constituent organizations, power and the purse were held by a single leader—Arafat, Habash, and Hawatmeh. The PLO had pluralistic appearances; the ANC was a unitary organization. But pluralism in the PLO was vitiated by personalism, while the ANC's unitary structure was subject to rules and accountability.

Thanks to Arab subsidies, the PLO was the best-financed liberation movement in history. The ANC remained a spartan outfit. Starting in 1974, the ANC actually received donations from the PLO. Ironically, wealth worked to the PLO's disadvantage. Arafat used money to find short cuts to protracted political effort and to manipulate colleagues no less than rivals. The PLO created a diplomatic corps, bureaucracy, standing army, and welfare system. It built an apparently opulent quasi-state before it had matured as a liberation movement. As money began to substitute for politics, the PLO became a magnet to opportunists from all over the world. As corruption seeped in, the most committed cadres were demoralized. Above all, availability of outside funds relieved it of the necessity to consolidate its constituencies. The ANC, by contrast, depended largely on membership contributions. For it, keeping members committed, cadres accountable, and finances in order was an objective necessity. Dependence on external financing also rendered the PLO vulnerable to shifts in Arab politics. Arafat's glittering but fragile edifice collapsed when he angered his beneficiaries by siding with Iraq during the Gulf War.

The most significant contrasts between the two are political. They explain the ANC's victory and the abject collapse of the PLO. For the ANC, politics never lost primacy. The fifties, sixties, and seventies were decades of dramatically successful armed struggles. From China to Algeria, Cuba to Vietnam, armed revolutions achieved liberation against impossible odds and powerful adversaries. Armed struggle had captured the imagination of youth and was widely viewed as the motor of liberation. Yet the ANC did not surrender to pressure or temptation. There existed an armed wing of the movement; Mandela himself had been part of it. But the ANC never let the balance of its effort shift in its favor. In 1975, a few days after the Vietnamese had liberated Saigon, I asked Regis September, a respected ANC leader now dead, why the ANC had not chosen the path of armed struggle. "The objective conditions in South Africa are very different," he had said, describing them convincingly. "We shall win primarily by political means."

The PLO was born to armed struggle and remained devoted to it until its catastrophic defeat in Lebanon in 1982. To make matters worse, all PLO factions perceived armed struggle in militaristic rather than political terms. Beginning with the battle of Karameh in 1968, when Palestinians fought valiantly against intruding Israeli forces in Jordan, armed struggle came to be viewed in the PLO as a matter merely of giving and taking lives. I recall sadly that I warned a large gathering of Arabs in May 1969 against this kind of romantic fixation with armed struggle and argued that Palestinians needed instead to develop a radical political strategy and pursue it with some discipline of detail. The late Dr. Fayez Sayegh, an eminent Palestinian intellectual, had responded: "Karameh has changed our image from the fleeing Arab to the fighting Arab. There is no other way." This outlook endured. Today, the tactics and outlook of Hamas and Islamic Jihad are different but only marginally from that of the PLO in the 1970s.

The worst aspect of this attitude was that no one in the PLO leadership had a clear notion of what armed struggles were about. They made no serious attempt to analyze and exploit the contradictions and vulnerabilities of Israel. It had no strategy to protect Palestinian land in the Occupied Territories and no program of linking the struggle of Palestinians in exile with those under occupation. It paid little attention to creating fissures in Israeli society or between the US and Israel. Only half-hearted efforts were made to counter Israeli influence and propaganda in American and European countries. The PLO seemed committed to outfighting its adversary without outadministering it. Repeatedly, several of us, including Edward Said, Ibrahim Abu-Lughod, and Shafiq al-Hout, argued for the primacy of politics, offering specific suggestions. Arafat would hear us respectfully, nod, ask questions, and take notes. The ethos and structure of the PLO remained militarized. Posturing and public relations substituted for sustained and sophisticated politics, which distinguish successful liberation movements.

This fundamental difference between the PLO and the ANC was due to their differing antecedents and composition. During the greater part of its existence, the ANC maintained a meaningful association with the South African Communist Party. Many of the ANC's ranking leaders were Communists or sympathizers. This association had a lasting impact on the ANC. Its outlook and organizational style was deeply influenced by Communist Party traditions, which emphasize the centrality of politics in struggles for liberation, cadre-based and disciplined formation, consolidation of party support in the working masses, and avoidance of appeals to race, religion, and ethnicity. These characteristics also distinguished the ANC from other South African parties.

The PLO was a nationalist coalition; its style and rhetoric was an amalgam of various Arab nationalist traditions including the Nasserist and the Baathist. Marxist elements were marginally present in Habash's and Hawatmeh's fronts, but neither had the discipline and political rigor normally associated with conventional communist parties. Gradually, communists began to play a part in the Occupied Territories and are known to have had a significant role in organizing the underground network of the Intifada, undoubtedly a powerful though greatly undermined expression of Palestinian resistance.

There existed perceptible contrasts between South African and Palestinian cultural presence especially in the United States and Europe. Anti-apartheid activists had unquestioned cultural hegemony over their adversary. Their presence was ubiquitous—a lecture here, poetry reading there, art exhibitions, plays on Broadway and off Broadway, books, documentaries. On the Question of Palestine, the Zionist viewpoint held sway. This was not the PLO's fault. Zionists had laid the ground for seven decades and cornered the cultural market—the media, movie industry, campuses, and publishing. To challenge them was an uphill battle. Palestinians and their supporters did that with some success, but they had little support from the PLO. Its representatives were focused on governments, United Nations, the diplomatic rounds. Their employer had no agenda for isolating its adversary politically from public sympathy. Occasionally, Arafat would give away handsome amounts to a supplicant to do "political work," which normally amounted to a couple of advertisements in an American newspaper.

Finally, international solidarity worked better for the ANC than for the PLO. Two examples stand out: The first concerned the campaign for divestment from South Africa, which had its base on American campuses, support from liberal clergy and, most importantly, the black American middle class. It had unexpected success. As churches and universities divested, corporations, too, came under pressure. When Citibank pulled out of South Africa, a decisive blow to apartheid had been dealt. Soon thereafter sanctions followed. The second, equally lethal blow was dealt by Cuba in a unique gesture of solidarity. In 1975, Cuba successfully intervened to prevent the victory in Angola of the South African–supported army of Jonas Savimbi. The government of Agostino Neto was saved, but the war went on. South Africa's powerful army eventually entered the fray. In 1988, the predominantly black Cuban forces in Angola routed this dreaded army in pitched battles. The event changed the psychological environment for blacks as well as whites. I am tempted to transpose Lord Curzon's remark on Japan's 1905 triumph over Russia: "The reverberations of that victory spread like a thunderclap through the whispering galleries of Africa."

At Mandela's inauguration as president of South Africa, American vice president Albert Gore could not have been happy to see a million South Africans applauding the bearded islander with cries of VENCEREMOS! Yasser Arafat was also there, welcomed most warmly by the South Africans, who had forgotten neither the PLO's solidarity with the ANC nor mistaken the Palestinian people's lasting pain for liberation.

[1994]

# 6 / IRAN'S LANDMARK REVOLUTION
Fifteen Years Later

Iran's Islamic regime celebrated this week the fifteenth anniversary of the revolution which catapulted an old and austere cleric, Ayatollah Ruholla Khomeini, onto the world stage and brought to an end the reign of Reza Shah
Pahlavi, king of kings, light of the Aryans, patron of the world's "beautiful people," host to the high and mighty, and a most renowned tyrant. It was one of
the most dramatic and sensational events of the twentieth century, the first
fully televised revolution in history, one that caused great shivering in Washington and other capitals of the Western world. Yet only fifteen years later this
historic event is almost forgotten outside Iran. This reflects, of course, the
shortness of modern memory, but it also suggests that in the eyes of the
powers-that-be this revolution has been well nigh contained.

Historians are likely nevertheless to view the Iranian as a landmark revolution. It merits comparison with the French Revolution more than to any
other in modern history. Like the revolution of 1789, its importance may be
less in the results it produced and more in the trends that it announced and
the fears it aroused. As the French Revolution marked the beginning of a new
era in Europe, so has the Iranian, in the Middle East especially and generally
in the Third World. As the French Revolution augured a period of war and
strife in European politics, so did the Iranian in southwest Asia. As the French
Revolution at first threatened, then augmented the influence of imperial
Britain in Europe, so were American interests in the Middle East at first
threatened by the Iranian Revolution and vastly augmented thereafter.

In other, more significant respects, the Iranian was like the French a
unique and perhaps seminal revolution for the postcolonial era as the French

had been for the industrial age. The uprising that began in January 1978 and ended successfully on February 11, 1979, was the first major break in the post-colonial world from the revolutionary model of protracted armed struggle experienced in China, Algeria, Cuba, Vietnam, Laos, Angola, Mozambique, and Guinea-Bissau. Iran's, by contrast, was a mass insurrection, by far the most popular, broad-based, and sustained agitation in recent history. During a single year—1978—some thirty thousand protestors were killed in Iran while its economic institutions and public services were intermittently shut down. The movement was quite unparalleled for its militant but nonviolent character and for its discipline and morale in the face of governmental violence. As such, it deserves to be studied for its lessons in mass mobilization and agitational politics.

The Iranian Revolution pointed toward a shift in the focus of revolutionary struggle in the so-called Third World from the rural to the urban sector. Until 1978, almost all Third World revolution had been primarily peasant revolutions, centered in rural areas and involving guerrilla warfare. Even in those countries (e.g., Algeria and Cuba) where support of the urban population held great importance in revolutionary strategy, the rural population was from the outset viewed as being central to the revolutionaries' success.

The Iranian Revolution represented the first significant departure from this pattern. It was predominantly urban in composition and entirely so in its origin and initiation. Its cadres came from the middle, low middle, and working classes. Its following was swelled by the lumpenproletariat, mostly rural migrants driven to the cities by the shah's "modernization" of agriculture. The capital-intensive commercial farm strategy of economic development which the shah initiated in the 1960s—and which Ms. Bhutto's "agricultural task force" has now recommended for Pakistan—led to rapid urbanization, cultural dislocation, and grossly augmented and visible inequality. These conditions created the mass base for the uprising, and increasingly they are appearing in other Third World countries, especially in those which are seeking links with the commercial market as uncritically as they once sought to imitate socialism.

Iran yielded a textbook example of the general strike as a primary weapon in revolutionary seizure of power. The strike, which lasted nearly six months in Iran, was one of the longest and by far the most effective in history. The turning point in the struggle against the shah came during September and October 1978, when the oil workers in Abadan and Ahvaz proved the weapon of the general strike to be powerful beyond the dreams of nineteenth-century Marxists and syndicalists, who had viewed it as the lynchpin of revolutionary strategy. Subsequently, events in South Korea, South Africa, Nicaragua, and Brazil, among others, suggested that what we witnessed in Iran was a trend.

The Iranian Revolution caused a shift in US preference in the Third World for pliable dictators; thenceforth Washington began to seek peaceful transitions to democracy. For Iran revealed the vulnerabilities of authoritarian governments, which were greatly favored in the 1960s and 1970s by both the Communist and Western powers. Since the Cuban Revolution, it was the first successful popular revolution in a postcolonial state, and, unlike Cuba under Batista, Iran under the shah had become a prototypical pro-Western dictatorship. Like other "regional influentials" of the Nixon Doctrine, Iran was a highly centralized, repressive, and militarized state. "Oriental despotism" arrived in Iran in the twentieth century, with the first Pahlavi usurper [Reza Khan Pahlavi, 1925–1941] and in the guise of modernization. Its authoritarian arteries hardened from an interlinking of oil, imperialism, and the vested interests of a rootless dynasty.

The last decade of the Pahlavi rule witnessed the transformation of Iran into a "regional power." That was due to its augmented oil revenues, the shah's unrealistic ambitions, and the compulsions of American policy under Nixon and Carter. To the United States governments and corporations, Iran had seemed an ideal ally, an extravagant customer who paid cash for expensive American weapons while guarding the oil-rich Gulf, a pro-Western, autocratic "island of stability," as Jimmy Carter described it just a month before the revolution began. But as in many militarized Third World countries, the superstructure of the Pahlavi state bore little logical and no organic relation to the infrastructure of Iranian society. Hence it had no capacity to serve society's needs, accommodate its demands, or keep pace with changes within it. It became too heavy a burden for the Iranian people to carry. Hence the movement for overturning the regime obtained a national consensus quite unparalleled in history. These conditions exist to varying degrees in many other countries. Soon after Iran, they produced protests and revolts in South Korea, the Philippines, Brazil, and Argentina, among others. Today, they account for insurgencies in Algeria and Egypt.

The fall of the shah revealed that, in the Third World, deployment of advanced weapons promotes internal contradictions and subjects the state apparatus to unbearable strains. When confronted by a sustained popular uprising,

Iran's 450,000-strong, superequipped military establishment disintegrated. Significantly, the noncommissioned officers and technicians, whose numbers had swelled since 1972 as a result of large infusions of sophisticated arms, were the first to defect en masse; their defection proved crucial in the disintegration of Iran's armed forces. The military's open and mass defections, which began in December 1978, were spearheaded by technicians and cadets of the air force and armored divisions. They sealed the Pahlavis' fate.

Herein lies an extraordinary irony: In terms of its intensity, scope, and the social forces which were involved in it, the Iranian was by far the most modern and objectively advanced revolution in the Third World. Yet revolutionary power in Iran was seized by a clerical leadership of theocratic outlook, medieval culture, and millenarian style. Most scholars have attributed this remarkable phenomenon to the shah's repression (only in the mosque one found the freedom of association and speech . . . ) and to Iran's Shia traditions (of martyrdom and clerical power).

This recent emphasis on Iran's Shia avocation and its ulema's institutionalized strength is exaggerated and misleading. A clearer explanation of the hegemony which the ulema achieved in the revolutionary process may be found in Antonio Gramsci's argument about the power of cultural forces in a disorganically developed environment. This idea may also help us understand how so powerful a revolution in a country so rich in human and material resources has been so tragically derailed. But that is an altogether different and more complex subject.

[1994]

# 7 / THE MAKING OF *THE BATTLE OF ALGIERS*

Editors' Note: *At the time of this writing (summer 2004),* The Battle of Algiers *is in the midst of a revival. Recently rereleased with a new print, Gillo Pontecorvo's 1966 film has been making the rounds of art cinemas and even some commercial venues in the United States, apparently finding new and avid audiences. Reports in the press have noted that the Pentagon screened the film for its Special Operations (counterinsurgency) chiefs in August 2003. One wonders what the intended lessons are; how to fight an urban counterinsurgency campaign seems most probable. This is how the Pentagon screening was advertised: "How to win a battle against terrorism and lose the war of ideas. . . . Children shoot soldiers at point blank range. Women plant bombs in cafes. Soon the entire Arab population builds to a mad fervor. Sound familiar? The French have a plan. It succeeds tactically, but fails strategically. To understand why, come to a rare showing of this film." The "French plan," of course, included torture of civilians to extract information. With these tactics, they destroyed the revolutionary organization inside Algiers, but at the cost of mobilizing the entire Algerian population against the possibility of French rule. The battle of Algiers eliminated any last shred of French legitimacy, eventually ensuring their defeat.*

*Apparently, the American military has drawn only half the lesson. In April 2004, before the public revelation of American soldiers' actions at Abu Ghraib, an article in the L.A. Times called attention to the response of American soldiers to reports of misconduct in the treatment of Iraqi detainees: "It's a little like the French colonel in 'The Battle of Algiers.' You're all complaining about the tactics I am using to win the war, but that's what I am doing, winning the war" (Andrew Bacevich, "A Descent into Dishonor," L.A. Times, April 8, 2004).*

*Eqbal Ahmad helped research the script and was present during the filming of* The Battle of Algiers. *What follows is an edited transcript of a lecture about the making of the film that he gave to an undergraduate class at Hampshire College in fall 1998.*

The Battle of Algiers is the first film I know of that in a concentrated fashion emphasizes a primary characteristic of revolutionary warfare, the fundamental characteristic of revolutionary warfare: to be successful, the revolutionary movement must outadminister the enemy before it starts to outfight it. *The Battle of Algiers* gives you that insight from both sides, Algerian and French. The film closely follows the actual battle, but the emphasis is not on violence; it is on organization. Early in the film, we see the French commissioner of police working hand in glove with the colon/settler underground organization. He aids the French settler underground in blowing up two Arab houses in the Casbah. In that incident, 157 Algerians died. Until that day, there had not been large-scale revolutionary violence in Algiers.

When the historical battle of Algiers began, the real war was in the countryside, not in the city. The revolutionaries were using Algiers as their headquarters, as a source of supply, as the place from which to organize. Ali La Pointe, one of the chief characters in the film, is an example of this effort to organize. He is the quintessential lumpenproletarian: he is unemployed; he is from the ghetto; he has a criminal record; he is a vagabond; he participates in the numbers racket; he earns money by gambling; he is connected to the gambling/prostitution network in the Casbah. While in jail for petty theft and for hitting a French boy who had taunted him in the street as he tried to escape arrest, he begins his conversion to the cause of the revolution. When the French blow up the Casbah, he is in a hurry: he wants revenge—immediately. Ali is shown leading an angry mob, calling for blood in response to the bombing. In a critical early moment in the film, he goes to see the resistance commander, Colonel Mohammed Jafar, and has an argument with Jafar, saying, "We must strike back." Jafar answers, "No, Ali, not yet; we are not ready. We must first organize the Casbah before we engage in violence. We must clean up the numbers racket, the gambling racket, the prostitution; we must institute discipline; we must offer services to people." Ali then walks through the Casbah, telling the residents, "We must stop the gambling, stop the prostitution." The kids beat up an old drunk, and Ali shoots the man who controls gambling and prostitution, after apparently having warned him twice to disband his network.

A second critical moment in the film is the marriage scene, presided over by an FLN militant. It signifies that French rule is over inside the Casbah, that the revolution has outadministered the French. Colonial law stipulated that marriages must be registered with the French government. Yet this marriage is not performed by a French-appointed *qadi* [Muslim religious judge], and it is not registered with the French; it is performed instead by the revolution and registered with the revolution. The French have been cut out of the process.

In Vietnam, where they fought before Algeria and lost, the French had the insight to recognize at a certain point, "We are still here, but we're finished." A political officer in the French resident general's office wrote a memorandum to Paris in 1944 or 1945, after French rule was reestablished in Vietnam, saying, "We are the formal authority, but we are making laws in a void, we are legislating in a vacuum." The parallel administration of the revolution had taken over, had superimposed itself on the administration of colonial France in Vietnam. This is what you see happening in *The Battle of Algiers*. This is why Mohammed Jafar says, "We are not ready to retaliate because we must organize the people, we must outadminister the enemy, so that the enemy is cut out, even when it thinks it is formally ruling."

With Colonel Mathieu, the French leader, we get the view from the French side. He is coming from Vietnam; he is a veteran of Indochina; he knows revolutionary warfare better than the colons. He says, "You cannot fight this enemy unless you lick the political organization; you can kill them, but unless you lick the political organization, they are going to win." Mathieu makes charts of how the revolutionary organization is structured to identify the key organizers. The film shows how the French deconstructed the revolutionary organization—using torture—knowing that you could not lick the revolution without getting to the politics of it. What makes this movie so significant is that it shows analytically a very fundamental reality of revolution. You must outadminister before you can outfight the enemy.

*The General Strike*

A few more points about revolutionary warfare with reference to the film. First, the general strike and its context. John F. Kennedy, who was then a US senator and who wanted France to settle Algeria, called for a debate on Algeria at the UN. All the Africans, all the Arabs, and all the other Third World people supporting the Algerian Revolution, agreed. The debate took place in the General Assembly, not in the Security Council. The French argued, "These people [referring to the Algerian anticolonial revolutionaries] represent nothing; they are a bunch of terrorists." To prove to the world that they did represent the people of Algeria, the organizers of the revolution called for a general strike, all over Algeria and also in France. With the general strike, however, the Algerians broke a rule of revolutionary strategy; it was the biggest blunder the leaders could have made. From that blunder followed other ones.

What happened was, the conventional Marxist idea of the effectiveness of the general strike was superimposed on the situation of revolutionary warfare. But the principle of the general strike is totally contrary to a principle that informs revolutionary warfare that is almost as important as outadministering versus outfighting the enemy. That is, in revolutionary warfare, the mass of the population must be organized to support the revolution. But they must officially remain neutral.

Revolutionary warfare is different from conventional warfare. In conventional warfare, the sides are declared. Adversaries fight openly, sides are clearly chosen and drawn, conventional armies move and fight set battles. A revolutionary war, by contrast, is by definition a war between a static and well-structured state and determined revolutionaries. There is a massive discrepancy of power between the two. For example, in Algeria, at the height of the Algerian War, France deployed half a million troops; at the end of the battle of Algiers, there were 450,000 French troops in Algeria, including helicopter units, armored divisions, tank divisions, infantry divisions, all supported by a navy and air force. Algerians, at the highest point of the revolution, had 25,000 fighters. The revolution had only men in pajamas, a gun or grenade in hand, nothing else. In this situation, strength is the people. Chairman Mao's famous dictum was "the guerrilla is to the people what a fish is to water." The people are the sea in which the revolutionary swims. The Japanese, against whom the Chinese revolutionaries fought, responded to the Maoist dictum by pursuing a policy in Manchuria of "draining the water"—killing the people.

In order to protect people, revolutionaries must maintain the fiction of popular neutrality. The incumbent power (whether colonial or local) has the compulsion to say, "The people are behind *us*; the revolutionaries, the guerrillas, are merely terrorizing them. We are protecting the people," as indeed the French said. That rhetoric reduces their ability to attack the whole population. Therefore good revolutionary tactics always create an environment in which the people are overtly neutral, while covertly larger and larger numbers of them support the revolution by various means. In Algeria, therefore, you didn't do anything to expose the entire people to attack by the other side. But that's what the general strike did. No decent revolutionary movement would call a general strike in a situation of warfare until almost the end, when it was winning, and it just needed the last push.

This was not the case in Algeria. The film opens with the first communiqué of the FLN in 1954; they were just beginning to organize. When the FLN declares the general strike, Colonel Mathieu is very happy and says, "Now we can lick them. They have made their first bad move." Why? Because they are announcing themselves to be on the side of the revolution. He can plan his operation: arrest everyone who is on strike and torture the bloody lot. Interrogate them. Some of them will turn out to be activists, some of them will turn out to be neutrals. But now he has a large pool from which he can get information. He called the operation, Operation Champagne: he went outside, saw a billboard advertising champagne, and thought, "This is going to be easy; it will go down easy, like champagne." He smoked them out. Seventy-seven thousand people in a period of just about twelve days were tortured, badly, in the city of Algiers. He would, each time, mark on the chart one more person they had identified, one more cell broken, check, check, check, destroy, destroy, destroy. That's how they did it. Six of the French who carried out the operation were eventually censured for torture.

*Dividing the Revolution*

The battle of Algiers had a very bad effect on the revolution. In 1965, working on the film, I had not quite understood that. The battle of Algiers made it impossible for the leadership of the revolution to stay in Algiers. The general strike, in fact, caused the total destruction of the cadres; the leadership eventually had to move out of one of the safest places to hide, the city. In the countryside, the revolutionary cadres were constantly pursued because the countryside was a battleground. After trying to live there, unable to send out communiqués, unable to direct their units, the leadership went to Tunis. There it formed the Provisional Revolutionary Government (Gouvernement provisoire de la République algérienne—GPRA), which proceeded to direct the revolution from Tunis.

But 1958 witnessed another event: the French started to build the Morice and Challe lines. These were electrified barbed wire fences that ringed the frontiers of Algeria and Tunisia. The French idea was to cut the leadership off from Algeria and to make it impossible for them to supply arms to the revolution. Their third goal was to divide, to create discontent between the *wilaya* commanders inside Algeria and the leadership by cutting off communications and supplies from one to the other.[1] The French had some success: a division was created in the Algerian Revolution between the exterior leadership and the interior revolution. There was bitterness inside, where Algerians were fighting the battles and the French were increasing their pressure, while the leadership was sitting outside, making speeches at the United Nations, meeting with all the great leaders of Africa and Asia. Arms were not making it into Algeria. The Tunisian-based GPRA then, knowing that there was anger toward them from inside and feeling insecure, created an army on the frontier, called the ALN (Armée de Libération Nationale), under the leadership of Colonel Boumedienne. This army sat on the Tunisian and Moroccan frontiers. It was well trained; it had arms, even tanks; it had a small air force; it had armored battalions. It was a proper conventional army, sitting outside the electrified barbed wire that surrounded Algeria.[2] Occasionally, it would lose half a unit, sending forty men into Algeria and losing twenty or twenty-five of them, but it had made a symbolic gesture of going in and fighting. Otherwise, it was well rested, well trained, well equipped.

Then, in 1962, independence comes. France negotiates its withdrawal. At that moment, the army the GPRA had created, a conventional army, in order to have a strong bargaining mechanism and a coercive apparatus in case the interior was hard to control, turned on the GPRA, because it was not a revolutionary force; the ALN was a military force. The turn was made easier by Ben Bella, a particularly ambitious man, who sided with the army. From 1963 to 1965, he was the most famous man in the Third World. No one realized that this man, in the name of revolution, had brought a conventional army into power. The army ate him up. The GPRA created the ALN, and the ALN ate the GPRA up. If you are going to raise a tiger, the tiger can turn on you.

Everyone knew the Algerians were going to win. By 1960, one way or another, the people were going to win. Even by 1954, when the French were defeated at Dien Bien Phu, France was internally divided about the Algerian war, just as America would later be over Vietnam. These two revolutions defeated the collective presumptions of modern technology. They defeated massive powers. They were an extraordinary demonstration of the power of human will and of organization. Without that conventional army, the revolution would have been at least partially successful. It has not been even partially successful. It only succeeded in getting rid of France; it failed at building a democratic, revolutionary society.

## The Making of the Film

The film *The Battle of Algiers* is a historically accurate rendition of the battle. The script was written by Franco Solinas. I did research for it and consulted on the script. The role of the leader was played by the actual organizer of the battle of Algiers, Saadi Yacef, who was also the associate director of the film. The script was based on Saadi Yacef's book about the battle of Algiers, a book he wrote in prison. Gillo Pontecorvo directed the film. Pontecorvo had a rule that those people currently living played themselves but were assigned fictional names, while real names were used for the dead. In the case of Yacef, since he was living, playing himself in the film, he was given the name Mohammed Jafar.

The first time you see him in the film is when Ali La Pointe comes out of prison and is ordered to shoot someone and given a gun with no bullets. He has a meeting with Mohammed Jafar and asks him, "Why did you give me a gun with no bullets?" "To test your sincerity." The second time you see him, he is sending women out to plant bombs. The last time you see him, he is being arrested. He is in a car, on the way to prison, and Mathieu, the colonel (who in real life was Roger Trinquier), says, "I would have been disappointed if you hadn't surrendered." And he asks, "Why?" Mathieu responds, "Because I have been studying your profile, and our estimation of you is that you never make an empty gesture."

Two incidents stand out in my mind in relation to the filming of *The Battle of Algiers*. I recall with great emotion that every time people died or were killed, Pontecorvo had music playing on the sound track. Every time a French person died, he used Beethoven; every time an Algerian died, he had the Algerian Arabic dirge. As the film was nearing completion, Saadi Yacef said to Pontecorvo, "This is something I don't like. You have to have the Algerian dirge for both of us. Otherwise, we are separating even the dead according to nationality." Of course, Pontecorvo made the change.

By conscious choice, Pontecorvo shot the film in black and white. He wanted to give it the texture of a documentary without using documentary footage. He wanted to give the film a sense of crude urgency, and he felt that using color would take away the feeling of intimacy and urgency. The choice to do it in black and white was contrary to the wishes of those funding the film. By this time (1966), nearly all films were made in color. His concern with immediacy was such that one time during the filming process something suddenly got into his head. He was filming the torture scene with which the film opens. When the torture scene was being taped, the cameras were on tripods (three cameras, 16 mm). Pontecorvo said, "Get them off, get them off, get those cameras off the tripods, hold them in your hands, approach the subject." And holding the cameras in their hands, they shot the torture scene. After that, all intimate scenes, such as the marriage, were shot with the camera in hand, to give a sense of extreme proximity and intimacy with the subject. He used a remarkable set of techniques.

One last historical note about the film. Do you remember Ben M'Hidi? He is the one who says to Ali La Pointe on the rooftop, "The general strike is a mistake, but we must do it." The lines were entirely his. He was one of the seven historic chiefs of the Algerian Revolution. He was the only one in the central committee of the Algerian Revolution who assiduously opposed the general strike. And, ironically, he is the only one who got killed.

He appears again in the film; he's the Algerian who is arrested and brought by the French to a press conference. The French then take him back into custody and announce later that he has died, he has committed suicide. And the general feeling, all over the world, including among us, was that Ben M'Hidi had died under torture. At the next press conference, you may remember, following the announcement of his death, there were questions about torture. Several years later, while doing the research for *The Battle of Algiers*, I interviewed Roger Trinquier (who is still alive, by the way), and one of the last questions I asked him was, "What happened to Ben M'Hidi?" And he answered, talking and looking just the way Matthieu did—that tall, lean, killer figure, but very sharp and intelligent. "I know that all of you think we tortured him to death, but we did not." I said, "What happened?" He said, "We shot him, but we gave him a guard of honor before we shot him." And I asked, "Why did you do that?" "Parce que M. Ben M'Hidi était un chef." "Because

M. Ben M'Hidi was a leader." And then he talked about Ben M'Hidi for almost an hour. He said, "I didn't want to shoot him. I had never met anyone like that. I would have liked to see him as *le président de la France*. So, once I was ordered to shoot him, I gave him a guard of honor first."

[1998]

# 8 / ALGERIA BEGAN BADLY
## Remembering Sidi Mohammed

Mohammed Boudiaf, president of Algeria, was killed on June 29, 1992, allegedly by Algerians in revolt against their government. It is hard to imagine a more ironic victim of rebellion. It is at least as likely that he was murdered by elements of the corrupt Algerian establishment.

Sidi Mohammed, as he was known by the cadres of the FLN [Front de Libération Nationale] was one of the historic chiefs who, on November 1, 1954, launched the epic war of Algeria's liberation. It was a landmark guerrilla war in modern history which lasted for seven years and a half, caused France's Fourth Republic to fall, brought Charles De Gaulle to power, and gave birth to the Fifth Republic and to independent Algeria. One out of every ten Algerians fell in this war; and three out of ten were displaced.

Boudiaf had been a motor of this revolution, a brilliant, methodical, and fearless organizer. A man of unassailable integrity, he commanded trust among comrades. When the FLN was formed in June 1954, it was Boudiaf who was chosen by common consent to head its highest body—the five member Committee of Coordination and Execution [CCE]. He fulfilled this enormous responsibility with competence and courage. In the revolution's preparatory phase, it was Boudiaf who consolidated the FLN's support among Algerian workers in France. There were half a million Algerians in France at the time, and their contributions—not Cairo's or Moscow's, as French propaganda used to allege—provided the financial backbone of the revolution. Under the FLN's leadership, they also participated in the revolution with workers' strikes and selective armed attacks on the French mainland. The FLN had divided Algeria into six politico-military districts—*wilayas*; its cadres used to call France *Le Septième Wilaya*—the Seventh Wilaya.

Boudiaf played a central role during the most formative years of the Algerian struggle. On October 22, 1956, the French air force intercepted a plane in flight from Morocco to Tunisia; they had information that five of the FLN's historic chiefs were on board. Sidi Mohammed was taken prisoner along with Rabah Bitat, Ait Ahmed, Mohammed Khider, and Ahmed Ben Bella. All five remained in prison until Algeria became independent in the summer of 1962.

It was then that I met him for the first time, in Tunis. Rugged, working-man's face; strong handshake; a man of few words. "Marhaba," he had said simply. "We go to Algeria. You are an honorary citizen [*citoyen d'honneur*]." "I am an Algerian," I had shot back, and he had smiled, an austere smile.

We met one more time, in Paris. Ben Bella, as president, had sentenced him to death, forcing him to choose exile. Perhaps it was not safe for him to have visitors where he lived; we met in a friend's apartment. We shared a sadness for Algeria; anger over the consumerism and careerism which had overcome its governing elite; and concern for its long-suffering and brave people.

In France, Boudiaf tried again to mobilize Algerian workers for his newly founded Revolutionary Socialist Party [PSR]. This time he had little success. Algerians were not inclined to again stake out their lives and livelihoods to another cause. They were weary of war, hopeful that life would gradually improve, and suspicious that the ousted revolutionaries were settling personal scores. When I said this to him, he merely nodded.

We both knew though that Algerians are an insurrectionary people, and the next generation shall rise up to demand an accounting of sorts. For, as Boudiaf put it sadly: *Algérie est mal partie*—Algeria had a false start, a phrase I would repeat some years later to Colonel Houari Boumedienne, the military chief with whose help Ben Bella came to power and who later overthrew his ally to become president himself.

The major portion of the blame for the false start goes to Ahmed Ben Bella and to Houari Boumedienne, his forceful ally and tormentor. They drained the mainsprings of the Algerian Revolution. Ben Bella violated its commitment to collective leadership. Boumedienne ignored the revolution's participatory legacy and imposed upon it a centralized, bureaucratic scheme of industrial development. Algeria's contemporary predicament has its roots in that time.

History had willed Algeria's revolution its uniqueness: unlike Russia, China, Vietnam, and Cuba, it did not have a charismatic leader. Rather, it was ideologically opposed to personalism in politics and explicitly committed to collective leadership. From that fateful day, November 1, 1954, when the nine declared war on France, to independence in July 1962, the Algerian Revolution was run by committees. There were powerful figures in it like Krim Belkacem, possibly the most brilliant Arab soldier in several centuries, but no one became the uncontested leader of the FLN.

There were reasons behind this obsession with collective leadership: Nearly all of the FLN's front-rank leaders had been activists of the PPA [People's Party of Algeria], which was founded and dominated by Messali Hadj. Messali's passion and power became legend in France no less than Algeria. Historians regard him as the father of the Algerian nation. The younger men left him because he had become autocratic and would not heed their urging for a call to revolution. The split was stormy and bloody. The FLN had to fight its way not only into French garrisons but also through the well-organized thickets of PPA militancy. In this primordial struggle, their primary weapon against the historic hero was his autocratic personality and their collective one.

Ben Bella betrayed the principle of collective leadership. He had but a limited role in the revolution, yet he projected himself as its most authentic leader. He was helped by good looks and good luck. Ben Bellaism started to build soon after the French captured him in October 1956. When the revolution broke out, he had been sent to Cairo to get Abdel Nasser's help. He had less success in obtaining material help from Egypt than in befriending the Arab leader to his own advantage.

Meanwhile, the French were portraying the FLN as an Egyptian proxy, paid, trained, and guided from Cairo. After capturing the FLN leaders, French propaganda emphasized Ben Bella's Cairo connection. More importantly, Radio Cairo made much of him. For the next five years, the Voice of the Arabs projected Ben Bella as Algeria's Abdel Nasser. In those days, beleaguered Algerians used to listen to *Sawt al-Arab* [The Voice of the Arabs] as though it were an oracle. Thus, for opposite reasons, France and Egypt participated in the making of the Ben Bella myth.

Ben Bella was a credible hero, and not averse to his own mystification. He was good-looking, a soccer player, a decorated veteran of the French army, and a nationalist who had robbed a post office to finance the revolution. He was one of the historic chiefs. As the most publicized prisoner of France, he began to symbolize to Algerians their ever-growing community of suffering.

All this seemed quite harmless while he was in prison. Once independence had been negotiated and he was freed, his ambition played out. At the time, there was no individual claimant to power in Algeria; there were five loci of power. The revolution had been fought and won through interaction between the following:

First, the Provisional Government of the Algerian Revolution [GPRA]. This government in exile, based in Tunis since 1958, was responsible for directing the armed struggle inside Algeria, procuring armaments, caring for refugees and families of cadres, and conducting international relations. The GPRA negotiated Algeria's independence from France. As the representative body of the revolution, it commanded legitimacy both internationally and among Algerians. All major leaders, including Boudiaf and Ben Bella, held high positions in it, although some, like Krim Belkacem, exercised more power than others. Yet, as we shall presently see, in the course of that long and harsh struggle it had also incurred political and psychological liabilities. Based in Tunis, it directed the armed struggle, conducted international relations, and eventually negotiated independence.

Second, there were the six wilayas, military regions under commanders inside Algeria. They were respected by the people among whom they had lived through the hard years of resistance and French reprisals. Since mid-1959, when the French effectively closed the Tunisian frontier with electrified barbed wire fences, they had suffered especially from shortages of arms supplies and nourished resentments of their leaders in exile. In 1962, they led forces that were weary of warfare.

Third, there was the external army of liberation based on the Tunisian and Moroccan side of the border under the command of the austere Colonel Houari Boumedienne. It was organized like a conventional army, with heavy arms, including tank and armored battalions. It had been created in 1959 by the Provisional Government in the expectation that, like the Vietminh forces in Indochina, the Algerian National Army one day would engage its adversary in set-piece battles. That opportunity was denied it by, among other factors, the electrified boundary wall, the Morice and Challe lines. So in Ghardimou and Oujda its units trained, exercised, received political indoctrination, awaiting an opportunity for combat and to become the elite of independent Algeria's national army. This ALN (Armée de Libération Nationale) wielded force more than any other group, but it lacked legitimacy and a constituency in Algeria.

Fourth, there were the prison people. Some 250,000 Algerians experienced incarceration of one sort or another during the seven years of armed struggle. There is hardly a family in Algeria that did not suffer the loss of a son/daughter and barely one that did not have one in prison.

Fifth, FLN–France, which represented half a million adult Algerians and had provided the financial backbone of the revolution.

On the eve of independence, the last two became irrelevant to the postindependence jockeying for power. Upon being released, the prisoners lost group cohesion and took differing sides. Similarly, in the absence of the political and military exigencies of armed struggle, the metropolitan branch of FLN lost importance.

The other three remained central to the political transition in Algeria. Of these, the Provisional Government, which led Algeria to independence, had legitimacy but no coercive power. Sensing this weakness and judging the wilayas to be a potential source of dissent, it had created the ALN under Boumedienne, presumably a loyal commander. This turned out to have been the Algerian leaders' fatal mistake.

The wilayas had legitimacy and linkages with the populace. But they lacked coordination with each other, and their fighters were weary of war. They had outfought France and had but little inclination to enter a civil strife for power.

The ALN was a well-armed, well-trained, and well-rested standing army. As the Algerian Revolution gained prestige, it acquired more and better arms. Since the border was virtually sealed by the French, it did but little fighting. It was a conventional/political army under an austere and ambitious command. It had power but no legitimacy. This is where Ben Bella came in.

Boumedienne knew that the Provisional Government's leaders would not permit the ALN's primacy in politics. He also understood that by electing an authentic revolutionary, Ben Khedda, as its president, it had rid itself of those moderates, like Ferhat Abbas, who might seek the ALN's partnership. To overthrow the revolution's political leadership, Boumedienne needed an instrument of legitimation. Ben Bella, a vice president of the Provisional Government, became an enthusiastic instrument.

At independence, the FLN was paralyzed, split, and confronted by the ALN, its own creation. Algeria was virtually without central authority for nearly four months. This at war's end and while the French settlers were destroying factories and farms—they controlled 75 percent of Algeria's productive enterprises—as they departed. In the days when the two armed contenders for power finally confronted each other outside Algiers, the Algerian people did what history had rarely before witnessed: they literally stood in the thousands between the warring factions with signs that said: "BARAKA, SAB'A 'SNEEN BARAKA" (enough, seven years were enough) and "LE SEUL HERO, LE PEUPLE" (the only hero is the people). They stood there until the leaders swore to make peace. Those who had the will to fight a civil war won the peace. Ben Bella came to power and held it until 1965, when Colonel Boumedienne thought fit to dispense of him and put him in prison.

During the months of nongovernment, citizens, with the help of the FLN's cadres, formed self-management committees all over Algeria and took over the abandoned, sabotaged French factories and farms. Some two million Algerians, from a population of nine million, were organized in the self-management movement. They kept Algeria's economy running. In March 1963, several months after taking power, Ben Bella legalized the self-management system and, in one speech after another, extolled it as the crowning achievement of the revolution. But the process of strangulating and bureaucratizing the self-managed enterprises had already begun. It was completed under Boumedienne.

Houari Boumedienne was an authentic nationalist, honest and austere. But his outlook was essentially militaristic. He ruled by command not consensus and held outdated and authoritarian ideas of economic and political development. He believed that rapid industrialization was essential to attaining economic independence and prosperity; investment in heavy industry was the best method of industrialization; socialism was the best guarantee of industrialization; and socialism meant centralization of power and the ownership of industry by the state.

Algeria followed a proto-Stalinist model of development without Stalin, without the resources or the level of Russian development, without having to fight a big war, but with its economy deeply and unequally linked to the capitalist market. Bureaucracy grew exponentially, fatter and more corrupt. The FLN, one of the marvels of twentieth-century political organization, collapsed under its weight. Repeated attempts to resuscitate it failed. Lacking skill and also motivation, the oligarchs preferred the "turnkey" concept of industrialization, which augmented both unemployment and Algeria's dependence on the West. Agriculture was neglected. Critics were suppressed.

Meanwhile the population grew exponentially; it stands now at twenty-five million. So did unemployment, which is 23 percent. Fifty percent of Algeria's people remain illiterate. Seventy-five percent were born after independence; they have no sense of either the struggles of the past or the relative improvement in national life. Many have attained literacy in the *madaris* [religious schools] which have proliferated in Algeria much as they have elsewhere in the Muslim world.

I visited Algeria for the last time in 1967, five years after independence. I had a foreboding that the promises of that extraordinary movement of liberation had been decisively betrayed. "How did you find it?" President Houari Boumedienne had inquired. He appeared displeased with my response: "Algérie est mal partie" (Algeria began badly.)

After that I lost touch with Algeria, and my interest in it did not revive until 1990, when I read that the Front for Islamic Salvation [FIS] had swept the municipal elections. I was glad, not because I think the neo-Islamists are an answer to our predicament but because Algerians had finally registered their protest against their unjust postcolonial order.

The Islamic movement did not do well holding municipal power and was beginning to lose popularity when the government began foolishly to crack down on it. Its unexpected success in the first round of national elections in 1991 was an outcome of the crackdown and the Algerian people's greater rejection of the militarist regime. The majority vote for FIS was merely a barometer of popular discontent. In panic, Algeria's insecure establishment suspended the final round of elections, eased out President Chadi Benjedid, who had wisely followed a policy of liberalization, banned FIS activities, and imprisoned its leaders. A French daily caught the mood. Algerians were fevered by an excess of disillusionment; as a cure, wrote *Le Monde*, they broke the thermometer.

The ruling junta brought Mohammed Boudiaf back from twenty-seven years of exile to replace Benjedid. The old warrior began by invoking the principle of collective leadership. So the junta put him at the head of a "collective presidency." The junta had needed Boudiaf. His stature as a founding father, his reputation for integrity, his humble origins, and his austere style promised them excellent cover in a time of crisis. But why did he accept their invitation into so dubious an environment? I do not know the answer; I can only guess.

Sidi Mohammed was a patriot, still in exile at seventy-two. He must have thought this was his last chance to serve Algeria. He was a devout Muslim, a secularist, and a socialist. He considered the contemporary Islamic movement as regressive and neototalitarian; it distorted Islam and violated the best values of Islamic civilization. A committed anti-imperialist, he had once sided with colonial France to resist German fascism. Why not side again with the bad against the worst? He may have fancied himself as rescuing Algeria from a menace, as being able to eradicate corruption in government, as restoring the FLN to a popular, democratic organization, and as returning Algeria to a program of sustainable, participatory development.

After all, he had once been a dreamer, and right. This time the old revolutionary may have miscalculated, not realizing that the enemy within is always the more dangerous. Whatever the reasons, Algeria shall remember him fondly and mourn him deeply.

*Postscript*

*DAWN*, SEPTEMBER 20, 1997

It is painful to witness Algeria's tragedy. More than sixty thousand, mostly innocent Algerians, have been killed since 1992,[1] when the military government annulled the outcome of the elections that had yielded a governing majority to FIS, the Islamic Salvation Front, and war began between the army and the Islamists.

A lame justification was offered for annulling the election results. It was alleged that the Islamic Front sought an authoritarian system of government. The allegation was correct insofar as the Islamic Front's leaders held ambivalent and opportunistic attitudes toward parliamentary government. But the Algerian establishment's suppression of the election results, a move welcomed by the governments of France and the United States, was itself undemocratic and undesirable morally and politically.

To begin with, Algeria's authoritarian ruling establishment is not a credible defender of democracy. Furthermore, the Islamic Front could not transform Algeria into a theocracy. In government in 1992, the Front would have wielded power partially at best. Secular forces would have remained in control of the state apparatus. The bureaucracy is largely secular in outlook and by training. The army retains ultimate mastery over the state. Algeria's economy is linked to France. In brief, the government of the Islamic Salvation Front would have resembled in 1992 the prematurely dissolved government of the Islamic Welfare Party in Turkey. Had the Algerian establishment been wiser than the Turkish army and permitted the Islamic Front to run its course in government, it would most likely have stumbled out of political prominence. Instead, the Islamic Front was denied a nearly certain opportunity to fail. Jihad ensued.

The violence has grown increasingly worse. Radical, hawkish factions have hardened in the army no less than in the Islamic movement. Neither side shows mercy even toward the innocent people who are used as pawns in their savage warfare. Each side appears determined to punish people for their views and to push citizens "by force if necessary" into its camp.

Singers have been silenced, writers and journalists are murdered, and unveiled women's faces have been slashed and disfigured by militants of the Islamic movement. For its part, the government imprisons and tortures with cruel impunity. In the last year, a new horror has appeared: masked men arrive and massacre entire villages—men, women, and children. On August 29, they massacred ninety-eight persons in Reis, a village to the south of Algiers, the capital. A week later, the killers arrived in Beni Messous, a village close to a military barracks, just a few miles from Algiers, and massacred a hundred children, women, and men. Yet another masked killing of eighty-five persons occurred on September 23. Private sources put these official figures three to four times higher.

Who are these killers? The government blames the Islamists. FIS leaders accuse the government. No one can be sure. They could be from either side or from both. Some observers believe these massacres are organized by hawks in the armed forces. Senior military officers are said to be divided between "eliminationists," i.e., those who advocate total elimination of the Islamic movement, and the "accommodationists" who favor negotiation with FIS moderates. The release on July 15 of FIS leader Abbasi Madani is reported to have increased the tension inside the ruling junta. As a compromise, Mr. Madani has now been placed in house arrest. Speculation is that the massacres were aimed at discrediting the moderate army leaders led by General Mohammed Bechine, former director of military security. Mohammed Lamari, the army chief, holds the hard line. There is also a counterspeculation: the Islamists committed the latest atrocities in order to sabotage elections, which are scheduled for October 23.

Victims of both sides, Algeria's people are caught between the devil and the deep sea—the self-styled Islamists and the militarists. The roots of this tragedy lie in the history that immediately followed the long war of Algerian liberation. When France withdrew in July 1962, an ugly struggle for power ensued among Algerian nationalists. The winners—Ahmed Ben Bella supported by Colonel Houari Boumedienne and his troops—favored one-party, authoritarian, and populist rule, which was then in vogue from Egypt to Ghana. Both men failed to comprehend that authoritarian rule kills creativity, breeds corruption, and distorts society. The democratic option was thus closed to Algeria at the moment of its liberation. The stage was set for the establishment of a military-bureaucratic oligarchy which rules the country to this day.

[1997]

# PART II
# THIRD WORLD POLITICS

## PATHOLOGIES OF POWER,
## PATHOLOGIES OF RESISTANCE

# INTRODUCTION

Carollee Bengelsdorf and Margaret Cerullo

The old is dying and the new cannot be born. In this interregnum, there arises a great diversity of morbid symptoms.

—Antonio Gramsci, *The Prison Notebooks*

In the articles in this section, written almost entirely in the 1980s, Ahmad lays out in detail his analysis of the crises of postcolonial societies. This analysis is framed and informed by the defeated hopes of those who lived under colonial rule and were involved in anticolonial struggles for independence and national liberation. Ahmad confronts directly the near-total failure of political transformation toward democratic constitutional statehood, let alone any meaningful alteration of social, economic, political, and cultural relationships and dependencies. His purposes in undertaking these analyses are manifold. His intent is to examine the authoritarian legacies of colonialism that, he argues, were not dismantled or eroded with decolonization but relentlessly, and, when necessary, violently, expanded in new "indigenous" forms. Like the postcolonial theorists, he insists that the postcolonial condition is inaugurated with the onset rather than the end of colonial occupation: there is an unbroken history of colonial consequences. If postcolonial studies examines the argument largely in cultural terms, Ahmad insists on the institutional and political legacies: he details how these legacies are reorganized and encrypted in distinct postcolonial configurations of power.

Despite his devastating analysis of the "pathologies of power" in the Third World, Ahmad's purpose remains always to seek the openings, to search out the possibilities, to reveal what cannot be thought because certain other things have been imposed on thought instead.[1] It is not to create yet another system of analysis but to look for avenues of movement, even as he recognizes and speaks of a level of "discontent" "unparalleled" among Third World peoples or of a "trauma" in Muslim societies more encompassing than at any moment in their fourteen-century history. Severe "pathologies of power" have in every case marked the transition from agrarian to industrial societies. Europe's prolonged transition was accompanied by brutal colonization, the genocide of ancient civilizations, and fascism, as well as epochs of revolution. It is impossible to confront the devastation that accompanies the most fateful transition in recorded history (no less in Europe than in the contemporary Third World), he once told an undergraduate audience, without a sense of counterpower, of the possibilities of intervention and transformation.

Ahmad begins each of these articles by dismantling the conventional frameworks and undermining the dominant and layered mythologies within which the Third World has been studied and interpreted in the major Western traditions of social science and political theory. Thus he challenges both mainstream modernization and neomodernization literature, as well as classical Marxism and dependency theory. Despite the fact that they represent opposing lines of thought within the Western tradition, as Ahmad points out over and over again, each deals with the Third World in hierarchical binary terms—traditional/modern; despotic/democratic; religious/secular—in which the implicit referent is always the West.

This strategy of dismantling permeates his three famous *Arab Studies Quarterly* articles. In "From Potato Sack to Potato Mash," his classic article on the peasantry, he unsettles entirely the idea of stagnant, unchanging, timeless, precolonial peasant civilizations. He substitutes a picture of societies marked by continual tensions that frequently erupted into violence. Indeed, he characterizes "traditional societies" as more often than not "insurrectional cultures." The picture he paints is of decentralized and brittle superstructures where the legitimacy of ruling elites depended on their limited incursions into the routines of daily life. Oriental despotism, he argues, arrives with modern colonialism; it is alien to the precolonial Third World.

In "Postcolonial Systems of Power," he challenges the abstractness and generality of the lens through which the state in the Third World has been interpreted by analysts of both the Left and the Right as dependent, peripheral, petit bourgeois, and uniformly undemocratic and corrupt. Such abstractions in his view lack the rich empirical grounding of the first Marxist analysts of the postcolonial state, preeminently, for Ahmad, Fanon. Ahmad's own analytical approach to the "pathologies of power" in the postcolonial world builds on these earlier Marxists (Fanon, Halavi, and Roger Murray) but also, critically, on Gramsci, whom he takes in unexpected and unconventional directions. He extends

Gramsci's framework for examining the autonomy of politics, the distinct varieties of power that develop within similar social and economic conditions, to examine how culture, morality, ideology, and specific histories shape the character of postcolonial states. He sets up what at first glance appears to be simply a political science typology to characterize the empirical variety of state formations in the Third World. But the purpose of this typology is not to freeze and keep stationary; to the contrary, he is intent on showing the fluidity of his categories. Displacing notions of linear political development, he elaborates on these "modes" [versus "systems" ] of power as "tentative," "changing," and, at moments, "circular." His goal is to understand these shifts, to clarify their likely directions and the reasons they will take such directions. His major concern in the essay is to analyze the trajectories of what he calls the "radical-nationalist" regimes toward "radical-authoritarianism" and even neofascism. The rightward drift of these self-proclaimed nonaligned, populist, anti-imperialist regimes is especially crucial to understand since they historically had some genuine claim to embodying the authentic hopes of Third World radicalism.

In "The Neofascist State: Notes on the Pathology of Power in the Third World," he makes precise the meaning of the label "fascism" when applied in the context of the Third World. It becomes not an arbitrary, loosely used, and therefore almost meaningless term but rather one invested with specific characteristics, specific roots, and specific vulnerabilities. He carefully examines similarities to fascism in the developed world but points to critical differences, above all, the absence of ideological nationalism, the dependence of those in power on metropoles (and therefore their autonomy from their own civil societies), and their roots in the old war national security state. These differences are exactly what make the Third World neofascist state so vulnerable.

Underlying all these analyses is his preoccupation with the possibilities for democracy in postcolonial states. In "The Challenge of Democracy," an unpublished paper delivered in Malaysia in 1984,[2] he takes apart the notion that the Third World is not prepared for democracy (as the two major schools of Western thought on the subject—modernization theory and Marxism—argue) and decimates the assertions of authoritarian Third World ruling elites who question the suitability of "Western" institutions to the distinct contexts of their countries. In this same vein, he criticizes the Marxist Left, traditionally suspicious of so-called bourgeois democracy as a cloak for class rule.

In the course of his analysis, Ahmad lays out his basic framework on the colonial legacy of antagonistic political traditions—"command and consensus, the vice-regal and the republican, the imperial and the democratic"—and explores why one has consistently triumphed over the other. Using a contrast between India and Pakistan to develop and illustrate his analysis, he points to the role of absorption into the US security system and the development of the postcolonial national security state in ensuring the triumph of one tradition and set of institutions (the army and bureaucracy) over the other (democratic and popular). He identifies the fragmentation of the masses as a crucial condition for the maintenance of formal democratic institutions in the Third World (India). As he has shown in the *Arab Studies Quarterly*, even democratic regimes have moved rapidly to the Right, in an authoritarian direction, in response to genuine popular mobilization and challenge.

In "Islam and Politics," he challenges another unholy alliance of scholarship: this time the "traditionalist *Ulema*" and the "modern Orientalists," both of whom, by different paths and for different reasons, collapse politics into religion in their static portrayal of Islam. Ahmad makes a starkly contrasting argument. Moving across the sweep of the historical Islamicate, he argues that Islam's roots are counter-traditional and linked with social and political revolt by those subject to unbearable oppression; that religion was effectively separated from state power within Islamic societies "from Indonesia to Spain" since at least A.D. 945; and that there is no better evidence of the nonsectarian, pluralist values within Muslim civilization than the (forgotten) centuries of collaboration with other cultures, especially the West. This secularism "at the heart of Muslim political praxis" for eleven of its fourteen centuries, whatever its textual ideals, is, he contends, more relevant to understanding Islam's relation to politics than the antics of any current Islamic leader.

Ahmad's intention is not by any means to ignore the rise of fundamentalist Islamic movements (although he argues elsewhere that fundamentalism, while clearly evident in multiple contemporary religions, is a term by and large reserved in the current period to describe its Islamic manifestation, in an equation intended to connect it irrevocably with terrorism.[3] To the contrary, his goal is to lay out the sources in the experience of colonialism, and in the grotesque inheritance and inheritors of postcolonial Muslim states, of what he sees as the darkest, and most shameful, period in Islamic history.

Fundamentalism is, for him, an aberration in this history, but it is an aberration largely resultant from the traumas of colonization and the failure of disfigured, dependent, postcolonial states to defend national sovereignty or meet basic needs, leaving their populations "stranded . . . in the middle of the ford . . . haunted by the past, fevered with dreams of the future."[4] Traditionally, Muslims had extra local, extra territorial identities and allegiances: "The passport is inimical to the spirit of Islam." Colonialism "territorialized" Islam, absorbing all loyalty into the nation-state. If the goal of traditional insurgent Islamic movements had been to reform the secular state in the name of "universal" Islamic values, in the postcolonial period the goal has become to take state power to restore an idealized Islamic past. It is, then, to modernity/colonialism that we must look to understand Islam's contemporary "peculiar, disjointed" relationship to politics, not to its textual precepts.

The articles in this section make clear Ahmad's debt to Antonio Gramsci. Ahmad both extends Gramsci's framework for analyzing configurations of power in the Third World and expands it to take account of imperialism. Why does Gramsci become so interesting to him?

First, it was perhaps Gramsci's outsider status, the "outsider within," the Sardinian "stranger" in Italy that resonated with Ahmad's own position. He, too, brought the unfamiliar perceptions and insights of the stranger into the heart of an activist commitment that knew no national borders, no conventional confinement.

Perhaps most important is Ahmad's interest in the extent and character of the links between civil society and the state, the mechanisms for the expression of popular will and accountability. Like Gramsci's, Ahmad's analyses of "modes of power" take as their central focus the question of legitimacy, the balance of force and consent in the relationship between the rulers and the ruled. They are guided by an expansive notion of democracy, as "active consent." Active consent, the democratic ideal, "excludes any bureaucratic repressive relation between leaders and led, any corporate integration of the led, any reduction of democracy to its legal aspect." The latter represent passive consent from above to below, in which "politics is identified purely with the statist and instrumental domain of domination."[5]

"Passive revolution" is the second Gramscian concept resonant in Ahmad's work. For Gramsci, passive revolution describes forms of politics in which the political class relies primarily on the state, substitutes itself for the people, and sustains itself in power through bureaucratic and military links with society, an encompassing of society by the state.

Finally, Ahmad is drawn to Gramsci's efforts to understand the roots of Italian fascism in the particular kind of national state that emerged from the Risorgimento. In this project, Ahmad recognizes a theoretical framework within which to elaborate his own preoccupation with the sources of the radical-authoritarian and neofascist regimes that predominate in the Third World.

Ahmad is hardly alone in noting the extent of the impact of nineteenth- and twentieth-century colonization by the industrial West on the agrarian Third World. But his stress on the reconfiguration of economic and political structures leads him to focus on the way in which institutions, both traditional and modern, of these agrarian civil societies were overwhelmed by modern centralized states. That is, again extending Gramsci to the Third World, his major concern in these articles is the relationship between state and civil society and most specifically the balance between coercion and consent. The centralized state is, for him, the key colonial legacy. Its postcolonial inheritors, whether they follow directly in the "vice regal" tradition or commandeer the state in the name of radical nationalism, inevitably move in the direction of its expansion. Foreign aid—and here he means in particular US security assistance—feeds what he once referred to as Third World governing elites' "addiction to the arms habit."[6] It serves both to keep them in power and to expand the state and its most authoritarian aspects, always at the expense of the institutions of civil society, always in the end involving a concerted attempt to crush its creative dynamic.

In the case of radical nationalism, the leadership's inability to realize and build on its ties to civil society leads inevitably in the direction of radical authoritarianism or neofascism. It is, in the end, characterized by a shallow legitimacy; its appeals to the heart rather than to the head cannot sustain it. Ahmad goes beyond the notion of the autonomous state of the Marxist tradition to describe the pathology of this severance of civil society and state in the Third World, whose instability he captures in the image of a "suspended state." This image recurs in his blistering and incisive dissection of the Iran-Iraq war, the "War of the Rentier States," which follows the *Arab Studies Quarterly* articles in this section. A rentier state, for Ahmad, is a "regime [that] doesn't need its people . . . an entity suspended in time, detached from politics, disengaged from history." Such states are vulnerable to personalism, to the extent that the Iran-Iraq war is best seen as a "Saddam-Khomeini war."

This leads directly to the second theme that resounds through these pages: Ahmad's critique of the ruling elites of Third World countries. Here he is without mercy. At the heart of his identification of the pathologies of power in the Third World is a derivative and dependent bourgeoisie that does not create the state to serve its own purposes, as Marxists would have the bourgeoisie do. It is instead the outgrowth of a native class of civil servants and soldiers, generated first by the colonial and now by the dependent state. For Ahmad, these ruling classes are literal power elites whose primary vocation is to exercise power. His scathing analysis traces the multiple paths along which these ruling elites, whether the carriers of the vice regal or the nationalist traditions of colonial rule, move to suppress popular participation and substantive and procedural freedoms.

Here a third theme becomes vital: the ties between these ruling elites and the dominant world hegemonic power in the postcolonial world: the United States. The arms habit is one aspect of these ties. The Cold War ideal of the national security state—an ideal that, he will later note,[7] survives the Cold War—serves both Third World ruling elites and US economic and political domination of the societies they rule. These ties have functioned, everywhere, to expand the state: he points out that this is as true for radical–nationalist states (once the initial shock of the rhetoric of these states dissipates) as it is for states of a more outright, dictatorial form. Ties to the United States play a major role in determining the triumph of neofascist modes of power.

Finally, he sets about analyzing why democracy has been so fragile in postcolonial societies. If, as he writes, the Third World of the 1980s was indeed unfavorable to democratic development, it was not because democracy had failed; rather, it had been ruthlessly suppressed. Ahmad argues powerfully that there is nothing in the cultural traditions of Third World societies that makes them more inherently adverse to democracy than any Western country. Indeed, in one of his most original analyses, he argues in "Postcolonial Systems of Power" that democracy in Europe was integrally tied to colonial expansion. Those nation-states that could export their surplus populations developed in democratic directions (Britain, France), whereas those states stripped of colonies after World War I (Italy and Germany) responded to the threat of popular challenge by moving to the extreme Right. Here he suggests the centrality of a non-Eurocentric analysis of European fascism.[8]

In the prophetic essay "Islam and Politics," he outlines his explanation for the rise of politicized Islamic fundamentalism, the "time bomb" that he identifies already in 1984. In this explanation, all the themes that he has developed in this section come into tragic focus, as he identifies the roots of what we might call a specific "pathology of resistance." Not only did the Muslim world suffer the trauma of capitalist development under foreign auspices and for foreign benefit, as did the rest of the Third World, it was also newly conquered and colonized precisely at the end of World War II and the beginning of the great epoch of anticolonial resistance and decolonization. The subsequent Arab-Israeli conflict brought one humiliation after another, culminating, as he writes in 1984, in Israel's terrorization and efforts to disperse refugees in occupied Lebanon, with no resistance from Arab governments, except to suppress their own people. It is in this breach between civil society and political power in the Arab world, a separation greater than at any other point in the history of Islamic peoples, that Ahmad locates a time bomb. The "moral explosion of the masses," he tells us, when it comes, will have a referent to the past but its objective will be the future. The present will be judged morally in terms of the past, materially in terms of the future. However, Ahmad implies, certain pathologies of perception will blind the "manipulative and malevolent" Cold War orientalists (and even more, it will turn out, their post–Cold War inheritors)[9] to any understanding of the roots of revolt in the Muslim world. Rather than aim at understanding Islam and its relationship to politics, their opportunist deployment of expertise will present Islam as an alien Other, unchanging, backward-looking, and defined particularly by the repressive inseparability of religion and politics.

It is this theme that he revisits in his three critical journalistic articles on the rise of religious fundamentalism, written a decade and a half later.[10] By 1999, Islam and fundamentalism had become virtually indistinguishable in the Western imagination. (Terrorism would later be added to this equation.) Ahmad's goal in these articles is to historicize fundamentalism, to understand it as a modern phenomenon, and to get at its commonalties, across multiple religions, its "shared roots and similar patterns of expression" in reaction to the "crises of modernity and identity," which he addressed in "Islam and Politics" as well as the *Arab Studies Quarterly* articles. In "Roots of the Religious Right," he argues that there has been a resurgence of "restorationist" fundamentalism in almost every religion in the last two decades—among Hindu mosque-smashing militants, right-wing Christians in the United States, nationalist Christians in Serbia, and Jewish settlers in Israel—although generally only the Islamist variety merits the name "fundamentalist." He focuses on the shape that "restorationist fundamentalism" has taken in Islam, challenging these modern Islamists, who "distort, debase and reduce the politics, culture, society, history *and* religion of Islam." The various Islamicist movements, he argues, cannot be understood as a return to traditional Islam: they have little to do with Islam. Rather, they select, out of the entire corpus of Muslim beliefs, those that suit their political purposes and invest these with the aura of the sacred. They are absolutists of religion who assert one decontextualized aspect of it and disregard the rest. He explores, as a prime example of the selective instrumental and distorted use of religion, the rich Islamic precept of jihad, which has been reduced, in its current usage, to a single meaning: engagement in "holy" warfare, entirely divested of any conditions or rules. (Indeed, the most famous contemporary jihad, in this sense, was waged against the Marxist government of Afghanistan, sponsored, funded, and turned into a transnational project by a non-Muslim power, the United States. It was the success of this war, above all, he argues, that gave current force to the Islamicist movement.) Today, he writes in 1999, everything is claimed as a holy war, and not only in the Muslim world.

Finally, he offers a systematic account of the threads that tie these fundamentalisms together: their "ideology of superior difference" that requires an actively demonized Other against whom a "cult of violence" can be mobilized; their appeal to "people caught in the 'middle of the ford' between tradition and modernity"; their grim humorlessness; their misogynistic obsessions; their definitionally undemocratic, absolutist nature (despite a marked ability to make "Faustian deals" in pursuit of power). All fundamentalisms, he concludes, reduce complex religious systems to one or another version of modern fascism

He understands fundamentalism, and the movements and parties it has spawned, as a decidedly limited phenomenon, without staying power, precisely because of the nature of its distorted hold on the past, the present, and the future. But it is in these very limitations that he locates its disastrous potential: here, again, his image of a "time bomb" has such tremendous resonance.

Ahmad's articles in this section meticulously dissect the reasons for the near-total absorption of the democratic hopes of national liberation movements by triumphant authoritarian regimes in the postcolonial Third World. In activist fundamentalism, he locates a form of pathological resistance to these regimes and to the postcolonial order that sustains them, a resistance that grows out of and reflects the distortions of desire and expectation experienced by Third World peoples and the trauma these distortions have entailed. These essays stand as a systematic attempt to unmask that trauma: to locate it, to protest against the manner in which it has been employed, and to revivify democratic and popular traditions.

# 9 / FROM POTATO SACK TO POTATO MASH

The Contemporary Crisis of the Third World

The small-holding peasants form a vast mass, the members of which live in similar conditions but without entering into manifold relations with one another. Their mode of production isolates them from one another instead of bringing them into mutual intercourse . . . . In this way, the great mass of the French nation is formed by the simple addition of homologous magnitudes, much as potatoes in a sack form a sack of potatoes.

—Karl Marx, 1852

This essay deals with three interrelated questions.[1] It (1) outlines the contemporary crisis of the Third World; (2) suggests a set of criteria for judging the extent to which the crisis is being faced in a manner that contributes toward the development of an even, equitable, and democratic society; and (3) identifies the attributes which best equip a government, party, or a political movement to meet this unprecedented challenge. As such, it moves from description and analysis to normative statements and judgments. It is not possible to include exhaustive definitions of concepts or to add the needed caveats to some broad generalizations, for this essay summarizes the main themes of the introductory part of a longer, and unfinished, work. Its purpose is to outline my argument in order to elicit reactions while work is still in progress.

## 1. Precapitalist Society

Any discussion concerned with the future of the Third World ought to begin with an inquiry into the past, because the past is very present in these so-called transitional societies. That it is a *fractured* past invaded by a new world of free markets, shorn of its substance and strength, incapable of assuring the continuity of communal lives lived for millennia does not make it less forceful. Its power derives from the tyranny of contemporary Third World life and the seeming absence of viable alternatives. For the majority of Third World peoples, the experienced alternative to the past is a limbo—of alienation from the soil, of living in shantytowns, of migration into foreign lands, and, at best, of permanent expectancy. Leaning on and yearning for the recovery of an emasculated but idealized past is one escape from the limbo, breaking out in protest and anger is another. At times, the two are mixed; at others, they are separated in time but historically, organically linked. In our time, peasant millenarian rebellions have often been the harbingers of modern revolutions. "The process of modernization begins," writes Barrington Moore Jr., "with peasant revolutions that fail. It culminates during the 20th century with peasant revolutions that succeed."[2]

Here is a remarkable irony: since Neolithic times, peasants constituted the world's overwhelming majority and were its sole providers. Yet they were treated as objects, insignificant in the view of history. John Berger writes: "Rather, they were thought of as a continuous given, a kind of anonymous historical raw material which, like the soil itself, was given form—used, controlled, and finally rendered historical by the identifiable social forces of the minority. . . . They only acquired a temporary mass identity when the means of control over them failed or had to be changed."[3] That happened with some frequency; world history is studded with meagerly recorded peasant rebellions.

The class which had long made up the vast majority of mankind has almost vanished in the Western world; it is diminishing in the Third World. It is often said that the majority of people in the world today are still peasants. Yet this fact masks a more significant one. For the first time ever it is possible that the class of survivors may not survive. Within a century there may be no more peasants. Peasants, as they disappear, can confront the present. And in doing so they both provoke and represent a question: how much does the future now being constructed correspond to the popular hopes of the past? Capital, concerned with its own reproduction, cannot ask this question. Nor will it make any sense to the academic Marxist because it evades the problem of ideological illusion.[4]

As they disappear, peasants have transformed themselves from being the objects to becoming the subjects of history; in the twentieth century, they have been the primary, historic instruments of revolution from China to Cuba, Algeria to Vietnam. In thus confronting the present, they provoke and represent, as Berger says, a question which capital cannot ask and conventional

Marxists do not entertain: to what extent do society's plans for the future represent the popular hopes of the past?

Any serious discussion of "alternative development"—one that seeks to go beyond technocratic social engineering—must attempt a meaningful answer to this question. It is necessary, however, to qualify that the "hopes" are not really of the "past." Their expression is frequently, and inextricably, laden with the values, yearnings, and images of the past, but they are intrinsically existential hopes, induced and augmented by the contemporary crisis. For example, the often publicized ideological traditionalism of Third World peoples (the media spoke as much about "resurgent" Buddhism in the early 1960s as it does of Islam now) is a product of excessive, uneven "modernization." In the "transitional" societies, one judges the present *morally* with reference to the past, to inherited values, but *materially* in relation to the future. Therein lies a new dualism in our social and political life; the inability or unwillingness to deal with it entails disillusionment, terrible cost, and possible tragedy. One mourns Cambodia, fears for Iran.

Romantic writers and artists have viewed the precapitalist societies as marked by peace and social harmony, devoid of change and conflict. Scholars have often presented them as being inhabited by fatalistic peoples who were contented with, or at least resigned to, a life of misery, sickness, tyranny, ignorance, and uncertainty. In reality, life in the precapitalist world was marked by a variety of social, economic, and political tensions; these often culminated in violent and costly feuds, uprisings, civil wars, and sometimes in the total overthrow of a ruling group. More often than not, the traditional societies were insurrectional cultures. But the manner in which collective grievances were expressed and resolved was quite distinctive. For example:

1. Traditional insurgents were often effective in defending their immediate, local interests; they were most deficient whenever faced with the need to pull their forces together and coordinate their struggle around a common purpose across villages and tribes.

2. Their ideological intent was normally restorationist, that is, far from questioning the legitimacy of the existing order, they sought to restore it to its accepted, authoritative norm. One attacked the ruling king, not the institution of monarchy. Rather, in protesting a tyrant, one defended and sought the good king. In precapitalist times, the peasant revolt was a corrective mechanism; it frequently served to reaffirm the established order.

3. Traditional insurgents were hostile to state power; their primary drive was for less, not more, government. Frequently, peasant rebellions were protests against the expansion of the state's role and the excessive presence of external authority in the local community.

4. The objectives of traditional insurgents were concrete and limited. With rare exceptions, they struggled to put certain limits upon intolerable injustices—extortionist lords, excessive conscription, arbitrary exercise of coercive power—not to suppress them altogether. They generally sought to preserve their hard-won margins of security, not to renovate the entire society or remodel it after a new fashion. They were rebels, not revolutionaries.

5. Whence the perennial contrast in precapitalist societies between an unstable superstructure and a very hardy infrastructure. Rebellions followed one another in endless succession; even dynasties were overturned; but the primary institutions governing political and economic life persisted and were often strengthened after each period of turmoil.

This state of affairs was perpetuated by the economic, political, and social realities of the preindustrial, precapitalist society—a milieu which will now be briefly described.

## THE PREVALENCE OF A GENERALIZED LOGIC OF CAUTION

Access to the basic necessities of life in precapitalist societies appeared to the people as being dependent upon natural and social forces which were impervious to human needs, unyielding to human effort or reasoning (e.g., floods, storms, droughts, pestilence, raids, invasions, and the lord's extortions). Faced with such persistent and unpredictable dangers, people were only too aware of the frailty of all things human; thrift, hard work, and perseverance helped one survive when things were good, but the threat of calamity hung over all, even the unsleeping. These conditions made people cautious; they created small spaces of security and predictability around them, strove for concrete and limited goals, and sought to propitiate the occult forces by means of prayers, offerings, and incantations, beliefs and rituals which also helped strengthen communal solidarity. Having experienced power primarily as a vehicle that caused suffering, peasants distrusted it. Peasants could be betrayed. "Once firmly mounted, the rider begins to spur the horse" runs one proverb. If co-opted into power, one was corrupted and betrayed one's community:

"He has just become a Muslim, and already claims descent from the Prophet." Peasants worked with, not against, the elements and did not hesitate to bend with the wind that could not be resisted. Whenever faced with bold and new schemes, peasants were wary and cautious lest they put themselves in the position of the proverbial fool who jumped in the river in order to avoid the rain.

This did not prevent peasants from dreaming about an ideal world in which justice prevailed. After all, their lives were marked by a fundamental, systematic economic injustice; they suffered from the "permanent handicap" of having their meager surplus taken from them. To cite John Berger again: "For the producer of food, to have to feed others before one could feed one's own seemed a total reversal of good order. Such an injustice, the peasant reasons, cannot always have existed; so he assumes a just world at the beginning."[5] Whence came the drive toward the utopian, millenarian movements which occasionally but powerfully swept through peasant societies. These movements conceived of a transformation from the real to the desired world by means of a sudden, thorough, and apocalyptic upheaval. They were extravagant outbreaks of shared dreams, not a consistent, much less functioning, program of action. In our time, these millenarian and primordial uprisings have been the forerunners of revolutionary movements, thus linking, as the earlier quotation from Barrington Moore Jr. suggests, the dualism of the past with the dualism of the present.

LEGITIMACY AND DISPERSION OF POLITICAL POWER

The ruling minority's elitism and injustices notwithstanding, precapitalist systems of power enjoyed a certain legitimacy among their subjects. Legitimacy is a crucial though badly defined and vastly misused term. As used here, legitimacy is not merely a matter of beliefs and sentiments; even less is it a question of popularity of government. It refers to that crucial and ubiquitous factor in politics which invests power with authority. It comes to states and other institutions of power when their constituents recognize their claim to authority in some principles or sources beyond their mastery of the means of coercion or when citizens actively or meaningfully participate in the process of government, i.e., when there is a maximum of self-government. Above all, legitimacy is assured to the extent that the political relationships and processes promoted by the system of power are responsive to the forces created by the system of production. In order to be legitimate, power must find an operative ideological justification—in the divine right of kings, the mandate of heaven, the sanctity of priests, or the superiority of lords; in constitutions stressing the principle of democratic consent or in the dictatorship of the proletariat. But its functional validity comes from the concurrence of economic and social forces and needs with political institutions and relationships. The erosion of legitimacy generally marks the increasing shift of citizens from obeying authority to rebelling against it. Its breakdown always heralds the pressure toward revolution. Unlike rebels—who normally protest the failures and excesses of existing authority rather than question its right to exist—revolutionaries challenge a system's very title to rule. They question the legitimacy of the entire system and seek new bases of authority in new values as well as in new political and economic arrangements.

In no small measure, the precapitalist systems enjoyed a certain legitimacy because in relation to what centralism implies today, state power in these societies was invariably decentralized. Even in such "centralized" systems as the Chinese, Mughal, or Ottoman, power was pluralistically distributed among more or less autonomous tribal and religious leaders, landed lords, provincial governors, and other state officials. When excess of discontent led to an outbreak, the rebels' targets were normally the local authorities. Central authority was often too remote to be deemed responsible ("If only the king knew!"). The kingship or the caliphate was invested with enough ascriptive legitimacy for the office not to come into question (thus the restorationist thrust). The centralized, repressive state backed by a well-organized bureaucracy, a nationalist-deployed police force, and a large standing army is a contribution, by and large, of Western imperialism. "Oriental despotism" arrived in the Third World in the guise of "Westernization," a crucial part of the colonial baggage; in the postcolonial period, it prospered and strengthened under the cover of modernization.

## DISCONTINUITY BETWEEN LOCAL PROBLEMS AND SOCIETYWIDE ISSUES

Precapitalist societies were usually composed of a multitude of small, cohesive, self-absorbed, autonomous, often mutually hostile units whose integration into a larger whole was markedly deficient. This lack of integration had important consequences: people devoted the greatest part of their lives to the conduct of local affairs; groups living outside the village community or kinship group appeared to them either as irrelevant strangers to be avoided and ignored, or as potential enemies to be feared or courted, or as potential victims to be used and exploited. Cooperation across the boundaries of clan and community was a compact of defense entered into only in times when the survival of all was threatened by an external enemy or a natural calamity. Being so dispersed and disconnected, the mass of the people were unorganized and—given the pretechnological means of communication and conditions of work—unorganizable on a large-scale or sustained basis. Hence local problems rarely merged to become societywide issues. Karl Marx noted this phenomenon while discussing the lack of revolutionary potential in the French peasantry and concluded that "insofar as millions of families live under economic conditions of existence that separate their mode of life, their interest and their culture from those of the other classes, and put them in hostile opposition to the latter, they form a class. Insofar as there is merely a local interconnection among these small-holding peasants, and the identity of their interest begets no community, no national bond and no political organization among them, they do not form a class."[6] Less than a hundred years later, peasants constituted the backbone of protracted and successful revolutionary struggles in the Third World. This is because these nonindustrialized countries have undergone, and are still undergoing, a shift in the fundamental equation of human condition. This change marks the Third World's transition from rebellion to revolution.

## II. The Revolutionary Challenge

In the Third World today, history and technology have intensified and accentuated the injustices and tensions which, in precapitalist times, produced peasant rebellions and millenarian movements. The social and political milieu which had, in the past, circumscribed discontent within the boundaries of religiosity and rebellion has been drastically altered by: (1) the forced integration of Third World economies into the international market system; (2) the externally determined superimposition of modern technology upon precapitalist social and economic infrastructure; and (3) the consequent transformation of land and labor into commodities (in the capitalist, market sense of the word).

These fundamental, if uneven and exogenous, changes define the contemporary crisis of the Third World. Past grievances remain; in fact, they have vastly augmented. Yet what underlies the passage from rebellion to revolution is not so much the augmentation of grievances as the creation of a political milieu which compels collective action toward a different, better world. The basic drive, the inner logic of this situation is not merely the fulfillment of limited goals, like raising the per capita income and level of food consumption, but the transformation of society and, within it, of all relationships between classes and individuals, between the elite and the masses, between national minorities and the dominant majority, between men and women.

## THE DIFFUSION OF THE LOGIC OF DARING

The appeal of the old logic of caution has weakened because of changes in economic, social, and political relations upon which this logic was predicated. Analysts have written extensively and generally agree on the circumstances which have forced the mutation of traditional societies: (1) the colonial encounter which, among other things, weakened and often destroyed altogether the legitimacy of the traditional systems of power and was also the primary instrument of forcing an uneven integration of the colonized countries into the international capitalist market; (2) commercialization of the rural sector, which had the effect of destroying the economic, social, and demographic equilibrium of traditional societies—"Where previously market behavior had been subsidiary to the existential problems of subsistence, now existence and its problems became subsidiary to marketing behavior";[7] (3) pauperization of the peasantry caused largely by the commercialization of agriculture and uneven infiltration of technology, which produced a demographic explosion unaccompanied by a corresponding growth of production; (4) urbanization, which has involved the uprooting and encampment of rural peoples into the limbo of shantytowns; and (5) cultural dislocation. The cumulative effect of these realities has been the disappearance of the traditional societies in the Third World.

The vast majority of people still live in structurally archaic societies, but they are organically linked with the modern, industrial, often metropolitan world. They are the men and women whom Germaine Tillion has vividly described as "living on the frontiers of two worlds—in the middle of the ford—haunted by the past, fevered with dreams of the future. But it is with their hands empty and their bellies hollow that they are waiting between their phantoms and their fevers."[8] One of Aimé Césaire's poems provides the appropriate profile of this Third World majority:

> My name: Offended
>
> My middle name: Humiliated
>
> My status: Rebel
>
> My age: the Stone Age
>
> My race: the Fallen Race

The degree of discontent is quite unparalleled. The world is experienced as being both unjust and disorderly. Yet, surprisingly, the environment in the Third World today is far from hopeless; it produces anger more often than despair. There is a diffusion of a new set of perceptions, beliefs, and expectations.

1. Relativism—the discovery that one's traditional way of life was only one among several possible social arrangements and that these others often yield more prosperity and justice; that traditional beliefs do not embody the answer to all fundamental problems; that many traditional practices were arbitrary, absurd, and therefore highly questionable.

2. Optimism—the emergence and diffusion of a feeling of hope and power, of the belief that what exists does not have to exist, that people can improve their lot if they try. The diffusion of this belief has been furthered by revolutionary activists who, thanks to modern means of communication, are able to transmit a program of hope and a call to action to millions of people. "It is the passionate and unflinching attempt to make people understand that everything depends on what they do," wrote Franz Fanon, "that if we stagnate it is their fault, and if we make any progress it is thanks to them."[9] Similarly, every popular movement in the Third World today impresses upon its militants the conviction that there is no such thing as an insoluble problem, that there is no difficulty which cannot be eradicated.

3. Rationalism—the logic of daring owes much to the spread of the presumption that planning, organization, and the use of scientific knowledge will resolve social problems. The extravagant, unprogrammatic hopes of traditional peasant life—the miraculous means of shortening distances, cutting down forests in minutes, shearing a flock of sheep in hours—have given life's real

possibilities a new meaning. It is thus that the gateway has opened to what has come to be called "the revolution of rising expectations."

## THE DISENCHANTMENT WITH AUTHORITY

Colonial powers developed a state system in the colonies which differed, in terms of its roots as well as its social composition, from the precapitalist monarchical, feudal, and tribal systems of power. This fact, as well as the commercialization of rural communities and the consequent demographic and cultural dislocation, has undermined the traditional bases for legitimacy and has produced a crisis of authority. Unlike precapitalist rebels, contemporary Third World people do not seek to restore the old order. The basic thrust of their discontent is toward overthrowing rather than renovating. "Gone are the times when one could say, 'Oh, if the king only knew!'" wrote an Algerian. "We now know that the king knows."[10] As mentioned earlier, the title to authority comes into question when changes in the system of production (including technology) alter the basic configuration of economic and social relationships. New knowledge, values, and classes destroy the presumptions of the old. Also, for the first time in centuries, there are concrete alternatives. Foreign rule gave one example of the alternative to the existing and inherited system; new ideologies offer other, more attractive alternatives. As old institutions and processes inevitably fail to fulfill new needs and satisfy new forces, the crisis of legitimacy augments. Under propitious circumstances, the crisis may be resolved through reformist renovations. More often, revolutions produce new legitimacy for new systems of power.

## THE TRANSFORMATION OF PRIVATE PROBLEMS INTO PUBLIC ISSUES

When the autonomy of the precapitalist local community is destroyed, when its economy ceases to be self-reliant, and when it begins to lose its basic functions—administrative, legal, educational, and economic—to newer and more powerful agencies, there are several ramifications:

1. Nationalization of the Peasantry. Peasants and former peasants begin to view themselves as part of a larger society and no more as isolated collectivities whom the good ruler left alone and upon whom the tyrant imposed. They begin to iden-

tify with groups and communities they never saw before. Peasants who knew each other only as enemies come to regard each other as fellow sufferers. They begin to see that their private and local problems are caused by and constitute an integral part of a wider system which hinders the improvement of their lives; that other individuals and communities suffer similar wrongs under the same system. It is thus that Marx's "sack of potatoes" becomes mashed potatoes.

2. Radicalization of Political Conflict. As large numbers of people previously outside the political realm force their way into national politics, the common man becomes increasingly relevant to politics. For many newcomers in politics, the mass constitutes a viable clientele, their only political capital. Thus politics ceases to be a mere struggle for the spoils of power within a privileged minority. It becomes, progressively, a contest between the contenders of different social systems and political ideals. When politics becomes a contest not merely for offices but for the power to transform or not to transform a society, between revolution and the maintenance of a status quo of privilege, it becomes a matter of life and death for the participants. The tension generated by the clash between the fears of the few and the frustrations of the many comes to permeate social life and radicalizes political conflicts. Progressively, then, the choice in the Third World narrows down to reaction or revolution.

3. Emergence of an Invitational Outlook. As mentioned earlier, traditional insurgents were "isolationists" in that they generally protested the augmented, oppressive presence of the external, state authority. In conditions of modern asymmetry, contemporary popular sentiment demands the contrary. Today the mass political environment is invitational in that it invites the state to intervene forcefully to reorder social and economic life. This phenomenon puts a very high premium on the rapid, often untrammeled expansion of the state's power. Yet, ironically, the state which expands is generally the state whose antecedents lie in colonialism and whose survival often depends on its continued links with the imperial metropolis.


*III. Requisites for Endogenous, Alternative Development*

The Third World is facing a revolutionary situation which cannot be understood merely in terms of anticolonialism, national independence, or economic development. As a triple revolution—political, social, and economic—which has forged in telescopic time with an unprecedented, actual and potential, involvement by a majority of the people, it is unique in history. The success of a regime in such a situation can be tested not so much by its seeming stability, for stability may only denote stagnation; nor can it be confirmed by the evidence of constant motion, for motion does not always mean progress; nor by lusty "growth," which often involves augmented inequality and exploitation; nor by the displacement of a privileged aristocracy by a managerial middle class; nor by the modification of traditional or colonial authoritarianism into single-party oligarchies.

Economic growth must serve to satisfy the demands for distributive justice; new institutions must be instruments not only of mobilization and control but also of accountability.

We argue that in order to grapple successfully with the contemporary challenge of the Third World a political elite, government, or movement must be able to respond creatively and meaningfully to six major crises: legitimacy, decolonization, democracy, development, distribution, and integration.

Furthermore, we argue, on the basis of empirical record no less than normative preference, that the following are the minimum requisites for achieving a measure of success in meeting the challenge of the Third World: (1) a coherent, consistent, and functioning ideology; (2) a revolutionary, radical political leadership; (3) ideological and leadership commitment to the principles of accountability and democracy; (4) institutions and mechanisms designed to ensure adherence to the democratic practices and the accountability of the government to the governed; (5) congruence of new institutions, styles of politics, and political symbols with the historical inheritance and culture of the people; and (6) operative commitment to self-reliance and endogenous development as bases for planning and organization.

Those countries which conform closely, even if not entirely, to these criteria stand the best chance of undergoing social transformation with a minimum of violence and political constraints. Those societies which, due to the strength of vested local or foreign interests, reject the radical, democratic option may live with the challenge a while longer, at a high cost to the common people and ultimately to face an explosion of much greater intensity.

[1980]

# 10 / POSTCOLONIAL SYSTEMS OF POWER

Third World countries share only a few, negative attributes—economic underdevelopment, dependence on a foreign metropolis, an undernourished, underemployed, poverty-stricken populace largely deprived of basic educational, housing, and health services. Political life in all but a few countries is characterized by centralization of power, government by Westernized elites with extremely constricted or no exercise of popular power, an absence of functioning institutions which allow for even a modicum of governmental accountability to the public, and executive infringement upon human rights without recourse to an independent judiciary.

Within this general framework of underdevelopment, unequal distribution, and undemocratic politics, there is a wide range of differences among the Third World countries. There exists but a negligible body of literature which attempts to identify and explain the contrasting developments. The focus of comparative research on the Third World has been on similarities rather than differences. Theoretical formulations compel emphasis on uniformities in the patterns of development while short-circuiting empirical evidence of significant differences between seemingly comparable states (e.g., Nasserite Egypt-Iraq; Tanzania-Uganda-Kenya; India-Pakistan-Sri Lanka) and socioeconomic formations (petite bourgeoisie, comprador bourgeoisie, the new middle class, the military-bureaucratic elite, etc.).

This has been true of the liberal "modernization" literature as well as the more recent and less numerous "Marxist" writings. Thus the "dependency" theory, which made an important beginning toward the study of neocolonial relations, has been applied so generally and mechanistically that important distinctions have been blurred between various forms and levels of dependency and their effects on the development of given societies. Similarly, in recent years there has been a welcome surge of interest in the nature of state in postcolonial societies. But, so far, the literature on this subject remains too broad, abstract, and detached from reality to be very meaningful. The first set of formulations on the postcolonial state—for example, by Franz Fanon, Roger Murray, and Hamza Alavi[1]—was remarkable for its empirical grounding and intellectual rigor. Unfortunately, subsequent literature on the subject has done little justice to these seminal attempts. Formulations about Third World states under the controlling interest of the petite bourgeoisie and the imperial metropolis, about the peripheral state being an "economic" and "political reproduction institution," are often so rarified and fragmented as to have little value as theory and less as a framework for analyzing specific situations and trends.

The following essay summarizes some of the general conclusions of a larger, unfinished work on "Development and the State in Dependent Societies." A critical survey of contemporary literature on Third World politics is beyond the scope of this essay. Here, it is relevant only to state that I avoid seeking a unifying theory of causation and linear conceptions of political development. My approach is eclectic. It owes a special intellectual debt to Antonio Gramsci's concepts of "hegemony," "relation of forces," and "dual perspectives" in the "analysis of situations."[2] Its aim is to identify and understand the varieties no less than the uniformities of developments in the Third World. As such, while regarding the interplay of imperialism and class struggle as the fundamental and decisive reality in the modern history and contemporary life of Third World peoples, it acknowledges the importance of historical experience, culture, morality, and ideology in defining the specificity and autonomy of politics.

On an empirical basis, taking into account their historical antecedents, formal-legal status, ideological preferences, economic policies, conduct of politics, and international links, the majority of Third World states can be divided into the following systems of power:

1. The elective-parliamentary system (e.g., India, Sri Lanka, Malaysia, Jamaica, Singapore);
2. The ascriptive-palace system (e.g., Morocco, Nepal, Saudi Arabia, Kuwait);

3. The dynastic-oligarchic system (e.g., Nicaragua under Somoza, Haiti, Paraguay);

4. The pragmatic-authoritarian system (e.g., Ivory Coast, Senegal, Tunisia, Zambia, Cameroon, Egypt under Sadat);

5. The radical-nationalist system (e.g., Algeria, Tanzania, Mexico, Iraq, Syria, Somalia, Libya, Indonesia under Sukarno);

6. The Marxist-socialist system (Cuba, Mozambique, Guinea-Bissau, Vietnam);

7. The neofascist system (e.g., Brazil, Indonesia, Chile, Uruguay, Argentina, Iran under the shah, Zaire).

A few clarifications: first, this classification is not the only one possible; using different criteria one may group the states quite differently. Its purpose is limited: to draw attention to the varieties of politics in the Third World and to establish a framework for comparison in order to better understand the process of change, including sudden shifts from one system toward another. Second, taken together the seven categories are not comprehensive. There are states—Burma and Ethiopia come to mind—which at a given time may not fit any of the descriptions.

Third, the Third World is so replete with mixed political systems and states in flux as to defy rigorous typologies. For example, under Sukarno, Indonesia was formally an elective system and, unlike most radical-nationalist countries which are governed by single parties, it had multiple political parties. Yet for its other dominant features I have regarded it as belonging in the radical-nationalist category. Senegal has a few characteristics of the radical-nationalist and not a few of the traditional-ascriptive system; I have placed it in the pragmatic-authoritarian mode. Egypt and Tunisia, which were (under Nasser and during a decade of planned development by Tunisian minister for planning Ahmed Ben Salah) leading members of the radical-nationalist mode, have moved rightward to join the pragmatic-authoritarian category. Since its founding by Colonel Reza Khan in 1924, the Pahlavi regime in Iran was, like those of Somoza, Batista, and Trujillo in Latin America, a dynastic-oligarchic one until the mid-1960s, when Western, primarily US, strategic interests and augmented income from oil began its full transformation into the neofascist mode. For two decades, Pakistan has been swinging dramatically back and forth between democracy and dictatorship. This typology, then, is a methodological device to help understand these circular no less than linear developments. Perhaps "modes of power" might better suggest their tentative, changing character than does the more conventional word "system."

Lastly, of the seven systems, only one—the Marxist-socialist—represents a total break from the colonial state and its replacement by a new and different state system. From Cuba to Vietnam, there is a wide range of important differences in the manner in which the new apparatus of statehood has been (and is being) created in these countries—their actual and potential linkages with the masses, the extent to which they envisage meaningful exercise of popular power and public accountability, and the manner in which the governments are run. Comparative analysis of these countries is crucial to an understanding of the promises and pitfalls of Marxist-socialist development in postcolonial societies.

*The Elective-Parliamentary System*

The parliamentary system, the most dominant form on the morrow of decolonization, has stabilized in a few countries after yielding in most others to radical-nationalist (e.g., Egypt—1952; Syria—1954, Pakistan—1958) or neo-fascist (Iran—1953, Brazil—1964, Indonesia—1965, Chile—1973). The list of survivors, led by India, suggests that among the major factors contributing to the success of multiparty democracy in the Third World are: heterogeneity (ethnic, religious, and linguistic diversity), the existence of a sizable national bourgeoisie relatively independent of the state and exercising some control over the productive sector of the modem economy, a development policy which allows for the growth of a production-prone indigenous capitalist class, and limited penetration of US economic and strategic interests.

Human rights violations occur because special security laws authorize limited but arbitrary power which the government often misuses. Mrs. Gandhi's declaration of the emergency was an extreme case of misuse. More commonly, a relatively independent judiciary, a free press, and parliamentary debates ensure a degree of *procedural freedoms*—of speech and association, from arbitrary incarceration and systematic torture—not known in the other systems of power. The margin of *substantive freedoms*—from hunger and dispossession, illiteracy and vagrancy, etc.—tends to be extremely narrow under this system. Yet it enjoys a measure of legitimacy because periodic elections under universal suffrage give a promise of the accountability of the government to the electorate and also help maintain and enlarge a political class which links the civil society with political power and because the existence of a relatively independent judiciary invests the system with a certain assumption of being rational and reformable. Above all, the system appears susceptible to popular demands and amenable to organized politics. As discussed later in this essay, the democratic polity is replaced by a military, frequently neofascist government precisely at the time when organized popular interests begin to gain ascendance through the electoral process.


*The Ascriptive-Palace System*

The palace system of power, the oldest extant form in the Third World today, is also receding—a traditional victim of the social forces and tensions produced by "modernization." In some countries (Morocco, Jordan, Nepal), it survives by virtue of the fact that it still enjoys a measure of legitimacy (generally ascriptive) among large numbers of citizens and an important segment of society views its continuation to be necessary for the maintenance of social balance and political order. In others (Saudi Arabia, Kuwait, Abu Dhabi), the advantages of tradition have been vastly augmented by the sheer excess of sudden wealth among a relatively homogeneous and small population so that a certain affluence has accrued to nearly all citizens and substantive freedoms have expanded considerably.

The rulers keep a tight grip on the reins of power by a combination of traditional and modern methods of bargaining, co-optation, shifting alliances, manipulation and coercion of allies as well as opponents. Violations of human rights are often serious and periodically widespread; legal norms are rarely enforced by independent judiciaries. But the political system's sense of legitimacy, its links with and respect for the norms of civil society, and an environment of political bargaining mitigate and limit the boundaries of repression. A significant increase in the government's coercive capabilities and a qualitative shift toward systematic violations of human rights occur when the system begins to lose its legitimacy. Such shifts normally mark the beginning of the system's end.

The economic and social policies of these states tend to be conservative, favoring large landholders, the private sector, and foreign investment. Resistance to land reform and redistribution of wealth freezes the narrow margins of substantive freedoms (except, as already noted, in the smaller states inundated by oil income); paternalistic concern for the welfare of common people is generally expressed through symbolic gestures. In some cases (Yemen, Libya, Ethiopia, Afghanistan, Nepal), the rulers kept a tight lid on social change, but in all these instances except Nepal they have been unseated by an augmented, modernized corps of army officers. A notable feature of their demise: since the start of the decolonization process, the palace system of power has yielded to the radical-nationalist coup d'état, not to the populist or socialist movement or to the neofascist junta.

### The Dynastic-Oligarchic System

The oligarchic system, most commonly found in Latin America, is in many ways a precursor of the neofascist regimes of the 1960s and 1970s. As such, it shares many structural and behavioral traits with the latter. The primary differences between the older and newer right-wing tyrannies of the Third World lay in the organization and use of terror (being, at the start, less widespread, systematic, and anticipatory than in the neofascist regimes), resources (fewer), and importance to the hegemonic power (relatively less important). Symbiotically linked to metropolitan power and multinational capital, the system commands no legitimacy, and it eventually collapses under pressure from organized, popular, often revolutionary, movements.

### The Pragmatic-Authoritarian System

The pragmatic-authoritarian system, most commonly found in Africa, has so far evinced a remarkable degree of durability. Of some forty-four founding fathers of the contemporary African states, only ten (Julius Nyerere, Ahmed Sékou Touré, Ahmadou Ahidjo, Habib Bourguiba, Félix Houphouet-Boigny, Léopold Senghor, Kenneth Kaunda, Samora Machel, Agostino Neto, Luis Cabral) survive in power; of these, five lead countries in this category, while three (Machel, Neto, Cabral) have been independent only a few years. Only five (Gamal Abdel Nasser, Sir Milton Margai, William Tubman, Leon Mba, and Jomo Kenyatta) died in power; of these, three (Margai, Mba, and Kenyatta) were from this category. (All the others were overthrown, but not by the electorate.) This highly personalized system of power enjoys a certain legitimacy and the support of significant sections of the population by virtue of the historical nationalist credentials of the leader. The support of rural notables and the urban bourgeoisie along with the role of the ruling party as an agent of communication and control reinforces the stability of the regime. The legitimacy of the regime begins to erode when it starts to rely on a managerial political elite and an expanding state bureaucracy for its links with the civil society and the political party begins to neglect its participatory mechanisms and representational functions.

The economic policies of these states generally favor the private sector, encourage foreign investments, rely heavily on external technical and economic aid, and envisage a minimum of reforms in the traditional or colonial system of land tenure and labor relations. However, the state plays, on the patterns established by the colonial regime, some regulatory role, especially in management-labor relations, and often provides an expanded and improved infrastructure of public services, especially in health and education. Civil liberties are quite restricted; specially constituted courts often render relatively independent judiciaries irrelevant in politically motivated cases. Extreme violations of human rights (torture, imprisonment without trial) occur but remain limited both in intensity and in scope. Two noteworthy characteristics: these deeply pro-Western regimes tend to prefer strong political, economic, and cultural ties with the ex-colonial metropolis rather than the United States. The strength of the armed forces remains circumscribed, and, in comparison with civilians, military officers are assigned lower status in the official hierarchy. Often, a regime is protected from internal military threat by the dominant power; thus French troops are stationed in Senegal and the Ivory Coast, and British troops intervened in Tanzania and Uganda to suppress army mutineers in 1964. (In 1971, Idi Amin staged a coup d'état after Milton Obote had followed Nyerere and made his much-publicized "move to the left"; after this point, far from intervening on behalf of the civilian regime, the British are believed to have encouraged the coup by the Israeli-trained General Amin.)


*The Radical-Nationalist System*

Ascendant in the 1950s and through much of the 1960s, the radical-nationalist countries collectively dominated the Organization of Nonaligned Nations.

They claimed to represent an independent, noncapitalist, non-Marxist, yet socialist path to the self-reliant development of Third World societies. Led by charismatic, "heroic" leaders (Gamal Abdel Nasser, Kwame Nkrumah, Ahmed Sukarno, Ahmed Ben Bella, etc.), aroused by anti-imperialist slogans, stirred by populist rhetoric, and enthused by promises of reform and renovation, these regimes were viewed—with fear in some quarters, admiration in others—as authentic expressions of Third World radicalism. But, by 1970, they appeared to have lost their élan. In several countries, radical-nationalist regimes began to drift rightward (e.g., Tunisia, Egypt, Sudan); in others, they succumbed to military, frequently neofascist coups d'état (e.g., Indonesia, Ghana, Uganda, Cambodia). In most countries, immobilism has become the primary characteristic of these erstwhile "mobilization" regimes. Only rarely, as in Algeria, do they show signs of revitalization.

The radical-nationalist is the broadest of the seven categories. It encompasses a wide variety of states with differing levels of achievements and stability. State-sponsored, rapid industrialization was a stated policy goal in Ghana, Guinea, and Indonesia as it later was in Algeria and Iraq. Yet, Nkrumah's and Sukarno's premature grandiosity thwarted Ghanaian and Indonesian development; if mineral extraction is excluded, Guinea's economy has also stagnated. On the other hand, in Algeria and Iraq, planning and implementation have been more rational, and their rates of growth, aided by oil income, have been impressive; but the "turnkey" model of industrialization has generated little indigenous skill and employment. Only in resource-hungry Tanzania, when Julius Nyerere saw a contradiction between rapid industrial growth and the development goal of self-sufficiency, was the growth of the rural sector over the urban one emphasized. There are differences, too, in their antecedents. Some, like the regimes in Algeria, Tanzania, Guinea, and Mexico, are directly descended from popular, national revolutions; the political parties in these countries have at least a history of organizing and representing the masses and in many countries still play some role in linking the civil society with the state. Others, like those in Iraq, Syria, Somalia, and Libya, were founded by military coups d'état. While they enjoy varying degrees of legitimacy and popular acceptance, the political parties and trade unions sponsored by the regimes have had little success in developing into popular and participatory organizations.

The similarities among these states—in terms of their structure, ideology, and composition of the ruling elite—are more striking than their differences. They are governed by authoritarian, generally single-party regimes committed to rapid economic growth through centralized planning, redistribution of income through radical land reform, nationalization and state control of basic industries (and, in some cases, agricultural cooperatives), and equity through the universalized distribution of such basic services as public health, education, transportation, and housing. Ideologically eclectic, their leaders are nationalist in outlook and populist in rhetoric. While rejecting the notions of class domination and class struggle, they claim to be socialists and justify this claim on the basis of their economic program and their proclaimed commitment to the creation of independent, egalitarian, socialist republics.

With power centralized in the executive branch and in the absence of independent judiciaries and assertive elected bodies, the margins of civil liberties tend to be quite narrow in these states. But the intensity and scope of their violations vary and depend on the antecedents, ideological appeal, and social-ethnic links of the leadership. For example, in Iraq, where the majority Shia population and the largest non-Arab nationality (Kurds) are inadequately represented in the ruling Baath party, severe violations of human rights—including imprisonments without trial and frequent executions of dissidents—have occurred. On the other hand, in Algeria, where the leadership has commanded some authority on the basis of its role in the war of national liberation, where regional and ethnic interests are better represented in the structures of power, and where a well-rooted, progressive opposition does not threaten the ruling elite, violations of human rights have been few, infrequent, and progressively declining. On the whole, political repression in these states tends to be limited and rarely becomes as massive or as systematic as in the neofascist countries. Popular pressure on these regimes builds slowly; in reaction, the system either moves rightward in economic and social policy (Tunisia, Egypt), or else it yields to a militarist or neofascist takeover from within (Ghana, Uganda, Indonesia).

Further theoretical arguments on the causes of the failures of these regimes and their ultimately right-wing, repressive destiny appear in a later essay in this series which deals with the neofascist system of power. Here we note the peculiar contradictions which underlie this phenomenon. First, after acceding to power, these regimes command a certain legitimacy and the support and consensus of the governed. Their populist rhetoric, reformist program, developmental ambitions, advocacy of social justice, and anti-imperialist posture arouse expectations and elicit an enthusiastic public response. Their popularity takes root as economic and social reforms and the nationalization of national resources promise to restore the nation's sovereignty and to expand the substantive freedoms of the common people. Their progressive and patriotic image is often confirmed by the manifest hostility of the imperialist metropolis. The idiom of politics under these regimes shifts to seek a mass constituency and, in the process of achieving it, radicalizes popular consciousness and the collective esteem of the toiling masses. Yet neither their class composition and ideology nor their structural preferences equip these regimes to meet their mission. When they face pressure from the disillusioned masses, they turn down the rightward, repressive road. Whether the turning is gradual or abrupt, in a conventional rightist or a neofascist direction, depends on a number of factors including the nature of the opposition and of the hegemonic external powers' strategic and economic interests in the country. In either case, the distinction between the ostensibly benevolent and the crudely repressive radical-nationalist breaks down in the face of popular challenge.

Second, the rhetoric, claims, and political stances of these regimes give them an appearance of being quite ideological. Yet they invariably lack a coherent, consistent, and functioning ideology. Conscientism, Nasserism, Bourguibism, Peronism, and Baathism are all ideologies remarkable for their lack of ideological content. They are amalgams of sentiments, generalized hopes and preferences, slogans and clichés borrowed—or rather rented—from diverse sources but expressed uniquely, sometimes mystically, with an uncanny sense of opportunity. They go right to the heart, bypassing the head, with the power to mobilize without being able to guide or sustain. Hence personalization of power and political spectacles rather than principles and values—the preambles upon which the ultimate authority of a political system rests—generally describe the shallowness of the system's legitimacy. Their ideological flabbiness, along with the shallow roots and managerial character of the ruling class, also define these regimes' propensity to shift abruptly and opportunistically in their international alignment (Egypt, Somalia, Sudan) and development strategies.

Third, a prominent characteristic of the radical-nationalist regimes is that they vastly expand the functions, size, and power of the inherited, colonial state apparatus. They are produced by and continue to rely heavily and progressively on an expanding bureaucracy and national security apparatus. In countries where mass political parties had existed and enjoyed some roots among the people, they have declined, conceding their functions to government agencies and bureaucrats. Where such a party did not exist and the radical-nationalist regimes were established by coups d'état, government-sponsored parties have typically failed to take root. In either case, participatory and representative institutions have declined in these countries in direct proportion to the growth of oligarchic power and the state apparatus. Disengagement from mass politics is a necessary product of this process. In the absence of a consistent, coherent ideology, the justification for the expansion of the state apparatus comes from the two interrelated notions of "development" and "national security." Together, these two make up the ideologically rigged concept of modernization, which emphasizes a high rate of capital formation and growth and the state as the primary development agency.

In a separate essay, we shall argue in some detail that the contemporary Third World state was a colonial creation, controlled by and conditioned to serve the imperial metropolis. As such, it was an extension of the metropolitan capitalist state, which developed in response to the needs of an ascendant commercial and industrial European bourgeoisie and provided a framework of laws and institutions essential to the development of capitalist relations of production. As colonizing entities, these European states were the instruments of corporate expansion abroad—a process which served the double purpose not only of exploiting the colonized but also of exporting to the colonies the social and political tensions produced by the shift from feudalism to capitalism. The ability to export the tensions associated with social change made possible the growth of liberal democracies involving a subtle and complex balance between institutions of coercion and consensus. This perspective on the link between colonial expansion and the development of bourgeois democratic systems requires a renewed examination of the forces which led to the development of European fascism, for it is not incidental that fascism took hold in countries which underwent the process of industrialization while they were largely denied the colonial raw materials and markets, as well as the ability to export their tensions. (Germany and Italy are prime examples.) It also helps [one] understand, at least partially, the roots of despotic (socialist, radical-nationalist, and neofascist) development in the Third World.

Scholars have noted that the colonial state was centralized and endowed with a well-organized, modern military, police, and administrative apparatus. The colonial powers gave only minor attention to the growth of representative institutions. Hence it was from inception a modern despotism in that the quotient of coercion was much greater than that of consensus. More importantly, in the colonial state the process of modern state formation was reversed: far from being the creation of an ascendant national bourgeoisie, it was merely an extension of the metropolitan state. A native class of civil servants and soldiers—the state bourgeoisie of the Third World—was created to serve the colonial state. From the start, then, the creation of the modern state in the Third World involved the imposition of a well-developed military bureaucratic superstructure of power over an underdeveloped infrastructure of participation.

However, unlike most other analysts, we argue that the colonial state cannot properly be described as an "overdeveloped" one in the relative sense of the word. By and large, it maintained itself by limiting its interventions in society, by a network of alliances with the traditional ruling classes, and by exercising constraints in the expansion of the native sector of the state bureaucracy and security services. It was also characterized by the subordination of the newly created native state bourgeoisie to the higher-echelon members of the metropolis. In short, the colonial state maintained a sizable traditional upper class whose legitimacy and power were emasculated through expropriation by and collaboration with colonialism, along with a subordinated state bourgeoisie created and sustained by it. After decolonization, the former lacked the will and the capacity to subordinate the latter. Hence the civilian political leadership tends to be overthrown or bypassed by the state sector when it (1) has outlived its usefulness in the consolidation of power following decolonization; (2) becomes an impediment to oligarchic growth; or (3) seeks reinforcement of popular institutions and the exercise of popular power. Only in exceptional Third World societies such as India, where an indigenous capitalism began to develop in the nineteenth century and expanded significantly between the two world wars, has a national bourgeoisie (that is, one outside of the state sector) developed that is capable of establishing its hegemony over, or at least becoming an equal partner with, the state bourgeoisie.

The power of the state bourgeoisie was derivative from the state; its expansion depended on the expansion of state power and functions. Hence its vested interests and compulsions would be toward expanding the state machinery. Under colonial rule, this urge was subject to the control and the needs of the metropolis; the metropolis's needs required an efficient, despotic, but relatively limited and defined government. Decolonization involved a handing over of the state apparatus to the erstwhile subordinate state bourgeoisie and brought with it the freedom to expand. After recovering from the initial shock of seeing this subordinate class take power and use strident nationalist rhetoric, the metropolitan powers, and particularly the United States, contributed heavily to the expansion of the state in postcolonial societies.

The ruling class which dominates the radical authoritarian regime has been described rather inaccurately as issuing from the petite bourgeoisie, for this description denotes a class accustomed to a modest middle position in an established social order. The liberal academic description of it as a new middle class is more suggestive of its roots as well is its disposition. It is a unique Third World phenomenon which owes its existence to colonialism and uneven development: a modern, educated managerial elite isolated from the productive process, alienated from its culture, and, in the face of continued dependency on external know-how and capital, unable to expand into a productive national bourgeoisie. It is a class torn out of its original petit bourgeois and, to a lesser extent, bourgeois roots and placed in a modern bureaucratic, national security setting. There it nourishes aspirations and attitudes which depend on continuing expansion of the sectors which require servicing, management, and control. It is a "power elite" in the literal sense of the word, in the sense that its primary vocation is the exercise of power; it owes its very existence to the task of management. In a nationalist environment, it discovers nationalization and state control of the economy as an effective way to expand its own size and power. Statism often provides an independent material base to this oligarchy, and foreign development aid links this base to the metropolis. Hence, wherever the foreign capitalist sector is weak and the servicing bourgeoisie is not divided between the state and corporate bureaucracy, its quest for self-aggrandizement produces the self-proclaimed socialist regime. In those countries where imperial, particularly US, strategic hegemonic interests have been large and deep rooted, it turns easily toward neofascism.

When separated from the legitimizing support of the "heroic" national leader or the original nationalist political class, the ruling state bourgeoisie of the radical authoritarian regime exercises no legitimacy. It lacks not only a coherent and functioning ideology but also the history and the symbols capable of invoking the consent of a significant section of the masses. It exercises power without hegemony, deploys force without consent, dominates the state while remaining isolated from the civil society. The state in these societies undoubtedly exercises, as some Marxist scholars have argued, a certain autonomy—an autonomy born out of isolation from society. And it is an autonomy which necessarily involves the maintenance of an unequal relationship with an external metropolis. Such a state is not merely a subsidiary but a suspended state, inherently incapable of endogenous development.

*Bibliography*

Alavi, Hamza. "The State in Post-Colonial Societies." *New Left Review* 74 (1972): 59–81.

Amin, Samir. *Unequal Development: An Essay on the Social Formation of Peripheral Capitalism.* New York: Monthly Review Press, 1976.

Apter, D. *The Politics of Modernization.* Chicago, 1965.

dos Santos, Teotonio. "Socialism and Fascism in Latin America Today." *Socialism in the World*, no. 1 (1977).

———. "The Structure of Dependence." In *Readings in US Imperialism,* ed. K. T. Farm and Donald Hodges. Boston: P. Sargent, 1971.

Fanon, Franz. *Les Damnés de la terre.* Paris: François Maspero, 1961.

Freyhold. Michaela von. "The Post-Colonial State and Its Tanzanian Version." *Review of African Political Economy* 8 (1977).

Hoare, Quentin, and Dennis Nowell Smith, eds. *Selections from The Prison Notebooks.* London and New York: Lawrence and Wishard International Publishers, 1971.

Hughes, Arnold, and Martin Kolinsky. "Paradigmatic Fascism and Modernization: A Critique." *Political Studies*, December, 1976.

Huntington, S. P., and C. H. Moore, eds. *Authoritarian Politics in Modern Society.* New York, 1970.

La Palombara, J., and M. Weiner, eds. *Political Parties and Political Development.* Princeton, 1966.

Leys, Colin. "The 'Over-Developed' Post-Colonial State: A Re-evaluation." *Review of African Political Economy* 5 (1976).

Murray, Roger. "Second Thoughts on Ghana." *New Left Review* 8 (1967).

Organski, A. F. K. *Stages of Political Development.* New York: Knopf, 1965.

Rokkan, S., and S. N. Eisenstadt. *Building States and Nations.* Beverly Hills, 1966.

Saul, J. "The State in Post-Colonial Societies: Tanzania." *Socialist Register* (1974).

———. "The Unsteady State: Uganda, Obote and General Amin." *Review of African Political Economy* 5 (1976).

Wallerstein, I. "The State and Social Transformation: Will and Possibility." *Politics and Society* 1 (1971).

Ziemann, W., and M. Lanzendorfer. "The State in Peripheral Societies." *Socialist Register* (1977).

[1980]

# 11 / THE NEOFASCIST STATE

Notes on the Pathology of Power in the Third World

Through the 1960s and 1970s, while our attention was focused on the Indochinese War, an ominous development was occurring in the Third World. These two decades witnessed the emergence and/or maturing of regimes which one may describe, for lack of a better term, as neofascist. In the 1950s, some of these countries—for example, South Korea, Iran, and Nicaragua—were already authoritarian states, whose survival required widespread repression of political opposition and social institutions outside state control (religious, educational, and professional associations, labor and peasant organizations). The 1960s and 1970s witnessed the hardening of the authoritarian arteries of these states, the systematization of terror, the "modernization" and "rationalization" of their repressive institutions. Other states—for example, Brazil, Indonesia, Greece, the Philippines, Uganda, Zaire, Uruguay, and Chile—changed in the mid-1960s and early 1970s from being democratic, protodemocratic, or radical-authoritarian regimes to militarist states. In the second half of the 1970s, the ranks of these states continued to swell: Argentina and Thailand were among the new members. However, with the possible exception of Brazil, none of these states had consolidated its tyrannies; that is, they had not acquired the economic wherewithal to sustain themselves without continued external support, and they had not forged meaningful political links with significant sectors of the civil society.

At the same time, the second half of the 1970s revealed, first in Greece, then in Iran and Nicaragua, these neofascist regimes to be extremely vulnerable and brittle; when faced with a major challenge, they collapsed totally and with a speed which surprised most observers. This paper attempts to summarize (1) the characteristics of this type of regime in the Third World; (2) the roots of neofascism; and (3) the vulnerability of these regimes and the sources of resistance to them.

*General Characteristics of Neofascist States*

Some variations among them notwithstanding, the following are the common characteristics of the neofascist state.

A FUNDAMENTAL SHIFT IN THE USE OF ORGANIZED TERROR

These states are by far the most blatant contemporary violators of human rights in both substantive and procedural matters. Most of them have developed highly sophisticated and complex machineries of repression. They are ever experimenting with new methods of terrorizing the people and eliminating their opposition while reducing the "visibility" of their excesses. Increasingly, people are tortured in "safe houses," in civilian quarters rather than identifiable prisons or concentration camps. Actual and potential dissenters disappear more often than they are imprisoned. The lucky prisoner who, because of international pressures on his behalf, gets released from captivity often becomes unusually and fatally accident-prone. Thus, in 1976–1977 in Argentina, some eighty-five hundred members of the opposition and independent bodies such as labor unions were officially acknowledged to be missing; officially, too, six hundred were killed and fifteen wounded in "combat." Amnesty International, on the other hand, established some fifteen thousand persons to have disappeared; eight to ten thousand were in known, official prisons, that is, the figure did not include the secret detention camps. Argentineans and foreign journalists widely believed that about fifteen thousand people were killed between the coup d'état of March 1976 and early 1978. Similar figures and discrepancies between official and independent body counts can be cited for the other countries in this category. The scales of violence exercise credulity. Some 350,000 people went through the torture chambers of the shah of Iran. An estimated 500,000 to 1 million alleged Communists were killed in Indonesia after the coup of 1965; 750,000 people were arrested by official count; of these, not one was brought to trial, and

Amnesty International did not find a single case of acquittal. Martin Ennals, the head of Amnesty International, reported that "about 30,000 people have disappeared in the last ten years in Latin America after being seized by official security forces or their sympathizers."[1]

What is striking about these gruesome violations of human rights is not only the increase in their scale but a qualitative shift in their administration and purpose. As Amnesty International's *Report On Torture* of 1974 put it, "there is a marked difference between traditional brutality stemming from historical conditions, and the systematic torture which has spread to many Latin American countries within the past decade." More importantly, the purpose of governmental coercion appears to have shifted from punishment to prevention. Torture is increasingly administered not so much to obtain information or punish a member of the opposition but literally to discourage people from linking with each other politically and socially; its purpose is to prevent a political process and the formation of relationships among people.

There is a historical irony to the emergence of these regimes; it occurred in a period when elsewhere in the world the margins of procedural freedoms and of substantive human rights had started to widen. In Spain and Portugal, for example, the fascist states had begun since the early sixties to experience a process of liberalization, and, by the midseventies, they had changed into social democratic polities. Since the start of de-Stalinization, the margins of procedural freedom in Eastern Europe and the Soviet Union had been widening significantly—although not enough to warrant satisfaction. For example, the 1974 Amnesty International *Report on Torture* noted that "although prison conditions and the rights of the prisoners detained on political charges in Eastern Europe and the Soviet Union may still be in many cases unsatisfactory, torture as a government-sanctioned, Stalinist practice, has ceased." By contrast, the same report noted that torture had "shown phenomenal growth in Latin America"; it explained further that "institutional violence and high incidence of political assassinations has tended to overshadow the problem of torture."

It is noteworthy also that the neofascist states show a qualitative as well as quantitative shift toward the worse in the area of human rights. Violations of human rights had been occurring, and still occur, in the other Third World systems of power discussed in an earlier paper.[2] Yet in these other countries the practice of terror is neither as systematized nor as widespread, nor does repression constitute the mainstay of the regime. Furthermore, in some of those states (e.g., in the radical-authoritarian, and the Marxist-socialist systems), the margins of substantive freedoms (e.g., improvement of health, education, and nutrition) have widened for the population at large; hence these regimes enjoy a measure of legitimacy which correspondingly diminishes the need for repression. Similarly, the regimes that belong in the ascriptive-palace or the pragmatic-authoritarian systems enjoy a measure of ascriptive and/or historical legitimacy and a lingering traditional style of government and conflict resolution. They, too, violate human rights, sometimes excessively, but repression has not quite become the mainstay of these regimes. By contrast, the neofascist states command, at best, the support of a microscopic, generally praetorian, minority. As such, they enjoy no title to authority and must depend on organized state terror as the primary means of staying in power.

## FASCISM AND NEOFASCISM

The neofascist state shares several characteristics with conventional fascism as witnessed in Europe in the 1920s and 1930s. These include: a repressive terrorist state apparatus; state control over the economy and labor; and its origins in petit bourgeois and propertied classes. But it differs from the classic model in many ways: unlike conventional fascism, the neofascist state in the Third World evinces but little ideological nationalism. To the contrary, it appears largely as a product of dependence and is sustained by its symbiotic relationship to the external metropolis. Unlike Nazism, neofascism is not anti-Semitic; the only exception is Argentina, where the junta's pronouncements were explicitly anti-Semitic during its most brutal years. To the contrary, almost all the neofascist states, including Argentina, maintain close links to Israel—a phenomenon which underlines their common links with imperialism and the United States.

Neofascist states are remarkable also for their inability to produce the "charismatic leader" capable of achieving any degree of mass mobilization or of invoking popular support. Furthermore, while the neofascist state exercises totalitarian powers, unlike the historical fascist system, it is unable to perform the political functions of aggregation, communication, and socialization. Above all, unlike Germany and Japan—where low wages, combined with restraint on consumption, produced high rates of gross national investment and industrialization—the economies of the neofascist states are based primarily on extraction and are characterized by growing dependence on the multinational corporations. As such, these states are not the instruments of "modernization" which liberal social scientists often describe them to be. It is true that they produce a measure of uneven industrialization, but at the same time they dislocate and disinherit the majority rural population, lower the living standards of the working classes, mortgage the country's future to foreign investors and debtors, and generally produce economic ruin; Iran under the shah, Brazil since 1964, and Indonesia since 1965 are examples.

## IDEOLOGICAL BASE OF THE NEOFASCIST STATE

While the neofascist state lacks a consistent and pronounced ideology, its origins lie in, and its existence is defined by, a pervasive ideological environment which favors the national security state. The doctrine of national security has its roots in the ideas, institutions, and policies associated with the Cold War. Ironically, it is nourished at the same time by the seemingly opposing heritage of modern nationalism and colonialism. It views the state as absolute, the individual as unimportant. It emphasizes a continual war between communism and freedom, stability and subversion, national security and anarchy. Instead of seeking mass manipulation and public control through political institutions such as parties, youth and labor organizations, it posits the armed forces to be, as Nelson Rockefeller put it, "a major force for constructive social change." Next to the armed forces, secret police organizations—SAVAK, DINA, KCIA, etc.—permeate the society. Their highest officials rank among the countries' most powerful men.

What A. J. Langguth says of Latin America holds true of practically every neofascist state: "The main exporter of Cold-War ideas, the principal source of the belief that dissent must be crushed by every means and any means, has been the United States. Our indoctrination of foreign troops provided a justification for torture in the jail cells of Latin America. First in the Inter-American Police Academy in Panama, then at the more ambitious International Police Academy in Washington, foreign policemen were taught that in the war against international communism they were the 'first line of defense.' The US training turned already conservative men into reactionaries."[3]

Predominant among the leaders of the neofascist system are military officers who have been trained in the counterinsurgency academies and programs run by the US government; Generals Papadopoulous of Greece, Pinochet and Leigh of Chile, Geisel of Brazil, Massera of Argentina, Zia ul-Haq of Pakistan are among the many examples. These training programs invariably steeped the officers in the anticommunist dogma that subversives and infiltrators could be anywhere and the latter undermine national security in a variety of ways, through student protest, labor strikes, and peasant demands. Deep fear of and hostility to populist movements and expressions of popular demands is therefore basic to the national security outlook.[4]

The concept of national security completely transcends military considerations; it is enmeshed with political, economic, and social issues and constitutes the basis for the armed forces' broad, all-pervasive mission. Furthermore, there exists a negative correlation between the perceived security problems of a country and its actual power and privileges on an international scale, to wit: the more powerful and richer the state, the less secure it is believed to be by the ruling elite.

A "MODEL" OF DEVELOPMENT

Closely related to the idea of national security are the ideologically rigged notions of "development" and "modernization." Typically, the neofascist state is deeply committed to economic development; we might even describe this neofascism as "developmental fascism." It views "development" in terms of rates of growth. "Growth" involves the concentration of wealth and of power, for both are necessary to the required rate of capital formation. Thus profit = investment = growth = power. The preferred development model favors return to the "free market." But the return is always selective: it does not involve curtailment of monopoly power or of untrammeled investment incentives; it does entail strict controls over wages, labor unions, and prohibition of strikes. A cheap labor force is offered as a primary incentive to capital; the internal market does not expand except for luxury goods. The economy becomes increasingly export-oriented; raw materials, including fancy food products, become the primary export items.[5] Income inequality multiplies. Any resistance to corporate and foreign interests is treated ipso facto as a police problem; anyone questioning this model of development is viewed as a subversive, a terrorist.

Hunger stalks the impoverished people while Western economic experts and institutions extol the "economic miracles" of their allies and clients. Thus a decade after coming to power, the government of Suharto had turned Indonesia, formerly self-sustaining in rice, into the world's number one rice importer, and famine broke out only a few miles from Jakarta. the capital. Similarly, in Brazil the real incomes of the lowest 80 percent of the population dropped steadily during the decade following the coup d'état of 1964, despite "the tripling of the GNP to $80 billion."[6] In May 1973, eighteen Catholic bishops of northeast Brazil issued a heartrending statement which said, among other things, that "hunger in the northeast has taken on the characteristics of an epidemic"; the statement noted that infants (that is, the half who lived to age five) and children were the primary victims of malnutrition, which contributed to an alarming rate of feeblemindedness among those who survived.[7] Social services decline while prestige projects—such as communications satellites and domestic communications networks, to which Indonesia allocated $840 million in 1978 alone—benefit foreign contractors and native contacters. Poor peasants are hurt or wiped out by agribusiness and large landed proprietors. State monopolies provide fiefdoms for the powerful; in every neofascist state a dozen or so family names become hated household words signifying the corruption, the callousness, and the brutality of the system. If there exists in a country an excludable minority (e.g., Amazon Indians, Baluciis, the Aches, Timoris), the regime follows a policy of dispossession and even genocide.[8] These realities add up to a sordid picture of substantive denials and violations of human rights, in comparison to which the better publicized procedural violations appear insignificant.

SYMBIOTIC EXTERNAL TIES

Almost without exception, these regimes began as clients of the United States and, with the exception of Uganda and Ethiopia, remain tied to the Western metropolis, economically, strategically, and psychologically. The largest and the richest of them (e.g., Iran, Brazil, Indonesia, South Korea) were among the Nixon/Kissinger doctrine's original choices for leading the regional constellations of pro-Western power—a strategy and preference which remained, with minor adjustments, US policy during the Carter administration. They are also the objects of corporate concentration as "export-platform countries" of the Third World. They are attractive to American policy makers and international corporations for obvious reasons. Their strategic locations and natural resources are highly valued. More to the point is the fact that these economic-growth–seeking tyrannies tend to be extremely hospitable to foreign capital. The denial of distributive justice under these regimes secures a high rate of profit. Their repressiveness assures stable, low wages for a quiescent labor force.

By enriching a small but highly consumptive indigenous bourgeoisie, they provide lucrative markets for Western consumer products as well as the transfer of "excess capital" to the financial institutions of the West.

There exists, then, as Noam Chomsky and Edward Herman have pointed out, a "systematic positive relationship between United States aid and human rights violations." Using ten selected countries as examples, Chomsky and Herman show a remarkable correlation in this regard. A typical example is Brazil, where "overall aid and credits by the United States and multinational leading organizations went up 112 percent . . . in the three years following the *coup* [1964] as compared with the three years preceding the *coup*." From the ten examples, they conclude that "for most of the sample countries United States–controlled aid has been positively related to investment climate and inversely related to the maintenance of a democratic order and human rights."[9] Similarly, Michael Klare has shown that from 1973 to 1978 the ten worst violators at the top of the list of human rights organizations such as Amnesty International were the primary recipients of US economic and military aid. During this period, they received economic aid of over $2 billion and military aid and credits of $2.3 billion; they were sold armaments in excess of $18 billion, and 12,723 military officers from these countries had been trained in American schools and programs. In his well-documented study, Klare concluded that the United States stood "at the supply end of the pipeline of repressive technology."[10]

### The Roots of Neofascism

Almost all the neofascist states have succeeded populist and reformist governments, most of them belonging in the radical-authoritarian category discussed in an earlier paper.[11] The emergence of the neofascist regimes was premised on the nature of the postcolonial state, its symbiotic relationship to a national bourgeoisie which was predominantly a state bourgeoisie, and the expansion of this bourgeoisie under populist and reformist slogans. In the previous paper I argued that:

> 1. The contemporary Third World state was a colonial creation designed to serve the imperial metropolis. In it, the process of modern state formation was reversed: far from being the creation of an ascendant national bourgeoisie, the colo-

nially created state gave birth to a native class of civil servants and soldiers—the national bourgeoisie. From the beginning, the development of the modern state in the Third World involved the imposition of a well-developed military bureaucratic superstructure of power over an underdeveloped infrastructure of participation.

2. After formal decolonization, the less-developed civic political class tended to be overthrown or bypassed by the state bourgeoisie when it became an impediment to oligarchic growth and/or sought the reinforcement of popular institutions and the exercise of popular power.

3. The overthrow of the civic, generally parliamentary, system was effected by the state-related power elite, which legitimized itself on the basis of populist, reformist, and nationalist slogans. Yet it was in the nature of these regimes that they should vastly expand the powers and the membership of their class (state employees) without being able to improve the welfare of the masses. Ultimately, it had to face a disillusioned and expectant mass. And when that moment of truth arrived, the most powerful and privileged group within that class carried out the protofascist "counterrevolution."

Hence, in almost all cases, the neofascist system emerged in reaction to organized popular demands for fundamental economic and social change. In Iran, Guatemala, Brazil, the Dominican Republic, Chile, Zaire, and Indonesia, the counterrevolutionary coup d'état occurred at a time when popular discontent was becoming vocal and visible. These coups also followed a trend toward the institution of desired reforms concerning taxes, profit repatriation, and nationalization of national resources—steps taken in response to popular pressures. In some cases, the praetorian reaction occurred after expressions of institutional threats against international vested interests. For example, the 1972 coup in the Philippines followed the Supreme Court's ruling against foreign ownership of land; the Brazilian coup of 1964 coincided with a major dispute over mineral concessions to the Hanna Mining Company; the nationalization of Iranian oil in 1953 was followed by the overthrow of Mohammed Mossadegh; and, of course, the story of Allende's Chile is well-known.

It is noteworthy that the neofascist system has emerged in societies which have developed a measure of economic stratification and class consciousness. The initial move of the praetorian putschists was often successful because it was able to rally the forces of order—particularly among the petite bourgeoisie, the conservative landed and the foreign corporate sectors—against the working class, peasants, and their progressive political allies. In this respect, the neofascist states bear some resemblance to European fascism. Yet the differences with European fascism are more significant: the Third World nonstate bourgeoisie which initially supports the praetorian reaction is more commercial than industrial, more comprador than indigenous, and thus different in character from its European counterpart. Similarly, the state bourgeoisie is somewhat more autonomous of the civil society because it is linked with and sustained by the foreign metropolis; as such, it is less dependent on the civil society and has fewer incentives to maintain meaningful links with any part of it, and in fact tends ultimately to lose its erstwhile allies. At the same time, in conjunction with foreign corporations, it exercises greater control over the nation's economic resources. Thus it becomes easily and completely isolated from the civil society while it becomes symbiotically linked and identified with foreign vested interests.

The ascension of the neofascist system does not involve the establishment of the power of a precolonial, indigenous class which, under colonialism, was either destroyed or weakened and reduced to a peripheral status. Nor does it mean the accession to power of an indigenous entrepreneurial class, for the dependent and underdeveloped economy remains dominated by the metropolis and subject to continued penetration by the multinational corporations. The advent of neofascism entails merely an enlargement of the colonial, national-security bourgeoisie whose power was based on its control over the modern state and its managerial and military skills. In other words, the social roots of the neofascist states are quite different from those of European fascism. European fascism was produced by severe limitations on colonial expansion while the neofascism of the Third World is a product of colonialism and neocolonialism.

*Resistance and Instability*

In the United States and Europe, the neofascist state was generally viewed as promising stability in an unstable Third World. By the end of the 1970s, this myth of stability had exploded. During the Greco-Turkish war over Cypress, the remarkably quick collapse of the US-supported Greek junta should have led to a closer examination of the extreme vulnerabilities of these regimes. But the event was ignored, and no examination of the assumed stability of these regimes was undertaken until after the shah went down in Iran. The

Nicaraguan Revolution followed closely on the heels of Iran. The regimes in South Korea and El Salvador are badly shaken. A more detailed analysis underlying the weaknesses of these regimes is needed; here we briefly mention the possible lines of inquiry.

First, the neofascist state, more than any other in the Third World, is characterized by what A. Sivanandan has aptly described as "disorganic development." The economic model which it follows superimposes on a Third World country a capitalist economy "unaccompanied by capitalist culture or capitalist democracy." The result is an economic system "at odds with the cultural and political institutions of the people it exploits," a system "not mediated by culture or legitimated by politics."[12] Political power and civil society, far from complementing and linking with each other, exist in a relationship of fundamental conflict. Since political institutions are severely repressed, culture and religion provide the strongest expressions of resistance. Hence the revolutions that emerge in such societies, as in Iran, are not necessarily class-oriented revolutions. They are mass movements that cut across class lines and contain within them elements of cultural and religious affirmations.

Second, the apparatus of the state in the neofascist system grows more rapidly than the society's capability to sustain it. Since the superstructure of the state bears little logical, much less organic, relationship to the infrastructure of the society, it has no capacity to serve society's needs, accommodate its demands, or even keep pace with the changes within it. It was thus that the Pahlavi state became too heavy and dry a burden for the Iranian people to carry; hence Khomeini's call for overturning it obtained a national consensus quite unparalleled in history.

Third, the specific contradictions of the neofascist model of development should be noted:

1. Being highly centralized and involving the state as the link between foreign corporations and a microscopic local elite, it focuses mass discontent on the state and the governing elite.

2. The economic model which favors collaboration of state and international capital relegates the local business class to a secondary position in times of expansion; it produces their socioeconomic deterioration in periods of economic downturn. Thus the increasingly marginalized indigenous business class joins in the forefront of the opposition's demand for democracy—a phenomenon observable both in Iran and Nicaragua.

3. The ruling elites in these states are remarkable for narrowing, rather than broadening, their base; an increasingly clannish exercise of power and concentration of privileges ultimately alienates a broad array of even the propertied classes. These, too, end up abandoning their erstwhile allies when the latter are faced with a serious challenge.

[1981]

# 12 / WAR OF THE RENTIER STATES

During all the years of war between Iran and Iraq, there has been one element of common ground between the combatants: in both countries, there is a pretense that this is a war against imperialism and a war of imperialism. This is a lie. For whatever one may call the Iran-Iraq war, it stretches anti-imperialist reasoning to call it an imperialist war. It is evidently true that the US initially encouraged Iraq in its aggression. But encouragement should not be confused with involvement. None of the great powers—whether the Soviet Union, Britain, France, or the US—appears to have had any role in initiating the war or for that matter in conducting it. That the capitalist countries have profited from it and are continuing to profit from it does not make it an imperialist war.

There are several points which need to be made. First, this is a war of local ambitions: President Saddam Hussein's opportunism and regional reaction to Iran's revolutionary promise were responsible for Iraq's initial aggression in 1980. The primary responsibility for this war, then, must lie with at least two people and two governments. The horrors of the war and its losses must be attributed to two generalized forces and to two individuals. The two generalized forces are nationalism and the postcolonial state, which have more to do with the Iran-Iraq war than does imperialism. And the two individuals, namely, Saddam Hussein and Ayatollah Khomeini, have a great deal to do with the war, one for starting the aggression and the other for prolonging the agony.

Second, the great powers have undoubtedly played a significant role in prolonging the war. While they did not initiate it, they have alternatively leaned toward each side as it appeared to be losing, in order to avoid an outright victory for either. That was true, for instance, of the US at the beginning of the war: sensing that Iran was in deep trouble and that the Iraqi forces were pushing ahead, Washington looked the other way as US operatives sold supplies to Iran and in fact promoted and gave a certain monopoly to the Israelis in supplying spare parts and small arms to Iran, just enough to keep the war going and prevent Iran's defeat. When Iran made its rebound (which was by no means because of the support from Israel or the US, as the Iraqis would have us believe; the primary reason was that Iran had a well-mobilized and revolutionary mass, its territories were under attack, and it fought back) and the tables were being turned, all the great powers—the Soviet Union, the US, France, and everybody else—became very interested in helping Iraq, so that it would not be defeated. Thus it is clear that by merely trying to prevent the defeat of either side, the superpowers have helped to prolong the war. One could conclude from this, and also from the example of the 1965 war between India and Pakistan, that in the Third World imperialism does not like to see a winner.

Third, the logic of regional politics and geopolitical realities in the Middle East have severely limited, though not eliminated, the role of the great powers in the Iran-Iraq conflict. The United States, the most activist of the great powers, has refrained from intervening because it does not have a sure client in either Iran or Iraq; because its logistical lines would be dangerously extended in case of a substantive riposte from the USSR; and because American congressional and public support for such an intervention is lacking. The Soviet Union, still involved in Afghanistan, anxious over events in Poland, and skeptical of the left forces in Iran, has been acting with its customary combination of opportunism and caution. Hence the basic logic of the war remains regional and local.

What, then, are some of the lessons of the war? One basic lesson to be drawn is that we, as Middle Eastern peoples, live in societies which suffer from a disastrous separation between political power and civil society. And when such a separation occurs, it produces societies which are not productive, creative, democratic, or lively. Personalism has reached a hitherto unexperienced pinnacle in our countries, so that the war is not really a war between Iran and Iraq; it is a Saddam-Khomeini war. It is a person-to-person war in which entire nations, entire peoples, are being made to pay the price of the criminal ambitions of one minority government and crazy individual and the mindless stubbornness of another. That is the fact, but why are such individuals able to get away with it? They are able to get away with it because both men, for different reasons and in different ways, have been able to establish a total separation between their power and the civil society. Muhammad Ja'far was correct in saying that the two defining symbols of this war have been the human wave attacks by Iran and the use of chemical weapons by Iraq. Both refer to one tragedy, and both define one attitude—the attitude of not caring about the cost of their ambitions and their ideological arrogance as regards the common people, especially the young. Both indicate moreover a lack of thought; they cannot figure out a strategy, they cannot figure out diplomatic manipulations or intelligent maneuvers, so they turn to brute attack: human waves and chemical weapons. Both reveal a certain callousness toward the mass of humanity with whose lives these men are playing—and I use the word "men" specifically.

Another noteworthy fact is that the Middle Eastern states have evinced deep, if unworthy, interest in the outcome of this war. From Morocco to Pakistan, Middle Eastern governments have shown greater interest in preserving the status quo than in defending national sovereignty and independence or serving the common good. So Saudi Arabia has expended much greater sums of money in saving the precious skin of Saddam Hussein than it has been willing to do to save the lot of the Palestinians in the West Bank and Gaza. Or to protect the sovereignty and territorial integrity of an Arab country called Lebanon. Or even to protect the sovereignty of Jerusalem and assure access for both Muslims and Christians to the sacred city. While it was Saddam's ambition that initiated the war, it is the Arab states, Egypt, Jordan, Saudi Arabia, and Morocco, which have sustained him through these years of senseless conflict. Their solidarity betrays the simple fact that the fear of upsetting the status quo is much greater than the question of history, or of sovereignty, or the question of humanity and the costs to common people. It is clearly not their love for Saddam Hussein but their fear of change, their anxiety over the consequences of a ruler having to pay for his mistakes, that have kept the Iraqi president in power, thereby prolonging this personalized war.

We have also seen through this war the harmful effects of the emergence of rentier states in the Middle East and North Africa. By the rentier state, I mean the state that has become rich on the basis of one product or, rather, one source of profit, since in the Middle East only the peasants and some artisans produce anything. The elite profit a great deal without producing. They buy machines without technology. They have oil, gas, and other minerals. Some foreign company comes and extracts it for them. It puts a rentier regime in power; that regime doesn't need its people. Its elite doesn't need to work even to exploit the people properly, because it doesn't need a tax base. And when a regime doesn't need a tax base, it loses literally all organic links to the civil society. And it loses any reason for maintaining accountability to the people, to society, to history itself. A rentier state is an entity suspended in time, detached from politics, disengaged from history.

Fourth, I wish to underline that, with dramatic intensity and at the highest cost, this war has demonstrated the damage inflicted on the Third World by the merchants of death, namely, the armaments industry of the first world. The Iran-Iraq war has yielded a sobering demonstration of the harm done to us by the arms trade. The arms trade in our time is the twentieth-century equivalent of the slave trade in the seventeenth and eighteenth centuries. We have to find ways to stop this horror, to ban it. The arms trade and the arms habit of our leaders must be abolished. The two sides in this war have poured billions of dollars into killing each other; the same regimes dread the typewriter. It is not widely known that the possession of a typewriter in Iraq requires a special license. In Iran, on the other hand, you cannot sing an ordinary song and even the words of Ferdowsi, for centuries the greatest of Persian poets, are banned and censored.

This takes me to the fifth point. There is a frightening absence on the world scale of any mechanism to pursue or ensure peace in the world. This senseless war has been going on for six years, and the world has watched callously and with indifference. The United Nations, which pretends to be concerned (and probably is concerned), has been reduced to an expensive cipher. Because it lacks the support on this issue, both of the superpowers and of the constituted governments that make up its membership, it is entirely dependent on the mutual interests of the Iranian and Iraqi governments. After countless trips, the UN delegation was finally able to get both sides to agree—which is a very great achievement under the circumstances—not to hit each other's civilians. At present, the UN is sitting tight, hoping that it will be in the interest of both sides to reach at least those minor agreements that would give us a no-war, no-peace situation, a kind of institutionalized stalemate.

The world will not be safe to live in as long as, through the power of public opinion and the power of movements, we do not produce new institutions and new ways of ensuring peace between madmen who drag in large numbers of decent people, because they are powerless.

What interests has the war served? First, the regime in Iran has profited. As of 1980, it had nothing to show for the great revolution that had occurred in Iran. The Nicaraguan Revolution occurred at about the same time as the Iranian Revolution—Somoza went to Paraguay at about the same time as the shah left Iran. By 1980, that is, a year and a half to two years later, Nicaraguan revolutionaries were able to show UNESCO that the Nicaraguan literacy rate had risen from roughly 35 percent to 85 percent, a full-fledged land reform had been implemented, a viable agrarian policy had been instituted. The Iranian Revolution, in comparison with the Nicaraguan Revolution, was richer and had a highly mobilized population, but its accomplishments did not compare either then or now with those of the Sandinista regime. Well-endowed Iran not only did not compare favorably with scarcity-ridden Nicaragua's accomplishments, but, worse, Iran had no program. The Islamic Republic of Iran is still without a viable program of social reconstruction. The Iraqi invasion helped Ayatollah Khomeini and his mullahs to mobilize popular support around nationalism: the regime can now claim that it has succeeded, at least temporarily, in consolidating power.

Second, the war has helped the elite in Iraq to profit from the war. The massive spending on war is going into buying arms, into infrastructure, into contracting and contacting—which is the business of Third World bourgeoisies. Businessmen on both sides of the war are getting rich. But the Iraqi elite has probably profited the most from subsidized war profiteering. The Arab world is paying the bill.

Third, great profit has accrued to Israeli contractors, acting on behalf of the Israeli government. The Israelis, very intelligently and with skilled American help, have cornered the market in spare parts and small arms to the Iranians. This is another irony of the Islamic Republic.

Fourth, the war has profited the superpowers and their multinational corporations, for obvious reasons. The losers are the two countries and their inhabitants. Their resources depleted, their cities destroyed, and their economies in ruins, Iran and Iraq are countries of orphans and widows, of sacrificed youths whom those in power have entitled martyrs.

How long is this killing to go on? What are the prospects, and what are our obligations? I think the present prospect is one of less-war, no-peace. Iran, in particular, would like to see a kind of stalemate that it could marginally institutionalize. Given Iran's population and resources, in the long run it stands a better chance to endure a stalemate. The Iraqis probably have no alternative to the stalemate, either. Saddam Hussein's power is obviously more precious than Iraq's peace, and Ayatollah Khomeini won't grant peace unless President Hussein departs. What can we do? I think we ought to recognize several facts. One is that our responsibilities are greater than our capabilities. Our responsibility is great because the civil society in our part of the world has been suppressed. There used to be a saying in the old days of feudalism and the monarchies that there are two types of poet in the Muslim world, *sha 'er al-imama* and *sha 'er al-khelafa*: the poet of prophecy and the poet of power. In other words, there was a literature of dissent and there was a literature of conformity to power—the poets who were located in the power establishment and those who belonged in the civil society. In a double entendre, the phrases also meant "the poet behind" and "the poet ahead." The saying used to go further: the *sha 'er al-imama* will usually be found in the "provinces"; he is not likely to be found in the *dar al-khelafa* (capital; literally, the seat of power).

Our problem is that they have now abolished the "provinces." Modern communications, the capitalist economy, modern management techniques have all brought the "provinces" within easy reach of the repressive state. Earlier, Muhammad Ja'far was saying that politics has been abolished in Iraq and the Baathists presided over its abolition. To a large extent, Ayatollah Khomeini is doing the same in Iran. The "provinces" are not there, and the actual and potential "poets of the provinces" have gone into exile, mostly to the capitalist metropolis, or are in prison if they are spared execution, or have been forcibly silenced. Our responsibilities are therefore very great. We must analyze, innovate, dissent. We need courage, which we have, and patience, which we do not always have. We must work very hard to keep the civil society alive and to make alternatives appear viable and necessary. This meeting is a beginning. If we can get together, we may keep pushing forward, critically and honestly.

[1986]

## 13 / ISLAM AND POLITICS

In writing about Islam and politics, one faces special difficulties. The field of Islamic studies, strewn with ancient potholes and modern mines, is dominated by apparently different but complementary adversaries—the "traditionalist" ulema and the "modern" orientalists. Their methods are different; so are their intentions. Yet, with few exceptions, both tend to view Islam's relationship to politics in fundamentalist and textual terms. Both emphasize the absence of separation between religion and politics in Islam. Both hold an essentially static view of Islam and interpret change and innovations produced by social and economic forces as impingements on established, therefore ordained, religious standards. Both treat Muslim history, especially its most creative periods—that is, the Umayyads in Spain, the Moghuls in India, the Safavids in Persia—as deviations from the norm. The interplay of the Westerners' academic orthodoxy and the ulema's theological orthodoxy has set the terms of prevalent discourse on Islam.

A second problem concerning perceptions and prejudices should be put forth. The Islamic civilization is the only one with which the territorial, religious, and cultural boundaries of the West have fluctuated for fourteen centuries. Islam's relationship with the West has been continuous, frequently intimate, marked by protracted and violent confrontations and fruitful, though often forgotten, collaboration. During the century that followed the prophethood of Muhammad, the dramatic expansion of Islamic dominance occurred largely at the expense of Christendom. Subsequently, the West and Islam remained locked in a relationship of antagonistic collaboration that included seven centuries of Muslim rule in Spain, an unsuccessful invasion of France, and an inconclusive occupation of Sicily. The long and bitter confrontation during the Crusades and later the Ottoman domination of the Balkans further solidified in the West the adversarial perceptions and menacing images of Islam and Muslims. Even the prophet Muhammad and the Quran were not spared several centuries of vilification and abusive misrepresentation. In turn, medieval Muslim writers misrepresented and misjudged Judaism and Christianity. However, because Islam venerates biblical prophets as predecessors of Muhammad, their polemics fortunately stopped short of vilifications in extremis. To the Western world's credit, the "medieval canon" of Christian discourse on Islam (up to the eighteenth century) has been admirably documented.[1]

This unique history of the West's encounter with a non-Western civilization undoubtedly left on both sides a heritage of prejudice and resentment. Yet, in this pattern of hostility, there were periods of accommodation. While our cultures were traditional, agrarian, and medieval, there existed a structural symmetry between them which accounted for a degree of equality in the exchange of ideas as well as products. Winners and losers manufactured and used the same weapons, traded in comparable goods, debated on familiar intellectual premises. There was a certain congruence of class interests and shared attitudes among the aristocrats, craftsmen, traders, and scholars. The commonality of outlook between Saladin the Great and Richard the Lionhearted is known to almost every Muslim and Christian child even today. Students of European and Muslim history can recall numerous such examples. But the symmetry which had constituted the basis of an intimacy and antagonistic collaboration between Islam and the West disappeared in modern times. Nothing in the past was as damaging to Muslim-Western understanding as has been the structurally unequal encounter of traditional, agrarian/pastoral Muslim societies with the industrial and capitalist West. Its many ramifications include, as we shall presently see, modern Islam's peculiar, disjointed relationship to politics.

A dramatic reversal in the relationship between the Muslim world and the West began with Napoleon Bonaparte's invasion of Egypt in 1798 and the establishment of British dominion over Moghul India during the eighteenth and nineteenth centuries. It ended with the breakup of the Ottoman Empire, which was the last of the Muslim empires, and the colonization by European countries of virtually all of the Muslim world from East Asia to West Africa. It was a traumatizing development for the Muslims. This was not merely due to the fact that for the first time in the confrontation between Islam and the West they were the colonized, not the colonizers; rather, this latest encounter of Islam with the West was felt as a deeply dehumanizing and alienating experience. Modern imperialism was unique in history in that it was a complex and highly integrated system in which preindustrial and pastoral civilizations were either destroyed (as was the case with the great civilizations of the Western hemisphere) or subjugated (as were the countries of Asia and Africa) to serve the needs of the mercantilist and industrializing Western metropolis. The legitimizing principles of this system (that is, the white man's burden, the *mission civilisatrice*, or the Manifest Destiny) were based on the assumption of the inferiority of "native" peoples, their lesser existence and diminished humanity. Devaluation of the colonized civilization, debasement of its cultural heritage, and distortion of native realities have been part of the moral epistemology of modern imperialism. These were important elements of the "corporate institution" which Edward Said and others have recently analyzed as "orientalism."[2]

As the process of decolonization began, the Western need to justify domination over the "natives" was lessened. A certain detente in the organized libel against Islam and Muslims was expected. The expectation was credible, given the growth of ecumenical sentiments in the United States and Europe and the ease in communications provided by technological development and international exchange. After centuries of interruption, the possibility had reappeared that Western scholars and their Muslim counterparts would begin to recognize and reassess the limitations and biases of their intellectual work and also begin to examine critically but positively the meaning of the Islamic experience in history and society. The trend that emerged between world wars, first in France, then in Britain and the United States, suggested that a change in this direction had started. In France, the works of Louis Massignon encouraged the rise of a "revisionist" school which included scholars of Islam such as Jacques Berque, Maxime Rodinson, Yves Lacoste, and Roger Arnaldez. In Britain and the United States, their counterparts were to be found in H. A. R. Gibb, Wilfred Cantwell Smith, and Norman Daniel. Unfortunately, this welcome trend was overwhelmed by those with vested ideological interests.[3]

Far from producing a detente in the postcolonial era, the Cold War and the Arab-Israeli conflict added to the Western discourse on Islam an element of manipulation and malevolence. Cold war academic functionaries and pro-Israel Middle East "experts" have rendered difficult an appreciation of contemporary Muslim problems. These include distortions, misrepresentations, and libels, not merely criticism. Critical writing needs to be distinguished from racial and ideological hostility. There is a desperate need for critical analyses of the Muslim world's contemporary predicament. From Morocco through Syria and Iraq to Pakistan and Indonesia, Muslims are ruled by armed minorities. Some describe themselves as socialist and democratic, others as Islamic, yet others as Islamic, socialist, and democratic. Nearly all Muslim governments are composed of corrupt and callous elites more adept at repressing the populace than protecting natural resources or national sovereignty. They are more closely linked to foreign patrons than to the domestic polity. The recent rise of fundamentalist, neototalitarian Muslim movements is an aberration, not a norm in Muslim history. However, it is predicated upon the failure of the current regimes and the absence of visible, viable alternatives. These are hardly the times for expert praise and paeans. But a critical scholarship is the opposite of heartless and opportunistic employment of expertise.

It is a nemesis of biased scholarship that the societies and systems they serve ultimately suffer from their distortions. An understanding of Muslim politics and the anguish and aspirations of Islamic, especially Middle Eastern, peoples has slipped beyond the grasp of most "experts." Hence historic trends toward major developments—that is, the outbreak of an epoch-making revolution in Algeria, an Arab military rebound in October 1973, or Anwar Sadat's dramatic and disastrous démarche for peace—went unnoticed by them until events hit the headlines. In 1978, big men in the United States, from Jimmy Carter to Walter Cronkite, were surprised by the failure of the experts to perceive the revolutionary process in Iran, which had been long in the making. The failure, nevertheless, was as predictable as the Iranian Revolution. The shah was deemed a friend of the United States as well as of Israel; he was "modern," anti-Islam, and generous to the experts. Foremost Iranian experts explained the shah by distorting Iran and its history. Thus Professor Leonard Binder, a distinguished professor at the University of Chicago, wrote, "Here is a nation, Iran, that has not ruled itself in historical times, that has had an alien religion (Islam) imposed upon it, that has twisted that religion (Shi'ism) to cheat its Arab tormentors, that can boast of no military hero . . . that has been deprived by its poets and mystics, of all will to change its fate."[4]

Professor Marvin Zonis, another well-known expert on Iran, found the "kingly grace" of the "Shahanshah" (King of Kings) toward "foreign scholars . . . both courageous and laudable . . . the monarch's control over the internal situation is at its zenith. It is undoubtedly true that no Iranian ruler however exercised as much power or commanded as responsive a political system as does Mohammed Reza Pahlavi in 1974, 'urban guerrillas' and censorious foreign critics notwithstanding."[5] Examples are nearly as numerous as experts. Superficially trained, attached to disciplines and methods in flux, governed by the preferences of governments and foundations, and lacking empathy with the objects of their study, the area experts of the postcolonial era have all the limitations of conventional orientalists but few of their strengths.

A historically rigged intellectual tradition, then, continues to dominate Western perspectives on Islam. Its impact on Muslims, too, has been considerable. It has made the traditionalist ulema more obdurate and closed to new methods of critical inquiry. It has led educated Muslims to neglect substantive contributions of Western scholarship to theological ideas and historical interpretation. Above all, it has stunted the creative and critical impulses of modernist Muslims by activating their defensive instincts.

In writing about Islam for a largely Western audience, a Muslim faces hard choices between explanation and exploration. One's instinct is to explain the errors, deny the allegations, and challenge the overwhelmingly malevolent representations of Muslim history, ideals, and aspirations. For a century, since Syed Ameer Ali wrote *The Life and Teachings of Mohammed*, most modernist Muslim writers have, to varying degrees, surrendered to this instinct.[6] There is a certain poignancy to their effort, for these colonized, Western-educated Muslims were desperate to communicate to the West, in Western terms, pride in their devalued culture, distorted history, and maligned religion. For their labors, they have been dubbed modern Islam's "Apologist" school. Thus another vast body of contemporary literature on Islam merely symbolizes the futility of corrective and defensive responses to the orientalists' representation of Islam. This is reason enough to resist giving in to this urge.

It is commonly asserted that in Islam, unlike in Christianity and other religions, there is no separation of religion and politics. In strict textual and formal legal terms, this may be true. But this standard generalization is not helpful in comprehending Muslim political praxis either historically or contemporaneously. In its most fundamental sense, politics involves a set of active links, both positive and negative, between civil society and institutions of power. In this sense, there has been little separation, certainly none in our time, between religion and politics anywhere. For example, Hinduism played an important role in the ideological and organizational development of the

Indian national movement. Mahatma Gandhi's humanitarian and idealistic principles of passive resistance and nonviolence drew on Hindu precepts like ahimsa. The Mahatma was challenged by fundamentalist religious parties like the Arya Samaj and the Hindu Mahasabha and died at the hands of a Hindu fundamentalist political assassin. In Southeast Asia, including Vietnam, Buddhism and Buddhist institutions have been a potent force on both sides of the political divide.

In the United States, where the two major political parties have become increasingly indistinguishable on the basic issues of war and peace, the Christian churches have emerged as the primary platforms of political discourse, disputations, and even militancy. The political activism of Christians in the United States ranges widely from the right-wing Reverend Jerry Falwell's Moral Majority, through the centrist liberalism of the National Council of Churches, to Dorothy Day's populist humanism and Father Daniel Berrigan's militant pacifism. In Latin American countries—including Argentina, Chile, El Salvador, and Brazil—government-sponsored assassination squads have been carrying out their murderous missions in the name of preserving Christian values and virtues. On the opposite side, bishops are killed and nuns are raped for their advocacy of justice and democracy.

As for Judaism, we have witnessed its full-fledged politicization with a fundamentalist ideology successfully staking out its claims over Palestine on the Bible's authority. The Bible is still being invoked to justify the expansion of Israel into "Judea and Samaria" (that is, the West Bank and Gaza) and further dispossession of Christian and Muslim Palestinians from their ancient homeland. Since the outcome of the struggle for power in revolutionary Iran remains uncertain and since in Pakistan a self-proclaimed "Islamic" dictator rules in isolation, Israel and Saudi Arabia must be counted as the two truly theocratic states in the Middle East. Both have a contradictory existence: one as an "Islamic" monarchy; the other as a sectarian "democracy" whose Christian and Muslim subjects are treated, under law, as second-class citizens. Given these facts, it is obviously tendentious to ascribe to Muslims, as media commentators and academic experts so often do, a special proclivity to engage in religiously motivated politics.

In a narrower perspective, the relationship of politics and religion may be discussed in terms of the links between religion and state power. In this sense, separation between state and religion has existed in the Muslim world for at least eleven of Islam's fourteen centuries. The organic links between religion and state power ended in A.D. 945 when a Buwayhid prince, Muiz al-Dawla Ahmad, marched into the capital city of Baghdad and terminated the Abbasid caliph's dual role as the temporal and spiritual leader of the Islamic nation. For a time, the caliph served in various parts of the Muslim world as a legitimizing symbol through the investiture of temporal rulers—sultans, amirs, and khans—among them, successful rebels and usurpers. The Buwayhids, who ruled over Iraq and Fars as amirs, kept the caliphate in subjection for 110 years, until they were displaced in A.D. 1055 by Tughril, the Seljuk warrior. In 1258, the Mongols sacked Baghdad, killed the caliph and his kin, and terminated the Abbasid Caliphate, which had been for two centuries a Merovingian cipher. Although the caliphate was revived and claimed—at different times in various places, by a variety of rulers—it never quite mustered the allegiance of a majority of Muslims. Power, in effect, remained secularized in Muslim practice.[7]

One is generous in dating the effective separation of religion and state power from the Buwayhid intervention of A.D. 945. The fundamentalist ulema take a somewhat more conservative view. They believe that no Muslim state has been Islamic since the accession to power of the Umayyad dynasty in A.D. 650; to them, the Islamic state effectively ended with the first four caliphs who had been companions of the Prophet Muhammad. However, the minority Shiite ulema, who believe that legitimate succession belonged only to the blood relatives and descendants of the Prophet, definitely do not regard two of the four caliphs (Umar and Uthman) as legitimate rulers. The orthodox ulema's rejection of the Islamic character of Muslim states after 650 is based primarily on three factors. The first concerns the presumed impiety of all but a few exceptional rulers (that is, Umar Ibn Abd Al-Aziz, 717–720). The second relates to the historic prevalence of secular laws and practices in Muslim statecraft. The third involves the actual fragmentation of the Islamic world into multiple political entities historically: sultanates, emirates, khanates, sheikhdoms, empires, and, now, republics. All theologians agree on the principles of a single ummah (Muslim nation) and a single caliph (or imam) as essential to a truly Islamic polity governed according to divine laws and the example of the Prophet.

Lacking all three conditions of the ideal Islamic polity, Muslim peoples have for more than a millennium accepted as legitimate the exercise of state power by temporal governments, as long as they observe the basic norms of justice and fair play and rule with some degree of consent from the governed. This generalization applies also to the overwhelming majority of ulema and local religious leaders. In fact, the most renowned theologians of Islam—that is, al-Mawardi (974–1058), al-Baghdadi (d. 1037), al-Ghazzali (1058–1111), and Ibn Jamaa (1241–1333)—have developed a large body of exegeses to justify, explain, and elaborate on this historic compromise between the Islamic ideal and Muslim political realities. Thus, as in all religious communities, there is a repository of millennial traditions in Islam that tend to surface most forcefully in times of crisis, collective stress, and anomie.[8] Times have rarely been as bad, as stressful, or as disorienting for the Muslim peoples as they are now. Hence all the contrasting symptoms associated with deep crises of politics and society—the rise of religious fundamentalism, radical and revolutionary mobilization, spontaneous uprisings, and disoriented quietism—characterize Muslim politics today.

A fusion of religion and political power was and remains an ideal in the Muslim tradition. But the absence of such a fusion is a historically experienced and recognized reality. The tradition of statecraft and the history of Muslim peoples have been shaped by this fact. The many manifestations of this reality are important in comprehending the Muslim polity. A few of these need to be mentioned here. As a religious and proselytizing medieval civilization, the Islamic ummah evinced a spirit of tolerance toward other faiths and cultures that has been rare in history. It is important for us to acknowledge—for the sake of historical veracity as well as for a desperately needed reinforcement of nonsectarian and universalist values in Muslim civilization—that non-Muslims, especially Christians, Jews, and Hindus, have been an integral part of the Islamic enterprise. In the precolonial period, Muslim law and practice reflected a certain separation and autonomy of religious and social life along confessional lines. Admittedly, there were also instances of excesses against and oppression of the non-Muslim population under Muslim rule. Yet the greatest achievements of Islamic civilization in science, philosophy, literature, music, art, and architecture, as well as statecraft, have been the collective achievements of Christians, Jews, Hindus, and others participating in the cultural and economic life of the "Islamicate." In fact, the most creative periods of Muslim history have been those that witnessed a flowering in the collaborative half of our ecumenical relationships. This secular fact of Muslim political praxis, from Indonesia and India through the Fertile Crescent and Egypt to Spain, is generally neglected in the writings both of the ulema and the orientalists. Yet, it is more relevant to understanding Islam's relationship to politics than the antics of any current "Islamic" political leader.

Throughout history, Muslims, like other people who live in complex civilizations, have evinced paradoxical tendencies in relation to politics. In dissident movements, Islam has sometimes played a crucial role by galvanizing group support for opposition leaders around a reformist, often puritanical creed, attacking the corruption and profligacy of a ruling class. The latest case in point is Ayatollah Khomeini's Islamic movement in Iran. An early example is the austere movement of Ibn Tumart, which in the twelfth century gathered enough support in North Africa to displace the Almoravid dynasty in Morocco and Spain. A later example is the puritanical Wahhabi movement of the eighteenth century, which gained tribal support in the Najd, especially of the tribe of Saud, and thence spread to the Arabian peninsula. In power, such reformist movements have betrayed a proclivity to softening and secularization. The Almohad, for example, patronized the rather secular and speculative philosophical school including Ibn Rushd, known in the West as Averroes (1126–1198).

On the other hand, the Muslim community has resisted state sponsorship of a creed or even a school of religious thought. Thus two of the greatest Muslim rulers encountered popular resistance when they unsuccessfully attempted to sponsor an official creed. The Abbasid caliph, al-Mamun (786–833), son of Harun al-Rashid (of the Arabian Nights!) and founder of the House of Wisdom in Baghdad (where many of the translations and commentaries on Greek works were completed and later contributed to the European Renaissance), adopted the Mutazilite doctrines as official creed. This rationalist school of religious thought in Islam was beginning to flourish when it received the sponsorship of the state. At the time, the caliphate was in its prime. Resistance to it mounted rapidly in the Islamic community. It was thus that the Mutazilites acquired the dubious distinction in Muslim history of engaging in the first significant practice of repression on theological grounds. Similarly, Akbar the Great (1542–1605), the most illustrious of the Moghul emperors in India, met with widespread resistance from his Muslim subjects when he promulgated his own eclectic creed *Dine Ilahi* (1582). Fortunately, Akbar was skeptical and open-minded enough to refrain from forcing his eccentric, ecumenical creed on the populace.

Historically, the ulema as a class prospered and played a conservative role as mediators between political power and civil society, much like the clergy in Christendom. During the first two centuries of Islam, a significant number of theological scholars abjured any identification with power, declining to serve even as judges. Thus Imam Abu Hanifa (d. 767), founder of one of the four schools of Sunni Islamic law, was flogged for refusing the judgeship of Baghdad. In later years, many served as legal advisers to governments and as judges. The institution of Waqf (private and public endowment of property to mosques and schools), which were invariably administered by the ulema, and their role as educators and as interpreters of religious law ensured for them a lucrative and prominent place in society next to the military and bureaucracy. As a class, therefore, they betrayed a certain bias in favor of stability and obedience to temporal authority. Thus al-Mawardi, al-Baghdadi, and al-Baqillani—great theological authorities to this day—held that an unjust and unrighteous ruler should not claim obedience and that the community would be justified in transferring its allegiance to a contender. However, they opposed rebellion and civil war. The great philosopher-theologian al-Gliazzati—the equivalent in Islam of Thomas Aquinas—and his successor Ibn Jamaa invoked the Doctrine of Necessity to counsel that public tolerance of even a bad ruler was preferable to anarchy and civil strife. Professor Anwar Syed has rightly concluded that the theologians "endorsed the secularization of politics in return for a pact of mutual assistance between the government and the Ulema."[9]

Recognizing their historical role as well as their present discontent, most contemporary Muslim governments have tried various schemes that offer a modicum of security and status to the ulema; in almost all instances, they have been successful in co-opting the clerical class. It is noteworthy that the most iconoclastic of contemporary Muslim rulers—Habib Bourguiba (1903–) of Tunisia, has encountered the least resistance from the ulema. This is so not only because he has enjoyed considerable popularity among the masses as the liberator of Tunisia but also because, unlike Kemal Ataturk (founding father of modern Turkey) or Mohammed Reza Khan (1877–1944, founder of the Pahlavi dynasty in Iran), Bourguiba did not attempt to suppress forcibly religion and traditional Muslim institutions. Rather, while instituting modernist reforms, he allowed the ulema a certain visibility and status as religious leaders.

The political quietism of the ulema has not been shared by all sections of the Muslim intelligentsia and by no means by the majority of the Islamic community. There has, in fact, been a perennial tension between the moral imperatives of Muslim culture and the holders of power. It is difficult to recall a widely known Muslim saint who did not collide with state power. Popular belief may have exaggerated the actual confrontations with contemporary rulers of men like the Persian saint Mevlana Jalaluddin Rumi (1207–1273)—best known to the West as the founder of the mystic order of "whirling dervishes"—the Indian Khwaja Muinuddin Chishti (1142–1236), and the Moroccan saint Sidi Lahsen Lyusi (1631–1691). But, in this case, popular belief is the more significant indicator of political culture. It is equally important to emphasize that in each instance the collision was not incidental, a mere adding of luster to the growth of a legend. Rather, it was a principal landmark in the making of a saint, in distinguishing the exceptional Muslim from the ordinary. In this conception of sainthood, there is an admission, on the one hand, of the difficulty of achieving an alignment of piety to power and an affirmation, on the other hand, of a Muslim's obligation to confront the excesses of political authority.

The political culture of Islam is, by and large, activist and insurrectionary. Scholars have described the Muslim heartland from Pakistan to Mauritania as lands of insolence. Historically, rebellions have been as endemic here as were wars in Western Europe, and the target of insurrection has often been the state's authority. Until recently, all but a few Muslim polities were typically divided between what the Maghrebins ("Western" Arabs of North Africa) aptly named *Bilad al-Siba* (the Country in Rebellion) and *Bilad al-Makhzan* (the Country of the Treasury). There are exceptions to the rule, but normally both popular rebellions and dynastic movements of opposition have been led by temporal figures. When involved in dissident politics, religious figures and groups were generally associated with the mystical schools, that is, with the pietist and populist rather than the orthodox, theological tradition in Islam. However, as with state power, Islam has played a certain role in the legitimization of revolt. If the state-oriented ulema cited religious injunctions against disobedience and contumacy, rebels, too, invoked the Quran and the Prophet's traditions, calling upon Muslims to struggle (jihad) against tyranny and oppression.

An explanation for the perenniality of the insurrectionary strain in Muslim societies lies, at least partly, in the fact that, wherever Islam took hold, it had its origins in a countertradition, a dissident point of view. In many regions, such as North Africa and Central Asia, the spread of Islam was dialectically linked with social revolt. In other places, such as the Indian subcontinent, Islam's egalitarian precepts and emphasis on social justice (both widely violated in practice) offered an escape to the disinherited from the harsh realities of oppression. In its exemplary form, Islam is a religion of the oppressed. Hence, to this day, it retains a powerful appeal among the poor and oppressed throughout the world. It is currently the most rapidly growing faith in Africa and the East Indies. In the black communities and prisons of the United States, too, Islam has a significant presence. Even in independent India it is still finding new converts among the Harijans (literally, Children of God, Gandhi's preferred name for the Untouchables). The religious and cultural force of Islam continues to outpace its political capabilities.[10]

Historically, then, the Islamic community has lived in separate polities ruled by a wide variety of temporal authorities ranging from tribal chieftains to modern republics. These secular political entities have been ethnically, linguistically, and often religiously diverse. They have been subject to constant change brought about by dynastic challengers and popular insurrections and, occasionally, by somewhat religiously motivated reformist movements. Given its heterogeneity, observers of the Muslim world are impressed by the evidence of unity in Islamic peoples' cultural, social, and political life. There is evidence also of a strong Islamic affinity across territorial and linguistic divides. This sense of solidarity has been based not merely on religious beliefs and practices but on a shared consciousness of history and a commonality of values. In this respect, the Islamic civilization was, and to a lesser extent, remains inherently political. The values and linkages that defined the unity of the historically diverse Muslim community have been political in the deepest sense of the word. It should suffice here to mention only a few factors that produced, over the centuries, the patterns of unity in diversity—what scholars have called the "mosaic" of Muslim cultures.

For centuries, a complementary tension, creative in its impact on society and individuals, had existed between particularist and universalist loyalties and loci of Muslim political life. Typically, a Muslim held two sets of identity: one—immediate, social, and spatially particular; the other—historical, ideological, cultural, and global. Almost all Muslims lived in intensely community-oriented societies which, paradoxically, eschewed isolation. The paradox had a political dimension. The interests and demands of local authority—that is, the extended family, tribe, city, guild, and ethnic or linguistic group—in principle competed with the universal expectations of the ummah, the vast Islamicate, that is, the worldwide community of people who embrace the teachings of the Quran and practice Islam. The stability and quality of Muslim life had depended on the extent to which these two identities were reconciled. The achievement of such a reconciliation had been a preoccupation of politics in the Islamic civilization. Its attainment was by far the greatest accomplishment of civil society in the Muslim world. The processes by which this was achieved included a certain decentralization of power, a toleration of differences, and pluralism in religious and cultural life. Thus, while the ummah was one and ideally united, its diversity was presumed. Rather, it was honored and extolled, for indeed it was the sign of God's mastery and creativity (S. 30:22). Also, the prophets had declared "differences within the Ummah to be a blessing."

A complex web of laws, activities, and institutions had contributed to the development of a common identity and culture in the Muslim world. A shared system of law, education, aesthetics, and religious organizations (especially religious fraternities or mystical orders) had assured the growth and continuity of a unifying ethos that cut across the political, ethnic, and linguistic boundaries of the Islamicate. For example, the divided and diverse ummah was assured a certain structural unity by a common adherence to laws (sharia) which were based on the Quran, the sunna (traditions of the Prophet), and ijma (consensus of the community). Typically, the sharia served less as a guide to governmental conduct than as a regulator of societal relationships—of property, business transactions, marriages, and public morals.

For centuries, Muslims from the Pacific to the Atlantic oceans were not merely born and buried according to similar rituals; more importantly, they were likely to be punished for crimes or failure to honor a contract, to have a grievance redressed or a property dispute settled, get married or divorced, and make business transactions in accordance with similar, though not always identical, laws and codes of conduct. Similarly, the educational system of the Muslim world was based on a shared tradition of jurisprudence, philosophy, mathematics, ethics, and aesthetics. Hence it was not uncommon for jurists and scholars to serve in more than one country in a lifetime, for artists and architects to have lived and worked in various kingdoms, for elites to intermarry across political boundaries, for nomadic tribes to move from one ruler's domain to another. The passport was inimical to the spirit of the Islamicate. The phenomenon provided the framework for a sharing of values, the growth of an extraterritorial ethos, a source of collective identity.

This state of affairs lasted until the eighteenth century, when Western imperialism started to "territorialize" the Muslim world. Thereupon began its parceling out into colonies and spheres of British, French, and Dutch influence. The differences and hostilities of European nation-states came to be mirrored in Muslim lands. For the first time in its long and eventful history, Islamic civilization began to be defined by reference to another. Neither its wars nor peace, neither prosperity nor sufferings were of its own making. A people habituated to a history of success were reduced to serving another's history. The myriad links which had assured the Islamic culture its unity in diversity were severed. Its fragmentation, institutionalized in multiple ways, was completed by the creation of highly centralized, "independent" nation-states governed by the postcolonial military-bureaucratic elites, each a disfigured copy of its colonial predecessors. The "mosaic" of Muslim culture was destroyed. The remarkable continuity which, over centuries of growth and expansion, tragedies and disasters, had distinguished Islamic civilization was interrupted. This change, labeled modernization by social scientists, has been experienced by contemporary Muslims as a disjointed, disorienting, unwilled reality. The history of Muslim peoples in the last one hundred years has been largely a history of groping—between betrayals and losses—toward ways to break this impasse, to somehow gain control over their collective lives, and link their past to the future.

In discussing the role of religion in contemporary Muslim politics, four points should be emphasized. First, the contemporary crisis of Muslim societies is without a parallel in Islamic history. Second, throughout the nineteenth and twentieth centuries, the role of Islam in politics has varied in time and place. Third, the evidence of continuity with the patterns of the past has been striking. Fourth, in the 1980s, the trend is toward the growth of fundamentalist, neototalitarian Muslim movements. The phenomenon is contrary to the political culture and historical traditions of the Muslim majority. The still limited but growing appeal of the fundamentalist parties is associated with the traumas of Muslim political life and the absence of viable alternatives to the existing state of affairs. A brief discussion of these points follows.

When a civilization reaches a point of fundamental crisis and perceptible decline, we see three responses. One may identify these as: (a) restorationist, (b) reconstructionist, and (c) pragmatist.

The restorationist is one that seeks the restoration of the past in its idealized form. This is the thrust of fundamentalism, of such movements as the Muslim Brotherhood in the Arab world, the Jamaat-i-Islami in Pakistan, the Sharekat Islam in Indonesia, and the Islamic government of postrevolution Iran. So far, these have been minority movements in the Muslim world. Without an exception, they have failed to attract the large majority of workers, peasants, and the intelligentsia. This was true even in Iran, where the shift toward the current fundamentalist ideology began after the seizure of power.

The reconstructionist is one that seeks to blend tradition with modernity in an effort to reform society. This is the thrust of the modernist schools which have, intellectually and ideologically, dominated the Muslim world since the middle of the nineteenth century. The most influential writers and thinkers of modern Islam—Jamaluddin Afghani, Shibli Nomani, Syed Ameer Ali, Muhammad Abduh, Muhammad Iqbal, Tahir Haddad, among others—have belonged to this school of thought; in political life, their influence had been considerable until the rise of military regimes in many Muslim countries. This was true also in Iran, where until after the shah's fall no significant group of ulema had openly challenged the eminent Ayatollah Naini's formulation in support of the democratic and constitutionalist movement (1904–1905), a position that was endorsed by the leading theologians of the Shia sect of Islam. For five decades, successive generations of Iranian religious leaders had reaffirmed this position. During the 1977–1978 uprising against the shah, all the politically prominent clerics of Iran, including Ayatollah Khomeini, had claimed to favor a pluralistic polity and parliamentary government. The first appointment by Khomeini of a social democratic government with Dr. Mehdi Bazargan as prime minister had seemed to confirm this claim. Above all, it should be noted that the mobilization of the Iranian Revolution toward Islam had been the work of such lay Muslim intellectuals as Dr. Mehdi Bazargan, Jalal Ale-Ahmad, and Abdul Hasan Bani Sadr. The most important populizers of Islamic idealism were Ali Shariati, a progressive layman, and the Ayatollah Mahmud Taleghani, a radical religious leader. Although the Ayatollah Khomeini had been an important opposition figure since 1963, he was far from being the central figure he became in 1978. In January 1978, as the revolution began to gather momentum, the shah's regime did Khomeini the honor of singling him out for its most publicized and personal attack. From this point on, he became the counterpoint to the hated but central figure of the shah. An explanation of his meteoric rise to charismatic power lies in the complex character of Iran's disorganic development, which lent one of the objectively most advanced revolutions of history a millenarian dimension.

The pragmatist denotes an attitude of viewing religious requirements as being largely unrelated to the direct concerns of states and governments and of dealing with the affairs of the state in terms of the political and economic imperatives of contemporary life. The regulation of religious life is left to civil society and to private initiatives. This approach has not been opposed by the reconstructionist school of intellectuals. As discussed earlier, it parallels the historical Muslim experience; as such, it is accepted both by the masses and the majority of the ulema. Thus, wherever popular attitudes have been tested in open and free elections, pragmatist political parties and secular programs have gained overwhelming victories over their fundamentalist adversaries. In this realm of real politics, one finds the resonances of the historical patterns discussed earlier. A few examples follow.

The paradoxical historical pattern involving, on the one hand, a preference for the temporal exercise of power and for a this-worldly political exchange and, on the other hand, popular vulnerability to religious symbols and slogans in times of social stress and collective anxiety is replicated in modern times. Thus, throughout the twentieth century, the political heroes of the Muslim world, the liberators and founding fathers of contemporary Muslim nations, have been secular, generally Westernized individuals. To name only a few and the familiar, Kemal Ataturk (1881–1938), the founder of modern Turkey, Muhammad Ali Jinnah (1876–1948), the founding father of Pakistan, Ahmad Sukarno (1901–1970), first president of Indonesia, Gamal Abdul Nasser (1918–1970), first president of the republic of Egypt, Habib Bourguiba (1903–), of Tunisia, and the seven historic chiefs of the Algerian Revolution are regarded as the most popular and decidedly historic Muslim leaders of this century. The movements and political organizations they led were secular and heavily influenced by modern, largely Western, ideas. Today, the most popular movement in the Arab world, the Palestine Liberation Organization, claims a "secular and democratic" polity as the basis of its program; two of its three most prominent leaders are Christians.

By contrast, religious sectarianism is being most aggressively displayed in the Near East by two exclusionary ideologies and movements, the Phalangists and Zionists—one Maronite Christian, the other Jewish. Their shared antipathy to the secular, democratic, and universalist ideal underlay the ironic alliance between Israel and the Phalange, that is, between the Jewish state and the first fascist movement to make a successful bid for power in the post–World War II period. This same phenomenon also explains, perhaps, the fact that in the Occupied Territories Israeli authorities have been particularly harsh on the Christian population, and, in an effort to destroy the unity of Christian and Muslim Palestinians, the government of Israel has been encouraging the growth of fundamentalist Muslim groups in the Occupied

Areas, allowing them considerable freedom to organize. This freedom is denied the ecumenical and secular Palestinian nationalist movement.[11]

Another historical pattern repeating itself in our time is the resistance to state-decreed religion in the two countries where an official version of Islam is being imposed on citizens by the state. In Iran, thousands of people have been executed and jailed for their opposition to Ayatollah Khomeini's Islamic regime. Significantly, the Iranian resistance today is made up primarily of former activists and supporters of the opposition to the shah. It includes the youthful mujahideen movement, influenced by Islamic radicals Ayatollah Mahmud Taleghani and Dr. Ali Shariati, the followers of Abdul Hasan Bani Sadr (first president of Iran after the revolution), the nationalists who had previously supported the constitutional regime of Prime Minister Mohammed Mossadegh, and many disillusioned former supporters of Ayatollah Khomeini. Were they to be given the freedom of choice, a majority of Iranian people would probably rid themselves of the fundamentalist tyranny in favor of a pluralistic and democratic regime of the sort the Iranian Revolution, including the leaders of its Islamic wing, had promised them. In Pakistan, there is a certainty that if General Muhammad Zia ul-Haq were to fulfill his promise of a free election, the secular political parties would win it by an overwhelming majority—a certainty which has led General Zia to violate for more than six years the solemn promises he made to hold free elections within ninety days of his coup d'état.

The centrality of Muslim peoples' predicament lies in the nature of their latest encounter with the West. The colonial encounter was unique in history in that it entailed the transformation of land and labor into commodities, in the literal, capitalist meaning of the word. Inevitably, it caused the erosion of economic, social, and political relationships which had contributed the bases of traditional Muslim order for more than a thousand years.

Unlike capitalist development in the West, in the Muslim world it occurred under foreign auspices for the benefit largely of the metropolitan power. Hence it involved uneven and disorganic change. Consequently, the vast majority of Muslim people still live in structurally archaic, increasingly impoverished societies, but they are organically linked with the modern, industrial, metropolitan world. They are the men and women—the Mustazafeen, the weakened ones—among whom the Algerian and Iranian revolutions had the strongest appeal. Germaine Tillion, a French anthropologist, who worked among the Algerians, has described them as "living on the frontiers of two worlds—in the middle of the ford—haunted by the past, fevered with the dreams of the future. But it is with their hands empty and their bellies hollow that they are waiting between their phantoms and their fevers."[12]

The trauma of Muslim life today is augmented by the fact that the resource-rich, strategically important heartlands of Islam are still subject to conquest and colonization. For the Palestinians, the era of decolonization opened in 1948 with the loss of the greater part of their ancient homeland. Now, they are being systematically dispossessed from its remnant, the West Bank and Gaza. In Lebanon, the refugees who fled in 1948, mostly from the Galilee, are being terrorized in Israel's pursuit of its policy of "dispersion." Jerusalem, a holy city and touchstone of Arab cultural achievements, has been unilaterally annexed, as has been the Golan Heights. Since the creation of the United Nations, only three of its members lost territories without being able to regain them. All three were Arab states. Only at the cost of betraying others and of isolating itself from its Arab/Islamic milieu did Egypt reclaim in 1982 the territories lost in 1967. Now Lebanon has joined the list of occupied countries; its ancient cities—Tyre, Sidon, Nabatiyyeh—are ruins. Beirut, the cultural capital of the Arab world, became the first capital city in the world whose televised destruction was watched by the world week after week. No Arab, no Muslim government budged except to suppress popular support at home. Their lucrative business with the United States, the sole sustainer of Israel, continued as usual. Never before had been so tragic the links between wealth and weakness, material resources and moral bankruptcy. Never before in the history of Islamic peoples had there been so total a separation or political power and civil society.

In the breach, there is a time bomb. When the moral explosion of the masses occurs, it will undoubtedly have a reference to the past. But its objective shall be the future. The past is very present in the postcolonial Muslim societies. That it is a fractured past invaded by a new world of free markets, shorn of its substance and strength, incapable of assuring the continuity of communal life does not make it less forceful. Its power derives from the tyranny of contemporary realities and the seeming absence of viable alternatives. For the majority of Muslim peoples, the experienced alternative to the past is a limbo of foreign occupation and dispossession, of alienation from the land, of life in shantytowns and refugee camps, of migration into foreign lands, and, at best, of permanent expectancy. Leaning on and yearning for the restoration of an emasculated, often idealized past is one escape from the limbo; striking out, in protest and anger, for a new revolutionary order is another. Occasionally, as in Iran, the two responses are merged. More frequently, they are separated in time but historically, organically, linked. Hence, in our time, religiously oriented millenarian movements have tended to be harbingers of revolution.

The "hopes" that underlie popular support of religious movements in our time, Islamic or otherwise, are not really of the "past." The slogans and images of religio-political movements are invariably those of the past, but the hopes that are stimulated by them are intrinsically existential hopes, induced and augmented by the contemporary crisis, in this case, of the Muslim world. The often publicized ideological resurgence of Islam (social scientists and the American media spoke as much of "resurgent" Buddhism in the 1960s) is a product of excessive, uneven modernization and the failure of governments to safeguard national sovereignty or to satisfy basic needs. In the "transitional" Third World societies, one judges the present morally, with reference to the past, to inherited values, but materially in relation to the future. Therein lies a new dualism in our social and political life; the inability or unwillingness to deal with it entails disillusionment, terrible costs, and possible tragedy. One mourns Iran, laments Pakistan, fears for Egypt.

[1984]

# 14 / ROOTS OF THE RELIGIOUS RIGHT

They belong to differing, often contrasting religious systems—Hinduism, Judaism, Christianity, and Islam. Yet their ideas and behavior patterns bear remarkable similarities. In India, they have burned down churches and destroyed a historic mosque. In Palestine, they describe themselves as "pioneers," desecrate mosques and churches, and with state support dispossess the Muslim and Christian inhabitants of the ancient land. In Algeria, they are engaged in savage warfare with a praetorian government. In Serbia, they attempted genocide and ran rape camps. In Pakistan, they have hit Christians, Ahmedis, and Shia Muslims and also each other. They wage holy wars and commit atrocities sanctimoniously, yet nothing is truly sacred to them. They spill blood in bazaars, in homes, and in courts, mosques, and churches. They believe themselves to be God's warriors, above man-made laws and the judgment of mankind.

They are the so-called fundamentalists, an epithet reserved by the Western media for the Muslim variety who are invariably referred to as "Islamic fundamentalists." Others of the ilk are assigned more neutral nouns. The Jewish zealots in Palestine are called "settlers" and, occasionally, "extremists." The Hindu militant is described as "nationalist," and the Christian is labeled "right wing" or "messianic." The bias in the use of language obscures an important reality: they are reflections of a common problem, with shared roots and similar patterns of expression. Here we briefly review first the environment that gives birth to these political-religious movements, then the commonality of their style and outlook.

The mistakenly called "fundamentalists" are a modern phenomenon, a response to the crises of modernity and identity. Modernity is a historical process. It refers to the development of societies from one mode of production to another, in our age from an agrarian/pastoral mode to the capitalist/industrial mode of production. The shift from one to another mode of production invariably brings revolutionary changes in society. It compels a new logic of social and economic life, threatens inherited styles of life, and forces transformations in the relationship of land, labor, and capital. As such, it requires adaptations to new ways of being and doing and demands drastic changes in human values and in the relations of sexes, classes, individuals, families, and communities. It transforms the correlation and arrangement of living spaces, requires change in how the workplace is organized, how new skills are gathered and distributed, and how people are governed.

When this process of change sets in, older values and ways of life become outdated and dysfunctional much faster than newer, more appropriate values and ways of life strike roots. The resulting social and cultural mutations are experienced by people both as threat and loss. For millennia, humanity had experienced this unsettling process, for example, when it moved from the Stone Age to the Age of Iron or when it discovered fire and shifted from hunting and gathering to agriculture. But never had this process been more intense and more revolutionary than it became with the rise of capitalism and the industrial mode of production. This latter development has been more revolutionary in its impact on societies than any other event in history.

The industrial mode threatened nearly all values and institutions by which people had lived in the agrarian order. A transformation so systemic was bound to threaten old ways of life. It destroyed the autonomy of rural life lived for millennia, shrank the distances that had separated communities from each other, forced diverse peoples and individuals to live in urban proximity and compete with each other, undermined the structures and values of patriarchy as it had prevailed for centuries, and threw millions of people into the uncertain world of transition between tradition and modernity. In brief, the phenomenon puts into question, and increasingly renders dysfunctional, traditional values and ways of life. Yet cultures tend to change more slowly than economic and political realities. All societies caught in this process undergo a period of painful passage. How peacefully and democratically a society makes this journey depends on its historical circumstances, the engagement of its intelligentsia, the outlook of its leaders and governments, and the ideological choices they make.

The capitalist and industrial revolution started in Europe. European responses to its dislocating effects offer meaningful variations that scholars have not yet examined with sufficient rigor. The Western and non-Western experiences are, nevertheless, comparable in that they reveal that when faced with a crisis so systemic, people have tended to respond in four ways. We might call these restorationist, reformist, existential, and revolutionary responses.

The restorationist wants to return somehow to an old way of life, reimpose the laws or customs that were, recapture lost virtues, rehabilitate old certainties, and restore what he believes to have been the golden past—Hindutva and Ramraj, Eretz Israel, Nizam-e-Mustafa. Restorationism invariably entails rejection of the Other—e.g., Muslim, Arab, Hindu, Christian, Ahmadi—and what are construed to be the Other's ways, which can range from women's dress and men's beards to song, dance, and such symbols of modern life as the television and radio.

The restorationist ideology and program can range from relatively moderate to totally extremist. Mr. Atal Behari Vajpayee offers a "moderate" example of Hindu restorationism, Mr. Bal Thackeray is an extremist, and Lal Krishna Advani falls somewhere in between. Similarly, the Jamaat-i-Islami's amir, Qazi Hussain Ahmed, may be viewed as a moderate Islamist while Mulla Omar, the Taliban leader, occupies the extreme end.

The reformists are of modernist disposition, men and women who care deeply about preserving the best and most meaningful in their religious tradition while adapting them to the requirements of modern life. The obverse is also true: they seek to integrate modern forms and values into inherited cultures and beliefs. An early reformist in India was Raja Ram Mohan Roy, founder of the Brahmo Samaj movement. The first great Indian Muslim reformist was Sir Syed Ahmed Khan, and the last to be so regarded is Mohammed Iqbal, whose "Reconstruction of Religious Thought in Islam" is a quintessential example of reformism in modern Islam. In the Arab world, the al-Manar group led by Mufti Mohammed Abduh and, in the Maghreb, Shaykh Ben Badis, Tahir al-Haddad, and Abdel Aziz Taalbi were influential reformists. Like the restorationist, the reformist trend emerged as a response to the perceived decline of Muslim power and the encounter with the colonizing Western powers. From the second half of the nineteenth century, it gained hegemony in the Muslim world but stagnated in the postcolonial period.

Reformism suffered an initial setback in the Ottoman Empire, where successive attempts at reform failed, mainly because they were feebly attempted. The Turks' revolutionary turn was premised on the failure of Ottoman reforms. Mustapha Kemal's was the first revolutionary response in the Muslim world. He abolished the caliphate, established an uncompromisingly secular republic, suppressed many religious institutions, proscribed the veil, prohibited polygamy, and enacted secular laws regulating property rights and women's rights on the basis of equality. No other Muslim country has so far equaled Ataturk's radical break from tradition and from the association of Islam with state power. Yet, in the 1980s and 1990s, Turkey did not escape the resurgence of Islamism.

In Iran, the ulema legitimized the constitution of 1906, of which the promise and premises were secular. Shaykh Mohammed Husayn Naini (1860–1936) delineated the doctrinal justification for the ulema's support for constitutional government, a position later affirmed by the Ayatollah-e-Uzma Husayn Burudjirdi (1875–1962), who was the sole marja of his time and remains a figure of great authority among contemporary Shia clerics. But the coup d'état led first by Reza Shah Pahlavi and another engineered by the American CIA in 1953 put an end to what might have been the most successful experiment in democratic reformism in the Muslim world. Under partial reformist influence, the nationalist regimes in a number of states—Tunisia, Algeria, Egypt, Syria, Iraq, Indonesia, and Malaysia, among others—instituted secular constitutions without effecting a radical break from the tradition of associating religion and power. Many of these secular authoritarian regimes are now being challenged by Islamist movements.

With Pakistan's exception, the secular alternative has been favored in postcolonial South Asia. Under Jawaharlal Nehru's leadership, India adopted a secular constitution so that lawmaking in India is not required to conform to religious beliefs. However, as the official restoration of the Somnath temple indicated soon after independence, India's Congress Party governments evinced a special sensitivity toward the feelings of the majority population, a fact widely criticized by left-leaning Indians. In recent years, the rise of the Hindu nationalists to power in several provinces and recently in the federation has greatly undermined the secular character of the Indian republic, a problem to which I shall return later. In Pakistan, on the other hand, the issue of the relationship between religion and the state has remained a source of confusion, instability, and misuse of Islam in politics, a phenomenon that contributed greatly to the violent separation of East Pakistan in 1971.

The dominant feature of the postcolonial period has been the existential style of deploying religion whenever it suits the political convenience of those in power and of ignoring the challenge of defining the relationship of religion and politics when governments and the ruling elites feel secure and contented. This posture came under assault with the rise of Islamic militancy in the 1980s and 1990s, a period that witnessed accelerated globalization of the world economy. The Islamists were further propelled by the Iranian Revolution (February 1979) and more importantly by the Afghan jihad, which, thanks to the generosity of the United States, became a transnational project. Ironically, the pro-US governments of Egypt and Algeria later became the prime targets of the Afghanistan-trained Mujahideen.

The resurgence of right-wing religious movements in the 1980s and 1990s was worldwide. They have played a particularly violent role in Israel, where the state-armed Zionist zealots became especially oppressive toward the Arabs of Palestine. In India, the Hindu movement launched a campaign against the Babri mosque as part of its effort at mobilizing mass support. It ended in the destruction of the sixteenth-century mosque, widespread communal violence, and the rise of the BJP to national power. After the Russians withdrew, the victorious and faction-ridden Mujahideen of Afghanistan tore the country apart. In Sudan, an Islamic government imposed a reign of terror, and mismanagement, that has yielded a horrific famine. Christian "fundamentalism" linked with Serb nationalism and Milosevic's diabolic opportunism has aided a reign of terror and ethnic cleansing in Bosnia-Herzegovina, and now it battles on in Kosovo.

*Religion in Politics*

Having suggested the common roots of contemporary religious fundamentalism in modern times and its unique tensions, I now wish to discuss how these so-called fundamentalists, in particular the Islamist variety, relate to the religious tradition they claim to cherish and represent.

The religious idiom is greatly favored in their discourse; its symbols are deployed and rituals are observed. Yet no religio-political movement or party has to my knowledge incorporated in a comprehensive fashion the values or traditions of Islam, Christianity, Judaism, and Hinduism in its programs and activities, nor have they set examples of lives lived, individually or collectively, in accordance with the cherished values of the belief system they invoke. What they do is to pick out whatever suits their political purposes, cast these in sacred terms, and invest them with religious legitimacy. This is a deforming though easy thing to do.

All religious systems are made up of discourses that are, more often than not, dialectically linked to each other, as in light and darkness, peace and war, evil and goodness. Hence it is possible to detach and expropriate a part from the whole, divest it of its original context and purpose, and put it to political uses. Such an instrumentalist approach is nearly always absolutist, that is, it entails an absolute assertion of one, generally decontextualized, aspect of religion and a total disregard of another. The phenomenon distorts religion, debases tradition, and twists the political process wherever it unfolds. The idea of jihad is a case in point.

It is an Islamic precept with multiple meanings that include engagement in warfare, social service, humanitarian work, intellectual effort, or spiritual striving. The word is formed from an Arabic root *jehd* that denotes an intense effort to achieve a positive goal. Jihad entails then a striving to promote the good and overcome the bad, to bring light where there is darkness, prosperity where there is poverty, remedy where there is sickness, knowledge where there is ignorance, clarity where there is confusion. Thus mujahada (as also jihad) in early Islamic usage was an engagement with oneself for the achievement of moral and spiritual perfection. A mujtahid is a religious scholar who does ijtihad, i.e., strives to interpret religious texts in the light of new challenges and circumstances.

In early Islamic history, when the need to defend and also enlarge the community of believers was deemed paramount, jihad became widely associated with engagement in warfare. Following a prophetic tradition, some early theologians divided jihad in two categories. The "physical jihad"—participation in religious wars of which the rules and conditions were strictly laid down—was assigned the "lesser jihad" category. Its premises were strictly defined.

As Muslim power and numbers increased and pluralistic patterns of life and outlook emerged, there were clashes between points of view no less than personal ambitions. Similarly, wars and dynastic conflicts frequently involved convergences of interests and alliances between Muslims and non-Muslims, and battles were fought. Traditionally, these were described variously as harb, Jang, qital, or muqatala but not as jihad, a tradition that has been all but jettisoned by contemporary Islamists.

The greater jihad was that which one undertook within the self and society—to conquer greed and malice, hates and anger, ego and hubris, above all to achieve piety, moral integrity, and spiritual perfection. The great sufis invested in the concept an even deeper meaning of striving to subjugate the self (*jihad bi nafsihi*) to the service of the creator and his creation. Many of them dedicated their lives to the service of the weak and needy, by their example attracted millions to embrace Islam, and in such places as India continue to be revered by Muslims and Hindus alike.

It is a rare Islamist party today that devotes itself meaningfully to the mission of helping peoples and communities. To the contrary, contemporary Islamists view with disfavor those who would follow the example of the sufi saints who in their time had waged the greater jihad. Two such figures in Pakistan today are Dr. Akhtar Hamid Khan and Maulana Abdul Sattar Edhi. Both are deeply influenced by the Sufi tradition, both are continuing to build social institutions that assist millions of people, and both have been persecuted by those who claim to be champions of Islam.

Without a hint of doubt, contemporary Muslim ideologues and militants have reduced the rich associations of jihad to the single meaning of engagement in warfare, entirely divested of its conditions and rules. Thus the war against a Marxist government in Afghanistan and its Soviet ally became the most famous jihad of the twentieth century even though it was armed and financed by the United States, a non-Muslim superpower. Today, such activities as terrorism, sectarian strife, and the killings of innocent people are claimed as holy warfare. This reductionism is by no means unique to the Muslim world.

Next door in India, Hindu militancy is doing much the same despite the very different religious tradition. These militants have cast Hinduism as a religion of violence, warfare, and force. There are, of course, elements of violence in the Hindu tradition. Mahatma Gandhi was a reformer who recognized that violence had a part in India's religious and cultural tradition but also viewed ahimsa as the essence of Hinduism. In his study on Gandhi, Rajmohan Gandhi mentions that when his friend C. F. Andrews observed that "Indians had rejected 'bloodlust' in times past and non-violence had become an unconscious instinct with them, Gandhi reminded Andrews that 'incarnations' in Indian legends were 'bloodthirsty, revengeful and merciless to the enemy.'"[1]

But Gandhi was a humane and imaginative leader. So he understood the essential lesson of the Mahabharata, which ends in a handful of survivors, differently—that "violence was a delusion and a folly." By contrast, in the discourse of militant Hindu parties, one scarcely finds a mention of ahimsa as a Hindu value while the emphases abound on violence, force, and power. The same obsessions occupy the Jewish and Christian variants of religious-political movements. Not long ago, a ranking rabbi of Israel ruled that in the cause of expanding Israeli settlements in Palestine the killing of Arabs was religiously ordained.

In the Islamist discourse, I am unable to recognize the Islamic—religion, society, culture, history, or politics—as lived and experienced by Muslims through the ages. The Islamic has been in most respects a pluralistic civilization marked with remarkable degrees of diversity and patterns of antagonism and collaboration. The cultural life of the traditional Muslim was formed by at least four sets of intellectual legacies. Theology was but one such legacy. The others were philosophy and science, aesthetics, and mysticism.

Contemporary Islamists seek to suppress all but a narrow view of the theological legacy. Professor Fazlur Rahman was arguably the most eminent scholar of Islamic philosophy in our time. I knew him to be a devout Muslim who was more knowledgeable about classical Arabic, Persian, and Ottoman Turkish than any Islamist scholar I have known. When Mohammed Ayub Khan proposed to establish an Institute of Islamic Studies in Pakistan, he resigned his position at McGill University to lead this institution and make it into a world-class academy. A few years later, a sustained campaign was launched against him, and he was forced to leave the country.

Religious scholars, artists, poets, and novelists, including Nobel Laureate Naguib Mahfouz, have suffered persecution and assault at the hands of self-appointed champions of Islam. Complexity and pluralism threaten most—hopefully not all—contemporary Islamists, because they seek an Islamic order reduced to a penal code, stripped of its humanism, aesthetics, intellectual quests, and spiritual devotion. Their agenda is simple, therefore very reassuring to the men and women who are stranded in the middle of the ford, between the deep waters of tradition and modernity.

Neither Muslims nor Jews nor Hindus are unique in this respect. All variants of contemporary "fundamentalism" reduce complex religious systems and civilizations to one or another version of modern fascism. They are concerned with power not with the soul, with the mobilization of people for political purposes rather than with sharing or alleviating their sufferings and aspirations. Theirs is a very limited and time-bound political agenda.

*Profile of the Religious Right*

Given what I have been arguing are their shared roots in the shift from the agrarian/pastoral to the capitalist/industrial mode of production and the many forms of dislocation that it entails, the so-called fundamentalist movements bear remarkable similarities that are outlined in the following paragraphs.

The Jew as well as the Christian, the Hindu no less the Muslim "fundamentalist" plies an ideology of superior difference. Each confronts an inferior and threatening Other. Each engages in the politics of exclusion. Hence each poses a menace to the minority communities within its boundary. The Jewish ones regard the Arab, especially the Palestinian Arab whose land they covet and colonize, as the Other—violent, wily, dirty, uncivilized, oversexed, and dangerous. Notably, the Jewish zealots enjoy the full support of their state in dispossessing the Arabs, and they alone are officially armed amid the unarmed natives. For long, the Hindu militants' sole Other was the Muslim; Christians have now been added to their enemies' list. The Christian bigot had long regarded the Jew as the conspiratorial, grasping Other. In the decades after World War II and the Holocaust, anti-Semitism became a widely decried prejudice and receded into the interstices of Christian societies. Gradually, Muslims and colored immigrants are taking the place of Jews in the Western world. For the Muslim militants, the Others are the Jews, occasionally Christians, and, in South Asia, the Hindus, Christians, and Ahmedis. I know of no religio-political formation today that does not have a demonized, therefore threatened, Other.

The Other is always an active negation. All such movements mobilize hatred and often harness unusual organizational effort to do so. The Ram Janam Bhoomi campaign lasted nearly two years, during which the BJP leaders and their partners reached out to thousands of villages and towns throughout India with their mobilizing rituals of preparing bricks to build a temple where then stood the sixteenth-century Babri mosque. The campaign ended in December 1992 in a national march to Ayodhya where the mosque was violently demolished by a frenzied mob. Riots and massacres inevitably followed.

Hate pays, however temporarily. The mobilization contributed to the dramatic transformation of the BJP from a marginal political grouping to one of two largest parliamentary parties in India. In Israel, the right-wing Likud and its extremist allies began their rise to national power as they mobilized a campaign of hate and colonization of Palestinians under occupation. In Bosnia, the Serbs' campaign of ethnic cleansing preceded and accompanied a mobilization of Christian hatred of Muslims. In Kashmir, where despite the maharaja's harsh and discriminatory rule Hindus and Muslims had coexisted peacefully, the Hindu Mahasabha and the RSS played an important role in alienating the Muslim population. In recent years, "Islamic" militants have assaulted Hindu homes in villages in Kashmir and committed atrocities that are strictly forbidden in Islamic laws of war.

The cult of violence and proliferation of enemies are inherent in ideologies of difference. All express their hate for the Other by organized violence. All legitimize their violence with references to religion and history. In nearly all instances, the enemy multiplies. At first, the Indian Parivar had the Muslim Other as its target. It has now turned on Christians. The Dalit, Sikh, and tribal communities will most likely be its future targets. The Jewish militants are increasingly turning on the liberal and secular Jews of Israel. They have already assassinated one prime minister and caused growing internal strife. In Pakistan, Christians have been hit, and Ahmedis. At the same time intramilitant violence has proliferated in Pakistan, and wanton killings occur even inside mosques and imambarahs. In Algeria, brutalities have become so complex that it is nearly impossible to identify the perpetrators and, occasionally, even the victims.

Since all religio-political formations bear but little relationship to lived religious traditions and histories, they tend to invent and, in the process, distort their own history and tradition. "I see but only shadows of Judaism and Jewish history in their writings and statements," Moshe Menuhin, a great Jewish scholar and father of the famous violinist Yehudi Menuhin, said of Zionist ideologues during a meeting I had with him in 1972. In recent decades, an eminent group of Israeli historians has been documenting the ahistorical character of Zionist historiography. When I pointed out to M. R. Malkani, a well-known theoretician of the RSS and currently a member of the Lok Sabha, that India's most respected historians had questioned the validity of their historical claims, he responded with an exclusionary declaration: "Aisay ittihaasiyon ke liye Hindustan mein koii asthan naheen hai" (For such historians, there is no place in India). In Pakistan, as Dr. K. K. Aziz has amply doc-umented, in the heyday of the "Islamization" process, even the school and col-lege history texts were contaminated with historical inaccuracies and sectar-ian claims. They still await a cleaning-up that is an essential requirement of the educational enterprise.

All such movements share a patriarchal outlook and to varying degrees discriminate against women. Amrita Basu has shown that a hostile attitude to-ward minorities parallels in the parivars' literature a patriarchal outlook and discriminatory practices toward women.[2] One may add that the religious Right's misogynic outlook parallels an unusual degree of obsession with sex, a deep-seated fear of seduction, and a tendency to regulate sexual behavior. In these regards, the Islamists outdo their Hindu, Jewish, and Christian counter-parts for they alone aim at full segregation and veiling of women and insist on laws that perpetuate gender inequalities in nearly all walks of life.

The cadres and constituents of all religio-political movements present comparable profiles. They appeal to urban more than rural people, to the lumpenproletariat and lower middle class more than the working or upper classes, technical more than the liberal professionals, and to the expatriate bourgeoisie more than the national one. The pattern suggests that they attract especially those persons and classes that are caught in the "middle of the ford" between tradition and modernity and who, in differing ways, feel marginal, socially uprooted, and insecure about their place in their social environment.

Given their transitional social standing, leaders and cadres of the contem-porary religio-political parties evince ambivalence toward products and sym-bols of modernity. They love the products of technology and put it to politi-cal and personal uses. But they evince a negative attitude toward science, with its emphasis on rationality and causation. Nearly all have a proclivity to find, post hoc, the evidence of scientific discovery in religious texts and proclaim the existence of an Islamic, Hindu, Jewish, and Christian science that predates the modern discovery of it. Invariably, they find a scientific discovery in their religious texts or tradition only after it has been discovered by modern science.

All tend to be grim and humorless. All, to varying degrees, frown on joy and pleasurable pastimes. They have few positive links to culture and knowl-edge and regard these as dangerous sources of corruption. Hence the control of educational institutions and regulation of society's cultural life become the primary objective of these movements. This tendency has climaxed with the

Taliban, who have prohibited chess, football, the homing pigeon, kite flying, singing, dancing, and leather jackets as un-Islamic.

All religio-political parties are inherently undemocratic even when they operate in a democratic framework. In theory and practice, they reject basic democratic values (acceptance of pluralism, emphasis on reason as the organizing principle of social and political life, commitment to the resolution of differences by dialogue, and secular legislation). Nearly all favor a centralist and absolutist structure of governance.

As movements and political parties, they are nevertheless quite normal in hankering after power. For power's sake, they make compromises and, when necessary, strike Faustian deals. The BJP leaders had no problem coalescing with the Janata Party even when it was led by the very secular prime minister V. P. Singh. Ironically, it was Mr. Singh who risked the dissolution of his government rather than compromise with the BJP's campaign to demolish the Babri mosque. The Jamaat-i-Islami, currently a champion of democracy, happily embraced Mohammed Zia ul-Haq, a military dictator. Similarly, in 1948, when Pakistan's foundations were shaky, Maulana Abul Aula Maudoodi, the Jamaat's founder and theoretician, declared that combat in Kashmir cannot qualify as jihad. Yet, in 1999, its amir, Qazi Hussein Ahmed, claims that it is *jihad fi sabi-lillah* and must be carried on till total victory. In Sudan, the National Islamic Front was part of the coalition against Jaafer Nimeiri's dictatorship. When opportunity occurred, it became an ally of the dictator and later ousted the ally that had catapulted it to power. Morals have not been an encumbrance in any religio-political pursuit of power.

What then is the future of these "fundamentalist" movements and parties? I think it is limited and quite dim. The reasons for it are multiple: Their links to the past are twisted. Their vision of the future is unworkable. And their connections to contemporary forces and ideals are largely negative or opportunistic. Yet in their limit lies the reason for us to fear. Between their beginnings and end, right-wing movements are known to have inflicted great damage upon countries and peoples. So help us, God!

[1999]

# PART III
# ON THE CUSP OF THE COLD WAR
## PORTENTS OF A NEW CENTURY

# INTRODUCTION

Carollee Bengelsdorf and Margaret Cerullo

In every era the attempt must be made anew to wrest tradition away from a conformism that is about to overpower it. . . . Only that historian will have the gift of fanning the spark of hope in the past who is firmly convinced that . . . even the dead will not be safe from the enemy if he wins. And this enemy has not ceased to be victorious.

—Walter Benjamin, "Theses on the Philosophy of History," VI

The articles in this section focus largely on Ahmad's assessment of the world at Cold War's end. His vision of this period is distinctive not only for its characteristic challenge to dominant interpretations but for its increasing darkness. Ahmad's view of the post–Cold War world depends on the interpretation of the Cold War he held to for the entirety of his life: as the latest mechanism for organizing and legitimizing a four-centuries-old system of imperial domination. If bipolarity represented a brake on the US free hand, the end of the Cold War presents the prospect of a freer play of US-defined imperial interest.

Its termination is not for him a reason for optimism about the future but the most dangerous moment the world has yet faced. The end of the century in an uncanny fashion echoes its beginning: the naked pursuit of Western interests and the naked display of Western power, now enhanced by unrivaled military might and unrestrained by competition among rival colonial powers or Cold War ideological struggle. It is, in the minds of its celebrants, the final triumph of the American Imperial Century.

Yet Ahmad understands US hegemony in Gramscian terms, as a project, not simply a result of the collapse of the Soviet Union. His attention therefore turns repeatedly in this section (in "Political Culture and Foreign Policy" and "The Cold War from the Standpoint of Its Victims," both of which reprise the Cold War itself) to the legitimating myths that secured (with one great rupture: the Vietnam War) and continue to secure domestic consensus for its imperial mission.[1]

First, he underscores the crusading, apocalyptic, Manichaean, and (in Hofstadter's words) "paranoid" cast of US actions on the world stage. The ideological dimensions of American expansionism, he argues, have far exceeded the demands of economic domination. It is this irrational excess that has resulted in a characteristic escalation of violence out of any proportion to resistance and beyond legal and human limits that, for Ahmad, defines "American exceptionalism." History, for those who made and make US foreign policy, is a conspiracy set in motion by demonic forces against which not political give-and-take but an all-out crusade is required. If the manner in which the regime of George W. Bush has framed the stakes in the war on terror seems uniquely excessive, Ahmad recalls for us Richard Nixon's assertion, during the Vietnam War, that "if the Vietnamese win, the right of free speech will be extinguished forever."[2]

Second, his dissections of US imperial culture return again and again to the power of naming, a power that encodes the desire to control the future as well as the past. This theme is most present in "The Cold War from the Standpoint of Its Victims," his answer to diplomatic historian John Gaddis's interpretation of the Cold War as the "long peace." The United States, throughout the Cold War, Ahmad reminds us, termed its interventions "limited wars" (when they occasionally got out of hand, as in Vietnam, they were "aberrations"). The question of their effects on those peoples in the Third World who suffered their full impact is thus negated. The label "limited wars," Ahmad asserts, continues the colonial tradition of sanitizing the decimation of peoples from the point of view of those doing the decimating through such euphemisms as "exploration," "pioneering," "expeditionary wars," "interventionary wars." So, too, Gaddis's new name for the Cold War, the long peace, "suppress[es] reality and obscure[s] history."[3] Naming thus constitutes a power/ knowledge system that effectively excludes non-Western humanity from the central concerns of world politics and simultaneously protects the dominating power from the intellectual and moral consequences of its own history.

The power to name is at the heart of Ahmad's critique of Henry Kissinger's obituary for Richard Nixon. Kissinger takes the opportunity of Nixon's demise to rename the ex-president (and, in the process, of course, himself) a "moral man" and to celebrate Nixon's achievements (and, in the process, his own). He lists among these "achievements" the termination of the war in Vietnam and the initiation of the Middle East peace process. For Ahmad, and for all those who remember the history surrounding these events, this is nothing short of obscene. Ahmad insists, by the very process of writing his own obituary for Nixon, that those subject to hegemony must interrupt this process of (re)naming as it is happening and assert a countermemory. He therefore names for us Nixon's role, both domestically (as a McCarthyite before McCarthy) and in the world (as a war criminal who, along with Kissinger himself, massively escalated the bombing of Vietnam, extended that bombing to Cambodia, and thereby both prolonged the war and deepened the agony it caused and who also armed Israel to a degree no other US administration had done, transforming it from a typical client state to a subimperial power). Death cannot change this history, nor can it be a tool in its rewriting.

Third, racism acquires a prominence in these articles that it did not have in his writing on counterinsurgency. In his 1981 genealogy of the popular culture of US imperialism, "Political Culture and Foreign Policy," he explicitly draws out the connections between US domestic and foreign policy in relation to nonwhite people, suggesting that cowboy and Indian movies prefigure the dominant view of the Third World, that "Indian fighting" is the template through which imperial policies are filtered and made sense of in US culture. As a newcomer to the US, Ahmad recalls being struck by the portrayal of Indians as an invisible elemental enemy, arriving in screaming hordes—with no family life, hopes, fears, or grievances. "Wipe them out," "smoke them out"—it is hard to deny that these representations have enormous staying power in the US popular (and presidential) imaginary or that the combination of racism and belief in the efficacy of violence, along with a tendency to miscalculate the will and tenacity of presumably inferior people, are abiding influences on the character of US foreign policy.

In "Racism and the State: Coming Crisis of US-Japanese Relations," an article not included in this volume,[4] Ahmad links the likelihood of resurgent racism in the US to the paradox of its position following the Cold War: as the preeminent strategic and military power but not, at the time of his writing, the leading economic power. The threat to US economic preeminence at the beginning of the 1990s was popularly identified (with racist overtones) more with Japan than with Germany. In times of uncertainty and instability, he argues, US settler/colonial mentality comes to the fore, in both domestic and international policy. The settler state, committed to dispossession if not annihilation of the natives, is haunted by its own genocidal tendencies and by fear of the return of the repressed native.

A critique of racism also informs "Cracks in the Western World (View)," Ahmad's scathing analysis of the Western Left's massive nuclear disarmament movement of the 1980s. He raises the question of why the movement that was apparently so relevant to the peoples of the Third World (the most likely locales of nuclear exchange) nonetheless had little resonance in the Third World or among Third World people in the West. His answer centers on the movement's acceptance of the same assumptions as the mainstream Cold War historians: the assumption of bipolarity as the defining axis of world politics and of nuclear warfare as the major threat to peace. That is, the movement assumed the "long peace" and named superpower rivalry, and the nuclear arms race, its direct offshoot, as the major threat to this peace. By focusing on what he labels "the white triangle" (the United States, Europe, and the Soviet Union), the disarmament movement failed completely to make the crucial "deadly connection" between the arms race and imperialism; this was nowhere more clearly demonstrated than in its refusal, in the very moment of its greatest triumph, the June 12, 1982, million-people march in New York City, to address, or even to permit speakers on the podium who would address, the Israeli invasion of Lebanon that, on that very day, besieged and began the destruction of Beirut. Ahmad's insistence on attention to the Middle East within the agenda of the peace movement was not a call for a dilution of its focus but rather, given the history of nuclear alerts, recognition of where such warfare would likely begin.

If the Cold War represented, for Ahmad, not a "long peace" but a "war system," the post–Cold War world is marked, above all, by the removal of (almost) all checks within this system. The remainder of the articles in this section are devoted to his writings about US foreign policy during the last decade of the twentieth century, written during the last decade of his own life. He sees this decade as the darkest moment of the century, a cruel reversion, and his voice becomes angrier as his frustration grows—with the unfettered dominance of the US and the decline of all movements that might challenge the manner of exercise of this dominance in the form of resistance to it either in the Third World or the first. Given his analysis, the end of the Cold War is signaled, for him, not by the fall of the Berlin Wall (the salient event for the "white triangle") but by two other events: Nixon's welcome in China and the Soviet Union in 1972 (while he continued and escalated the bombing of Vietnam) and the 1990–1991 Gulf War, the first postwar US intervention in the Middle East without Soviet protest. This world of unfettered US hegemony is what he sketches out so somberly in his key *Boston Review* essay, "At Cold War's End: A World of Pain." The comparison to the nineteenth-century "long peace" in Europe is now even more telling, and the meaning of this "long peace" for the peoples of the Third World even more threatening. He provides us with only two caveats to this comparison, both of which increase the danger. Britain's dominance in nineteenth-century Europe was based on the related facts of imperial rule and economic prosperity. The United States, as it entered the post–Cold War world, at least at the moment Ahmad was writing, was a declining economic power. Even the opening act of its New World Order, the Gulf War, had to be financed by others. Second, the world itself was and is an unruly place—witness the Pakistan-India dispute over Kashmir or Israel's refusal to rein in, even for show, its violence against the Palestinian people and the consequent ever-escalating war in the Middle East. "A World of Pain" focuses on three key arenas for the performance of the New World Order, arenas that, for Ahmad, reveal its nature with brutal clarity.

The first of these is the 1990 Gulf War. The second is ex-Yugoslavia, in particular the West's refusal, sustained over several years, to intervene in Bosnia, while the Serbs freely battered and destroyed it. The third is the selective nature of US policy on nuclear arms proliferation, specifically its refusal to sanction either India or Israel, which, he argues, suggests "a frightening vision of imperial arrangements of domination." He sees these as dangerous, potentially disastrous indications that the post–Cold War world will not be characterized by peace but by the escalation of violence and insecurity. As always, he looks not to states to check the escalation but to civil society—to ordinary people—and here, too, in his observation of a pattern of increasing "passivity in the face of genocide," he sees no reason for optimism.

"A World of Pain" is followed by articles that elaborate on his analysis of the first Gulf War and Western policy toward ex-Yugoslavia. The Gulf War (or, for Ahmad, clarifying its nature, the "Hundred-Hour War") brought together the strands of his frustration, anger, and despair—at the corruption and decadence of Third World leadership and at Western imperialism in its most dangerous incarnation. Of the Muslim world, he noted poignantly, "We live in scoundrel times. This is the dark age of Muslim history, the age of surrender and collaboration, punctuated by madness. . . . I have been a lifelong witness to surrender and imagined at so many times—as a boy in 1948, a young man in 1967, again in 1971, and approaching middle age in 1982— . . . that the next time even if we go down we would manage to do so with a modicum of dignity. Fortunately, I did not entertain even so modest an illusion from Saddam Hussein's loudly proclaimed 'mother of battles.'"

For the United States, it was a "war of restoration"; that is, a war to ensure the continued existence of the sheikhs of Saudi Arabia and the Gulf, those "heads of tribes with flags," as Tahseen Basheer, an Egyptian diplomat, described them,[5] and to make explicit their dependence on US military might. For Ahmad, what was perhaps most startling and most depressing about the Gulf intervention were the questions that were not being asked by US civil society—in the debates at universities, even in the movement that grew up to oppose the war, and particularly in the press. He asks exactly these questions and provides some critically suggestive answers in "America's Gulf War: Neglected Perspectives."[6] The first question concerns what compelled Saddam Hussein's invasion of Kuwait. In a far-reaching interpretation, Ahmad argues that the roots of the Gulf War lie in the 1976 Camp David Accords between Israel and Egypt. The diminishment of Egyptian authority with its perceived defection to the American camp, confirmed by the subsequent advance of Israeli settlements, created a power vacuum in the Arab world. It was this vacuum that Saddam Hussein hoped to fill, first by his ten-year war with Iran and then through his invasion of Kuwait.

Second, while oil is always mentioned as a reason for the intervention, the politics of oil in the Gulf itself is never discussed. Why is it, Ahmad asks, that by and large the states with the largest populations in the Gulf control no oil, while the sheikhdoms with minuscule populations literally sit on oil? The roots of this arrangement lie in the way that colonialism redrew the map of the Middle East. The manner in which the oil states have employed their wealth, including their investments and subsequent stakes in the Western economies, explains their openness to the US-staged invasion.

Third, why was it that half of all Arab states, including those traditionally on the best of terms with the US such as Jordan and Tunisia, opposed the intervention? Here Ahmad explains the way the Gulf War was seen by Arab populations, elaborating why Middle Eastern peoples had little reason to think the US was acting in the defense in Kuwait. The US had displayed unflagging support for Israel as it occupied the land of four Arab states. US intervention was, then, feared as logically part and parcel of this process, the definitive beginning of the recolonization of the Arab world.

Finally, Ahmad challenges the conflicting stated goals of the first Bush administration in the Gulf and argues that the US had two other objectives, both longstanding and both faltering in key aspects. Saddam Hussein's greatest achievement, Ahmad states, was to open the door for the successful realization of these long planned-for and long-held American aspirations. The first was the resuscitation of the twenty-year old Nixon Doctrine, vis-à-vis the Gulf, shattered temporarily by the Iranian Revolution. Saudi Arabia, which had historically refused all requests for US bases on its territory, has now become the site of key, seemingly permanent, US bases.

The second driving US objective was staying number one. US control of Middle East oil was aimed not at the Arabs but at Europe and Japan, over which the US had lost strategic and economic domination, and at the Third World, over which it sought to ensure its imperial dominance.

But the much-celebrated US triumph, Ahmad cautions, will not equip it "to confront the logic of its own ambitions." The war in the Gulf and the subsequent decade of sanctions and military strikes against Iraq were justified respectively as a response to Iraq's unlawful seizure of land and the threat to its neighbors of its nuclear weapons potential—both charges the US refuses to make against Israel. The failure to deal with this reality, Ahmad argues, would make the Gulf War not the triumphant launching pad for the next American Century, as the first President Bush declared it, but something else entirely. Blatantly contradictory, violent US actions would "turn up the heat of Islamic outrage."[7] This would be the "nightmare victory" he foresees in all his articles about the consequences of the war in the Gulf and its aftermath. The peoples of the Middle East would inevitably look to some state or person to fill this power vacuum. Ahmad first suggests as a possible candidate the radical fundamentalist Saudi cleric, Sheikh Safar al-Halawi, who vigorously denounced the ongoing US deployment in Saudi Arabia in popular taped speeches that circulated throughout the region.[8] In assessing "Operation Infinite Reach," the 1998 US double strike against an alleged nuclear weapons facility in the Sudan and suspected terrorist camps in Afghanistan, Ahmad underlines the emergence of Osama bin Laden "from an obscure figure stalked by undercover agents" to a "world famous adversary of the sole superpower . . . his lean figure restlessly shifting as he holds a wireless phone in each hand, . . . imprinted in a billion memories."[9]

The second defining arena in this new period of hope and its betrayal is the ex-Yugoslavia, particularly the West's endless refusal to do anything to help put an end to Serbian genocide in Bosnia and the delay and ultimate futility of the West's response to Serb aggression in Kosovo. In a series of columns written for the Pakistani weekly *Dawn* and the Egyptian newspaper *Al-Ahram*,[10] Ahmad elaborates the ongoing politics of the argument he laid out in "A World of Pain." In these, his voice is at its angriest and most frustrated. It is clear to him that the politics of race and anti-Muslim sentiments explain the West's refusal even to end the arms embargo on Bosnia that might have given it some capacity to fight for its own survival. He argues that the post–Cold War world, much like the pre–World War I world, will be governed purely by pragmatic Western interests, a realpolitik unmasked, with little consideration either for ideological justifications or conditions of peace and international security. In a "world system so rigged in favor of the rich and powerful,"[11] the international human rights regime, the Universal Declaration of Human Rights, the Convention on Genocide, and other international laws are useless. In this "world out of balance and without order,"[12] in which nation-states have long ago surrendered their sovereignty to international financial institutions—the IMF, the World Bank—a policy of strict anti-interventionism is outdated, an ideological cover for brutality, fascism, and genocide.

The West's actions and inaction in Bosnia and Kosovo symbolized for Ahmad the yielding of a spirit of solidarity that crossed ethnic and national borders to a "cult of ethnicity and narcissism."[13] Civil society on a world scale has been contained in national, ethnic, and other narrow and self-interested boundaries. If, during the Cold War, self-interest promoted the recognition that small wars could lead to big ones and resulted in international concern, now citizens of advanced countries can regard local wars, as in the Balkans, as unconnected to their futures and ignore them. The 1990s, in his summary verdict, would be the sectarian decade in which civil society was reduced to a contract of mutual indifference.

In a stunning and prophetic talk, "Terrorism: Theirs and Ours" (delivered in October 1998) that gained prominence in the US after September 11, 2001, Ahmad addresses terrorism as another key phenomenon of the post–Cold War world, a world in which ideology receded, not only in imperial realpolitik but also in the resistance to it. "Terrorism" in his analysis is a floating signifier attached at will to our enemies to evoke moral revulsion. The vagueness and inconsistency of its definition, he insists, is key to its political usefulness. Official discussion will eschew, indeed disallow, any search for causes or motives, to the point where former secretary of state George Schultz, asked about the causes of Palestinian terrorism, insisted "there is no connection with any cause. Period." The key link Ahmad makes in exploring the causes of modern terrorism is to the decline of revolutionary ideology in the 1980s and 1990s and the emergence in its stead of the globalized individual. He insists on the distinction between terrorist organizations and liberation movements, in which social problems are addressed by political mobilization rather than by individual acts of violence. Drawing on his vast knowledge of the great revolutions of the twentieth century, he refers back to his writings on revolutionary warfare to distinguish the selective character of revolutionary violence from indiscriminate terror against civilian populations.

For Ahmad, the "transnational activist,"[14] national, ethnic, communal, or religious borders never confined his thought or the scope of his activity. What communism represented to him, in theory if not in practice, was the expansion of solidarities beyond particularistic confines. In a dark period, he calls on the memory of solidarities to face and challenge a world that so deeply lacks and needs them.

# THE COLD WAR FROM THE STANDPOINT
## OF ITS VICTIMS

# 15 / POLITICAL CULTURE AND FOREIGN POLICY

Notes on American Interventions in the Third World

At the close of World War II, the United States enjoyed, in the words of Wendell Wilkie, an "inexhaustible reservoir of goodwill," particularly in Asia and Africa. For the colonized people of the world, America symbolized the possibility and the promises of liberation. Americans had waged the first successful struggle against colonialism, had declared their unequivocal commitment to the right of self-determination, had asserted as inalienable the people's right to revolution and charged them with the duty to exercise that right, had founded a prosperous republic dedicated to the exciting proposition that all men are created equal, and had even engaged in bloody civil war to uphold that principle.

Subsequent developments tended to confirm in these distant lands the image of America as a unique Western nation dedicated to the universal application of democratic and republican ideals. Anti-imperialist idealism continued to characterize the popular culture and political rhetoric of the United States, reflecting the origins of the nation as well as the clash of interest between it and the old colonial powers. American rivalry with British, French, and Spanish colonialism in the Far East and Latin America was often constructed in the non-Western world as an expression of anti-imperialism. The Open Door policy, for example, was hailed by most Asian nationalists as a triumph of anti-imperialism. Hardly anyone noted Woodrow Wilson's candid admission that America's concern was "not the Open Door to the rights of China, but the Open Door to the goods of America."[1] Similarly, Woodrow Wilson's Fourteen Points, with their ringing support for self-determination, had an enormous impact in Asia and Africa. American entry in the war against German fascism and Japanese militarism further confirmed our *préjugement favorable* for the United States. The only exceptions to the Third World's Americophilia were some Latin Americans made wiser by experience.

Historically, in the development of Asian and African national movements and during the crucial years of our struggle for independence, America served as an inspiration and an example. Faith in its friendship and support was part of our rising expectations. As a schoolboy in British India, my first act of rebellion had been to substitute the phrase "American Rebellion" for the "American War of Independence" in a history reading class. George Washington was a popular hero among us. Words from the Declaration of Independence adorned the constitutions of several new republics in the Third World, including the Democratic Republic of Vietnam. Belief in an anti-imperialist America was part of our nationalist mythology. The persistence of this belief through more than a century of counterrevolutionary American interventions in the Third World is a poignant witness to the universal appeal of the principles upon which this republic had been founded.

*The End of an Illusion*

The realities of American foreign policy stood in sharp contrast to the myths we had nourished. For over a century, successive American governments and major American corporations abroad have flagrantly betrayed the principles embodied in the Declaration of Independence, in the Bill of Rights, and in George Washington's first inaugural address. Their policies have been consistently antinationalist, opposed to revolutions, supportive of dictatorship and fascist states, and violently interventionist in the American sphere of influence (which, until World War II, was limited to Latin America and parts of the Pacific). Between 1900 and 1917, for example, the United States intervened militarily on more than twenty occasions, from Columbia to China, in an attempt—so Woodrow Wilson would have the world believe—"to make the world safe for democracy."

After World War II, when the United Stated emerged as the paramount world power, there occurred a Latin Americanization of the Third World. The rhetoric of American policy makers has been dominated by images of bipolarity. The public is told that the policy is concerned with national security, as it is directed at rival powers such as the USSR. However, the reality is different. Since 1945, United States forces have engaged more frequently, lost more lives, inflicted more suffering, and expended greater amounts of arms and money in suppressing social revolutions in poor countries than they have in defending America's security from enemies or rivals. Between 1947 and 1970, as America stood "watch," in the ringing phrase of John F. Kennedy, "over the walls of world freedom," Washington intervened against local revolutions and nationalist regimes on an average of once every sixteen months. During this period, the United States spent more than fifty times more money on its military operations in underdeveloped countries than on its so-called economic aid to them. At the same time, its investments abroad grew from 7.2 billion dollars in 1947 to more than 60 billion in 1970; the Pentagon and the armaments industry collaborated to make the United Stated the biggest merchant of death in the Third World (11 billion dollars in United States arms sales to the Third World in 1975); the United States, representing less than one-fourteenth of the world's population, consumed an estimated 40 percent of the world's resources; and each successive year its war budget increased until, in 1976, it surpassed every defense budget in American history. Yet, except for a handful of pacifists and Marxists who suffered severe reprisals for exercising their right to dissent, few Americans protested and fewer challenged the assumptions and objectives of this policy. Total consensus on matters of policy may be an anomaly in a liberal democracy, yet it lasted until the relentless escalation of an undeclared aggression, and the Indochinese peoples' heroic resistance to it, put intolerable strains on the country as a whole, and particularly upon the young. To us, in the Third World, America began to appear as a status-quo–seeking, interventionist monolith whose allies were the Saudis and the shah, the Samozas and the Trujillos, and the Phnom Penh, Vietnam, and Saigon generals who had once collaborated with colonial France and then sanctioned the systematic destruction of peoples and countries they pretended to represent. The war in Vietnam laid to rest the Third World's myths and illusions about the United States.

## A Profile of Interventions

Americans interventions in the Third World have been noteworthy for the following characteristics:

First, there has been a tendency to escalate the violence out of proportion to the natives' resistance. Two examples should do. The American colonization of the Philippines was the bloodiest in colonial history, followed closely by the French colonization of Algeria, involving the massacre of an estimated two-thirds of the native population. In Indochina, United States intervention entailed widespread crimes against humanity that were surpassed in our times only by the Nazis.

Second, these interventions have been carried out in support of unrepresentative, dictatorial regimes, against revolutionary and popular movements, and often against constitutional regimes such as those of Mossadegh in Iran and Allende in Chile. This is understandable because right-wing dictatorships tend to be especially attractive to foreign capital. The denial of distributive justice under such regimes assures a high rate of return on investments; their repressiveness secures a quiescent labor force; their ruling class, being antagonistic to and fearful of the masses, covets external support, and thus they become dependable allies.

Third, the United States, the protestations of its leaders and academic functionaries notwithstanding, has been opposed to Third World nationalism, historically in South America and in recent years throughout the world. However, this opposition has been clearly expressed not in the initial stage of a country's demand for formal independence from Spanish, French, or British colonialism but in the stage when a particular nationalism begins to acquire economic and social content. For good reason: radical nationalism (that is, one not contained by the mere transfer of formal power from the metropolitan to the indigenous bourgeoisie) threatens the interests of those who shape United States foreign policy. For example, nationalization of natural resources is the primary economic expression of nationalism. It appears to threaten American corporations, which exercise a near monopoly of influence over United States foreign policy and which continue to have a stake in a policy characterized by militarization at home and interventions on behalf of right-wing oligarchies abroad. Similarly, an independent foreign policy and rejection of foreign military ties are expected of radical-nationalist governments; this displeases the American national security establishment, whose growing power is based on the accumulation and expansion of military power and political leverage over other nations.

Fourth, Washington's tolerance for Third World governments which seek to exercise their full sovereignty appears to be inversely proportional to its business investments in a country. In client states like Guatemala, Iran, the Dominican Republic, Brazil, and Chile, the United States has preferred exploitative elites and dictatorial governments. American-sponsored coups d'état or sharp, swift armed interventions have suppressed radical expressions of nationalism or any efforts to overthrow an oppressive regime. In nonclient states, a radical expression of nationalism is tolerated if it occurs unexpectedly or if change occurs gradually under a popular leader. Egypt under Gamal Abdel Nasser was an example of the first type; Tanzania of the second. But relations with such regimes remain reserved, often strained. When conditions permit, subversion is encouraged, as it admittedly was in Indonesia (1957–1958) and British Guiana (1962–1963). In the decade of 1965 to 1975, there was an inclination to tolerate radical governments in zones of French influence, in response to De Gaulle's national ambition to free France from American tutelage. But only in eastern Europe has America consistently welcomed and encouraged assertive nationalism.

*Roots of American Foreign Policy*

In locating the sources of American foreign policy, I should first acknowledge the argument of those American historians and economists (William A. Williams, Paul Baran, Harry Magdoff, Gabriel Kolko, and others) who situate the roots of American foreign policy in monopoly capitalism and identify it as a policy in the service of corporations rather than of the public at large. Their argument on the historical relationship between the corporation and the state in America is by no means dated. To the contrary, the multinationals' need for imperial states may be greater now than in the past, for their investments abroad are increasing rapidly, and today they have no better candidate for policing the globe than the United States.

Foreign investments of the international corporations, a majority of which are United States–based, are increasing rapidly. The more famous of the giants—IBM, Uniroyal, Squibb, Coca-Cola, Mobil, Gillette, Reynolds, Pfizer, and others—draw over 50 percent of their profits from outside the United States. And, as a study of the Business International Corporation shows, profits abroad are increasing at a much faster rate than at home. American corporations have also been shifting their assets abroad. According to Barnet and Muller, about one-third of the total assets of the chemical industry, two-fifths of the consumer industry, and three-fourths of the electrical industry have moved out of the United States.[2] More, in every sector, are on the way. As labor costs have risen in the United States and Western Europe, the Third World countries from which the metropolitan corporations have historically extracted a bulk of their raw materials are now becoming a source of cheap labor also. The richer among them are the targets of corporate concentration as "export-platform countries."

It is understandable that partisans of big business should herald the dawn of a new era of corporate globalism. The chiefs of the capitalist giants are being portrayed, and portray themselves, as transformers of the world—the new internationalists. They pronounce the nation-state an anachronism. A 1967 research report of the Business International Corporation warns that "the nation-state is becoming obsolete; tomorrow it will in any meaningful sense be dead—and so will the corporation that remains essentially national."[3] Jacques Maisonrouge, the articulate president of IBM World Trading Corporation, relishes pointing out that "Down with Borders," a slogan in the Paris uprising of 1968, is also a company slogan of IBM. He views the world as an "extension of a single market" and contemplates the making of "one world" under the aegis of international business.[4] Aurelio Peccei announces the corporation to be the "most powerful agent for the internationalization of human society."[5] Courtney Brown, dean of Columbia University Business School, rhapsodizes them as "the prologue to a new world symphony."[6] And Roy Ash, Nixon's budget director, affirms that the multinationals represent "transcendental unity."[7]

Yet, like Henry Kissinger's, Gerald Ford's, or Jimmy Carter's professions of peace, the internationalist cant of business magnates is no Orwellian hoax. Their claims to internationalism and transcendence are belied by a mundane reality: big businesses have much to protect in the world, especially from the forces of national liberation, but few means of doing so except to employ the coercive capabilities of certain states. No corporation owns an army, air force, or navy. Yet one knows from three centuries of experience that these military forces are ultimately necessary to protect corporate investments and perpetuate the exploitation of peoples and their resources. Nothing has changed this fundamental reality which, since the advent of modern imperialism, has defined the symbiosis between monopoly capitalism and imperial states.

It is not surprising, therefore, that such seemingly diverse entities as ITT, the State Department, CIA, Naval Intelligence, and the World Bank collaborated to destroy Allende's government or that David Rockefeller's way to Egypt was paved by his brother's protégé, Henry Kissinger. Or that a majority of the countries chosen to be regional marshals under the Nixon Doctrine (for example, Iran, Indonesia, Brazil, South Africa) are precisely the ones which are targeted to be the "export-platforms" of the Third World.

## Culture and Diplomacy: The Making of Consensus and the Logic of Intervention

Although its motives have been imperialist, United States foreign policy has generally enjoyed popular support because its ideology and practice have been in harmony with some dominant features of American political culture. The language of realpolitik offers a poor basis for constructing a popular consensus behind a corporate ideology. Hence modern imperialism has needed myths to legitimize itself. A policy which responds to the interests of the few but needs the support of the many must necessarily invoke a people's sense of mission and fear. The British carried the white man's burden; the French had their *mission civilisatrice*; and America stood watch over the world's freedom. Each, in its mission, was threatened by the forces of evil—the yellow, the black, and the red perils. Take the myth away, and domestic support for imperialism will begin to disintegrate—unless a new, equally effective set of myths replaces the old. This is what Kissinger meant when he complained that every former colonial power of Europe, except fascist Portugal, had lost its imperial avocation not so much because it lacked power but because it had lost "a certain view of its own destiny" and with it the will to play a "global role."[8]

## An "Extraordinary" Conception of Mission

A sense of power is congenial to any people. Its exercise becomes morally acceptable when it is believed to be employed on behalf of a noble cause and against a mortal enemy. In the United States after World War II, the doctrines of necessity and moral responsibility combined to produce a compelling ideology whose most important single component was the invocation of the threat of conspiratorial communism. From Truman and Acheson to Nixon and Kissinger, officials have contended that the United States was reluctant to assume the stewardship of the world, but the nation, come of age, could not shirk its historical responsibility of defending itself against communism. History and metaphysics had crowned America to become the world's watchman. "We did not choose," explained President Johnson helplessly, "to be the guardians at the gate."[9] Yet the stake in the struggle, as President Kennedy put it, was nothing less than "sway over the destiny of man." The principal battleground is said to have shifted in the late 1940s to the underdeveloped countries. Hence every local area acquired a global significance; countries became dominoes.

The globalist, destiny-ridden outlook feeds on what Edward McNall Burns has described as America's "extraordinary" conception of mission. It is a product, at least in part, of a deeply and popularly held belief in the uniqueness of America and its perfection as a political model. The American Revolution gave the world, Abraham Lincoln contended in 1842, the final "solution" to political problems; hence it must "grow and expand into the universal liberty of mankind." His contemporary William Seward contended that if America were weakened mankind's hopes would be "disappointed," and all progress would be "indefinitely postponed," for it was the "ark of safety in which are deposited the hopes of the world" and the "key to progress of freedom and civilization." Since 1945, no president, secretary of state, or secretary of defense in the United States has failed to repeat and exploit this theme.[10]


*America's Self-Image as an "Island Power"*


William Appleman Williams attributes the Americans' "intense consciousness of uniqueness" to the "colonial achievement of founding and consolidating a society on the edge of a vast wilderness; the deep religious convictions and intensity of the early settlers; the secular pride in having purified the tradition of the 'Rights of Free Englishmen': the country's rapid economic growth; and the Founding Fathers' awareness that by establishing a Republic in such a large state, they had carried out a theoretical breakthrough."[11] A more important, if less obvious, reason for the American sense of uniqueness, but also of isolation and insecurity, may be that, despite their large population, vast territory, and historic position as a hemispheric power, Americans view themselves as an island nation. It is a major source of the American's deep-seated and recurring, if ever suppressed, isolationism; aggressive globalism draws on it as well.

For two centuries—from George Washington's first inaugural address through the Monroe Doctrine to the Nixon Doctrine—the self-image of island America had conditioned Washington's diplomatic and military policies. For example, among the few basic and commonly held concepts to which Henry Kissinger adhered for two decades is the distinction between "island power" and "continental power." For this reason, he, like other American policy makers since 1917, was obsessed with the challenge of the Soviet Union. The USSR, being the largest, richest, and politically the most integrated land mass in "Eurasia," was viewed as the leading "continental power." As such, it was the natural enemy and permanent threat to the United States, which Kissinger described as the foremost "island power" (that is, one in need of access to the resources of Europe, Asia, and Africa). Hence he argued that in relation to the USSR the United States was confronted by the traditional problem of an island power—"of Carthage with respect to Italy, of Britain with respect to the continent."[12]

This perception produces a compelling domino theory and an unavoidable role for America as the guardian at the gates. "If Eurasia were to fall under the control of a single power or group of powers and if this hostile power were given sufficient time to exploit its resources, we should confront an overpowering threat."[13] This view of America's geopolitical predicament also defines the American concern with preventing the emergence of Western Europe as an independent and cohesive center of power. Similarly, for nearly two decades, the policy of halting the imagined rise of China as the Pacific power conditioned American policy in Indochina. At the popular level, it reinforced the sense of national anxiety and insecurity which the salesmen of militarism and intervention were adept at exploiting. "Everything that happens in the world affects us," said Lyndon Johnson in a typical justification of the intervention in Vietnam, "because pretty soon it gets on our doorsteps."

*A Conspiratorial View of History*

What Richard Hofstadter has described as the paranoid strain in American politics is undoubtedly related to the feelings of uniqueness and insularity. It constitutes the most important component of a conspiratorial view of history, a Manichaean outlook which panics over imagined subversions by the forces of evil of the forces of good. Hofstadter states: "The distinguishing thing about the paranoid style is not that its exponents see conspiracies or plots here and there in history, but that they regard a 'vast' or 'gigantic' conspiracy as the motive force in historical events. History is a conspiracy, set in motion by demonic forces of almost transcendent power, and what is felt to be needed to defeat it is not the usual methods of political give-and-take, but an all-out crusade."[14] This phenomenon contributes to the crusading zeal which realists like Morgenthau, Kennan, and Fulbright have bewailed. It may also account for the tendency to escalate violence beyond rational limits. The deep hold among the people of an almost theological anticommunism becomes more understandable when viewed in this light; so does the easy acceptance of the official ideology of foreign policy.

The habit of viewing historical events in ad hoc, technical terms also derives in part from the conspiratorial view of history. The bulk of recent American writings on revolution is a case in point. Revolutionary warfare is viewed as a technical problem—of plotting and subversion, on the one hand, and of intelligence and suppression, on the other hand. As the chief conspiratorial group, the communists are believed to be the most likely initiators and beneficiaries of revolution. This belief produces a pessimistic posture toward a transforming world and underlies America's obsessive commitment to maintaining the status quo in the countries under its influence.

A logical extension of this attitude is the puppeteer view of the world. In complete disregard of the forces of nationalism as well as revolution, it assumes that any revolution and every radical movement is inspired, directed, and controlled from abroad. Dean Rusk's colorful description of the People's Republic of China as a "Slavic Manchukuo on a large scale" expressed a view commonly held in the 1950s.[15] Similar to it were the claims made by senior officials in three successive American administrations that the northern Democratic Republic of Vietnam was a puppet of Russia (or China, in some versions), the NLF was a puppet of the DRV, and the Cambodian and Laotian national fronts were the puppets of the Vietnamese. Such assertions often fly in the face of facts and eventually prove wrong, but the attitude which produces them persists tenaciously, and, when they are made, the allegations are popularly accepted.

The combination of globalism and paranoia yields a rhetoric so senseless and a vision so apocalyptic that were it not coming from serious and successful politicians one would tend to dismiss it as insane. Thus, at the beginning of his remarkable second campaign to win the presidency, Richard Nixon warned in a letter to the *New York Times* that "victory for the Vietcong . . . would mean ultimately the destruction of freedom of speech for all men for all time not only in Asia but in the United States as well. . . . We must never forget that if the war in Vietnam is lost . . . the right of free speech will be extinguished forever."[16] Three years later, while the war still raged, he was elected president after announcing only—and rather conspiratorially—that he had a "secret" plan for peace. Whatever opinion one may hold of the role of the military-industrial complex or of corporate influence on American foreign policy, it would be difficult to deny that such a statement by a serious aspirant to the presidency, and the Republican Party's and public response to it, reveals more about the political pathology of America than it reveals about the economic interests of America's ruling class.

## A Tradition of Bargaining and Co-optation

Owing, perhaps, to its immigrant character, which required the successful integration of diverse groups, the American political culture is management oriented. Historically, group demands have been met through the process of political bargaining and selective rewards. Ideological and political dissent has been managed by the co-optation both of individuals and ideas. The politics of management within a pluralistic framework was made possible by expanding resources (largely through territorial aggrandizement and colonial exploitation) and an extremely mobile social structure. It was further facilitated by the existence of a national consensus to which all aspiring groups tended to subscribe.

Yet the same forces which produced a flexible tradition of bargaining and co-optation also encouraged an emphasis on consensus so strong that the system would admit differences but not an agreement on how society was to be organized. Unmanageable dissent has therefore encountered swift and ruthless repression in America. The case of the Industrial Workers of the World immediately comes to mind. Furthermore, those groups which were defined as being outside of the political boundary either faced extermination, as did the American Indians, or were forcibly kept on the outer limits, as were the blacks. The result is an authoritarian superstructure, allowing for a well-defined but extremely permissive infrastructure. This characteristic has important ramifications for American response to the stresses of social change in the Third World countries.

First, there is the expectation that the African, Asian, and Latin versions of robber barons and political bosses will, out of self-interest, get around to introducing reforms and achieve an orderly resolution of conflicts arising from the pressures for political participation and income distribution. Hence the tendency to cling obstinately to the hope that political institutions shall be promoted and social progress shall be achieved under a shah, a Diem, the Thai generals, or Philippine politicians. This view misconstrues the value systems and class characteristics of what the social scientists fondly call "elites" in the traditional feudal societies. It is one reason for America's alliance with reactionary, status-quo–oriented regimes whose legitimacy erodes as social pressures mount and foreign involvements increase.

Second, since bargains and rewards are essential aspects of this tradition, the United States increases its economic and military commitments to client states in the hope of using these as leverage to press for political and economic reforms. Yet students of American foreign aid have noted that in most countries American pressures for reforms backed by United States economic and military aid inducements fail to produce the desired reforms, often promote the expansion of the American presence, and sometimes culminate in United States military intervention on behalf of the defaulting client. This phenomenon, called "incrementalism" in academic parlance, obviously results from transposing American style and expectations of behavior to relationships with feudal elites and comprador bourgeoisies, whose interests, motivations, and techniques of ensuring political and economic survival are quite different from those of the mercantilist and capitalist Americans.

Third, the consensus upon which the American system of bargaining and boundary management is predicated does not exist in the client states; foreign alignments tend to exacerbate internal divisions. There is a growing trend in our part of the world toward the radicalization of conflict. The superimposition and infiltration of modern technology and values are drastically altering the social and economic configurations which had, in traditional societies, circumscribed discontent within the boundaries of religiosity and rebellions. Third World countries are witnessing a fundamental shift in the equation of the human condition, and this change marks their transition from rebellion to revolution. The basic drive becomes not merely the fulfillment of limited goals such as raising the per capita income and the level of food consumption but the transformation of all relationships—political, economic, and social— between groups and individuals. As new groups of people, previously outside the political realm, force their way into politics, the common man becomes politically relevant. For many newcomers in politics, this mass constitutes their only capital. Politics thus ceases to be a mere struggle within a privileged minority for spoils of power. Politics becomes, progressively, a contest between the contenders from different social systems and political ideas. The opposition in such societies is frequently unmanageable because it does not share the values of an often ill-defined and sometimes illegitimate authority.

When faced with unmanageable dissent in countries within its paramount influence, the United States tends to intervene, responding in a traditional American style. The opposition is defined as being outside the legitimate political boundary (it often does not matter if legitimacy as well as a defined boundary are absent). Paranoia seeks plausible enemies: radical nationalists, socialists, all become communists; repression against "outside agitators" is carried out. If the clients are unable to defeat the opposition with American aid and advice, then direct intervention appears to be a necessity. After listening to a State Department official's defense of Vietnam at Tougaloo College, Mississippi, a black woman remarked that he spoke exactly like the white leaders in the South: there was the assertion that people in the South were generally satisfied; trouble began only when agitators from the North infiltrated; there was communist subversion. For the same reason, Ambassador Nolting in Saigon came to "remind" the *New York Times*'s correspondent, David Halberstam, "of some white community leaders in Mississippi and Tennessee."

### The Legacy of Latin America

Before becoming a superpower, the United States had exercised power outside of its own boundaries mainly in the Latin American countries, and this seems to have shaped its attitudes and methods of dealing with weaker nations. "What the C.I.A. has done in Indo-China, Iran, and Chile is no different in kind from the way Marines turned patriots into bandits and puppets into presidents in Central America and the Caribbean."[17] There, radical nationalism had been the greatest threat to vested American interest; there, the pattern of alliance with right-wing oligarchies was established and paid economic and political dividends. Even the practice of labeling radical nationalists as "communists" developed in Latin America long before the Cold War had begun. For example, in 1933, the American ambassador in Cuba found the ill-fated Grau San Martin government "communistic"; in 1937, Cordell Hull condemned the Mexican government intent on nationalizing oil interests as "those communists down there." The dialectic of American intervention developed in that hemisphere. There, too, was confirmed the belief in the efficacy of violence as an instrument of foreign policy.

*Belief in the Efficacy of Violence*

There has been some discussion in recent years of the role of violence in American culture. However, I have not seen a sufficient analysis of the extent to which a belief in the efficacy of violence appears to be an important aspect of the historical outlook and socialization in the United States. As a newcomer, I was struck by the thematic consistency of films on American colonization and the audiences' reaction to them. The whites are depicted with human emotion and failings. Tension builds up around the pioneer group united by a common enterprise, threatened by an invisible, elemental enemy. The Indian is an outsider and dehumanized. One does not learn of his family life, hopes, fears, and grievances. Indians come in hordes. They are screaming primitives. Wipe them out. They fall in stylized movements which bring smiles or laughter to the audience. Efficiency and superior technology in the service of a mission overcomes the Indian; violence is seen as an instrument of national purpose, with culturally and racially alien groups perceived as being inferior and expendable. One is reminded of Mark Twain, when Huckleberry Finn was asked if anyone was hurt in the steamboat accident. "No'm," he replied, "a couple of niggers was killed though." An Asian people were the victims of American atomic bombs. And it was in Southeast Asia that crimes against humanity were committed (in the opinion, among others, of the chief American prosecutor at Nuremberg)—while the men responsible for these crimes are being honored at and preside over the Bicentennial celebrations. When reinforced by racism, the belief in the efficacy of violence augments interventionist tendencies and brutalizes the resulting conflict beyond legal and human limits. It also produces a tendency to miscalculate the will and tenacity of the presumably inferior people. It is not surprising that the United States has experienced a significant stalemate (Korea) and its first defeat (Indochina) in Asia.

[1981]

# 16 / THE COLD WAR FROM THE STANDPOINT OF ITS VICTIMS

Allen Hunter's call to this conference and his accompanying letter render it difficult for me to write this essay as I might otherwise have done—without reference to the current academic debate on the Cold War. Allen recalls specially Professor John Lewis Gaddis's 1986 essay "The Long Peace: Elements of Stability in the Postwar International System." I am persuaded to use this influential work as a starting point for this essay on the Cold War from the standpoint of its victims.

I should refrain from detailing the extent and costs of victimhood and also the varieties of wars to which nonmembers have been subjected by members of the "bipolar" club. My colleagues on this panel—Professors Walter LaFeber and Charles W. Kegley Jr.—have already noted the salients. An estimated 21 million people died, uncounted millions were wounded, and more than a hundred million were rendered refugees by what have been variously described as the limited, invisible, forgotten, and covert wars of the 1945–1990 period.

Professor Gaddis, too, is sensitive to the anomaly of describing a time so fraught with war and violence as a period of "long peace." "To be sure," he writes, "the term peace is not the first that comes to mind when one recalls the history of the Cold War. That period, after all, has seen the greatest accumulation of armaments the world has ever known, a whole series of protracted and devastating limited wars, an abundance of revolutionary, ethnic, religious and civil violence, as well as some of the deepest and most intractable ideological rivalries in human experience. . . . Is it not stretching things a bit, one might well ask, to take the moral and spiritual desert in which the nations of the world conduct their affairs, and call it 'peace'?"[1]

"It is of course," he answers, "but that is just the point. Given all the conceivable reasons for having had a major war in the past four decades . . . it is worthy of comment that there has not in fact been one." Professor Gaddis's essay is an attempt to "comprehend how this great power peace has managed to survive for so long in face of so much provocation, and for thinking about what might be done to perpetuate that situation."

Professor Gaddis does not formally define peace; its meaning is subsumed. In the subtitle of his essay, peace is identified with the "stability" of the "postwar international system." In the text itself, he perceives peace variously as "great power peace"; the absence of "great power conflict," "major war," or "World War III"; and "survival" of the post–World War II system of international relations. He cites two mainstream political scientists, Karl Deutsch and David Singer, to support his central argument that during the four decades following World War II the international system remained stable and yielded a peace that has "approximately equaled in longevity the great 19th century international systems of Metternich and Bismarck."[2] This parallel between the nineteenth and twentieth centuries' periods of "long peace" is, we shall later see, noteworthy, for it underlines the continuity of a dominant tradition in diplomatic historiography.

After noting that a disproportionate amount of scholarly attention has been given to the causes of war, Professor Gaddis devotes the rest of his erudite essay to an investigation of the causes of the "long peace."[3] For the sake of clarity in the proceeding discussion, a summary of his six-point finding follows: (1) Elements of stability were present in the bipolar structure of the post–World War II international system. Specifically, (a) it "realistically reflected" the loci of military power; (b) as a "simple system," the bipolar did not require sophisticated leaders to maintain it; (c) simple structure rendered alliances more stable; and (d) stability of alliances rendered defections more tolerable and hence less disruptive. (2) The USA and USSR were independent of and remote from each other, hence too much familiarity did not breed contempt. (3) The domestic structure of neither superpower impeded the maintenance of a stable international system. (4) Nuclear deterrence provided the mechanism for avoiding war. (5) The "reconnaissance revolution" enabled both sides to evaluate each other's capabilities, reducing the risks of miscalculation and surprise attack. And (6) both Moscow and Washington had developed an overriding interest in "preserving the existing international system."[4]

Those who accept the notions of peace as synonymous with international stability, of international stability as the absence of "great power conflict," and this latter alone as constituting "major war" will find Professor Gaddis's essay erudite, persuasive, and, above all, reassuring. But no one who recognizes the existence and structures of modern imperialism as a defining force in world history can be persuaded of the usefulness of these and ancillary concepts in comprehending the realities of international relations in the past four or, for that matter, forty decades.

My aims in this brief and, I regret to admit, unfinished essay are threefold: to raise some questions about the language and concepts that dominate the literature on international relations; to place in a historical perspective the savage wars of the "long peace"; and to inquire into the future of the United States' policies toward the Third World—that majority of international community that lived, by and large, beyond "bipolarity"—after the formal end of the Cold War.

The issue at hand is the nature of the Cold War, the era that began after World War II and may be presumed to have terminated at the decade's end. For, if it ever existed, "bipolarity" may be construed to have ended somewhere between 1989, when the wall that divided Berlin was dismantled, and the fall of 1990, when the United States led a multilateral military expedition to the Middle East, the first such campaign to be waged by Washington without Moscow's protestations.

Central to this debate are differing notions of war, peace, and the contemporary international system. There are two simple ways of approaching a definition of peace—the positive and the negative. A positive view of peace presupposes an international system based on cooperation between major powers, their operative commitment to resolving international disputes collectively and by peaceful means, and their respect for the sovereignty and independence of weaker countries. The concomitants of these assumptions, which are embedded in the charter of the United Nations, are that peacetime activities and expenditures shall take precedence over preparations for war, fear of war shall recede as a global anxiety, the use of force shall be an exception rather than the rule in relations among nations, and international laws, rather than coercive capabilities, shall govern the behavior of the powerful no less than the weak.

Hardly anyone who holds this view of peace would regard the last forty-five years as a period of peace. The arms race that was unleashed upon us had no parallel in history. One superpower became so concentrated on inventing and producing weapons that it lost to junior partners, like Japan and Germany, the art of peacetime production. Another superpower—or so it was designated—literally went broke trying to play catch-up. Miraculous Arabian Nights fantasies materialized, nevertheless, as killing machines.

Addiction to armaments spread beyond the great powers to poverty-stricken Third World countries and to the indulgently rich petroleum producers of the Middle East. The habit spawned, as habit often does, violence, civil strife, dependency on suppliers, indebtedness, crime, and delusions of grandeur. Furthermore, the proliferation of sophisticated armaments raised the costs of the Third World's multiple—ethnic, religious, revolutionary, and counterrevolutionary—strifes to astronomical proportions. Iraq was the latest casualty of the post–World War II addiction to arms.

The sovereignty of weak nations was frequently violated. Resistance to these violations caused one superpower to brandish the Bomb, according to one estimate, on twelve occasions between 1946 and 1986.[5] As if to underline America's debt to its imperial predecessors, Professor Henry Kissinger described these nuke rattlings as the "twentieth century equivalent of showing the flag."[6] Fear stalked our lives, and "End Time" attained the status of an ideology, especially in America, where high politics was reduced to the art of selling the latest "family" of weapons.

The negative definition of peace is less demanding and more congenial to "realists" of both the scholarly and "crackpot" variety. It views peace merely as an absence of war and in the interest of realism focuses on "major wars." Even from this narrower perspective, the Cold War did not yield a "long peace." It is true that there was no nuclear war, and humanity was spared global holocaust. This may be a cause for thanksgiving but does not justify the analytical elevation of scoundrel times to peacetime. For, if peace is to be construed as avoidance of the ultimate catastrophe, then war has been peace for centuries, at least for every one except the Mayas, Incas, Aztecs, American Indians, gypsies, Jews of Europe, inhabitants of Hiroshima and Nagasaki, and possibly the Palestinians.

It may be argued that in the complex, ideologically charged, and nuclearized international environment, it is unhelpful to view the problems of war and peace in a reductionist, positive-negative perspective. One ought to focus on the dominant characteristics of the international system, not on its disturbances, deviations, and injustices. This is not an unfair demand. In evaluating the many wars that came in from the cold, the central question to ask is whether they were incidental or integral to the postwar international system. If they can be shown to be incidental, then it is obviously correct to treat them as having been generated outside the dominant system of great-power politics. On the other hand, if these wars were integral to international relations, then the international system that spawned such widespread and continuous warfare ought to be viewed as a war system, that is, one that relied on militarism and warfare in order to sustain itself.

The relationship of the so-called limited wars to the international system may be examined in terms of three criteria: (1) whether the conflict began in the context of international relations involving one or more of the great powers; (2) whether a superpower directly engaged in warfare, deployed its advanced weaponry, and caused large-scale casualties; and (3) whether the war had a global significance in that it significantly affected international relations and a superpower's international standing and future policies. Judged by these very conservative criteria, at least the Korean War [1950–1953], Indochina War [1945–1975], Afghan War [1979–1988], and the Gulf War [1991] would qualify, not at all as limited wars but as major wars of historical importance.

A more liberal and, I believe more accurate way of drawing up the balance sheet would be to include the complete repertoire of the wars of intervention—full-scale invasions, covert wars, proxy wars, and surgical strikes—in which one or the other of the superpowers and their surrogates engaged in the Cold War era. Taken together, the scope, intensity, and frequency of these wars suggest that they were systemic in nature and not merely a series of provocations that the superpowers could not evade but kept limited. That is to say, they were integral to the international system, were deemed necessary to system maintenance, and were tolerated by its other members irrespective of their differences with the warring power or coalition of powers. We begin, seemingly, to describe a war system.

The arms race was not merely a wasteful enterprise. All the high-tech weapons, except the big one, were tested on human beings in the real-life battlefields of Korea, Vietnam, Laos, Lebanon, Afghanistan, and Iraq. Wars in these unfortunate countries alone took the toll of an estimated twelve million lives. During the "long peace," the great powers gave us no less than one "limited," or "invisible," war every sixteen months. It is a tribute to the power of ideology and tradition that in the last quarter of the twentieth century reputable historians can dismiss as "limited" or as mere "provocations" wars like those in Korea, Vietnam, Lebanon, Afghanistan, and the Middle East. After all, each of these was destructive beyond imagination, and to each a superpower was organically linked. They also shaped the diplomatic, military, and economic posture of one or both superpowers and in many ways guided the course of contemporary world politics. I can appreciate the perception of stability on the part of those who identify with the Western metropole. But it hurts one's sense of history, no less than fair play, to find this era of intermittent and multi-pronged war of the strong upon the weak described as a period of "long peace."

There is a more painful recognition to be made: the roots of this debate do not lie in either differences over facts or the degree of moral sensitivity. We, Professor Gaddis and I, to cite two immediate names, are unlikely to differ over what actually happened in the last four decades, and we are most probably equally committed to a peaceable environment of international relations. The defining factors in this debate are methods not intentions.

Those among us who suppose, as William Appleman Williams did, that imperialism constitutes the modern world system and empire is also an American way of life view international politics as being shaped by hegemonic relations in their triangular aspects of competition, collaboration, and resistance. Peace is not construed in terms of stability of a real or imagined international system. War is categorized less in terms of power equations and more with respect to the intensity and scope of its impact, internationally, on peoples and their histories. Notions of balance of power and international equilibrium have but a tertiary value for this school of thought, and "bipolarity" appears to describe, at best, an aspect of international relations—a subsystem within the system—not the defining feature of it.

Then there is the school of thought, albeit dominant, that has viewed world politics in terms primarily of relations among great powers; bipolarity, I shall later argue, was merely a piece of this tradition. Because the West has dominated the world for several centuries, its focus of analysis has been on Western powers. The international system was allotted to them as a permanent holding. World politics was viewed and interpreted from their vantage point, in terms of their ententes and their wars. Methodologically—and habitually, as the tradition took roots—scholars perceived the world and its history in terms, to borrow a phrase from Edward Said, of "a higher mission and a humble reality."[7] The latter, of course, were the realities of people destroyed in their entirety and of continents subjugated.

As Edward Said has argued, devaluation of non-Western cultures and history has been integral to the epistemology of imperialism. The language no less than the methods of history, especially diplomatic and military history, offers ample support for his argument. What have been labeled by scholars variously since the sixteenth century as "expeditionary," "colonial," "interventionary," and—the latest euphemism—"limited" wars suppress reality and obscure history. They were named for their meaning to the dominant powers or, rather, to imperialism, which may be accurately described as a war system. The history of the past four centuries is a history of barely recorded holocausts. For the peoples and nations under assault, those belittled wars were always "systemic" and often total wars that had profound historical consequences. They transformed, in every sense of the word, the American, Asian, African, and even the European environment.

Great civilizations—the Mayas, Incas, Aztecs, and the so-called civilized nations of the Americas—mere impediments to the process of pioneering and exploration—were wiped out by "expeditionary" warfare. "Colonial" and "interventionary" wars yielded slavery as a modern institution and also the conquest and/or subordination of Asia, Africa, and the Middle East. Yet historians rarely interpreted these universal, world-transforming wars as anything more than a series of milestones on the road to progress. Recordings and remembrances were reserved for the occasions when the humble inflicted injury on the high—when a Custer was killed or a Gordon besieged.

The international system that gave these wars a continuous, unrelieved reality was seldom described, or understood, as a war system. The dominant school of historians continued to interpret world history largely in terms such as "balance of power" and "international equilibrium." These concepts, much like "bipolarity" during the "long peace," addressed the Western experience as the hegemon wished it. The method and the body of knowledge that flowed from the dominant historiography had two primary consequences: they excluded, as the central concern of world politics, the rest of humanity, and they protected key civilizations of the West from confronting the intellectual and moral consequences of their own history.

Yet in the twentieth century something changed. The wars of greed and expansion came seriously home to roost. The colonial have-nots of the Western world took on the haves. World War I was the last truly popular war in the

West. The innocent populace in Paris and London, no less than in Berlin and Rome, toasted and danced at its start; young men sang their way to battle-fields. But it was a devastating war in which air and chemical warfare made their debut. Europeans, who were so unaccustomed to total wars, called them world wars and gave them numbers—I, II.

When the First World War was over, a new time began, a time of yearning for peace. Perhaps for the first time in the Western world, war lost its appeal as a great game—so Winston Churchill, then a young subaltern on a military campaign in India, had described it less than twenty years earlier—to be played out in exotic, alien lands in the service of a "civilizing mission." A significant opinion—mostly of socialist and anti-imperialist provenance—emerged in the Western world that evinced revulsion from war and considered peace a necessity. It was a time in which peace associations proliferated and peace became a best seller in Europe. It was this environment that gave birth to the League of Nations and Woodrow Wilson's Fourteen Points.

I should not dwell here on the causes of the failures of the postwar peace settlement or the dynamics of fascism's successes in Germany, Italy, and Spain, even though both subjects are underanalyzed by dissenting scholarship and deserve attention. However, two points merit passing mention because they suggest the intellectual and practical costs of ignoring both the contradictions of imperialism and its capacity to undermine international mechanisms for peace.

Few scholars have investigated the correlation between the ascendance of fascism and the absence of large colonial safety valves. After all, both Germany and Italy were the only colonial have-nots among the major countries of Europe, and in the age of industrialization Spain had become a receding colonial power. Adolf Hitler himself made quite a stink and won quite a few followers in the German aristocracy and business class who would otherwise have recoiled from him.

Similarly, I have seen but little analysis, or narrative, of the ways in which the great powers undermined the League of Nations and betrayed promises to the subordinated majority of the world. The league lost its legitimacy, as the United Nations is losing its now, because it became a blatant instrument of power, not of peacemaking. In the Middle East, for example, the mandate of the league was twisted beyond imagining; the West's Arab allies were divided up as spoils; and Palestine was promised to Jewish militants whose mission was to create a biblical Eretz Israel where a native people had dwelled and built civilizations for millennia. We are reaping still the harvests of those betrayals.

The limited wars of the long peace occurred in a postcolonial international environment that differed significantly from what Winston Churchill had called "the great game" of the previous centuries. Conquests and colonization ceased to be the objectives of warfare. In the post–World War II period, ensuring control over actual or desired clients became the primary objective of interventions. The only exception to this rule may be the Israelis, whose pioneering zeal has survived the nuclear age. Yet the continuities in imperialism's outlook and style are more noteworthy than the changes in its structure. Like the more recent American wars in the Third World, these wars were "limited" only in their consequences for the intervening power, "covert" only for the citizens of Western democracies, and "forgotten" by the ensurers of democratic accountability: the press and parliaments.

A survey of this centuries-long history of systemic, occasionally genocidal, wars reveals a pattern: they have been waged on a large scale, with greater frequency, and at enormous costs to defenseless and weak peoples precisely during periods of international stability, that is, of relative peace between the great Western powers.

[1991]

# 17 / YET AGAIN A NEW NIXON

It is customary for the living to praise the dead. That is a harmless practice, because the rights and wrongs of private lives do not normally affect the public interest. But to extend this courtesy to public figures is to distort history and deny the benefits of truth and analysis to future generations. The death of Richard Nixon has provided grist to the mill of right-wing revisionists intent on putting the ex-president in the pantheon of this century's greatest statesmen.

Henry Kissinger leads the pack. In a eulogy published in hundreds of dailies the world over (see *Dawn*, May 3, 1994), he credited Nixon with: (i) ending the Vietnam War; (ii) initiating the peace process in the Middle East; (iii) starting negotiations and the process of arms control with the Soviet Union; (iv) resuming relations with China; and (v) contributing to the collapse of the Soviet Empire. "Beyond all this," writes Kissinger, "Nixon's most impressive accomplishment was as much moral as political: to lead from strength at a moment of apparent weakness; to foster the nation's resilience through the nightmare of Vietnam and thus to lay the basis for victory in the Cold War."

Both the assertions and the sweeping prose are quintessential Kissinger. But how much truth is there? Whatever adjectives one may use to describe the remarkable career of Nixon, the word "moral" is most unlikely. Richard Milhous was a devious, venal, and violent man. He began his political career as a witch hunter, in 1946, falsely charging his electoral opponent, Jerry Voorhis a five-term Democratic congressman, of being a communist sympathizer. His next quarry was Alger Hiss, a State Department official whom Nixon hunted on behalf of the House Un-American Activities Committee. After purportedly discovering a hollowed-out pumpkin containing microfilms of State Department papers, Nixon had himself photographed studying the films with a magnifying glass although it is impossible to read microfilms with magnifying glasses. Nixon manufactured an image to substantiate a false charge, an art he would perfect in later years.

His career was built on red baiting and image making. During the 1950 congressional campaign, he labeled his opponent, Helen Douglas, "the pink lady." She fought back with "Tricky Dick," which stuck forever. To Stephen Ambrose, historian of the Cold War, Nixon "was a McCarthyite before McCarthy." He appealed to the dark side of the American psyche—its capacity to be mobilized by the demons of manifest destiny and imagined menaces to life, liberty, and property. Nixon fed also on what Richard Hofstadter has described as the paranoid style in American politics. The Cold War, with its facile bipolar division of the world between the evil empire and enlightened free world, provided fertile soil for his brand of politics.

The Vietnam War broke the spell of the Cold War in America. It exposed anticommunism to be a cover for imperialism; as such, it brought forth some of the liberal and the humanist in American culture. Richard Nixon was the first victim of this change just as Jimmy Carter was its first undeserving beneficiary. The connections between Vietnam and Watergate—the extralegal habits associated with covert and illicit war making, the paranoid view of domestic opponents that led to illegal break-in and wiretaps, the chickens of counterinsurgency returning home to roost—were close and, in some respects, direct. Nixon's conduct had been unbecoming of a politician in a democracy ever since he entered politics in 1946. But it became intolerable only in the 1970s because Vietnam exposed him full-blown to a critical public. He lied, manipulated, cheated, played dirty tricks, broke laws, obstructed justice, created the first constitutional crisis in the US since the Civil War, and became in 1973 the only president in American history who resigned in order to escape impeachment.

It is obscene to credit Nixon—or Kissinger—with ending the Vietnam War. The war ended long after Nixon had resigned and only because the Vietnamese won and the Americans lost it. To claim anything else is to do injustice to the dead and wounded. If justice were to prevail, both Nixon and Kissinger would have been tried under the Nuremberg Laws for crimes of war and crimes against humanity. Nixon campaigned for president in 1968 claiming that he had a "secret plan" for peace. He continued—rather, escalated—the war on becoming president. Under Nixon and Kissinger's government alone, the American war machine used on Indochina more TNT than the total expended during World War II. Their excessive violence included the secret bombings and invasion of Cambodia, the mining of Haiphong harbor, the indiscriminate and unbelievably heavy Christmas bombings of North Vietnamese cities and villages, and repeated attempts at nuclear blackmail. Millions perished. Anthony Lake, now the national security adviser to President Clinton [1994], was an aide to Kissinger at the time. When he and a colleague protested the illegal attacks on Cambodia, security taps were put on them. They resigned.

This is not the first time Henry Kissinger has claimed for himself and Richard Nixon the kudos of initiating the Middle Eastern "peace process." Nothing is further from the truth. What they did do was to transform Israel from an ordinary client state into a strategic ally in the Middle East. American arming of Israel began under them. From 1949 to 1968, total US arms flow to Israel was just below $500 million. Between 1969 and 1976, Israel received from America a whopping $22 billion worth of sophisticated arms. In the largest logistical operation in history, Washington airlifted $1.5 billion in arms to Israel during the most crucial week of the Arab-Israeli War in October 1973. Israel felt free thereafter to proceed with its ambition of colonizing parts and dominating all of the Arab world. The nearly total dispossession of Palestinians in the Occupied Territories, the multiple invasions and occupation of Lebanon, annexation of Golan and Jerusalem, expulsion and incarceration of thousands upon thousands of hapless people had for the coming decades the full material support of Washington. With such a "peace process," who needs peace?

The claim that Nixon and Kissinger initiated a process of arms control is not new. Both men asserted it repeatedly and assigned it a name—détente. In fact, the process began earlier, under Dwight Eisenhower. Summitry was already a feature of US-Soviet relations when Nixon became president. What he and Kissinger did was to give détente a high profile and, under its cover, escalate the arms race. It was under them that the American nuclear doctrine shifted from Mutual Assured Destruction (MAD) to Flexible Targeting Options. The shift signaled a race, on the one hand, for first-strike capabilities (counterforce weapons), from B-1 bombers to the Strategic Defense Initiative

(Star Wars), and, on the other hand, battlefield weapons—tac nukes, mini-nukes. The escalation in the arms race had an unintended consequence: it put additional burdens on both the strong American and weak Soviet economies; gradually, the one slid into a protracted recession, and the other fell into virtual depression. It is only in this context that one may credit Nixon's policies with the collapse of USSR, and also with America's economic decline. And, yes, Nixon and Kissinger did finally end America's irrational boycott of China. For that, all the doughnuts they want!

Given his administration's criminal record and the harm his policies did especially to the Muslim world, it is amazing how widely Nixon was praised in our media as a statesman and friend of Arabs and Muslims. One after another, columnists and editorialists in Pakistan have mentioned his support for them, especially with reference to his professed pro-Pakistan "tilt" during the East Pakistan crisis in 1971. Beyond repeating whatever Kissinger and Nixon conveyed through calculated gestures and leaks such as the Anderson papers, none of the commentators offered any evidence of Nixon's lasting friendship toward Pakistan. In fact, during the East Pakistan crisis, Nixon and Kissinger played a sickeningly manipulative game with Pakistan's deluded leaders. They withheld from Pakistan significant material support but with their verbal tilt fed the worst illusions of Yahya Khan and his generals. For months in advance, they knew of India's plan to invade; two weeks before the invasion, they even knew its timing and did nothing to prevent it. When the deluge came, Pakistan's foolish leaders waited for the Seventh Fleet to rescue them. But the *Enterprise* did not sail until the Pakistan army had surrendered in Dhaka. Washington then claimed that it had saved West Pakistan from being conquered by India. Unbelievably, there are still Pakistanis, educated ones, who believe this falsity to be the truth.

Hegemony entails the dominance of a given discourse even among those who are not its beneficiaries. It is the cultural arm of imperialism. Nixon's passing brought, as the London weekly *Economist* put it, "the first revisionist phase of Nixonology to its climax." It would be a shame if it is perpetuated by the very people—Vietnamese, Cambodians, Arabs, Pakistanis—who were victims of Nixon's and his deputy's immoral and inhuman "grand design."

[1994]

# 18 / CRACKS IN THE WESTERN WORLD (VIEW)

Questions for the US and Europe

In this essay, I wish to raise some critical issues for the European and American disarmament movements. I recognize that there are diverse currents within the European disarmament movement and that it is therefore hazardous to generalize. It is my belief, nonetheless, that by and large the European movement's approach and outlook do not significantly differ from its American counterpart's. In any case, my comments are based on what I know directly of the American disarmament movement and on the dominant politics projected by the European movement in its literature, including the writings of Professor E. P. Thompson, and in the public presentations of its leaders/activists.

I begin by affirming my solidarity with the movements, in Western Europe no less than in the US. In the last decade, their achievements have been many and worthy of the gratitude of a menaced world. I shall mention only two. Collectively, the movement in Western Europe can take credit for introducing an independent, European dimension to the debate over the "defense" of Europe. Its break from the assumption of America's centrality in assuring European security may prove to be a most lasting contribution of the European movement to contemporary international politics. The crack in the Atlantic consensus was first opened by the Algerian War and Charles de Gaulle's subsequent withdrawal from NATO in the early 1960s. European reluctance to support Washington's massive logistical effort on Israel's behalf during the Arab-Israeli war of 1973 and cynical US manipulation of the oil boycott had widened the growing divergence of interest between Europe and America.

But it was not until popular opposition had surfaced against the deployment of the Cruise and Pershing missiles that the American "security umbrella" came to be viewed by many Europeans as a liability. Now, Western Europe could be in a frame of mind to seriously contemplate the extraordinary advantages, to its own future and to world order, of its becoming an independent, nonaligned bloc.

The antinuclear movement also helped remobilize the progressive sectors which, lacking consistent and functioning ideologies and organizations, had become steadily fragmented and demoralized following the United States' withdrawal from Indochina. The peace movement was apparently demobilized by the end of the Vietnam War; it needed another issue, simple and compelling like America's blatant and costly aggression in Indochina, to refocus its energies. Feminism proved one such focus, but it is neither a simple issue nor, unfortunately, a very compelling one to a large majority of people. The antinuclear movement, on the other hand, seemed to pose a more urgent, starkly simple question of survival.

The general response, in Europe, in Japan, and in the United States, to its call to "protest and survive" testifies to its broad appeal in the advanced capitalist countries. The concerns of the disarmament movement have also penetrated the consciousness of the Western world's liberal and social-democratic center; thus even such Cold Warriors of American politics as Gary Hart and Walter Mondale sought, during the last presidential elections, to align themselves with the freeze campaign. Rich American foundations, which had in the previous decades not deemed it fitting to support moderately radical institutions like the Institute for Policy Studies, have started funding disarmament-related research groups. One enterprising foundation—the MacArthur—has even conferred upon a movement personality its highly lucrative, hence coveted, "Genius Award" for inventing, I am told, the "concept of freeze." Even such luminaries of the American defense establishment as Robert MacNamara and Harold Brown have been moved by the movement.

I do not take purity in isolation as a politically commendable posture. The broadening of concern over the arms race should be regarded as a positive achievement of the disarmament movement in the 1980s. However, an estimation of its costs is in order. In the United States, "social responsibility" has, at least for now, become synonymous with opposition to the nuclear arms race. Groups like Physicians for Social Responsibility, Architects for Social Responsibility, and Social Scientists for Social Responsibility have sprung up.

They are concerned solely with disarmament. Such issues as health, housing, or education for the mostly black and brown poor are relegated, if they figure at all, to a tertiary place in their organizational priorities. A few months ago, I addressed a weeklong national symposium of peace activists in Boston. During the two days I attended, there was scarcely a mention of the enormous problems of hunger, homelessness, and illiteracy in the United States; nor did my proddings induce the participants to confront the question of the nuclear threat in the Near and Middle East. Perhaps it is this lack of involvement with inequality and injustice domestically and, internationally, the failure to focus meaningfully on the deadly connection between imperialism and the arms race that have rendered significant sectors of the disarmament movement so attractive to the establishment. The same phenomenon might also explain another noteworthy fact: that unlike the anti–Vietnam War and the feminist movements, the disarmament campaign has so far produced no reverberations in the Third World or Third World sectors in the first world. Since the movement professes the global objective of human survival, its failure to reach out to a majority of humanity must be regarded as serious.

The roots of this failure do not lie, obviously, in the irrelevance of the disarmament movement's concerns to the Third World. After all, the threat of war hangs over all; nuclear holocaust, if it occurs, is unlikely to be racially or ethnically discriminatory. Rather, it may be argued, as I do later in this essay, that while its use, however "limited," may engulf the globe, the first locales of nuclear exchange are more likely to be in the third than in the first or second worlds. Nor does the explanation for the movement's failure to reach Third World constituencies lie in indifference and insularity or ignorance of the "underdeveloped." After all, since the late eighteenth century, Western ideas and movements have influenced the intellectual and political life of the Third World. Since midcentury, nearly every significant political trend in the West— of the Right, Center, and the Left—has been reflected in non-Western societies. Sometimes, as in the case of nationalism, Marxism, and statism, the non-Western derivations have had as great or greater impact on modern history than their Western originals. The antinuclear movement is one of the rare Western movements to have had no influence in the Third World—intellectually, politically, or morally. An explanation for this is to be found in its own limitations. It is, in effect, a woefully narrow and parochial response to a universal challenge.

*The disarmament movement in Western Europe and in the United States is, by and large, ahistorical, technocentric, nukocentric, ethnocentric, and phobocentric.* I mean this: it is so obsessed with the technology of war, specifically nuclear war, that it ignores the causes of it. By viewing the arms race as an aspect merely of superpower rivalry and ideological psychopathology, it misapprehends the nature of the Cold War and embraces the erroneous assumption of bipolarity. By focusing exclusively on the white triangle—the United States, Europe, and Russia—it bypasses the ignition points of nuclear conflagration. By concentrating primarily on nuclear weapons, it overlooks the fueling functions and trip wires of the conventional arms race and of escalating weapons sales to the Third World. Finally, in its educational and organizational work, the disarmament movement has come to depend so heavily on invoking the fears of nuclear holocaust that it has become practically bereft of a positive vision of the future.

In a brief essay, it is not possible to fully discuss this estimation. What follows are a few observations offered in the hope that the argument shall be joined, and I shall have another day to elaborate and refine. First, I should admit to an initially uncritical support for the disarmament movement. I began to question its dangerously narrow approach only gradually. Ironically, the high point of my disenchantment was reached on June 12, 1982, the day of the largest disarmament rally in the United States. Nearly a million people had gathered in New York's Central Park to protest the arms race and especially the production of the MX and the planned deployment of Cruise and Pershing missiles in Europe. That was also the eighth day of Israel's massive invasion of Lebanon; besieged Beirut, one of the world's major financial and political capitals, center of Middle Eastern artistic and intellectual life, had already been heavily and indiscriminately under bombardment for a week. The horror was televised; in fact, since neither Dresden nor Tokyo were so privileged, the world was witnessing for the first time in history the systematic destruction of a city. Only one of the more than a score of speakers at this rally thought fit to mention and protest this outrage and the United States' part in it. When approached, the organizers of the rally declined to include either a Middle Eastern speaker or a resolution on the subject. The peace rally in Central Park ended without acknowledging even the existence of the wanton war in one of the most strategic areas of the world. I suffered physically that day, from nausea.

The failure which so shocked me was both moral and political. Here, I am concerned with the politics, not the morality. The event suggested the rally's technocentric and Eurocentric bias; it was protesting certain weapons—the MX, Pershing, and Cruise missiles—and their deployment—in the US and Europe. Its organizers betrayed a studied avoidance of connecting their concerns to imperialism and war in the Middle East particularly and generally in the Third World. The tendency is reflected in the disarmament movement's literature. For example, a very popular and mobilizing work *Protest and Survive,* edited by E. P. Thompson and Dan Smith, has a selection of eleven articles.[1] Not one of them deals with intervention, the arms race, or regional conflicts in the Third World. One may cite other such examples. In a moment, I shall note the extraordinary irony of the omission in the Thompson-Smith anthology.

I hope I am not being understood as engaging in Third Worldism. I do not believe that every injustice in the world should be the organizational concern of the disarmament movement or that every national or regional conflict has a deadly connection to nuclear politics. However, if the disarmament movement's goals are to prevent nuclear war, reduce world tension, and end the strategic arms race, then both its biases and its avoidances are self-defeating. For these do not conform to the realities of contemporary international politics. Thus, in the introduction to the book by Thompson and Smith et al., Daniel Ellsberg, in an attempt to pry out the "hidden realities of the nuclear dimension to U.S. foreign policy," documents twelve instances of "actual nuclear crises" after Hiroshima and Nagasaki. *All,* repeat, *all* except two of the twelve instances of nuclear diplomacy cited by Ellsberg occurred in the Third World. The two relating to Europe occurred over Berlin—in 1948 and 1961—an issue which has since been effectively defused. The editors must have read the introduction to their book. Then why did they not include at least one or two articles on superpower policies in—may I call it—"the Third World theater"? I read Professor E. P. Thompson's very long and very scary "Letter to America" in vain for an answer.

It seems that so limiting is the preoccupation with the ever-proliferating nuclear technology and so numbing the fear of holocaust that one tends to neglect the lessons of history. One such lesson is that great wars often have small beginnings; another is that great-power involvement and clash of interests define the link between small wars and their internationalization. Today, no region is more central to superpower interests than the area bounded by the Mediterranean and Indian oceans, and no conflict is more susceptible to internationalization than the one between Israel and the Arabs. Hence this region has witnessed the most numerous instances of nuclear brinkmanship. Daniel Ellsberg's count is conservative. A Brookings Institution study by Barry Blechman and Steven Kaplan lists nineteen instances between 1946 and 1976 in which "strategic nuclear weapons were involved."[2] Of these, thirteen occurred over conflicts in the Third World; five, leaving out the controversial case of Azerbaijan in 1947, took place in the Middle East. The last known instances of nuclear flag showing, during the Arab-Israeli war of 1973, involved a worldwide alert of US strategic forces and brought us up to DEFCON-3, two steps away from thermonuclear war.

These facts reflect not merely the psychopathology of policy makers but also the realities of superpower interests. We need to recognize the logic behind two related developments in the last one and a half decades: a qualitative shift in the nature of the arms race and the dangerous augmentation of superpower, especially US, interest in the Middle East and southern Africa. Since ancient times, the Mediterranean and the Indian oceans have served as imperial seaways; their hinterlands provided the human and material resources of the Roman, the Byzantine, the Arab, and the Ottoman empires and allowed their outreach to the French and British. Lacking originality of mind and autonomy from vested interests—conditions which are necessary to break from the strategic assumptions of the past—American policy makers regard this area as central to their interests. Their view of America's geopolitical predicament as an "island power" does not center on the USSR alone. Already, in the 1950s, strategic experts like Henry Kissinger believed that conflict between the US and USSR was now less likely in Europe; the greater risk lay in the gradual erosion of American power in the "grey areas" of the Near East, Western Asia, Indochina, and Korea.[3]

Dr. Kissinger attached a special importance to the Near and Middle East, for, "if Eurasia were to fall under the control of a single power or group of powers . . . and if this hostile power were given sufficient time to exploit its resources, we should confront an overpowering threat." This perception was accentuated by US failure to suppress the revolutionary movement in Indochina, by the collapse of the Baghdad Pact, and by Soviet advances in strategic weapons which rendered thermonuclear war "repugnant," according to Kissinger, and created a stalemate in which its ideological adversaries could subvert the influence and interests of the United States. More important, as the Soviet Union attains strategic equivalence and war becomes unthinkable, force loses its historic role as a balancing mechanism. The classic rules of balance-of-power politics do not apply, and this adversely affects the credibility of American power. Friends cannot ultimately count on American might, and local adversaries shall not sufficiently fear it. If the credibility of superior American power were to be restored with friends no less than adversaries, war will have to be rendered thinkable again.

The goal, in Dr. Kissinger's words, was to restore the link "between power and the willingness to use it." It required a lowering of the threshold on the threat and, in case that did not work, on a limited, graduated use of nuclear weapons. "The United States," Kissinger wrote, "requires a twentieth century equivalent of showing the flag, an ability and readiness to make our power felt quickly and decisively, not only to deter Soviet aggression, but also to impress the uncommitted with our capacity for decisive action."[4] Like his colleagues of the "realpolitik" school so favored in Washington, Henry Kissinger was not entirely unaware of the risks inherent in this doctrine; as safeguards, he stressed the need for graduated increments of nuclear escalation and a negotiating posture to persuade the enemy that a "settlement is possible on reasonable terms." But what if the adversary is not amenable to this subtle combination of terror and diplomacy? Answers Dr. Kissinger: "*It requires strong nerves.* We can make a strategy of limited war stick only if we leave no doubt about our readiness and our ability to face a final showdown."[5]

C. Wright Mills had aptly described this sort of thinking as crackpot realism. Yet a decade later it was decisive in defining America's global design. The DEFCON-3 worldwide alert of October 25, 1973, like Israel's and the United States' bomb-brandishing jingoism over Jordan in December 1970, was faithful to Dr. Kissinger's 1950s blueprint for linking nuclear arms to American diplomacy. One wonders over the consequences had the Soviet Union responded in 1973 with an attempt to intervene directly on Egypt's behalf. Its failure to do so contributed to the success of Dr. Kissinger's "shuttle diplomacy" and to Egypt's total break with Moscow, a lesson that may, unfortunately, not have been lost on the cautious but reactive decision makers in Moscow. More important than the tactical expressions of this neorealism were the structural changes it entailed in the United States—and quite rapidly in the Soviet—strategic planning and deployments. Starting in 1969, following the accession of Richard Nixon and Henry Kissinger to power, the White House and the Pentagon (the State Department, then under William Rogers, was largely ignored in this matter) employed language similar to that used in the 1950s to justify a momentous shift in America's nuclear strategy. Kissinger was appointed to head a "top level interdepartmental group" with a commission to "come up with additional nuclear war options."[6] On January 10, 1973, the United States secretary of defense officially announced a new policy of "Flexible and Selective Targetting Options." Henceforth, all-out nuclear war will "not be the only option and possibly not the principal option open to the National Command Authorities."[7] This would eventually entail not only the worldwide deployment of a new generation of tactical nuclear weapons and a reprehensible augmentation of superpower military presence in the Middle East and Africa but also the deployment in NATO countries of such "intermediate"-level strategic devices as the Cruise and Pershing missiles. The two developments are strategically and organically alike. For the disarmament movement to ignore the origins and implications of the shift, briefly outlined here, in favor of concentrating almost exclusively on the production and deployment of certain weapons in the US and Europe, is somewhat like piling up sandbags without clearing the mines.

Between the rejected flexible options and limited nuclear war advocacies of the 1950s and their adoption as official policy in the 1970s, there intervened a decade of perceived decline in American power. As American policy analysts saw it, the postwar paramountcy of the United States had been based on four primary factors: (1) its unquestioned strategic superiority over adversaries; (2) its economic and security leverage over allies in Western Europe and Japan; (3) its will and capacity to carry out successful interventions, at reasonable costs, in the Third World; and (4) the existence of an overriding Cold War national consensus in favor of a forward American foreign and military policy. By 1968, all four pillars supporting the United States posture as the world's number one power had disappeared or diminished. The Soviet Union had, by 1968, effectively gained strategic parity with the United States. America's two leverages over its capitalist allies—that of economic superiority and security umbrella—had diminished. Washington's will and capacity to intervene in the Third World, to ensure allies and protect investments, was weakened by the protracted war and defeat in Indochina. Finally, with the rise of a dissenting, progressive sector in American society and the general affliction of the America public with the "Vietnam syndrome," the national consensus was cracked. The perception, in United States policy-making circles, of a serious decline of American power was pervasive. What had been heralded, following World War II, as the American Century seemed to be ending in its third decade.

The mood was to attempt a restoration of the slipping "century." As always with restorationist attempts, this, too, would entail some disregard of history, of costs and consequences, as often it was approached as a technical, managerial problem. The restoration of strategic superiority involved both a search for counterforce weapons and a doctrine of flexible targeting. The revitalization of America's interventionist capabilities would entail the "regional influential" alternatives of the Nixon Doctrine as well as nuclear flag showing, the Rapid Deployment Force, and preparedness to use tactical nuclear weapons in nonnuclear "theaters." And gaining new leverages over capitalist allies would necessitate, among other things, a shift in the centrality of the world struggle for power from the Atlantic and the Pacific in the 1950s and 1960s to the areas bounded by the eastern Mediterranean Sea and the Indian Ocean. After all, from 60 to 80 percent of raw material, including the energy supplies of Western Europe, come from this region; an unquestioned American hegemony over this region cannot but assure the US a powerful new leverage over its old allies.

I should, at a later time, like to discuss in some detail the deadly connection between Western Europe and the Middle East and between big wars and their small beginnings. Here the following reminders should suffice: since 1969, the heaviest concentration of superpower competition has been in the Middle East. This region was the centerpiece of the Nixon and Carter doctrines. Outside of NATO and the Warsaw Pacts, it has been the largest single market for Western and Eastern armaments; by now, this volatile region of multiple tensions is bustling with advanced weaponry. Three countries of this region—Israel, Egypt, Syria—have been the world's largest recipients of American, and Russian, military and economic aid. The region has also witnessed the most dramatic expansion of superpower military presence, including the astronomical jump in the size of the Rapid Deployment Force to more than 400,000. After the Vietnam War and until the US invasion of Grenada, all US combat casualties occurred in this area (specifically in Iran and Lebanon), and only here (Afghanistan) are Soviet forces engaged in combat today. The Near and Middle East have been the scene of the last three instances of nuclear diplomacy, and, in addition to its highly modernized and expanded naval presence, the US has acquired new land bases in this region. Israel, an insecure and expanding settler state, has acquired nuclear capability; so has its ally, South Africa; so may its adversary, Pakistan. Since 1973, the Middle East has become integral to US, and presumably Soviet, strategic planning.

In addition to tactical weaponry and navy-based nuclear deployment, the missile systems in Sicily are believed to be aimed at this region.

Starting with Nixon, every American president has publicly identified the Middle East as the likely theater of nuclear exchange. All four have explained their choice in geopolitical and strategic terms. President Ronald Reagan also cites religious grounds for it. When asked to justify his contention that the Middle East was the most probable locale of nuclear war, he said he was thinking of the Bible and "of Armageddon and so forth." In a recent pamphlet—"Nuclear War and the Second Coming"—the Moral Majority of the Reverend Jerry Falwell affirms the religious basis for President Reagan's belief and promises on Armageddon day the body's rapturous ascent from Jerusalem.

Undoubtedly, there are groups and individuals in the American and European peace movement who have taken these signs and warnings seriously and who have spoken out on issues relating to militarism, intervention, and denial of people's right to self-determination. Yet, by and large, the disarmament movement on both sides of the Atlantic has chosen to stay within the boundaries of its Eurocentric and technocentric bias. Given the realities of international politics, one can only agree with Noam Chomsky that the disarmament movement in the Western world "dooms itself to near irrelevance" if it continues to duck the question of Palestinian rights and the issues arising out of Israel's transformation as a major military power allied to the United States.[8]

[1985]

# AFTER THE COLD WAR

Worlds of Pain

# 19 / AT COLD WAR'S END

## A World of Pain

Mikhail Gorbachev effectively renounced the Soviet Union's role as a global rival of the United States. The fall of the Berlin Wall symbolized the end of the Cold War. The breakup of the USSR into a loose confederation of independent states lent it finality.

These developments have enlivened long-standing controversies about the nature of the Cold War and generated intense debate about the implications of its end for the future of international relations and world order. This essay is concerned with such implications. A few observations on the Cold War itself may, nevertheless, be useful in situating the discussion.

*Bipolar Rivalry or Imperial Domination?*

There are two contrasting perspectives on the Cold War. The first sees it in bipolar terms: as a product of great-power rivalry with ideological and strategic aspects. According to this view, the arms race, military alliances, competition for influence over Third World countries, superpower engagement in foreign wars (e.g., Korea and Vietnam), and interventions abroad were all aspects of bipolar competition.

This perspective is apt to yield a relatively optimistic outlook on the prospects for world politics after the Cold War. The arms race will end; peace dividends will accrue to socially beneficial enterprises; economic aid and arms supplies to Third World countries can be rationally determined; in a non-competitive environment, great powers can cooperate in resolving regional and local conflicts and reinforce peacekeeping institutions like the United Nations. Reflecting an allegiance to this optimistic outlook, George Bush, many media pundits, and some scholars saw the Gulf War as heralding a world order of collective peacemaking, signaling how aggression would be treated without the overlay of bipolar rivalry.

The dissenting view holds that superpower rivalry was only a part of the larger framework of international relations which is shaped by imperialism, a centuries-old phenomenon with deep economic, institutional, and cultural roots. The Cold War served as the latest mechanism for organizing and legitimizing a world system of domination.

From this perspective, the end of the Cold War may relieve some tensions, but it does not represent a fundamental change in international relations. To the contrary, the removal of a countervailing power and the development of a unipolar international system may allow for a freer play of imperial interests in world politics and a monopolistic shift of power over world security to the West. The international environment today resembles the imperial century which followed the end of Napoleonic war in 1815, the period of British pre-eminence in world politics. Europeans saw it as a period of "long peace." Asians and Africans experienced it as a time of torment. Like Britain earlier, the United States now holds world power. And, as a rule, those who control the status quo do not like to change it.

Analogies are, of course, rarely exact. Unlike Britain after Waterloo, the United States is a declining economic power. The Cold War has taken its toll here, too. The homeless sprawl our cities. Educational standards have fallen. Productivity has decreased. Citizens wish to turn now to the long neglected tasks of national reconstruction and economic recovery. Bill Clinton's election was but one expression of this hope. Also, the world is more disorderly than before. It will not yield to unipolar management.

Still, this second outlook provides reasons for deep pessimism. Recent instances—in the Middle East, the Balkans, and South Asia—suggest that, as during the century preceding the First World War, perceived Western interests rather than larger considerations of peace and international security will be the chief determinants of which aggressions will be punished and who will be deemed to have violated international law.

These competing perspectives on the Cold War suggest two questions about the current period: What trends can we identify in the post–Cold War security environment? And if, as the more pessimistic outlook indicates, the trends suggest increasing violence and insecurity, what steps might be taken to create a safer international environment? To answer the first question, I examine three recent security issues: the Gulf War, the Bosnian conflict, and nuclear proliferation. I will conclude with some reflections on the second question.

## The Gulf War

Iraq invaded Kuwait on August 2, 1990. The oil-rich sultanate fell easily to superior Iraqi forces. The sheikh and most of his family fled the country. Amnesty International reported on December 2 that the Iraqi invaders had brutalized Kuwaiti civilians, killed hundreds, jailed and tortured thousands. They also ransacked banks and vandalized private homes and public places such as museums.

It was aggression. Reaction from Washington was immediate, authoritative, and uncompromising. There could be no reward for aggression; no violation of the UN Charter; no appeasement; no Munich. The UN Security Council met on the same day, condemned Iraq, and ordered its immediate withdrawal from Kuwait.

The US government prepared to punish Iraq. It shaped the UN resolutions, defined the means of their enforcement, and pursued member countries' support of them. On August 6, the Security Council met for a second time and imposed comprehensive international sanctions against Iraq, traditionally a friend of the USSR. The council, it seemed, was no longer hostage to a rival veto.

From then on, the council met repeatedly, tightening the noose and widening the scope of intervention against Iraq in no less than eleven resolutions. The twelfth, Resolution 678 of November 29, 1990, authorized "Member States cooperating with the Government of Kuwait" to "use all necessary means to uphold and implement Resolution 660 (1990) and all subsequent relevant resolutions" if Iraq failed to withdraw from Kuwait by January 15, 1991.

Barring the occasion when the Security Council—acting in the absence of the Soviet delegate—approved US intervention in Korea, the UN had never issued so open-ended a license to wage what Rudyard Kipling might well have described as a "savage war of peace." Washington's confident and activist leadership stood in striking contrast to its diffident posture on Bosnia, where it ceded to Britain and France virtual control over the Western response to the crisis.

The countdown to January 15 was a long morality play. The script was written by Bush, Baker, and Cheney, but a host of legislators, scholars, and pundits—including Henry Kissinger, Stephen Solarz, Michael Walzer, A. M. Rosenthal, and Charles Krauthammer—played supporting roles as President Bush prepared to "kick Saddam Hussein's ass." Prominent Americans who argued for giving sanctions and diplomacy a chance—Jimmy Carter, Zbigniew Brzezinski, the World Council of Churches, and Admiral William Crowe, not to mention dissenting intellectuals like Noam Chomsky and Edward Said—were all but ignored. And Bush spurned or undermined all openings for a negotiated withdrawal of Iraq from Kuwait.

Proposals by Jordan, Algeria, France, Iran, and the USSR toward a negotiated end to the crisis died untested. The president did not mellow even after Saddam Hussein unconditionally released several hundred Americans whom he had held hostage as shields against a US aerial assault on Iraq's urban and industrial infrastructure. President Bush's "no concession, no compromise" posture had, nevertheless, one positive aspect: it insisted that the UN Charter was not negotiable.

There was extended debate in Congress. It was extolled in the media as a model of democratic process. The legislators did not pursue the historical, economic, or ideological roots of Iraqi-Kuwaiti conflict; they did not explore issues related to the interaction of nationalism, imperialism, and Islam in the region; they did not discuss the nature of Iraq's grievances and possible objectives in invading Kuwait; nor did they consider the recent history of US-Iraq dealings. The congressional debate was narrowly focused on the effectiveness of economic sanctions, and costs of war to the United States. On January 12, the debate culminated in a joint House-Senate resolution authorizing the president to use US armed forces. Public opinion polls showed a steady rise in popular support for President Bush.

I emphasize that throughout the period leading up to the war, Congress, the public, and foreign allies did not lead the American executive into intervening against Iraq; they were led by it.

On January 16, 1991, war started. Its defining symbols were "smart" weapons. Their accuracy and effectiveness in disabling Iraqi air force, tanks, and artillery were pointedly televised. Within days, they accomplished not just the liberation of Kuwait but also the destruction of Iraq's economic infrastructure. Allied losses were notably low. Some half a million Americans were deployed in the Gulf; 183 are reported to have been killed, 35 of them by "friendly fire." (Iraqi fatalities are estimated at seventy to one hundred thousand.)

A final point: revulsion against Iraqi atrocities in Kuwait is claimed to have played a central role in shaping American resolve against Iraq, turning public opinion toward a forceful solution. President Bush himself was said to have been decisively influenced by Iraqi atrocities. In a letter to students, he had written that "there is much in the modern world that is washed in shades of gray. But not the brutal aggression of Saddam Hussein. . . . It's black and white." Elizabeth Drew, writing in the *New Yorker*, quoted a White House aide as saying that Iraq's behavior had touched in George Bush a "deep inner core."


*Bosnia*

Bosnia apparently did not get to George Bush's core. In fact, the responses to Bosnia and Iraq are different at every step.

Questions which were rarely asked during the Gulf crisis—about roots of the conflict, its complex history, and enduring psychological dimensions—are now in fashion concerning Bosnia and Herzegovina. They are good questions. But in the present context, they serve not as vehicles of analysis but as instruments for evading responsibility. And they ignore the recurrent lesson that movements based on hate serve to twist, warp, and invent history.

The stark reality is that the people of Bosnia face genocide. Yet the United States, the European Community, and the United Nations have dithered for one year in a posture of complicity and appeasement.

Genocide is a battered word. Misuse has vitiated its grim significance. Genocide—the willed extermination of a people—remains nevertheless the most horrific crime against humanity. It is rarely meaningful to raid the past for images. Yet in this instance, as the organizers of the Holocaust Museum in Washington, D.C., understood, the past imposes itself on our consciousness. Bosnia's tragedy bears many of the searing signs of the insane brutality visited on Jews and Gypsies earlier in the century—emptied villages, hurriedly abandoned homes, millions fleeing, tortured children, and, yes, death camps. In the

"Year of the Woman," Serb fascism also gave us its distinctive signature—mass rape.

The perpetrators of this crime are driven not by a sense of lived history but, in Hannah Arendt's phrase, by a "banal evil," an ideology of difference which drives them to the neo-Nazi quest for "ethnic cleansing." In a year's campaign, they have "cleansed" more than 70 percent of Bosnian land of its Muslim inhabitants. Uncounted thousands are dead; the survivors are gathered mostly in the shrunken remains of Bosnia—homeless and exposed to death by hunger, disease, cold, and more ethnic cleansing.

The horror is widely reported and officially acknowledged. The UN has condemned aggression against Bosnia, a member state. But for a year its resolutions have remained mild and indulgent by comparison with the Iraq sanctions. And as I write (mid-May), the UN has not taken any measures to enforce these resolutions.

In April of this year, President Clinton gave "firm" indications that he finally was moving to tighten and enforce them. But at the Vancouver summit meeting he granted Boris Yeltsin an extension on genocide to April 25. No substantive measure was to be taken against Slavic Serbia until after the presidential election in Slavic Russia. Encouraged by the indulgence, the Serbs launched a final assault on Srebrenica. The town's sixty thousand inhabitants are now under precarious UN custody.

The Security Council has authorized the creation of a tribunal to conduct trials for crimes against humanity. But high UN officials and world leaders such as Douglas Hurd of Britain and UN Secretary General Boutros-Ghali have been shown—smiling, hand shaking, even banqueting—with the worst of the known criminals. So who will prosecute whom?

Verbal denunciations of Serbia and of the Bosnian Serbs are now commonplace. But the words are not backed by deeds. What is worse, Western policies do amount to intervention—on the side of the aggressor. They provide a dismal picture of complicity in crimes against humanity. Consider three examples:

1. The UN has a large presence in Bosnia, including a military contingent of eight thousand. But the rules of engagement make appeasement a necessity. UN humanitarian aid is hostage to Serb military units who expropriate 25 to 40 percent of the relief supplies. To evacuate sick and wounded civilians, the UN seeks Serb permission, which is often granted only to be violated. Bosnia's foreign min-

ister was murdered under UN escort. Women and children have been massacred in its custody.

In October 1992, the UN declared a no-fly zone in Bosnia, but, unlike the practice in Iraq, it did not enforce the ban. By December 15, UN observers had reported 225 aerial infringements by the Serbian air force, which included bombing of Muslim villages and towns. Serbs have repeatedly broken cease-fires and safe-passage agreements. The United Nations has never appeared more ineffectual or pitiful.

2. The great powers have denied to Bosnians the means of their own defense. By May 1992, "ethnic cleansing" had emerged as a systematic Serb goal. As Bosnians lost ground, Serbia's rival Croatia also began to grab Bosnian territories. But the Western powers insisted on maintaining an embargo on arms to Bosnia.

Technically, the embargo applies equally to Serbia, Croatia, and Bosnia. But it is damaging only to Bosnia. Serbia inherited the bulk of the former Yugoslav army, and its impressive arsenal. Croatia got much of the remainder. Both have coastlines, neutral or friendly frontiers, and plenty of suppliers. In fact, arms are so plentiful in Serbia that it was exporting weapons to, among others, Somali warlords. Bosnians, by contrast, were lightly armed. The military gap between Bosnia and Serbia is one to ten in light weapons, one to three hundred in heavy armaments including tanks and artillery. Landlocked and encircled, Bosnians cannot get arms unless the embargo is lifted. Their easy slaughter has been made possible by the arms embargo of the great powers and in effect ratified by the UN.

From summer 1992, the Bosnian government pleaded not for Western intervention but for lifting the embargo. A majority of the elected members of the Security Council supported this demand. The permanent members, however, led by Britain, France, and Russia, have still rejected it. They say that lifting the arms embargo will intensify the conflict; that it may provoke the Serbs to attack UN forces, which include British, French, and Canadian troops; and that the armaments will fall into Serb hands. Any secondary school student can see the implications of these arguments for the future of world order.

3. After months of unsuccessfully urging a forceful Euro-American posture, Lord Owen and Cyrus Vance, mediators of, respectively, the European Community and the UN, produced a peace plan which proposes dividing Bosnia into ten autonomous units. Two features of this plan are noteworthy: First, it rewards aggression and ethnic cleansing. For this reason, the Clinton administration opposed the plan during its first month in office. Its second aspect is equally disturbing: by dividing Bosnia along ethnic lines, the Vance-Owen plan legitimizes Serbia's and

Croatia's sectarian program. Croatia welcomed it. Bosnia agreed to sign on US urgings. Serbs rejected it.

The fate of Bosnia has not yet been completely sealed. Some cities remain; people also remain. America's official conscience appears to be moving. Threat of military action by President Clinton has temporarily persuaded the Serbian government to accept the Vance-Owen plan. Given the past record, this acceptance may be tactical, not real. Still, one may hope that at least partial justice shall now be done.

What are we to make of these contrasts between Bosnia and Iraq? They reveal the cynicism with which great powers use peace conferences and the United Nations as instruments of national policy. Aggression was predictable in Bosnia; it could have been prevented. In March 1992, when Bosnia's application for membership was before the UN, several countries warned that Serb aggression was imminent and requested that UN observers be sent to Bosnia. Even a small UN presence at the time might have deterred the Serbs. In June 1992, President Mitterand made a dramatic visit to Sarajevo in order to "seize the world's conscience toward helping an endangered people." Britain's foreign minister, Douglas Hurd, then moved in to stall the resulting momentum with his London Peace Conference and its equally worthless sequel in Geneva. And so it went month after month.

*Nonproliferation*

The problem of nuclear proliferation is less dramatic than the previous two and thus less in the public eye. It is precisely for this reason that it serves to highlight the patterns of post–Cold War policy making that we have seen in the cases of Iraq and Bosnia.

In the fall of 1989, US officials signaled an active interest in pursuing a policy of arresting and, in some cases, rolling back the proliferation of nuclear weapons. Washington's nonproliferation policy justifiably focused on regions where nuclear proliferation had occurred, where its pace was believed to be picking up, and where there existed a conflictual environment which increased the risk of wartime use of nuclear weapons.

These areas of concern were the Korean peninsula, where North Korea was believed to be engaged in the development of nuclear weapons; South

Asia, where India and Pakistan had achieved nuclear capability but were not known to have actually built weapons; and the Middle East, where Israel possessed both a significant arsenal of nuclear weapons and systems capable of delivering them and Iraq was attempting but had not yet achieved material capability.

Few would question either the risks inherent in weapons proliferation or the value of controlling, and possibly reversing, the race to nuclear arms. The question of interest here is: has the United States pursued its antiproliferation policy in a manner which advances the specific goal of a nuclear-free environment in the regions in question or at least fulfills the general objective of promoting a stable nuclear environment? If the answer is negative, then where are these policies leading us?

The details of nuclear politics in each of the three regions are Byzantine. Cumulatively, they convey a deadly sense of seriousness and the conviction that the stakes are nothing less than survival itself. In this environment, the United States has started vigorously to pursue a nonproliferation policy based on discrimination and double standards—not a promising strategy for preventing nuclear proliferation. Consider how this policy has been implemented in South Asia and the Middle East.

India carried out a successful nuclear test in 1974. Since then, its program has broadened to include the development of short- and long-range missile systems. It is virtually a nuclear country. The United States has mildly rebuked India, but apart from a belated embargo of the Indian Space Research Organization, it has not significantly pressured Delhi.

Pakistan's nuclear quest began after India's test. Under Zia ul-Haq, the military dictator from 1977 to 1988, the program made significant progress. Pakistan became capable of manufacturing up to five or six Hiroshima-type nuclear bombs. During this period, Pakistan was coordinating the US-financed covert operation in Afghanistan; its targets were the USSR and the Afghan government. The United States ignored the nuclear issue. In fact, the White House annually certified to Congress that Pakistan was not engaged in nuclear weapons development.

By the end of 1989, however, the Soviet Union had withdrawn from Afghanistan, and US pressure on Pakistan to roll back its nuclear program and open its installations to international inspection began to mount. Islamabad offered to do so but only as part of a regional agreement including India. The alternative was for the United States to enter a defense treaty with Pakistan.

The Pakistani government also floated a five-point proposal for control of nuclear arms in South Asia.

These maneuvers failed to satisfy Washington, and in 1991 all US aid to Pakistan was terminated. Today, the pressure on Pakistan continues to mount. The United States now threatens to declare its former ally a "terrorist state," presumably for its alleged support of Sikh dissidents in India and guerrillas in Kashmir—a state over which India and Pakistan have had a dispute since 1947.

In the case of the Middle East, destruction of Iraq's nuclear program was declared by President Bush to be a primary aim of the Gulf War. This goal was achieved. Yet UN inspectors remain, sniffing out components, including dual-purpose technologies, which might be used by Iraq in a future nuclear program. This, of course, means that Iraq will be denied access to a range of industrial technology.

Israel's nuclear program has not been subject to congressional scrutiny or pressure from the US government. US antiproliferation laws have not been invoked against it. Congress has passed country-specific legislation such as the Pressler and Solarz amendments, which do not apply to Israel. The full extent of Israel's nuclear capability is not known. What we do know is that Israel's nuclear arsenal is awesome and that its advanced delivery system is provided largely by US arms and technology.

The double standard of US nonproliferation policy suggests a frightening vision of imperial arrangements of domination. The policy evinces no sense of history or of the anxieties, fears, and ambitions which compel governments to seek awesome weapons and peoples to welcome them. As such, it is a policy doomed not only to fail but to be counterproductive. As long as Washington maintains its current approach to nonproliferation, it will practice double standards, cause fear, and promote an intolerably unstable nuclear environment. A viable alternative is to support nonpartisan, multilateral, regional approaches implemented under the umbrella of an authoritative international organization.

## What May We Hope For?

At Cold War's end, people sense opportunities as well as dangers. In particular, there is growing interest in strengthening the peacemaking and peacekeeping capabilities of international institutions. That interest appears now to be crystallizing in a consensus among scholars and diplomats on five basic reforms of the international system:

- The UN Security Council needs to be democratized. The veto ought to be abolished, the Security Council enlarged, and nongovernmental organizations representing public interests included on the Council.
- The UN should have a permanent pool of armed forces at its command. This is essential if it is to act forcefully as an autonomous world organization.
- The International Court of Justice ought to be linked organically to the UN. The court should, for example, have powers of judicial review over Security Council and General Assembly resolutions.
- The International Atomic Energy Agency should be vested with additional powers to play a significant role in ending nuclear proliferation and the strategic arms race.
- The structure of development aid should be democratized, and bilateral aid discouraged.

These are admirable suggestions. If implemented, they would be of real benefit. But is it realistic to expect them to be adopted? The three situations I have explored here suggest that the answer is "no." The problem is that the big powers are status quo powers. They have no apparent interest in changing the distribution of international power. At the same time, the former Eastern bloc countries are dominated by economic hardship, ideological confusion, political disintegration, and ethnic warfare; they are unlikely to work for constructive reform of international relations. And Third World governments are mostly corrupt, inefficient, undemocratic, and dependent postcolonial clones. Incapable of practicing democracy or promoting justice internally, they are ill suited to seeking it internationally.

In the case of Iraq, the UN was forcefully mobilized because the United States viewed the Gulf region as central to its interests. In recent decades, while US economic and strategic leverage over Europe and Japan declined, Washington has sought to increase its hold on the Middle East as a means to acquire new leverage over old allies. Saddam Hussein opened the door. Saudi Arabia, Kuwait, and the United Arab Emirates have now become virtual American protectorates. With a controlling hand over the world's largest reserve of oil, the United States has achieved a goal defined more than twenty years ago by Richard Nixon and Henry Kissinger.

The West's indifference to Bosnia reveals the same basic logic of power. Britain has led an appeasement policy, engineered diversions when the international outcry threatened to compel action against Serbia, and provided the arguments for keeping the arms embargo on Bosnia. France has gone along. America has nodded.

Policy in this case was fueled in part by distrust of Germany. Reunited and economically powerful, it promises to become increasingly politically assertive. Germany's support of Croatian independence aroused suspicion. Other European nations saw a strong Serbia as a counterweight. There is a second, related consideration: Britain, France, and the United States share the objective of wooing Russia, whose sympathy for Serbia is well-known. Why, then, be tough on the beloved cousin of a future ally? Serbs understand this. Unless American force refutes their presumptions, they are likely to remain flexibly obdurate. Here we have a classic case of realpolitik.

US nuclear indulgence of Israel, and efforts to prevent another country in the region from becoming Israel's atomic equal, is also comprehensible. In the Middle East, the "Vietnam syndrome" compelled a search for "regional influentials" to serve as proxies for American power. Iran and Israel were picked to play this role. Despite $20 billion in American arms, the shah fell. Israel remained an acclaimed "strategic ally." When a peace settlement is reached with its remaining Arab adversaries, Israel's role as regional power can become legitimate with Arab allies—unless another nuclear country emerges to upset the arrangement.

As ever, then, the basis for hope lies not in the policies of states but in the sensibilities of ordinary people—in their unwillingness to tolerate intolerable violence or to be silenced by the unspeakable cruelties that define the international system. But here, too, the signs are not good. Throughout the Bosnian tragedy, the peace movement has been nearly inert. For three decades, activist coalitions in the United States and Europe have manifested a certain will and resourcefulness in organizing morally compelling protests on significant foreign policy issues—from the Vietnam War and apartheid to Central America and the nuclear arms race. Their passivity in the face of genocide provides grounds for deep pessimism about the current period.

[1993]

# 20 / TERRORISM

Theirs and Ours

By 1942, the Holocaust was occurring, and a certain liberal sympathy with the Jewish people had built up in the Western world. At that point, the terrorists of Palestine, who were Zionists, suddenly started to be described, by 1944–1945, as "freedom fighters." At least two Israeli prime ministers, including Menachem Begin, actually had bounties on their heads. You can find copies of posters with their pictures, saying "Terrorist, Reward This Much." The highest reward I have noted so far was one hundred thousand British pounds on the head of Menachem Begin, the terrorist.

Then from 1969 to 1990, the PLO, the Palestine Liberation Organization, occupied center stage as *the* terrorist organization. Yasser Arafat has been described repeatedly by the great sage of American journalism, William Safire of the *New York Times*, as the "Chief of Terrorism." That's Yasser Arafat.

Thus, on September 29, 1998, I was rather amused to notice a picture of Yasser Arafat to the right of President Bill Clinton. To his left is Israeli prime minister Benjamin Netanyahu. Clinton is looking toward Arafat, and Arafat is looking literally like a meek mouse. Just a few years earlier, he used to appear with a very menacing look about him, with a gun appearing from his belt. You remember those pictures, and you will perhaps also remember the next one.

In 1985, President Ronald Reagan received a group of bearded men in the White House. I was writing about these bearded men in those days in the *New Yorker*. They were very ferocious-looking bearded men with turbans who looked as though they came from another century. After receiving them, President Reagan spoke to the press. He pointed toward them, I'm sure some of you will recall that moment, and said, "These men are the moral equivalent of America's founding fathers." These were the Afghan Mujahideen. They were at the time, guns in hand, battling the Evil Empire. They were the moral equivalent of our founding fathers!

In August 1998, another American president ordered missile strikes from the American navy based in the Indian Ocean to kill Osama bin Laden and his men in the camps in Afghanistan. I do not wish to embarrass you with the reminder that Mr. bin Laden, whom fifteen American missiles were fired to hit in Afghanistan, was only a few years ago the moral equivalent of George Washington and Thomas Jefferson! He got angry over the fact that he was demoted from "moral equivalent" of your "founding fathers." And he is taking out his anger in different ways. I'll come back to that subject more seriously in a moment.

I have recalled all these stories to point out to you that the matter of terrorism is rather complicated. Terrorists change. The terrorist of yesterday is the hero of today, and the hero of yesterday becomes the terrorist of today. This is a serious matter in the constantly changing world of images in which we have to keep our heads straight to know what is terrorism and what is not. But, more importantly, to know what causes it, and how to stop it.

The next point about terrorism is that a posture of inconsistency necessarily evades definition. If you are not going to be consistent, you're not going to define. I have examined at least twenty official documents on terrorism. Not one defines the word. All of them explain it polemically, to arouse our emotions rather than exercise our intelligence. I give you only one example that is representative. October 25, 1984. George Shultz, then secretary of state of the US, is speaking at the New York Park Avenue Synagogue. It's a long speech on terrorism. In the State Department bulletin of seven single-spaced pages, there is not a single definition of terrorism. What we get is the following:

Definition number one: "Terrorism is a modern barbarism that we call terrorism."

Definition number two is even more brilliant: "Terrorism is a form of political violence." Aren't you surprised? It is a form of political violence, says George Shultz, secretary of state of the US.

Number three: "Terrorism is a threat to Western civilization."

Number four: "Terrorism is a menace to Western moral values."

Do these "definitions" tell you anything? Or do anything other than arouse your emotions? This is typical. They don't define terrorism because definitions involve a commitment to analysis, comprehension, and adherence to some norms of consistency. That's the second characteristic of the official literature on terrorism.

The third characteristic is that the absence of definition does not prevent officials from being globalistic. We may not define terrorism, but it is a menace to the moral values of Western civilization. It is a menace also to mankind. We are assured that it's a menace to good order. Therefore you must stamp it out worldwide. Antiterrorist policies therefore have to be global. Same speech of George Shultz: "There is no question about our ability to use force where and when it is needed to counter terrorism." There is no geographical limit. On a single day, missiles hit Afghanistan and Sudan. Those two countries are 2,300 miles apart, and they were hit by missiles belonging to a country roughly 8,000 miles away. Reach is global.

A fourth characteristic: claims of power are not only globalist, they are also omniscient. We know where they are, therefore we know where to hit. We have the means to know. We have the instruments of knowledge. We are omniscient. Shultz: "We know the difference between terrorists and freedom fighters, and as we look around, we have no trouble telling one from the other." Only Osama bin Laden doesn't know. He was an ally one day and an enemy another. That's very confusing for Osama bin Laden. I'll come back to his story toward the end.

Five. The official approach eschews causation. You don't look at why anybody becomes a terrorist. Cause? What cause? Looking for causes might make us sympathetic to these people. The *New York Times*, December 18, 1985, reported that the foreign minister of Yugoslavia, you remember the days when there was a Yugoslavia, requested the secretary of state of the US to consider the causes of Palestinian terrorism. The secretary of state, George Shultz, and I am quoting from the *New York Times*, "went a bit red in the face. He pounded the table and told the visiting foreign minister, there is no connection with any cause. Period." Why look for causes?

Number six. The moral revulsion that we must feel against terrorism is selective. We are to feel revulsion and the terror of those groups that are officially disapproved. We are to applaud the terror of those groups of whom officials do approve. Hence President Reagan, "I am a contra." He actually said that. We know that the contras of Nicaragua were by any definition terrorists. The media heed the official view of terrorism.

The dominant approach also excludes from consideration, more importantly to me, the terror of friendly governments. To that question I will return because it excused among others the terror of Pinochet, who killed one of my closest friends, Orlando Letelier, and it excused the terror of Zia ul-Haq, who killed many of my friends in Pakistan. According to my rough calculations, the ratio of people killed by the state terror of the Zia ul-Haq, Pinochet, Argentinian, Brazilian, Indonesian type versus the killing by the PLO and other nonstate terrorists is literally, conservatively, one hundred thousand to one. That's the ratio.

History unfortunately recognizes and accords visibility to power and not to weakness. In our time, the time that began with this day, Columbus Day, a time of extraordinary unrecorded holocausts, great civilizations have been wiped out. The Maya, the Inca, the Aztecs, the American Indians, the Canadian Indians were all wiped out. Their voices have not been heard, even to this day, fully. Now they are beginning to be heard, but not fully. They are heard, yes, but only when the dominant power suffers, only when resistance has a semblance of costing, of exacting a price. When a Custer is killed or when a Jordan is besieged. That's when you know that there were Indians fighting, Arabs fighting and dying.

My last point of this section—US policy in the Cold War period has sponsored terrorist regimes one after another. Somoza, Batista, all kinds of tyrants have been America's friends. You know that. Nicaragua, the contra, Afghanistan, the Mujahideen, El Salvador, etc.

Now the second side. There isn't much good on the other side, either. You shouldn't imagine that I have come to praise the other side. But keep the imbalance in mind and first ask ourselves, What is terrorism? Our first job should be to define the damn thing, name it, give it a description of some kind, other than "moral equivalent of the founding fathers" or "a moral outrage to Western civilization." Let us turn to *Webster's Collegiate Dictionary*: "Terror is an intense, overpowering fear . . . the use of terrorizing methods of governing or resisting a government." This simple definition has one great virtue, that of fairness. It focuses on the use of coercive violence, violence that is used illegally, extraconstitutionally, to coerce. And this definition treats terror for what it is, whether the government or private people commit it. Have you noticed something? Motivation is left out. We're not talking about whether the cause is just or unjust. We're talking about consensus, consent, absence of consent, legality, absence of legality, constitutionality, absence of constitutionality. Why do we keep motives out? Because motives differ. Motives differ and make no difference. In my work, I have identified five types of terrorism.

First, state terrorism. Second, religious terrorism; terrorism inspired by religion, Catholics killing Protestants, Sunnis killing Shiites, Shiites killing Sunnis, God, religion, sacred terror, you can call it, if you wish. Third, criminal terror. Think of the Mafia. All kinds of criminals commit terror. Fourth, there is pathological terror. You're sick. You want the attention of the whole world. You've got to kill a president. You terrorize. You hold up a bus. Fifth, there is political terror of the private group, be they Indian, Vietnamese, Algerian, Palestinian, Baader-Meinhof, the Red Brigades. Political terror of the private group. Oppositional terror.

Keep these five in mind. Keep in mind one more thing. Sometimes these five can converge on each other. You start with protest terror. You go crazy. You become pathological. You continue. They converge. State terror can take the form of private terror. For example, we're all familiar with the death squads in Latin America or in Pakistan. Government has employed private people to kill its opponents. It's not quite official. It's privatized. Convergence. Not only is there the political terrorist who goes crazy and becomes pathological, but there are also the criminals who join politics. In Afghanistan, in Central America, the CIA employed drug pushers in its covert operations. Drugs and guns often go together.

Of the five types of terror, the dominant focus is on only one, the least important in terms of cost to human lives and human property—the political terror of those who want to be heard. The highest cost is state terror. The second highest cost is religious terror, although in the twentieth century religious terror has, relatively speaking, declined. If you are looking historically, however, these are massive costs. The next highest in terms of cost is crime, then pathology. A Rand Corporation study by Brian Jenkins, for a ten-year period up to 1988, showed 50 percent of terror was committed without any political cause at all. No politics. Simply crime and pathology. So the official focus is on only one, the political terrorist, the PLO, bin Laden, etc. Why do they do it? What makes the terrorist tick? I would like to lay out some reasons quickly to you. First, the need to be heard. Imagine, we are dealing with the political, nonstate terrorist. Normally, and there are exceptions, there is an effort to get your grievances heard by those with power. They're not listening. A minority acts. The majority applauds.

The Palestinians, for example, the superterrorists of our time, were dispossessed in 1948. From 1948 to 1968, they went to every court in the world. They knocked at every door in the world. They were told that they became dispossessed because some radio told them to go away—an Arab radio, which was a lie. Nobody was listening to the truth. Finally, they invented a new form of terror, literally their invention: the airplane hijacking. Between 1968 and 1975, they pulled the world up by its ears. They dragged us out and said, Listen, Listen. We listened. We still haven't done them justice, but at least we all know. Even the Israelis acknowledge. Remember Golda Meir, prime minister of Israel, saying in 1970, "There are no Palestinians"? They do not exist. They damn well exist now. We are cheating them at Oslo. At least there are some people to cheat now. We can't just push them out. The need to be heard is essential. One motivation there.

Mix of anger and helplessness produces an urge to strike out. You are angry. You are feeling helpless. You want retribution. You want to wreak retributive justice. The experience of violence by a stronger party has historically turned victims into terrorists. Battered children are known to become abusive parents and violent adults. You know that. That's what happens to peoples and nations. When they are battered, they hit back. State terror very often breeds collective terror.

Do you recall the fact that the Jews were never terrorists? By and large, Jews were not known to commit terror except during and after the Holocaust. Most studies show that the majority of members of the worst terrorist groups in Israel or in Palestine, the Stern and the Irgun gangs, were people who were immigrants from the most anti-Semitic countries of Eastern Europe and Germany. Similarly, the young Shiites of Lebanon or the Palestinians from the refugee camps are battered people. They become very violent. The ghettos are violent internally. They become violent externally when there is a clear, identifiable external target, an enemy where you can say, "Yes, this one did it to me." Then they can strike back.

Example is a bad thing. Example spreads. There was a highly publicized Beirut hijacking of a TWA plane. After that hijacking, there were hijacking attempts at nine different American airports. Pathological groups or individuals modeling on the others. Even more serious are examples set by governments.

When governments engage in terror, they set very large examples. When they engage in supporting terror, they engage in other sets of examples.

Absence of revolutionary ideology is central to victim terrorism. Revolutionaries do not commit unthinking terror. Those of you who are familiar with revolutionary theory know the debates, the disputes, the quarrels, the fights within revolutionary groups of Europe, the fight between anarchists and Marxists, for example. But the Marxists have always argued that revolutionary terror, if ever engaged in, must be sociologically and psychologically selective. Don't hijack a plane. Don't hold hostages. Don't kill children, for God's sake. Have you recalled also that the great revolutions, the Chinese, the Vietnamese, the Algerian, the Cuban, never engaged in hijacking-type terrorism? They did engage in terrorism, but it was highly selective, highly sociological, still deplorable, but there was an organized, highly limited, selective character to it. So absence of revolutionary ideology that begins more or less in the post–World War II period has been central to this new terrorism.

My final question is this: these conditions have existed for a long time, but why then this flurry of private political terrorism? Why now so much of it, so visible? The answer is modern technology. You have a cause. You can communicate it through radio and television. They will all come swarming if you have taken an aircraft and are holding 150 Americans hostages. They will all hear your cause. You have a modern weapon through which you can shoot a mile away. They can't reach you. And you have modern means of communicating. When you put together the cause, the instrument of coercion, and the instrument of communication, a new kind of politics becomes possible.

To this challenge, rulers from one country after another have been responding with traditional methods. The traditional method of shooting it out, whether it's missiles or some other means. The Israelis are very proud of it. The Americans are very proud of it. The French became very proud of it. Now the Pakistanis are very proud of it. The Pakistanis say, "Our commandos are the best." Frankly, it won't work. A central problem of our time, political minds rooted in the past confronting modern times with their new realities. In conclusion, what is my recommendation to America?

First, avoid double standards. If you're going to practice double standards, you will be paid with double standards. Don't use them. Don't condone Israeli terror, Pakistani terror, Nicaraguan terror, El Salvadoran terror, on the one hand, and then complain about Afghan terror or Palestinian terror. It doesn't work. Try to be evenhanded. A superpower cannot promote terror in one place and reasonably expect to discourage terrorism in another place. It won't work in this shrunken world.

Do not condone the terror of your allies. Condemn them. Fight them. Punish them. Please eschew, avoid covert operations and low-intensity warfare. These are breeding grounds of terror and drugs. Violence and drugs are bred there. The structure of covert operations, I've made a film about it called *Dealing with the Demon* that has been very popular in Europe. I have shown that wherever there have been covert operations, there has been a major drug problem. Centers of covert operations have also been centers of the drug trade. Because the structure of covert operations, whether in Afghanistan, Vietnam, Nicaragua, or Central America, is very hospitable to drug trade. Avoid it. Give it up.

Please focus on causes and help ameliorate causes. Try to look at causes and solve problems. Do not concentrate on military solutions. Do not seek military solutions. Terrorism is a political problem. Seek political solutions. Diplomacy works.

Take the example of the last attack on bin Laden. You don't know what you're attacking. They say they know, but they don't know. They were trying to kill Gadhafi. They killed his four-year-old daughter. The poor baby hadn't done anything. Gadhafi is still alive. They tried to kill Saddam Hussein. They killed Laila bin Attar, a prominent artist, an innocent woman. They tried to kill bin Laden and his men. Not one but twenty-five other people died. They tried to destroy a chemical factory in Sudan. Now they are admitting that they destroyed an innocent factory. One-half of the production of medicine in Sudan has been destroyed, not a chemical factory. You think you know. You don't know.

Four of your missiles fell in Pakistan. One was slightly damaged. Two were totally damaged. One was totally intact. For ten years, the American government has kept an embargo on Pakistan because Pakistan is trying, stupidly, to build nuclear weapons and missiles. So we have a technology embargo on my country. One of the missiles was intact. What do you think a Pakistani official told the *Washington Post*? He said it was a gift from Allah. We wanted US technology. Now we have got the technology, and our scientists are examining this missile very carefully. It fell into the wrong hands. So look for political solutions. Do not look for military solutions. They cause more problems than they solve.

Please help reinforce and strengthen the framework of international law. There was a criminal court in Rome. Why didn't they go to it first to get their warrant against bin Laden, if they have some evidence? Get a warrant, then go after him. Internationally. Enforce the UN. Enforce the International Court of Justice. This unilateralism makes us look very stupid.


## Q&A

I mentioned that I would go somewhat into the story of bin Laden, the Saudi in Afghanistan, and didn't, so could I go into some detail? The point about bin Laden is roughly the same as the point to be made about Sheikh Abdul Rahman, who was accused and convicted of encouraging the blowing up of the World Trade Center in New York City. The *New Yorker* did a long story on him. It's the same as the case of Aimal Kansi, the Pakistani Baluch who was convicted of the murder of two CIA agents. Jihad, which has been translated a thousand times as "holy war," is not quite that. "Jihad" is an Arabic word that means "to struggle." It could be struggle by violent or nonviolent means. There are two forms, the small jihad and the big jihad. The small jihad involves violence. The big jihad involves struggles with the self. Those are the concepts. The reason I mention this is that, in Islamic history, jihad as an international violent phenomenon had disappeared in the last four hundred years, for all practical purposes. It was revived suddenly with American help in the 1980s. When the Soviet Union intervened in Afghanistan, Zia ul-Haq, the military dictator of Pakistan, which borders on Afghanistan, saw an opportunity and launched a jihad there against godless communism. The US saw a God-sent opportunity to mobilize one billion Muslims against what Reagan called the Evil Empire. Money started pouring in. CIA agents starting going all over the Muslim world recruiting people to fight in the great jihad. Bin Laden was one of the early prize recruits. He was not only an Arab. He was also a Saudi. He was not only a Saudi. He was also a multimillionaire, willing to put his own money into the matter. Bin Laden went around recruiting people for the jihad against communism.

I first met him in 1986. He was recommended to me by an American official who may have been an agent. I asked the American, "Who are the Arabs here who would be very interesting to interview?" By "here" I meant in Afghanistan and Pakistan. He said, "You must meet Osama." I went to see

Osama. There he was, rich and bringing in recruits from Algeria, from Sudan, from Egypt, just like Sheikh Abdul Rahman. This fellow was an ally. He remained an ally. He turns at a particular moment. In 1990, the US goes into Saudi Arabia with force. Saudi Arabia is the holy place of Muslims, Mecca, and Medina. There had never been foreign troops there. In 1990, during the Gulf War, they went in, in the name of helping Saudi Arabia defeat Saddam Hussein. Osama bin Laden remained quiet. Saddam was defeated, but the American troops stayed on in the land of the kaba (the sacred site of Islam in Mecca), foreign troops. He wrote letter after letter, saying, Why are you here? Get out! You came to help, but you have stayed on. Finally, he started a jihad against the other occupiers. His mission is to get American troops out of Saudi Arabia. His earlier mission was to get Russian troops out of Afghanistan. See what I was saying earlier about covert operations?

A second point to be made about him is these are tribal people, people who are really tribal. Being a millionaire doesn't matter. Their code of ethics is tribal. The tribal code of ethics consists of two words: loyalty and revenge. You are my friend. You keep your word, I am loyal to you. You break your word, I go on my path of revenge. For him, America has broken its word. The loyal friend has betrayed. The one to whom you swore blood loyalty has betrayed you. They're going to go for you. They're going to do a lot more.

These are the chickens of the Afghanistan war coming home to roost. This is why I said to stop covert operations. There is a price attached to them that the American people cannot calculate.

[1998]

## 21 / A TIME TO REMEMBER

Today, at Cold War's end, as the West celebrates the collapse of the "Evil Empire," Muslims of Bosnia are the objects of "ethnic cleansing." In a world inhabited by nearly a billion Muslims, this is a euphemism for religious genocide. For, like their Serb tormentors, Bosnia's Muslims are ethnic Slavs whose ancestors had converted to Islam following the Ottoman conquest in 1463 A.D. Then, too, Christian intolerance had provided the backdrop to their conversion. A majority of Bosnian converts to Islam had belonged to a Christian sect, the Bogomil, that was cruelly persecuted by both the Western Catholic [Croat] and the Eastern Orthodox Church [Serb]. At Communism's end, they are victims again of revived religious hatred, territorial ambitions, and an indifferent world.

Muslims are targets today of a two-pronged genocidal drive from Serbia and Croatia. The Croats, victims themselves of Serbian aggression, were until recently allied to Muslims. But after attaining independence, in a deal with Serbia that was calculated to isolate the Muslims, Croatia's president, Franjo Tudjman, has begun a murderous drive to slice some territories off tiny Bosnia. Two and a half million people have already been displaced. Countless persons have been killed, 850, 000 survivors remain besieged. Stories abound, each more horrifying than the other, of the agonies of survival. The world, Western no less than Islamic, looks on, the one callously, the other helplessly. It is a mockery of the so-called World Order and ad nauseam shamelessly touted solidarity of the ummah.

Four questions arise: Where is the United States, whose president, and Congress, and secretaries of state and defense had been so loudly proclaiming, barely eighteen months ago, that aggression shall go unpunished never again? Where are the powerful European governments, members all of NATO, on whose continent a holocaust is happening again? Where are the governments of key Muslim countries—Egypt, Pakistan, Saudi Arabia—ummah invokers all whose shamelessness matches only their boundless greed for wealth and power? Answer these questions, and you shall get a realistic portrait of World Disorder in the Age of the Market.

George Bush's quietism over naked aggression in the Balkans appears in sharp contrast to his activism in the Gulf. As excuse, he cites the absence of public opinion in favor of forceful American policy against Serbia. We all know, and to their credit most American commentators have pointed out, that he is lying. Public opinion did not influence US policy in the Gulf. To the contrary, policy mobilized public opinion. Moreover, American people are not at all averse to a forceful American role in putting an end to Serb atrocities. That is why Bill Clinton—no humanist, he—has taken up Bosnia's cause.

The explanation for the Gulf/Balkans contrast lies in the crisis of American power and the importance Washington attaches to the Middle East as a vehicle of overcoming that crisis. More than a decade ago, scholars had argued that the causes of American decline lay in the changing economic rather than strategic balance. Therefore the weakening of Soviet power cannot substantially resolve the crisis of American power.

US policy makers also understood that their real difficulty lay in the loss of economic and strategic leverage over Japan and the Common Market countries. When strategic equations change, they are not easily altered. Similarly, it is extremely difficult to reverse global economic trends like the rise of Japan and Germany as economic giants. It seemed relatively easier, on the other hand, to establish American domination over the Middle East on whose energy resources depended the economies of Europe and Japan.

The quest for new leverage over old allies led Washington to seek new configurations of pro-American power in the Middle East. Its buildup of Israel and Iran as primates of Pax Americana was an aspect of this quest. So were its promotion of the Camp David Accord, its massive arms sales to Saudi Arabia, its secret dealings with Iraq, and its hostility to revolutionary Iran, which alone appeared to challenge its Middle Eastern agenda. The Balkans, by contrast, cannot serve as a leverage over Europe or Japan. Rather, instability in the Balkans can only expose Europe's vulnerabilities and its shortage of political will. If it moves under public pressure to help end the tragedy of Bosnia, Washington will do so only after the yellow underbelly of Western Europe has been fully exposed.

If the exposure of Europe's collapsed will is what the US has so cruelly waited for, it is time for it to move forcefully. For we can all testify that Western Europe is prostrate, satiated by consumerism and fattened by affluence. Countless wars of colonial conquests, two world wars, the concentration camps and gas chambers of Auschwitz and Dachau have obviously inured it to new faces of fascism. Europe is too exhausted, it seems, from centuries of imperialism and war to assume a responsible role in a changing world. And it is much too contented to care.

As for the well-touted ummah, it is difficult to recall a more demoralized and corrupt community in the annals of history. Each of the thirty-odd "Islamic" governments is dominated by self-serving rulers and country sellers. With the exception perhaps of Iran, all are beholden to a foreign power more than to their own people. All are addicted to armaments and to dependence on suppliers. All are littered with machines but command no technology. Not one is home to a university or research center of repute. They lack the will no less than know-how necessary to transform wealth into capital, importance into influence, resource into power.

Above all, those "Islamic" dictatorships and monarchies have, by and large, sapped the will and morale of the people. There were more demonstrations against Israel's invasion of Lebanon in 1982 in Israel than there were in the Muslim world, and more concern is being expressed over Bosnia's fate in the US and Europe than by the ummah. Under the circumstances, we are acted upon regularly in places as far apart as Kashmir, Palestine, and Bosnia. We are not actors. Iran has called for an emergency meeting of the Organization of Islamic Countries to decide a course of action concerning Bosnia. As a tactical move to expose Muslim bankruptcy, it will work. A decisive meeting of OIC is not imaginable in these scoundrel times.

Is there any hope then for Bosnia? There is only a slim hope. It lies in the arousal of public opinion worldwide. We need to pressure individual governments to take concrete steps to save Bosnia. We must protest the criminal negligence of the great powers and condemn their selective use of the United Nations.

We must demand: that a UN-sponsored force immediately intervene to end Serbian and Croatian aggression; that if the UN fails to act, the OIC must expeditiously constitute an expeditionary force to rescue Bosnia unilaterally; that Serbia's leaders be tried under Nuremberg Laws; that reconstruction of Bosnia be started immediately upon the cessation of hostilities.

Other ominous crises loom if the world fails to save Bosnia and Bosnians: The ethnic mosaic of Eastern Europe, the former USSR, and the Balkans has come unglued with the end of Communism. Far too many majority governments are poised to oppress and obliterate minorities. Their dark designs shall be encouraged if Serbia continues to enjoy immunity. Above all, Israel may be emboldened to fulfill its long-held dream of "ethnic cleansing" and begin the process of what Zionist zealots call "transferring the Palestinian" from the remnants of their occupied homeland.

[1992]

## 22 / WELCOME WAR IN BOSNIA

War has finally begun in Bosnia. It is a development most humanists should welcome. For thirty-one months, the world had been witness to genocide. It carried all the insignia of an earlier holocaust—an exclusionary nationalist ideology, the stated goal of ethnic cleansing, concentration camps, emptied towns and burnt villages, refugees in the millions, and ceaseless suffering. It carried also its own special signature—rape camps—that were discovered in the United Nations Year of the Woman. The great Western powers that had sworn, for five uninterrupted decades, to let it happen "Never Again," acknowledged that a genocide was in progress but let it go on at the center of their enlightened world. At Cold War's end, supreme moment of the triumph of the free world, humankind was given a long plunge into the heart of darkness.

As though indifference was not enough, in this instance the world powers effectively aided the aggressor by maintaining an arms embargo on the landlocked victims. Their studious waffling has been worthy of a comic opera. Take note of these howlers: The UN Security Council passed resolutions while ensuring that they shall not be enforced. URNA peacekeeping forces were sent to Bosnia without a mandate to stop even open slaughter of civilians. Western leaders and UN officials have described the Serb assault on Bosnia, a UN member, as "aggression" and, also officially, proposed rewarding the aggressor a hefty 49 percent of Bosnian territory. Bosnia's besieged government accepted this unjust peace proposal. The Serbs rejected it. This is where things stood on October 25, 1994, when war miraculously began in Bosnia.

For one who has brooded over the Bosnian tragedy, this has been a week of relief. In the northwest, the Bosnian army's V-Corps has been gaining dramatically in pincer moves. It has reclaimed more than a hundred miles of territory from the Serbs in the Bihac pocket. The Serb forces are reported to be fleeing in disarray, abandoning significant amounts of weapons in an unusual display of panic.

Success improves relationships. By November 2, the Croats had joined the Bosnians in capturing the strategically important town of Kupres which Serb forces had captured and "cleansed" in April 1992. When the Bosnian army consolidates this gain, it will open the strategic highway between central Bosnia and Croatia's major seaport at Split, thus ending Bosnia's crippling handicap: its logistical isolation.

The rebound of the Bosnian army's V-Corps offers a lesson to defeatists who abound in the contemporary Third World. Ill equipped and ill trained, it had been fighting desperate rearguard battles in the Bihac area. The town of Bihac, where thousands of people from the neighboring villages have taken refuge of sorts, was declared a safe haven by the UN. But the Serbs continued to shell it from surrounding hills they held.

The V-Corp's story is especially dramatic, but the improvement in Bosnia's fighting capability is broad based. Its training and morale have improved. It has improvised backyard factories to produce arms and ammunition. It has taken initiatives to capture enemy weapons. Above all, since last March when US officials helped restore the severed alliance between Croatia and Bosnia, landlocked Bosnians gained some access to supply routes and received modest amounts of arms.

For those countries and peoples who care for the fate of Bosnia, it will be a mistake to assume that these developments assure an end to Bosnian suffering. Their survival as a sovereign people remains in question. Serb leaders have threatened a forceful counteroffensive; the threat should be taken seriously. As they lose ground, the Serb forces shall most likely receive renewed support from Belgrade. If the Bosnians are starved for supply, they could again be facing genocide rather than ending the war successfully.

In this context, the Muslim world has a special responsibility to aid the Bosnians, who are victims not only of fascist aggression but also of liberal callousness that has roots in the Western world's anti-Muslim prejudices. It is thus that it has permitted aggression and genocide against the most multicultural and universalistic among contemporary Muslim states. During 1991–1993,

Muslim governments failed abjectly to challenge and break the European powers' unjust and irresponsible arms embargo on Bosnia. In a post–Cold War world in which the great powers are probing for vacuums and vulnerable world spots, that failure has been costly already, not only to the Bosnians but also to the future of the Middle East and, possibly, South Asia. The rebound of Bosnian resistance offers Muslim governments a second opportunity to help Bosnia. On our part, people the world over have a moral and political responsibility to organize, on as large scale as possible, aid to Bosnia.

At the UN, there is talk again of lifting the arms embargo. The United States favors it. France and Britain do not. And Russia opposes militantly. It is a can of worms better left to the big powers, who at best will keep the embargo for another year. What is desperately needed is the immediate start of quiet and unpublicized aid to Bosnia. Recent Bosnian territorial gains have made the passage of aid possible for the first time. It would require a modicum of organization, which Bosnians have; modest amounts of arms and money, which Muslim governments do have; and a certain will to sovereignty and solidarity that our rulers lack and will have to muster.

[1994]

# 23 / AMERICA'S GULF WAR

Neglected Perspectives

Few countries mobilize against the "other side" as quickly and thoroughly as docs the United States. This culture of belligerent conformity was weakened during the Vietnam War when a handful of enlightened dissenters, aided by mounting American costs and casualties, shattered the Cold War consensus. The age of dissent lasted, alas, for barely a decade and a half.

President Ronald Reagan's military intervention in Grenada and George Bush's invasion of Panama marked the end of America's splendid affliction with the "Vietnam Syndrome." Their responses to the latest crisis in the Middle East suggest that Congress and the media have decisively overcome the nascent habit of casting a critical eye at flexed American muscles. The costs, apart from injury to Arab and Muslim sensibilities, are disturbed perspectives and misleading analyses.

In order to establish the uniqueness of Iraq's aggression, the press has repeatedly stated that in the contemporary period, no Arab country had invaded another. The statement obfuscates the more relevant fact that in recent decades invasions and annexations have been routinely carried out in the Middle East. Until it reacted to the Iraqi adventure, the United States had aided and condoned them all.

The United Nations has been widely praised in the US for its resolution condemning Iraq and imposing sanctions against it. In the Middle East, it was remembered that in 1982 similar sanctions against Israel's immensely more destructive invasion of Lebanon were vetoed by the United States. President George Bush could not be credible to any Arab when he spoke, on August

7th, of his standing up "in the American tradition" for national sovereignty, self-determination, and the "inadmissibility of territorial acquisition by force."

For the Arab people, this has been an era of grief and humiliations. Never before had they experienced a similar combination of wealth and weakness, material resources and moral bankruptcy. In the age of decolonization, they alone are subject to conquest and colonization. Since the end of World War II, five Arab countries—Palestine, Jordan, Syria, Lebanon, and Egypt—have lost all or part of their land to Israel. Egypt finally regained Sinai but at the cost of betraying the others and isolating itself from its Arab milieu. All Arab states, including those that have united under American leadership to oppose Iraqi aggression, stood by when Israel invaded Lebanon in 1982 and destroyed even Beirut, the Middle East's financial capital. Bitter cynicism now greets their avowedly "principled" stand against Iraq.

Saddam Hussein's ambitions, and the ambivalence with which Middle Eastern people have greeted his Kuwait adventure, are better understood in the context of Arab politics than as a function of his paltry gains in the war with Iran. Throughout the 1980s, a power vacuum existed in the Arab world. With the decline of the Ottoman Empire late in the eighteenth century, Egypt had emerged as the leader in Arab politics. With Cairo as its cultural and economic metropolis, it held the balance of power and influence in the region. In the era of decolonization, its role as the ideological leader and power broker pre-empted the ambitions of lesser players like Syria and Iraq. Its championship of nonalignment and sacrifices for the Palestinian cause conferred upon it legitimacy and authority. The Camp David Accord drastically altered this equation.

In signing a separate peace with Israel, Anwar Sadat had put his faith in a step-by-step but comprehensive settlement of the Israeli-Arab conflict. The actual results were the opposite of Egyptian expectations and American promises. After making peace with its most populous and powerful Arab enemy, Israel proceeded to colonize and conquer the others with ruthless impunity. There were two invasions of Lebanon; the second, in 1982, was more far-reaching and destructive than the other. It took three years of bloodshed and violent resistance to obtain Israel's partial withdrawal. A portion of Lebanon remains under Israeli control. Syria's extensive Golan Heights were annexed, as was Jerusalem earlier, into Israel. The complicity of the United States, Israel's provider, in these developments was self-evident. It does not take Arab xenophobia or Muslim fundamentalism to be skeptical about President Bush's assertions of the inadmissibility of territorial acquisition by force.

Of Camp David's commitment to autonomy in the West Bank and Gaza, Gayez Sayigh, the Palestinian historian, had written bitterly: "A fraction of the Palestinian people (under one-third of the whole) is promised a fraction of its rights (not including the national right to self-determination and statehood) in a fraction of its homeland (less than one-fifth of the area of the whole)." Soon after it had been made, this meager commitment became a dead letter when the Israeli prime minister declared that the "autonomy" will apply to the people, not the territories. Only days after the treaty had been signed, Israel announced the establishment of new Jewish settlements in the Occupied Territories; it was a violation, so President Jimmy Carter would confirm, of promises made at Camp David. The Israeli announcement heralded a campaign of accelerated colonization, a systematic assault on the four elements of Palestinian life—land, water, leaders, and culture—without which no community can long survive.

After Egypt's alienation, popular expectations had turned, unreasonably but understandably, toward Saudi Arabia and its clients in the Gulf. They had glitter and gold. Multinational corporations sought their favors. Bankers relied on their investments. The dollar owed its hegemony to their preferences. They should have been able to translate their economic power and strategic value into political and diplomatic leverage and bring some relief to the beleaguered and dishonored region.

Saudi Arabia responded to popular expectations with military buildup and active diplomacy. It entered the American arms bazaar, an extravagant buyer. Its diplomatic efforts led to the ceasefire brokered by a US official, Philip C. Habib, between the PLO and Israel that the latter broke when it invaded Lebanon.

The sheikhs, led by Saudi Arabia, pleaded with Washington to save Arab face and their dynastic future. But they are prisoners of dependence and uneven development. They have acquired wealth without working and make enormous profits without producing. Their countries are littered with expensive machines, but they have no technology. Their economies are run by foreigners. Their investments have tied them symbiotically to America. They own billions of dollars but control no capital. They lack the will and capacity to translate wealth into power. Their diplomacy was reduced to buying favor and pleading fairness. As expectations failed, they became objects of contempt. The power vacuum in the Arab world came to be increasingly and palpably felt.

The first clear signal that Iraq, not Syria, was keen to fill the vacuum in the Middle East came when Saddam Hussein invaded Iran. Instead of discouraging his adventure, the United States quickly helped Saudi Arabia and Kuwait supply Iraq with no less than US $60 billion in aid. The monster, if that is what Saddam Hussein is, was made by them.

Iraq has unquestionably committed aggression. It would be unwise, especially for the Arab states, to acquiesce in Saddam Hussein's annexation of Kuwait. The problem may have been susceptible to a regional solution. Until the American intervention invested him with the glow of heroism, Saddam Hussein was an isolated dictator, in deep debt especially to Saudi Arabia, and desperately in need of access to the world market. Major Arab states—Egypt, Jordan, Syria, Algeria, even Morocco—favored a regional approach. But the deposed sheikh was disheartened, and the Saudis were worried enough to have yielded to US suggestions that their forces be invited in.

The United States was keen to intervene. Since the late 1960s, it has viewed the control of oil as a necessary leverage and balancing mechanism in its increasingly contradictory relations with Europe and Japan. Iraq offered an opportunity to increase the American stranglehold in the Persian Gulf. George Bush was keen to grasp it. The media aided him, immoderately comparing Hussein to Hitler, raising the specter of Munich, and of the West's economic collapse.

[1990]

We live in scoundrel times. This is the dark age of Muslim history, the age of surrender and collaboration, punctuated by madness. The decline of our civilization started in the eighteenth century when, in the intellectual embrace of orthodoxy, we skipped the Age of Enlightenment and the scientific revolution. In the second half of the twentieth century, it has fallen.

I have been a lifelong witness to surrender and imagined so many times—as a boy in 1948, a young man in 1967, again in 1971, and approaching middle age in 1982—that finally we have hit rock-bottom, that the next time even if we go down we would manage to do so with a modicum of dignity. Fortunately, I did not entertain even so modest an illusion from Saddam Hussein's loudly proclaimed "mother of battles."

The hundred-hour war is over. It was a status quo war, a war of restorations and vindications. The al-Sabahs and their "disco Arabs" have reclaimed their kingdom. *Ahlan wa Sahlan*! [Thanks for coming! Be sure to come back!] Iraq and Kuwait are ruins strewn with uncounted dead and unclaimed wounded. The house of Saud, which in Islam's name prevents Muslim women even from driving automobiles, has been "saved" by, among others, thirty-five thousand uniformed and—*na 'uzu billah* [God save us]—unveiled American women.

The United States claims victory. "By God," exclaimed George Bush, president of the United States, "we've kicked the Vietnam syndrome once and for all," as if Iraq's was a revolution or its defeat would discourage authentic revolutions from challenging imperial power. Saddam Hussein—no Ho Chi

Minh, he—still rules his "republic of fear." Israel remains firmly in occupation of south Lebanon, Syria's Golan Heights, the West Bank, Gaza, and al-Quds (Jerusalem). And Prime Minister Nawaz Sharif declares that Pakistan's policy—if a posture of half pregnancy can be called policy—has been "vindicated." It is now open season for the contractors, contactors, and country sellers of the Middle East. To the detriment of our long-term national interest, much of Pakistan's ruling elite openly salivates on the sidelines for a piece of the pie.

But the status quo cannot hold. The Gulf War is not likely to yield, as George Bush so ingenuously promised, a "new world order" or a "second American Century." Washington is undoubtedly seeking to extend into the twenty-first the "American Century" that, thanks partly to the Vietnamese, ended in a mere twenty-five years. But it is likely to fail because the rest of the world is neither as softheaded nor as subservient as the dictators and monarchs of the Middle East. More importantly, America's flexed military muscles rest on declining economic arms. This has been a common ailment of imperialism throughout history. From Thucydides to Paul Kennedy, historians have diagnosed it to be a violence-inducing but terminal affliction.

War, Karl Marx once said, is the midwife of history. New realities are born after decisive wars. World War I marked the abolition of the Ottoman caliphate, the formal end to the Islamicate, and the colonization and division of the Middle East into nation-states; it impelled the October Revolution and the creation of the USSR and provided the environment for another great war. World War II decimated nations and peoples, dismantled the empires that had dominated the world for three centuries, inaugurated the nuclear age, and led to the rise of the USA and USSR as rival powers.

The Gulf War may prove less momentous. After all, it was from the beginning the winner's war, and absolutely avoidable. Also, British and American propaganda notwithstanding, Iraq is not Germany and Saddam is no Hitler, which is why even his defenses collapsed so precipitously, and he is still there. In fact, this was less a war than a technological massacre. It became a world-scale conflict because the United States chose to make it so, involving the United Nations, other Western powers, and a majority of abject Middle Eastern governments.

Furthermore, Washington elected to assert its paramountcy at a crucial point in history, when the USSR had opted out as a competing world power, and the world awaited alternatives. By intervening with a force out of proportion to Iraq's challenge, the US wanted to affirm its paramountcy as a unipolar global power. To a great extent, it succeeded. Now, it bears a burden more political than military. Failure to carry it will involve decisive and lasting costs.

The United States is ill equipped to confront the logic of its own ambitions. It is noteworthy that, in America's national security establishment, the pro-Israeli personalities, like Henry Kissinger and Stephen Solarz, stood out as active hawks both before and during the war. Prominent members of the American establishment who argued against the military option were concerned not about the war's outcome but about their government's capacity to meet the obligations of collectively waged conflict. If Washington fails now to uphold in the Middle East international laws and principles, which it invoked to justify the war option, it will undermine its Arab clients and sow the seeds of disorder, resistance, and revolution in the world's most strategic region.

The American approach to a single challenge will define its standing in the Middle East and ultimately in the world: the challenge of Israel. There are two dimensions to this challenge—territorial and nuclear. Both involve the security and sovereignty of all the states in the Middle East. President George Bush has himself defined the issues in simple, stark terms. He rejected compromise with Iraq and virtually destroyed an Arab country arguing that nuclear proliferation and acquisition of territory by force are absolutely unacceptable. The UN Charter and Security Council resolutions were not negotiable. His government must now deliver on these principles in relation to Israel. If it does not, there will be protracted ideological and political warfare throughout the region.

This was a war between Third World insanity and aggressive imperialism. Saddam Hussein betrayed demented ambition barely two years after becoming Iraq's president, in 1981, when he invaded Iran. His protracted and costly aggression received American encouragement and the unqualified support of Saudi Arabia and Kuwait. He failed to comprehend both the resiliency of Iran's revolutionary order and the danger to the region's future in America's anti-Iran stance.

Following his ill-conceived invasion of Kuwait, he showed no understanding of American objectives in the region, or its style of politics, or decision-making process. He bluffed himself and his people into destruction and defeat. He was too arrogant to heed advice and too insecure to tolerate dissent. Eventually, Iraq and Kuwait suffered as much from the distortions of dictatorship as from imperial violence.

There is a hidden history of America's Iraq war that awaits telling. It is to America's credit that its historians, like William Appleman Williams and Howard Zinn, have shown its past wars to be fraudulent and its commitments unreliable. But the consensus tends to prevail in times of war, including wars of aggression. The American media often accords priority to patriotism over principle and serves as an instrument of propaganda rather than of news and analysis. Thus the media hoodwinked the world with its biased stories of the origins and conduct of the Korean War. I. F. Stone, dissenting journalist and indefatigable investigator, exposed the lies in his obscure weekly and wrote *The Hidden History of the Korean War.*

The untold story of the Gulf War is available in fragments. Sometime soon I should piece it together for this space. The preparation for America's Gulf adventure began fifteen years ago when American forces began to train for desert warfare, when the Gulf became a primary focus of the modernized American navy, when the Rapid Deployment Forces were created, and when Israel was chosen to be a strategic asset. Specifically, the campaign against Saddam Hussein began in August 1988 and led in September of that year to the first congressional sanctions against Iraq. And the military preparation for intervention in the Gulf began in July 1990 well in advance of Saddam Hussein's invasion of Kuwait.

The United States had been ready and eager to enter when Saddam Hussein opened the door. That is the difference between rational and irrational exercise of power, collective planning and individual enterprise, between adventure and war, above all, between Western imperialism and Third World insanity. It is hardly surprising that discipline has prevailed over indulgence; insanity has been defeated, and imperialism has won.

[1991]

## 25 / COVERING THE MIDDLE EAST

In previous articles, I have discussed how biased were the American media generally, and particularly the *New York Times*, in covering the crisis and war in the Gulf. Today, we consider the price of the bias. Here is a list of nine crucial failures that, taken together, amounted to denying the public a perspective on the crisis.

One: Virtually no explanation was offered of President Saddam Hussein's extraordinary ambition. After all, he has been effectively in power for two decades, as president of Iraq since 1979. Yet he became identified as a villain only recently. If this question were allowed, the Camp David Accords would inevitably have emerged as a defining event. Camp David worsened the plight of the beleaguered Palestinians and isolated Egypt—since the early nineteenth century, the political center of the Arab world—from its Arab milieu.

Smaller players attempted to fill the resulting vacuum. Saudi Arabia tried to buy American arms worth billions of dollars and, in partnership with the UK, mediated a cease-fire between the PLO and Israel. It failed when Israel invaded Lebanon in 1982, killing more than twenty thousand people and destroying cities, including Beirut, the cultural and commercial capital of the Middle East. Saddam Hussein betrayed his ambition to lead the region when he invaded Iran. The US encouraged and the Saudis and Kuwaitis financed his aggression. The monster, if that is what President Hussein is, was helped to grow by US policies in the region. His latest crime was not that he committed aggression but that he did so without Washington's approval.

Two: The media noted that there existed popular Arab-Muslim sentiment against the US-led intervention in the Gulf. But scant attempt was made to explain why. On the rare occasion when an explanation was sought, most reporters relied on the so-called experts, who spout supercilious bromides about Arab insecurity, xenophobia, and fundamentalism. The simple answers were strenuously avoided: no Middle Easterner could possibly take seriously President George Bush's assertions about the unacceptability of territorial acquisition by force or the necessity of upholding the UN Charter. After all, the US has been sustaining Israel's occupation of Palestinian, Syrian, and Lebanese territories and has continually frustrated UN efforts to uphold its charter in the Middle East.

Furthermore, few informed Middle Easterners were unaware that for two decades the US had been enlarging its military presence in the Gulf and seeking a permanent presence there. Saddam Hussein merely opened the door to it.

Three: Hardly any attention was accorded to Middle Eastern governments that opposed the military option. The media praised the Bush administration's "masterly" diplomacy in gathering international consensus behind its intervention in the Gulf. But scarce attention was given to those who did not share that consensus. They included such historic pro-American "moderates" as Jordan, Tunisia, and Algeria, which had brokered the US out of several difficulties including the Iran hostage crisis.

King Hussein and the PLO did receive media notice, but they were grossly misrepresented. King Hussein in particular was portrayed as being pro-Iraq, a callous allegation in view of the fact that, with its new slogan of "Jordan is Palestine," powerful segments in Israel want the king eliminated and inhabitants of the Occupied Territories "transferred" to Jordan. In fact, the king opposed Iraq's invasion of Kuwait but argued that Iraqi withdrawal was better achieved by political means. It was not until the sixth week of US bombings that, responding to inflamed Jordanian opinion, King Hussein expressed solidarity with Iraq.

Four: Equally curious was the dearth of media attention to the politics and economics of oil that underlay the conflict. Oil is among those rare commodities whose price has consistently fallen since 1980, reaching a low in 1989 of $14 a barrel. Iraq wanted a higher OPEC price at around $25 per barrel; Kuwait resisted. Why? How could the interests of Kuwait, Saudi Arabia, and the Emirates be better served by low oil prices? One answer is that they have to feed fewer people, and plentiful oil is only one of several sources of their wealth. They are small countries with large reserves. They also own offshore refineries and massive investments in the Western, especially American, market.

Similarly, there was no discussion of oil pricing. It was acknowledged that Saudi Arabia and other producers were compensating for the shortfall from Iraq and Kuwait. Yet, while the supply and demand remained unchanged, prices rose. No major newspaper investigated the mechanism by which consumers' alleged anxieties translated into high prices, and no commentator asked why President Bush, who dispatched half a million soldiers to defend the "West's lifeline" in the Gulf, took no steps to punish the price fixers.

Five: The media ignored this obvious Middle Eastern anomaly: the more populous countries have small oil reserves, and the small sheikhdoms control vast reserves.

The rulers of the Gulf know the significance of this issue, which is one reason why many, including Saudi Arabia, do not conduct censuses and do not publish population figures. Could there be any truth in the popular belief that the imperial powers that drew the boundaries of nation-states in the region purposely delinked the wealth and the people of Middle East?

Six: There was an absence of inquiry into the purposes of America's unusually forceful intervention in the Gulf. It is common knowledge that starting in the early seventies the focus of American military and diplomatic attention shifted toward the Middle East. With Iran on its eastern flank and Israel to the west playing the role of Kissinger's much-vaunted "regional influentials," the Middle East became the centerpiece of the Nixon Doctrine.

Throughout the eighties, some eighty percent of total American military and economic aid went to three countries—Israel, Egypt, and Pakistan—in the region. The deployments of the modernized US Navy were concentrated in the Mediterranean and Indian oceans; the Rapid Deployment Force was created and remained geared for intervention in the Middle East. Old military bases in the region, like the one at Diego Garcia, were expanded; and new ones were sought in Bahrain, Oman, and Somalia. These decades-long planning and investments suggest purposes greater and more complex than were allowed in the public discourse.

Seven: There was no discussion about the meaning and uses of America's much-invoked "strategic alliance" with Israel. More than fifty billion dollars worth of US aid went into making Israel the world's third strongest military power, and all of it was justified on the grounds that Israel was a "strategic ally" in the Middle East.

The media reported at the outset of the Gulf crisis that Washington requested Israel to please do nothing, and Israel complied. In gratitude, President Bush promised significant increases in Israel's military aid. Praise for Israel's "restraint" reached a crescendo when Iraq's cynical Scud strikes failed to draw Israel into the conflict. As a reward for its "restraint," Israel requested another $13 billion in US aid. This unique situation presented the possibility of a revolutionary redefinition of the concepts both of strategic and alliance and deserved at least some discussion in the media.

Eight: President Bush claimed that he exhausted the possibility of negotiated settlement before going to war. The media failed to question this claim. In fact, George Bush spurned several opportunities for diplomacy. The only time he made a diplomatic gesture—when he invited Iraq's foreign minister to Washington and offered to send his secretary of state to Baghdad—Saddam Hussein responded with a dramatically generous, and stupid, gesture: he allowed all Americans to leave Iraq, giving Bush a free hand to bomb Iraq.

Nine: Officials invoked and the media repeatedly emphasized the menace to world security in Iraq's imminent possession of nuclear weapons. They have yet to discuss soberly the issue of nuclear proliferation.

Nuclear arms threaten human survival. A superpower that possesses an awesome nuclear arsenal bears a special responsibility to deal with this issue honestly and equitably. And this is precisely what is not happening in the US either at the governmental or public level. Official and academic experts generally agree that Iraq was years away from acquiring an operational nuclear capability. Pakistan is closer. India is nuclear capable, i.e., while it may not have manufactured the bombs, it can produce and deliver them. In all of South Asia and the Middle East, Israel alone actually possesses a nuclear arsenal estimated to contain between one hundred and two hundred boosted fission weapons and, thanks to US arms supplies, the capacity to deliver them to distant targets.

When American laws prohibiting aid to countries engaged in proliferation were invoked in the fall of 1990, American dailies including the *New York Times* praised the congressional action against Pakistan. Yet none even noted that the biggest violator, Israel, remains above the law or that unequal application of rules devalues law as well as its enforcer.

Volumes have been published on the effects of nuclear weapons on the Western psyche both at the conscious and subconscious level. No major newspaper or magazine in the West has thought it important to ask how the people of the Middle East feel about living, without any deterrence, under the shadow of Israeli nuclear weapons, the only country in the world without declared boundaries.

In thus ignoring our anxieties and aspirations, America's officials and its media have but one justification: a majority of Middle Eastern governments also ignore them and seek unconditional collaboration with an unjust and discriminatory imperial power.

[1991]

## 26 / AFTER THE WINTER BOMBS

As deadly missiles rain down on Baghdad, six verities ought to be restated. First, the target of the Anglo-American bombing campaign is not Iraq's arsenal of mass destruction. Chemical and biological weapons are nearly impossible to destroy from the air. The job UNSCOM inspectors could not do, bombs will not finish. The intent behind the bombing is murder—of Saddam Hussein, his family, and staff—and the destruction of his security services.

Among the targets hit on day one of the missile strikes were his daughter's home, the presidential palace, the Directorate of Military Intelligence Services, and the headquarters of the Republican Guards, an elite force that serves as Saddam Hussein's personal security force.

Second, the Vatican, of which the sentiment is normally pro-American, has told the truth in plain words. "This is aggression," said a statement issued from the Holy See. The American president and British prime minister invoked UN resolutions on Iraq to justify their violation of international laws and the UN Charter. The big lie nearly always accompanies aggression. The UN secretary general spoke thus: "It's a sad day for the United Nations and for the world. It is also a very very sad day for me personally."

In a rebuke rare from any secretary general, Kofi Annan said, "My thoughts tonight are with the people of Iraq and with the 370 UN humanitarian workers who remain in Iraq." In February 1991, Saddam Hussein committed aggression when he invaded Kuwait. For that crime, the Iraqi people were severely punished. Clinton and Blair have now equaled the score. No retributions await them except of history.

Third, denials notwithstanding, the bombings are linked with Bill Clinton's personal predicament. The surprise aggression occurred days before the House of Representatives was to vote on his impeachment. The bombs on Baghdad deflected attention from it, brought a reprieve of sorts by a few days, and possibly raised the already high public rating of the president. Whether he likes it or not, in the eyes of the world, Saddam Hussein and Monica Lewinsky hold hands with Bill Clinton. It is not a linkage the chief executive of the superpower should relish.

Fourth, the American proclivity to excessive violence is again on display. The phenomenon finds bipartisan expressions. Two administrations—one Democratic and the other Republican—dropped more bombs in Indochina than were used in World War II, killing an estimated four million peasants. In 1991, under Republican president George Bush, 2,600 American warplanes dropped 88,500 tons of bomb on Iraq. In 1998, a Democrat is emulating him, without, hopefully, matching the earlier levels of mass destruction.

Five, at the end of 1998 it is clear that even without the legitimizing framework of the Cold War, American interventionism is alive and thriving. With the exception of Britain's symbolic participation, the United States has committed this aggression alone, as it did when Clinton ordered the missile attacks on Sudan and Afghanistan. Therein lies a great danger to world peace and sovereignty of nations. Moral rhetoric cannot hide the fact that caprice and self-interest rather than concern for international law or justice informs American policy and interventions.

Israel's occupation of the West Bank, Gaza, and South Lebanon violates UN resolutions, its annexation of Jerusalem and the Golan violates the UN charter, and its colonization activities in the Occupied Territories violate the Geneva Conventions. Far from intervening to prevent its client from committing these unlawful acts, Washington aids and abets Israel. It is known also that Israel has stockpiled weapons of mass murder, including nuclear, chemical, and biological weapons. Yet not a word from Washington.

What will the US and Britain gain from this assault? Britain's gain is obvious and already made. It has earned American goodwill; the "cousinship" is affirmed yet again. On the American balance sheet, there appear to be many losses and no gain. The primary US objective in the Middle East is to maintain its hegemony there. That requires a measure of legitimacy for American power in the region and an environment relatively free of instability and popular discontent. The missiles of December will surely add to anti-American sentiments and political instability in the Middle East.

In the unlikely event that Saddam Hussein is killed, an American obsession will have been satisfied. Captain Ahab will get the great white whale. But fulfilling an obsession is not a viable policy objective. In fact, President Hussein is the likely winner, live or die. If he survives, he will be a hero to the Arab masses. Dead, he will be a martyr. Not that people are pathologically inclined. Rather, American double standards anger them. Moreover, they sense the great danger of living in the shadow of Israel's nuclear weapons. In a PR initiative just before the assault on Baghdad, Bill Clinton turned up in Gaza and spoke sympathetically of the Palestinians. Later, his war statement mentioned the holy month of Ramadan and his concern with Muslim sensibilities as a justification for hitting Baghdad now. Such palliatives cannot work while Jerusalem continues to be "Judaized" (an Israeli term), Jewish settlements expand onto Arab lands, and Israeli weapons of mass destruction hang over the Arabs.

Dictators rarely leave behind them an alternative leadership or a viable mechanism for succession. Saddam Hussein is not an exception. Disarray and confusion shall certainly ensue if Saddam Hussein is eliminated. Iraq is a greatly divided country, with the rebellious Kurds dominant in the north and Shias in the south. With the one linked to the Kurds in Turkey and the other to Shiite Iran, their ambitions in post-Saddam Iraq can cause upheavals in the entire region. It is not clear that the United States has either the will or the resources to undertake the remaking of Iraq. If it does not, the scramble over Iraq may ignite protracted warfare involving Turkey, Iran, Syria, Saudi Arabia, Israel, Kurd, Arab, Shia, Sunni, and, in one form or another, the United States.

The fundamentalist brand of Islamism may thrive in such an environment. Islamism will find at least two major sponsors in the struggle for Iraq. Iran borders on southern Iraq, which is home to the most sacred shrines of Shia Islam and is populated largely by Shia Muslims. Iran's influence may easily fill the post-Saddam vacuum, a development Saudi Arabia, the sheikhdoms of the Gulf, and the US shall find intolerable. Since none of America's conservative Arab allies like Arab nationalism (it favors secular government and Arab unity), they may counter Iran by promoting Sunni fundamentalism. Sectarian groups thrive in this brand of Islamism. Like Afghanistan today, Iraq may turn into a battleground of war parties backed by several states.

During and after the Gulf War I, I had argued that Islamic movements are likely to find fresh opportunities in the postwar Middle Eastern environment. The argument was that the political culture of the Middle East is message oriented. In the region where three great religions were born, the success and failure of dynasties, leaders, and movements have been defined often by their links to a legitimizing ideology. For many centuries, the struggles for power revolved around differing interpretations of Islam. In the nineteenth and twentieth centuries, secular nationalism gained hegemony. Secular nationalist movements led the founding of most nation-states and until the Iranian Revolution in 1979 dominated every state except Saudi Arabia and the Gulf sheikhdoms.

In the 1950s, the United States was alarmed by the assumption of power by nationalists like Mohammed Mossadegh in Iran, Abdul Nasser in Egypt, and the Baath Socialist parties in Syria and Iraq. Their rhetoric of nonalignment and anti-imperialism and nationalization of such multinational enterprises as Iranian oil and the Suez Canal were viewed as harmful to American and Western interests. Thence began the effort to undermine them. With the overthrow of Mossadegh in 1953 and defeat of Abdul Nasser in 1967, the influence of nationalism began to wane first in Iran and then in the Arab world. As the pro-Western alternative, like the shah's dictatorship, was unattractive to much of the populace, Islamism began its gradual rise.

One high point of the Islamic movement came when Iran's popular revolution, led by Ayatollah Khomeini's clerical followers, founded the Islamic Republic. Another historic watershed occurred when the United States and Saudi Arabia sponsored from Pakistan an international jihad against the evil empire. A third moment of opportunity may occur when the Iraqi dictator departs, the secular Baath regime collapses, and the struggle for Iraq begins.

[1998]

# PART IV
# THE PALESTINIAN-ISRAELI CONFLICT
## COLONIZATION IN THE ERA OF DECOLONIZATION

# INTRODUCTION

Noubar Hovsepian

In this section of the book, Ahmad focuses historically and thematically on what would become an abiding center of his attention from the 1970s until his death in 1999: the Middle East and in particular the Palestinian/Israeli conflict. For Ahmad, Palestine was the quintessential cause for the Third World: "Our painful colonial past, neocolonial present, and the dangerous perspective for our future" converge on the question of Palestine ("Pioneering in the Nuclear Age"). He viewed the dispossession of the Palestinians as *the* powerful symbol of the postcolonial tragedy of the Middle East: "at the dawn of decolonization, Palestine was colonized" ("An Address in Gaza"). The irony and paradox of this fact permeates his writing, engagements, and thinking about the Middle East. This historic setback was not just due to the power of imperialism but is a function of a compromised postcolonial Arab elite that excelled in issuing many empty words but lacked insight or foresight. "The locus of pessimism," he insisted, "is in the Middle East, not at the center of imperialism."[1] The indifferent and incompetent Arab leadership was unable to comprehend the character or extent of the challenge posed by imperialism in the postcolonial era. Instead, they deposited "Arab eggs" in the "American basket" ("'A World Restored' Revisited"). Ahmad skewered these leaders as "country sellers" ("An Address in Gaza").

The articles in the section cluster along several interconnected themes. The first of these is the crisis of postcolonial Arab states, captured particularly in the bankruptcy of their leadership; second is the failure to grasp the complexity of the Zionist movement, its "discipline of detail," and its special relationship to the world powers. Third comes the place of the Middle East in post-Vietnam US foreign policy, and, finally, there is his critical solidarity with the Palestinians themselves. Ahmad's contribution was not only to frame the contemporary Middle East historically and politically but also to try to intervene at every point to reverse the PLO's failures to live up to its promise as a movement of national liberation and to reverse the Arab leadership's state-centric view of power. Like his friend Edward Said, he was an insistent and often lonely voice challenging the overwhelming assumptions that flowed naturally from the singular and dominant understanding of the Arab world in the West—as backward, irrational, inferior. This view has only become more dominant as the US digs into the quagmire it has created in the wake of its 2003 invasion and occupation of Iraq. It is captured, seemingly conclusively, in Samuel P. Huntington's "clash of civilizations," which centers on the differences between the "Islamic world" and "the West," exclusively in cultural terms. Ahmad here will retell the story historically and politically, to undermine that pervasive interpretation,

In "Pioneering in the Nuclear Age," the essay that opens this section, he lays out his classic interpretation of Zionism, as an extreme form of settler colonialism, whose violent dynamics he lays bare.[2] Paralleling Zionism with the settling of the Americas and the elimination of the native inhabitants (and perhaps suggesting one root of the US's almost instinctive sympathy for the Israelis),[3] Ahmad emphasizes its basis in the myth that there were no inhabitants (and therefore no place in the collective memory of the West for the Palestinian experience of loss). He underscores how, haunted by its exclusionary policies and in pursuit of its own security, Israel enters into an "inexorable dialectic of anxiety, violence, and expansion." Hence, he argues, like other settler colonialisms, it tends to "reproduce its own risks." Committed to expelling and replacing the native inhabitants, Israel sought to diminish its dependence on a native workforce by encouraging successive waves of immigration by Jews in the diaspora. Beginning with those living in Arab states (aided by Arab rulers' willingness to expel rather than protect them); passing, from the 1970s on, to Soviet Jews; and continuously encouraging a steady stream of settlers from the US, the Zionist "discipline of detail" and systematic and creative pursuit of objectives contrasted tragically for Ahmad with the Arab states' and PLO's failure on both counts. He relates, for example, that during his first meeting with Arafat in 1979 he brought up what he called "the superbly orchestrated and multi-layered campaign" to get Soviet Jewry to Israel. "[Arafat] looked bewildered, as though wondering what the hell it had to do with Palestine . . . told an aide to look into the matter, and said to me Soviet leaders will not let this happen. There it was—a faith in leaders, a disregard of politics, of organized militancy, and the processes it can unfold."[4]

Besides his interpretation of the dynamics of settler colonialism, Ahmad's other major contribution to the analysis of the contemporary Middle East derives from his understanding of US foreign policy and its managerial technicians. In "'A World Restored' Revisited," his major piece on Kissinger in this book, he dissects the crucial role of Israel in Kissinger's strategy for post-Vietnam US dominance. More than any other article in the book, this essay brings together his strategic and military understanding (in this case of the 1973 war) with his broader analytical interpretation of world politics. His chief question is why, in the face of the 1973 war, did Sadat capitulate and sign the 1975 Sinai accord. He is merciless in his critique of Arab acceptance of the US (in the person of Kissinger) as evenhanded arbiter. For Ahmad, Kissinger is neither evenhanded nor Golda Meir's "miracle worker" but the "confidence man of modern diplomacy," the master manager, always "logical and wrong." His shuttle diplomacy for Ahmad was "shuttl[ing] around the basic issues."

In contrast to those who believed that Sinai opened the way to a genuine settlement between the Arabs/Palestinians and Israel, Ahmad is unsparing in his critique, as he will later be of Camp David and Oslo. The flaw in each case for him was basic: based not on justice or equity, the accords "restored the equation of occupation and war."

Yet "'A World Restored,'" is an optimistic piece. Ahmad is convinced that, given the centrality of oil to world power, unless Arab leaders "succeed in snatching failure from the jaws of success," Kissinger's design will not hold. But in fact his strategy has held—splitting Egypt from the rest of the Arab world and, with Egypt, putting to rest militant Arab nationalism, which no Arab state has been able to revive. For Ahmad, the fatal flaw in Arab strategic perception, which he sought to correct, was the view that the Arabs' deployment of the weapon of oil in the 1973 energy crisis "diminished US commitment to maintaining Israel as a regional gendarme."

Ahmad continues his unsparing critique of the Arab states, which "lack the will and capacity to translate their wealth into power," in the *New York Times* at the time of the Israeli invasion of Lebanon ("On Arab Bankruptcy"). In "The Public Relations of Ethnocide," he is the chronicler of outrage. His voice is at its sharpest as he critiques the official commission that exonerated

Israel of responsibility for the Sabra and Shatila massacres. Finally, in "Peace of the Weak" and "Peace in the Middle East: A Lost Opportunity," he delivers his scathing verdict on Oslo: Having retained for itself the crucial elements of sovereignty, "Israel absolved itself of responsibility for the occupied population while keeping the occupation."[5] As Edward Said put it upon hearing the terms of Oslo, "[The PLO] will end up guarding the world's largest prison, Gaza."[6] Moreover, Oslo heightened internal tension among the Palestinians, between pro- and anti-Oslo factions, between the PLO and Hamas. Subsequent accords tightened the noose, but Ahmad already in 1995 anticipated the future: "In effect Arab and Jew in the Occupied Territories will be two distinct and unequal humanities—one's existence being privileged and the other's precarious, one enjoying the rights of citizenship and the other existing in a gray area between occupation and autonomy, one deeply and hopelessly dependent on the other both politically and economically."[7]

A starker contrast with Ahmad's own vision of a future for the Middle East is hardly imaginable. Along with Said, he abhorred racialist, exclusionary, and separatist values. More than any other reviewer, he recognized Said's *The Question of Palestine* as "an essay on reconciliation" between what Ahmad often referred to as two communities of suffering.

The selections on the Palestinian/Israeli conflict only suggest the extent of Ahmad's engagement with the question of Palestine. He wrote numerous private letters and memos to many Palestinian leaders offering advice and critical solidarity. I served as the courier for several letters, including one dated September 17, 1982. It is wisely addressed "Dear Comrade." In the wake of the 1982 Israeli invasion of Lebanon, he urged Palestinian leaders to exercise "great discipline of detail and flexibility in struggle."[8] What did (does) this entail?

Though the PLO had sustained a severe setback as a result of the 1982 war, Ahmad saw room for guarded optimism. He outlines three conclusions he had reached concerning where the PLO "might go following this Lebanon war." He advised that the post-1982 struggle should be carried out on a three-pronged basis and "with utmost subtlety and coordination." First, he advised the promotion and methodological organization of an underground resistance in Lebanon. Second, he favored the organization of a militant (not militaristic), creative, nonviolent political struggle in occupied Palestine. He emphasized that this struggle should involve Israelis, Europeans, and Americans, "even at the cost of tactical compromises," and that it should be expressly political. Third, he urged the launching of a well-orchestrated effort to bring about the moral isolation of Israel and to create multiple levels of solidarity organizations in the West, especially the US.[9]

To pursue his three-pronged strategy, Ahmad insisted on the need for maximum political flexibility. He noted that the Israeli government, after the 1982 invasion of Lebanon, under Begin's leadership had become "rigid and brittle." This weakness, he advised, should be exploited. He gently added: "I feel that quite frequently Palestinian failure to distinguish between tactical and strategic objectives, and between a war of movement and a war of position (I speak politically) has been its greatest liability."[10] Then and now, the Palestinian resistance movement failed to comprehend the difference between militant resistance and militarism. Were Ahmad to write today, he would vehemently oppose the adopted tactics of suicide operations, as he earlier criticized terrorism ("An Essay on Reconciliation") in discussing highjacking. Highjacking and suicide bombing, while certainly a measure of Palestinian desperation, are uncreative and counterproductive, as well as unethical. "Between a weak strategy of diplomacy and terrorism, there are many untried options," most important for Ahmad, militant nonviolence. The point is never for him to contrast Palestinian violence with the "completely asymmetrical record" of Israeli terror against Palestinians.[11] While true, it is "neither good morals nor good politics." The point is rather to suggest what other lines of action are lost in a sterile debate over suicide bombings. He would surely emphasize that the Palestinian movement and its leadership, until now, have failed to weaken the moral resolve of the Israeli polity. Instead, this leadership has succeeded in unifying the majority of the Israeli public behind the brutal leadership of Ariel Sharon. At the same time, Palestinians have finally begun to create a militant nonviolent movement (virtually uncovered in the US media) and to mobilize international solidarity in their support, politics of the sort Eqbal Ahmad called for his entire life.

# 27 / PIONEERING IN THE NUCLEAR AGE

An Essay on Israel and the Palestinians

Future historians are likely to view the rise of national liberation movements and the start of the strategic arms race as the most momentous developments of the twentieth century. Viewed together, the two represent contrasting realities. One is a weapon of the weak, the other an affliction of technologically advanced, globally ambitious powers. If the arms race betrays the contemporary nation-states' propensity to destruction, the movements for liberation reveal the power of hope, of people's readiness to resist injustice and seek self-determination against seemingly impossible odds, invariably at extraordinary cost. Underlying the unprecedented rise of liberation struggles following the Second World War and formal decolonization is the increasingly perceptible gap between the sorrows of the majority in Third World countries and the contentment of the few, between the coercive military apparatus of governments and the determined resistance of the governed. It is this gap that some strategic thinkers and policy makers would fill, with the augmented interventionist capabilities—including the tactical use of nuclear weapons in situations of "limited wars"—of a superpower and its regional surrogates.

The arms race is conclusive evidence of the harm caused by the links between power and technology, between militarism and profit making. Equally conclusive have been the demonstrations by national liberation movements of people's will and capacity to defeat the destructive presumptions of modern technology and the manipulative power of management techniques. Thus two small, underdeveloped nations—Algeria and Vietnam—engaged and defeated two of the most advanced war machines and most highly developed national security states of our time. And Fidel Castro made the first clear-cut revolution in Latin America just about ninety miles away from a hostile United States. Since the end of the Second World War, liberation struggles have been the primary force in defining conflict and change in the international system. The Chinese, Algerian, Cuban, and Vietnamese struggles each had an impact on the international balance of power, marking the end of one period in world politics, inaugurating another.

Rarely in recorded history has the status quo felt more threatened than in our time. Hence it is the status quo power's interventionist responses to this perceived threat, rather than mere superpower rivalry, that poses the ultimate risk of Armageddon. Of the fifteen documentable instances of active nuclear diplomacy, nine were occasioned by the United States' confrontation with either a national liberation movement or a regime issued from it.[1] When one adds to this another reality, viz: that the centrality of the international struggle for power has shifted in the last quarter of the twentieth century to the Middle East and southern Africa, one can only agree with Noam Chomsky that the disarmament movement in the Western world "dooms itself to near irrelevance" if it continues to duck the question of Palestine and the issues arising out of Israel's transformation as a major military power allied to the United States.[2]

Since the 1950s, the movements for liberation in the Third World have been proliferating. Twenty-two armed movements were reported by the United States Department of Defense in 1958, and forty-two in 1965.[3] In 1969, some fifty were under way. A decade later, several of these, including the movements in Algeria, Vietnam, Angola, Mozambique, Guinea-Bassau, Zimbabwe, and Nicaragua, had won their protracted struggles, against heavy odds and contrary to expert predictions.

In this cauldron of armed struggles, the Palestinian Liberation Organization (PLO) stands out for its uncommon characteristics. It elicits the solidarity of and arouses deep emotions among perhaps the largest mass of people in the Third World. It has been the most successful in obtaining worldwide attention and formal recognition from governments and international organizations. It is the only political movement in recorded history that is formally recognized by more governments throughout the world than its governmental adversary. Financially, it is believed to have been at best strikingly unsuccessful not only in achieving its objectives but even in denying continued success to its adversary's expansionist and colonizing goals. It has, nevertheless, been one of the most enduring liberation struggles of our time. Its durability, despite continued losses, is a tribute to the persistence of the Palestinian people and a measure of the legitimacy the PLO commands among them.

No other liberation struggle in history presents so many paradoxes. For an explanation of its uniqueness, one must view the Palestinian movement in terms of:

1. The historical significance of the struggle for Palestine not only for the Palestinian people but also in its international, Third World, and Arab contexts.

2. The complexity and discipline of the Palestinians' primary adversary—the Zionist movement and its product, the Israeli state.

3. The special relationship that Zionism and Israel developed with the paramount world powers during the periods of its [Israel's] expansion and active confrontation with the Palestinian Arabs (1915–48; 1967 on).

4. The crisis of Arab nationalist ideology that resulted from its antagonistic collaboration with the Arab state system (Nasserism, Baath) and the centrality of the Palestine question in maintaining an ideologically and structurally paralyzing relationship between Arabism and Arab governments.

5. The failure of Palestinian leaders to grasp the significant details in 2, 3, and 4 above and to develop a winning strategy of struggle that would help evade the dangers and exploit the opportunities presented by friends no less than enemies.

6. The failure of the PLO to offer a consistent, coherent, and functioning program based on a meaningful vision of the future but informed also by courageously and creatively drawn lessons of the past, especially the lessons of their own earlier encounter with Zionism and of the theory and practice of revolutionary warfare.

All these points are touched on in this essay; the primary focus, however, is on the last point.


*I. The Question of Palestine in the Context of the Third World*

Edward Said once talked of why the question of Palestine so stirs the emotions of people throughout the world. He spoke of the animating role of ideas and values of liberation, equality, and fraternity; of the power of the simplicity of a people's quest for a home, the right to live outside refugee camps free from the daily terror of settlers and soldiers; of the persistence of a people's inalienable claim to dignity, equality, and self-determination. One might add that the Palestinian experience, like the South African, affects a majority of mankind at a deeper, more primordial level. Our painful colonial past, neocolonial present, and the dangerous perspective for our future converge on the question of Palestine.

August 1947 marked the beginning of decolonization, when British rule in India ended with a last spasmodic human carnage. In January 1948, Burma became independent; in February, Ceylon; October 1949 witnessed the exhilarating final liberation of China. It was in those days of hopes and fulfillments that the colonization of Palestine occurred. It was formalized in 1948 by the establishment of Israel cosponsored by the postwar superpowers, consecrated by the United Nations, and conceded by the abject failure of Arab governments. Thus, at the dawn of decolonization, we were returned to the earliest, most intense form of colonial menace—the exclusivist settler colonialism that had dealt genocidal blows to the great civilizations and peoples of the Americas. As if to compel our historical memory, Israel's sectarian, racialist character was ensured by the expulsion of the native Palestinians from their homeland. The tragedy occurred as a counterpoint to contemporary history, a reminder that all was not well with the era of decolonization.

There were in the Palestinian example some dire warnings, some terrible lessons for the Third World. The conduct of "independent" Arab governments in relation to the British role in the transformation of Palestine provided alarming insights into the culture and political mind of the postcolonial elites, the bureaucratic legalism, mindless formalism, and petty opportunism of their diplomacy of dependence. When the belated showdown finally came in 1948, the performance of the Arab armies was the first dramatic indication one had of the meaning of independence, the nature of the postcolonial state, the corruption of our ruling classes. Similarly, since 1967, Israel's expansionism, the United States' all-out support of it, and the Arab governments' responses toward both Israel and its sustainer have been daily reminders of the meaning of disorganic development in the Third World and the consequences of accommodating ourselves to dependent, undemocratic minority governments.

We have in the Middle East also a testing ground of imperial design, the centerpiece of Washington's post-Vietnam strategic architecture; of nuclearization; of addiction to unusable and dependence-inducing weapons; of regional surrogates armed to the teeth; and of plans and preparedness for intervention. In short, we have here, organically linked to the state of Israel, the wherewithals of recolonization. To anyone who is willing to see, it should be clear that Israel and the United States are together engaged in shaping the future of the region from Pakistan to Morocco; unless they are stopped now, and isolated from each other, the sovereignty and integrity of the entire region will have been mortgaged for centuries to come. Thus the question of Palestine, to which has now been added the question of Lebanon, transcends the question of Palestinians' right to peace and self-determination, fundamentally important as it is.

In the absence of viable partners in the Arab world, the PLO has been saddled with a heavier burden than any other liberation movement in contemporary history except one: following the Korean war, US policy placed the Vietnamese in a similar predicament. Their response—historically rooted, tactically flexible, strategically consistent, and politically virtuous—changed the premises of world politics and sent Washington scurrying in several directions at once, including, as we shall later see, into the arms of Israel. A movement in exile, an integral part of the Arab nationalist environment but excluded from its system, itself dependent on the goodwill of others who lacked not merely vision and wisdom but also principles and commitments, confronting an expansionist, settler-colonial adversary, the PLO was not equipped structurally, ideologically, organizationally, or demographically to carry this burden. Only a few of its leaders thought that it was; most were wiser. Their modest lives and limited objectives testify to their understanding. Yet all have made the mistake of allowing accommodations, pretenses, ambiguities, and claims that prevented the evolution of a clear and consistent political program responding to Zionism's unusual, unorthodox challenge and the Palestinians' special realities. It should, nevertheless, be underlined that it is the unique fate of the Palestinian and Arab people that they have encountered a remarkable phenomenon: a settler-colonial movement in the twentieth century, an infinitely better organized, more desperate, more disciplined, more complex, if inherently weaker, movement than its predecessors.


*II. Settler Colonization and Its Zionist Paradigm*

Unless one counts the centuries-long, largely unrecorded, and dispersed resistance of the vanished native people against white settler colonialism in the Americas, no liberation movement in modern times has encountered an adversary like the one the Palestinians have faced. Israel obviously shares many similarities with South Africa and may in time come to resemble the apartheid state more than most liberal Zionists suspect. However, structurally and substantively the Zionist movement and state share significant similarities with the early form of colonial movements that transformed the Western Hemisphere into the "New World" of the West. They destroyed the Aztec, the Mayan, the Inca civilizations and the Indian cultures and peoples, including the five "civilized nations" of the United States and Canada. It is a pioneering colonialism, one that seeks to exclude and eliminate the native inhabitants rather than to occupy and exploit them. Although produced by the process and power of imperialism, it is a form of colonialism that offers refuge to the disinherited, to persecuted minorities and to the surpluses, marginals, and misfits created by industrialism and modernization in the metropolis. A colonialism committed to replacing the native people, it is racist and extremist by nature. Yet, a product of the Western metropolis, constituted mostly of the dispossessed, of dissidents and the persecuted, it is often liberal in ideology and humane in rhetoric. Hypocrisy, the compliment paid by vice to virtue, is the hallmark of the exclusionist settler style. It is invariably hardened both by appropriating the colonial ethos that assumes the inferiority of the natives and by producing a moral epistemology uniquely its own, involving the negation of native realities, the myths of an empty land, of swamps reclaimed and deserts blooming. Settler moralism is compounded with messianic complexes of manifest destinies and promised lands, and with an ethic of work without which the exclusion of the native is rendered difficult. It is a colonial form that produces a paranoid strain in the colonizing culture, an instrumental attitude toward violence and a tendency to expand. Naturally, the exclusionist settler society develops a dynamic of its own in the promised land, so to say, and occasionally comes to exercise a certain autonomy, sometimes even full independence from its metropolitan sponsors.

All settler societies share certain vulnerabilities. Basic weaknesses and insecurities tend to characterize them until three conditions have been fulfilled:

(a) until the "solution" of the native "problem" has been found and finalized;

(b) until the settler state has decisively established its hegemony over or at least achieved normal relations with its neighbors;

(c) until it has obtained a measure of independence from its metropolitan sponsors by acquiring the ability to sustain itself economically and militarily, because until it has fulfilled the first two conditions, the settler society must remain a garrison state, dependent on foreign military aid and logistical support.

The historic settler societies of the era following the industrial revolution, the United States, Canada, and other countries of the Western Hemisphere, easily crossed the danger point a long time ago, aided by an overwhelmingly imperialist environment; the absence of concerted resistance by the fragmented, unsuspecting, and unprepared native civilizations; their access to the vast resources of the New World; their distance from the metropolitan country; and a steady stream of immigrants from the Old World. The white settler societies in Africa (there was no significant settler community in Asia until the Zionist implantation of the European-Jewish community in Palestine) did not fare so well. They lacked each of the three attributes of permanence. The settler colonial states of Kenya, Algeria, Angola, and Zimbabwe experienced the more violent form of decolonization; liberation from white rule was achieved by the indigenous inhabitants who had remained a majority, if an extremely dispossessed one.

Of the two remaining settler societies outside the Western Hemisphere, South Africa, by and large, fulfills the third condition. It has control over enough financial and technological resources and raw materials to afford a certain independence from and bargaining power in relation to the metropolitan countries. But despite many attempts to discard and quarter the native people, the African majority has held; and although several of its neighbors remain economically dependent on it, South Africa has not been able to ensure their conformity and recognition. To the contrary, the future of South Africa is more uncertain today than ever before. The failure of apartheid has become increasingly apparent as resistance among the black people has spread and become bolder than most observers were able to imagine only a decade ago. The establishment in Angola, Mozambique, and Zimbabwe of independent governments has heightened the white regime's sense of insecurity and extended the frontiers of its overt and covert aggression. There is no apparent pool of potential white immigrants on which the racist regime could draw in order to overcome its demographic and political predicament. And the alternative of expelling or liquidating the native population is not available to it because:

(i) Its economy has become structurally dependent on a sizable African labor force;

(ii) the black population, now numbering some 16 million, is much too large to be disposed of;

(iii) world opinion is far too mobilized against the regime to permit the exterminist solution, even if the white regime were willing to under take it.

Israel, still far from reaching these goals, is trying to fulfill all three conditions simultaneously. It does not have access to resources comparable to South Africa's or the advantages of being surrounded by weak, landlocked, and, until recently, colonized neighbors. Yet in each of the three areas it has made dramatic and unexpected gains, thanks to its own initiatives, careful planning, and resourcefulness; thanks largely to Washington's enormous economic, military, and diplomatic support; but thanks also to the inept conduct of Arab governments and to the distracted, piecemeal responses and badly chosen priorities of Palestinian leaders. It is noteworthy that in its dual quest for expansion and consolidation Zionist strategy and style have changed but little. A more striking fact is that although the international environment and the position of the Arabs in it has drastically changed, Arab responses to the Zionist challenge have not done so significantly. There is a qualitative and meaningful increment in the mobilization of Palestinian identity and resistance, yet there remains, in the conduct of the Palestinian struggle, a certain absence of learning from the past.

## III. The Past Revisited

In order to comprehend how much of history is being repeated during Israel's attempt, since 1967, to complete the transformation of Palestine, it may be helpful briefly to recapitulate the past. Zionism's successes in the first struggle for Palestine may be summarized as being due to the following factors:

(a) It successfully linked itself to the paramount imperial power (Britain). While maintaining this link, it developed the institutions, alternatives, and leverage needed to exercise a certain autonomy from its British sponsor. The Zionist movement did not confine itself merely to lobbying or to currying Britain's favor.

Rather, it attempted to link its interests organically with those of the imperialist power; yet, wherever the necessity arose, it confronted Britain by directly threatening its interests. In other words, the Zionist movement evinced then, as Israel does now in its relations with the United States, an operative understanding that relations with other states—be they allies or adversaries—must be based not on ingratiation and appeals but on an exercise of power and the principle of mutual exchange. The Arabs responded generally by trying to compete with Zionism for Britain's favors but never quite linking their favors—economic or political—to British policy. Without genuine evidence of British goodwill toward Arabs or the will to make good on stated policy, Arab governments conceded Britain the role of an arbiter.

(b) Zionist settlement and expansion policy was characterized, in Edward Said's apt phrase, by a remarkable "discipline of detail." The expansion crept slowly, inch by inch, step by step, "another acre, another goat"—as Chaim Weizman put it.[4] And the final Judaization of the greater part of Palestine occurred "coterminously" with its de-Arabization. This was no happenstance. Early Zionist leaders' plans to "reconstitute" Palestine were marked by cold calculation, circumspection, and a salami-slicing approach. In 1895, Theodore Herzl saw the necessity of "spiriting the penniless population . . . across the border," noting that "both the process of expropriation and the removal of the poor must be carried out discreetly and circumspectly."[5] Forty-five years later, in 1940, Joseph Weitz, then director of the Jewish National Fund, would note in his diaries that "there is no room for both people in this country. . . . There is no room for compromise on this point. . . . We must not leave a single village, not a single tribe."[6]

(c) Demographic expansion of Jews in Palestine was achieved by a highly organized campaign to obtain the exodus (aliyah) of European Jews to Palestine. This campaign included both a collaboration with the Nazis, especially in the early phase when the Germans were seeking a solution to the "Jewish problem" by the expulsion of Jews from Nazi-occupied territories, and a discouragement of the transfer and resettlement of the victims of European fascism in the United States, Canada, and elsewhere. Both policies on the part of Zionist organizations caused undoubted augmentation in the number of Holocaust victims, but they provided the legitimacy and the manpower needed for the transformation of Palestine into a Zionist state.[7]

(d) Emerging out of a nineteenth- and early-twentieth-century European, especially Russian, milieu, the Zionist movement, though ideologically primitive and retrograde, organizationally had the characteristics of a revolutionary movement. It built institutions and propagated values, and it proceeded to outadminister the enemy (in this case, the Palestinian people) before it began to outfight them. Alienation of land, access to water, strangulation of the indigenous economy, and devaluation of Palestinian culture were the primary goals of Zionist strategy. The Palestinian peasants and workers responded as beleaguered, oppressed people always do: with protest and resistance involving sporadic, mostly uncoordinated violence. Their violence invariably served as an alibi for Zionist aggression and expansion.

The Palestinian elite met Zionism's specific, organized challenge not only in the context of general Arab politics but, more importantly, also in the Arab governments' institutional frame of reference—with official representation and legal briefs, invoking general principles (right to self-determination, legal claims to Palestine, British promises) and moral appeals for justice. They had no parallel organizations capable of mobilizing and leading the Palestinians' collective resistance, no program of assisting the besieged Palestinian communities and of shoring up their defenses and morale. They had weak institutions for popular participation and leadership accountability and no strategy to hold the land. Hence the 1948 confrontation occurred in an environment permeated with a mood of failure, demoralization, and dependence; and the people—some 780,000 of them—were driven out of or fled from their homes, hoping to return after the Arab armies liberated their land.

(e) The Zionist movement grasped the crucial importance of keeping its Palestinian adversary morally and politically isolated, especially in the Western world, where lay the focus of world power. It did so by employing multiple techniques of propaganda and manipulation; of these, two are noteworthy. It successfully portrayed itself as an underdog, striving for Jewish survival, outgunned, outnumbered, and mortally menaced by a populous and powerful enemy intent on "throwing the Jews into the sea." It portrayed the Palestinians either as nonexistent or as a backward, undifferentiated part of a larger entity called the Arab world. The rhetorical flourishes and verbal violence of Arab and Palestinian leaders and various Arab governments' pretenses to represent the Palestinian people lent credence (and to a much smaller extent still do) to Zionist claims. It is in this latter aspect that, by incontrovertibly asserting Palestinian identity and its right to self-representation, the PLO made its most significant departure from the past and came closest to resembling the classical model of national liberation movements.

This gain was the primary target of Israel's war in Lebanon—an Israeli objective that the Reagan Plan attempted to consecrate by asking King Hussein to represent Palestine.

(f) International support, especially the support of Western public opinion and of the Jewish diaspora, played a crucial role in Zionist successes. The Zionists appreciated the crucial role of cultural institutions, religious organizations, and professional associations in linking civil society to political power and thus in creating the political climate and long-range trends in policy making. Arabs, on the other hand, did little to affect public attitudes in the West, neglected the centers of political pressure and institutions of civil society in favor of communicating only with political power.

(g) The Zionist movement was nonconformist, unorthodox, and audacious in narrowing the gaps between its objectives and the immediate opportunities. In doing this, it correctly evaluated and put its bets on Arabs' responses, counting heavily on the rejectionist strain in Arab politics; its tactical acceptance of the UN partition plan (to which the Zionist leaders were in fact opposed) is a case in point.

(h) The Zionists used diplomacy tactically, as a weapon to exploit opportunities, consolidate gains, and isolate the Palestinians. The Arab side viewed diplomacy strategically and lost opportunities and flexibility of posture as a result.

It was the combination of a complex and relentlessly pursued Zionist strategy and a disjointed, piecemeal Arab and Palestinian response to it that made possible the first victory of Zionism over the Palestinians and Arabs. But it was a victory made decisive by the many failures of Arab governments. (Between 1947 and 1967, they had assumed entirely the responsibilities of representing Palestinian interests and of defending the Arab "fatherland.") These governments' decisions and policies made possible both the creation and Judaization of Israel and later its consolidation as a state. Israel's unilateral declaration of independence might eventually have proved as illusory as the Rhodesian UDI of Ian Smith. And had the Arab governments made a viable effort to prevent another aliyah, this time of Arab Jews into Israel, the history and contemporary character of Palestinian/Israeli confrontation would be significantly different.

*IV. Exodus and Expulsion: A Dialectic*

In 1948, Israel resolved its "native" problem in a single masterstroke by expelling the Palestinians from their homeland. It was a "miracle" rendered easy by the ill-timed and impulsive rejection of the United Nations partition plan,

ill-prepared and corrupt conduct of the war by participating Arab governments, and the inverted priorities of both the Palestinian and Arab leaders,
e.g., Hajj Amin, Al-Husseini, and King Abdullah. Having rid itself of the Palestinians, Israel needed to shore up its demographic strength; its predominantly
European population and economy also needed a pool of cheap labor. From
1950 to 1965, the Israel aliyah program concentrated not on Russian, American, or European Jewry but on including the immigration of Arab Jews from
their native lands to Israel. Again, no Arab government or Palestinian leader of
the time—Ahmad Al-Shukury being the most prominent among them—
grasped the significance of the Zionist campaign, and no effort was made to
discourage the massive immigration of "Oriental Jews" to the sectarian settler state. After the conquests of 1967, Israel again faces the classic dilemma of
the exclusionist settler society. It needs more Jews to settle the occupied lands
and fewer Arabs under occupation in order to ensure the "Jewish character"
of Eretz Israel. Thus a well-orchestrated campaign was launched, after the 1967
war, to induce immigration, especially of Russian Jews to Israel, and a systematic policy gradually escalated of alienating and expelling the Palestinians
from their land. Again, there has been no organized and sustained Arab/Pales-
tinian effort to stop Israel on these two crucial tracks.

Israel's problem is real; its preferred solutions involve obvious and serious
dangers for the Palestinian/Arab inhabitants of the Occupied Territories and
a continuing denial of their fundamental rights to Palestinians in the diaspora.
They also point at other contradictions and vulnerabilities of settler states. I
had earlier mentioned the ethnocentric ethics of work, without which the
exclusion of the natives becomes difficult. But all settler communities are by
nature modern, industrializing, and capitalist. As such, when an alternative
pool of racially "pure" labor is not available, then the ideologically claimed
ethics of work (e.g., Jewish labor—Jewish land; Jewish factory—Jewish hands)
yield to the profit motive, and relations of production tend to determine policy toward the native inhabitants. Economic and political change gradually
pushes the settler economy toward dependence on native labor; the exclusionist settler state becomes also an exploitative one. When a settler society is
forced—by economic and political processes—to abandon its ethnocentric
ethic of work, it must choose between genocide and slavery, apartheid and as-
similation. In the United States, the Indians were virtually wiped out and, in
order to replenish labor, the Southern states turned to slavery. Mexico became
assimilated. South Africa chose apartheid.

Today, Israel is at a crossroads, relying more on Arab labor than before, yet far from depending on it. Sensitive to long-term trends, given to planning in detail, and fixed in its sectarian ideology, Israel appears to be simultaneously pursuing four routes to escape the demographic and structural dangers to its exclusivist character:

(a) It seeks more Jewish immigrants, aiming its aliyah campaign especially at Russian Jewry.
(b) There is a concerted policy of dispossessing and driving out the Palestinian population, especially from Jerusalem and the West Bank.
(c) Israeli industry is expanding most rapidly in the armaments sector that is inclined to be the most capital intensive.
(d) There are discussions and plans to introduce foreign—including Lebanon (and Gaza Strip)—based workers into Israel.

The heart of the Israeli scheme is the first two—Jewish immigration and Arab dispossession.

In 1968, Israel launched an elaborate campaign to alienate the Soviet Jewry from its patrimony and to induce the immigration of Russian Jews to Israel. Another "exodus" aliyah is obviously deemed necessary to achieve the goal of colonizing "Judea and Samaria" without incurring the risk, as the term goes in Israel, of "levantinizing" Eretz Israel. Although Zionist leaders and Israeli officials understate their success, the campaign has, in fact, made impressive gains. Between October 1968 and October 1982, a total of 261,994 Jewish citizens left the Soviet Union with Israeli visas. Approximately 180,000 of them actually went to Israel; the 82,000 "dropouts" have been a cause of bitter controversy within the Zionist movement. There is much concern in the Israeli government also over the immigrants who eventually leave Israel, although only about 3 percent of the 180,000 have emigrated, and a total of 162,000 have stayed in Israel.[8]

During the same period, 125,000 Jews settled in the Occupied Territories, and an estimated 650,000 Palestinian Arabs were expelled or emigrated from the Israeli-occupied territories.[9] Among the zealots who are settling the Occupied Territories, right-wing American Jews, not the Russian immigrants, figure most prominently. But the point is Israel's quest to dominate Eretz Israel demographically, not the exact location of its new immigrants. Furthermore, the pressures created by the influx of immigrants on Israel's housing have provided an impetus and justification for the construction of settlement housing, especially in Jerusalem and the West Bank.[10] The subsidized good life being offered in the suburban Jewish settlements, especially on the West Bank, can only add incentives to future immigration.

The Soviet immigrants are also believed by some observers to have become a key factor in Israel's burgeoning, economically and strategically significant armaments industry. They are well educated, technically qualified new arrivals. By 1981, Soviet-trained engineers constituted an estimated 35–50 percent of all qualified Israeli engineers, and the new Russian arrivals constituted a fourth of Israel's medical staff. Their participation in the weapons industry is believed to be significant. According to an April 1981 report, in the Israeli aircraft industry alone, three thousand Jews from the USSR work as technicians and engineers. Their number in all the weapon-exporting industries must be much greater, and probably it is their help alone that allowed these industries to expand phenomenally in recent years. In only two years, 1979–1980, the Israeli export of weapons increased by 371 percent.[11]

By 1982, Israel had become, thanks mainly to technology transfers from and coproduction deals with the United States, the sixth largest exporter of arms in the world.

The significance of this development cannot be overstated. It has created new and organic linkages between Israel and its metropolitan sponsor, and it has given Israel greater leverage in its relations with the United States. For Israel's expanding arms industry is being linked by multiple ties to the "military-industrial complex" in America. In addition, for the American policy makers, Israel's arms-supply capability has become a viable instrument of overcoming the "Vietnam Syndrome," i.e., the post-Vietnam popular opposition to interventionist US involvement against liberation movements abroad, and of evading congressional or diplomatic prohibitions against providing military aid to such countries as South Africa, Chile, Guatemala, Argentina, and the counterrevolutionary Nicaraguan saboteurs in Honduras.

More impressive than the numerical gains of its post-1967 aliyah campaign has been Israel's success in institutionalizing, legitimizing, and internationalizing its goals of obtaining the immigration of Jews from the USSR to Israel. A network of institutions and activities, both open and clandestine, inside the USSR has been created to encourage and support this aliyah. The legitimacy of this campaign has been quietly established. Under United States pressure, the USSR agreed to regard Israel as the sole legitimate destination for departing Russian Jews. Although its rationale is the unification of families, and it occurred in the absence of counterpressures or even mild open protests from Arab quarters, it remains, nevertheless, an ironic socialist concession to a sectarian, theocratic concept. Even more striking has been Israel's success in formally linking the question of Soviet-Jewish immigration with US-Soviet relations. Since the commitments given Israel by the Nixon administration, the passage of the Jackson Amendment (1969), and the signing of the Helsinki Accords (1975), the matter of Jewish immigration has become an integral part of superpower diplomacy. It is considered routine now for US officials and negotiators to bring up, with their Soviet counterparts, demands for more visas to Israel. Hence the rate of immigration fluctuates in accordance with the state of US-Soviet relations: in 1982, "détente" hit its worst year since 1968, and, at 2,700 persons, the figure of Soviet immigration to Israel was the lowest.[12] The Israeli goal is to get the entire Russian-Jewish population of three million. If this goal is a quarter filled, the boundaries of Eretz Israel could easily expand beyond the West Bank, Gaza, and the Golan Heights.

*V. A Second Transformation of Palestine?*

It was mentioned earlier that while in the fifteen years following the 1967 war the Israeli campaign produced the immigration of 180,000 Russians and an estimated 35,000 other Jews (American, Latin American, and European) into Israel, more than half a million Arabs were expelled from the Occupied Territories. A high death rate (15 per 1,000) and enormous infant mortality (at least 82 per 1,000) have been adding to the demographic depletion of the Arab people in occupied Palestine. Thus, in a 1982 report, Meron Benvenisti, a former Israeli deputy mayor of Jerusalem, concludes that: "A comparison of the annual growth rate indicates that the so-called *demographic threat*, i.e., the gradual increased proportion of West Bank and Gaza inhabitants versus Jews in Western Palestine, is not upheld by the data. While it is true that there are more Arab children (Israeli, West Bank and Gaza) in the 0–7 years age group, the aggregate Arab growth rate is almost half the Jewish rate."[13]

Given what humanity has already suffered from another ethnocentric ideology, one had a right to hope that such ethnic body counts shall not concern the survival and freedom of a people. It is, nevertheless, a fact that, unlike classic colonialism, Israel has put into question not only one's sense of justice but the very commitment of a people to their soil. For the Palestinians, then, it is a question literally of survival. Hence the numbers are important both to the victimizers and the victim. The extreme balance in Jewish/Arab demographic growth, which Mr. Benvenisti has noted in his fine study, is a product of Israel's policies, not of moral forces. Much on the subject has already been written, and the question of Israeli settlements has been a focus of international attention.[14] Here we need only point out briefly that Israel's policy, complex in planning, cold-blooded and methodical in execution, once again aimed at dispossessing the Arabs of Palestine of the four fundamental elements—land, water, leaders, and culture—without which an indigenous community cannot survive. It is a policy of ethnocide, in the strict, legal sense of the word.

Israel has expropriated more than a third of the total land in the Occupied Territories—in the Jordan Valley the figure exceeds 60 percent. Stringent Israeli controls over water and electricity render the remaining land vulnerable to Israel's will, which is being consistently exercised to the detriment of the native population. Arab wells go dry when deep-bored wells are sunk in nearby Israeli settlements; permission to sink new wells is generally denied the Arabs. Meron Benvenisti reports that "the settlements today are 2–3% of the West Bank population and use 20% of the total water consumption of this area."[15] It is thus that orange groves, tended for generations and vital to Palestinian livelihood, die as swimming pools are built in the Israeli settlements.

About 18 percent of the West Bank's total area has been incorporated in the annexed Jerusalem district. Its 120,000 Arab inhabitants have become disenfranchised nonpersons. These annexed areas are excluded from the "autonomy" envisaged in the Camp David Accords (and, by a sleight of words, from the Reagan Plan). So are the "settlement" lands, "absentee" properties, and properties in the "security" zones.

The Palestinians have been demographically "cut off" by 122 strategically situated settlements, says Matityahu Drobles, head of the Jewish Agency's Settlement Department and author of the Master Plan for the Development of Judea and Samaria (1978), to render it "difficult for the minority Israeli Arab population to unite and create territorial and political continuity." The Drobles Plan of October 1978, calling for 125 settlements, has nearly been completed. Enlargement of the settlements and large housing projects are in progress. Israeli planning now envisages, in thirty years, a population of one million Jews on the West Bank. Throughout the world, pioneers are being recruited for this purpose and are being trained and armed in Israel. These vigilantes are a law unto themselves. The Arabs under occupation today live in the nightmarish world of a thousand and one Kristallnachts.

For a people to become demoralized and for its resistance to be weakened, it must lose its local leaders, its cultural institutions, and identity. An estimated 3,000 Palestinians in the Occupied Territories are political prisoners; another 1,500 have been expelled by the occupying power. Municipalities have been denuded of power. Elected mayors have been dismissed. Quislings have been imposed on Arab villages as Israeli-appointed "leaders" of the "Village League." Libraries are regularly shut down. Books, including translations of Western works and classics, are banned. Documents are destroyed. Schools and colleges, including the Bir Zeit University, the principal institution of higher education, are perennially closed by military order. Even the use of the word "Palestine" is proscribed, and the law is selectively enforced. Curiously, like the fascist government of Germany, the Israeli government has been extremely legal minded in going about its ugly mission. It has created an elaborate set of new laws and resuscitated or reinterpreted some old ones to use against the indigenous inhabitants.[16]

For more than a decade now, we have been witness to the second transformation of Palestine. The process bears a certain similarity to Zionism's earlier enterprise. The colonization of the West Bank began slowly; at first, "security" was its only stated raison d'être, then its pace accelerated and the justification became ideological. As before, the eventual solution of the demographic problem of finding a sizable number of non-Jews in the Jewish state is assumed. "We should not be afraid of Arab demography," says Mordecai Tzipori, the Israeli minister of commerce, "there are ways and means to counter this." The proposed solutions to Israel's expansionist dilemma range from allowing the "minority" autonomy instead of citizenship to the outright "expulsion of 700,000–800,000" persons. That this latter was contemplated at high official levels was disclosed by General Aharon Yariv, Israel's retired chief of military intelligence.[17]

Similarities with the past are more striking on the Arab side. The possibilities of Israel obtaining another exodus of foreign Jews and expanding even farther into the fertile crescent seemed as remote in the 1960s and 1970s as had the prospects of the creation of a Zionist state in Palestine appeared to the Arabs in the early 1900s. There are other parallels: the complicity of the contemporary superpowers, then of Britain and now of the United States, in the transformation of Palestine (add Lebanon!); the ease with which the Arab rulers conferred on the British and then the American governments the role of just and evenhanded arbiters; the formalistic legalism, mindless rejectionism, the political opportunism, and the diplomacy by ingratiation that lost the Arabs the first struggle for Palestine are still there. Thus, so far, no Arab government has seen the necessity of linking its economic relations with the United States to the latter's military and economic support for Israel's expansionist drive. None has taken one substantive step to oppose Israel's well-planned drive toward further expansion. As they did following the Balfour Declaration, Arab and Muslim governments confine themselves to issuing statements and making ineffectual representations against an aggressive and ambitious adversary.

There are, to be sure, differences with the past. This time, the World Zionist Organization has at its disposal the power of an occupation army and the protection and support of the United States. This time, the Zionist drive is not motivated by the search for a state; nor is it joined by a desperate, driven people. Its motor is a state; its motivation is power; its goal, domination of the region from "Morocco to Pakistan." Israel's avocation now is merely imperial, as John Chancellor, the NBC anchorman understood in a fleeting moment of anguish. "One of the strangest features of the conflict over Palestine," the great historian Arnold J. Toynbee wrote, "is that it should be necessary to demonstrate that the Arabs have a case." Zionism's greatest kudos had been its ability to convince the Western world and an overwhelming majority of Jews of its goodness as an ideology, its moral validity as a "liberation movement." It did so not merely by misrepresenting itself but also by representing the Palestinians first as nonexistent, then as nonhuman, "two-legged beasts" (in Prime Minister Menachem Begin's description). "There is a nemesis for committing wrongs as well as for condoning them," Toynbee had warned a decade ago in a statement that was controversial at the time.[18]

Today, the goddess of retribution has begun to haunt Israel. No one except its die-hard right-wing supporters can defend its policies, from South Africa, Argentina, and El Salvador to the West Bank and Lebanon. Bereft of its moral egotism, Israeli society is more susceptible to self-doubt now than ever before, to divisions from within, and to substantive pressures from without. Since the relationship is defined ultimately in terms of metropolitan interests, distrust of the supporting metropolis is basic to settler mentality. Israel's power is still largely derivative; it depends heavily on the bounties of an uncertain, distrusted ally. What has aided it so far has been the Arab failure to open and widen this potential breach. Finally, like other settler states, Israel has evinced a tendency to keep its frontiers in a state of hostile flux. Israel suffers from an inexorable dialectic of anxiety, violence, and expansion. Hence it tends to re-produce its own risks. Thus Israel's demographic "problem," resolved after the 1948 Palestinian exile, has returned following the conquests of 1967. Thus it is in the process of denormalizing its relations with Egypt, its most important and populous neighbor. Thus it has invaded Lebanon, which, given a certain policy on Syria's part and some planning by the Lebanese, could turn into a quagmire for Israel.

There are differences with the past, too, on the Arab side. The Palestini-ans are led today by a national liberation movement that, even in its divided state, commands their support. The experience of dispossession, of exile and repression, above all, of suffering and resistance has endowed them with a last-ing identity as Palestinians. As such, they are the most likely contributors to the development of a humane and universalist program for which the mod-ern Middle East has yearned for so long. The PLO, like other successful liber-ation movements of our time, has built institutions, renders services, offers participation, produces culture, and is led by a trusted and popular leader. The Palestinian milieu today is qualitatively different from what it was in 1948. It is a lively, creative, combative milieu. In this post–Second World War world, the Palestinians are the only Third World people to learn two languages in a single generation, the language of the conquerors and the language of resis-tance. In the Occupied Territories, they have daily demonstrated their persis-tence and their will to stay on in their ancient homeland. And the unaided Palestinians, joined by the Lebanese patriots opposed to the ethnocentric vi-sion of Phalangists and Israelis, have given Israel its longest war to date. The Israeli invasion of Lebanon ended certainly in major losses to the Palestinians and the Lebanese. Analogies are approximations of contemporary to histori-cal experiences. In this sense, the PLO's losses in Lebanon may be compared to that of the FLN in the battle of Algiers. After the battle was "lost" (1957), the leaders of the movement dispersed; its headquarters moved out to Tunisia, from where they returned in July 1962 to an independent Algeria. Another comparison, and one that may have more valuable lessons to offer the PLO, is with the Chinese liberation movement, which thrice during its protracted struggle suffered crippling defeats, bringing it close to total annihilation. Each of these disasters led to radical innovations in the strategy and tactics of the Chinese struggle for liberation. The best known of these setbacks—the annihilation of the Kiangsi Soviet and other bases in 1934—led to the epic Long March. More important, the lessons of the encirclement, fighting, and retreat from the Kiangsi Soviet led Mao Tse Tung to abandon the strategy of "agrarian revolution and armed insurrection in favor of the formation of the anti-Japanese United Front of the reform program of the New Democracy."[19]

Most liberation movements in contemporary history had their turning points after a major setback. Historically, crises and defeats have served creative functions in struggles for liberation. However, there are fundamental requirements for a turning around. They entail critical evaluation of errors and weaknesses in the preceding assumptions and conduct of the struggle, a dispassionate analysis of available options, willingness to innovate, and, above all, the creative adherence to the basic precepts of revolutionary struggle.

[1984]

# 28 / "A WORLD RESTORED" REVISITED

## American Diplomacy in the Middle East

The Arabs believe in persons, not in institutions. They saw in me a free agent of the British government, and demanded from me an endorsement of its written promises. So I had to join the conspiracy, and, for what my word was worth, assured the men of their reward. In our two years' partnership under fire they grew accustomed to believing me and to think my government, like myself, sincere.

—T. E. Lawrence, *Seven Pillars of Wisdom*

Kissinger is a man of his word. I trust him completely. He is the first U.S. official who dealt with our problems who has proved himself to be a man of integrity—direct, frank and far-sighted. . . . Kissinger, under the guidance of President Nixon—and you cannot separate the two—has revolutionized the thrust of U.S. policy in our area and before that in the rest of the world. . . . They are now doing the unthinkable in the Mideast. Kissinger is a man of vision, imagination, and perhaps most important of all, trust.

—Anwar Sadat, interview with de Borchgrave in *Newsweek*, March 25, 1974

We are trying to get a [Middle East] settlement in such a way that the moderate regimes are strengthened, and not the radical regimes. We are trying to expel the Soviet military presence.

—Henry Kissinger, background briefing at San Clemente, June 26, 1970

It is the dilemma of conservation that it must fight revolution anonymously, by what it is not, not by what it says.

—Henry Kissinger, *A World Restored*

A quarter peace in Vietnam for which he received half a Nobel Prize is another matter, but with respect to the Middle East it is hard to deny Golda Meir's description of Henry Kissinger as a "miracle worker."[1] One may use a phrase less divine, but the accomplishment certainly establishes Dr. Kissinger as the confidence man of modern diplomacy.

It is difficult to imagine a more unlikely mediator between Israel and the Arabs. As a special assistant at the White House and later as secretary of state, he was a party to the conflict—on Israel's side. To say this is not to accuse Kissinger of inventing either US imperialism or its support for Israel. The two have been linked since before the Zionist state became a reality. Yet Kissinger has made unique contributions to that relationship. The promotion of Israel from a protected state to becoming the best armed primate of Pax Americana in the eastern Mediterranean is due entirely to Kissinger's strategy. Understandably, he helped sabotage the Rogers Plan after it had gained, through the promulgation of a cease-fire, the tactical objectives of achieving a stalemate along the Suez Canal and of isolating the Palestinians from the support of Egypt in the battle with King Hussein.

During the October War, he played the decisive role in the massive resupply of Israel (to date history's biggest operation of this kind, involving an estimated $1.5 billion of military supplies in less than two weeks) without which Israel could not have launched the offensive to cross the Suez Canal and reconquer the Golan Heights. Thanks also to Kissinger's manipulations and Arab ineptitude the cease-fire was achieved only after the Israelis had crossed the canal, secured a bridgehead, and created an enclave on the western side. Then it was violated until Israel had isolated Egypt's Third Army. These violations had the cover of a global nuclear alert initiated by Kissinger—the first since the Cuban missile crisis of 1962. A few weeks later, he appeared before the world in the arms of Anwar Sadat, who proclaimed him a "friend" and a "brother." Stunned, people spoke of him as the miracle man, the magician, the untier of knots. This extraordinary development appears to support T. E. Lawrence's statement that "Arabs believe in persons, not in institutions." However, evidence suggests that President Sadat and the sultan of Arabia are wise men, no less dedicated to their class and dynastic interests than were the sharif of Mecca and his sons. They had compelling reasons to welcome Henry Kissinger to the center of the stage.

The Egyptian-Israeli interim agreement of January 1974 and the Sinai Accord of September 1975 are the landmarks in Kissinger's "step-by-step" road to peace in the Middle East. Both agreements were generally acclaimed as historic achievements. Despite the unusual commitments Kissinger made to win Israeli acceptance of the Sinai Accord, it obtained overwhelming congressional ratification. In Western Europe no government has voiced objection to it. Even in the Middle East opposition was initially cautious and muted, although it is likely to become increasingly open and intense as the full impact of the accord is felt. Two assumptions underlie the broad support for Kissinger's Middle East diplomacy from people the Western press like to describe as "moderates." The first assumption is that his step-by-step approach has been bringing Israel and the Arabs closer to a settlement and provides the best chance for averting another war. Second, it is assumed that in view of the Middle East's enhanced economic importance and the Arab leaders' demonstrated will to use the "oil weapon," the US has begun to play a positive role as an honest and evenhanded arbiter.

Both assumptions are inaccurate. Far from constituting the best chance for peace, the two accords squandered the opportunities for a negotiated settlement that had been created by the October War. Like the Paris agreement on Vietnam, the Sinai Accord (that has superseded the January agreement) is distinguished by its vulnerability to violations. Far from constituting a step toward peace, it is likely to yield an interregnum for the accumulation of violence. And far from being an honest arbiter, the US government has progressively become a party to the Middle East conflict—on the side of entrenched interests and to the detriment of the Jewish, Arab, and American people.

### A Squandering of Opportunities: The Accord at Kilometer 101

Of the two Egyptian-Israeli agreements, the second, involving Israeli "withdrawal" from the Ciddi and Mitla passes and from the Abu-Rudeis oil fields in the Sinai, is generally regarded as the more significant and substantive step. One might argue for the opposite conclusion: the disengagement accord of January 1974 entailed the squandering of the opportunities for peace after the October War and locked the Egyptian government into a compromising and dependent relationship with the United States. The Sinai Accord followed logically from the January disengagement.[2]

The agreement at Kilometer 101 satisfied Kissinger's requirements of a meaningful accord: it had the appearance of being a compromise by both sides and of rendering satisfaction to both. Egypt gained its entrapped Third Army, the withdrawal of Israeli forces from both sides of the canal, and the possibility of augmenting state revenues by opening it. Israel obtained an arrangement that permitted military demobilization, granted it a cease-fire line along the most favorable strategic formation in the Sinai, left for two more years the depleting Egyptian oil fields under its occupation, and interposed a UN buffer zone between the contending armies.

Far from being equitable the January disengagement yielded Israel primary gains and conceded Egypt benefits of secondary importance. If President Sadat's objective is to obtain the total evacuation of the Occupied Territories, then he is further from it as a result of the accord. Not since 1945 had the belligerents and their backers in the Middle East been confronted with as much incentive to reach a negotiated settlement (e.g., Israeli need for demobilization, Egyptian concern for the Third Army, the risk of superpower confrontation, and the effects on Europe and Japan of the oil boycott disposed all parties toward a settlement). The January disengagement removed those incentives and restored the equation of occupation and war.

In explaining Egypt's acceptance of the agreement, many commentators stressed its military predicament and Sadat's need to rescue the Third Army Corps. These undoubtedly played a part, but Cairo's predicament was less serious and one-sided than American and Israeli propagandists would admit. True, in a brilliant display of bold maneuver and fast movement, aided by incredibly slow and disjointed Egyptian reaction, the Israelis crossed the Suez Canal and trapped some twenty thousand well-equipped Egyptian soldiers. But in the process they also trapped themselves. Tactically Israel enjoyed an advantage because its forces held an offensive position at the edge of Egypt's interior and to the rear of advance Egyptian columns. Strategically, however, the situation favored Egypt. The haphazard cease-fire line, with its interlocking pattern of territorial control, rendered the Israeli enclave on the West Bank extremely vulnerable to surprise attack. The mettle of Egyptian soldiers having been tested, the Israelis could not afford to underestimate the risk. To stay on the West Bank they would have had to remain on alert—allowing at best only partial demobilization of their reserve units. This, Israel could not afford.

In the event of another outbreak of war, the thirty thousand Israelis on the western side would have been subject to pounding by some two hundred thousand well-equipped and easily supplied First and Second Egyptian armies to the west and north. Even if the latter failed to improve on their past performance and fought in their usually sturdy, conventional manner, the Israelis would have needed more than ingenuity and boldness to meet them. They might have had to bring reinforcements. Reinforcing and supplying these troops would at best have been difficult, for Israel's supply lines were extended, and it held only about eight miles of the bridgehead on the eastern bank. That could easily be lost to a determined enemy willing to make sacrifices, as the Arabs obviously were. In that event, the Israelis could have found themselves in a situation worse than that of the Egyptian Third Army. Given the smallness of Israel's population and the needed skills of its reservists, the entrapment of so large a force—a setback for Egypt—would have been a disaster for Israel.

The isolation of Egypt's Third Army, while serious, was by no means as hopeless as the Western press and analysts portrayed. It had access to sweet water, and some supplies were reaching it clandestinely from the mainland. Above all, the entrappers were subject to attacks from the north and west while commanding only a narrow bridgehead connecting them with their forces in the rear. In warfare, psychological factors are of crucial value. The Israelis were likely to encounter their toughest adversary in the Third Army because the latter was confronted with that rare combination of risk and hope that has historically produced heroic breakthroughs.

Most importantly, the October cease-fire line was intolerably costly for Israel. It required a state of mobilization that reduced the Israeli workforce by an estimated 20 percent. According to Itzhak Ben Aharon, former general secretary of the Hista'drut (Israel's trade union confederation), the defense mobilization since October 1973 deprived the Israeli economy of 30–40 percent of its skilled technical workers, reduced production by 30 percent (comparative base being September 1973), and canceled out the equivalent of two years of economic growth.[3] These realities were beginning to be reflected in the daily lives of people. The cost of basic staples—like bread, milk, and butter—was up 30–70 percent; transportation by 50 percent; and dislocations in the servicing sector—mail, phones, deliveries—were reported to be widespread.[4] The political and social costs of stalemate along the post-October line were incalculable.

Israel could probably have maintained the required level of mobilization with massive amounts of economic and military aid and a large influx of skilled people from abroad. The US is the only source of both. One doubts that Washington would have been meaningfully forthcoming. Rushing $1.5 billion in arms to save an ally from defeat was one thing; keeping it in a precarious military posture at the cost of $8 or $10 billion a year was another, especially for a Watergated president and a troubled economy. Similarly, American Zionists who live vicariously off the Jewish state were unlikely to leave the comforts of the US in large numbers in order to serve in the Middle East. On the contrary, had the situation been prolonged, Israel would have had to contend with growing pressure to modify its negotiating position.

## Israel's Options: An Appraisal

For these reasons, the Egyptian-Israeli cease-fire line of October 1973, unlike those after the wars of 1948, 1956, and 1967, was untenable. It could not be frozen. Israel had three options: (a) start another war; (b) negotiate agreement on separation of forces based on a commitment of withdrawal from the Occupied Territories and a negotiating timetable toward a peace settlement (at the beginning of the Kissinger rounds this was stated to be the minimum Egyptian condition for disengagement); or (c) withdraw unilaterally from the area west of Suez to a more rational and defensible line, which most Israeli and American strategists had designated, since 1968, to be the Giddi and Mitla passes.

Israel was unlikely to start a full-scale war. It had no rational political or military target left in Egypt. The rhetoric of Israeli generals notwithstanding, the "destruction" of the Egyptian army was not a practical proposition either militarily or politically. On the contrary, the chances were that even in the event of full-scale war it would suffer a major setback. Secondly, without massive support from the US Israel could not wage the war. It is doubtful that Washington would have sanctioned a project so fraught with the risk of a superpower confrontation and potentially so costly to US interests. Thirdly, a flexible but firm Arab posture, favoring a negotiated settlement but continuing the oil boycott, would have isolated Israel and the US and made the resumption of war difficult to justify.

The second option (Egyptian-Israeli military disengagement as a first stage in the fulfillment of a commitment to relinquish the conquests of 1967) represented the test of Israeli and US intentions. If Israel were at all willing to make peace with the neighboring states on the basis of complete withdrawal it would have accepted this option. It had the obvious virtues of assuring the Arab governments of peaceable Israeli intentions, of making the accord with Egypt a model attractive to Syria and Jordan, and of linking military disengagement to the process of peacemaking. It would have permitted Israel the time to negotiate the terms of its security and freedom of navigation—the time to test and be assured of the intentions of the Arab states. Finally, since it was obviously attractive to the Arab governments involved, this option might have served a primary Israeli purpose: the isolation and abandonment of the Palestinian people's demand for the restoration of their national rights.

Similarly, if Kissinger were disposed to promote peace on the basis of complete Israeli withdrawal he would have exerted the considerable influence of his government on behalf of an accord that definitively linked military disengagement with a peace settlement. For someone who has consistently emphasized the necessity of linking negative military and economic pressures with positive diplomatic initiatives, Dr. Kissinger performed rather strangely in the Middle East; he violated his own norms of negotiation, acting more as an adversary than a mediator.

Given their annexationist position (even the "doves" have declared Jerusalem, Sharm el-Sheikh, and the Golan Heights to be nonnegotiable), Israeli leaders needed special inducements to admit the necessity of complete withdrawal. In the wake of the October War, which shook their presumption of invincibility, underlined their isolation, and emphasized their utter dependence on the US, they might have been more amenable to reason, in particular because their national interest demanded early demobilization. Had Egypt held, and Kissinger assisted with friendly advice and firm warnings, Israel might have been induced to accept completely withdrawal as a basis for disengagement and negotiation. If it had refused, the third option (unilateral withdrawal from the west of Suez Canal) might have proved to be the only feasible course for Israel. Its one-sided character may have been disguised by an escalation of clashes resulting in an agreement allowing for a new cease-fire line along the Giddi and Mitla passes. The predicament of the Third Army was serious and the recovery of the canal was important enough to make such an arrangement attractive to Egypt. But then Egypt would have gained what it did from the disengagement accord without setting the precedents that paved the way for Israel to become Egypt's cosovereign in the Sinai.

Reason and rules of diplomacy led one to assume that while maintaining a posture of moderation Egypt would reject a fourth option (disengagement from the post-October cease-fire lines to a new military frontier that Israel could hold without full mobilization) unless it were tied to a commitment and a negotiating timetable for complete Israeli withdrawal. In the Israeli-

American game plan this option must have figured as a good counter but a bad bet. Eventually Israel would have had to choose from the other three options. But, as Dr. Kissinger told newsmen, Anwar Sadat pulled a pleasant surprise on him. The US and Israeli governments were spared the necessity of choice. In accepting the terms of the January disengagement, President Sadat relinquished his strategic and political advantages in a gamble that could, at best, yield limited gains to Egypt—and Egypt alone. The Sinai Accord underlined the limits of those gains.

*The Sinai Accord*

Like the January 1974 disengagement, the Sinai Accord has the appearance of being a compromise by both sides and of rendering satisfaction to both, while conferring upon the US the special privilege of policing the peace. Egypt gained formal Israeli withdrawal from territories (the Giddi and Mitla passes and the Abu-Rudeis oil fields) which were symbolically and economically important. Israel obtained from the US the assurance of long-term economic aid and oil supplies that will more than compensate it for Egypt's drying oil wells and a promise of advanced, offensive weapons that will significantly augment its military superiority in the Middle East. Egypt was also offered a package, though minuscule in comparison with Israel's, of US aid. Israel gained for its cargoes the right of passage through the Suez Canal even before the state of belligerence between it and Egypt had ended—a privilege without precedent in international law—and a renunciation by Egypt of its right to blockade the Red Sea. Finally, the US was accorded the sole responsibility for monitoring and supervising the agreement and the exclusive opportunity to penetrate the Middle East politically and economically. Since each side is being viewed as having gained from the accord and the world's "number one" power has assumed the role of overseer, their interest in respecting its terms is presumed. In fact, though, the accord is likely to put unbearable long-range strains on Egypt, stimulate the Israeli quest for a permanent stalemate, augment the arms race in the Middle East, and accentuate divisions within the Arab world.

By "withdrawing" from the Giddi and Mitla passes, Israel undoubtedly relinquished an advantage. However, US and Zionist propaganda notwithstanding, Israel's "loss" is limited and minor, for the "withdrawal" did not include the key Israeli air base in Rifidim. That is a significant exception. Since the 1967 War, the Israeli Defense Force has relied primarily on its air superiority over Egypt; the Rifidim base in the Giddi-Mitla region has been the westernmost anchor of this superiority. Israeli fighters and bombers based there can strike at any target along the entire Suez Canal front and beyond at the bases and stockpiles in the rear. Furthermore, the most important observation post (Umm Khisheib) in the passes has also stayed under Israeli occupation. The accord obviously strains to minimize Israel's strategic losses in the Sinai.

Egypt, on the other hand, has not gained militarily from Israeli withdrawal. It does not even have the right to build an air strip in the evacuated territories. Rather, it has accepted severe limits on its sovereignty. For example, it is forbidden to place any military personnel in the strip along the Suez including the Abu-Rudeis oil fields, and, under UN supervision, Israel and Egypt share the road along the strip. Entry to the area is only through UN checkpoints. Similarly, Israel and Egypt are treated as equals in the passes; each is allowed a surveillance post manned by no more than 250 persons and monitored by the presumably neutral Americans. In effect, Israel has achieved the status of *primus inter pares* in the Sinai, with the United States and the UN overseeing the unequal terms of cosovereignty.

If the Middle East conflict had primarily concerned Israel and Egypt, one might have just managed to view this agreement as a step toward peace. But Egyptian-Israeli hostility has been a reflection of the fundamental conflict over the national rights of Jews and Arabs in Palestine, a conflict with its origins in the Middle East's colonial past, and that continues to be exacerbated by foreign interests. No peace is possible until this basic issue is resolved, and its resolution is unlikely to be aided by augmented foreign presence and increased militarization of the belligerent countries—the two most tangible results of the Sinai Accord.

Dr. Kissinger seeks to manipulate Middle East realities. His negotiating strategy is intended to produce a durable stalemate by further dividing the Arabs, by separating Egypt—the largest and historically an important Arab state—from the mainstream of radical Arab nationalism and by isolating the Palestinians. In a fundamental sense his quest for peace in the Middle East suffers from the same problem that marked American pursuit of pacification in Vietnam—the failure to come to grips with the nature of a nationalist movement and a people's aspirations. There is no hint in the Sinai Accord of confronting the real issues that evoke anxieties and anger in the Middle East—of Jewish security and Palestinian rights, of Israeli frontiers and Arab sovereignty.

In effect, these issues have been bypassed in a manner that stimulates contradictory expectations. The Israeli leaders share Kissinger's presumption that once Egypt's primary grievances are removed it will shun another war. The Palestinians, Syria, and even Jordan will then be isolated and accept a dictated peace. Israeli officials believe that except for minor territorial adjustments they can hold on to the territories they have declared as being basic to either Israeli security or the Zionist mission. These include Sharm el-Sheikh, the Golan Heights, the lands constituted by the hills of Latroun and Judea, and Jerusalem—that monument of ecumenism over which the Zionists have declared their messianic monopoly.

The Sinai Accord as well as the US-Israeli agreement accompanying it have reinforced Israeli expectations. There is a noteworthy absence in the accord of a commitment or even a promise by Israel to enter into negotiations over the Golan, the West Bank, or Palestinian rights. Furthermore, clause 12 of the US-Israeli agreement contradicts the claim that the Sinai Accord is only a step toward peace linked to overall settlement. It reads: "It is the United States Government's position that Egyptian commitments under the Egypt-Israeli agreement, its implementation, validity and duration are not conditional upon any acts or developments between the other Arab states and Israel. The United States Government regards the agreement as standing on its own." Let us suppose that two years from now lack of meaningful progress toward a settlement leads the Egyptian government (under pressure from the Syrians, Palestinians, and its own Arab nationalist elements in the army and bureaucracy) to close the Suez Canal to Israeli cargoes as a means of pressuring it to withdraw from the occupied lands. The situation would then parallel the events of June 1967. Israel would undoubtedly describe it as a violation of the Sinai Accord and probably launch a "preemptive" attack. In such an event, the US is clearly committed to supporting Israel, notwithstanding its avowedly neutral presence in the Sinai.

Israel is not the only country to have been given "understandings" and "assurances"—by now familiar illusions in Dr. Kissinger's magic bag. President Sadat and the Saudi king have been assuring Arab leaders of private US commitments to bring about a speedy peace settlement on the basis of Israeli withdrawal and a modicum of justice for the Palestinians. A leaked memo of "assurances" to Egypt makes no mention of Palestinians or of Jordan but promises "serious" US efforts to bring about "further negotiations between Syria and Israel." That may occur during this next year, for the credibility of Sadat and the sheikhs requires the tranquilizing of Syria. Arms supplies will be used as the incentive for Israel to make adjustments on the Golan. In addition, its leaders are assured of further augmentation in Israel's role as a Mediterranean power allied to the US—a prize much greater than the Golan Heights. In anticipation of American pressure, Israeli leaders have been preparing for what Prime Minister Rabin has termed "cosmetic surgery" in the Heights. More facts (i.e., more Zionist settlements) have been created in the Golan. The Israeli position has hardened. "Israel will not go down from the Golan," says Rabin. "None of the Zionist settlements shall be dismantled as a result of interim talks with Syria," pledges Defense Minister Shimon Peres. Then a softening is indicated; "cosmetic" adjustments are possible. They mean the outlying fields around Quneitra and a few minor border corrections. If Washington were to insist, which is unlikely until after the 1976 presidential elections, Israel may also withdraw from the strategically unimportant southern part of the Heights.

Neutralize Cambodia, cut off North Vietnam, and the NLF will go away. Disengage Egypt, tranquilize Syria, restore a bit of King Hussein on the West Bank, and the Palestinians will not matter. It is a typically Kissingerian construct: logical and wrong, likely to crumble after an impressive opening. In seeking to manipulate realities Kissinger misinterprets, underestimates, and distorts them. His game plan is destined to fail with possibly disastrous consequences for the Jewish, the Arab, and, perhaps, the American people. He confuses peace with US predominance, and in his eagerness to maintain the latter he ignores local realities. For example, since neither he nor Israel is offering much to Syria, one wonders why Damascus will be tranquilized by minor concessions. Similarly, the thrust of US policy in the Middle East has been provocatively anti-Russian; Kissinger has sought to exclude the USSR from the process of negotiations. Hence Moscow is unlikely to aid him in a region where its leverages are still strong. Of the anguish and aspirations of the Palestinian people and the moral force they represent in the Arab world, no one in Washington appears to have a clue. Above all, the US government evinces as little understanding of Arab nationalism as it did of the Vietnamese. Otherwise, it would not still assume—as it did earlier in creating the Baghdad Pact—that its efforts at isolating "radicals" and strengthening "moderates" will yield "stability." In fact, they will have the contrary effect of accentuating inter-Arab differences and subjecting the moderates to mounting radical pressures. Nor would Washington expect, as it has done since 1967, that Arabs will ultimately acquiesce in a peace settlement that would leave the Palestinian question unresolved and at least Jerusalem, parts of the Golan Heights, and Sharm el-Sheikh under Israeli occupation.

Since Kissinger has shuttled around the basic issues, the prospects of a negotiated settlement in the Middle East are slim. A hardening by both sides is likely; and bitterness will be increased by the resulting disappointments. Having offered to reach a negotiated settlement, the Arabs will become more convinced of Israeli expansionism. And having relinquished some conquests in the Sinai, the Israelis will be convinced of Arab treachery when Egypt joins the dissatisfied eastern states in putting tangible pressures on Israel. Another war may become unavoidable.

### When the Fifth Arab-Israeli War Starts

The next war is likely to be more widespread, for a number of states that have previously stood on the sidelines will probably become direct participants. Historically Israel's enemies have multiplied in direct proportion to the increase in its military strength. A major difference between the Arab-Israeli war of June 1967 and that of October 1973 was that in the latter the Arab countries that do not border on Israel played a more substantive economic and military role than they had in 1967. Nadav Safran, Harvard's pro-Zionist Middle East expert, has pointed out that this phenomenon was "the consequence of the vast growth of Israeli power in the years since 1967." "As the military capabilities of Israel multiplied in these years," Safran wrote, "the radiation of that power began to be felt directly by these countries for the first time. . . . Their concern began to rest no longer solely on pan-Arab considerations but also on the considerations of precaution; and their support for countries of the 'first circle' became an investment in their own security."[5] Weapons such as Pershing missiles or the F-16, that range over Saudi Arabia, Kuwait, and Iraq, can only expand the military coalition of Arab states against Israel.

The fifth Arab-Israeli war is bound to be more destructive and might involve nuclear weapons, for the Sinai Accord will vastly accelerate the vicious arms race in the Middle East. Over the next four years Israel is to receive from the US an estimated $10 billion worth of armaments, much of them the most advanced and lethal offensive weapons—such as the long-range Pershing missile (with its range of 450 miles and designed to carry a nuclear payload of 10,000 pounds), the F-16 fighter bombers, and the Lance surface-to-surface missile (also equipped to fire nuclear warheads). The Arabs will undoubtedly catch up—a few with Russian help, while others will spend oil money on Western weapons. After all, it is the dialectic of imperialism that the sheikhs should subsidize the Pentagon and the armaments industry that together maintain the military "balance" in Israel's favor.

When the next war comes the Arab governments will, nevertheless, find in Israel an adversary more aggressive, intensively mobilized, and better equipped than in October 1973. The advantages they enjoyed in the last war cannot be duplicated. In conventional wars one can rarely achieve surprise more than once; in any case, the UN buffer zone in the Sinai guarantees against it on the Egyptian front. Moreover, next time Israel is likely to strike first, especially if the Arabs supply (as in 1967) a credible rationale for it. Israeli armed forces are better prepared today than at any time before. US supplies have more than compensated for the losses suffered in the October War so that both the quality and quantity of Israeli armaments have vastly improved.

Nor would the Arabs have the advantage of wielding superior weapons unknown to the enemy, as was largely the case in October 1973 with the SAM 6 antiaircraft missiles, the Sagger antitank missiles, and the Sukhoi 7 close-support fighter planes. Since the USSR did not make these sophisticated weapons available to the Vietnamese, the US had no chance to crack their electronic secrets. However, during the October War the US devised countermeasures within weeks of Israeli capture of these weapons.

In addition to the countermeasures and jamming devices, Israel is now equipped with new weapons of comparable or superior quality. For example, massive US supply of Maverick and Tow antitank missiles is designed to off-set Arab possession of Saggers (the Tow, especially designed against Russian T-62 tanks, was first rushed to Israel during the October War and was used in the Israeli thrust across the Suez). Similarly the deployment by Israel of the latest Standard surface-to-air missiles (developed by the US Navy) will make it harder for the Sukhoi 7s to support the ground forces. It can be safely predicted that Washington will continue to supply Israel with more and newer weapons. If the past (in Vietnam and Middle East) is a guide these supplies will be justified in terms of a leverage, an inducement for peace.

Strategically Egypt's position is hardly better. Its one weapon against the Israeli effort at normalizing the situation was the threat of resuming what was grandiosely described as a "war of attrition"—heat up the front lines, force a degree of mobilization on Israel, and arouse enough global concern to induce a measure of diplomatic movement toward a negotiated peace. However, the October War was, in effect, the last of the genre—a war of "limited objectives" (although in the process of succeeding beyond their own expectations the Egyptian leaders appear to have forgotten first the limitation and then the objective). The terms of disengagement have removed that possibility.

Those who know him testify to the shrewdness of President Anwar Sadat. His diplomacy and military planning preceding the October War also suggest an astute and cautious man not prone to eccentric behavior. How then can one explain his bold, rather reckless investment of the Arab world's political and military assets in the goodwill of the United States? It is as unhelpful to credit it to Kissinger's manipulative genius as it is incorrect to ascribe the January disengagement to the plight of the Third Army. Nor is it particularly valuable to explain it in unilinear terms of Saudi Arabia's influence, or ARAMCO's assurances, or Egypt's unremitting if unrequited love affair with the US, or everybody's ill-founded fear of the Palestinians serving as a catalyst of an Arab revolution. All these are realities but only as parts of a complex mosaic of neocolonialism and counterrevolution in the Middle East. A meaningful answer to the question demands an inquiry into the nature and aspirations of the Arab ruling elites; into the corrupt colonial components of Arab nationalist ideology; into the consequent degeneration of radical nationalist groupings such as the Nasserites; and into the remarkable resurgence of reactionary forces in the Middle East. It also requires an inquiry into US global strategy, i.e., the "structure for peace" in which Arab governments are seeking integration. To discuss the first set of problems is beyond the scope of this article. In the second part we examine the outlines of the US global strategy.

*US Foreign Policy in the 1970s: The Kissinger-Nixon Doctrine*

With the defeat of US power in Vietnam, Washington has launched a new strategy designed to restore the position of global paramountcy it had enjoyed in the 1950s and appears to be losing in the 1970s. As such, the Kissinger-

Nixon doctrine represents neither a redistribution of power nor a retreat from imperialism's forward position. Its aims are restorative, conservative, and aggressive.

Since the end of the Second World War the emergence and acceptance of the US as the paramount world power had been predicated upon five factors:

(a) the overwhelming superiority of the US in strategic weaponry;

(b) the decline of Western European countries and Japan as centers of power;

(c) successful US military interventions against real or imaginary social revolutions in the Third World;

(d) the dominance of US capital over the world economy; and

(e) the existence of a national consensus on behalf of a bipartisan foreign policy.

Throughout this period certain ghosts have haunted Henry Kissinger as he has groped for a stable international system under US hegemony. Three of them are of long standing: the existence of a powerful USSR, national liberation movements in the Third World, and the possible loss of a domestic consensus for a forward foreign policy. Time has diminished but little of his apprehensions regarding the Soviet Union; the US defeat in Indochina has increased those regarding the liberation movements; and the specter of a broken-down consensus has become a reality. To these has been added a fourth problem: that of restoring America's leverage over Western Europe and Japan.

In order to understand a policy, one must inquire into the assumptions of its makers. And for Henry Kissinger, as for most other makers of America's postwar foreign policy, power is above all a question of who controls the land. His geopolitical assumptions, so much a part of the realpolitik tradition to which Kissinger subscribes, have led him to direct his focus not on Southeast Asia but on the Middle East as the most appropriate field on which to combat his ghosts.

*Detente: The Politics of Antagonistic Collaboration*

More than any other US strategist, Henry Kissinger has been obsessed with the challenge of the Soviet Union. The USSR, being the largest, richest, and politically the most integrated land mass in "Eurasia," represents the only power capable of competing successfully with the United States. As such, it is the natural enemy and permanent threat to the US, which Kissinger views as inferior in resources and therefore in need of access to those of the Eurasian land mass.

This geopolitical view of the US strategic predicament also defines Kissinger's concern with preventing the emergence of Western Europe as an independent and cohesive center of power. Given the strategic importance of the Middle East and the primacy of its resources to industrialized states, Washington gives the highest priority to preventing an expansion of Russian influence in the area, as well as to controlling the character of Europe's ties to it.

Compared with the 1950s, however, the contemporary US view of the USSR is more rational and discerning. Then, even Kissinger had regarded it as a threat not only in geopolitical but also in ideological terms. The Soviet Union and China were viewed by him equally, as "revolutionary powers" who "do not accept the framework of the international order or the domestic structure of other states or both." Today he views both as potentially status quo powers, i.e., those who can be induced to respect the "framework of the international order" and leave the policing of "disorder" to the US and its clients. Hence US policy toward the Soviet Union is best described as one of antagonistic collaboration. It combines elements of co-optation and selective cooperation in some areas; of confrontation and containment in others. In the Middle East the Americans put relations with the Soviet Union squarely in the antagonistic half of the détente. In order to fully comprehend and predict the parallelisms of antagonistic collaboration, it is necessary to remember that Kissinger attaches high value to the concept of "linkages." This defines Washington's view of the links between confrontation and collaboration, war and negotiations, and, above all, between show of force and retention of power. For Kissinger all international crises exist on a single continuum in that their resolution is ultimately determined by the balance of power between the US and the Soviet Union. Hence the resolution of each issue in America's favor depends not so much on the individual merits of the case ("we committed blunders in Vietnam") but on the overall balance of power. A demonstration of will and strength in one area, of flexibility in another, is expected to contribute to a favorable outcome in the third. Here is how Kissinger described the connection between the US invasion of Cambodia and his objective in the Middle East in 1970: "It is of course nonsense to say that we did what we did in Cambodia in order to impress the Russians in the Middle East. But we certainly have to keep in mind that the Russians will judge us by the general purposefulness of our performance everywhere. What they are doing in the Middle East, whatever their intentions, poses the gravest threats in the long term for Western Europe and Japan and therefore for the U.S."[6]

*The US and the Third World:*
*In Quest of a "Legitimizing Principle of Social Repression"*

A fundamental objective behind détente with the Soviet Union and China has been to isolate the revolutionary movements from the support of socialist powers. There was little or no military logic to the dramatic increase in the bombings in Indochina (37 percent) immediately preceding Nixon's journey to China and the mining of Hanoi and Haiphong just before his visit to the USSR. Their targets were psychological and political. The objective was to establish a link between détente (acknowledgment of the legitimacy of "revolutionary" power) and counterrevolution (violent denial of it to revolutionary movements). The intent was to reaffirm the presumption of paramountcy and the premises of "limited war" that concede to the superpower the right to intervene with unlimited inhumanity—against social revolutions.

The forces for liberation in the Third World continue to be regarded in Washington as primary and the least manageable—hence ultimately the most serious—menace to American interests.

For good reasons: all revolutionary—and in some respects radical nationalist—movements seek to overthrow the existing system of power, production, and distribution. When victorious, they tend to replace the old order with new, sovereign, popular, or national institutions of power and socialist modes of production and distribution. In other words, they challenge the legitimacy and threaten the existence of the three basic and interlinked elements that support and perpetuate the structure of imperialism: the international corporations, the pro-Western and procapitalist indigenous bourgeoisie, and the state's apparatus of coercion and control (such as the bureaucracy). The accession of a revolutionary movement to power normally results—as it did in China, North Vietnam. and Cuba—in the severance of the ties of dependence on the dominant centers of Western industrial power.

Washington regards maintaining the "stability" of the "international system" as the primary goal of policy. International stability depends, according to Kissinger, on there being a "generally accepted legitimacy," that he defines as an international consensus, "about the permissible aims and methods of foreign policy . . . the acceptance of the framework of international order by all major powers." Revolutionaries, who threaten the status quo, are not amenable to the dictates of diplomacy because, he says, "it is the essence of revolutionary power that it possesses the courage of its convictions."[7]

Whence comes the unsettling characteristic of revolutionary movements and leaders? Unlike established socialist powers, they evince stubborn indifference to material incentives. "Revolutionaries are rarely motivated by material conditions," remarks Kissinger, "though the illusion that they are persists in the West. If Castro or Sukarno had been principally interested in economics, their talents would have guaranteed them a brilliant career in the societies they overthrew."[8]

According to Kissinger, the revolutionaries of "pre-Newtonian" cultures such as Vietnam, Cuba, and Oman enjoy unusual advantage over the statesmen of the Western world. The "real world being almost completely internal to them," they can be impervious to "empirical" realities in starting a revolution, immune to "external" stimuli (such as torture, saturated bombings, and pacification programs) in stopping it. "To revolutionaries," says Kissinger, "the significant reality is the world they are striving to bring about, not the world they are fighting to overcome." This enables them to "override conditions that had seemed overwhelmingly hostile."[9] Thus Kissinger perceives the Third World liberation movements as threatening the "psychological balance of power" that in another of his crucial analytical distinctions he regards as being equal, if not greater, in importance to the "physical balance of power."[10] The deepest problems of equilibrium, he explains, "are not physical but psychological or moral. The shape of the future will depend ultimately on connections that far transcend the physical balance of power."[11]

Finally, insofar as the revolutionary forces question the justness of the present system of power, they accentuate the already critical problem of "legitimacy." And, as Kissinger has rightly insisted throughout his writing, without legitimacy no stability, no orderly change, is possible. Of the Third World in this context he wrote some time before he came to power: "The problem of political legitimacy is the key to political stability in the regions containing two-thirds of the world's population. A stable domestic system in the new countries will not automatically produce international order, but international order is impossible without it. An American agenda must include some conception of what we understand by political legitimacy."[12]

The above truism might have been worthwhile had Kissinger attempted to offer a conception of political legitimacy—how it is gained and why it is lost. Such an exercise might have helped him to recognize that the matter is not susceptible to political engineering, that it concerns fundamental problems—of authority not administration, of consent not obedience, of morality not management—that belong in the realm of political processes rather than diplomatic or military manipulation.

The tendency to recoil from facing an admittedly fundamental problem is necessary to the search for managerial solutions. The cumulative effect of Dr. Kissinger's discursive references is logical: if stability is the goal of policy and revolutions the main threats to stability, then these latter must be contained, confronted, and destroyed. And this he knows requires international acquiescence to a "legitimizing principle of social repression."[13] The war in Vietnam wrecked the one "principle of social repression"—the unilateral American doctrine of limited wars—to which the world had acquiesced through two decades of military intervention in the Third World. "Every war in which we have been engaged in the Western Hemisphere," wrote Henry Kissinger, "was a limited war."[14] And he called them "productive." No one would ever make that statement on Vietnam. What was supposed to be a "limited war"—i.e., limited in terms of its impact on the aggressor, not in its consequences for the invaded people—cost more than a quarter of a million American casualties and an estimated $200 billion. The "invisible" war—so visible to the beleaguered populace—became manifest to the world. The "forgotten" war—so remembered by its victims—impressed itself on the consciousness of the American people. The touchstone of contemporary revolutions—Vietnam—defeated the collective presumptions of modern technology and put into question the impregnability of US power. An exponent of "limited war," wars not of "conquest," as he would say, but of "conservation"—Kissinger understood the meaning of Vietnam. "Whatever the outcome of the war in Vietnam," he wrote just prior to his accession to power, "it is clear that it has greatly diminished American willingness to become involved in this form of warfare elsewhere. *Its utility as a precedent has therefore been importantly undermined*" (emphasis added).[15]

The "low-profile, low-cost" strategy of the 1970s seeks to overcome the constraints of domestic opposition to interventionism, while attempting to exploit the expanding riches of allies and clients. It entails the promotion of regional constellations of power in strategically important areas of the world; the reorganization of US armed forces into, in Admiral Zumwalt's phrase, "high technology capital-intensive services . . . to support the indigenous armies of threatened allies";[16] and a lowering of the threshold on the use of nuclear weapons in order to make its threat credible in situations of "limited wars."

## New Leverages, Old Allies

For two decades after the Second World War Europe and Japan were America's pliable allies because the United States enjoyed the leverage of economic dominance over them and provided an umbrella of security. But by the mid-1960s it was in the process of losing both. Today, détente has reduced the value of America's security umbrella, and subservience to the US now offers but little economic benefit to Europe or Japan. On the contrary, they are now America's competitors as sellers of finished products and buyers of raw materials. Hence one of Washington's primary aims is to acquire new leverages over old allies, who, Kissinger explained to a group of congressmen's wives (on March 11, 1974), are a bigger problem for the US than its enemies. The long-range goal is to prevent the emergence of Western Europe as a unified and independent power in world politics.

In Kissinger's strategic design NATO was destined to be depreciated from a glorified system of global alliance to a regional constellation of pro-American power. Hence his declaration on April 23, 1973: "The U.S. has global interests and responsibilities. Our European allies have regional interests." Bipolarity is better suited to Kissinger's balance-of-power approach; it also simplifies the task of staying number one. Hence he has been an early and consistent proponent of denying Europe a global role in world politics.

As stated earlier, Dr. Kissinger's estimation of America's geopolitical predicament as an "island power" does not center on the USSR alone. "If Eurasia were to fall under the control of a single power or group of powers and if this hostile power were given sufficient time to exploit its resources, we should confront an overpowering threat."[17] As geopoliticians see it, nowhere in the world is such a threat more apparent than in Europe's potential relationship with the countries south of the Mediterranean where some 70 percent of the world's energy reserves and much of its mineral resources are to be found.

Since Phoenician times the Mediterranean has served as the imperial seaway to the riches of Africa and Asia. Its hinterlands provided the human and material resources of the Roman, the Byzantine, the Arab, and the Ottoman empires and allowed their outreach to the French and the British. In recent years the actual and potential shortages of those raw materials (such as oil, gas, phosphates, copper, etc.) that are essential to industrial economies have enormously enhanced the strategic importance of the countries bounded by the Mediterranean and Indian oceans. Control over the production and distribution of these raw materials can only be viewed as a decisive factor by a major power straining to maintain its position of predominance. Hence the focus of the world struggle for power has shifted in the 1970s from the Atlantic and the Pacific to the Mediterranean and Indian oceans.

Three of the four ghosts we have mentioned as haunting Henry Kissinger—the USSR, national liberationist forces, and loss of leverage over Europe and Japan—converge to the south of the Mediterranean. According to his admiring biographers (Marvin and Bernard Kalb), Dr. Kissinger has an "apocalyptic vision" of a possible "change in the strategic balance of power" in that region.[18] Washington views with extreme apprehension an enhancement of Russian influence there. Thus in June 1970, when the presence in Egypt of Russian pilots and missiles was reported, Kissinger blew his whistle on détente and in two successive background briefings threatened to "expel" them. He considers the existence of radical and revolutionary forces in the area as being equally reprehensible. Washington threatened to intervene directly in the Middle East and put on its most elaborate arms rattling in September 1970 during King Hussein's war with the Palestinians. Its most dramatic displays of brinkmanship, including a worldwide nuclear alert, occurred in the region where America's strategic interest (and potential military involvement) was expanding.

In relation to Europe the lands bounded by the Mediterranean and Indian oceans hold both a promise and a threat to the devotees of US paramountcy. If the US can preserve its dominance in that region and assume the role of guardian over the production and distribution of oil and other raw materials essential to European and Japanese economies, then it would have maintained an effective leverage over its allies. In addition, it would have been assured of the energy supplies needed for American consumption. On the other hand, potential association of Middle Eastern countries with the European Economic Community is likely to be at the expense of American capital. Besides, it raises the specter of another "continental power."

Historical and economic forces favor such a development. European governments have compelling reasons to seek close ties with the producing countries of the Middle East and Africa. They fear the effects on their monetary system of the vast outflow of cash to other regions; and they cannot feel assured of stable supplies of raw materials until their economies are fully interdependent with those of the producing countries and until the Arab-African elites have acquired vested interests in the European Economic Community. The Lome trade convention represents an important step in that direction.

The emerging Euro-Arab and Euro-African economic cooperation is viewed by the leaders of the "island power" as a serious threat. In his policy-setting speech of April 23, 1973, Kissinger candidly stated that: The prospect of a closed trading system embracing the European Community and a growing number of other nations in Europe, the Mediterranean, and Africa appears to be at the expense of the United States and other nations that are excluded. The concern is understandable, for a Common Market comprising some 600 million people, Europe's advanced industrial base, a large pool of labor, and the world's richest deposits of energy and mineral resources will inevitably become a formidable locus of power. In order to remain paramount Washington must somehow maintain a controlling role in the Mediterranean and Indian Ocean regions.

As one would expect, the most serious Euro-American differences have been over matters of trade, investment, and monetary relations. These divergences surfaced dramatically in "the year of Europe" during the Arab-Israeli war when such close allies as West Germany publicly protested the use of its ports for US arms supplies to Israel and the British government barred the use of its base in Cyprus for reconnaissance. With the exception of fascist Portugal they all acted, Kissinger bitterly complained to a group of European parliamentarians, "as though the alliance did not exist." His policy of employing the strategic advantage of the US to ensure European conformity had its limits. So did invocations of Western fraternity.

Throughout its first term and in the second, at least until the Arab-Israeli war of October 1973, the Nixon administration pursued a policy of ensuring Europe's and Japan's subordination. It sought to exclude them from the rank of world powers by focusing its quest for a stable balance on the primary military powers—the United States, Russia, and the People's Republic of China. The choice allowed, in the words of Professor Stanley Hoffman, a former colleague and friend and now a critic of Kissinger, "for the neo-Bismarckian tour de force of manipulating all relationships—a feat neither Moscow nor Peking can perform due to their own antagonism."[19] Détente, then, serves as an instrument for perpetuating a situation of "bipolarity" in which the US remains strategically ahead of the USSR.[20] In this there exists a conjunction of Russo-American interests, for bipolarity is congenial to both. Moreover, Russia is also wary of European association with the countries south of the Mediterranean. Hence it may be expected that while seeking to expand its own influence in the Middle East, Moscow will cooperate with Washington in frustrating an independent European role there.

Nor should one overestimate Europe's will to act independently of the US. Alfred Grosser of France calls Europe a "community of malaise" vis-à-vis the United States because its yearning for independence is genuine but its military dependence on the US is fundamental.[21] Europe's security needs, as perceived by its policy makers, require continued military alliance with the United States. A Europe without strategic defense is unacceptable to them because they fear it will lead to dominance by Russia. Yet a European defense policy is inconceivable because it can neither exclude nor admit Germany's nuclear participation. This Kissinger knows and is determined to exploit as his carrot and stick in Europe. Détente may have enhanced America's security leverage over Europe because, says Stanley Hoffman, "the direction of the 'linkage' can now be reversed; as long as our security dilemma was as acute as our allies' we had to accept certain economic disadvantages in return for their military subordination; now we can exploit their security needs for economic redress."[22] It should be noted that since his speech on a new Atlantic Charter Kissinger has been unambiguous in linking the issues of security with those of economic relations with Europe and European complicity in America's Middle Eastern and Southern African policy.

*Kissinger's "Southern Strategy"*

Kissinger's strategic design aimed not only at containing the USSR and creating effective instruments of "social repression" in the Third World but also at outflanking US European allies. One of its primary thrusts was the creation of an informal yet cohesive military alliance in the Mediterranean and Indian Ocean regions to supersede the role in that area previously assigned to NATO and to the ill-fated Baghdad Pact (CENTO). Spain, Portugal, Turkey, Greece, Israel, Iran, and Saudi Arabia were chosen as the primates of Pax Americana. The weaker clients, such as Ethiopia, Jordan, and Pakistan, were to serve as secondary surrogates. It was the Mediterranean version of Nixon's "Southern strategy" that, at home, implied the realignment of the Republican Party with the forces of the Right and exclusion from it of centrist elements.

The basic elements of Kissinger's design became clear by the autumn of 1970 during Nixon's visit to the Mediterranean and were also discernible in the seemingly contradictory developments associated with the 1969 cease-fire along the Suez Canal. The Rogers Plan (that in fact was drafted by Joseph Sisco working with Kissinger's staff in the White House, not by Rogers's men in the State Department) was promoted to obtain some tactical gains rather than to achieve a Middle East settlement. Evidence also suggests that as Secretary of State Rogers became serious about the plan, he was sabotaged by Henry Kissinger, whose intimate working relations with the Israeli government had remained, until recently, a closely guarded secret.[23]

Nixon's 1970 visit to the Sixth Fleet underscored the importance he attached to the Mediterranean—especially as the presidential visit concentrated on the aircraft carrier *Saratoga*, which had been poised, in a well-coordinated plan with Israel, for possible intervention in Jordan. Meanwhile, Defense Secretary Laird was the guest of the junta in Athens, giving what he called "high priority" to the "modernization" of Greek forces. Subsequently US-Greek military relations grew closer, and the American navy acquired "home" ports in Greece. Similar developments occurred in relation to Turkey and Spain. With Portugal the US reached over the Azores one of its most comprehensive defense deals.

If these states were being prepared to act as sentinels, Israel and Iran were allotted the role of chief marshals. Israel fitted all the specifications of an ideal surrogate. Its military performance in 1967 had been a matter of unabashed envy to the Vietnam-frustrated chiefs of general staff. Its air force was regarded as an effective deterrent against Syrian, Iraqi, or Libyan attacks on America's allies. Between France and India it was the only power to enjoy the nuclear option. Its technological sophistication reassured American officials who, despite Vietnam, retained deep faith in the decisive power of machines. Above all, its economic and military dependence on the US was viewed as being permanent; hence its durability as an ally was presumed. The image was of Sparta in the service of Rome—an irresistible opportunity.

The military buildup of Israel was also viewed at the White House as an asset in assuring the complicity of Congress, where Israel commands virtually unanimous support, in the Indochina war and its consent for the ever-increasing defense appropriations. In relation to Israel itself Congress gave the president in September 1970 what the *New York Times* described as the "most open-ended arms buying program in the world." (September 29, 1970). The Honorable John McCormack, the Speaker of the House, sounded a little amazed: "I have never seen in my forty-two years as a member of the body of Congress language of this kind used in an authorization or an appropriations bill." In its first five years the Nixon administration provided Israel with nearly twenty times as much military aid as did its predecessors in twenty years.[24] Armed with the most advanced offensive weapons in the conventional arsenal of the US, Israel seemingly became the great power of the Middle East. The efficacy of its US-backed threat to intervene in the Jordanian civil war confirmed this status and consecrated the US-Israel strategic alliance.

Iran emerged swiftly on the eastern flank to equal Israel as a major regional power in Southwest Asia. Since the CIA's overthrow of Prime Minister Mossadegh's nationalist government in August 1953, the shah had been an exemplary ally. In the 1950s and early 1960s he used US military and security assistance effectively to consolidate power. Then, while remaining hospitable to international corporations, he combined totalitarian methods for maintaining "stability" with what McNamara's men in the World Bank call a "successful" program of economic development. Motivated by a strong sense of "regional responsibility" he has developed excellent relations with Israel while maintaining meaningful links with Saudi Arabia and the sheikhs in the oil-soaked Gulf. He has filled the "security gap" allegedly created by British withdrawal from the Persian Gulf and deploys his armed forces to suppress the liberation struggle of Arab peoples in Dhofar and Oman. His armaments expenditure has soared annually from some $10 million in 1950 to $5 billion in 1974. The self-styled "light of the Aryans" has, by a large margin, displaced West Germany as the biggest buyer of US arms. With his annual oil earnings now totaling some $20 billion he is able to pay for the weapons and the US advisers who teach how to use them. For the US it is good diplomacy and excellent business.

Kissinger's design had an impressive "conceptual" coherence—an imaginative and logical scheme based on classical balance-of-power precepts. But beneath the brilliance of Kissinger's construct there were pitfalls that a managerial mind could not perceive, for such a perception (or the admission of it) would cost it its raison d'être. A conservative outlook is necessarily closed to the future. The policy suffered from the same fundamental defects that contributed to US failures in Southeast Asia and to the early demise of the Baghdad Pact in the Middle East: it ran counter to the ongoing course of history, underestimated the power of emerging social forces, sought stability in times of change, and looked for client states in a century of national liberation. Its future was linked to the dying status quo of injustice which had developed mainly in the direction of tyranny. Fascist Spain and Portugal, militarist Greece, monarchical Iran and Ethiopia, and Zionist Israel—in the second half of the twentieth century these are falling dominoes.

By mid-1974, as the pro-American regimes of Portugal, Ethiopia, and Greece fell, the backbone of Kissinger's structure for peace, already strained by the October War, had broken. Its restoration would require a great deal of subversion, violence, and diplomatic manipulation—and a shift in US policy toward Europe, in the direction of seeking greater European participation in the Mediterranean and Indian Ocean regions.


*Egypt on the Road to "Moderation"*

Kissinger's design had one obvious flaw that, in the opinion of many power brokers in Washington (e.g., the oil lobby, some banking and investment establishments like the Chase Manhattan Bank, and prestigious law firms representing oil interests), needed correcting: its linkages with America's Arab allies were extremely weak. Even Saudi Arabia, the world's largest oil producer and the Arab state most intimately tied to American capitalism, was imperfectly integrated in the new "regional grouping." Thus the primary objects of this strategy were inhibited from full participation in it.

For the Nixon Doctrine to work in this region the integration of some Arab states in the Mediterranean constellation of power was a necessity—or rather it was a part of the design that had not yet been fully realized. "What we decided," Joseph Sisco testified in 1973, "was that we would try to stimulate and be helpful to two key countries in the area of the Persian Gulf—namely Iran and Saudi Arabia—that to the degree that we could stimulate cooperation between these two countries, they could become the major elements of stability as the British were getting out."[25] Washington's Arab friends understood this well. They repeatedly emphasized to US officials that only continued Israeli occupation of Arab territories stood in the way of an uninhibited Arab-US embrace. Facts supported their contention. The Saudis, for example, extremely generous with gifts to the Nixon family and other officials, were nevertheless linking their arms buying to Washington's role in promoting a peace settlement. The Zionists also opposed large-scale arms sales to Arab countries fearing that some might reach the belligerents.

The peninsular rulers played the key role in persuading President Sadat to satisfy American demands for demonstrations of good faith and moderation. "We think that Saudi Arabia has been a voice of moderation in the area," Joseph Sisco, assistant secretary of state and Kissinger's chief aide on the Middle East, told the congressional subcommittee in 1973. "We believe that it is in the mutual interest of the United States and Saudi Arabia for the forces of moderation to retain the upper hand in this area."[26] Sadat did the utmost to prove his pliability and pro-Western disposition. On the day of Abdel Nasser's funeral, while Nixon and Kissinger, fresh from the triumph of their brinkmanship over Jordan, were provocatively flexing their muscles aboard the *Saratoga*, Sadat assured Elliot Richardson, the official American mourner, of Egypt's eagerness to resume negotiations under the Rogers Plan. To no avail! Undeterred, the Egyptian leader started openly to snub the USSR. In May 1971, two days before Rogers's visit to Cairo, Ali Sabri and other high officials publicly identified in the West as being pro-Moscow were purged. That same summer Sadat actively aided Numeiry's bloody repression of the left in Sudan (including the execution of the secretary general of the Sudanese Communist Party). A year later Russian military advisers were precipitously asked to leave Egypt, thus fulfilling the White House's wish.

"We are trying to get a Middle East settlement," Kissinger explained at the beginning of this process to his special coterie of journalists, "in such a way that the moderate regimes are strengthened and not the radical regimes. We are trying to expel the Soviet military presence."[27] In a sense he succeeded. By the end of 1972 neither the ascendancy of "moderation" in the Arab world nor the elimination of Russian military presence was in doubt. Yet the arming of Israel continued at an accelerated pace, no effort was made to induce a negotiated settlement, not even after Nixon's second term had begun, and neither Jewish money nor Jewish votes (in reactionary Arab belief, the determinants of US foreign policy) stood in the way of his being "evenhanded."

In Egypt, however, "moderation" had acquired momentum. Washington noted with satisfaction the repression of the leftist student movement, the purging of radical writers and journalists from the Arab Socialist Union and from their jobs, and the steps toward economic "liberalization"—the granting of exploration contracts to Exxon and Mobil Oil and a multimillion dollar pipeline deal with the Bechtel Corporation. Egypt, the most populous and influential of Arab states, was obviously offering itself as a pro-Western "export-platform" country in the oil-rich region, asking in return an end to occupation.

During the three years preceding October 1973 the White House received Egyptian entreaties through Arab emissaries. One of these was Hafez Ismail, President Sadat's special envoy, who came in February 1973 to convey Cairo's sense of desperation for a negotiated settlement, only to be followed at the White House by Golda Meir and news leaks of more Phantoms for Israel. Kissinger would call the slap a "signal." The US wanted the terms of negotiation to be more "realistic," i.e., more acceptable to Israel than was the Rogers Plan. In March 1973 Sadat is reliably reported to have indicated his willingness to accept an "interim solution" involving the international control of Sharm el-Sheikh. The White House showed interest but did not move. Six months later the Arabs went to war—essentially to get Washington moving. The "limited objective" (Sadat's phrase) of the October War was not so much the armed liberation of occupied lands as to end the stalemate and start negotiations. Under the circumstances Kissinger's appearance at the center of the stage was hardly a feat of diplomacy.

Why did the US procrastinate for more than three years despite the entreaties of its Arab friends and President Sadat's signal of a pro-Western shift in Egypt? One answer is Kissinger's faith in the stability of stalemate. In his view the cease-fire produced by the Rogers Plan, plus the ascendance of a "moderate" regime in Cairo, rendered the Israeli-Arab stalemate more durable than it was before Abdel Nasser's death. Kissinger and Nixon understood power more than the human urge for intangibles such as the liberation of one's land. They were convinced of the efficacy of their *force de frappe* in the Middle East, of Israel's overwhelming superiority and its converse—Arab incompetence. They did not expect that Egypt under the pragmatic Sadat would be suicidal enough to start a war, and Syria could not do it alone. And after Hussein's impressive victory in Jordan, the PLO hardly counted in Washington except as an occasional airborne nuisance.

Nor was there much fear of losing allies like Saudi Arabia whose rulers hate socialists and radicals with a passion few can match, even in Washington. They had not only increased their investments in the US but by 1971 were also ordering costly US weapons (the Zionist lobby had also relaxed its opposition to US arms sales to Saudi Arabia and Kuwait). Kissinger obviously believed that Israel could get a settlement on its terms (that he believes ought to be generous) by holding out a bit longer. Realism favored such a settlement, not war. And if the Arabs went to war, another Arab defeat would open an opportunity for Israel and the US to be magnanimous (a Kissinger favorite) in victory.

*Arab Eggs, American Basket*

The October War ended the complacency with which Washington had regarded the stalemate. It destroyed the assumption of Arab equanimity in accepting protracted occupation and of their incompetence in war. It demonstrated Israel's power as too derivative to be totally dependable. The oil embargo underscored the dependence of Japanese and European (and to a lesser extent American) economies on Arab oil, dramatized the contradictions in Atlantic relations, and underlined the importance of the Middle East in perpetuating America's global predominance. It also confirmed the argument of Washington's Arabists that Egypt is the pivot of the Arab world. Without it no war can be fought, and no political arrangement can be stable. Under the circumstances Kissinger's bid to act as the mediator was inevitable. Given the objectives that motivated Egyptian recourse to war and conservative Arab support for it, President Sadat's capitulation to Kissinger's blueprint for peacemaking was equally predictable.

The mutuality of perceived Arab and American interests and a common vision of the future, rather than the Arab's alleged belief in individuals—a T. E. Lawrence or a Henry Kissinger—explain the latter's remarkable rise as the magician of the Middle East. President Sadat and his advisers, much like the rulers of Saudi Arabia and the sheikhs in the Gulf, believe that their interests will be best served if they can develop close ties with the US and the international corporations. For Sadat it is a vision of Egypt becoming the industrial and commercial center of the Arab world. A combination of Egyptian manpower, American corporate and technological skills, and Arab petrodollars could yield Egypt the kind of prosperity and power its bourgeoisie has long craved. This hope has been stimulated skillfully by men like Sheikh Yamani, Richard Nixon, David Rockefeller, and Henry Kissinger, for it entails a shift in Egypt's role from the vanguard of radical Arab nationalism to becoming an ally with the Arabia of the sultans. In Washington it is believed that Egypt's defection will emaciate the radical and progressive elements in the Arab world and bring about the restoration of a neocolonial order there.

The paradoxes of post-October diplomacy underline Egyptian and Saudi obsession with the corporate, neocolonial vision of an Arab future. One need mention only a few examples, some banal, others of greater importance: the adoption by President Sadat as a brother and friend of the one cousin who bore the primary responsibility for overarming Israel before, during, and after the October War; or the acceptance of a disengagement plan that removed the immediate incentives toward a negotiated settlement; or the decision to apply the oil embargo in a manner that hurt countries (like France) friendly to the Arabs, alienated potential allies (such as Germany that in a remarkable assertion of independence had refused the use of its port facilities for US supplies to Israel), and aided the one country it had pretended to punish (the dollar as well as the US balance of payments was strengthened in the wake of the oil embargo that severely affected the European economy). Thanks mainly to official Arab ingratiation a major contribution of the October War was to affirm, however temporarily, the paramountcy of the United States as the world's number one power—the "untier of knots."

The Arab leaders who decided to put their eggs in the American basket assumed that the "energy crisis" had increased their importance in Washington. That is correct. They also thought that their enhanced importance had correspondingly diminished US commitment to maintaining Israel as a regional gendarme. That is incorrect. The extent of the US arms buildup in Israel since the October War is a measure of US commitment to maintaining Israel as a major power in the region. The setbacks that the US policy has suffered in Cyprus and Greece may have increased, in Kissinger's view, the importance of Israel as the guardian of the "western flank." Nevertheless, he would wish Saudi Arabia and Egypt to become full partners with the shah in securing the "eastern flank" and stabilizing the Arab world.

In the aftermath of October 1973 Washington's notion of a just peace is different from that of Israel. But not much. Israel wants to keep Sharm el-Sheikh. The US is expected to advise a compromise, e.g., a formula involving Egyptian sovereignty and Israeli occupation. Israel will not withdraw from

Jerusalem but is willing to concede Muslim and Christian sovereignty over their holy places (which is not much more than a euphemism for your right to pray in al-Aqsa and the Church of the Holy Sepulchre). Dr. Kissinger is likely to counsel a further concession—a thin corridor (a Cadillac path!) to the Harem al-Sharif so that Emir Feisal may reach there without treading on Jewish soil. Israel wishes to annex the pockets constituted by the hills of La-troun and Judea. Washington may induce it to be content with demilitariza-tion there. As for the Palestinians, the PLO's official elevation as their sole rep-resentative is unlikely to constitute a lasting hindrance to the creation of a Palestinian state in the Gaza and a truncated West Bank. Officials in Washing-ton believe—and once their guilt-ridden hysteria is allayed Israelis may share the belief—that as it is constituted today the PLO commands neither a revo-lutionary ideology nor a mass organization, hence its leaders are likely to be as corrupt and co-optable as the many nationalist regimes that came to power on formal decolonization.

If the belligerents can be induced to accept a settlement along these lines, a negotiated peace may be possible or at least the expectation of it could be prolonged. Kissinger's game plan promises Egypt the most and would prefer to deliver there first. Syria will then be isolated. Negotiations over the West Bank of Jordan may be protracted and, as the ultimate arbiter, the United States will remain at the center of the stage.

The prospects of a negotiated settlement being slim, another war may be unavoidable. The fifth round, however, is likely to be initiated by Israel, not by the Arabs. For obvious reasons: the costly and inconclusive character of the October War has put a psychological burden on Israel. A clear-cut victory over the Arabs must appear as a necessity to a leadership that sincerely believes that Israel's national security lies in keeping the Arabs permanently defeated.

Secondly, Israelis understand, if most Arabs do not, that ultimately Amer-ican interests (as the ruling class perceives them), rather than humanitarian considerations or the Zionist lobby, determine the size and quality of US aid to Israel. The October War has shaken the faith of some in the United States, including senior generals in what used to be described as Israel's "swift sword." Israelis may want to reassure Washington of its effectiveness as a *force de frappe*.

Thirdly, time does not favor Israel. Unless Arab leaders succeed in snatch-ing failure from the jaws of success, they will be in a very favorable position. Oil is now a primary element in defining power. If the Arabs use it wisely this decade will witness their emergence as a center of world power. Israel, on the other hand, is likely to suffer from increasing international isolation, and diminishing US interest in satisfying its massive economic and military requirements. A stalemate, therefore, is not as attractive for Israel as it was before. New developments, accentuating its domestic and international difficulties and strengthening the Arab position, may tempt Israel to strike out while it still has the means to do so and attempt to impose a settlement with Syria.

Yet Israel cannot initiate a war unless it is assured of US support. Washington is unlikely to let Israel loose unless it plans to use a second oil embargo as an excuse for military intervention. Its aim will be to establish undisputed US control over the production and distribution of oil—the one privilege expected to ensure the paramountcy of American power. This is considered a serious option in Washington. President Ford and Dr. Kissinger have already issued warnings, but vaguely. The Pentagon's planning indicates rather clearly that the US defense forces have been preparing for possible intervention in the Middle East. The Arabs will be wise to develop a strategy to discourage and, in case of necessity, defeat this kind of adventurism.

[1976]

No one interested in the Arab-Israeli conflict can ignore Edward Said's *The Question of Palestine.* It is by far the most impassioned and morally compelling book by an Arab since George Antonius wrote his classic, *Arab Awakening,* in 1938. But unlike Antonius, who documented imperial Britain's betrayal of its World War I Arab allies and foresaw the tragedy of Palestine, Said is profoundly optimistic. In the awesome uncertainties and violence of Middle Eastern politics, he knows two things to be certain: "the Jews of Israel will remain; the Palestinians will also remain."[1] Therein lies the uniqueness of this book, for Professor Said, a member of the Palestine National Council and one of the most influential Arab intellectuals today, is the first Palestinian writer to argue for the necessity of a full-scale political encounter between the Jews and the Palestinians "whose past and future tie them inexorably together" [p. 238].

Since he is likely to be attacked by die-hards and apologists on both sides, it should be stated at the outset that Said's is an essay in reconciliation. He writes with apparent conviction that "both Palestinians and Jews in Palestine have much to gain—and obviously something to lose—from a human rights view of their common situation, as opposed to a strictly national perspective on it" [p. 52]. He argues that a political settlement requires the recognition of some fundamental realities by the parties to this conflict. He contends that while "most Palestinians fully realize that their Other, the Israeli Jewish people, is a concrete reality with which they must live in the future" [p. 174], it is Israel's refusal to recognize the reality of Palestinian existence that prevents a resolution of the conflict. This is a contention that Said's adversaries shall undoubtedly challenge, but he shows, quite convincingly, that historically and ideologically, in politics no less than in law, in diplomacy and war, "negation" of the Palestinian reality is the "most consistent thread running through Zionism" [p. 82].

How did the Jews, who constituted less than 10 percent of Palestine's population in 1919, succeed in establishing there in 1948 a Jewish state from which the majority of the natives became exiled while the remainder were made by law second-class residents? And why did the secular and liberal West give its unquestioning support to so obvious and monumental an injustice, such overt discrimination based on religion and ethnicity? To answer these questions, Said draws heavily on his resources as a literary critic and returns to the themes of his much-acclaimed book *Orientalism*. His answers are difficult to summarize, for he knows that the creation of Israel resulted from a "complex, many-sided struggle, and a full-scale war" [p. 100]. Yet, because they bear on the present situation, that includes the Zionist attempt to colonize the West Bank of Jordan, the Golan Heights, and Gaza as part of Eretz Israel, one must note his major themes.

First, having "internalized imperialist perspective on the 'natives' and their 'territory'" [p. 70], the Zionist movement leaned heavily on the West's racism, and its deep prejudices about Islam, the Arabs, and the Orient, in order to establish the Palestinians' inferiority, to dehumanize them, render them dispensable, and ultimately deny their very existence. Thus the Zionist slogan about Palestine as "a land without people, for a people without land" was not an expression of sheer ignorance; rather, it was an ideological statement, the declaration of a political program totally congruent with the contemporary ethos of imperialism. Using a wide range of writers from Alphonse de Lamartine and George Eliot to Reinhold Niebuhr and Edmund Wilson, Said shows that it was the dominant ethos of *mission civilisatrice*—based on the notion of inequality between races and cultures—that turned the Zionist-Palestinian struggle into a conflict between a "higher" mission and a "humble" reality [p. 17]; it helped the Zionist interpretation of Palestine to triumph over the Palestinian "presence" [p. 8].

It was thus that Lord Balfour, Britain's foreign secretary, could write in 1919 that Zionism's "present needs" and "future hopes" were "of far profounder import than the desire and prejudices of 700,000 Arabs who now inhabit that ancient land" [pp. 16–17]. Said shows that in time, the language changed, but the mission did not. After World War II, when the United States inherited much of Britain's imperial reach, Niebuhr, jointly with six other

American notables, would proclaim that American interests "dictate speedy modernization of the Middle East"; that the Muslims present a "hopeless" picture of backwardness and despotism, and that "there is only one vanguard of progress and modernization in the Middle East, and that is Jewish Palestine." Gentiles and Jews thus became united in denying the native Palestinians "their status as sovereign and human inhabitants."[2]

As Westernized and emancipated Semites, the Zionists sought to be and increasingly became the interpreters of Arabs and Islam in the West. Said gives ample evidence of Zionist leaders and ideologues from Theodor Herzl through Chaim Weizmann to David Ben-Gurion and Yehoshafat Harkabi interpreting the "treacherous," "devious," "cruel," "despotic," "greedy," "backward," "cunning," and "medieval" Arab and his culture to the West. Idealism also yielded omniscience; since 1917, Zionists have been claiming to know better than Arabs the wishes of the backward Palestinian mass. To anyone who follows the US media's discussion of Islam and Arabs or the "progress" of the Israeli-American-Egyptian talks on Palestinian autonomy, the argument must be obvious. For those who need convincing, Said offers ample evidence that, an occasional dissenting voice notwithstanding, the Middle East is still seen in the United States "from the Zionist perspective" and in more than one way the Palestinians still await a fair hearing and the right to self-representation.

The strength of Zionism lay in combining its messianic drive with extraordinary attention to detail. From the beginning of the movement, Zionist leaders spoke of "reconstituting" and "rebuilding" Palestine, and they knew that this was to be done "on the ruins of the Palestinians' homeland." Thus, in 1895, Herzl wrote in his diaries of the eventual necessity of "spiriting the penniless population . . . across the border," noting that "both the process of expropriation and the removal of the poor must be carried out discreetly and circumspectly" [quoted on p. 71]. Forty-five years later, in 1940, Joseph Weitz, then director of the Jewish National Land Fund, would write in his diary that "there is no room for both people in this country"; that "the only solution is Eretz Israel, or at least Western Eretz Israel, without Arabs. There is no room for compromise on this point. . . . We must not leave a single village, not a single tribe" [quoted on pp. 99–100].

Doing this with "discretion" involved a complex, well-organized, and institutionally backed policy leading to the encirclement and emaciation of the native communities by the technologically advanced Jewish pioneers. Said describes it as "a discipline of detail," a colonization that creeps "inch by inch, step by step, 'another acre, another goat,'" as Weizmann put it [p. 95].

The Palestinian peasants and workers responded as beleaguered, helpless people always do—with resistance in the form of sporadic and generally uncoordinated violence. Said is especially critical of the Palestinian elite for meeting Zionism's institutionalized challenge with insipid representations and legal briefs invoking general principles—their right to self-determination, legal claims to Palestine, moral appeals for justice. He notes also that they made no effort to form parallel organizations and institutions capable of responding to Zionist colonization; they never explored militant nonviolence; they had no strategy to hold the land, no program of assisting the besieged Palestinian communities and of shoring up their defense and morale. Hence, when the final confrontation occurred, the people—780,000 of them—fled the war zones in a "psychological mood of failure and terror" [p. 101], hoping to return home after the fighting subsided.

Said notes, unfortunately without fully exploring their fateful implications, the many parallels between 1917–1948 and the new stage of Zionist colonization that began after the Israeli-Arab War of 1967. By 1978, when Said was writing, 27 percent of the West Bank's Arab-owned land had been confiscated by Israel; nearly half a million Arabs had evacuated the Occupied Territories; there were seventy-seven illegal Zionist colonies, and twenty new ones were announced on the day the Camp David agreement was being signed. More ominously, by means of a series of land sales regulations, discriminatory distribution of water supplies, a psychologically and sociologically selective policy of deportation, and sometimes by naked force, Israel has begun to strangle the occupied native population. Neither Egypt, nor Syria, nor Jordan, nor Saudi Arabia, nor even the Palestine Liberation Organization has so far countered this fateful development. Assuming the Israeli occupation lasts two more decades—and there is no reason to doubt this assumption—the land alienation and dispossession of a majority of the Arabs in the West Bank, Gaza, and Golan is virtually assured.

Said, who supports the PLO's demand for a separate state on the West Bank and Gaza, obviously knows but does not openly state the tragic fact that what the Palestinians are demanding today is not so much the restoration of lost rights but the prevention of a final round of dispossession and another choice between exile and servitude.

Said knows also that despite its organizational strength, Zionism's messianic compulsions would have found little support among the Jewish people had they not been traumatized by fascist crimes. Notwithstanding a systematic, four-decades-long campaign, it was not until the mid-1930s that the Zionist movement began to elicit the support of the world's Jewish majority. He realizes, too, that support for Israel now transcends not only morality and justice but even the needs and interests of the Jewish people. This institutionalization of support for Zionism as an exclusionary ideology concerns him, for it renders impractical his hope that eventually Jews and Arabs may live in peace as equal and fraternal communities.

The encounter with Zionism has defined for the Palestinians their contemporary experience and distinguishes them from other Arab and Third World peoples. "To us," writes Said, "Zionism has meant as much, albeit differently, as it has to the Jews." For "it has been the Palestinian who has borne Zionism's extraordinary human cost, a cost not only large but unacknowledged" [p. 54]. Since he considers such an acknowledgment basic to reconciliation, he dwells not only on the Palestinians' physical and material losses but also on the more painful and permanent psychological and moral costs. His chapter "Zionism from the Standpoint of Its Victims" is by far the most powerful; it is also likely to be the most controversial. Its power lies not merely in his analysis of the collective humiliation and sorrow of the Palestinians as they experienced ideological depreciation and dehumanization, physical dispossession, and ultimate exile. Rather, it derives from the fact that Said evinces a compassionate understanding of his victimizer as well.

He believes, as do all Palestinians, that there is an inherent racialism in the exclusionary idea of a Jewish state, in the discriminatory land regulations, in the much-admired "socialist" kibbutzim that effectively practice a system of apartheid, and in a law of return that guarantees to Scharansky of the Soviet Union the right to settle in Jerusalem while denying it to Said, who was born there. Yet he does not subscribe to the familiar equations of Zionism and racism, South Africa and Israel. Such parallels "get badly shaken," he says, when a Palestinian "reflects seriously upon the differences between white settlers in Africa and Jews fleeing European anti-Semitism" [p. 119]. He understands "the meaning of Israel for the Jews," the "terror and exultation" that have nourished Zionism [p. 60]. Indeed, he seems to know the sorrow of being a Jew so well that inadvertently at times the Palestinians appear in this book like reflections of the Jews. And he writes sadly of his people's "extraordinary bad luck" in having to resist dispossession and colonization by "the most morally complex of opponents, Jews, with a long history of victimization and terror behind them" [p. 119].

This important book is marred by repetitions, lack of economy, and a loose structure. Toward the end, it begins to sag, as though the last chapter— "After Camp David"—were an afterthought. There is much that is missing in Said's analysis of Anwar el-Sadat's policies and their potential impact. His critique of Camp David is familiar, and he does not show an awareness of the Arabs' many lost opportunities. In places he judges hastily. In discussing terrorism, for example, Said contrasts Palestinian violence with the "completely asymmetrical records" of Israeli terror against Palestinians. This is true but unhelpful in the sense that balance sheets of this kind add to neither good morals nor good politics. That he is "horrified at the hijacking of planes . . . by the terror in Palestinian men and women who were driven to do such things" attests to his humanity [p. xxxviii]; that a committed partisan of the Palestinian resistance openly expresses his feeling also shows courage. But there is in this also a failure to examine the complex and pivotal role that the PLO's violence played in focusing world attention on the question of Palestine. After all, for two decades before the hijackings, the Palestinians had tried no means of resistance except diplomatic initiatives; more than a dozen ineffectual United Nations resolutions were all they had to show for it. To this extent, and in its limited way, the violence succeeded. But between the Palestinians' initial and weak strategy of United Nations diplomacy and their later recourse to terrorism there lies a broad range of political activities (among them militant nonviolence) that were left untried. In part this may be because the link between popular militancy among the Palestinian people and the political strategies of the leadership was and is weak, so that the alternatives in the form of effective mass movements did not emerge. But to assess Palestinian terrorism we need to know more about what these alternatives were.

Lastly, Said's book is distinguished by its insightful and sharply critical discussion of the Arab states and inter-Arab politics. These parts, welcome and refreshing to the Western reader, will undoubtedly produce controversy in the Middle East. Said has a good eye for the paradoxes of elite politics. Although every Arab government champions the Palestinian cause, "the number of Palestinians dead at Arab government hands is appallingly high" [p. 170]. He is hard on the "antiquated and oppressive structures of most of the Arab countries" [p. 59] and condemns Arab rulers' "minority cast of mind," their "uncritical commitment to state power for its own sake" [p. 53], and their "perpetuation of police states in the name of fighting Zionist aggression."

He is also critical of Palestinians for making "historical appearances largely in the form of refusals and rejections" [p. 119] and for the "mindless" violence that costs innocent lives. He is at his best, though, when he draws on Palestinian literature to portray a striking picture of a self-conscious and determined people whose will to recover their national sovereignty increases with adversity, leading them to challenge their enemies, embarrass their friends, and unsettle many a grand design in the Middle East.

[1980]

## 30 / ON ARAB BANKRUPTCY

Bad times have visited the Arabs before. From 1096 to 1204, Crusaders ravaged the Fertile Crescent. In 1258, the Mongols sacked Baghdad—then, like Beirut today, Islam's cultural and commercial metropolis. In 1492, the Arabs were expelled from Spain after seven centuries of brilliant rule. Past catastrophes provided occasions for renewal and change, investing Moslem civilization with unusual resiliency. The Arabs' current predicament is without parallel. Never before have they experienced a similar combination of wealth and weakness, material resources and moral bankruptcy.

Economically, the Middle East is the richest region in the Third World; strategically, the most important. Multinational corporations seek Arab favors. Bankers rely on their investments. Great powers covet their cooperation. The dollar owes its continued strength to Arab preferences. Yet Arab governments have not been able to translate economic power and strategic value into political and diplomatic leverage.

The Arabs are still subject to conquest. As the era of decolonization began in 1948, the Palestinians lost the greater part of their homeland. They are now experiencing systematic dispossession from its remnant: the West Bank, Gaza, Jerusalem. In southern Lebanon, the refugees are the target of Defense Minister Ariel Sharon's declared policy of expulsion.

In 1976, Lebanon started disintegrating with the complicity of some Arab states, the indifference of others. Exhausted after six years of Syrian depredations, private armies' violence, and Israel's relentless raids, Lebanon now is fully invaded. Its besieged capital burns.

The pro-Western Gulf states have pretense neither to military prowess nor radicalism. Led by Saudi Arabia, they plead with Washington to save Arab face and their dynastic future. But they are prisoners of dependency and uneven development. They have acquired wealth without working and make enormous profits without producing. Their countries are littered with expensive machines, but they have no technology. Their economies are run by foreigners. Their investments have linked them symbiotically with America. They own billions of dollars but control no capital. They lack the will and capacity to translate their wealth into power.

Their diplomacy is reduced to buying favors and pleading fairness. For three months, Israel's invasion of Lebanon had been imminent, yet the Saudis could not prevail on Washington to prevent it. Now the Saudis watch Philip C. Habib seek the Palestine Liberation Organization's departure from Beirut without linking it to Israel's withdrawal or to the disarming of its Phalangist allies. American diplomacy, which Arab "moderates" can do little to influence, obviously wants for Israel a free hand in reordering Lebanon's future.

During Lebanon's devastation, "radical" governments who comprise the confrontation front have tucked their tails. Some have excuses: On his long march to Jerusalem, President Saddam Hussein of Iraq got stuck in Iranian sands. Mu'ammar al-Gadhafi of Libya could not reach Beirut on time via Chad. Despite its revolutionary past, even Algeria remains mute. At last, Arab "rejectionism" is exposed as rejecting all responsibility.

After forcibly preventing the left-leaning Lebanese National Movement from taking power in 1976, Syria's Arab deterrent force continued to deter a political settlement in Lebanon. But it refrained from deterring Israel until Syrian redoubts in the Bekaa Valley were attacked. As the invading army approached Beirut, senior Syrian officers slipped out in the dark; typically they escaped combat in commandeered cars. Syria's ally Iran has remained engaged in fighting Iraq's "infidelity" and in slaying domestic devils who range from innocent Bahais to opposition leftists. Gen. Mohammad Zia ul-Haq, Pakistan's self-anointed president and "Soldier of Islam," nurses his infected liver and newly acquired American weapons.

Without radical democratization, the Middle East cannot escape recurrent defeats and recolonization. Its rulers are too cautious to wage war except on their own peoples, too insecure to initiate peace, too dependent to protect state sovereignty, too corrupt to reclaim national honor. Its soldiers lack the motivation to fight; its civilians, a stake in the existing order. There have been more protests in Europe, the United States, and Israel against the invasion of Lebanon than in any Middle Eastern country. State power has rendered Muslim societies impotent. The "strongmen" of the Middle East are on display as toy soldiers; "strongmen" invariably produce weak nations.

The besieged inhabitants of Beirut and the beleaguered Arabs under Israeli occupation alone redeem the self-respect of Middle Eastern peoples with their courage and persistence against a powerful, pitiless enemy.

[1982]

## 31 / THE PUBLIC RELATIONS OF ETHNOCIDE

Imperial democracies have a history of performing absolution by judicial bath. Among the dozens of examples are the trial of Robert Clive (1725–1774), a founder of the British empire in South Asia and the first English governor of Bengal; the impeachment of Warren Hastings (1732–1818), the first governor-general of the British dominion in India; the conviction of General Michael O'Dwyer, author of the 1919 massacre of Jalian Wala Bagh; and the court-martial of Lt. Calley, whose US army unit carried out the My Lai massacre in Vietnam. The infractions of each were products of an ideological environment and of policies for which the responsibilities lay with a political system and with men who occupied higher positions. In each instance, the legal exhibition helped provide a liberal covering for aggressive policies and served to calm disturbed popular conscience. On each occasion, they merely cleaned the slate for the next series of brutalities.

The appointment by Mr. Menachem Begin of the Commission of Inquiry into the massacres of Sabra and Shatila was undoubtedly a tribute to the 400,000 Israelis who demonstrated their outrage following the slaughter.[1] Yet one had feared its falling into the historical pattern. The report of the commission and the Western world's reaction to it suggest that the historical pattern does not merely hold; rather, it is now extended to cover up a policy of ethnocide. Uncritical approval for this ritual of absolution is widespread. Thus the verdict of the Western media on the Israeli Commission of Inquiry report has been favorable. David Shipler of the *New York Times* paid tribute to its "exacting standards of humaneness"; Trudy Rubin in the *Christian Science Moni-*

*tor* called it "a stunning moral triumph"; David Zucchino in the *Philadelphia Inquirer* describes it as "a unique democratic achievement." As for the editorialists, the *Los Angeles Times* declared: "Out of the tragedy and anguish and shame has come a certain redemptive honor"; the *Sunday Times* (London) called it "a fearless report"; the *Guardian* (Manchester) argued that "much credit flows to the state of Israel for the vigour of the Kahan Commission's enquiry and the rigour of its conclusions"; and the *Jerusalem Post* hailed it as a "splendid example of Israeli—not to say Jewish—justice at work." As for the *New York Times*, in total disregard of the illegality of Israel's annexation of the holy city, its editorial announced the advent of a "Jerusalem ethic." This pattern of praise was repeated with equal enthusiasm by American and European politicians including Jimmy Carter and Ronald Reagan.

A dispassionate and sober outlook would have suggested to these instant historians that the Kahan commission failed to fulfill its legal and human obligations in at least three fundamental respects: (i) it engaged in a politically motivated legal evasion unworthy of a commission which was, in principle, judicial in character; (ii) although it was charged with examining "all the facts and factors" connected with the massacre, it neither disclosed all the facts nor examined all the factors that led to the slaughter; (iii) most crucial, it did not assign legal and political responsibility in a way that could diminish the likelihood of a repetition of similar crimes.

The commission cited the unambiguous obligations that international law imposes on the occupying power to ensure the well-being of civilians, but in an exercise of legal sophistry, quite incredible under the circumstances, it went on to profess a "lack of clarity" on whether or not Israel was legally the occupier of West Beirut. The commission members recognized that fudging on this clear-cut question was necessary to legally absolve the Israeli government of criminal responsibility in the massacre: "If the territory of West Beirut may be viewed at the time of the events as occupied territory—and we do not determine that such indeed is the case from a legal perspective—then it is the duty of the occupier, according to the rules of usual and customary international law, to do all it can to ensure the public's well-being and security." After dubiously, and peremptorily, suggesting an invalidation of "legal norms . . . regarding the situation in which the Israeli government and the forces operating at its instruction found themselves at the time of the events," the commission proceeded to invoke, in stern phrases to be sure, the vaguer and unencumbering moral precepts of civilized societies. It is from this base of legal evasion that the Israeli commission enunciated its own doctrine of "indirect responsibility"—an original but judicially spurious and morally reprehensible doctrine.

A recurring theme in the media's comments has been the contrast between Israel's willingness to investigate the massacre and Lebanon's failure to punish the Phalangists who actually did the killing. It is disingenuous to blame dismembered Lebanon for not punishing the Phalange since the Israeli government, not the Lebanese, controls the Phalange militia. Revelations to this effect are interspersed throughout the commission's report; yet their impact is minimized by the decision to keep secret the details of Israel's relationship with the Phalange. Not included in the published sections of the report are the facts that the Phalange militia commanders receive salaries from Israel and take orders from its officials and that many have been trained in the Jewish state. According to undenied reports, this information is included in the commission's secret appendix B. Typical of the commission's surrender to Israel's official sensibilities is that it does not even identify the paymasters of the killer militias, much less establish their culpability in this and other crimes still being committed in Lebanon. Nevertheless, the facts disclosed by the commission— and by its own admission it did not disclose those facts which could be injurious to Israel's "national security"—warranted a conclusion other than that of "indirect responsibility." Consider, for example, the following:

1. Menachem Begin and Ariel Sharon decided upon the invasion of West Beirut—in violation of an international accord guaranteed by the United States— at about 11 PM on Tuesday, September 14, 1982, i.e., within a few minutes of receiving word of Bashir Gemayel's death.

2. Before the break of dawn on Wednesday, September 15, the Israel Defense Forces moved into West Beirut. The official reason given for this violation was Israel's concern over the dangers of widespread civil violence. Nevertheless, Generals Sharon and Eitan made arrangements for the Phalangist assault on the refugee camps simultaneously with their invasion of West Beirut.

3. General Eitan flew to Beirut late on the night of Tuesday, September 17. There he met with General Amir Drori, commander of the Israeli forces in Lebanon, and General Amos Yaron, divisional commander for West Beirut. Together they proceeded to the Phalange headquarters, where Eitan "ordered the militia commanders to effect a general mobilization of all their forces." These Israeli chiefs of staff informed them that they were to enter the two refugee camps.

Neither Amin Gemayel nor his father, Pierre, founder of the Phalange Party, was informed of Eitan's orders or the subsequent movement of the militiamen into the camps. General Sharon apparently withheld this information when he met with them the following day.

4. From the Phalange headquarters, General Eitan moved to the forward command post overlooking the refugee camps and stayed there from the early morning hours of Wednesday, September 15, until Thursday morning, September 16. General Sharon joined him at the command post between 8 and 9 AM on Thursday, approved the agreement with the Phalangists, and from the roof overlooking the camps telephoned Prime Minister Begin. He is reported to have told Begin that there was "no resistance in Beirut, and all the operations are going well." Present on the scene were the chief of Mossad, the director of Israeli Military Intelligence, the deputy chief of staff (Moshe Levi, now chief of staff), General Drori, Brigadier General Yaron, the divisional commander, and other officers. General Sharon made another call to Begin: "The Minister of Defense spoke with the Prime Minister twice from the roof of the command post." It was in one of these calls that the wording of the belated Israeli announcement was decided on: "Israel Defense Forces entered West Beirut tonight to prevent possible grave occurrences and ensure quiet." From the command post General Sharon went to the Phalange headquarters and ordered the militias to coordinate their operations with the IDF.

5. At 11 AM on Thursday, September 16, General Amir Drori and General Amos Yaron met with the Phalange's officers to "coordinate" the militias' entry into the camps and to arrange for a "communications set" at the Israeli command post overlooking the refugee camps. Back in Israel, Chief of Staff Eitan was telling the Israeli cabinet of the possibility of impending revenge by the Phalangists: "I can see already," he is quoted as telling the cabinet, "in their eyes what they are waiting for . . . and it will be terrible."

6. The militias entered the camps at 6 PM on Thursday, September 16. Approximately one hour later, an Arabic-speaking Israeli lieutenant who was one of General Yaron's aides heard a conversation in which Elias Hobeika, head of the Phalange's "intelligence service," gave the signal to start killing "women and children" in the camps. The Israeli lieutenant immediately informed General Yaron who was present at the time.

7. This was possibly the earliest—but not the only—intimation of mass slaughter ignored by Yaron and other Israeli officials. At approximately 8 PM, another militia officer inside the refugee camp radioed the Israeli command post to ask what he should do with the forty-five persons he was holding. He was told to "do the

will of God." The Israeli intelligence officer in attendance withheld this information from his superiors (including Yaron) for about an hour "because an 'officers' briefing was scheduled to take place at field headquarters shortly afterwards." A little later, General Yaron and his staff were in the dining room of the command post when the Phalange's liaison officer walked in to inform that about "three hundred terrorists and civilians" had already been killed; this occurred "in the presence of many IDF officers who were there, including General Yaron." At 8:40 PM, during an update briefing, the intelligence officer who had withheld the information he had earlier received reported it. The Kahan commission report shows that he was interrupted and silenced by Yaron.

8. At 11:30 PM—it is still Day One, Thursday, September 16—a report circulated by the Israeli command in Lebanon to various intelligence units in Israel stated: "Preliminary information conveyed by the commander of the local Phalangist forces in the Shatila refugee camp states that so far his men have liquidated about 300 people. This number includes terrorists and civilians." On Friday, September 17, at 5:30 AM, this report from the previous night was delivered to Colonel Hevroni, *chef du bureau* of the director of Israeli Military Intelligence.

9. By Friday, September 17, reports of the massacre had started piling up and were, according to the commission's report, systematically ignored by the Israeli authorities. On Friday, General Eitan met with senior Phalange militia commanders at 4 PM (after he had received on-the-spot reports of the killings) and approved their continuing the "operations" in the camps "until tomorrow at 5 AM at which time they must stop their action due to American pressure." That same evening, General Eitan telephoned Defense Minister Ariel Sharon informing the latter that the "Christians" had "gone too far" and had "harmed the civilian population more than was expected." The slaughter continued until 8 AM, Saturday, September 18.

10. Throughout the forty hours of slaughter, the Israeli army provided logistical support, including night flares to light the murderers and tractors to dispose of the bodies.

With these, and more, facts at hand the Israeli Commission of Inquiry has concluded that any allegation of Israeli governmental complicity in the slaughter is a "baseless libel" and accusations that the Israel Defense Forces had knowledge of the killings are equally "unfounded." Let history judge the integrity of men who came to such a conclusion.

The finding of "indirect responsibility" is based on a single premise: Israeli soldiers did not pull the triggers, and Israeli officers were not present during the killings. Some witnesses have questioned the validity of this premise. These include Dr. Paul Morris, an English physician, who was then working at the Gaza Hospital, a Palestinian facility in Sabra. Dr. Morris has charged that the Kahan report deleted from his testimony evidence indicating that Israeli irregulars were among those who carried out the killings. But even if these doubts are set aside, by the logic of the Kahan commission's judgment, the Israeli government is exonerated of its surrogates' conduct so long as a few of its officers resign, are transferred, or retire—so the commission recommended in the case of General Raphael Eitan—on reaching the age of superannuation.

The doctrine of "indirect responsibility" is a legally dubious, morally reprehensible conception that has extremely dangerous implications, given the oft-expressed Israeli goal of eliminating the Palestinian population from the West Bank and South Lebanon. Israel already has a surrogate force in the West Bank—the Village Leagues—and it is arming and training more militias there. In South Lebanon, Israel has armed the forces of the Lebanese Army defector Saad Haddad and has organized other militias, too, drawing recruits from hoodlums and thugs living in the area. Continuing reports of Palestinians found murdered in South Lebanon—five bodies one day, seven another; sixteen in a mass grave discovered by the International Red Cross in the week of February 14—point out the danger in the principle of indirect responsibility. An appeal by Olof Rydbeck, the commissioner-general of UNRWA, for the "Israeli forces . . . to put an end to these attacks, which are terrorizing innocent refugees, including children," has gone unheeded. The role of Saad Haddad's forces has grown daily under Israel's protection. The doctrine of indirect responsibility has done nothing to discourage atrocities by surrogate forces carrying out Israeli government policy. The only consequence to the government could be a few reprimands, occasional transfer of officials for dereliction of duty, at worst some resignations.

Perhaps the compulsion to narrow its verdict to indirect responsibility explains the commission's failure to look into the political environment in Israel that made the Beirut massacre possible. The commission argues convincingly that the Phalangists' "hatred of the Palestinians" should have been taken into account by Israeli commanders and that the Phalange "leaders' plans for the future of the Palestinians when said leaders would assume power" should have been seen as a warning of what the militiamen might do in the camps. Specifically, taking a sectarian view common to Phalangist (and Zionist) thinking, the commission noted that the presence of the Palestinian refugees, "for the most part Muslims, endangered the demographic balance between the Christians and Muslims in Lebanon and (from other standpoints as well) the stability of the state of Lebanon and the status of Christians in the country. Therefore, the Phalangist leaders proposed removing a large proportion of Palestinian refugees from Lebanese soil, whether by methods of persuasion or other means of pressure." While emphasizing the record of sectarian attitudes and violence in Lebanon, the commission berated Israeli officials for not paying attention to this when they unleashed the militias into the camps. But it totally ignored Israeli enmity toward Palestinians as well as the strong current of Israeli policy seeking their expulsion and dispersal. An acknowledgment by the Kahan commission of the symmetry between Phalangist and Israeli perspectives on "solving" the Palestinian "problem" would have rendered difficult its ruling of "indirect responsibility."

The commission's failure to raise this issue is crucial. after all, Begin and Sharon espouse the absorption of what they call "Judea and Samaria" into Israel and also envisage the de facto retention of South Lebanon; both objectives endanger "demographic balance" between Jews and Arabs in Eretz Israel, a balance which Zionist ideology considers essential to maintaining the Jewish character of Israel. Hence Sharon's plan for the invasion of Lebanon, publicly known months in advance, had among its objectives not only the destruction of the Palestine Liberation Organization in Lebanon but also the dispersal of the Palestinian population. Menahem Milson, in the article in *Commentary* that won his appointment as civil administrator of the West Bank, had already advocated the removal of the Palestinians from Lebanon; so did the Israeli minister of religious affairs. More than one Israeli official is on record seeking the elimination and dispersion of the Palestinians in the West Bank and Gaza. Such attitudes are not limited to the supporters of the ruling Likud coalition. General Aharon Yariv, former chief of Israel's Military Intelligence, has reported high-level discussions on expelling 500,000 to 700,000 Arabs from the occupied West Bank and Gaza. Most recently, Maier Cohen, a prominent member of the Knesset from the ruling Herut Party, has openly regretted his predecessor's failure to drive out an additional 300,000 Palestinians.

Even some liberal leaders of the Zionist movement abroad are on record seeking the elimination and dispersion of the Palestinians. Thus, during the siege of Beirut, Rita Hauser, a well-known figure in the American Jewish community and vice president of the American Jewish Committee, proposed in a *New York Times* article (July 26, 1982) that the "400,000 Palestinians in

Lebanon be dispersed to various countries including the US, Canada, and France." But none of these were to be repatriated to their original homes (the large majority of the Palestinian population in Lebanon comes from the Galilee area incorporated into the state of Israel in 1948). "By dispersing them," Hauser wrote, "the problem would be pierced." Only after this has been accomplished would Hauser have Israel negotiate autonomy in a "generous spirit" at an international peace conference to which might be invited "freely selected [sic] Palestinian representatives from the West Bank and Gaza." Those who do not advocate a "solution" of the Palestinian problem through dispersion and expulsion promise the native inhabitants a grim future in their ancient homeland. Thus Lt. General Raphael Eitan recently told the Knesset's Foreign Affairs and Defense Committee that "when we have settled the land, all that the Arabs will be able to do about it will be to scurry around like drugged roaches in a bottle."[2]

The Kahan commission has evinced its awareness of this issue by focusing on sectarian hatreds in Lebanon; it has even dwelled, in somewhat racialist tones, on the record of sectarian violence there. Yet it has assiduously avoided applying the same standards of judgment to the attitudes and conduct of Israeli leaders and government. I believe it is wrong to expect, as some people do, a higher sense of humanity from Jewish people. But there is reason to think that Jews would know better than most people that dispersion and freely selected leaders are not the notions ever to be resurrected. Both had a crucial role in the Third Reich's blueprint for the solution of the "Jewish problem." Concentration followed the failure of dispersion to solve the problem; freely selected representatives assisted significantly in the final solution. The late Hannah Arendt described this inevitable but unthinking process of descent as the "banality of evil."[3]

In modern times, when the raison d'être of a state and its security are defined in exclusivist—ethnic, racial, or religious—terms, it must inevitably result in evil.

The commission's recommendations were not legally binding; but they carried an obvious political weight and could have established the norms needed to protect the beleaguered populace in the Occupied Territories. Its report could have underlined that evil results from ethnocentric ideologies and banal ideas and intentions—like dispersing an entire people. It could have found that allowing Palestinian civilians to be terrorized by Israeli surrogates is a matter of direct governmental responsibility; that Israeli-paid, -trained, and

-controlled troops should be considered Israeli soldiers even if they are remu-
nerated secretly; that officials who pay, lead, and order such surrogates are
guilty of any crimes the surrogates commit. Had the commission faced up to
its responsibilities concretely and paid less regard to public relations, its judgment might have struck hard at the Begin-Sharon agenda of dispossession and
expelling a people from the remnants of their homeland—the West Bank and
Gaza.

In effect, the furor over the massacre at Sabra and Shatila has not served
even to ensure the safety and well-being of the survivors in occupied
Lebanon. The commendable effort of the MacBride commission[4] to draw
world attention to the excesses of an ideologically motivated ethnocentric
power has been ignored by the US-dominated media. No official inquiry has
been made to investigate and censure such rare acts of barbarism as systematic
destruction of historical archives and libraries. An uncounted number of men
between the ages of fourteen and sixty have vanished (according to the International Red Cross, 15,000 is a "very realistic" figure) and are presumably
incarcerated in concentration camps. This, too, is a violation of the Geneva
Conventions (1949). The remaining Palestinians, many of them dependents of
those in captivity, are subject to constant terrorizing. Homeless again, they are
barely managing to survive. One has a right to demand that the Western
world, which evinced a tragic indifference to the fate of earlier victims of an
ethnocentric government, would act decisively to guarantee not only the sovereignty of Lebanon but also the national survival and self-determination of
the Palestinian people. One has a right also to expect that Middle Eastern and
Arab governments will not carry on business-as-usual in the face of this peril.
Finally, one must hope that the PLO leaders will not fail to adopt a strategy
of struggle that links the Palestinian people's survival needs with their right to
self-determination.

[1983]

## 32 / PEACE OF THE WEAK

Yasser Arafat's accord with the government of Israel has been in the news for more than a week. Western leaders and the Euro-American media, source of more than 90 percent of the world's flow of information and analyses, are greeting it as a final step toward peace in the Middle East. Arab leaders as well as journalists and experts associated with Arab regimes have also welcomed the accord as yet another milestone on the road to a "New Middle Eastern Order."

Villains and heroes change roles rapidly in the Middle East. Images are reversed: Yesterday's "terrorist" is now a statesman. Erstwhile "moderates"—Mahmoud Darwish, Shafiq al-Hout, Edward Said—are lumped with "extremists." We have been here before, in 1978–1979 and in 1990–1991. "Which side are you on?" the reporter who called last week from Beirut wanted to know. There was then, as now, no easy answer.

The accord is secret, though its purported text was published by an Israeli daily, *Yedioth Ahronoth*. Broadly, it envisages the following: (i) Within four months after the accord is signed Israel shall "withdraw" from Gaza and Jericho, a town on the West Bank, and Palestinians shall constitute autonomous governing bodies. (ii) Within nine months a Palestinian representative council shall be elected for a term of five years. It will exercise autonomy over all populated centers of the West Bank and Gaza in the spheres of education, culture, health, tourism, and the policing of Palestinian population. (iii) Israeli military shall withdraw from Palestinian-populated areas but will remain in the Occupied Territories to ensure its "external security" and the security of its Jewish settlements. (iv) This "transitional" period will last for up to five years during which Israel and Palestinians shall negotiate on such issues as the status of Jerusalem, future of Palestinian refugees, relations with neighbors, and security arrangements.

Secret covenants are rarely about peace or justice. The available text suggests that what is being bandied about as a treaty is in fact an instrument of surrender. The PLO's chairman has apparently submitted to Israel's unique definition of autonomy: it applies to people not to the territories. In the *Yedioth Ahronoth* version, there is no mention of Palestinian self-determination, sovereignty, or statehood. Palestinians are mentioned, Palestine not at all. More ominously, there is no provision for Palestinian control over their land and water resources, a question that is central to the very survival of Palestinians on their native soil. No restriction on continued Jewish colonization is stipulated, and no power to control or suppress the settlers' lawlessness is accorded to the Palestinian local governments stipulated in the accord.

During the five years of "transition," Israel shall remain the sovereign power with the PLO's consent—in charge of defense, foreign affairs, and the security of Zionist settlers. Palestinian local bodies will be responsible for keeping public order, a responsibility which Israel will undoubtedly interpret to include the suppression of Palestinian resistance to settler activities. There is mention of economic cooperation between Israel and Palestinians which, under foreseeable circumstances, can only add Palestinian economic dependence to Israel's overwhelming political and military presence in the Occupied Territories. It is possible that before the quinquennial "transition" is over, the Palestinian police force envisaged in this accord would become, if it does not revolt, the equivalent of Haiti's hated Tontons Macoutes.

The accord does not identify the goal of "transition." That is a matter left to negotiations over five years. Arafat and his aides declare the imminence of a Palestinian state as the outcome of negotiations. Israeli officials who are obviously keen to formalize the agreement do not publicly contradict them. But Palestinian statehood is not envisaged in the agreement. When negotiations begin Palestinians will certainly demand sovereign statehood. Israel shall offer, as it has since 1979, autonomy. Barring a vague reference to "arbitration," the PLO-Israeli accord does not prescribe a binding resolution of the inevitable impasse between Israel and the Palestinians. With the latter fragmented between pro- and anti-accord factions, Israel is likely to consolidate its conquest more easily than it has been able to do in the past twenty-five years. This is an optimistic scenario.

A pessimistic projection ends this accord where it begins—with Yasser Arafat presiding over Gaza and Jericho. The PLO chairman is relieving Israel of its colonial albatross. The Gaza Strip is a living hell. Soweto, South Africa's worst ghetto, looks good by comparison. Here, 800,000 Palestinians, nearly all refugees, are boxed into a barren, strategically useless piece of land some twenty miles long and six miles wide. Since its creation as a congested repository of Israeli inhumanity, it has been a cauldron of Palestinian nationalism and desperation. The PLO was born here; and here it first confronted Hamas, its Islamic challenger. The Intifada started here. For twenty-five years it has been the site of daily confrontations between Israel and Palestinian resistance.

The government of Israel has been wanting a way out of Gaza. During the Camp David negotiations Anwar Sadat was shrewd enough to decline assuming responsibility for it. In recent years, ranking members of Israel's government and political establishment have openly advocated its unilateral withdrawal from Gaza. And now comes the PLO to its adversary's rescue. Arafat has tied the burden to his back with the thin threads of Israeli commitment to "autonomy" in the West Bank and private promises of a better future five years later. To lend Arafat's hopes a symbolic weight, the Israelis have shrewdly thrown in Jericho, a small town (pop. 15,000) along Jordan's border. Historically, Zionists owe their successes to an extraordinary discipline of detail. Jericho was a predictable prize: the nearest Zionist settlement is thirty kilometers away.

The agreement is likely to be signed. There is no credible opposition to Arafat. He controls Fatah, the largest PLO organization. The smaller groups including the PFLP, led by Dr. George Habash, cannot effectively oppose him without support or connivance of their host, Syria. President Hafiz al-Asad, a shrewd tactician, is keen to recover the Golan Heights. Arafat's accord with Israel frees him from the burdens of solidarity, permits him greater room for maneuver, and turns the focus of negotiations on Syria. Asad may not approve, but he has no reason to oppose this accord. For differing reasons, King Hussein of Jordan will also be amenable. Egypt has played the midwife. So, beyond the differences which still exist between Arafat and Israel on its final terms, there is no serious obstacle to the signing of the accord.

Trouble awaits after the accord. Hamas will continue to question its legitimacy and may be joined by other nationalist elements. Attacks on Israeli occupation forces and other acts of resistance shall occur, giving Israel ample arguments against Palestinian statehood. It may stall even on extending limited autonomy to the West Bank. After all, its cooperation is premised on the PLO's ability to maintain order, especially in Gaza. No one should be surprised if Yasser Arafat ends up as the pasha of Gaza residing in Jericho.

Why is the PLO leader entering into an accord so patently unjust and sterile? Several factors have contributed to it. One, Arafat has been losing political ground. Disaffection has augmented internally, and from the outside the Islamic movement has been nibbling on the PLO. Two, the PLO's financial crisis worsened when thousands of Palestinians, who contributed handsomely to its treasury, were expelled from the Gulf as punishment for the PLO's support of Iraq. In addition, Saudi Arabia, Kuwait, and the Gulf sheikhs stopped the subsidies on which a large part of the PLO's vast bureaucracy and welfare program had rested. Arafat was desperate to restore the conjunction of politics and money on which his power had so long rested. Three, he understood that an accord with Israel might end the PLO's financial predicament because pro-US Arab regimes would view it with favor.

The most crucial factor in Arafat's capitulation, however, is the general collapse of the Arab establishment's will. There is among Arab ruling elites a conviction that their future lies in submitting to the mercies of the United States. In the Middle East today, this translates increasingly into a posture of submission to Israel's growing power. A pragmatist par excellence, Arafat may have been shaken also by the way Muslim governments let Bosnia be destroyed. Whatever the reasons, we are witnessing the removal of the last obstacles to Israel's rise as the dominant power in the Middle East. History may record this to be a momentous time.

[1993]

## 33 / BEYOND ARAFAT'S ANTICS

The media had never given Yasser Arafat such sustained and favorable coverage. His impish, stubby face peers out from dailies, weeklies, and the TV screen, kissing Palestinian soil one day, tasting Gazan juice another, smiling ear to ear, and making grand gestures of peace and civility—Yitzhak Rabin and Abu Ammar curtseying at an entrance: "after you." Arafat obviously knows he stands on shaky ground. So he is flying high and talking tall.

He rode in a black bulletproof Mercedes through foul-smelling, garbage-lined streets of Gaza. Emotions were apparently high; he whipped them higher. "We are going from here to al-Ibrahimi mosque," he intoned, "going to Nablus and Jenin and Tulkarm and Qalqilya and Bethlehem and Beit Sahur and Beit Jalla and Ramallah and shortly after to al-Quds, al-Quds, al-Quds, to pray there." The striking fact about this speech was not Arafat's rhetorical flourish or his extravagant promise; these, after all, are the hallmark of our leaders in these dark Muslim times. The noticeable fact was his caution, the little caveat he put at the end of his pledge to go to al-Quds—"to pray."

The grand gesture accommodated an ugly reality, which is that the "limited autonomy" he has accepted is no more substantive than limited pregnancy. Arafat had made a similar reference to Jerusalem earlier without the prayerful qualifier; the Israelis hit him over the head for it, and he retracted. This time they watched him on closed-circuit television and were obviously satisfied. When he went to Jericho days later, an Israeli air force helicopter escorted him. The leader of the Palestine Liberation Organization is now a dependent of Israel's rulers. They are the masters of his destiny, though, hopefully, not of the Palestinian people's.

The text of the Israeli-PLO agreement on "self-rule" in Gaza and Jericho has been released, significantly by the government of Israel, not by the PLO. It reads in part: "Israel shall continue to carry the responsibility for defense against external threats, including the responsibility for protecting the Egyptian border and the Jordanian line . . . as well as the responsibility for overall security of Israelis and Jewish settlements . . . and will have the powers necessary to meet this responsibility."

Translated in plain language, the PLO under Arafat has agreed that: (i) Israel is the sovereign power in all of Palestine including the territories covered by "self-rule"; as such it alone shall exercise the sovereign right of defense. (ii) Arab countries contiguous with Gaza and Jericho—Egypt, Jordan—are defined as foreign lands from where "external threat" might emanate. This principle when extended to the West Bank shall apply surely to Syria and Lebanon also. (iii) Israel shall guard the "overall" security of Israelis and Jewish settlements.

There are 110 settlements, strategically laid out throughout the Occupied Territories. Israel planned them carefully so each Jewish settlement delinks one significant Palestinian community from another, and each is situated to better command the area's resources and control its communications network. It follows then that the government of Israel shall continue to occupy the territories militarily, exercise administrative powers over large portions, and also control the area's resources, of which land and water are the most crucial. The settlers Israel shall protect are one hundred thousand in number, ideologically motivated, and regard the native Arabs as intruders. They are armed, given to killing Arabs and to asserting their claims on places holy and profane. In the last three weeks the so-called Palestinian police force has merely suffered helplessly and in utter humiliation their provocative behavior. Palestinian militants, increasingly under the banner of Hamas, have been fighting back, especially in Hebron. There is now in Palestine, as before, neither peace nor justice.

So what has changed? The answer is many things, and significantly. One, Israel's occupation has been "legitimized" by an agreement with the Palestinian leadership. Thus, following the declaration of principle on which the self-rule agreement is based, the US secretary of state declared it "unhelpful" to describe the West Bank, Gaza, and Jerusalem as Occupied Territories. Two, Israel has rid itself of the burden of administering Gaza, its most troublesome and least desirable conquest and a burden it tried and failed earlier to dump on Egypt. Three, a formula has been found whereby Arafat may assume the responsibility of administering the people—not the territories, as Israel had always insisted—under occupation. Four, it is possible for Israel now to make separate deals with other Arab states; it is close to an agreement with King Hussein; and negotiations with Syria have entered a serious phase. Above all, Israel is in a position now to concentrate on the central task of consolidating its conquests.

Jerusalem is at the heart of Israel's gobbling strategy. "Gaza–Jericho," Edward Said had warned Arafat early this year, "is a kind of elaborate distraction, so that Palestinian energies will be absorbed in administering the peripheries while the core is left to the Israelis."[1] Jan de Jong, a Dutch geographer, has been studying "the core." The Israelis are taking the "last open spaces that . . . might be claimed by Palestinians . . . to square the circle around the Old City," he says in a detailed study.[2] Two rings of settlements are envisaged in Israel's building plans: one primarily around annexed al-Quds; the other shall enclose the first ring, then expand to most of central West Bank, from Bir Zeit in the north to the outskirts of Hebron in the south—eighty-five square miles of prime territory surrounding al-Quds. The pockets of Palestinian population in the area shall presumably be offered "self-rule," and marginalized. Israel has confiscated no less than 10,000 acres of Palestinian land since Arafat signed the declaration of principle. The Israeli government is building a $600 million road system in the Occupied Territories that links the Jewish settlements and military outposts to Israel while bypassing major Palestinian towns and villages, turning them, in de Jong's words, into "islands, cantons, small spheres of containment."[3] There is no evidence anywhere of a counterstrategy.

All this has a familiar ring. Backwardness is defined by an absence of the habit of investigation, critical analysis, strategic planning, and sustained execution. The Zionists have been winning and the Arabs have been losing because the former have, in Said's apt phrase, the "discipline of detail,"[4] and the latter do not. Zionism set out on its ambitious, seemingly impossible agenda of transforming Palestine into a Jewish state with a clear definition of the objective before it: to establish its sovereignty over the land. And it set forth a straightforward strategy that required a complex course of action: another acre, another goat.

The consequences of Israel's continued successes shall be felt beyond Palestine unless, that is, a viable strategy emerges soon to counteract its growing power. For we are witnessing the emergence in our midst of an unusually dynamic, ambitious, and young nuclear power allied for the time being with the United States. Its near-term goal is to play the hegemon over the oil resources of the Middle East. As its population expands—it is feverishly gathering to it the Soviet Jewry while denying their natural home to the nearby Palestinian one—it will be tempted to take more territory and subjugate more people. The governments and leaders of the region from Morocco to Pakistan—that is Ariel Sharon's designation of Israel's "sphere of influence"— have neither the will nor the capacity to resist either Israel's extravagant imperial design or American complicity in it. The burden then falls still on the beleaguered Palestinians.

[1994]

It does little justice to your gracious gesture for me to say that I feel exalted to be speaking at this inauguration of Gaza's first human rights conference. I am honored and also very sad, for reasons unfortunately more than one. Courteously, the organizers of this conference have not informed you that I am here because Edward Said is not here. He is undergoing chemotherapy this month and will recover, insha Allah. He is pained and angry like most of you by the latest development concerning the question of Palestine. I bring you his warm and fraternal greetings.

The deepest reason for my sadness is that my first-ever visit to this wounded land occurs at a juncture that marks the moment neither of liberation nor of renewal through resistance but a time of tragedy as great and lasting in its consequences for the Middle East as the one that befell the Palestinian people in 1948. To this question, I shall speak tomorrow. But lest my judgments and concerns be misunderstood, I should begin by affirming my solidarity with you as fraternal.

In the marvelously universal terms in which Arab patriots defined Arabism, I should be counted as an Arab. Syed Haider Abdel Shafi shall surely recall the century-old definition offered at the outset of the Arab national movement: *Kullu munn kanu arabun fi lughatihim, va thaqafathihim, va valaihim fa hum al-arab* (All those who are Arab in their language, culture, and feeling are Arabs). In this age of sectarian and exclusionary nationalisms, this was an open invitation I could not resist. So, meant this way, I am an Arab and entitled to making harsh judgments on the man-made disasters that pile on us.

In the course of this conference, you shall hear me speak plainly ill of Arab and Muslim, including Palestinian, leaders and ruling classes, their slavish outlook, mental indolence, twisted ambitions, and failure of will. In the history of Arab people, of the Islamic civilization as a whole, I cannot recall a darker time than this. For never before had we experienced so catastrophic a combination of wealth and weakness, of material resources and moral bankruptcy. Our elites consume opulently and obsessively and contribute not at all to production. Our lands are littered with machines while we have no technology. Wealth is plentiful among us, but it does not convert into capital. Our greatest strengths—the concentration of vital resources in this region, its strategic location, and civilizational legacies—yield surrenders and misfortunes, national and regional tragedies. The most depressing fact of all is our long failure to ask why and our acceptance of indolent leaders who substitute money for politics, speech for action, and ingratiation of Western powers for policy making. Those country sellers are at the center of our disasters. To be fruitful, resistance, like charity, should begin at home.

No people symbolizes the Middle Eastern tragedy today as Palestinians do. Many of us know this suffering instinctively to be a sign of our times. Raja Sourani just gave us a list of the distant lands from where delegates have come to attend this conference. More important, from the moment of arriving at the Ben Gurion airport I have been meeting the young volunteers from England, America, Scotland, and Wales who are here sharing the risks and hardships of Palestinian life under occupation. I have asked, why? They are certainly not attracted to this place as they were to Cuba or Vietnam—by the integrity and style of the struggle for liberation. Palestine's appeal to them is obviously deeper. Two facts seem to me of fundamental importance:

First, the Palestinian experience holds a mirror to the Third World. The Middle East offers as does no other place in the world a metaphor for the postcolonial era. The abject lesson converges on the question of Palestine. As a boy, I witnessed the beginning of the era of decolonization. It was in the summer of 1947 that India and Pakistan waded in blood to independence. "Is it worth the price?" my eldest brother had asked as the subcontinent burned and twenty million people fled, fought, died, and killed. "Yes, yes, yes!" replied a chorus of family and friends. Just a year later, we were mourning for Palestine. Its people were dispossessed. At the dawn of decolonization, Palestine was colonized. I recall my utter confusion at this irony of history.

Later, I understood that this was a warning, not a paradox. The loss of Palestine was in fact an outcome of the postcolonial condition. Most Middle Eastern countries including Egypt, Iraq, Jordan, Iran, and Turkey were already "independent" when the major portion of Palestine was captured by Zionists, a majority of its native inhabitants were driven away, and a self-proclaimed "outpost of Western civilization" was implanted there with full Western support. Anyone who cared to think would have known that this extraordinary development would make an obviously lasting and adverse impact on the future of the entire region and beyond. It also made a mockery of the notion of decolonization. The postcolonial elite was an elite of words not thought.

The response of the "independent" states to this historic challenge was remarkable for its combination of incomprehension, indifference, and incompetence. All failed to analyze the historic significance of Israel's creation and the necessity to oppose it. The Turkish government was feverishly busy making Turkey a part of the West. Iran fancied itself as separate from the Arab world. Egypt went to war half-heartedly and ill-prepared and lost abjectly. Every Arab government appealed to and expected the West to do justice. In the age of decolonization, this was the first clear-cut reminder of the vulnerability of postcolonial states, the vacuity of the postcolonial intelligentsia, and a reminder also of the continued menace of Western imperialism to the well-being of the so-called decolonized peoples. The fate of Palestine symbolized the Third World condition. This latest Palestinian debacle suggests that the postcolonial environment is worsening, especially in the Middle East.

Second, the idea of Palestine is the universal counterpoint to the greatest evil of our time: the idea of exclusionary and sectarian statehood. The ideology of difference and superior claims is an evil most banal and menacing, one that caused a holocaust in Europe. Jews and Gypsies suffered the most from the German quest for Aryan statehood. Today, a similar presumption compels the Serbs to carry on "ethnic cleansing" in Bosnia while the Western powers keep their lopsided arms embargo on Bosnia's hapless Muslim victims. Zionism has been more circumspect in declaring its heartless mission. Theodor Herzl came close to it when he confided to his diary that "both the process of expropriation and removal of the poor [Palestinians] must be carried out discreetly and circumspectly."[1]

Facts reveal the ugly reality nevertheless. Palestinians have been victims of Zionism's exclusionary quest in a variety of ways. They were forcibly driven out in the hundreds of thousands in 1948 and again in 1967; an overwhelming majority in Gaza are refugees in this barren strip of land. Since 1967, they are victims again of a well-designed campaign of strangulation in the Occupied Territories that systematically deprives people of the elements of life—land and water—without which a nation cannot survive. The Zionist settlements, which continue to expand despite the so-called peace accords, are so situated as to cut off one major Palestinian habitation from another. Your brethren, the Arabs in Israel, are reduced to second-class citizenship, an oxymoron no Jew in the United States and Europe shall or should tolerate. Two million Palestinians in exile have been abandoned to the mercies of governments more harsh than hospitable. The Western world ought at the very least to be embarrassed to describe this state of affairs as democratic and liberal.

You are a besieged people, and the continuity of your community life has been broken. The most extraordinary and inspiring fact of Palestinian political life in the diaspora and under occupation is this: despite decades of suffering, you have by and large abjured sectarian alternatives. You still make the necessary distinction between Judaism and Zionism. Muslim and Christian Palestinians still struggle for a shared liberation, and unless one is in a church or a mosque, it is difficult to know a Palestinian's religious affiliation. This unity of secular purpose has been your strength, a national treasure I hope you shall retain.

Oppressed people often end up following their oppressors into exclusionary darkness. Should the Palestinian people yield to this temptation, your losses shall be even greater than you have experienced so far. We belong to a civilization that achieved its greatness through the universality of its appeal, respect for pluralism both cultural and religious, and an openness that allowed us to learn from China to Europe, Africa to India. We cannot renounce this heritage under the menace of an exclusionary ideology. Ideas that break boundaries and create bonds among people do not die. Struggles for justice and liberation are often protracted, but they are rarely lost if people persist. This conference at this dark hour of capitulation and continuing aggression is but one sign of your persistence.

I am saddened to be in Palestine because I see this monument to ecumenism disfigured by sectarian symbols. I am appalled at the sight of those armed zealots on the loose and of those settlements that rise like sores on native soil. But I am glad to be able to renew with you our commitment to the Universal Declaration of Human Rights.

[1994]

## 35 / KING HUSSEIN'S DUAL LEGACY

Hussein Ibn Talal, at sixty-three young by today's standards, has been buried. Among the powerful men who came to bid him goodbye were all the American presidents who are alive—Bill Clinton plus Gerald Ford, Jimmy Carter, and George Bush.[1] The Israelis arrived in force. The "bad" Arabs—Mu'ammar Gadhafi and Saddam Hussein—advisedly stayed back. So did Iran's Mohammad Khatami. The PLO leader turned good Arab was predictably there, wiping tears. Even Boris Yeltsin dragged his wobbly self into Amman.

The American media described it as the "diplomatic funeral of the century." The editorial in the *New York Times* eulogized the "power of the peacemaking man. . . . In death, King Hussein was able to do one more time what he often did while living—draw together divided men." "Forceful and compassionate advocate of Arab-Israeli peace," echoed the *Washington Post*. How sweetly diplomacy deals with death!

How cynical are the media in the great democracies, and how in tune with the purposes of power. Could they have really forgotten their governments' and their own denunciations of King Hussein? Jordan's monarch was in fact distinguished among Arab rulers for sustaining repeated punishments, administered intermittently each time he dared stray away from their preferences. To his credit, he did dare more than once. Yet as he was dying and after he was gone, all the presidents and their men lacked the simple humanity to recall or regret the punishments that they had inflicted upon him each time he revealed an Arab heart.

The last time was in 1991. He did not quite fall in line behind Washington's determination to invade Iraq and insert American forces in the Middle East. Boy, did George Bush, his aides, plus the reporters, editors, and pundits pile on him. As often happens in such cases, to pillory him they misrepresented, exaggerated, and lied. He was portrayed as an ally of Saddam Hussein, supporter of the aggression against Kuwait, an unstable potentate, autocratic monarch, and a born loser. The *New York Times* gave ample space even to its bête noire, the Saudi Arabian ambassador—a prince, what else?—to insult Hussein and accuse him of cowardice in failing to defend Jerusalem, an Islamic sanctuary under the guardianship in 1967 of the Hashemite dynasty.

The allegations that were repeated daily and for months were not true. Hussein did not support Saddam Hussein's invasion of Kuwait. He did not form an alliance with Iraq. On the contrary, he openly advocated Iraq's withdrawal from Kuwait. What he tried to avert was a full-scale American invasion of the Gulf. Variously, he sought an Arab solution to an Arab problem, a judicious and patient international effort to end the crisis, and time to let diplomacy prevail. The United States, on the other hand, viewed Saddam Hussein's aggression as an opportunity not to be missed. Since the early 1970s, the Middle East had become the primary focus of the American struggle to maintain its status as a world power. The region was targeted as the centerpiece of the Nixon Doctrine.

With modernized and mobile naval deployments, large bases in such places as Diego Garcia, Sicily, and Oman, large stockpiles of arms in Saudi Arabia, and a strategic ally as primed as Israel, Washington had waited for an opportunity to go in and assert the paramountcy of American power in the oil depot of Europe and Japan. Saddam Hussein opened the gates. In the smallest possible way, King Hussein appeared to stand in the way of Operation Desert Storm. For his impudence, Jordan's "plucky little king" was maligned and punished.

The United States government and its allies in Gulf added injuries to the insults. Jordan's lifelines—in financial aid, credits, arms, and spare parts, even the supply of oil—were cut off. The harsh economic embargo nearly broke Jordan's back. Unemployment rose to some 40 percent of the labor force, the number of Jordanians below the poverty line ($136.00 per month for a family of 6.5 persons) increased fourfold, and the health environment deteriorated so badly that in 1994 the World Health Organization warned of the "possible re-emergence of previously eradicated diseases." Read all the gushing editorials and obituaries, you will scarcely find a hint of the beating "the peace-maker" took from American officials and their mimickmen in the media.

The ruler of the kingdom which, from the time of its cesarean birth in March 1946 had suffered from dependency first on Britain, then the United States, was hardly in a position to withstand Washington's torture without even a pretense of solidarity from the rich Arab states. Eventually he crossed over to reach a formal peace with Israel, a crossing made easier by Yasser Arafat's simultaneous surrender to the Israeli-American agenda. Thomas Friedman, the *New York Times* columnist and Middle East expert, has nowhere any of these unpleasant details, yet he asserts deadpan that "when it came to the game of nation-building, King Hussein deserves to be remembered as an Arab superpower." "In a neighborhood of brutal thugs," writes Mr. Friedman, "he operated with a basic decency." Ironically, he is not referring here to George Bush and Jim Baker, Yitzhak Rabin or Benjamin Netanyahu, Abraham Rosenthal or Thomas Friedman. Some journalism!

A different treatment had been accorded to the much-eulogized Hussein of Jordan when he joined Gamal Abdel Nasser against Israel in 1967. On the other hand, his pro-American posture and CIA connections, his 1970 war with the PLO, and his secret dealings with Israeli leaders have caused many Arab radicals to denounce him bitterly. Hussein was often caught in the cross fire because he was a man in between, an heir to the dual legacy of Arab nationalism and Western imperial patronage. His tragedy and limitations have not been fully understood. He was a victim of two forces—imperialism and nationalism—which throughout this century have interacted in the Arab world in an unequal relationship of antagonistic collaboration. The unresolved equation between these two forces has contributed greatly to the crisis of state and society in the Middle East.

King Hussein operated at the center of this contradiction. The Arab revolt during World War I was the defining moment in the development of Arab nationalism. Its hated other was the dying Ottoman empire, not the strident British or French imperialism. Rather, the latter were the Arab nationalists' apparent benefactors and patrons who made large promises, delivered in meager pieces, not enough to satisfy the Arab players' political and territorial appetites but just enough to keep them compromised and dependent.

From the start of this debilitating process the Hashemites were entrapped in it. Hussein, the amir of Hejaz, shifted his loyalties from the Ottoman Empire to the British and helped ignite the Arab revolt in June 1916. The Brits were not given to keeping promises. At the war's victorious end Hussein did not become the unifier of the Arab world and passed his embittered last days as an exile in Cyprus.

The region was parcelized instead into little entities called mandates held by Britain and France. The Zionists, then leading a small settler movement, were promised a "homeland" in Palestine, a British mandate. The ascendant Saudis drove Hussein out of Hejaz. The British did not intervene on his behalf. Later they appointed his elder son, Faysal, as the king of Iraq, where he ruled until July 1958, when he was killed in the military coup that overthrew the monarchy. Amir Hussein's second son, Abdullah, King Hussein's grandfather and his role model, was assigned the emirate of Transjordan, which in March 1946 became the sovereign state of Jordan.

A pan-Arabist dependent on Britain, Abdullah participated in the Arab-Israeli war of 1948 (with a British commander, Glubb Pasha, leading his Arab Legion) and took a portion of the Palestine mandate under his control. His son, Talal, was incapacitated. So upon reaching majority in May 1953, grandson Hussein Ibn Talal became the king of Jordan. The declining British gradually passed their spheres of influence to their American cousins. In 1967, without American approval, King Hussein allied with Egypt and Syria against Israel and lost control over the remainder of Palestine, including Jerusalem. That's when he personally experienced the dark side of the free world and its media.

The compulsions which rendered Hussein punishable in American eyes were not only subjective and ideological. More than a half—by now some 67 percent—of the people in the desert kingdom are displaced Palestinians or their descendants. They know that Zionism alone is not the cause of their national tragedy. By instinct they are anti-imperialist and Arab nationalists. When the lines are clearly drawn, a cautious Jordanian monarch cannot afford to defy their collective feeling. King Hussein was a survivor by instinct and common sense. He knew when taking sides 1967 style and when dancing on the fence— as in 1991—was essential to the survival of his dynasty.

In 1991, many observers were surprised by his refusal to get behind American-led Operation Desert Storm. They did not take Jordanian realities into account: the Intifada was raging in occupied Palestine, children had their eyes gouged by rubber bullets, thousands of unarmed minors had been murdered by Israel's forces, and Palestinians of Jordan lived in shame and anxiety when Saddam Hussein defied their tormentors, whom they did not believe to be Israelis alone.

Abdullah II inherits an uneasy throne in an uncertain world of continuous and deep pain. He has inherited a false and unjust peace with Israel which the superpower expects him to keep while it lets Israel violate its terms with impunity. He has displaced a popular uncle who has been viewed by citizens as more capable of protesting Israel's expansions and withstanding American pressures. He rules a restive people who have now suffered a decade of economic downturn. He lives in a tormented neighborhood where in one country (Iraq) bombs rain while children and old people die of malnutrition and lack of medicines; in another country (Syria) a sick old dictator holds together a divided and discontented land; and next door bands of armed zealots are aided by a militarized state to dispossess and torment the hapless indigenous Arabs.

"He is a chip off the old block," assures an American pundit. "He clearly understands his mission," says the president of the United States. "Iran remains a threat to the security of certain Gulf states," said the new king on the eve of his coronation. "We are on the same sheet of music" is how he described his agreement with US policy on Iraq. That is too much pleasing, too openly and too soon. It is most unlikely that the wily old king would have done that at this time.

[1999]

# PART V
# SOUTH ASIA

# INTRODUCTION

Yogesh Chandrani and Radha Kumar

In this section of the book, we have included a selection from Eqbal Ahmad's extensive writings on South Asia. These articles were written over a period of almost three decades (1971–1999) and provide us with a glimpse of Ahmad's political and intellectual engagements in South Asia. They were mostly written after 1987, when Ahmad returned to Pakistan and became a regular columnist for *Dawn*, Pakistan's largest English-language daily, and they reveal his remarkable ability to put complex arguments both simply and succinctly. The theoretical frameworks that Ahmad developed in his works on postcolonial states (part 2) and the Cold War (part 3), especially in the Middle East, North Africa, and South Asia, are brought to bear on his analysis of Pakistani politics and society. Ahmad shows us that while colonialism's legacy to Pakistan was the vice-regal tradition of an overdeveloped and authoritarian state, this legacy gained new life from the Cold War and contributed to the rise of virulent sectarianism in the country. Pakistan's relationship to the United States during the Cold War, in particular, empowered the military and bureaucracy at the expense of the democratic aspirations of its peoples.

*Partition*

"Partitioned Lands, Divided Sentiments," the first article in this section, is based on a lecture delivered in New Delhi in 1998, fifty-one years after the creation of the two independent states of India and Pakistan.[1] Ahmad's own life was profoundly affected by the competing nationalisms and sectarian violence that accompanied partition. As a teenager, he made the long and weary trek from Bihar in eastern India to Pakistan with his elder brothers in 1947. Aspects of this journey are recounted in the BBC documentary *Stories My Country Told Me: Eqbal Ahmad on the Grand Trunk Road* (1996).

The partition of India was not inevitable, despite the British policies of divide and rule that were based on the antihistorical idea that India's Hindus and Muslims constituted two monolithic communities whose relations with each other were marked by antagonism, and violence. This idea, as Ahmad so eloquently suggests, contradicted the centuries-long history of interaction between the two communities—an interaction that is visible even today in the languages, literatures, and religious practices of the subcontinent's Hindus and Muslims. What began as the colonial strategy of divide and rule was soon transformed into "the two-nation theory" with the arrival of mass politics between the two world wars. Colonialism, mass politics, and nationalism enabled the consolidation of community identities on the basis of religion, with far-reaching implications for the new states of India and Pakistan.

Partition transformed what had been until 1947 a conflict over state power and representation between India's secular, Hindu, and Muslim nationalists. But it did not solve the problems that the two new states faced. Partition highlighted, and in many ways internalized, the unresolved issues of self-determination in both. Their largely colonized administrations proved unequal to building the independent democratic institutions that were promised by Nehru's "tryst with destiny" and Jinnah's vision of a secular Muslim state.

Ahmad interrogates the political, historical, and cultural legacies that partition bequeathed to the subcontinent. An article on the paradoxical figure of Mohammed Ali Jinnah attempts to rescue him from the grasp of the historiography sponsored by General Zia ul-Haq's dictatorship. Even though Jinnah's later political career was devoted to representing Muslim political demands in colonial India, he remained a committed secularist for his entire life. The creation of Pakistan in 1947 had left unresolved the question of whether Pakistan, with its heterogeneous population, would be a secular polity or one governed by religious principles. In a remarkable speech to Pakistan's Constituent Assembly, Jinnah stated: "You are free; you are free to go to your temples, you are free to go to any other place of worship in this State of Pakistan. . . . You may belong to any religion caste or creed—that has nothing to do with the business of the State. . . . We are starting with this fundamental premise that we are all citizens and equal citizens of one State. . . . Now, I think we should keep that in front of us as our ideal and you will find that in course of time that Hindus shall cease to be Hindus and Muslims shall cease to be Muslims, not in the religious sense, because that is the personal faith of each individual, but in the political sense as citizens of the State."[2]

By the time of General Zia ul-Haq's military coup in 1977, however, Jinnah's dream of Pakistan as an experiment in crafting a constitutional order that guaranteed the rights of all citizens regardless of religious beliefs had been abandoned, and the construction of Pakistan as an ideological state (i.e., a state for Muslims) had begun in earnest. In history textbooks (and in some sections of the press), the figure of Jinnah was recast as an upholder of Islam. Upon taking power in 1977, General Zia declared: "Pakistan, which was created in the name of Islam, will continue to survive only if it sticks to Islam. That is why I consider the introduction of [an] Islamic system an essential prerequisite for the country."[3] The ambiguities that surrounded the Muslim League's campaign were displaced by the claim that Jinnah's goal was the creation of an Islamic state and by representations of the ulema (most of whom had been marginal to the Muslim League or even rejected Jinnah's claims to speak on behalf of India's Muslims) as the vanguard of the Pakistan movement.

Pakistan has been ruled by the military for twenty-nine of its fifty-seven years of independence. And even when the military has not formally ruled, it has retained the power to dictate terms to civilian leaders. This dominant role is the product of the colonial encounter and American support for authoritarian regimes during and after the Cold War. Among Pakistan's military dictators, none was as repressive as General Zia ul-Haq, and none was the beneficiary of US and Saudi Arabian largesse on such a massive scale. It was under General Zia's rule, in the shadow of the American-sponsored "covert war" against the Soviet occupation of Afghanistan, that the construction of Pakistan as an ideological state was accelerated. Within this context, Ahmad argues that Jinnah ought to be remembered as a paradoxical figure, one who sought to speak for India's Muslim minority, appealed to Muslims as Muslims, and yet remained committed to secular, constitutionalist politics. Jinnah's vision of Pakistan represented not the sectarian ideologies of the nation-state and of nationalist movements but an attempt to realize the universalist and inclusive ideals that Ahmad believed are at the center of Muslim teachings and practices.

## Pakistan's Military

"Letter to a Pakistani Diplomat" was written during the Bangladesh crisis and while Ahmad was in the midst of the Kissinger kidnapping trial. The Bangladesh crisis was precipitated by the abrogation by the military, with the support of West Pakistani leaders, especially "the miserable Mr. Bhutto," of election results that gave a majority in the National Assembly to the Bengali Awami League. Ahmad's letter came at a time when few if any members of Pakistan's intelligentsia acknowledged the atrocities of the Pakistani military in East Pakistan. Soon after the article was published, India intervened militarily, and East Pakistan became the independent country of Bangladesh. Once again, the question of rights and representation of an underrepresented group—in this case, the rights of Pakistan's Bengali-speaking citizens—were at the center of the rebelling region's demands.

The letter is followed by an analysis of the military dictatorship of General Zia ("General Zia is Now the Law"), whose rise Ahmad traces to the antidemocratic and corrupt rule of Prime Minister Zulfiqar Ali Bhutto. In "Pakistan: Signposts to Police State," published in 1974, he argues that Bhutto's rule was characterized by the centralization of power, the suppression of demands for local autonomy, and the militarization of the state. The theoretical frameworks that Ahmad outlines in the articles on the postcolonial state are elaborated in the context of Pakistan. Here, Ahmad's analysis of what he terms "fascism" is quite specific to postcolonial Pakistan: the failure to respect the pluralist character of Pakistani society, the turn to antidemocratic and personalist politics, the expansion of the coercive arms of the state, and the resort to religious nationalism in legitimizing repression. It was during Bhutto's reign that the military was restored to a central role in Pakistani politics, when he called on it to suppress a revolt in Baluchistan. And it was Bhutto who encouraged religious nationalists within the military, promoting General Zia ul-Haq to the rank of chief of staff for his seeming loyalty and lack of interest in politics. As Ahmad points out, this was a dangerous policy: in 1977, General Zia carried out a coup and subsequently had Bhutto executed. During his reign, General Zia Islamized Pakistan's military as well as its legal and educational systems.

## Afghanistan

In the next section, we bring together some of Ahmad's critical articles on the Soviet invasion of Afghanistan in 1979, the American and Pakistani responses to that invasion, and the aftermath of the American-sponsored proxy war. The clarity and prescience of Ahmad's analysis of the Afghan war and its many legacies for the region and the world beyond is all the more apparent in light of the terrorist attacks on New York and Washington on September 11, 2001. "Bloody Games," an article that he coauthored with his friend and colleague Richard Barnet of the Institute for Policy Studies, is an analysis of the events leading up to the Soviet invasion of Afghanistan in 1979 and the formation of the American-Saudi-Pakistani alliance in financing a global "jihad" against the Soviet occupation. By 1987, American aid to the Afghan resistance had reached $660 million per year and was matched dollar for dollar by the Saudi government. Most of this aid was distributed by the CIA through Pakistan's Interservices Intelligence Directorate (ISI) to radical Islamist groups headed by the likes of Gulbuddin Hekmatyar, Yunus Khalis, Abdur Rasul Sayyaf, Barnahudin Rabbani, and one Osama bin Laden.

The American "covert" operation in Afghanistan was unique for at least two reasons. First, the Reagan administration attempted to extend the Islamic guerrilla struggle into Soviet Central Asia. This decision was made by then–CIA director William Casey in 1986 and subsequently reversed when the Soviet government threatened to attack Pakistan. Second was the decision to recruit Muslims from around the world to train in Pakistan and join the fight with the Afghan Mujahideen. Ahmad's writings on Afghanistan offer us an analysis of the hidden history of both America's "covert war" and the context that gave rise to al-Qaeda. As Ahmad argues, American sponsorship transformed the Afghan war of liberation into a pan-Islamic jihad against "godless communism" and legitimized the establishment of an Islamic state in Afghanistan:

> Ironically, [the rebels] had the support of Western powers as no liberation movement ever did. The United States and its allies supplied to the mujahideen an

estimated $10 billion worth of arms and aid. They also invested in this jihad the legitimacy of their enormous power and the luster of their media-made glory. On one especially memorable occasion, when Afghanistan's hard-line Islamists visited the White House, President Ronald Reagan described them as the Muslim world's "moral equivalent of our founding fathers." Similarly, the American and European media played up the war in Afghanistan as the greatest story of the eighties. Foreign correspondents combed the Hindu Kush for stories of "Mooj" heroism. Competition for jihad narrative was so great that in one instance a major network, CBS, paid handsomely to film a staged battle between Islam and communism.[4]

The global "jihad" that Ahmad writes about is the American- and Saudi-sponsored war against the Soviet occupation of Afghanistan. In these articles, it becomes clear that what Western officials and media now call Islamic fundamentalism emerged in the context of America's covert war against "godless communism" and is in fact a very modern mix of dollars, drugs, guns, realpolitik, and religious radicalism. The deployment of this global network of militant Islam, or what Ahmad aptly calls "Jihad International, Inc.," in the service of imperial policies has been the Afghan war's most devastating legacy, first and foremost for the peoples of Afghanistan and Pakistan and then for others all over the world.

The Soviet withdrawal from Afghanistan in 1989 was not followed by peace and stability for either Afghanistan or the region; instead, the Americans, having won the last battle of the Cold War, withdrew from the region and ignored it until September 11, 2001. Afghanistan was a land in ruins, awash in drugs and guns, and devastated all over again by civil war between rival factions of the Afghan Mujahideen. Pakistan was burdened with some three million Afghan refugees, a massive drug problem, a thriving gun trade, and widespread corruption in state institutions. Karachi, Pakistan's largest city and the engine of its economy, was engulfed by sectarian armed conflict between the *Mohajirs* (Muslim refugees and migrants from India) and the state. The Pakistan army and the intelligence services emerged from the war against the Soviet Union with even more power and autonomy in determining Pakistan's foreign policies and domestic politics.

The Pakistani security establishment interpreted the Soviet defeat in Afghanistan as *its* victory, and continued to sponsor Gulbuddin Hekmatyar's extremist Hizb-e-Islami Party in the civil war against rival militias of other ethnic groups sponsored by other neighbors of Afghanistan. The Pakistani aim was to control Afghanistan's political future by installing a friendly regime in Kabul in order to secure for Pakistan "strategic depth" against a much stronger India. In 1991, Ahmad warned that Pakistan's investment in the Mujahideen would be to its detriment and that "strategic depth" was a "mirage" and an idea that "would lead us into unrelieved darkness." In addition, he warned that Pakistani attempts to install a centralized regime in Kabul would fail in Afghanistan: "More importantly, the ideologies at war—Marxism and Fundamentalism— are alien to Afghan culture. Afghanistan is a diverse, pluralistic society; centralizing unitary agendas cannot appeal to it. It is a country surrounded by other, bigger neighbors, who would not let another shape its foreign and defense policies."[5] Pakistan's support for Hekmatyar indeed brought neither stability nor peace in Afghanistan. Instead, it fueled a civil war that further devastated Kabul, Jalalabad, and other cities.

Through the early nineties, a series of warlords was installed and then removed from power in Kabul. The Russians, the Iranians, and the Pakistanis all had their favorites, and civil war continued to wrack Afghanistan. The Pakistanis meanwhile continued to recruit, finance, and train Islamists and, by 1995, had sponsored the Taliban to invade and take power in Kabul. In 1996, the Taliban captured Kabul and instituted a regime that Ahmad describes as a "theocracy" unparalleled in Islamic history. The Taliban are products of the refugee camps and the *madaris* created in Pakistan during the US- and Saudi-financed Afghan war. In Pakistan, this covert war was managed by the ISI in partnership with such extremist movements as the Jamaat-i-Islami. In 1995, when the Taliban were in the midst of their assault on Afghanistan, Ahmad wrote of the dangers of Pakistan's policies:

> Nowhere is the distortion of political life more severe than here. Drugs, guns, sectarianism, violence, and crime. We experience them all. They can get worse. The Taliban's successes for example will hurt this country deeply. Products of Pakistani *madaris*, they have links here and spawn here. *Harkat-ul-Ansar*, their Pakistani counterpart is already born and growing. Like the Taliban, they too are a rabid anti-Shia party with an Islamic agenda the Holy Prophet (PBUH) would have found repugnant.[6] The chickens of proxy wars and manipulation politics always come home to roost. If we keep going this way, we cannot ensure peace or our place in Afghanistan. But as surely as night follows day, we shall lose ourselves and what is left in Pakistan of decency and civilization.[7]

*Kashmir*

The Pakistani military's betrayal of the secular, democratic promise is developed in a poignant way in the article on Kashmir. Despite the tremendous costs to the Afghan and Pakistani people, the security establishment persisted in its policy of backing *jihadi* groups and eventually deployed them in a proxy war against India over Kashmir. India and Pakistan have fought two wars over Kashmir, one in 1948 and another in 1965. Decades of misrule and repression in Indian-held Kashmir had led to a popular and armed uprising in 1989. In its initial stages, the uprising was dominated by the Jammu Kashmir Liberation Front (JKLF), a secular movement that demanded Kashmir's independence from Indian rule. The Indian government deployed the army and brutally suppressed the uprising. The Pakistani security establishment at first supported the JKLF and then began to seek more pliable allies. By the mid-1990s, the Indian forces had dismantled the JKLF's armed infrastructure, and the Pakistani military had switched over to backing jihadi groups such as Harkat-ul-Ansar, Jaish-e-Mohammed, and Lashkar-e-Jhangvi. These groups had proliferated as a result of the Afghan campaign and were sponsored by the ISI and the Jamaat-i-Islami as front organizations. The network of *madaris* that were integral to the Afghan campaign were now used to recruit fighters for a militant campaign to liberate Kashmir. Ahmad's "Beyond Mutual Destruction" reviews the history of the Kashmir uprising and focuses especially on the failures of both India and Pakistan to respect the dignity and the rights of the Kashmiri people. As in the selections on Afghanistan, what animates Ahmad's argument is the grave injustice done to the Kashmiri people by both the Indian and the Pakistani states. The other theme is Ahmad's search for ways to overcome the hostilities between India and Pakistan, hostilities that he believed were a legacy of the partition of the subcontinent. Kashmiri society, with its syncretism, represented the rich possibilities that were created by the intermingling of diverse religions and cultures in South Asia, and a peaceful Kashmir would, in his vision, serve as a model for the entire region to emulate.

*India-Pakistan Nuclear Rivalry and Dialogue*

In the last fifteen years of his life, Ahmad was actively engaged in promoting a dialogue between India and Pakistan. When, in 1998, the Hindu nationalist government of India tested nuclear weapons, Ahmad argued that Pakistan should not test its weapons and enter into a costly arms race with India. Nuclear weapons, he insisted, were "weapons of terror and deterrence." But, as in the Cold War, nuclear arms could function as an "umbrella for proxy warfare" and would not improve the security of either India or Pakistan.[8] His arguments were ignored by Pakistan's rulers. Instead, in the spring and summer of 1999, Pakistan infiltrated its troops into Kargil, and India and Pakistan were at war over Kashmir again. In 1998 and 1999, Ahmad wrote a series of prescient articles, with which we conclude this section. In "No Alternative to Dialogue," he argued that the possession of nuclear weapons by both India and Pakistan made it all the more urgent for the two governments to negotiate an end to the bloody and expensive conflict between them and that a failure to do so would be to the detriment of the peoples of the region and to the prospects for democracy in Pakistan. The visit to Pakistan by the former Indian prime minister, Atal Behari Vajpayee, in February 1999 offered such an opportunity.

Ahmad saw the dangers to Pakistan's democracy that were represented by the combination of conflict in Kashmir, the nuclear arms race between India and Pakistan, and the tense relationship between the corrupt civilian and military leaders of post-Zia Pakistan. In the last three essays of this section, each written at a moment of crisis of elected governments, Ahmad returns to these tensions and warns of the threat to democracy posed by Pakistan's generals. The first of the three, "No, Not Again," was written in response to the army's decision to launch a military operation against the MQM in Karachi, a coalition partner in then–prime minister Nawaz Sharif's elected government.[9] He observes: "We forget that there exists a dialectical opposition between rules of military organization and principles of governing a society. One relies on command; the other on consensus. One favors regimen; the other requires participation. One stresses discipline; the other values accountability. One rests on order; the other on participation. That is why, when they assume power, armies distort societies, repress politics, demoralize and corrupt themselves, and lose wars."

The military forced Sharif to resign, and in 1993 Benazir Bhutto returned to form her second government, this time with "enhanced powers." Bhutto's second term was characterized by repression and corruption, and by 1995 there was a sense that the army would intervene once more in Pakistan. In "The Signals Soldiers Pick," Ahmad returns to analyze the appeals as well as the profound dangers of turning to the military to resolve political crises.

In the final essay of this section and of the book, "Shotgun Governance," written in March 1999, two months before his untimely death, Ahmad returned to address the temptations of a military coup. Subsequent events in the summer of 1999 demonstrated that his fears were well founded. American pressure on Prime Minister Nawaz Sharif forced him to withdraw troops from Kargil in Indian-controlled Kashmir, and the withdrawal was followed by a military coup led by General Pervez Musharaf. Once more, Pakistan's democracy had been compromised by a corrupt civilian prime minister and a military committed more to its own privileges and prerogatives than to the well-being of Pakistan's peoples. Since September 2001, Musharaf's abrogation of democracy in Pakistan has been legitimized by the Bush administration.

We conclude this introduction by pointing to the larger significance and uniqueness of Ahmad's intellectual and political legacy for South Asia. In mainstream writings on postcolonial Pakistan, it is often argued that the absence of democracy is the result of a society that is resistant to modernization or that the incidence of sectarian violence is a product of ancient hatreds. The assumption in these arguments is that the fault lies within the beliefs, cultures, and traditions of the peoples of Pakistan (and of South Asia, in general). The abiding power and influence of Ahmad's life and work on South Asia is his insistence that it is not a people's attachment to their culture, their religion, or their tradition that stands in the way of democracy, justice, and peace. Rather, Ahmad's work reminds us that the crisis of postcolonial South Asia stems from the undemocratic practices of modern states, especially from their propensity to authorize and mobilize the most repressive aspects of religion and tradition in the service of power.

Ahmad himself was a courageous and untiring critic of these tendencies. He was an active participant in the struggles against authoritarianism and sectarianism in Pakistan in particular and in South Asia in general. In the later years of his life, he wrote weekly columns for the Pakistani press, gave many interviews to the press, delivered speeches to wide-ranging audiences, and organized and participated in campaigns for democracy and in civilian initiatives for peace and understanding between India and Pakistan. Perhaps the most poignant example of his endeavors to cross the boundaries between traditions and cultures, to show that modernity need not mean abandoning one's culture and tradition, can be found in his unfulfilled dream of founding an independent liberal arts college, Khaldunia University, named after the great Islamic philosopher Ibn Khaldun. In Ahmad's vision, Khaldunia would have brought together the best of Western and non-Western traditions of learning and knowledge so that young Pakistanis could imagine and work toward a democratic and just society—a vision that Pakistan's rulers could not bear to see realized.

# PARTITION AND INDEPENDENCE

# 36 / PARTITIONED LANDS, DIVIDED SENTIMENTS

Great anticipation preceded the fiftieth anniversary of India's independence and its division into two countries, India and Pakistan. But the anniversary passed quietly. Official celebrations were muted, and citizens in both countries expressed more doubt and discontent than patriotic fervor.

In this awareness of common failure lies perhaps the promise of a peaceable South Asian future. India divided on the eve of decolonization. What Pandit Jawaharlal Nehru called its "tryst with destiny" was marred by widespread violence and the largest known migration in human history, involving at least fifteen million people in just about ninety catastrophic days. Partition did not resolve the problems it aimed to solve. Rather, the problems—of ensuring the rights and representation of minority groups and of containing expressions of religious and cultural chauvinism—have been vastly augmented by a host of new impediments to the common weal. India and Pakistan have fought three wars and carried on an exorbitant arms race which now includes nuclear bombs and missiles. Full-scale war may break out again as the two countries' armed forces come to blows almost weekly across the Line of Control in Kashmir and their secret services engage in a savage exchange of sabotage and support for violent sectarian groups. Their open hostility barely masks the identical failure of India, Pakistan, and Bangladesh to provide for the basic needs of citizens for food, employment, transport, housing, and education. A rigid postcolonial order perpetuates a system of virtual apartheid to cushion the contented few from the sorrows of the overwhelming majority of the subcontinent's deprived people.

The ironic silence about Bangladesh at the fiftieth anniversary of partition is indicative of our anxieties about the future. Bengali support of the Muslim League played a crucial part in the partition of India, but within two decades Bengalis became alienated from Pakistan and, after violent convulsions and an Indo-Pakistan war, seceded in 1972 from the country they had helped create. India supported East Pakistan's secession. But it, too, has been beset by separatist demands in the northeast, in Punjab, and in Kashmir, where nationalist insurgency and India's efforts to suppress it have cost upward of sixty thousand lives. As did the Kashmiris under Sheikh Abdullah's leadership, the Sikhs had supported the Indian National Congress against the Muslim League and opposed the creation of Pakistan. Three decades later, Sikh nationalists sought Pakistani support in their struggle against the federal government of India. The case of Bangladesh, and also of Punjab Sikhs and Kashmiri Muslims, suggests that nationalist identity is fluid by nature. It is shaped less by history and "ancient hatreds" than by contemporary forces and events.

The post-Partition uprisings in East Pakistan, Punjab, and Kashmir suggest that both Indian and Pakistani ruling establishments ignored the lessons of partition, chief among which was the forest-fire speed with which ethnic and religious conflicts spread. Until almost the end of the 1930s, Muslims tended to support the Indian National Congress or provincial parties other than the Muslim League. Mohammed Ali Jinnah, Pakistan's founding father, was himself a prominent Congress leader once and widely regarded as an "ambassador of Hindu-Muslim unity." In the first Indian elections of 1937, the League garnered a mere 4 percent of Muslim votes. Yet three years later, it formulated the demand for Pakistan and in 1947 achieved it. An inquiry into how so dramatic a turnaround occurred suggests that the majority leaders' failure to comprehend the anxieties and insecurities of a minority people can speedily lead to its alienation. In the age of nationalism and mass politics, alienation is likely to translate into the demand for "self-determination" and separate statehood. There is a premium in heterogeneous environments not merely on goodwill but also on statesmanship.

The partition of India was a product of the key modern forces of colonialism, nationalism, the growth of a modern state structure, and the promise of representative government. Right-wing Hindu ideologues often portray Muslims as violent conquerors fundamentally alien to India. V. S. Naipaul is to my knowledge the first well-known writer to ply this view. In a lead article in *India Today*'s anniversary issue (August 18, 1997), he argues that India "was ravaged and intellectually destroyed" by Muslim invasions from about 1000 AD, and it was not until the "British period, and in the 50 years after the British period, [that] there has been a kind of recruitment or recovery, a very slow revival of energy and intellect."

Muslim hatemongers hold a similarly Manichaean view of India's history. But there is little in the centuries-long history of Hindu-Muslim relations to anticipate the demand and creation of separate statehood. An overwhelming majority of the subcontinent's Muslims were indigenous people who shared the languages, cultures, and historical memories of their Hindu or Sikh neighbors. They were converted to Islam not by the sword but by social movements including the Sufis, who were widely revered in the countryside by members of both communities.

Conquests, ancient or modern, are not pretty things. Tyrants—Rajput, Turk, Mughal, and English—did torment Indians at various times. Also, tension and conflict between Hindus and Muslims did occur, as they did within communities and across caste boundaries. Similarly, communal violence occasionally broke out especially at proximate sites of ritual observation. Yet organized communal violence was rare until the beginning of the twentieth century when it began to make its appearance in urban areas. Great Britain, the colonial power, pursued a policy of "divide and rule" and remained committed to it until it had lost the will to rule and decided to "divide and quit" in a haste that was irresponsible and costly in human lives, property, and sheer mayhem.

But divide-and-rule policies were not the only divisive factors associated with colonialism. There was also the contrast in Hindu and Muslim responses to the colonial encounter which placed them on differing scales of modernity. For a variety of reasons, Muslims shunned Western culture and education for nearly a century and did not begin to acquire modern knowledge until the latter half of the nineteenth century. After the suppression of the 1857 revolt, India formally became a crown colony. The event heralded, among other developments, the organization and expansion of a modern state and the steady growth of a native "salariat" to serve it. The state, not a growing capitalist economy, was the parent of India's middle class, its nurturer and provider. The culture of this middle class, its outlook and aspirations, jealousies and competitive spirit were shaped by the requirements and promises of serving the state. Muslims, who had earlier shunned modern education as Western and colonial, now eagerly sought it. Thus the first Western-influenced, reformist

Hindu movement, the Brahmo Samaj led by Raja Ram Mohan Roy, preceded its first Muslim counterpart, Sir Syed Ahmed Khan's modernist movement, by nearly a century.

The effects of this contrast in the nature of Hindu and Muslim responses to the West were dialectical; therefore, far reaching. In the colonial administration, Muslims were latecomers and underrepresented. It followed that they also lagged in founding and joining modern political parties and in articulating nationalist demands. Among the Muslim upper and middle classes of the 1920s and 1930s, there was a sense of anxiety at having fallen behind, an anxiety which accentuated as the promise of independence and democratic rule appeared increasingly realizable. Their first instinct was to seek guarantees of minority representation in government and politics. When these were not conceded sufficiently by the dominant party—the Indian National Congress—some Muslims would turn to alternatives, to class and confessional formations.

Maulana Abul Kalam Azad, two-term president of the Congress, was the most popular Muslim leader until Mr. Jinnah wrested Muslim support from him. The maulana would later ascribe this turnabout to the Congress leaders' failure to show generosity toward the defeated Muslim League in 1937 by inviting their participation in the many provincial governments which the Congress led. The failure of the Congress leadership lay also in not recognizing the class clout of the Unionist landlords in Punjab, the mobilizing power of A. K. Fazlul Haq's peasant populism in Bengal, or the Muslim League's ability under Jinnah's leadership to make tactical alliances and compound its power and influence.

In the period between the world wars, as the colonial state expanded and opened the doors of its superior civilian and military services to Indians, the competition for jobs became broader, more intense, and more political. The British policy of establishing quotas on the basis of religion and castes underlined the importance of jobs in the state sector and also legitimized the expectation of communal claims on the resources of the state. As the prospect of self-rule increased, so did the competition for representation in and control over the state.

Beginning with the Morley-Minto Reform Act of 1909, India made gradual advances toward representative government. By 1935, it had become obvious that within a decade or two India would be self-governing at least as a British dominion if not as an independent state. The Muslim minority viewed the prospect of self-rule and democracy with a mix of hope and anxiety. Broad-based Muslim support for the Congress in the 1937 election was an expression of the hope. Their rapid turn toward the Muslim League in 1939–1940 marked the arousal of anxiety. The gap between hope and anxiety was widened by rival nationalism, elements of which had become integral to the Muslim League as well as the Congress, although the latter was, in principle, a noncommunal party.

From its beginnings, Indian nationalism had three divergent streams: secular, Hindu, and Muslim. Such early nationalists as Aurobindo Ghosh and later Bal Gangadhar Tilak not only employed Hindu religious symbols but also portrayed the Muslim, along with the British, as the Other. Mother India, they claimed, had been the victim of both. Muslim nationalism, on the other hand, drew on the pan-Islamic rhetoric and symbols which were in vogue during the late nineteenth and early twentieth centuries throughout the Middle East and North Africa.

Secular and communal nationalism often resided in the same individual. Tilak was both a Congress leader and a Hindu nationalist. Mohammed Iqbal, the poet, wrote nationalist as well as pan-Islamic poems. In Pakistan, he is honored as a founding father, while in India's Republic Day celebrations, its armed forces "beat the retreat" to the tune of an Iqbal poem. The communal strains of nationalism coexisted for a time inside the Congress, converging under the umbrella of secular nationalism.

Mahatma Gandhi presented a most remarkable instance of such convergence when he joined Maulana Mohammed Ali to lead the Khilafat movement, an anti-British agitation in support of the Ottoman Caliphate which had hardly any defenders left even in Turkey. This political gesture was in complete harmony with Gandhi's style of deploying cultural and religious symbols and themes as a means to mobilizing the masses in the struggle against colonialism. Ironically, it was Jinnah who warned against such a spiritualization of Indian politics. He was right. For the amalgamation of religious and secular motifs and ideas reinforced a sectarian outlook among Muslims and Hindus alike. As India approached independence, leaders with a sectarian outlook and sentiments such as Sardar Vallabbhai Patel and Rajendra Prasad had gained commanding positions in the Congress. Mohammed Ali Jinnah was already leading the Muslim League, which formulated in 1940 the demand for a separate Muslim state.

Was the partition of India inevitable? It is too early for a definitive answer. I believe, nevertheless, that India could have remained united but the price would have been the centralized colonial state. Since the end of World War I, Jinnah had been proposing decentralization of power as a way to defuse minority fears and make independent India more governable. As nationalists everywhere have been prone to do throughout the nineteenth and twentieth centuries, India's leaders, too, equated national unity and good governance with centralized power arrangements.

The last opportunity to save India's unity was presented by the Cabinet Mission Plan of 1946 which envisaged a loose federation with a relatively weak central government. Both the Congress and the Muslim League accepted the plan. Then the Congress had second thoughts, expressed by Jawaharlal Nehru. Jinnah, known by then as the Quaid-i-Azam, decided to protest against this rejection with a "Direct Action Day" which passed peacefully elsewhere in India but in Calcutta ignited large-scale communal violence. Mass-level violence occurred next in the predominantly Muslim district of Noakhali, then a communal carnage happened in Bihar, a predominantly Hindu province. In all three instances, Congress and Muslim League leaders cooperated to end the violence. Mahatma Gandhi campaigned at length to restore communal peace in Noakhali and Bihar. But the fire spread with astonishing speed. Large-scale violence rendered the partition of India a certainty.

Barely half a year later, on June 3, 1947, the partition plan was announced. Congress and Muslim League leaders ignored the dire warnings of Calcutta, Noakhali, and Bihar when they acquiesced in Lord Louis Mountbatten's callous and mindless haste to become Britain's last viceroy in India. The fire spread then with astonishing speed, devouring all in its way, including Mahatma Gandhi.

Given the apparent hostility between India and Pakistan, people the world over view us as implacable enemies. Before the rhetoric of the "Middle East peace process" had emanated from Washington and New York, I often heard the Israel-Arab conflict compared with Indo-Pakistani relations. This I believe is a misconception.

Like the South Asian subcontinent, our sentiments remain divided. Like the traditionally undivided Indian family which separates when brothers and cousins quarrel and build walls along the family courtyard, Indians and Pakistanis make awkward, complementary enemies. While opposing nationalisms, which is for us a recent ideology, pit us against each other, history and nature are against the rivalry between us. So we feel and act in contrary ways as people do when they harbor mixed emotions and divided feelings. In this dialectic of feelings, there is an element of hope: the most creative among South Asians have not surrendered to the instincts that divide the subcontinent into hostile entities. I am inclined to tell stories.

Sadat Hasan Manto was the first among Urdu writers to portray the ambivalence and ironies of partition. One of his many partition stories, "Toba Tek Singh," is set in Lahore's mental asylum, which serves as a metaphor for India's partition. Britain's partition arrangements had included the division of all government assets between India and Pakistan. So the asylum's inmates were to be divided between the two countries. The news produced much excitement and confusion among the insane. The main character in the story, Bishan Singh, is a quiet old man who is fond of standing on one leg, speaks an incomprehensible gibberish, and remembers only that he came from Toba Tek Singh, a village in the divided Punjab, actually on the Pakistan side. Inmates speculate variously, but no one seems to know the location of his village on the subcontinent's new map, not until the day the inmates are to be transferred to their assigned countries. As his name indicated a non-Muslim, Bishan Singh was slotted to India. At the border, he asks one more time: "Where is Toba Tek Singh? In India or in Pakistan?" Upon not getting a satisfactory answer from the official, Bishan Singh took a stand on the strip of land that divides India and Pakistan: "This is Toba Tek Singh," he declared and refused to move.

Here is how Manto concludes this story:

> There he stood in no man's land on his swollen legs like a colossus. Since he was a harmless old man no further attempt was made to push him into India. He was allowed to stand where he wanted while the exchange continued. The night wore on.
>
> Just before sunrise, Bishan Singh, the man who had stood on his legs for fifteen years, screamed, and as officials from the two sides rushed towards him, he fell to the ground.
>
> There, behind barbed wire, on one side, lay India. And behind more barbed wire, on the other side, lay Pakistan. In between, on a bit of earth which had no name, lay Toba Tek Singh.

Manto, who is arguably the subcontinent's finest fiction writer, is by no means unique in expressing a sense of incoherence and deep loss over the divisions and conflicts between Pakistan and India. Faiz Ahmed Faiz is regarded with Rabindranath Tagore and Mohammed Iqbal as the greatest among South

Asia's twentieth-century poets. Unlike Tagore and Iqbal, Faiz, who died in 1986, is also a postcolonial poet. Millions of people hear and sing his verses throughout Pakistan, India, and Bangladesh as his imageries are drawn from our common history, aesthetic traditions, epics, religious symbols, and literary allusions. Above all, Faiz writes and protests the postcolonial condition—of continued poverty and neglect of the poor, inequalities and injustices, hunger and oppression—which afflict all of South Asia. But there was a special pain in his voice when war broke out between India and Pakistan in 1965, and again in 1971. During the 1965 war, Faiz wrote "Black Out" from Lahore, the Pakistani side of the front line. The translation is Naomi Lazard's:

> Since our lights were extinguished
> I have been searching for a way to see;
> both my eyes are gone,
> God knows where.
>
> You who know, tell me who I am
> who is a friend, and who an enemy.
> A murderous river has been unleashed
> into my veins; hatred beats in it.
>
> Be patient; a flash of lightning will come
> from another horizon like the white hand
> of Moses with my eyes, my lost diamonds.
> Only wait a while, the river will find its shores;
> my new heart purified in the acid-bath of poison
> will sail into a harbor.
>
> On that day, my dear one,
> I will take up my work again, the songs of beauty
> my epistles of love.[1]

Creative artists are repositories no less than creators of collective memory and emotions. I have cited a storyteller and a poet from Pakistan to suggest something of the deep and complex feelings which define our outlook on India, and Indian attitudes toward us. As Franz Fanon argued, decolonization like colonization is a violent process. South Asian leaders—Gandhi and Jinnah, Nehru and Liaquat Ali Khan—strained to avert it and nearly succeeded. Yet at the very end, in the hour of independence, violence did break out—massively and in an inverted manner, ruining friendships, as Faiz Ahmed Faiz wrote, and "centuries" of loyalties. These remain, nevertheless, embedded in our collective memory. Our sentiments divide when the realities of the past and present collide. Hence the need for other "texts of love" and new "translations of hope."

[1997]

ON JINNAH

# 37 / JINNAH, IN A CLASS OF HIS OWN

Mohammad Ali Jinnah is an enigma of modern history. His aristocratic English lifestyle, Victorian manners, and secular outlook rendered him a most unlikely leader of India's Muslims. Yet he led them to separate statehood, creating history and, in Saad R. Khairi's apt phrase, "altering geography."

Several scholars, among them H. M. Seervai, Ayesha Jalal, and Saad R. Khairi, help explain his shift from Indian nationalism to Muslim separatism, but the mystery of Jinnah's appeal remains. After all, neither Muslim nationalism nor the idea of Pakistan originated with him; he embraced them somewhat reluctantly.

There is another way of viewing the matter. In the twentieth century, two extraordinary personalities competed for the leadership of Indian Muslims. They were Abul Kalam Azad and Mohammed Ali Jinnah. As a point of departure in comprehending the aspirations of Muslims in India, we might review their biographical profiles.

The contrasts in their family background, education, culture, and styles of leadership were remarkable. Azad's ancestors belonged since Emperor Babar's time to the Persian- and Urdu-speaking Muslim aristocracy of India. His great-grandfather was one of the last Ruknul Mudarrasin, a position roughly analogous to today's "minister of education," in Mughal India. After the War of 1857 his family migrated to Medina where it intermingled with the Sharifian aristocracy. Azad's mother was a daughter of Sheikh Mohammed Zaher Watri, in his time Medina's best-known "*Alim*" [theologian]. His father, Maulana Khair al-Din, gained much fame in the Muslim world for his ten-volume work on Islam and for his central role in the restoration of Nahr Zubeida, Mecca's main source of water. Among Indian Muslims who were still wistful over a lost empire and reeling from the excesses of British colonization, it is hard to envision a family with better credentials than Abul Kalam Azad's.

Abul Kalam was a most worthy scion of an extraordinary family with roots deep in the duality—Indian and pan-Islamic—to which South Asia's Muslims have been historically linked both psychologically and culturally. Born in Mecca, he was fluent in Arabic, at ease in Persian, and a most gifted writer of Urdu prose. He was deeply immersed in the mystical tradition of Islam. As early as 1919 he wrote on Sarmad Shaheed and the grand dichotomy between state and civil society in Islam. His later commentaries on the Holy Quran are still regarded as among the best in the world.

"Who is your master among the mufassareen?" I asked the late Maulana Kausar Niazi some years ago. "Abul Kalam," he replied reflexively. *Al-Hilal*, the magazine Azad founded in 1912, at age twenty-two, marked the beginning of serious, mass-circulation Urdu journalism. With its successor *al-Balgah*, it remains a milestone in the development of Urdu as a popular vehicle of political and social discourse. Azad was a spellbinding speaker and, like Jinnah, an ardent nationalist. In 1923, at age thirty-five, he was the youngest man to be elected president of the Indian National Congress, a record Nehru would break later. An overwhelming majority of India's ulema supported him.

The man we shall later revere as the Quaid-i-Azam was a contemporary of Azad and a most unlikely contender for Muslim leadership. He was born in 1876; Azad in 1890. But beyond the proximity of age, the two stood in sharp contrast to each other. While Azad's aristocratic roots lay in the Muslim heartland of the United Provinces and Bengal, Jinnah was born to a middle-class business family in the port town of Hindu-dominated Karachi. At age twenty-one he moved to England, thence to Bombay, the modern gateway to British India. Unlike Azad, who belonged to the majority Sunni denomination of Islam, Jinnah came from the minority Shia community. He was the prototypical Westernized Indian, tutored at Lincoln's Inn, tailored at Saville Row, in his youth a Shakepearian actor, a constitutionalist barrister in the Anglo-Saxon tradition, married to a Parsi woman. More at home in English than his native Gujarati, Jinnah spoke little Urdu, which he would later designate as Pakistan's official language, knew neither Persian nor Arabic, and had only the rudimentary knowledge of Islam which is common to Western-educated Muslims. He was anathema to an overwhelming majority of the ulema of the subcontinent, including so grand a figure as Maulana Husain Ahmed Madani and such ideologues as Abul Ala Maudoodi.

Mr. Jinnah made little effort to overcome his obvious handicaps. Unlike Barrister M. K. Gandhi, with whom Jinnah shared similarities of language, class, and education and who donned the mahatma's homespun dhoti, Jinnah stuck to his Western ways and pinstripe suits. He bowed but rarely to populist symbols, appearing only occasionally at political rallies and shunning the display of emotion in public. Reasoned arguments and cold logic were the hallmark of Jinnah's discourse. He spoke at political rallies as though he were addressing a courtroom or a conference of lawyers. This is not the populist style anywhere, least of all in South Asia. Yet, in less than a decade of his return from London in 1935, he had eclipsed his political foes no less than colleagues in the Muslim League and successfully established himself and the League as the sole spokesman of India's Muslims. In the elections of 1937, the Muslim League barely survived as a minor political party; in 1940, it set Pakistan as its goal. Barely seven years later, the new state was born.

In the introduction to this first volume of Jinnah's papers, Professor Zaidi has asked this central question: "What then turned Jinnah into the embodiment of Muslim hopes and aspirations?" One answer, admirably documented by Saad Khairi and H. M. Seervai, is that the leadership of the Indian National Congress allowed Jinnah no alternative even though he constantly probed for one. But a deeper explanation offered in Professor Zaidi's introduction is worth quoting: "What distinguished Jinnah from his great contemporaries is that he was quite self-consciously a modern man—one who valued, above all, reason, discipline, organization, and economy. Jinnah differed from other Muslim Leaders in so far as he was uncompromisingly committed to substance rather than symbol, reason rather than emotion, modernity rather than tradition."

But how could this apparently modern figure so powerfully appeal to a people laden with tradition and religious inertia? I should summarize Professor Zaidi's answer to this question: Jinnah's peculiar appeal worked because collectively Indian Muslims had an instinctive if inarticulate grasp of recent history. It was a community conscious of its declining condition, and it had experienced the ineffectiveness of old remedies. After all, neither the revivalist prescriptions of Shah Waliullah, nor the fiery war cries of Syed Ahmed Shahid, nor the flamboyant, though confused, démarche of the Khilafat movement—

with which Abdul Kalam Azad had become associated and from which Jinnah kept a pronounced distance—provided relief from the ills which afflicted Muslim society in India. Restorationist alternatives had nearly exhausted when Jinnah reentered the second act of contemporary Muslim tragedy in India. On their part, leaders of the Indian National Congress were so overcome with hubris that they refused to open viable political doors to this wounded and bewildered people.

Significantly, by then the modernist view of the causes of Muslim decline and of the remedies it required, especially as articulated by Sir Syed Ahmed Khan and his ideological successors, including Iqbal, had seeped into the consciousness of the Muslim intelligentsia. There was to this phenomenon also a pan-Islamic context: in the 1930s, the Muslim world as a whole had entered what Albert Hourani has described as the Liberal Age, when Muslim nationalism grew exponentially on the premises of modernism and reform. Mr. Jinnah returned from England in 1935 to find himself swept to the crest of this wave.

In the four decades that have followed his passing, Pakistan has moved precipitously away from the country its founding father had envisioned and the people had created at costs beyond counting. The two volumes of Jinnah papers and the archives from which they are drawn do not tell the story of the cowardice and betrayals which followed the Quaid-i-Azam. What they do tell us is who he was, how he waged a difficult and deeply painful struggle for statehood, the vision he nourished, and the hopes he had for this country. I would like to recall him and remind us in passing of what we have done with his legacy. I am sorry if in the process I cause some discomfort to some of you readers.

[1995]

Before I recall Mr. Jinnah and the aspirations which inspired the subcontinent's Muslims to seek separate statehood, it is relevant to underline the price nations pay when the values and expectations on which a state is founded are systematically betrayed. Since Plato's time political theorists have acknowledged the centrality of legitimacy in the consolidation and continuity of states. Legitimacy refers not to the popularity of a government or given institutions thereof; rather, it entails the title to authority which a system of power enjoys among citizens. A subjective attribute, legitimacy, issues forth largely from objective factors—the values which shape state or government policies, predominance of the rule of law and prevalence of distributive justice in society, and, above all, the degree of coincidence between promise and fulfillment in terms of the rights of citizenship. It is for the lack of these attributes that Pakistan has been suffering from a growing crisis of legitimacy. The separation of East Pakistan was but the most dramatic outcome of this crisis. At the heart of this crisis has been our collective failure to resolve the central issue of the nature of the Pakistani state and the sources of laws which govern it.

During the decade which preceded India's partition, politics of the Congress no less than the Muslim League had become greatly laden with the language of religion and communal symbols. Mr. Jinnah, too, partook of it, most prominently when he enunciated the two-nation theory. Yet two facts stood out: one was that the ulema in their overwhelming majority opposed him, and he made scant effort to placate them. The other was that he remained uncompromisingly opposed to theocracy. Thus in the year of communal frenzy and high point of religious fervor—1946: "What are we fighting for? What are we aiming at? It is not theocracy, not for a theocratic state. Religion is dear to us. All the worldly goods are nothing when we talk of religion. But there are other things which are very vital—our social life and our economic life, and without political power how can you defend your faith and your economic life." Need I explain the relevance of this passage in these tormented times of blasphemy laws, *Hudood* and *Qisas* ordinances, and *Shariat* bills?[1]

Jinnah did invoke Islamic ideals often as informing the policies and practices of the state and its governments. Always, this was to emphasize the congruence of democracy, social justice, and rule of law to Islamic values. Thus to the Sidi Darbar in 1948: "Let us lay the foundations of our democracy on the basis of truly Islamic ideals and principles. Our Almighty has taught us that our decisions in the affairs of the state shall be guided by discussion and consultations." And again, "Islam and its ideals have taught us democracy. It has taught equality of man, justice and fair play to every body. . . . In any case Pakistan is not going to be a theocratic state, to be ruled by priests with a divine mission. We have many non-Muslims—Hindus, Christians, and Parsis—but they are all Pakistanis. They will enjoy the same rights and privileges as any other citizens and will play their rightful part in the affairs of Pakistan."

This, a sort of pledge given to all citizens, has been honored in the breach. In less than three decades we had four minorities, each a little less Pakistani than the so-called Muslim majority. During this year alone Christian citizens had to take asylum abroad because even after a court had acquitted them of blasphemy charges, their safety was not assured; an Ahmadi was beaten to death inside a government building,[2] and scores languish in prisons without trial. If he were to appear in my dream, how shall I convey our shame to the lean old man whose life and work we celebrate today?

Or hear him on the question of women: "It is a crime against humanity that our women are confined within the four walls of their homes like prisoners. Women are our companions and you should take them out with you to work shoulder to shoulder in all spheres of life." I have not asked, but Professor Zaidi may have been in the audience that day in 1944 when the Quaid spoke thus to students at Aligarh University. Four decades later, a dictator promulgated in this country the Zina and Hudood ordinances. Among their contributions to national progress is that one law provides a license of sorts to actual and potential rapists, and the other reduces the worth of a woman's witness to half of a man's. So far three elected governments have failed to remove this stain on our society and the state.

Mohammed Ali Jinnah had been anxious from the outset over the persistence of sectarian and exclusionary tendencies in our social and political life. In speech after speech, he warned of their menace to society and beseeched: "For God's sake give up this provincialism. Provincialism has been one of the great curses, and so is sectarianism, Shia, Sunni, etc. . . . You should live, act and think in terms that your country is Pakistan and you are Pakistanis." As I read this, I wondered if he might have foreseen that the country he founded shall break up from an excess of sectarian practices by those in power, his successors shall engage in creating minorities, upholders of law shall break the law in daylight and after dark, citizen shall kill citizen in streets, offices, and mosques, and terrorist factions shall be allies of the state!

Civilizations are built on the rule of law as are states and nations. There is ample evidence that the Quaid-i-Azam did not lose sight of this civic principle even in the darkest hours of 1947. He made no distinction of class, ethnicity, and religion when it came to the enforcement of law in defense of people and society. There is a rare note of admiration in Lord Louis Mountbatten's confidential memo of June 24, 1947, to Evan Jenkins: "I talked to Jinnah last night and he begged me to be utterly ruthless in suppressing trouble in Lahore and Amritsar. He said 'I don't care whether you shoot Moslems or not, it has got to be stopped.'" The death count mounts these days in the civil war born of sectarianism, terror, and crime. Tragically, politicians and governments are so enmeshed as part of the problem that they cannot be even a small part of the solution.

Who then is responsible? And where do we go from here? Frankly, we have no one to blame but ourselves—me and you who are in this hall—members all of the national intelligentsia. I am tempted one last time to quote Jinnah: "Corruption is a curse in India, and amongst the Muslims especially in the so-called educated and intelligentsia. Unfortunately, it is this class that is selfish, and morally and intellectually corrupt."

This straightforward estimation encapsulates our ultimate failure. It has been a failure of conscience not intelligence, of will not comprehension, of courage not imagination. We could read a long length of time the writing on Bengali walls. But we read in selfish silence with an indifference seeped in self-absorption. Acquiescence prevailed as the Pakistani establishment dealt blow after blow at our body politic, made a mockery of citizenship rights, turned murder and mayhem into a mission, and finally surrendered to a conquering adversary. A simple insight is alien to us: that power is prone to excesses, corruption, and miscalculations; that it is moderated only by a dissenting and assertive civil society; and that critical mass is constituted, at all except the revolutionary moment, by the intelligentsia. Inertia is ever immune to experience. So horrors follow upon horrors. And so we survey every day the killing fields of Karachi as we did those of Dacca and Noakhali. This must end. And it will not until our complicity comes to an end, and our silence is broken.

Postscript: Learned people have argued that the roots of the confusion which underlie Pakistan's crisis of ideology and statehood lie in its formative experience. Thus commenting on my last article in this space, Dr. Akbar Naqvi (*Dawn*, June 15, 1995, "Letters to the Editor") argues that it is "not true that the Muslim masses instinctively chose progress and democracy against theocracy, because the 1946 election, which was a referendum for Pakistan, was won on the cry of Islam in danger." He writes further on that: "The dilemma of two horns, one represented by the liberal and the other by Ulema was Mr. Jinnah's contribution to Pakistan. He needed it as an ambiguity which served well to make Pakistan a popular cause." Most historians would regard his argument about the 1946 election as much too moot. After all, the election served to confirm rather than to create broad-based Muslim support for the League. Also, to the best of my knowledge, the Quaid himself never used the "Islam in danger" slogan. Dr. Naqvi's more analytical argument over "Mr. Jinnah's contribution" is, nevertheless, worthy of reflection and debate, which I hope shall be joined by others.

[1995]

PAKISTAN'S MILITARY

## 39 / LETTER TO A PAKISTANI DIPLOMAT

After the publication of a letter in the *New York Times* (April 10, 1971) signed by me jointly with three other West Pakistani scholars and after subsequent statements of mine opposing the Pakistani military government's intervention in East Bengal, several Pakistani officials protested my position. They all pointed out that: (1) the army, under General Yahya Khan, is only protecting national integrity against a secessionist movement which would cause the 70 million people in East Pakistan to break away from the 56 million in West Pakistan; (2) the army intervened only after the Bengali nationalists had started killing West Pakistani residents in East Pakistan and the minority Bihari refugees from India; (3) since the leaders of the Awami League of East Pakistan have pro-Western sympathies and connections, and the Chinese "support" the federal government, anti-imperialist and radical elements should not oppose the military's action. The following is a reply to one such "friend."

Dear _____,

I hope you understand that it was not easy for me and my brother Saghir Ahmad to publish the statement you saw in the *New York Times* (April 10, 1971). First, I did not have any natural sympathy for the Bangladesh movement. In fact, I had a definite feeling of antipathy for Sheikh Mujib [East Pakistan's leader, whose party, the Awami League, won a governing majority in the National Assembly and 98 percent of Bengali votes]. He impressed me as being a limited man, impetuous and unimaginative. But then I have less regard for his West Pakistani counterparts—the miserable Mr. Bhutto who changes his politics like a lizard his color or the generals who, bred by colonial Britain and armed by the USA, appear bent on turning the country into a Muslim version of Greece and Spain.

Second, as you know, I am originally from Bihar, and most of my people had migrated to East Pakistan. Several of them were killed by Bengali zealots during the period immediately preceding the military's intervention. Furthermore, I grew up during the Movement for Pakistan, and it is hard not to cherish the idea of national unity. Last, as a radical and an internationalist, I do not believe that separatist movements constitute a forward step in the right direction. For these reasons, my inclinations should be to support a policy of maintaining the integrity of Pakistan.

However, as I see the facts surrounding recent developments, I am able to find neither a political and economic nor a moral justification for the current policy of military intervention. I have been examining the facts as closely as it is possible to do, given the censorship of news by the military regime and the resulting imbalances in news reports, some of which necessarily emanate from India.

My considered opinion is that:

1. The East Pakistanis had genuine grievances against the federal government, dominated by the military since at least 1957. Not even the most hawkish West Pakistanis deny the gross economic inequities and exploitation suffered by the Bengalis. Politically, twelve years of direct military rule deprived them of even a minor share in the exercise of power.

2. The nearly unanimous electoral support for the Awami League's demand for provincial autonomy was the result of the neglect of East Pakistan, climaxing in the example of the incredible negligence in the relief of cyclone victims last November. I recognize that the poor in West Pakistan have suffered also. The callousness of our rulers may be undiscriminating. Yet the more disadvantaged people of East Pakistan could only comprehend their condition as caused by regional discrimination.

3. Having failed to arrive at an extraparliamentary settlement, the military, supported by West Pakistani leaders, intervened on March 25, 1971, to offset the results of Pakistan's first freely held elections. Perhaps the army had little hope of obtaining the capitulation of Pakistan's elected representatives. It is now clear that the army used the negotiations between General Yahya and Sheikh Mujib as a cover to prepare for its intervention.

4. There is absolutely no popular base of support for the federal government. Even after four months of terror it has been unable to produce a group of political quislings capable of lending some legitimacy to the army's occupation.

5. While the military has the power to lord over East Pakistan, the cost of this colonization will be very high for the peoples of both East and West. For the latter it must include increasing economic hardships, militarization of our politics and society, and total denial of civil liberties. The closing of journals like *Asad* and *Lail-o-Nahar*, the recent jailing without trial in West Pakistan of eight hundred persons, including leaders like Afzal Bangash, Mukhtar Rana, and G. M. Syed, intellectuals like Abdullah Malik and Sheikh Ayaz, academicians like G. M. Shah, and the recent public floggings of dissenters against the government in Lyalpur and Sialkot are indicative of the shift toward totalitarianism.

Similarly, I worry over the statements and editorials which provoke public paranoia by suggesting an Indian–Jewish American conspiracy in this conflict. This, regardless of the fact that with arms and money the American government is underwriting the murderous mission of the military dictatorship. Above all, I am distressed by the promotion of religious fundamentalism and the systematic killing and harassment by the army of our Hindu citizens. I shudder when I think of the repercussions this policy may have for the eighty million Moslems in India.

6. Unless there is an immediate end to military rule in East Pakistan, famine and pestilence as well as periodic massacres by the army will cost millions of lives in the coming months. The intervention has already caused an estimated 250,000 deaths of unarmed civilians. Six million refugees have reached India. Between 60,000 and 100,000 are arriving daily and are facing infection from cholera and the hostility of poor Indians. Millions languish in the interior of East Pakistan, hungry and terrorized, potential statistics in what threatens to become the greatest holocaust in history.

As you know, the balance of survival is delicate in East Pakistan. Minor disruptions often cause major tragedies. Nineteen seventy and 1971 have been particularly hard years. The floods last August and September were the worst of the last decade and destroyed about half a million tons of rice. The cyclone in November, the most severe of the century, destroyed an equal amount of rice and rendered one thousand square miles of rice lands uncultivable for at least one year.

Then the army, in an effort to deny supplies to the Bengali opposition, started confiscating and burning the food reserves. Many displaced or frightened peasants in the villages have not harvested the winter crop. The combined losses, amounting to about 2.5 million tons of rice, must be replaced immediately if mass starvation is to be prevented. The recent survey by the World Bank, as well as the disclosures by Senator [Edward] Kennedy of suppressed State Department reports, indicate that Western and US officials in East Pakistan have been warning Washington of the "specter of famine."

Others have been more concrete in their predictions. Three months ago, Ian MacDonald, relief coordinator for Oxfam and other agencies, warned that 1.5 million persons may face starvation. Recently, the *Financial Times* of London estimated that possibly four million would die unless relief and reconstruction were speedily begun. Alan Hart, a BBC reporter, believes it "probable that twenty or more million East Pakistanis will be starving by September or October."

The dispatch of more supplies for relief is by itself unlikely to avert the impending tragedy. Only a quick restoration of civilian rule can prevent the use of food grains and medicine as military weapons; and only such a restoration can ensure both the distribution of relief and an effective role for international agencies in the administration of such relief.

7. Lastly, I should stress that no genuine restoration of civilian government will be possible until the East Pakistanis have been conceded their right to autonomy or even secession.

For these reasons, I believe that the only workable course for West Pakistanis is to insist on immediate and unconditional termination of martial law, the convening of the duly elected National Assembly, and a commitment that the majority decisions of that assembly shall be binding on all, even if these decisions dismember Pakistan as a state consisting of East and West. We must reject the army's absurd claim that it has intervened to protect the nation's "integrity" from the party that had just won, in Pakistan's only freely held elections, a governing majority in the National Assembly.

In fact, the elected representatives of East Pakistan had insisted only on fulfilling their mandate to achieve autonomy for their province. The proclamation by the East Pakistanis of the independent state of Bangladesh took place only after the army refused to convene the National Assembly and after it had brutally intervened in East Pakistan on March 25, 1971. In his speech of June 28, General Yahya denied the right of the National Constituent Assembly to draw up a constitution, and he harshly attacked all the leaders of the Awami League. This destroyed the possibility of any settlement based on the mandate of the elections.

I know that I shall be condemned for my position. For someone who is facing a serious trial in America, it is not easy to confront one's own government. Yet it is not possible for me to oppose American crimes in Southeast Asia or Indian occupation of Kashmir while accepting the crimes that my government is committing against the people of East Pakistan. Although I mourn the death of Biharis by Bengali vigilantes and condemn the irresponsibilities of the Awami League, I am not willing to equate their actions with that of the government and the criminal acts of an organized, professional army.

According to reliable reports, which were not challenged by the government, no more than ten thousand persons were killed or wounded by Bengali nationalists in the riots against the Biharis. At the beginning of August, however, West Pakistan military authorities issued a White Paper which claimed that one hundred thousand people were killed by the Bengali opposition. These and other exaggerated claims in the white paper were obviously intended to justify trials and possible death sentences for opposition leaders. As this letter is being written, the military government has announced that Sheikh Mujib will face a secret military tribunal on August 12, on charges of "waging war" against Pakistan. Since the white paper announced that seventy-nine members of the unconvened National Assembly will face criminal charges, Mujib's trial may foreshadow more secret prosecutions.

I know that the army did not intervene in East Pakistan to stop the killing of non-Bengalis, which went on for three weeks while the generals pretended to seek extraparliamentary deals with the politicians. Saving civilian lives was not the motive behind the vast repressions that have already cost countless Pakistanis their lives and property and forced millions to flee to India. Unequal bartering of brutalities is not a function of responsible government. The very fact that this military regime seeks justification for its behavior by referring to the excesses of the Awami League and the aroused masses is a measure of the steep decline in the civic standards of our army and civil services. Above all, criminality is not a commercial proposition: one cannot deposit the crimes of one into the account of another.

The Chinese rhetoric on this issue is irrelevant. They have offered Pakistan their support only against foreign interference and indicated their belief that this conflict is an internal matter. Much more alarming is the American government's decision to continue armaments sales and economic aid to the dictatorship, despite the unanimous opposition of its Western allies, of important men in the Congress, and of the World Bank. This is particularly striking in view of the longstanding loyalty to the West and to the US of Sheikh Mujib and his party.

Washington's assistance to the West Pakistan junta should be a lesson to those Pakistanis who believed that the US, given a choice between militarists and moderate democrats, would choose the latter. The leaders of the Awami League in East Pakistan failed to understand how important West Pakistan was to the Nixon-Kissinger strategy of building an informal anti-Soviet alliance of dependable clients around the Mediterranean and Indian oceans—from Spain and Portugal, through Greece and Israel, to Iran and Pakistan.

It has been said that General Yahya is now being rewarded by US support for having arranged Mr. Kissinger's recent mission to China. If this is so, then the Chinese-American détente will have started by being detrimental to the weak and poor in Asia. Whatever the reasons for US policy, however, one effect is clear: Americans have become silent accomplices in crimes against humanity in yet another part of Asia. But their obligations are not as urgent as yours and mine.

I should also stress that the recent developments strengthen the possibility of a war between India and Pakistan. The two countries are more and more becoming pawns in world politics. India and the USSR have now signed a twenty-year friendship pact in which Russia promises to give military assistance to India in the event of war with Pakistan. This treaty cancels the gains that Pakistan had made at the Tashkent conference in 1966, when the Russians promised both to give aid to Pakistan and to be neutral in India-Pakistan relations.

I do not know if my position would at all contribute to a humane settlement. Given the fact that our government is neither accountable to the public nor sensitive to the opinion of mankind, our protest may have no effect until this regime has exhausted all its assets and taken the country down the road to moral, political, and economic bankruptcy. However, lack of success does not justify the crime of silence in the face of criminal, arbitrary power.

[1971]

# 40 / PAKISTAN
Signposts to a Police State

Recent developments in Pakistan evoke growing concern. Although one could have anticipated the general trends two years ago when Bhutto came to power, the rate of deterioration has been unexpectedly rapid. The contradictions in which Mr. Bhutto and the PPP are enmeshed have been swiftly sharpened, and the country is moving toward a major, possibly decisive, crisis.

We are witnessing the emergence of two clearly identifiable, seemingly hostile, but symbiotically linked trends toward fascism and separatism.[1] Of these, fascism is the more serious threat although separatism is generally being viewed as the imminent danger. This is because the fear of separatism has been stimulated by the example of Bangladesh, by government allegations against opposition groups, the credibility accorded these allegations by the statements and conduct of some opposition leaders (e.g., Ajmal Khattak's choice of Kabul as a place for exile),[2] and by the start of an insurgency in Baluchistan.

The two trends complement each other no less than they are antagonistic. The separatists draw sustenance from the excesses of the emerging fascist elements and from the increasingly protofascist practices and attitudes of the present government. The fascist elements will expand and their values will become institutionalized through their growing participation in the repression of alleged "separatist" "subversive" "threats" to national security. Thus separatism would derive its increasing popularity from the growth of fascism, and fascism its justification from the existence of separatists. These complementary enemies, incapable of destroying each other, shall nevertheless damage the society and the peoples they pretend to serve. Symbiotically linked, they may sustain each other while devouring the healthier, progressive elements in Pakistani society.

Six main factors point toward the development of a fascistic governmental apparatus in Pakistan. They are:

(a) The contradictions of the PPP regime which impel it not just to revise its electoral promises and commitments (which is normal to parliamentary parties) but to renege on them. The result can only be a steady decline in popular support for the party and its government and the consequent defection of leftist, even social democratic elements from it.

(b) The class and ideological composition of the command ranks in the officers corps of the army and possibly even the air force.

(c) The attempt to terrorize, manipulate, and deprofessionalize the bureaucracy in order to make it an instrument of personal power. Its consequent demoralization and the end of its role as a relatively autonomous and, in relationship to the army, countervailing group within the ruling class. This, one must add, is more true of the civic and servicing sectors of the bureaucracy than of the "security" branches, which are being expanded, strengthened, and "modernized."

(d) Concentration of the opposition parties in non-Punjabi areas.[3]

(e) The commitment of the US, backed heavily by the shah of Iran, to promoting developmental fascism in Pakistan on the model of Iran, Brazil, Chile, Greece, and Indonesia.

(f) The personality traits and ambitions of Z. A. Bhutto who alone sets the style and makes the decisions in the PPP and the government.

*The Nemesis of the Peoples Party*

The contradictions of the PPP government are known. Their cumulative effects are also obvious. The increasingly perceptible gap between the ruling party's electoral promises and actual commitments can only grow into a chasm.[4] It is not that the masses were promised too much but that the government lacks the will and capacity to do the little that is required to satisfy even their modest expectations. It should, however, be noted that thanks partly to the PPP's preelection propagandizing, the disillusionment is less likely to produce apathy; more a moral explosion of the masses. And the distance between Bhutto and the betrayed, protesting masses will have to be bridged by the forces of law and order.

Yet the public's betrayal is unlikely to produce a clear-cut shift in favor of a modern capitalist economic policy in which the state assigns itself only the regulating responsibilities. The government's "socialist" avocation and its hunger for power preclude such an option. It is settling for the discredited, colonial bourgeoisie's brand of "mixed" economy which has spelled economic disaster and political doom in the Third World from Ghana to Indonesia.

Specifically, this will have the following consequences: the capitalist class will give this regime only qualified support, and invest but conservatively and selectively. The "nationalized" sector will not compensate for the slowdown since nationalization in its present form involves merely the substitution of profit-motivated, hence efficiency-prone entrepreneurs by a corrupt and indolent bureaucracy.[5] In effect, the managerial rank of the nationalized enterprises is likely to be even more corrupt and wasteful than the civil services because it will tend to become the Peoples Party's preserve for political patronage. Hence there will be at least a lag in "growth" if the economy escapes complete stagnation. This can only intensify the isolation of the regime and the pressures on it. It will tend to become increasingly dependent on a petit-bourgeois base and the security and defense institutions manned by it. Fascism has historically had its base in this social class.

*Profile of a Potential Junta*

Two institutions—the army and the bureaucracy—have been the primary instruments of power in Pakistan. They have ruled the country as partners although the terms of partnership have shifted in time. Until 1958, the bureaucracy enjoyed the role of senior partner; after Ayub Khan's coup d'état, the relationship was formally reversed although the bureaucrats continued to dominate decision making and administration. There undoubtedly existed a measure of distrust (civilians vs. soldiers syndrome) and tension between them. But these were easily mediated because there was between the two a certain balance of power and because at the top level both were manned by the same social class (haute bourgeoisie by preference when not by origin, landed, colonial loyalists, and anglicized), sharing identical interests and outlook. Both were proud of their "professionalism." Both derived their ethos from their colonial creators and belonged in the vice-regal tradition of British India. Both had pretensions to being liberal, utilitarian, and modern. Both liked associating with foreigners no less than with the rich capitalists. Both were pro-Western, pro-Islam, pro-order, prodevelopment, pro-guided democracy, and proprietors. Both were antipoliticians, antimullah, and anticommunist.

These bourgeois soldiers and bureaucrats of British vintage governed Pakistan from 1948 to 1971. Their primary concern was maintaining order, which meant the preservation of the status quo. It was a requirement also for a climate of investment and the enrichment of their kin and class. They regarded politicians contemptuously as fomenters of trouble and were disposed to locking them up—some lapses notwithstanding—in prisons appropriate to a man's economic status, as good colonial tradition demanded. They regarded the people callously, as the object of administration and a reservoir of labor. At best, some viewed the masses paternalistically and assumed their welfare as the natural consequence of the enrichment of the rich. Although excessively greedy and callous, they were nevertheless moderate men in the sense that politically they were neither revivalists nor zealots. Belonging to an entrenched upper class, proxies of Curzon and Kitchener, these retarded Tories had much stake in the old order, hence an inclination to eschew fascist solutions.

This class of officers has evidently lost power in the army and is being succeeded by another group, of petit bourgeois origin and fascistic outlook. As a result, the contradiction between the controlling elites in the army and the bureaucracy has heightened from tertiary to secondary level. At the same time, the balance of power is shifting—in the army's favor, not because the army is getting stronger but because the bureaucracy is loosing its morale and esprit de corp.

Available information on this matter is incomplete.[6] Hence the following should be seen as a statement of broad trends, and not as precise, statistically verified conclusions. It appears certain that over the years the social composition and ideological outlook of the officers corps has been changing. The Sandhurst and early IMA graduates are being replaced in command positions largely by those who received emergency or temporary commission during World War II. The attrition of the old guard has been due partly to the usual process of retirements and promotions. But the principal cause of the decline of the old army elite and ethos has been the politically motivated demotions and purges which began as early as 1954–1955 and accelerated in the aftermath of the 1965 and 1971 wars. The ascendant group today appears to have the following attributes:

(i) A majority of those who hold command assignments and occupy strategic positions in the GHQ—colonels, brigadiers, and some generals—are from the Punjab. When combined with the ranking officers of Indian Muslim origin, with whom they share many attributes, they constitute a formidable majority.

(ii) They come predominantly from petit bourgeoisie, that is from middle peasant, small landholder, or urban middle-class families. A sizable number are from the nonirrigated *barani* districts of Rawalpindi division where the petite bourgeoisie has derived little benefit from the "green revolution" and industrial expansion. The sons of those sturdy middle owners have reason to feel righteous and resentful since they believe they have contributed more services to the nation and received fewer rewards than the bureaucrats, senior generals, and businessmen. They harbor a particular dislike for the higher civilian bureaucracy, are contemptuous toward it, and blame it for the ills of the country in much the same way as their predecessors blamed politicians and parliamentary institutions.

(iii) Many had some college education and most were in school in the late 1930s and early 1940s, i.e., during the heyday of agitational politics in the subcontinent. Hence they may be presumed to have experienced a measure of politicization before joining the army.

(iv) Having been trained and socialized in the old tradition they share most of the authoritarian values and elitist attitudes of the old guard. However, being less acquainted with the liberal, British tradition they are more prone to viewing the world in straight lines, in terms of order vs. disorder, discipline vs. permissiveness, strength vs. weakness. The regiment would be their model for running the country, discipline their watchword, and regimentation and force the instruments of inculcating discipline.

(v) They tend to be more religious, at least in sentiment if not always in practices, than their more anglicized seniors. They view the ills of society in moral terms as having their roots not in the economic and social structure but in the indiscipline, corruption, and sinfulness of man. Given their class origin and earlier socialization, fundamentalism appeals to them. During the conflict in East Bengal they often betrayed an extreme degree of xenophobia and belief in religious nationalism. It seems likely that the Jamaat-i-Islami has strong sympathizers among this most strategic of power groups in Pakistan. If it does not yet, it soon will. For, if this analysis is correct, the Jamaat should be broadening its appeal and "modernizing" its program in order to provide the appropriate appeal and supply the ideology of a neototalitarian state.

(vi) A significant portion, if not the majority, of these ranking officers had some American training. Through training courses in America and contact with the MAAG (Military Assistance and Advisory Group, established in October 1954) and MAP (Military Assistance Program) operatives, they have come to respect American technology, crave contemporary weapons system, and favor alliances which promise hardware. More to the point is the fact that two decades of Pakistan-US military ties have created links between the Pakistani military commanders and the US institutions and individuals who, in recent years, encouraged the Brazilian, Greek, and Chilean coups. The profile of the Pakistan army today approximates that of the Brazilian and late Greek juntas. But that is not a sufficient cause for alarm. The officers' corps of many armies in the world resemble the above description. Those are important but not sufficient conditions for a fascist or protofascist takeover. The decisive factor is the political environment, the compulsions it creates, the opportunities it offers, the constituencies it promises, and the resistance it can produce. At this level, the situation in Pakistan is alarming, for the political environment appears to favor the growth of a right-wing, militarist dictatorship.

The perspectives and mood of the army officers are part of that environment. It is impossible to inquire systematically into their political preferences and attitudes. Nevertheless, informal conversations have revealed a pattern quite different from the one that had prevailed eighteen years ago. They still speak sincerely of "professionalism" as the highest virtue in a soldier, of the army as a "nonpolitical" institution, of their wish that the civilian authorities would govern the country, keep the armed forces in the barracks and on the frontiers, and provide it [the army] well. But underneath these sentiments and shibboleths, one senses resentment, extraordinary anxiety, and repressed anger. For an army proud of its traditions and convinced of its quality, the last twenty-five have been agonizing years. It entered an aborted war in 1948, fought an inconclusive one in 1965, and suffered a humiliating defeat in 1971. It consumed the largest share of the national budget but was unable to defend the country.[7]

This is bad enough. But insult is added to injury when people suggest, as they often do, that the army was somehow responsible for these failures. As the officers view it, the civilians ruled the country even while the army was allegedly in power from 1958 to 1971. Political decisions, not military mistakes, caused the events and the failures for which the army is blamed. A profound belief that their collective fortune was shaped by political decisions for which they are held responsible but over which they exercised no control is an existential necessity for these officers. They tend to believe that the army should not have taken over in 1958 but that if such a move by the commander-in-chief was required in the national interest, the army should have run the country instead of merely providing a cover for the corrupt civilian bureaucrats and politicians. After all, "We showed how to run things during the first three or four months of martial law," (i.e., after Ayub Khan's coup d'état in 1958).

In other words, one hopes it won't be necessary, but, if it is, the next time around won't be the same; the officers will fulfill their "mission" directly, with determination and discipline. If the present regime moves with speed and skill toward establishing a national-socialist police state in Pakistan, the "necessity" may not arise. If it were to reverse its present policies toward centralization of power, personalization of politics, and subordination of opponents, then the opportunity would have been denied. But if the continuation of the present course produces disturbances and sporadic resistance, which is very likely, then both the opportunity and the "necessity" for an army intervention will be deemed present.

### A Bureaucracy in Decline

The bureaucracy has rarely been a rooter for democracy or justice. That of Pakistan, in particular, is a colonial bureaucracy—authoritarian, arrogant, and indifferent. It scarcely deserves any praise. However, it had inherited from the British and from our own feudal tradition a conservative ethos and civilian outlook. This fact was probably important, though not decisive, in softening the character of Ayub's dictatorship. But now the bureaucracy is unlikely to play a role in civilizing military rule. To the contrary, it will increasingly become an instrument of militarizing civilian life for several reasons:

First, the homogeneity between the military-bureaucratic elite which had previously helped produce an easy alliance at the top has been severely damaged. There is now a greater divergence—of class origin, educational level, and outlook—between the senior bureaucrat and the ranking army officers. Previously the contradictions between the two were tertiary. Now they are of a secondary nature, hence harder to resolve and prone to produce subordination of one by the other rather than a partnership of equals. This is reflected in the accentuated anti–civil service mood of the army officers.

Second, the balance of power between the two institutions is shifting. The bureaucracy is rapidly losing its cohesion and esprit de corps, for Mr. Bhutto is packing it with a large, "nonprofessional," "political" element, that is, with party hacks and personal favorites of doubtful abilities and dubious politics. The bureaucrats are demoralized also because Mr. Bhutto has struck at them unpredictably and without due process as though the purpose was to terrorize all rather than to punish the few.[8]

Third, the imbalances and tensions within the bureaucracy as a whole will increase drastically as it splits more clearly between its civil service and national security wings. It should be noted that the latter is now the expanding, modernizing sector within the bureaucracy; its personnel, proficiency, and powers are being rapidly increased. This marks the trend toward using the bureaucracy as a vehicle for militarizing civilian life. The expanding national security sector will undoubtedly form the bureaucratic backbone of the emerging police state. They would be supported by a third, somewhat recent group of bureaucrats with a stake in the "new order"—the officials of the "nationalized" industries.

*The Opposition*

The opposition parties as they are constituted today do not offer much obstacle to the emergence of a police state. They are electoral parties given more to hyperbole and public meetings than to organizing and resisting. A large part of the opposition is either ideologically reactionary or indistinguishable from the party in power. Hence it is prone to mixing the tactics of protestations with those of accommodation rather than to developing a strategy of preemption and resistance. It makes an easy target for a ruthless regime. Bhutto is likely to continue to alternately cajole and coerce these opponents into compromises, isolation, and sporadic revolts.

That the opposition is concentrated in the non-Punjabi provinces renders the situation risky for it, and for the country as a whole.[9] A vicious logic is at work here, which, if permitted to develop, would cause much harm to Pakistan and more suffering to the people. It is doubtful that there is now a serious separatist movement in NWFP or Baluchistan. Yet separatism may increasingly come to be regarded there as a legitimate and ultimately a necessary choice. This will inevitably happen if politicians, particularly those in power, continue to exploit ethnic and regional diversity for personal political gains; if people are denied their rightful demands, and coercion substitutes for the constitution. The events of the last two years indicate that this has already begun. For this the responsibility is largely Mr. Bhutto's.

These judgments are not influenced by political party preferences. The NAP (National Awami Party) is no improvement over the PPP in terms of leadership, organization, or program. During my last visit (June 1972), I found its governments in the Northwest Frontier Province and in Baluchistan more committed to its feudal patrons than the rights and welfare of the people; obsessed with order, indifferent to justice. Yet, in fairness, it must be said that on the question of separatism NAP leaders are often being pushed to the edge by Mr. Bhutto and his men.[10] And to date they have displayed more sensitivity and greater wisdom than has the prime minister. Evidence does not bear out the serious accusations of separatist statements and activities against them.

It is irresponsible in the extreme to make such serious charges so lightly. The fact that such accusations have been made against prominent opposition leaders can only accord credibility and legitimacy to separatism as a political alternative.

Similarly, no honest person can justify as unifying and integrative Mr. Bhutto's clever maneuverings which smoked the NAP government out in NWFP. That the NAP ministry in Baluchistan was wrongfully forced out is hardly debatable. Both developments can only have increased Pakhtoon and Baluchi distrust of the national government and their grievance against it. The current military operations in Baluchistan can be viewed as a war against separatism only by those blinded by the government's propaganda or by belief in Mr. Bhutto.[11] At worst, these operations will become a festering wound in Pakistani society. At best, i.e., if they are terminated and a political solution is reached quickly, they will leave a scar. In the short run, Mr. Bhutto will be the beneficiary. In the long term, Pakistan will suffer for his petty political gains.

One might hope that Mr. Bhutto would realize that his expedient policies, which undoubtedly produce personal triumphs for him, may cause lasting damage to the country. There is a genuine regional and linguistic diversity in Pakistan, and its constituent cultures are insurrectional. Historical, and contemporary, examples—e.g., those of the Croations, Berbers, Nagas, Kurds, and Shans—show that governmental effort at coercing such people into submission has typically failed. Its human and material costs have been extremely high. And resistance keeps renewing until a fundamental shift in policy occurs. On the other hand, a policy of respecting local autonomy and cultural aspirations within the framework of economic integration and democratic participation (through national planning and reconstruction) helps produce progress and unity.

It is equally true that secessionist movements rarely succeed in attaining their announced objective. The Bangladeshis enjoyed unusual advantages; theirs is the sole instance of success in this century full of secessionist movements. Furthermore, the geopolitical, economic, and cultural configurations in NWFP and Baluchistan are particularly unfavorable to secessionism. Yet it is extremely dangerous and may even be disastrous for the country if the government and party in power conduct a policy of centralization based on divisiveness, confrontation, and violence. Similarly, one hopes that the opposition groups do not swallow the bait being offered. They ought to realize that nothing would serve the central government's narrow interests more, and their interests less, than for them to be boxed into a separatist or regionalist position.

Such hopes notwithstanding, the realities are stark and reprehensible. These include the facts that the opposition in NWFP and Baluchistan is being stimulated toward separatism, and when they go over the edge they might take a large mass with them; that since at least the Rawalpindi clashes of March 1973 and the earlier firing upon workers in Karachi, the federal government and the ruling party have been exploiting provincial (Punjabi-Pathan and Baluchi-Pathan, etc.) tensions; that an insurgency and army operations have begun in Baluchistan; that negative links are developing between politics and economics. (While the thrust of Mr. Bhutto's politics is to forge political conformity in the dissident provinces, the economic policies of the federal and provincial governments encourage fragmentation and provincialization.) Finally, there are actual and potential foreign interests—such as Afghanistan, India, USSR, and Iran—ready to support a promising separatist sentiment in Pakistan.

So far, the government and party in power have been the prime movers in these developments although the opposition cannot be entirely absolved of responsibility. The NAP has been the primary victim, but being regionally based it has been unable, on this issue, to elicit the understanding and support of the country as a whole. Consequently, it appears isolated nationally and outmaneuvered and frustrated in the provinces. If pushed further, its leaders might jump Mr. Bhutto's bait several steps further on the road to separatism.

Given the climate of provincial tension and distrust, they will not lack popular support. If that happens the country will divide into warring camps. Class struggle will be overshadowed by civil conflict. The voices of reason and revolution will be drowned by those of reaction and revolt. Nothing will grow except the defense and security services.

*Washington Sponsors Developmental Fascism*

The trend toward fascism is likely to be encouraged by the US. For it concurs with the preferences of American foreign policy under Kissinger and Nixon. Close analysis of the recent US role in promoting and aiding protofascist regimes in Greece, Turkey, Brazil, and Chile suggests a conscious preference in Washington for what may be described as developmental fascism. Spain, Portugal, and South Africa, and now Brazil and Iran, are viewed as examples of the success and suitability for underdeveloped nations of police states wedded to economic growth and endowed with "populist" appeal.

Washington's preference is pragmatic and stems from the quest for stability. Yet it inevitably has ideological ramifications. In order to attain stability, even the most repressive contemporary political system must find a constituency. Hence it needs an ideology and a program whose appeal may cut across social groups and justify its legitimacy to the masses.

In Pakistan today, fascism has two potential sponsors: religious fundamentalism and national socialism. In accordance with the policy of keeping options open, Washington, heavily aided by the shah of Iran, is likely to encourage both of them simultaneously. First, the present regime, being obviously attracted to creating a one-party state, may succumb to the temptation. If that happens—and there is some evidence to suggest that the process has already begun—the PPP will transform itself into a protofascist apparatus, while the state will become increasingly militarized through the enlargement of the police and the military's role and power. A reverse leftward shift is not to be expected, for, nomenclatures and rationalizations notwithstanding, neither its ideology, nor leadership, nor organization compels the PPP to move in a progressive, socialist direction. To the contrary, the party has in it the seeds of a contemporary, Third World version of national socialism.

The second possibility is that of another military government, which, as suggested earlier, is likely to be fascist in character. Bhutto's drive for absolute power coupled with deterioration in the people's living condition will inevitably produce disturbances and violent challenges to the government. These may create the climate and opportunities for a coup d'état. If that happens, the officers will look, as Ayub Khan had done, outside the army for preambles and constituencies. But given their socialization and social origins, they will discover it in Muslim fundamentalism rather than the Basic Democracies. The Jamaat-i-Islami is more likely to supply their ideology and propagate their legitimacy than the Tehrik-i-Istiqlal or any other ideological equivalent of the old Muslim League.[12] If this analysis is correct and the politicos—from Washington to Ichra (the headquarters of the pro-US, right-wing Jamaat-i-Islami is located in this petit bourgeois district of Lahore)—with their noses to the ground have smelled the rats right, then I would expect that the Jamaat already has or will soon be making an effort to "modernize" its doctrine, enlarge its appeal, and sharpen the "progressive" edge of its social and economic pronouncements. As part of this dialectic, the PPP, on the other hand, should be acquiring a more conservative, orthodox coloring.

*Bhutto as a Problem*

Mr. Bhutto's personality has significance in this crisis for he embodies the present and represents the future of the PPP and of the present government. Furthermore, he is in power at a crucial time; his decisions and moves will inevitably have a lasting impact.

He is a talented and proud man with sincere nationalist commitments. In the difficult days which followed the creation of Bangladesh, his accomplishments were many. Insofar as he was the only available man of national stature capable of heading the government of a defeated, dismembered Pakistan, he helped prevent confusion and possible chaos. In dealing with India, he displayed patience, flexibility, and skill. His approach to Bangladesh is realistic and imaginative. He has been quick to sense the shifts in Middle Eastern politics, and this sensitivity has enhanced Pakistan's position there.

But these achievements stand in sharp contrast to his myopia in domestic policies. Not without reason, for Bhutto belongs to a social class and ideological tradition notorious for producing paradoxes. He is a product of transition; a composite, technicolor personality—of feudal upbringing, bourgeois education; in politics fathered by a dictator; a self-proclaimed socialist. A man in the "heroic" mold of Sukarno and Nkrumah, of Ataturk and Abdel Nasser, he may bring more grief to Pakistan than they did to Indonesia and Ghana, Turkey and Egypt. For, while he cannot claim their historic roles as liberators, their contributions as iconoclasts, their humble origins, or their sacrifices and sufferings, he possesses the other traits—untamed hubris, ideological flabbiness, fixation with power, blindness to political processes—which accounted for their self-defeating policies. Nixon is a more apt comparison. Like Nixon, Bhutto has a pathological will to power; the instincts of a salesman; an uncanny sense of opportunity. Like Nixon, he likes to win, a gambler without stakes.

Bhutto is not a social democrat; nor is he a Tory. He is not a fascist, either. He is merely dedicated to himself and regards power as the best expression of self. He will use his considerable stamina to keep in the saddle while having fewer scruples over changing horses; will employ his remarkable cunning to manipulate, mislead, and misappropriate his friends no less than his enemies. He may thus succeed in keeping the opposition off balance, alternately compromised and confronted, while his allies remain uncertain, fearful, and hoping, and he himself acquires loyal cronies. In the process, he will emaciate or destroy the few existing countervailing forces within the bourgeois polity and administration; lose whatever links he has to political constituencies; and violate the remaining legal and judicial norms which have so far offered a modicum of protection against unlimited and unchecked political terror. Inevitably, the army and the national security bureaucracy will come to constitute his primary base of power; and he will become increasingly dependent on a yet unassertive, seemingly malleable praetorian elite.

Meanwhile repressive measures are increasing. They include the closing of newspapers and magazines, the mass summary dismissal of bureaucrats, the creation of a new Federal Security Force, the astronomical jump in the expenditure on special police establishment, the promulgation of an Anti-National Activities ordinance, the requirement that citizens must register and carry identity cards (with photographs), the dismissal of the opposition government in Baluchistan and consequent military operations there, the obvious indifference being shown to "unofficial" violence and terrorism against opponents of the government, and the emerging practice of systematic torture of prisoners. The most shameful is the recent National Assembly vote to declare the Ahmadiyya community a minority in Pakistan—an act of retrogradation without a parallel in Pakistan.[13]

The actual repression under the present government may not be worse than what Pakistanis have been accustomed to. Insofar as there may exist somewhat more freedom of speech and association than under Ayub Khan, some might even perceive the situation as better. But these developments constitute a qualitative shift toward regimentation and institutionalization of terror. These mark the transition from a bourgeois-democratic or feudal-authoritarian to a fascist polity. Unfortunately, the democratic and revolutionary groups in Pakistan to whom falls the responsibility of halting this trend are as yet only weakly developed.

*Appendix*

## Table 1

| Province Party | Punjab | Sind | Northwest Frontier | Baluchistan | Pakistan total |
|---|---|---|---|---|---|
| PML (Council) | 12.6 | 6.8 | 4.0 | 10.9 | 11.29 |
| PML (Convention) | 5.1 | 2.7 | 0.5 | Nil | 4.42 |
| PML (Qaiyum) | 5.4 | 10.7 | 22.6 | 10.9 | 7.19 |
| NAP (Wali) | Nil | 0.3 | 18.1 | 45.1 | 3.04 |
| Jamaat-i-Islami | 4.7 | 10.3 | 7.2 | 1.1 | 5.8 |
| Jamiat-e-Ulema-i-Pakistan | 9.8 | 7.4 | 0.0 | NIL | 2.18 |
| PPP | 41.6 | 44.9 | 14.2 | 2.3 | 40.00 |

Source: Adapted from Mushtaq Ahmad, *Politics Without Social Change* (Karachi: Space Publishers, 1971); and *General Elections 1970* (Karachi: Pakistan Economist Research Unit, 1973).

## Table 2

| Province Party | Punjab (60) | Sind (60) | NWFP (40) | Baluchistan (20) |
|---|---|---|---|---|
| PPP | 113 | 32 | 3 | |
| PML (Qaiyum) | 6 | 5 | 10 | 3 |
| PML (Council) | 15 | 4 | 1 | |
| PML (Convention) | 6 | | 2 | |
| JUT (Hazarvi) | 2 | 4 | 2 | |
| Jamiat-e-Ulema-i-Pakistan | | 4 | 2 | |
| NAP (Wali) | | 13 | 8 | |
| Jamaat-i-Islami | 1 | 1 | 1 | |

Source: Mushtaq Ahmad, *Politics Without Social Change* (Karachi: Space Publishers, 1971).

Table 3

| Year | Percentage of total revenue spent on defense | Percentage of GNP |
|---|---|---|
| 1949–1950 | 63.7 | 3.0 |
| 1957–1958 | 48.0 | 2.9 |
| 1964–1965 | 29.9 | 2.6 |
| 1965–1966 | 60.3 | >5.4 |
| 1966–1967 | 37.6 | 3.8 |
| 1967–1968 | 37.6 | 3.6 |
| 1968–1969 | 35.1 | 3.6 |
| 1969–1970 | 34.9 | 3.7 |
| 1970–1971 | 40.9 | 4.1 |
| 1971–1972 | 53.8 | 7.6 |
| 1972–1973 (revised) | 52.7 | 7.8 |
| 1973–1974 | 44.9 | |
| Average | 45.17 | 4.37 |

Source: Finance Division, Government of Pakistan, *The Budget in Brief, 1973–74* (Islamabad: Finance Division, Government of Pakistan, n.d.).

# 41 / GENERAL ZIA IS NOW THE LAW

At a recent press conference, Pakistani foreign minister Agha Shahi, on an official visit to Washington, appeared pleased, as did General Alexander Haig, with their "far-reaching, unusually cordial, and productive discussions." Despite General Mohammad Zia ul-Haq's virtual abolition of the rule of law in Pakistan and his obvious, if unrealistic, drive to produce nuclear bombs, the United States has offered him a five-year, multibillion-dollar armaments package. Unlike Jimmy Carter's $400 million "peanuts," Reagan's is an offer General Zia cannot refuse. Overriding legislative requirements on human rights and nuclear proliferation, Congress has approved an initial $100 million toward this package.

We ought to be clear, though, about the consequences: US military aid to Pakistan's praetorian regime is likely to augment political repression beyond endurance, heighten transnational tensions in the region, worsen India's relations with the United States, accelerate the arms race (including the nuclear arms race) in the region, exacerbate ethnic conflicts within Pakistan enough to jeopardize its territorial integrity, and create the conditions for an armed US-Soviet confrontation in Southwest Asia.

The last three months of improved Reagan-Zia relations have witnessed a serious deterioration of human rights conditions in Pakistan. To those, like UN ambassador Jeanne Kirkpatrick, who assume non-Western, "authoritarian" cultures to be alien to the traditions of rule of law, it may come as a surprise that Pakistan had long enjoyed an independent, thoughtful, and, at times, feisty judiciary. Over decades of military rule and erratic civilian governments, the higher courts of the country remained the ultimate legitimator of government authority and the final arbiter of conflicts between individual rights and state power. Confrontations between the judiciary and executive occurred, and compromises were made. But successive governments, including the military regime of Field Marshall Ayub Khan, always conceded the independence of the judiciary; when enjoined, they bowed to the orders of the court. No head of government had so far dismissed a High Court judge on political grounds and without the recommendation of Pakistan's chief justice.

Now, General Zia has virtually destroyed the only peaceful recourse citizens had against his untrammeled abuses of power. On March 25, he fired at least nineteen senior judges when they refused to endorse his "constitutional order," which restricts the civil courts, outlaws all political parties except the small, neototalitarian Jamaat-i-Islami, deems the advocacy of any secular ideology or program to be a crime, and empowers Zia to amend the 1973 constitution at will, thus allowing him to dictate the country's future.

Among the senior judges who declined to take the required oath of allegiance to this new "constitutional order" was Anwar ul-Haq, the chief justice of Pakistan, an appointee of General Zia, whose earlier compliances with the junta had done much to lower citizen respect for the judiciary. Three of the six sitting judges of the Supreme Court and a State High Court chief justice also refused. Another Supreme Court judge, Safdar Shah, had earlier fled the country on foot through the Hindu Kush Mountains. Twelve High Court judges, well-known for their judicial integrity, were not invited to take the oath and automatically lost their posts. Among them were Justice Khuda Bux Marri, chief justice of the troubled Baluchistan Province, and Justice K. M. A. Samdani who, as Pakistan's law secretary, had earlier opposed Zia's attempts to pack the judiciary and reduce its jurisdiction.

"A judiciary's job is to interpret the law and administer justice, not to challenge the administration," General Zia proclaimed at a March 27 press conference. As for lawyers, rule of law and civil liberties were none of their business. "They must mind their own business and not meddle in other affairs," said the general. The besieged legal community responded through a statement by the Bar Association: "A country can put up with laws that are harsh or unjust just so long as they are administered by just judges who can mitigate their harshness or alleviate their unfairness, but a country cannot long tolerate a legal system which does not give a fair trial. Nations fall when judges are unjust because there is nothing people consider worth defending."

For their defense of the rule of law, lawyers have been hit harder than the judges. A recent crackdown on the democratic opposition to the junta added another two thousand political prisoners, of whom a significant portion are lawyers. Since March, some two hundred senior High Court advocates have been jailed in Pakistan; the number of young attorneys in detention may be higher. They include Mahmud Ali Kasuri, a former law minister in the federal government and president of the defunct Pakistan Civil Liberties Union; Raza Kazim, a well-known international lawyer; the current as well as two former presidents of the Pakistan Bar Association; two former judges of the High Court, and two prominent women advocates. Two sons of a former law minister were thrown in prison because they agreed with their father.

The junta's assault on the legal profession has been general and indiscriminate. All of the lawyers save one were jailed without trial. The lengths of their sentences were not announced. Recourse to the courts of appeal is not allowed. The only exception was Yahya Bakhtiar, whose case exemplifies justice under Zia's regime—and yields a mordant little joke. The former advocate general of Pakistan was charged, convicted, and sentenced to five years at hard labor for allegedly tampering with the electoral votes of his district in the parliamentary elections of March 1977. In other words, the junta has severely punished him now for irregularities allegedly committed four years ago in connection with elections of a parliament which the junta illegally overthrew and abolished in July 1977. In fact, Bakhtiar was severely punished because he took his professional responsibility seriously: as an attorney, he had conducted a vigorous defense in the twice-rigged trial of Prime Minister Zulfikar Ali Bhutto.

Rarely in modern times have so many judges and lawyers shown such courage or suffered this much collective punishment in defense of the rule of law. The indifference of the Reagan administration was predictable; indeed, its support encouraged the junta's unconstitutional conduct. But the silence of the American media over these blatant violations by a government which is negotiating a formal alliance with the United States is astonishing. If Pakistan were Poland, its judges and lawyers would be folk heroes in America today. Even if the questions of human rights and democratic values were to be set aside, as the Reagan administration is prone to do, a realistic appraisal of the situation in Pakistan suggests that if the United States enters into a security pact, it will incur a major political and strategic liability. Pakistan's military dictatorship is isolated from its 175 million people; Zia's unprecedented assault on the judiciary, the only institution that commanded a modicum of legitimacy and public trust, is a measure of this isolation. Lacking even a semblance of legitimacy at home, Zia seeks support abroad. But foreign support, especially military aid, can only worsen the already serious crises of political legitimacy and national integration in that ethnically diverse and historically insurrectional land.

Central to the crisis of legitimacy is the unresolved tension between authoritarianism and popular demand for democracy. What is unique about Pakistan is not the military's interventions in politics but the constancy of public resistance to absolutism. The cycle of resistance and repression has progressively widened the gap between popular aspirations and elite power. It was in recognition of this reality that on July 5, 1977, General Zia told the nation that his "sole aim" in staging the coup d'état was "to organize free and fair elections," which would be held that October. He gave a "solemn assurance that I will not deviate from that schedule." The pledge was formalized when Zia swore allegiance to the constitution and again when Pakistan's Supreme Court invoked the Doctrine of Necessity in order to recognize the legality of the caretaker military government administration. The court stipulated the condition that the military government abide by the 1973 constitution and within a reasonable period restore representative government.

But Zia's nearly four years in power have been marked by betrayals and broken oaths. Initially he chipped away at the constitution and the nation's laws and traditions. Unlike previous military governments, Zia deprived the judiciary of its power to review the decisions of the military courts, which now exercise wide civilian jurisdiction. Similarly, in. a development hitherto unknown in Pakistan, the army's field investigation units became responsible for internal security; their powers, too, are unchecked by legal provisions. Four of the five known deaths under torture have occurred in military custody. Zia's Islamization plan, designed to win over the conservative clergy, revived a medieval penal code and outdated social practices. The civilian bureaucracy began to be militarized. Finally, in March, he abrogated the constitution and wrecked the judiciary. Terror and violence have increasingly become the only link between the people and the government. Even a child can guess on whom the promised American weapons will be used.

Decades of unequal development have compounded the problem of national integration. It is aggravated by contiguous Baluchi and Pakhtun populations in Iran and Afghanistan and by the fact that Bhutto, the executed prime minister, came from Sind, the most oppressed and potentially explosive of Pakistan's four states. Unless the minority provinces—Sind, Baluchistan, the Northwest Frontier—begin to get a fair share of power and wealth, separatist movements will gain ground, and a large-scale war may follow. Given the strategic location of these provinces—the long coastline overlooking the Persian Gulf and the mountain ranges along the border between Afghanistan and Iran—the possibilities of regional and international involvement in the ensuing struggle are enormous.

The military regime is ill suited to defusing the Pakistani powder keg, much less promoting national integration. Rather, military spending has long been a primary cause of undemocratic and unequal development in Pakistan. The military consumes 50 percent of Pakistan's budget; it is the largest employer in a country of 40 percent male unemployment. Status and privileges accrue to members of the army, yet Baluchis and Sindis have negligible representation in it; 80 percent are Punjabis largely from a few rural districts. For the non-Punjabis, 42 percent of Pakistan's population, the army symbolizes inequality and ethnic discrimination. General Zia's preference for a strong, centralized government stirs deep anxiety in the minority provinces, which regard a federal, parliamentary system as the best hope for redressing their grievances. Furthermore, the partiality of General Zia to the Jamaat-i-Islami's fundamentalist ideology worries not only the Christians but also the Shiite Moslems, who constitute 25 percent of the population.

The resumption of US military assistance will surely exacerbate Pakistan's internal crisis. It may also provide the external pressures that will cause Pakistan's disintegration. In return for military aid, Zia promises Washington greater cooperation in assisting the Afghan rebels. If he does, Afghanistan may retaliate by supporting Pakistan's increasingly militant dissidents in the Baluchistan and Pakhtun regions. The seeds of armed hostilities in the area are being sowed, and the harvest may be a great-power confrontation.

[1981]

# AFGHANISTAN

# 42 / BLOODY GAMES

Eqbal Ahmad and Richard J. Barnet

The invasion of Afghanistan—an impoverished, mountainous land of 15 million herders, traders, and peasants which is squashed up against Iran, Russia, China, and Pakistan—is the largest, longest, and costliest Soviet military operation since the Second World War. The Soviet pacification campaign in Afghanistan has caused civilian casualties in the hundreds of thousands and left more than a third of the Afghan people refugees. And the United States, in support of the Afghan resistance, has been waging its most elaborate and expensive covert war since the Central Intelligence Agency's operations in Laos and Cambodia in the early 1970s. This is the first time that the United States has supported a guerrilla army firing on Soviet troops.

In the fiscal year 1987 alone, according to the *Washington Post*, clandestine American military aid to the Mujahideen, the holy warriors of the Afghan resistance, amounted to $680 million—more than the total of American aid to the Contras in Nicaragua. Unlike aid to the Contras, however, the covert aid to the Afghan resistance has not been a matter of congressional debate. Indeed, Congress has on several occasions appropriated more money than the administration requested.

This is not the first time two world powers have clashed in combat over Afghanistan. From 1837 to 1907, the British and the Russians fought along the northwest frontier of British India—now part of Pakistan. British officers called these mountain struggles the Great Game, and the phrase was popularized by Rudyard Kipling in *Kim*. Today, Afghanistan is still the playing field for great powers, but there are more players now, and the games are bloodier.

"Afghanistan is the calf in this *buzkashi* between Moscow and Washington," remarked Professor Sayd Bahaouddin Majrooh, a former dean at Kabul University and director of the Afghan Information Center in Peshawar, just inside Pakistan. "Go see the game. We have brought it here to Pakistan. You will understand much about Afghanistan and about this war." With a group of Afghan friends, we joined a crowd of two thousand spectators scattered in the dusty outskirts of Peshawar below the Khyber Hills. To visualize the game, imagine American football, on horseback, with no protective gear, few rules, no limit on the number of players, and for the ball a headless calf weighing fifty to a hundred pounds. The objective is to get hold of the calf and carry it to a goal, which is usually a mile distant. It is a game that depends not on teamwork but on the skill of individual riders and their horses.

There were about a hundred horses—an unusually small number—being walked or exercised, but only a dozen or so looked well bred and well trained. As these horses and their riders passed the crowd, they drew soft exclamations of "Maasha Allaah!" These were the chapandazan—master players. The rest were camp followers or novices, who would provide the necessary obstacles for the real players. As the horsemen were lining up at the starting point—the chapandazan at the front and the rest behind them—four turbaned men carried the carcass of a calf to the center of the field, placed it there, and withdrew. A rapid volley of rifle fire signaled the start. With a powerful cry of "Allah-u-Akbar" ("God is great"), the horsemen galloped off, a fast-moving mass of color. Within seconds, some of them had moved to the sides, while others reached the center quickly, and struggled to gain access to the dead animal; the mass of lurching, rearing horses and jostling, yelling, hissing riders was hidden by clouds of dust. The melee broke suddenly, allowing us a view of the action. In the contest among the master players, we could see that each one had the support of clusters of horsemen—multiple teams organized around individual players. When a rider approaches the calf, he lowers his head and shoulders toward the ground, and then, the reins in one hand, the whip between his teeth, he reaches out with his free hand to grab the calf. (Hence the name of the game—*buzkashi*, or "goat grabbing"; sometime in the nineteenth century, calves replaced goats.) He gets pushed, shoved, hit; his horse may collapse under the weight of other advancing or rearing horses; and hooves can mangle his hands. Only the nimblest of riders on the best-trained horses, working in perfect coordination, can capture the calf. In badly played contests, the calf gets torn to pieces, and judges have a hard time deciding the winner. In the game we saw, one player—galloping with the carcass cradled in one arm, his whip still between his teeth, and blood trickling down his face—finally eluded his rivals and rode out of sight, to the finish line. Minutes later, he returned, and as the crowd cheered he deposited the calf in another circle, close to the first one. Then all returned to the starting point and resumed the game.

That evening, we discussed the analogy that had led us to the match. The game reflects a culture that places enormous value on physical courage and individual enterprise, allows untrammeled competition, and assumes that order will emerge from anarchy. "But there is more to it," one of our Afghan friends said. "It is not possible to play this game without sponsors. It involves great expense, prizes, payments to the chapandazan, horses—above all, good horses, which very few people have. It is a game that only the rich can afford to sponsor: no sponsor, no game. It is a game of dependency. That is how this war is. We are being torn to pieces by teams sponsored by outsiders."

Another man added, "The Communists and the fundamentalists are contesting Afghanistan as if it were a dead object. There are two sides, they say. That's wrong. There are twelve, maybe twenty, fifty political chapandazan on all sides. Each for himself. Our suffering is great." On February 11 of this year, Professor Majrooh was himself killed in Peshawar. He was associated with the moderate wing of the resistance and had advocated a negotiated end to the conflict.

The story of the Afghan people has been written largely by their adversaries, who have often become grudging admirers. In 1924, the Earl of Ronaldshay, then president of Britain's Royal Geographical Society, wrote of the borderland between Pakistan and Afghanistan, "The life of a frontier officer is hard, and he treads it daily on the brink of eternity. Yet despite its obvious drawbacks the fact remains that these endless ranges . . . do possess the power of inspiring in those whose lot is cast among them an extraordinary enthusiasm."

Afghanistan owes its unique culture to its towering peaks and a cruel absence of water. The Hindu Kush, the western end of the Karakoram range, stretches across Afghanistan for six hundred miles, cutting off the country's north from its south. The Pamir Knot, part of the Himalayan system of more than a hundred peaks rising from twenty to twenty-five thousand feet, dominates the northern region, along China and Soviet Central Asia. To the south are vast deserts—most notably Dasht-i Margo, "the wilderness of death."

Afghanistan's climate veers between extremes. In summer, there is sweltering heat, and dust storms sweep across the deserts; winters are bitter cold, and the winds are fierce. So little grows in the rocky soil that only the hardiest animals survive. In 1937, Rene Dollot, the former French envoy to the court of Kabul, wrote, "The lunar landscapes of the Hindu Kush, as if borrowed from prehistory, seem still to be waiting for the birth of the animal world, or perhaps to announce its end." But Afghanistan is also a land of surprises. The "assault on the spirit . . . of stark ugliness and discomfort" is often relieved by "beauty indescribable in its clarity and contrast with the barren emptiness that went before," Sir Olaf Caroe, former British governor of the Northwest Frontier Province and the author of *The Pathans*, writes. "The weft and warp of this tapestry is woven into the souls and bodies of the men who move before it. Much is harsh, but all is drawn in strong tones that catch the breath, and at times bring tears, almost of pain."

A large majority of Afghanistan's village settlements are linked only by narrow mountain paths. In winter, these become impassable—a circumstance that assures the autonomy of villages and tribes. Since ancient times, Afghan society has been largely a collection of inward-looking settlements that have resisted integration into a national community. Each village and tribe displays strong family ties and group loyalty. The center of politics is one's immediate community. Authority rests with a khan—a tribal chief—or with a religious leader. Outside the village or the tribe, most Afghans view one another warily, as strangers. This means that the outsider may be considered deserving of help and hospitality or that he may be seen as an enemy to be feared or fought—or he may turn out to be a benefactor, to be protected and exploited.

Just as geography has forced social fragmentation, so the barren economy has generated fierce competition for resources. Throughout Afghan history, cooperation beyond the boundaries of community and tribe, when it occurred at all, took the form of a defense compact, and then only when the independence of all parties was threatened by an external enemy or an intrusive government. Rebellions in Afghanistan have typically occurred not against feudal lords or oppressive tribal chiefs but against foreign invaders and centralizing, reformist governments. When the Soviets intervened militarily and lent their support to a centralized and reformist Communist government, they encouraged the two historic causes of rebellion in Afghanistan.

In the nineteenth century, Russia watched as the British pushed into the interior of the country and suffered their greatest imperial misadventure. *The*

*Cambridge History of the British Empire* describes that invasion as "a terrible mistake." Others have been less polite. Lord Auckland, the governor general of India, who ordered the expedition, was denounced by contemporaries as a "bumbling" weakling. Lord Auckland himself admitted that the first Anglo-Afghan war was a "horror and disaster of which history has few parallels." Lord Palmerston, the British foreign minister at the time, who was accused by political rivals of being led into the expedition by his Russophobia, was haunted by the disastrous outcome for the rest of his life.

A Soviet historian, Naftula Khalfin, recounts the story of the British failure in his 1981 book *British Plots Against Afghanistan*. In October of 1838, he writes, Lord Auckland announced that Britain's candidate to rule Afghanistan, Shah Shoja, would enter the country "supported against foreign interference and factious opposition by a British army." A British expeditionary force of more than fifty thousand, grandly named the Army of the Indus, marched into Kalat, a principality that is now part of Pakistan. In order to impress the local ruler, a British official bragged that his army had entered Kabul without firing a shot. The Khan of Kalat was silent. "You make no answer. You seem lost in thought," the official said. "Yes, I am thinking. You people have entered this country, but how will you get out?"

The British official recalled that the khan made his flesh creep with a prophecy: "Wait till sickness overtakes your troops—till they are exhausted with fatigue from long and harassing marches, and from the total want of supplies; wait till they have drunk of many waters; and wait, too, till they feel the sharpness of Afghan swords." By December 1840, the British had to all appearances won the Great Game. Dost Muhammad Khan, the Afghan ruler, whom the British had vowed to remove, had surrendered and been sent off to exile in British India. The British puppet, Shah Shoja, occupied the throne, and Lord Auckland told London that Sir William Hay Macnaghten, the envoy of the Crown, might be capable of "organizing an honest and friendly government, and . . . reconciling this wild and divided country." But while victory was being proclaimed in London, the British Army in Afghanistan was being destroyed.

In November and December of 1841, there was an uprising in Kabul; the British garrison there was besieged, and many senior British officers, including Macnaghten, were killed. British troops in Kabul finally broke the siege and started the retreat to India. Karl Marx, a correspondent for the *New York Tribune* at the time, re-created the scene for his readers: "On the walls of Jalalabad . . . the sentries espied a man in a tattered English uniform on a miserable pony horse and the man was desperately wounded; it was Dr. Brydon, the sole survivor of the 15,000 who had left Kabul three weeks before. He was dying of starvation."

A painting of the wounded doctor on the wretched pony was reproduced widely, and for a time people believed that Dr. Brydon was indeed the sole survivor of the Anglo-Afghan war. But when the British returned to wreak vengeance they found two thousand of their soldiers and camp followers begging in the streets of Kabul. After four years of death, hardship, and humiliation, the British left Afghanistan as they had found it, with Dost Muhammad Khan back on the throne.

The Great Game continued as British power expanded throughout India and into Iran and the Russians penetrated farther into Central Asia. From the first Anglo-Afghan war to the outbreak of the Second World War, the British carried out more than a hundred military operations against the Pashtun tribes on both sides of what is now the Afghan-Pakistani border. In November of 1878, Anglo-Russian rivalry led to another British invasion and another disastrous defeat. In Victorian England, meanwhile, Afghanistan had come to symbolize the risks and hardships of carrying the white man's burden. Winston Churchill, who participated in an 1897 "frontier war" as a "subaltern of horse," defended the British massacres and village burnings against the Gladstone liberals, who "seemed to imagine that the tribesmen consisted of a regular army who fought, and a peaceful, law-abiding population who remained at their business." The reality, he wrote, was that "every inhabitant is a soldier from the first day he is old enough to hurl a stone, till the last day he has strength to pull a trigger." Finally, the British concluded that the Afghans did not make good clients—that, given their history of isolation and their insurrectionary culture, it was better to subsidize the tribal chiefs than to attempt to pacify them.

For centuries, the people of Afghanistan have scratched out a livelihood by travel, trade, and combat. As late as 1929, only 2 or 3 percent of the land in Afghanistan was under cultivation; since the 1960s, various development projects have increased the figure to about 15 percent. But, having only ten inches of rainfall a year and four uncooperative river systems, Afghanistan offers few opportunities for farming. Two centuries before Christ, the Great Silk Road—the network of caravan trails through the difficult terrain and hazardous weather of Afghanistan—linked the civilizations of China and India to those of Egypt, Greece, and Italy. (Around 1940, French excavators discovered in two subterranean rooms, presumably storerooms, rare Buddhist art, vases, and lacquerware from China's Han Dynasty, carved ivories of ancient India, Phoenician glassware, and a vase bearing a scene from the Iliad.) Nomads, who until 1978 were still a sixth of Afghanistan's population, had the knowledge and the skills to guide the caravans along the trails. Warrior bands protected the travelers and their merchandise—for a price—or, failing to find protégés or looking for better returns, raided them. Tribes that controlled sections of the route and the mountain passes collected levies both from private traders and from governments. Merchants in the cities provided food, water, and pack animals. Only in the small urban centers, at the junctions of trails or close to border areas—Kandahar, Herat, Ghazni, Mazar-i-Sharif, Peshawar—did the government exercise authority. Elsewhere along this most enduring trade route in human history, the warriors' code prevailed. For the nomadic warriors, the most feared enemy was a central government seeking dominion over them.

By the middle of the second millennium, this commercial network, under the control of Muslim rulers and merchants, had expanded greatly. Then the rise of Western capitalism and the opening of maritime routes to the East destroyed the ancient trading network. The Dutch, French, and British East India Companies began to control the flow of trade between East and West. The Afghans were put out of business. But they were spared colonial occupation, and they remained largely outside the international capitalist economy. Only after the Second World War did Afghanistan begin a process of economic modernization, with Soviet and American aid.

The Soviet invasion, despite the destruction it has caused, has revived the trading life of Afghanistan, for it has produced a thriving commerce in consumer goods and contraband, mostly through Pakistan. Early last year, the state bank of Pakistan estimated that goods worth eighty-two billion rupees, or four billion six hundred and seventy million dollars, were being smuggled in and out of Pakistan each year. That is an eighth of Pakistan's gross national product. Narcotics are the major commodity of this underground economy, followed by arms. The center of the commercial activity is Peshawar. There Afghan peddlers sell Russian caviar, and in the markets are to be found canned fish, cheeses, jams, and jellies from the Soviet Union and Eastern European countries. The war has brought French, Norwegians, Americans, Englishmen, and Saudis to Peshawar, and they eagerly shop for East German cameras and binoculars, Russian scarves and woolen sweaters, Swiss watches, and Japanese calculators. A Pakistani customs official explained to us that West European and Japanese imports bound for Afghanistan from Karachi were trucked to the Khyber Pass, where the goods were inspected before crossing into Afghanistan. "But these days many trucks unload soon after the border crossing, and their cargoes are smuggled back into Pakistan," he said. "We can't control the border. There is so much traffic. It is nothing here in Peshawar. Go to Bara or Landi Kotal if you want to see."

Bara, a dusty patch of land divided by a broken, narrow road, is about fifteen miles north of Peshawar. Goods are sold in hundreds of shops made of corrugated metal and protected from the summer sun by cloth hangings. The traffic resembled that of any rural market in a small frontier town—carts, donkeys, goats, a couple of scrawny cows mingled with armed men in baggy clothes and turbans—except that there were Toyotas and Suzukis parked in clusters in front of the stalls. Middle-class families come here bargain hunting from as far away as Lahore, three hundred miles to the southeast. Smuggled goods are cheap in Bara, but prices mount as one moves farther from the Afghan border. The black markets in the tribal areas along the border where the Afghan refugees are concentrated have become popular shopping centers for northern Pakistan. An astonishing variety of merchandise is on sale. There are clothes, cosmetics, and weapons, but the best sellers are the household appliances: Russian irons, air conditioners, toasters, gas stoves; East German refrigerators, television sets, stereos. Young employees carry large boxes to the cars, and the customers scramble to make room.

Pakistan has replaced Lebanon as the world's largest open market in arms. A London television group was reported to have found a Blowpipe missile in the market at Bara—a British-made missile that the CIA supplies to the Mujahideen. Most of the weapons available in Bara are less advanced. We saw British Lee-Enfield .303s of Second World War vintage, an American M-1, and many AK-47 assault rifles of Chinese manufacture. Prices for such weapons range from a thousand to fifteen hundred dollars. Local, Khyber-made Lee-Enfield rifles, which used to be the standard weapon of the frontier tribesmen, were selling at forty to fifty-five dollars—200 percent below their prewar price. There is now a nationwide system of clandestine gun rentals; resourceful customers can find bigger weapons—occasionally even an antiaircraft battery. The frontier posts of Tor Khama, Miram Shah, Parachinar, and Chaman are bustling centers of travel and trade. Teahouses have sprung up along trails.

The trade in mules and horses is brisk. Bus owners ferry the Mujahideen for a price. The Great Silk Road has in part been revived.

When Soviet troops crossed the Afghan frontier in force, in December of 1979, many observers in the United States concluded that the invasion was the first move in a grand strategic plan. It was the first time Soviet troops had entered a territory not occupied by the Red Army at the end of the Second World War. President Carter quickly accepted the judgment of his national security adviser, Zbigniew Brzezinski, that the invasion was a threat to the rest of the region. Aides have recalled that Carter, disappointed by what he called the "misleading" response of the Soviet leader, Leonid Brezhnev, to his demand for Soviet withdrawal, became "almost apoplectic." He said that the Soviet invasion was "the greatest threat to peace since the Second World War," and on January 23, 1980, he announced a policy that came to be known as the Carter Doctrine: "An attempt by any outside force to gain control of the Persian Gulf region will be regarded as an assault on the vital interests of the United States of America, and such an assault will be repelled by any means necessary, including military force."

In the weeks following the invasion, there was speculation about Soviet objectives in the region, most of it highly alarmed. Brezhnev, many experts concluded, had taken up Peter the Great's quest for a warm-water port. By traversing the uncongenial mountain passes through landlocked Afghanistan, the Soviet Union might eventually arrive at the Persian Gulf. This would require invading either Pakistan or Iran, of course.

The end of the Nixon-Brezhnev détente, already in its death throes, was hastened by the Soviet intervention, which seemed to provide corroboration for the worldview of the hard-liners. Facing an election battle a few months hence in which softness on Russia and the neglect of America's defenses would be likely issues and Ronald Reagan the likely candidate, Carter withdrew the SALT II treaty from consideration by the Senate, announced that the United States would boycott the Moscow Olympics, and prepared a major military buildup, which included a Rapid Deployment Force, intended primarily for the Persian Gulf. The administration requested approval for a CIA covert operation in Afghanistan and offered Pakistan $400 million dollars in aid, which General Zia ul-Haq, Pakistan's military ruler, dismissed as "peanuts." Suddenly, Afghanistan had become the focal point of American global strategy.

Though the Soviet leaders undoubtedly expected criticism from the United States after the invasion, the strength of the reaction from Washington must have surprised them. The United States had appeared content to consign Afghanistan to the Soviet sphere of influence. In the Truman administration, as the deputy chief of mission in Kabul later wrote, "the State Department showed absolutely no interest in Afghanistan." Former assistant secretary of state George C. McGhee recalls that in 1951 Prince Naim, the Afghan ambassador to Washington, suggested that he would have to talk to the Russians if the United States did not come up with a little military aid. "I picked up the phone and asked my secretary to get me the telephone number of the Russian Embassy," McGhee writes in his memoirs. "I wrote it on a piece of paper and handed it to the Prince, whereupon we both laughed." In the Eisenhower era, Secretary of State John Foster Dulles also turned aside Afghan requests for American arms. Pakistan was the centerpiece of his Southeast Asia Treaty Organization, and the tension between Pakistan and Afghanistan over a disputed border ran high.

By contrast, the Soviet Union has had a long-standing interest in Afghanistan. After Lenin came to power, the Afghans were the first recipients of Soviet military and economic aid. In the 1920s, Soviet engineers put telephone lines in the country and established an air route from Moscow to Kabul. The Afghans remained suspicious of Russian intentions, yet when Britain left the region in 1947 after the withdrawal from India, and the United States showed no interest in becoming heavily involved, Afghanistan turned into the South Asian equivalent of Finland. At home, it was free to keep its traditional institutions; in foreign affairs, it had to accommodate Soviet interests. The level of Soviet aid to Afghanistan has fluctuated over the years and appears to have been responsive to the American commitment to Pakistan. In 1955, shortly after Dulles concluded the mutual security agreement with Pakistan, the Soviet leaders Nikolai Bulganin and Nikita Khrushchev visited Afghanistan, and thereafter the Soviets stepped up their aid, much of which was military. Soviet influence grew rapidly. When the United States sharply reduced its aid to Pakistan in a show of displeasure over the India-Pakistan war of 1965, the Soviets cut aid to their client, too. Between 1953 and 1963, Sardar Muhammad Daud Khan served as the prime minister of Afghanistan, and, with Soviet aid, he introduced reforms. For the first time, a university in Kabul began to train a few intellectuals, and in parts of the country a small start was made on public education. Daud's brother-in-law, Muhammad Zahir Shah, had been the king of Afghanistan since 1933. In 1963, he suddenly dismissed Daud. Ten years later, Daud staged a coup, returned to power, and abolished the monarchy. He dispatched his brother-in-law to Rome (where he still lives) and provided him with a pension. Daud's return to power was assisted by some army officers who later joined the Afghan Communist Party, and by Babrak Karmal, a well-known and reasonably well-liked leftist politician from an upper-class family. (Six years later, when the Soviets invaded, they installed Karmal as president of Afghanistan.) By all accounts, the Kremlin leadership was entirely satisfied with the state of affairs in the early years of Daud's rule. Soviet influence grew, and the Soviet Union became Afghanistan's leading trading partner as well as its leading arms supplier.

Afghanistan was an Islamic tribal society made up of four dominant nationalities and numerous smaller ones. With a small urban population, an annual per-capita income of less than two hundred dollars, a literacy rate of 10 percent, and a life expectancy of thirty-eight years, it was not a nation in the modern sense. It was an unlikely candidate for a socialist revolution. On this assessment, the containment strategists in Washington and the party ideologues in Moscow were in agreement. By abolishing the monarchy, however, Daud had removed the one symbol of legitimacy that had held Afghanistan together since its founding as a state in 1747. And by staging a military coup to seize power—an unprecedented tactic in Afghanistan—he had transformed the politics of the country. Two new players now appeared on the scene, and the country's fate was no longer entirely in the hands of the Soviet Union or the United States or the traditional ruling elite of Afghanistan.

In 1965, thirty men belonging to various Marxist study circles had formed the People's Democratic Party of Afghanistan. Nur Muhammad Taraki, who was the son of a Pashtun nomad and had served as press attaché in the Afghan embassy in Washington, had been elected general secretary, and Babrak Karmal also held a position of leadership. The People's Democratic Party, Marxist in organization and ideology and semiclandestine, was neither democratic nor popular. Over the next decade, a few hundred people were attracted to it, all of them from the intelligentsia—teachers, bureaucrats, students, and, most important, military officers, many of whom had been to the Soviet Union for training. Since there were no peasants or workers in the party, the Kremlin did not take it very seriously, but this disregard did not prevent Soviet leaders from trying to give it direction. As the parliamentary elections of September 1965 approached, Taraki and Karmal went to Moscow to get financial support to run eight candidates. Four of their party's candidates were elected, including Karmal. Both Taraki and Hafizullah Amin, his most devoted disciple, lost. The

Afghan secret police concluded, according to a former minister of the interior, that the leaders of the PDPA were "controlled, subsidized, paid, and ordered directly by KGB elements of the Soviet Embassy." Technically, the secret-police report was correct, but it missed what was in fact taking place. From the first, controlling this most unorthodox Communist Party had presented a nearly impossible task, because its leadership was seriously divided, with Karmal challenging Taraki for power. In May of 1967, a little over two years after its formation, the PDPA split into two factions, each named after its newspaper. Taraki's faction, which was called Khalq ("masses"), was made up mostly of Pashtuns from rural areas, but it aspired to be a Leninist working-class party. Karmal's faction, called Parcham ("banner"), aroused more Soviet interest, because it presented itself as a broad national democratic front ready to work within the system. (In 1982, a former major in the KGB who had defected to the West claimed that Karmal had been a KGB agent for many years and said, "He could be relied upon to accept our advice.") Hafizullah Amin, an instructor at the Teachers' Training School in Kabul, had just received an M.A. at Teachers College of Columbia University in New York. Reporting on Amin shortly before the Soviet invasion, the American chargé d'affaires in Kabul described him as "all charm and friendliness" and noted that these qualities might make it hard to realize that he had been "directly responsible for the execution of probably 6,000 political opponents." Babrak Karmal also had a devoted disciple—a former medical student named Najibullah. In each case, the disciple ousted his patron in order to assume the presidency of Afghanistan; Najibullah is the current president.

After Daud's coup, Soviet agents had little success in uniting the party's factions. The energies of the PDPA leaders were directed chiefly against their rivals within the party rather than against the state they were committed to overthrowing. The disagreements were personal, not ideological; one major issue was the color of the masthead for the party newspaper.

Nevertheless, in 1978, they were able to collaborate sufficiently to take over the country. The improbable Afghan Revolution would most likely not have happened without the entry of yet another major player, the shah of Iran. Under Nixon and Carter, the United States welcomed Iran as a surrogate capable of serving American interests in the region without direct American involvement. Under this arrangement, the shah was sold billions of dollars worth of advanced military equipment and was encouraged in his dreams of becoming a modern Xerxes. "It was the Shah of Iran, not Leonid Brezhnev, who triggered the chain of events culminating in the overthrow of the Muhammad Daud regime," Selig Harrison, a specialist on South Asia at the Carnegie Endowment for International Peace, wrote in the *Washington Post* in May of 1979. "Beginning in 1974 . . . Iran, encouraged by the United States, made a determined effort to draw Kabul into a western-tilted, Tehran-centered regional economic and security sphere embracing Pakistan, India and the Persian Gulf states." The shah offered Kabul $2 billion in aid over a ten-year period—more than Afghanistan had received in foreign aid since the end of the Second World War—and encouraged Daud to mend his relations with Pakistan and to lessen his dependence on Moscow by sending more military officers to Egypt and India for training. The shah also advised Kabul to improve relations with the other countries of the region, including China. In August of 1976, Secretary of State Kissinger visited Daud in Kabul, and an upbeat communiqué was issued after their meeting. Plainly, Daud was looking for new friends, because, in 1973, the Islamabad government had begun to train and arm the Mujahideen to harass the Afghan government.

At the same time, Daud moved to cut down the influence of the Left in domestic politics. In 1977, he announced a new constitution, which provided for only one political party—his own—and he began purging suspected members of the PDPA from the army and the bureaucracy. He appointed prominent anticommunists as minister of the interior and minister of defense. The party, its warring factions now uneasily reunited, began preparations, as Taraki's official biography puts it, "to wrest power through a shortcut," using the army "to topple the ruling class." On April 19, 1978, the PDPA organized a funeral procession for one of its leaders who had been murdered, probably on Daud's orders. When fifteen thousand people marched through the streets of Kabul crying, "Death to the US imperialists!" Daud was shocked at this demonstration of leftist power. A week later, he arrested the three leaders—Taraki, Amin, and Karmal—on charges of treason and conspiracy. The next day, tanks converged on the presidential palace while other units freed the PDPA leaders. President Daud died fighting; his family was killed in the palace.

At the time of the coup, at least a third of the Afghan army's officer corps was Soviet-trained. Nevertheless, nobody in power, in Afghanistan or outside it, foresaw the coup. Taraki boasted that "the news of our revolution took both superpowers by complete surprise." On the morning of April 27, the Soviet ambassador, unaware that the coup was in progress, was waiting at the office of the foreign minister to lodge a protest against the arrests of the PDPA leaders. (The next day, he delivered the protest to Taraki, who had become the new president, and—according to a report by the Pakistani journalist Raja Anwar, which was based on eyewitness accounts—"they both burst out laughing.") When Babrak Karmal was freed from prison by a rebel officer and put on a tank, he had no idea where he was being taken. The next day, he was Taraki's deputy prime minister. The commander of the Presidential Guard was a member of Karmal's faction of the PDPA; he died at his post, defending the palace against his comrades. For three days after the PDPA takeover, Tass kept referring to it as a "military coup d'état" rather than a popular revolution, which is what the Soviets would surely have called it if they had been behind it. But the Soviet Union quickly recognized the new government, and shortly afterward the American embassy in Kabul cabled Washington, "The Russians have finally won the 'Great Game.'"

In the revolutionary government that took over in April of 1978, the two factions were equally represented in the cabinet. Despite Soviet efforts to keep the rival factions united, however, a split began at once. Within three months, the Parcham leaders were purged. Karmal was sent abroad, as ambassador to Czechoslovakia, and other leaders of his faction were also posted abroad. Many were jailed and executed. Within Khalq, a bitter struggle for power developed between Amin and Taraki. Nevertheless, in December, they went to Moscow together to sign a Treaty of Friendship, Good Neighborliness, and Cooperation. One of its articles provided that Afghanistan could call upon the Soviet Union for military assistance.

Despite the cautionary advice of senior Soviet advisers in Afghanistan, the Afghan government pursued a course calculated to provoke resistance among the people. The traditional flag—of green, black, and red—was replaced with a red banner. Overzealous land reform carried out by inexperienced and imperious bureaucrats was resisted, and such innovations as coeducation and legal limitations on dowries aroused further opposition in the conservative rural population. It was almost as if the revolutionary leaders had decided, in the name of progress, to outrage every segment of Afghan society.

By the winter of 1978–79, there was armed resistance in virtually every province. In the fall of 1978, the Islamic fundamentalist guerrilla groups that had operated against Daud between 1973 and 1976 reentered Afghanistan with a force of about five thousand. There followed major armed rebellions, which the conscripts in the Afghan army were unable to put down. Many of them, horrified at being asked to kill their own kin, joined the resistance, bringing their weapons with them. Units of the Afghan army in the provincial capital of Asadabad defected en masse. In March of 1979, an uprising broke out in Herat, an ancient city near the Iranian border populated by Shiites, who were enthralled by the Khomeini revolution. These pro-Iranian rebels went from house to house looking for government collaborators and Soviet advisers. About a thousand people, including a number of Soviet advisers and their families, were killed; in reprisal, parts of the city were destroyed. In June of 1979, Tehran Radio broadcast the appeal of a senior ayatollah calling upon the people of Afghanistan to rise up against the Communists. The Shiite population of the Hazarajat region staged another uprising.

By then, the United States had concluded that the Soviets were "moving forward with plans to engineer replacement" of the leadership of the PDPA. In mid-July, the American embassy in Kabul reported that a high-level Soviet mission, headed by a special envoy, Vasily Safronchuk, had been charged with bringing about a "radical change," because "the regime has little public support and is losing control of the country." But Soviet efforts to regulate Afghan affairs succeeded only in exacerbating the discord within Khalq. The most complete account of the intrigue that led to the downfall of Taraki and Amin and to the Soviet invasion is in the forthcoming book *Revolution and Betrayal in Afghanistan*, by Raja Anwar, who interviewed many of the participants, including several cabinet ministers and the family of Amin. On September 4, 1979, Anwar reports, Taraki left for a visit to Havana, and in his absence one of his supporters, a man named Sarwari, drew up plans to assassinate Amin. However, Sarwari made the mistake of putting his nephew in charge of carrying out the plot, not knowing that the young man worked for the KGB. At that point, the Soviets had less drastic ideas for getting Amin out of the way, and he was informed of the plot. From that day, Amin's trust in Soviet goodwill was confirmed, and Taraki's fate was sealed.

Meanwhile, Taraki, stopping in Moscow to see the Soviet foreign minister, Andrei Gromyko, was advised to send Amin into exile and appoint Karmal as his deputy. But Amin, having foiled the assassination attempt, had no intention of leaving the country, and on the day Taraki returned to Kabul the two leaders quarreled bitterly in the palace. Summoned three days later to a second meeting, at which the Soviet ambassador was to mediate their differences, Amin arrived early, in the hope of seeing Taraki alone. When he climbed the stairs leading to Taraki's quarters, guards opened fire, but Amin rolled down the stairs and managed to escape. That evening, he ordered tanks into all key points in Kabul and had Taraki arrested and confined to his quarters. Three weeks later, the founder of Afghanistan's revolutionary party was murdered, on Amin's orders.

The Soviets were now becoming desperate. The Afghan leader whom Brezhnev had embraced was dead, and his rival, whom the Soviets had been trying to get rid of, was firmly in power. Though Amin moved quickly to placate the opposition, mostly by promising religious freedom, and though he was given increasing Soviet military help, he could neither put down the insurgency nor win wider political support. He turned to diplomacy to relieve the pressure, courting both Pakistan and the United States. Yet at the same time he kept asking for more Soviet military aid. By July, there were fifteen hundred Soviet military advisers assigned to the Afghan army, and a Soviet light-airborne battalion was deployed near Kabul for their protection. In late November, Amin asked the Soviets to bring in ten thousand soldiers to protect Kabul, so that he could free Afghan forces to attack the rebels in the countryside. Between November 29 and December 5, two additional Soviet battalions were flown into Afghanistan, and in mid-December one of them went into action to secure a key tunnel on the highway to the Soviet Union. At this point, Amin approached Pakistan. He invited President Zia to Kabul to discuss settling the disputed frontier on Pakistan's terms in return for Zia's agreement to end his support of the Afghan resistance. He also went out of his way to be conciliatory in a private conversation with the American chargé d'affaires. In interviews with American journalists, he appealed for aid from the United States and promised that "no Soviet military bases will be allowed in Afghanistan." In mid-December, Zia replied to Amin's invitation by agreeing to send his foreign minister; Amin was ecstatic and asked the Soviets to halt their troop movements into Afghanistan. Some American analysts have speculated that Amin was an Afghan Tito or, at least, was thought to be by the Soviets. But suddenly, on December 22, the Pakistani foreign minister canceled his trip. Amin thereupon offered arms to Pakistani dissidents fighting Zia and to Baluchi rebels in Iran fighting Khomeini. All this suggested that Amin was pursuing a strategy of widening the war to save his regime. The possibility that the entire region would be destabilized must have alarmed the Soviets.

On December 27, Soviet forces crossed the frontier in strength, and the Soviet pacification campaign began. That evening, a Soviet contingent arrived at a palace near the Defense Ministry, to which Soviet advisers had induced Amin to move a few days earlier, for "security" reasons. Unlike his previous residence, it had no protective walls and was almost totally indefensible. The day before the move, Amin had survived another attempt to get rid of him—a sophisticated plot that had almost certainly been engineered by Lieutenant General Viktor Paputin, the Soviet first deputy minister for internal affairs. Raja Anwar recounts how the plot went awry. The Soviet cooks at the presidential residence (the Afghan president evidently considered them more trustworthy than Afghans) laced Amin's lunch with drugs, and he lapsed into unconsciousness. Apparently, the plan was to take him into the custody of the Soviet Medical Corps, where, after a public declaration of gratitude for the Soviet troops, he would be given a choice of resigning or standing trial for Taraki's murder. But Amin, who ate only lightly, regained consciousness. "Don't worry, the Soviet Army should be coming to our rescue," he said to his wife just a few minutes before a Soviet unit made up of Tajiks arrived at the palace. Amin was later found at his desk, shot through the head. Lieutenant General Paputin, who had been charged with arranging a more discreet removal of the president, died shortly thereafter, probably by his own hand.

The overriding reason for the invasion was that the civil strife inside Afghanistan was viewed in the Kremlin as "a seat of serious danger to the security of the Soviet state," as Leonid Brezhnev put it two weeks later. Afghanistan has a thousand-mile border with the Muslim Central Asian republics of the Soviet Union, which are populated by Tajiks, Uzbeks, and Turkmens—peoples that also inhabit Afghanistan. In 1978, there had been a riot of Tajiks against the Russians in Dushanbe, a town on the Soviet side of the frontier. Toward the end of 1979, the Khomeini revolution in Iran was stirring up Islamic nationalism in the entire region, and the taking of American hostages at the American embassy in Tehran on November 4 increased the possibility of American military action against Iran within a few hundred miles of the Soviet border.

The Soviets thus faced two disagreeable choices. One was to allow a country on their border which had been within their sphere of influence for more than thirty years to continue to unravel and possibly end up in the hands of an anti-Soviet Islamic fundamentalist regime backed by conservative Arab nations, China, and the United States. The other was to invade. In short, the military operation was a desperate response to the failure of the Kremlin's political strategy. In a conversation on June 25, 1979, with the senior American diplomat in Kabul, Safronchuk had agreed that a Soviet invasion, about which there was already considerable speculation, "would very much complicate and harm Soviet-American relations." The East German ambassador in Kabul had told the same diplomat that "the entire Afghan nation" would rise up against a Soviet invading force, just as it did against the British in the nineteenth century. The recognition by Soviet and Communist-bloc diplomats in Kabul of the risks of a Soviet military move suggests that the Kremlin leaders did not lack expert advice. Rather, they chose to ignore it.

At the time of the invasion, much was made in the United States of the Brezhnev Doctrine—the policy enunciated after Soviet tanks ended the reformist experiment of Communist Party secretary Alexander Dubcek in Czechoslovakia in 1968. Now, by intervening in Afghanistan, the Russians appeared to be saying that they were prepared to "defend" with Soviet divisions even socialist revolutions that occurred outside their sphere in Eastern Europe. The use of military force to keep socialist countries from backsliding appeared to have become standard Soviet practice, and it confirmed the worldview of the hard-liners in both political parties in the United States that the Soviet Union was an openly expansionist power. Just as Munich stood for the follies of appeasement and Pearl Harbor for the ever-present danger of surprise attack, Afghanistan now became a metaphor for the Soviet Union's boundless appetite and unpredictable behavior.

Eight years later, however, it seems clear that the Soviet goals in Afghanistan have always been limited. First, unlike the Chinese in Tibet, the Soviets have neither claimed sovereignty over Afghanistan nor been willing to commit enough resources to subdue it. They were obviously aware after a few months that without large-scale reinforcements their army could not hope to eliminate the resistance. Second, within weeks of the invasion Soviet leaders had agreed in principle to the withdrawal of Soviet forces—a promise that they had never made with respect to Eastern Europe. Third, Soviet diplomacy over the last eight years has simply not embraced a strategy for the sort of regional expansion that aroused so much fear in the United States at the time of the invasion. True, military pressure on Pakistan has been stepped up, but the obvious motivation has been to discourage Pakistani support for the Mujahideen. Soviet policy toward Iran has been extremely cautious.

The Kremlin did expect the military phase of the "rescue" of Afghanistan to be over in short order. The Soviets may have really believed that it was Amin's personal style, rather than the offensive revolutionary policies of the

Afghan ruling party, that had aroused so much hostility. Certainly, they thought that Karmal, being a smoother and more popular figure, would elicit much more public support. Just as President Kennedy was persuaded in 1963 that the removal of Ngo Dinh Diem, coupled with the increased presence of American military advisers, would resolve difficulties in Vietnam, so the Soviets were deluded into thinking that Amin's removal and a Soviet military presence could stabilize the revolutionary regime. It was one of many Soviet miscalculations.

Despite great destruction and human suffering, the war in Afghanistan is, in comparison with, say, the Vietnam War or the Korean War, a limited operation. From the start, the Soviet Union has concentrated on four strategic objectives. The first is to control the northern plains and the mountainous areas along the road from the Soviet Union to Kabul and to control Afghanistan's other major cities and the roads linking them to Kabul. There is a large Afghan army base near the capital, and the entire area is actively patrolled by Soviet soldiers. The resistance has a significant presence in the northern region, but its strength is dissipated by rivalry between two Islamic organizations. The second objective is to guard the western frontier against Iran. The Soviets have maintained a large force along the border, but it is rarely deployed in offensive operations. Third, a consistent effort has been made to control access to the cities near the Pakistani border and to interdict by aerial strikes and commando raids the supply lines of the Mujahideen. Fourth, the Soviets attach great importance to building and protecting the infrastructure of the state, and troops are deployed around government installations, warehouses, hospitals, and so on, which are often attacked. Together, the four war zones constitute no more than 20 percent of the territory of Afghanistan, but about 70 percent of its food has been produced there. By and large, the rest of the country, though it feels the effects of the war, actually sees little of it. Most of Afghanistan continues to be under the control of local khans and maliks, as it has been for centuries. These local chieftains are opposed to the Soviet presence, but, though generally sympathetic to the resistance, they are independent of the Mujahideen.

Not until September of 1981, almost two years after the invasion, did the Soviet media report the death of a Soviet soldier in battle. And during the first five years of the war, the Soviet press tried to minimize the military commitment in Afghanistan and create the impression that Soviet troops were in Afghanistan for training. As was true of the Americans in Vietnam, the Soviets had originally believed that their troops would have to do little fighting—that the mere presence of their forces in Afghanistan would stiffen the resolve of the Afghan army and raise its morale. But, with recruits defecting in droves, the Afghan army melted away. It was so unreliable that the Soviets would disarm suspect units at night and return the rifles and machine guns only at daybreak. After five years of fighting, the Soviet force of more than a hundred and fifteen thousand, supported by thirty thousand additional soldiers just across the Soviet border, had achieved no more than uneasy control of the cities and about 20 percent of the countryside. At night, entire neighborhoods of even the larger cities were in rebel hands. Kabul itself was not secure from guerrilla rocket attacks. "There is no safe place to walk," Soviet soldiers complained on returning home. Hundreds of thousands of Soviet soldiers, most of them conscripts, have served time in Afghanistan. Over ten thousand have been killed in battle. The Soviets have limited their military objectives and modified their tactics in the hope of keeping their casualties low, but Pentagon intelligence analysts believe that their dead, wounded, and nonbattle casualties still number between four and five thousand a year and that more are the result of dysentery, cholera, and bad medical care than of enemy fire. In the Pentagon and the CIA, a number of trained observers are watching Afghanistan, for the war provides the only view anyone has had of the Soviet army in prolonged combat since the end of the Second World War. The Soviet military effort has become more efficient with experience, Pentagon intelligence analysts say, but they add that over all they are not impressed by the Soviet performance. The morale in the Russian fighting units in Afghanistan is low. Alcohol and drugs are a serious problem. Soviet tactics appear to be outmoded or inappropriate, and the forces are plagued by sloppiness and poor discipline. But some observers, such as the Defense Department intelligence specialist Elie Krakowski, have said that despite these problems and the rebels' access to more sophisticated weapons the Soviets have steadily "widened the gap in their favor." Another senior specialist in the Pentagon concludes that for the job the Soviets have set themselves in Afghanistan they have always been "seriously undermanned." He estimates that no more than thirty thousand fighting men can be sent into battle on any given day—not a great number in a country the size of Texas. The Soviets maintain about two million men under arms, and they could have put more troops into the war if they had chosen to.

When the Soviet forces intervened in Afghanistan, it was predicted in the West that the docile Soviet masses would be told nothing about the war except self-serving lies and the Kremlin would have a free hand to pacify Afghanistan: there would be no need to contend with either domestic opposition or the embarrassment of worldwide criticism. Things have not worked out quite that way. After eight years, the effects of the war are widely felt in Soviet society. In Armenia, Georgia, the Ukraine, and other Soviet republics, there have been public demonstrations against service in Afghanistan. Between four and five million Afghans are refugees, and the brutal character of the war is not lost on the Soviet soldiers who must fight it. Because returning soldiers bring home firsthand reports, Soviet citizens know enough of the war to raise some of the same moral questions that troubled many Americans during the Vietnam War. Even those Soviet citizens who accept the official explanation of the invasion—that it was provoked by Pakistani and American aggression—can see that the seemingly endless war is indeed a "bleeding wound," as Mikhail Gorbachev himself has called it, because it reinforces Soviet isolation and delays on internal reform. In each of the last eight years, the United Nations General Assembly has passed a resolution condemning the Soviet Union for the invasion of Afghanistan—in language much tougher than any used against the United States during the Vietnam War—and the resolution has now been endorsed by 123 nations. The invasion of Afghanistan has hurt the Soviet Union's relations not only with the United States but also with China and with Iran and other Islamic nations. Because of the decision of the Kremlin leadership to limit the number of troops in Afghanistan, the political costs are not as high as those which American political leaders incurred during the Vietnam War, but, over time, they have grown. Therefore, during a period of eight years, under four national leaders, the Soviet objectives have been scaled down, and the Soviet strategy has been modified.

In Brezhnev's time, the Soviet army conducted large-scale search-and-destroy operations in the Afghan countryside. Villages suspected of harboring guerrillas were bombed, and water supplies and food were deliberately destroyed to drive the guerrillas from their hiding places. In 1980, uprisings occurred in Kandahar, the second-largest city, and also in Herat and Jalalabad; some cities were under rebel control for as much as a week before Soviet sweeps were able to drive the rebels out. In 1982 and again in 1984, the Soviets launched major operations to destroy a center of fierce resistance in the Panjshir Valley, forty-five miles north of Kabul, but did not succeed. In April of 1983, Soviet bombers carried out "carpet bombing" attacks on Herat, and many civilians died. At the same time, Soviet political advisers in Kabul were counseling reforms to make the revolutionary government more acceptable to the people, for more than four million Afghans had left their homes, with three million ending up in camps in Pakistan, providing a vast pool of recruits for the resistance. Today, many of these refugees routinely go back and forth across the frontier, sometimes by hiding in trucks and vans that carry supplies to the guerrillas but mostly by mule or camel. Occasionally, a family catches a bus to Kabul.

Belatedly, the Soviets began to realize that as their attacks on the civilian population became more savage their difficulties increased. Traditionally, Afghan warriors do not venture far from their home territory, for they must guard the women and children. By driving so many dependents into refugee camps, the Soviets unwittingly liberated the Mujahideen from their family responsibilities and turned them into more mobile and formidable opponents. The Mujahideen themselves accelerated this process. Even before the Soviet invasion, they had declared a jihad, a holy war, against the Communist government, and, as custom prescribed, had moved their dependents to an "abode of peace," in Pakistan—some four hundred and seventy thousand of them. By the end of 1981, about two and a half million refugees were in Pakistan; the total increased by only four hundred thousand in the next seven years.

By the time of Yuri Andropov's accession as general secretary of the Soviet Communist Party, in late 1982, the prospect of a quick Soviet victory had faded. Military operations and air strikes were therefore reduced, and the Soviets evolved the strategy they have been following, with some interruptions, ever since. Soviet advisers began to insist that the Afghan government take political reform seriously, repair its relations with the merchants of Kabul, and improve its enforcement techniques. The KGB reorganized and built up the Afghan secret police. There was a new emphasis on unconventional warfare—subversion, infiltration, bribery, assassination—in order to break the Afghan resistance. In many cases, the Soviets succeeded in establishing a modus vivendi with local commanders. There was much more accommodation between the two sides, and many more local truces, than the sporadic coverage of the war on the nightly news suggested. Under Andropov, there was also a new emphasis on political strategies to exploit tribal rivalries and battles for turf among competing groups of Mujahideen. And when cities were attacked or Soviet convoys were ambushed merciless punishment followed.

From time to time, accounts of Soviet atrocities appear in magazines and newspapers in the United States. A typical story appeared in *Reader's Digest* in

November of 1985. It described how Narainjan, a ten-year-old shepherd boy, had picked up a doll-like object on a grassy hillside and had his hand blown off. Arthur Bonner, a sixty-five-year-old retired television journalist who made seven trips into Afghanistan in 1985 and 1986 as a correspondent for the *Times*, traveling thirty-five hundred miles throughout the country, remembers seeing a Soviet "toy bomb" in the shape of a vase. Others have reported seeing lethal devices shaped like tiny pistols or horseshoes. Most of these booby traps were dropped in the mountain passes in the early years of the war. Stories about them appear to be more widely distributed than the weapons themselves are today.

The Mujahideen spare nothing in their efforts to impute genocidal intentions to the Soviets. There are eyewitness reports that Soviet troops have committed war crimes by taking reprisals on unarmed villages following guerrilla attacks in the area. On one such occasion, on September 13, 1982—an incident that J. Bruce Amstutz, the former United States chargé d'affaires in Afghanistan, considers "particularly well documented"—Soviet forces swept into a village thirty-five miles from Kabul, forced 105 of the inhabitants, including women and children, into a tunnel, and massacred them. On another occasion, after a Soviet sweep, a Swedish official who was in a guerrilla-controlled area reported, "Russian soldiers shot at anything alive in six villages—people, hens, donkeys—and then they plundered what remained of value." But Pentagon officials question the charges that the Soviets are deliberately destroying the country. "There is a Belgian Baby Syndrome at work here," one senior Pentagon official told us, referring to the British propaganda campaign to stir up feelings in the United States against the Germans in the First World War.

In the early 1980s, the State Department repeatedly charged the Soviets with using chemical weapons. In 1982 alone, according to one official United States report, there were "several dozen chemical attacks in Afghanistan resulting in over 300 agent-related deaths." Amstutz says that Western correspondents, a hospital director in Peshawar, and at least one Soviet deserter have offered eyewitness corroboration of specific uses of chemical warfare. The Soviets deny any use whatever. Volunteer doctors and nurses serving the Mujahideen inside Afghanistan whom we interviewed all reported seeing civilians and animals killed by mines and aerial attacks but not by gas attacks.

The Soviets accompanied their new military strategy under Andropov with stepped-up diplomatic efforts to end the resistance. Diego Cordovez, the United Nations undersecretary general for political affairs, who is in charge of the peace negotiations, believes that in 1983 the Soviets made the decision to withdraw from Afghanistan but then Soviet diplomacy was stalled during Andropov's illness and through the brief interregnum of Konstantin Chernenko, his successor. Under Chernenko, Soviet military strategy appeared to be harsh but confused and ineffective. Mikhail Gorbachev, upon becoming general secretary, resumed the Andropov strategy and took it further. The Soviets made more use of special commando units, which they deployed to strike suspected centers of the resistance. Increasingly, they attacked, with devastating effect, suspected rebel positions and supply routes with light counterguerrilla forces supported by helicopter gunships.

Since 1986, however, the Mujahideen have been receiving Blowpipe and Stinger ground-to-air missiles from Britain and the United States, and these make the use of the helicopters costly. The Mujahideen claim that the missiles have destroyed more than four hundred Soviet planes, or over a third of the Soviet Union's annual production. This figure may be exaggerated. Still, there is no doubt that the missiles have been a boost for the morale of the Mujahideen; moreover, they have forced the Soviets to shift their tactics once again. The use of aircraft has been curtailed, and as air support has become less certain Soviet and Afghan army ground forces have become more vulnerable to ambush and less aggressive.

The Soviet invasion served to unite hundreds of scattered guerrilla groups into a national effort against the Communists, and within a little over a year the Mujahideen grew to eighty thousand full-time warriors, who have since demonstrated remarkable military prowess. Pentagon analysts say that the Mujahideen have "matured" into an effective fighting force. Still, it is not possible to describe the resistance as if it were an army; it is a mosaic of fifteen hundred separate "fronts" in which a hundred and fifty thousand guerrillas participate. The Mujahideen exhibit solidarity but also carry on intense competition within their ranks, and as many as a dozen guerrilla groups often coexist in a single area. Each group not only has its own tribal or ethnic membership but is further separated from other groups by its political affiliation with one of eleven Mujahideen organizations—seven in Pakistan and four in Iran. Groups may unite to repel attacks by Soviet forces but only rarely to initiate combat. On the contrary, when the enemy is not pressing them their internal conflicts accelerate. The commanders say that while a group is transporting weapons from Pakistan to its base it is more likely to be attacked by a rival than by the enemy. Hizb, the Islamic Party, led by Gulbuddin Hekmatyar, is the largest resistance organization and the one most frequently accused of confiscating the supplies of other groups. There are other kinds of intra-Mujahideen violence, too. In 1984, Zabiullah, a legendary commander of Jamaat, the Islamic Society, based in the strategic northern area, was killed, reportedly by a rival organization. Two years later, Muhammad Salim, a popular Hizb commander, was murdered—by members of his own party, it is said—because he had responded positively to a call from the Jamaat commander, Ahmed Shah Massoud, for a unified command. Large-scale defections normally follow factional warfare; the International Institute for Strategic Studies, in London, reported in 1986 that after Zabiullah's death most of his people joined the government's militia.

The disunity and the absence of a common strategy cause most commanders to limit their military operations to defending their own territory. In his book *Islam and Resistance in Afghanistan*, Olivier Roy, a French academic who has made six trips into Afghanistan, writes, "The resistance has not deployed its troops in line with strategic considerations. Soviet disposition of troops and strategy determines the military activity of the resistance, who become involved in fighting only when Soviet units appear inside their territory. When there are only government troops, a modus vivendi is soon established between the two sides." Military observers have documented the shortage of technical skills and training among the Mujahideen. Though a number of well-trained former officers of the Afghan army have joined the resistance, many more have offered their services but have found the doors closed. "The most active organizations are Islamic fundamentalists," said a Soviet-trained major who was a member of Afghanistan's Defense Planning Council in 1978 and is now a refugee in Pakistan. "They do not trust us." Another officer remarked, "There is a social gap between us and the commanders. They are interested in fighting, which to them is a question of honor and Islam. They have no use for our ideas of discipline, training, and organization. To them, modern warfare means fighting with modern weapons. Nothing more." An artillery commander who had been trained in the United States agreed. "The resistance is extremely tribalized," he said. "The leaders do not understand the outlook of professional military men."

Like their Communist adversaries, the Mujahideen talk a great deal about the need for unity, but each effort to cooperate seems to leave them more bitterly divided. The foreign sponsors—the Saudis and the CIA—are reported to work hard at trying to unify the rival factions, much as the Soviet advisers did to unify the PDPA before the invasion, and with similar success. Senior American officials tell Congress—usually when the vote on covert aid approaches—that the Mujahideen commanders are now working together and coordinating their activities. The favorite example is Ahmed Shah Massoud, who in 1986 did make substantial progress toward building a unified command in four northern provinces. But in recent months, as the possibility of an imminent Soviet withdrawal has become more credible, fighting among the Mujahideen has intensified, as have politically motivated assassinations within the Afghan community in Pakistan.

The Mujahideen are too disunited to win the war, but they are too spread out to lose it. The Soviets face more than a thousand separate armies that depend not upon a central command, which could be wiped out, but upon the initiative of thousands of individual leaders and the bravery of tens of thousands more. Afghans fight because their code of honor instills the warrior spirit and their sense of religious obligation demands their participation in the holy war. The Quran exhorts all Muslims to take part in a rigorous effort to combat evil and promote good, not necessarily through war. Sufi philosophers have written that the personal struggle for enlightenment and the conquest of passion are forms of jihad. The ayatollahs in contemporary Iran call the struggle for economic development a jihad. Ever since the expansionist period of Islam, however, the word has usually connoted a just war against an evil enemy. Once the war has started, it becomes a religious duty to fight in it.

Until Gorbachev's February 1988 announcement of Moscow's intention to withdraw Soviet troops before the formation of a coalition government, the Soviets had openly worried about a bloodbath if they abandoned the Afghan government. This concern is not a frivolous one. A decade of war has undermined the old Afghan ways of managing and limiting violence. These traditional methods rested on a set of shared values and customs, which have been weakened by revolution, war, and exile. Furthermore, to the ancient ethnic and tribal divisions of Afghanistan have been added the conflict of ideologies and the irreconcilable ambitions of armed political organizations. In the Afghan code of honor, *badal*—the obligation to take revenge—has an important place. Kinsmen of someone who has been killed by an enemy must discharge the "debt" of retribution, which is handed down from one generation to the next. Neither time nor space limits the obligation. Unless a truce is made and compensation is paid, harm done in Peshawar or Kabul may be avenged years later in New York or Moscow.

Afghanistan's guerrilla war has spawned a significant network of private enterprise. Arthur Bonner describes life among the Mujahideen in his book *Among the Afghans*. As in the olden days, he reports, Afghans are making money by controlling roads and mountain passes. Guerrilla commanders collect tolls from one another. "The route was divided into sections, each under the control of a single commander or an alliance of commanders," he writes. "For each section there was a fixed rate for passengers and freight although there seemed to be no relationship between the rates in different areas." Bonner relates moving instances of the Afghan people's commitment to the holy war—their keenness to join, their willingness to die. As a convoy is assembled for the war zone, clerks read out letters from families offering their sons: "We are a poor family and have little land. Please take our youngest son to fight the Jihad." A village mullah recommends another: "This man is Sadiq, son of Mustafa. He is honest and wishes to serve God." An individual who joins the Mujahideen is as likely to buy his personal weapon as to draw it from an armory. We met families who had sold their jewelry to pay for a son's Soviet-made weapon.

Arms and heroin are the mainstays of what cynics in Pakistan call the jihad enterprises. The resentment among Pakistanis who are not involved in the illicit trade is understandable, for the jihad in Afghanistan has brought their country corruption, addiction, and crime. In 1986, according to the International Narcotics Matters Bureau of the State Department, Afghanistan produced as much as five hundred metric tons of opium—almost four times the amount produced two years before. In 1987, Afghanistan had a bumper crop of poppies, and some experts estimate that it may now be the biggest single source of heroin in the world. Among large landowners in Afghanistan, nearly all of whom are opponents of the regime, opium has superseded wheat, corn, and fruit as the principal crop. Recent refugees with whom we spoke reported widespread food shortages in the poppy-growing areas—a condition contributing to migration to the cities. Nangarhar, the eastern province, adjacent to Pakistan, is the center of poppy cultivation. But visitors to all parts of Afghanistan—Badakhshan, in the north; Herat, in the west; and Kandahar, in the south—have reported seeing the unmistakable blaze of white and purple flowers. Officials of the Pakistan Narcotics Control Board estimate that opium poppies are now grown as a primary crop in thirteen of Afghanistan's twenty-nine provinces.

In Kandahar Province, Bonner says, extensive opium fields belong to Ahmad Akbar, a commander affiliated with the National Islamic Front, which is one of the resistance groups in Peshawar. (The head of that organization, Pir Sayed Ahmad Gailani, a traditionalist and a moderate, also heads a major religious order.) The family of the commander Ali Ahmad, who belongs to the fundamentalist Jamaat, has several hundred acres that in 1986 were being used for opium production. Both commanders told Bonner they needed the money "for the Jihad." Younis Khalis, then the chairman of the seven-party alliance of Islamic unity of Afghan Mujahideen, told us last November that, in accordance with Islamic law, he had prohibited opium growing and ordered military commanders to enforce the prohibition strictly. The leaders deny that opium is cultivated in Afghanistan on a significant scale. The United States embassy in Islamabad supports their denial; in a 1985 report it stated that "there is no evidence indicating that the Afghan Mujahideen freedom fighters have been involved in narcotics activities as a matter of policy to finance their operations." The statement is almost certainly true in a literal sense. There is no evidence showing that much, if any, of the proceeds from narcotics are used to finance guerrilla operations. Clearly, opium production does not help the Mujahideen's cause. By reducing Afghan food resources, it enhances dependence on the government, which imports food and controls the cities. Also, in the poppy-growing areas both growers and dealers seek stability and secure transportation; hence the Mujahideen come under pressure to reach an accommodation with the government.

Guerrilla commanders make frequent trips to Pakistan for weapons and supplies. We spoke about the drug business with four of them. Each acknowledged the existence of the trade in narcotics but denied any personal involvement in it. The growers' price for the harvested crop of opium, they said, ranges from forty-five to fifty-five dollars a pound. Virtually all the refining used to be done in Pakistan, but now, as the fighting has subsided and an undeclared truce exists in many areas, opium is increasingly refined in Afghanistan itself. It is transported out of the country by the Mujahideen, who cross freely into Pakistan and less freely into Iran. Once opium shipments reach Pakistan, they disappear into a complex of businessmen, smugglers, and government officials. Recently, members of elite Pakistani families, including graduates of Oxford and Cambridge, have been arrested at airports on charges of smuggling narcotics. In June 1987, General Zia ul-Haq told a Norwegian journalist that he favored the death sentence for offenders in "the holy war against drugs," and the joke went around the country that the president was preparing to liquidate the General Staff. The suspicion is widespread in

Pakistan that the money to be made from the war is no small obstacle to its settlement.

With funding from Saudi Arabia and the United States, Afghanistan's resistance movement is one of the best-financed such movements in history. Yet a majority of the guerrillas inside Afghanistan lack arms, food, and medical supplies. The Mujahideen accept their hardships with astonishing stoicism. According to Aaron Karp, writing in the September 1987 issue of *Armed Forces Journal International*, 1,150 Stinger and Blowpipe ground-to-air missiles were sent to Pakistan for the use of the resistance between September of 1986 and August of 1987. Of these, 863 actually reached commanders inside Afghanistan. At least 60 were captured. The first shipment went exclusively to the fundamentalist wing of the resistance; that is, the three groups headed by Hekmatyar, Khalis, and Dr. Sayed Burhanuddin Rabbani. Reports indicate that the fundamentalists continue to be favored over the more traditionalist (and moderate) wing of the Mujahideen. One of the most successful commanders belonging to the traditionalist National Islamic Front told us that he had never seen a Stinger.

Some time ago, a top Pakistani intelligence official confided his concern to us that once Americans got to know their Afghan clients better they would become less enthusiastic about supporting the war. Leading figures in the seven resistance groups in Peshawar, which receive more than half a billion dollars a year in covert American support, have not disguised their feelings about America. Gulbuddin Hekmatyar, whose Mujahideen organization is a major recipient of CIA aid, is well known for his outspoken contempt for the United States. But he is not alone. A poster outside the office of Dr. Rabbani was noted by an American reporter in 1982. It carried the message "In point of us conquerist America and blood-thirsty USSR are both enemy of the great revolution of Iran and Afghanistan," and it was signed "Rabbani." Younis Khalis was in Washington last November as the chairman of the alliance of resistance groups. He is a theologian and a warrior of considerable repute. We asked him what was the most important thing that Americans should know about the war in Afghanistan, and without hesitation he said, "You are a materialistic country, and your leader should take you in hand and give you spiritual direction."

Afghanistan is an Islamic country, and religion pervades rural life. Traditionally, Islam has coexisted with Afghan tribal customs, which are pre-Islamic and secular, although the two frequently conflict. For example, custom forbids women to inherit property, while Islamic law requires that women receive a share; and custom states that blood feuds are a matter of honor, while religious law forbids them. Traditionally, Islam in Afghanistan has been compatible with secular rule under tribal chiefs, the khans and the maliks, and tribal assemblies, the jirgas. The Islamic traditionalists wish to live like their grandfathers. The most powerful among them are large landowners, who have no interest in disturbing existing social arrangements.

Islamic fundamentalism, on the other hand, is heavily influenced by the Muslim Brotherhood of Egypt, a twentieth-century phenomenon, and by the Khomeini movement in Iran. Not unlike some strains of Christian fundamentalism in the United States, it searches the scriptures for authority to support radical change in the social order. It uses an imagined golden age of scriptural times to support a modern ideology at odds with Afghanistan's past. Theocracy is the heart of the fundamentalist ideology, but it goes against the Afghan grain. The country has never had a theocratic government or a centralized state. The fundamentalists appear to be intent on introducing both.

The basic split in Afghan society is not between capitalism and communism but between traditionalism and modernism. The fundamentalists are much like the Communists, and neither can govern Afghanistan, for much the same reasons. While some of the leaders of the movement are religious teachers, many of them are products of secular education and, by profession, are doctors, technocrats, engineers, and entrepreneurs. Gulbuddin Hekmatyar, whose fundamentalist group is the most politically extreme, studied to be an engineer. Like the Communists, the fundamentalists are mostly from rural families and were converted by coming into contact with the modern world at the university in Kabul. The radical Right and the radical Left each sees itself as the savior of Afghanistan from the other. At the same time, each sees its own ideology as the instrument for challenging entrenched power and for moving a beloved, backward country into the modern era.

From the day the Soviets invaded, American diplomatic strategy was to mobilize world opinion against the Soviets and at the same time minimize the appearance of American involvement. "We are interested in Afghanistan only because the Soviets are there," a senior State Department official told us last November. It was all part of the game of nations for the Soviets to "exercise paramountcy" over Afghanistan, in the discreet imperial phrase of nineteenth-century British diplomats, but sending an army across an international frontier into territory previously unoccupied by Soviet forces was breaking the rules. What aroused American concern was not the particular victim but the act of aggression itself and what it portended for the future. The day the Soviets invaded Afghanistan, Afghanistan became a domino.

It might be thought curious that such a militantly anticommunist administration as Ronald Reagan's has focused so much more attention on the role the "evil empire" has played in Central America, where the Soviets are giving limited military aid, than on Afghanistan, where the Soviets are fighting a war against the people. The president has never given a television speech devoted to the Soviet invasion of Afghanistan. As a State Department official explained to us, American leaders had no need to say much about the invasion once they had expressed their outrage, because the invasion spoke for itself. The Soviet Union, which had claimed to be the champion of the nonaligned nations, was making war on a poor, nonaligned, Muslim country. The more visible the American interest in the future of Afghanistan became, the more the Soviets might be able to divert attention from their own aggression. It was not to the advantage of the United States to do anything to convert this North-South struggle into an East-West confrontation. The support for the Afghan resistance by the United States and Saudi Arabia is public knowledge, but it is technically clandestine, on the theory that Pakistan's involvement will be less of a provocation to the Soviets if it is not officially proclaimed. The whole purpose of keeping "secret" something that was reported in major newspapers around the world was to preserve "plausible deniability." For this reason, in the early years of the war the CIA went to great expense to procure non-American arms, even manufacturing simulated Soviet weapons in a secret factory. Thus, if the Soviets should publicly protest the American involvement the President could say, "Prove it." The same considerations prompted this country to minimize its role in the peace negotiations as well.

Pakistan has played a key part in encouraging the American commitment to the Afghan resistance. The resistance began six years before the Soviet invasion, as an expression of a long-standing border dispute between Pakistan and Afghanistan. In 1973, when Daud, a Pashtun, took over the government in Kabul for the second time, he renewed encouragement to the Pashtuns of Pakistan to secede and join their blood brothers under the Afghan flag. At that point, the government of Pakistan fought back by organizing the Pashtuns into a guerrilla movement to harass the Afghan government. Younis Khalis told us that he went to Pakistan in 1973 to organize resistance forces to fight Daud, whom he considered a dangerous modernist, even a Communist. For fifteen years, two very different Pakistani governments—the civilian government of Zulfikar Ali Bhutto and the military regime of Zia ul-Haq—have used the Afghan resistance first as a way of exerting pressure on Kabul, then as a means to strengthen the often-wavering American commitment to Pakistan. The more the United States involved itself in the Afghan cause, the more Pakistan would emerge as the indispensable staging area for the fight against communism, and the more secure the flow of American aid to Pakistan would be.

Pakistan's Interservices Intelligence Directorate, whose size and influence are believed to have vastly increased in recent years, has been in charge of distributing the weapons; that is, the government of General Zia has had the most to say about what sorts of arms should be sent to which resistance organizations and in what amounts. Zia, who when he seized power, in 1979, was supported only by the Jamaat-i-Islami, Pakistan's right-wing fundamentalist party, has used the weapons flow to build up the Islamic elements of the Afghan resistance at the expense of the more moderate and secular elements. But as shipments of arms from the United States have increased and become more visible over the past two years, American intelligence officials have assumed greater responsibility for weapons distribution and, according to a journalist in Pakistan, are "more closely involved in the day-to-day running of the war than ever before."

The United States' covert military aid program has been pushed in several different directions, because high officials have clashed over its objectives. From the start, leading American officials have believed that the Soviet invasion was a blunder and that it has served American interests. An early end to the war seemed implausible from the outset, and, moreover, Washington did not make ending the war a priority. In the Carter administration, Brzezinski was the leading advocate of the "make the Russians bleed" school, and in the Reagan administration the most forceful exponent of this view was William Casey, the late director of the CIA. But within the CIA there have been important disagreements. John McMahon, the former deputy director of the CIA, considered it both bad form and dangerous to supply American weapons in a covert operation. Was the program meant to serve as an inducement to negotiate, or was it designed primarily to punish the Soviets? The size of the covert aid operation, the character of the weapons, and the choice of recipients would differ depending upon the answer.

Congress has seen the guerrilla war in Afghanistan as a struggle for freedom with none of the moral ambiguities that surround the Contras in

Nicaragua, and a number of members who have opposed the covert American war in Nicaragua have embraced Afghan aid to demonstrate their commitment to fighting communism. In 1983, Senator Malcolm Wallop, of Wyoming, led a fight to throw off the restraints on the Afghan policy. "It's so damn obscure what the policy is," the senator said. Other congressional supporters of the Afghan resistance, claiming that the United States was supplying "just enough aid for Afghans to fight and die but not enough to win," introduced a joint resolution calling for "material assistance, as the United States considers appropriate, to help the Afghan people to fight effectively for their freedom." In an executive session of the Senate Foreign Relations Committee, CIA and State Department witnesses repeated their warnings that increased American involvement would endanger Pakistan, and for almost a year Senator Charles Mathias, of Maryland, led a fight to kill the resolution, which he considered an open-ended license to intervene, in the tradition of the Tonkin Gulf Resolution. In 1984, when President Reagan was trying to persuade Congress to give $24 million in aid to the Contras, the CIA had no trouble getting an appropriation of $30 million for the Afghan resistance. Shortly thereafter, a Texas representative, Charles Wilson, who had made frequent trips to Pakistan and had once crossed into Afghanistan in the company of the Mujahideen, decided that this was too little. "There were fifty-eight thousand dead in Vietnam and we owe the Russians one," he noted, and his single-minded efforts resulted in the addition of $40 million to the Pentagon budget for the well-advertised secret war in Afghanistan. In October of 1984, the resolution on Afghanistan passed. The following April, President Reagan signed National Security Decision Directive 166, which called for American efforts to drive Soviet forces from Afghanistan "by all means available." After secret debates in the congressional intelligence committees, appropriations for the increased commitment to the war in Afghanistan were approved. The prohibition against supplying sophisticated weapons to the Mujahideen was overcome.

Until recently, the "bleeders," as those who advocate this policy are known around Washington, usually carried the day. The more ideological foreign-policy officials, such as former assistant secretary of defense Richard Perle, have regarded Afghanistan not as the locale of a harsh and dangerous conflict to be ended but as a place to teach the Russians a lesson. The Soviets had an ideological explanation for why they could not lose in Afghanistan— history was on their side, because Communist rule was by definition "progressive"—and the "bleeders," driven by their own ideology, came to the same conclusion by a different route. The Soviets were too evil to withdraw. They had never pulled their troops out of any place they had pronounced to be "socialist" and under the rule of a Communist Party. It followed that the Russians could never be induced to negotiate a settlement. The most the United States could accomplish in Afghanistan was to make sure that the resistance would be kept alive and substantial numbers of Soviets would be killed. Thus the more modern the weapons supplied to the Mujahideen, the better. As the war dragged on, it would reveal to the world not only Soviet brutality but also Soviet impotence—and American resolve.

Support for the Mujahideen was the cornerstone of what soon came to be known as the Reagan Doctrine—a global package of widely publicized covert aid for anticommunist guerrillas fighting the established governments in Nicaragua, Angola, Kampuchea (Cambodia), and Afghanistan. In most cases, the United States continued to recognize the target government while paying for its overthrow. (A shell of an American embassy still operates in Kabul.) The Reagan Doctrine was an ideological statement of a global war against communism, and its aim was to establish the United States as a player in the global game of guerrilla politics. What the Soviets had done in the 1960s and 1970s, when they were encouraging wars of national liberation and providing at least moral support in successful leftist revolutions, the United States would do by sponsoring right-wing guerrilla movements in the eighties. For the president's right-wing supporters, the symmetry and the poetic justice of the Reagan Doctrine were irresistible. But a number of specialists in the foreign-policy establishment and some veterans of counterinsurgency wars were skeptical, for they understood how deceptive the symmetry was. In none of the four countries selected for major American military aid did the freedom fighters have any chance of winning. The real question was whether the benefits of harassing the Soviets and "showing the flag" were worth the costs and the risks of further involvement. A week after the interagency meeting at which the decision was made to send Stinger missiles with American markings to guerrilla forces fighting the leftist government in Angola and to the Mujahideen, John McMahon resigned from the CIA.

The decision to send Stingers was popular in Congress, because it almost certainly prevented the Soviets from crippling the resistance—and after Soviet sweeps in 1984 and 1985 it had begun to look as if the resistance might collapse. But the more sophisticated the weapons flowing through the Pakistani pipeline to the resistance, the greater the likelihood that the weapons would end up in some other war and the money in some unauthorized pocket. In October of 1987, fragments of American-made Stinger missiles were found in the wreckage of two Iranian gunboats: the missiles had supposedly been captured by the Iranians in a border clash with the Afghan rebels but almost certainly had been sold to them. Unknown but significant quantities of other weapons supplied to the Afghans have found their way onto the world arms market. One reason the CIA's covert operation in Afghanistan has been so expensive is that the weapons, mostly of Soviet origin, are bought from former Soviet-aid recipients, such as Egypt, or from arms traders. As in the Iran-Contra affair, millions of dollars can disappear in exorbitant markups, middleman fees, and sloppy accounting.

Some members of Congress feel that one important declared foreign-policy objective of the United States has been a casualty of the Afghan war: for most of the past eight years, the United States has suspended the operation of Section 669 of the Foreign Assistance Act, which is aimed at preventing nuclear proliferation, and has continued to aid Pakistan despite widespread suspicion that it is secretly building a nuclear bomb. Under legislation passed last December, the Pakistani government—apprehensive that when the war ends it will come under intense American pressure to curb its nuclear program—is assured that for at least two years the nuclear issue will not be used by Congress to disturb the flow of United States aid. The administration had urged that this assurance be given, presumably to ensure Pakistan's cooperation in the covert war.

Diego Gordovez is a professional peacemaker. He is an Ecuadoran lawyer who has spent most of his career as an international civil servant. For six years, he has been traveling back and forth among Geneva, Moscow, Kabul, Islamabad, and Washington, seeking to define issues and narrow differences among the four principal parties involved—the governments of the United States, the Soviet Union, Pakistan, and Afghanistan. Only Pakistan and Afghanistan are formal participants in the Geneva negotiations, but Moscow and Washington have been regularly consulted. The Mujahideen have officially denounced the negotiations, and Iran has kept aloof. In Geneva, Cordovez shuttles between two nearby conference rooms in the old League of Nations Palace, taking messages back and forth between the Afghan and Pakistani officials, who will not sit in the same room. The areas of agreement are embodied in carefully phrased, lawyerly prose in four draft instruments bound in a handsome leather folder. Cordovez is a resourceful, elegant draftsman, with a gift for finding the useful ambiguities that propel agreement. He is an incurable optimist—optimism being a temperamental requirement for this line of work—and is known affectionately among skeptical diplomats in Pakistan as the Señor of the Tunnel at the End of the Light.

The United States formally endorsed the United Nations mediation, but for the first three years it showed little enthusiasm for the negotiations to end the war in Afghanistan. After the 1985 Geneva summit, Washington began to change its public position. On December 13 of that year, Deputy Secretary of State John Whitehead declared that the United States would agree to be a guarantor of a settlement. The hope that the hard-liners had nourished—that the United States would recognize the alliance of Mujahideen groups as a government in exile—collapsed after a widely publicized meeting between a prominent resistance leader and President Reagan, at which the idea was firmly rejected.

Three of the four instruments on which the peace is to be erected were virtually completed more than three years ago. (A fifth, which provides for the monitoring of the agreement by the United Nations, was agreed upon in 1986.) The first of the documents includes a mutual pledge of noninterference. The second provides for international guarantees of the settlement. The third is an agreement for the voluntary return of the refugees in safety. In 1985, these three agreements were accepted by the governments of Pakistan and Afghanistan, and Iran ended its public denunciation of the peace talks. The fourth instrument, which specifies the timing for the withdrawal of Soviet troops, had been the sticking point, but in February of this year the Soviet Union suggested completing its withdrawal in a ten-month period and set May 15 as the date when the process would begin. Acceding to the insistence of the United States, Gorbachev agreed to remove half the Soviet troops within ninety days and to complete the withdrawal by March 15, 1989. The Soviet Union has made its withdrawal conditional on the cessation of outside aid to the resistance, and that principle is embodied in the draft agreements.

For six years, the Soviet Union had sought to engage the United States and Pakistan in a negotiation for a coalition government for Afghanistan as a precondition for the withdrawal of its troops. From the first, American officials had made it clear to Cordovez that the United States would not be drawn into such a negotiation. A senior official told us after Gorbachev's visit to Washington last December that the superpowers should not be in the business of inventing a government for Afghanistan. As far as the United States was concerned, there was only one issue: Soviet withdrawal. For six years, the Pakistani government had adopted the same posture, which it called a principled position of noninterference, a way of saying, "Let Afghans settle their own affairs." It had also been widely regarded in Washington and Islamabad as a nonnegotiable position, for it seemed inconceivable that the Soviet Union would walk away from Afghanistan without some assurance of a friendly government in Kabul. But in February the Soviets announced that they no longer insisted on making their withdrawal conditional upon the establishment of an acceptable government.

The switch in the Soviet position provoked an immediate switch in the position of Pakistan. Like the "bleeders" in Washington, Pakistani military and intelligence officials had far more invested in fighting the war than in ending it. The Soviet capitulation to the American and Pakistani position that Soviet troops simply withdraw without a political settlement struck Zia as a betrayal of Pakistan. He spoke bitterly to newspaper editors in Islamabad. "America and Russia have reached an understanding," he said. "By brokering in coal, we have blackened our face." In the absence of a coalition government including the Mujahideen, refugees, and the ruling PDPA, he said, "Soviet withdrawal would only lead the country into chaos, bloodshed, anarchy, and civil war." In such a situation, millions of refugees in Pakistan would resist being returned to their homes. Zia's concerns are understandable. Unless there is a broad political settlement inside Afghanistan, supported by the superpowers, there will be no peace in the region. And Pakistan, though it may continue to receive enormous revenues from the war, will also feel its devastating effects—crime, addiction, and violence caused by the drug trade, the refugees, and the bombings in every major city. Nevertheless, Zia is reported to have dropped his insistence that a transitional coalition government be established in Kabul before the withdrawal agreement is signed, provided that Cordovez continues "private" efforts to arrange one after the Soviets leave.

But there is one remaining serious obstacle to a negotiated end to the Afghan war. As the talks in Geneva moved toward what appears to be their final phase, a coalition of supporters of the Mujahideen in Congress, rightwing activists, and skeptical columnists mounted an attack on the settlement. The two strongest supporters of the Mujahideen in Congress, Representative Charles Wilson, of Texas, and Senator Gordon Humphrey, of New Hampshire, condemned the Geneva agreements as a sellout of the Afghan "freedom fighters," because the accords called for a cessation of aid to the Mujahideen without committing the Soviets to stop giving aid to the Kabul government. Humphrey characterized the Geneva agreements as "indecent," "scandalous," and "dangerous." Wilson suggested that it was not necessary to sign the agreements, for the Soviets were "defeated" and would have to withdraw militarily in any event.

Seventy-seven senators, led by Majority Leader Robert Byrd, went on record in opposition to the agreements, and President Reagan claimed that he was personally unaware of the commitment—although it had been announced in 1985—that the United States would be a guarantor of the agreements. He wrote Byrd that a cessation of United States aid "must be matched by a cessation of similar aid to the regime in Kabul." The Soviets have rejected the principle of reciprocity on much the same ground used by the United States in the past. (Aiding recognized governments is an established prerogative of sovereign governments; supplying armed guerrillas fighting the government is normally regarded as subversion.) At no time during almost seven years of negotiations had the United States ever brought up the matter of government-to-government aid to Afghanistan. As hopes faded for an early agreement in Geneva, the Soviet Union, as some of the "bleeders" in Washington had predicted and hoped, announced that it would withdraw its troops from Afghanistan even without an agreement, but in its own time and in its own way.

A unilateral Soviet withdrawal would not mean an end to the war; it would mean a new kind of war. Even with a political agreement on a coalition government, which is still possible, Afghanistan faces continued fighting—wars of retribution between the Mujahideen and those who have collaborated with the Russians and fights among the different factions within the resistance movement. Gulbuddin Hekmatyar, who was recently elected chairman of the alliance of resistance groups in Peshawar, vows that he will not stop fighting until he has established a fundamentalist order in Afghanistan, and he has promised to continue the fight from Iran if Pakistan closes its doors. (He has also boasted to interviewers that he plans to liberate the Muslim republics of the Soviet Union.) But without a political settlement subscribed to by the United States and the Soviet Union, the war in Afghanistan will be bloodier. It will become a two-sided proxy war between the superpowers. Covert aid will continue to the Mujahideen, and the Soviets will continue to supply aid, advice, and military hardware to the Kabul regime. It is widely believed in Washington that the Communist regime cannot survive the departure of the Soviet troops. That is probably true, although the Mujahideen are politically weaker and the government is stronger than is generally assumed in Washington.

The Afghan government has stepped up its efforts to woo guerrilla leaders by cease-fires, amnesties, promises, and bribes. A few local commanders, some nominally loyal to Hekmatyar, the most extreme fundamentalist leader, have shown an interest in cooperating. A new constitution provides for local elections, a popularly elected parliament, and considerable autonomy for local tribal leaders, whose cooperation has been further encouraged with liberal payoffs. More than a thousand mosques have been constructed or rebuilt. Religious leaders have been given the power to review textbooks. Land owned by religious institutions is exempt from taxation. The markets in Communist Kabul are as free as those anywhere.

According to Selig Harrison, of the Carnegie Endowment for International Peace, who visited Kabul most recently in 1984, there is a hard core of Communist activists, about forty-five thousand strong, who still believe that despite its unhappy history the party is the only vehicle for modernizing their country. That is not an insignificant force in a country as divided as Afghanistan and in a society in which a politically committed individual can count on the loyalty of many family and tribal members. Moreover, many people in the middle class, though they are strongly anticommunist, fear the fundamentalists almost as much as they loathe the Russians.

In the United States, the war in Afghanistan has been seen across the political spectrum as the good fight against communism. Few Americans are aware that the most strongly supported elements of the "freedom fighters" bear a remarkable resemblance to the fundamentalists of Iran, who, of course, have a quite different reputation in the United States. Nor are most Americans aware that the United States is committed, under a 1959 mutual-security agreement, to take "appropriate action, including the use of armed forces," in the event of an attack on Pakistan. Such an attack, inspired and organized by the Soviet Union, has been under way for almost two years. In January of 1986, a bomb exploded in the Pakistan International Airlines office in Peshawar, killing several people, and since then there have been terrorist bombings in all the major cities, which are assumed to be the work of the Soviet-controlled Afghan secret police. Soviet planes regularly conduct air attacks along the frontier. The message seems clear. Pakistan is a fragile nation, and the Soviets are in a position to inflict even greater punishment.

Regrettably, the establishment of a stable peace in South Asia has not been a high priority of the Reagan administration. The prime objective has been to humble the Soviet Union and force it to withdraw its troops. The withdrawal is almost certain to take place; without the establishment of a government in Kabul more acceptable to the Afghan people than one dominated by either the Communists or the fundamentalists, though, the war will enter a new stage when the Soviets leave. How costly and brutal the war will continue to be will depend on the outside powers. The Geneva agreements provide the essential framework for Soviet-American collaboration in the reconstruction of Afghanistan and the creation of a stable peace in the region. At a critical moment in United States–Soviet relations, they offer an unprecedented opportunity to test the possibilities of positive common action. The alternative is another round of bloody games. As the Soviets pull back, the specter of Lebanon—another once-peaceful country caught up in other people's struggles—hangs over Afghanistan.

[1988]

# 43 / STALEMATE AT JALALABAD

The Islamic Mujahideen's full-scale assault on Jalalabad began on March 6, three weeks after the last Soviet soldiers left Afghanistan. On March 8, Sibghatullah Mujaddidi, the president elect of the interim Islamic government of Afghanistan, announced that his cabinet would convene there in three days. More than seven months later, the struggle over the historic city continues. It could become bloodier. During June, July, and August, when the fighting was light, the United States sent vast quantities of heavy weapons to the Mujahideen.

It is a costly, merciless battle. Western journalists who have visited Jalalabad have reported on the devastation caused by Mujahideen rocket and mortar attacks. John Burns of the *New York Times* found the city "a sad, crumbling shell," alive with "blossoms of mimosa, jasmine, and bougainvillea." "But little else," he wrote, "resembled the Jalalabad of prewar years, a city celebrated for its palaces, orchards, and gardens." Less visible than the rubble are the dead: an estimated 12,000 to 15,000 killed since the assault began. Mujahideen deaths alone are believed to be 4,000. Across the border, in Peshawar, Pakistan, hospitals that I visited in April were so crowded with the wounded that tents had to be erected outside. Since the Soviet withdrawal, another 100,000 Afghans have joined the more than 3 million refugees there.

Destruction of cities is not uncommon in our time, but only rarely have people destroyed their own cities. In wars of liberation, patriotic forces are known to have taken special risks to safeguard their country's heritage and resources. Irrespective of whether Jalalabad capitulates, its ruin has already discredited both those who ordered and those who executed the attack.

We leave, for now, the question of who gave the order. It is more important to ask why the siege has lasted longer and proved bloodier than the experts had predicted. Some analysts have blamed the lack of unity of purpose and command among the Mujahideen. They have also pointed to such "mistakes" as the wholesale slaughter of prisoners and defectors—actions that have stiffened the resolve of the defenders. Pakistani and American officials, who are responsible for the Mujahideen, do not dispute these claims but offer what they call a more fundamental explanation for the stalemate. Pakistan's foreign minister, Sahabzada Yakub Khan, himself a reputed former general, told the BBC on March 22 that the type of tactic required for set-piece battles "does not come naturally to guerrillas." The "Mujahideen had to come up with fixed defenses, mine fields, dug-in tanks . . . and were subjected to bombs and rocket attacks which they were unable to deal with." Two weeks after the siege of Jalalabad had begun, I spoke to Gen. Hamid Gul, then head of Pakistan's Interservices Intelligence, which has been advising and arming the Mujahideen. He, too, impressed upon me the alleged limitations of guerrilla fighters. The Mujahideen, he said, needed time to adjust to the exigencies of conventional warfare.

Purely as explanations of the Mujahideen's failure to knock out government forces quickly, despite considerable deployment of firepower, these statements have some truth. But as general commentaries on guerrilla warfare they belong to the nineteenth century, when Spanish irregulars led by Francisco Mina harassed Napoleon's army without defeating it. Liberation then was ultimately achieved by conventional armies. This view of guerrillas was reinforced during World War II, when Italian partisans and French Resistance fighters sabotaged Mussolini's and Hitler's forces but could not mount battalion-sized attacks. In our time, however, the guerrilla army is also the army of liberation, and so the standard of comparison arises not from the European battlefield but from the fighting grounds of revolution. What comes to mind is Dien Bien Phu, and its memory offers lessons for those who would wish to understand Jalalabad.

History has rarely recorded a victory more dramatic, decisive, and momentous. The 10,000 men, French and Vietminh, who died at Dien Bien Phu "may have done more to shape the fate of the world than the soldiers at Agincourt, Waterloo, or Stalingrad," concluded Bernard Fall in his classic history of the battle. Among its many consequences—the start in November 1954 of the Algerian war of liberation, France's eventual exit from NATO's military command, the beginning of the US war in Vietnam—Dien Bien Phu put to rest the myth that guerrilla forces are ill suited for set-piece battles.

In seven years of classical guerrilla fighting, the Vietminh had nearly depleted France's treasury, costing it $11 billion by the end of 1953, when Gen. Henri Eugène Navarre, the French commander in chief, decided to lure them into a conventional showdown. The assumption was that a war of siege "does not come naturally to guerrillas." Vo Nguyen Giap, the Vietminh commander, watched as the French dug in with their tanks and mortars, laid the mines, stocked the bunkers, and mobilized the air force to support their ground troops. Then, on March 13, 1954, he attacked.

The strangulation lasted only six weeks; by April's end, 13,000 well-armed French forces were huddled within two square miles of the fortress. For the colonial army, in the words of Fall, Dien Bien Phu had become "hell in a very small place." Gen. Christian de la Croix de Castriès appealed insistently but in vain to the United States for aerial intervention. On May 7, 1954, he came out of his bunker and, with 10,000 of the surviving men under his command, surrendered to the Vietnamese.

Strictly in military terms, the Mujahideen outside Jalalabad are at a considerable advantage compared with the Vietminh at Dien Bien Phu. In all battles, especially those involving siege, logistics have primary importance, and the Vietminh faced a logistical nightmare. Their supply lines extended across six hundred miles of uncharted jungle, swamps, and rivers. Along those lines tens of thousands of volunteers hurriedly built a network of roads and ferries that were hazardous for the Vietminh's Soviet Molotova trucks; hence bicycles became the mainstay of the supply system. With their seats replaced by bamboo sticks, each one carried up to four hundred pounds. The French air force was able to concentrate its interdiction raids on this well-circumscribed and arduous route, yet in the course of the battle, these "liberation trucks" delivered 6,286 tons of weapons, food, and gasoline to the fighters in the mountain redoubts. Another 2,000 tons were consumed by the carriers. The French received daily supplies: in the end, a total of 6,900 tons for a force one third the guerrillas' size. This was considerably more than besieged forces had received anywhere in World War II, including Stalingrad.

In Afghanistan, only about fifty miles of paved highway separate the Mujahideen's supply sources inside Pakistan from the Jalalabad front. Transport vehicles are plentiful and move easily; there is little interdiction by the enemy's air force and none by its commando units. By contrast, Kabul has difficulty keeping its forces supplied. The Mujahideen have intermittently closed the Kabul-Jalalabad road and shut the airport; helicopter landings and airdrops are rendered hazardous by ground fire, especially from the deadly Stinger missiles.

It might be argued that this logistical advantage is more than offset by a balance of forces that does not favor the Mujahideen. There is a rule of thumb that for a successful siege the attackers ought to outnumber their enemy by a minimum of three to one. At Dien Bien Phu, more than 60,000 Vietminh guerrillas surrounded the 16,000 French forces. In Jalalabad, the ratio is extremely lopsided: the government's forces are estimated at about 20,000, and the Mujahideen's have fluctuated between 6,000 and 12,000. However, given their lack of coordination, a more favorable ratio may not have helped the Mujahideen. Early during the siege, when volunteers swelled their numbers, the confusion was great, and the casualties were higher. "It is not an army; it is a mob outside Jalalabad," said one man wounded in the second week of fighting. Since then, the mob has been subjected to some military discipline, but the number of volunteers has declined, suggesting that either the spirit of jihad has dampened or, as the expectation of victory fades, the hopes of *maali ghaneemat*, or booty, have dimmed among the characteristically poor refugee volunteers.

Still, what is lost in manpower is consistently accommodated by the sophisticated destructiveness of the Mujahideen's weaponry. By contemporary standards and in comparison with the adversary, the Afghan rebels are better equipped than were the Vietminh. They have excellent weapons, including the latest-model Kalashnikovs and M16s, RPG 7 antitank rockets, highly accurate artillery, and antiaircraft batteries. The Mujahideen are brave and intuitive fighters. Their weaknesses lie in the political, not the military, domain. The strength of the Vietminh, by contrast, lay not in the quality of their arms but in their standing with the masses, their political organization and strategic planning.

Here we begin to unravel the riddle posed by Jalalabad's endurance. In sponsoring the war in Afghanistan, American advocates of the doctrine of "low-intensity conflict" have once again ignored the lessons of Mao Tse tung, who rewrote the theory and practice of revolutionary war, distinguishing it from simple guerrilla warfare. Wars of national liberation, he argued, involve four stages of development: essentially, organizing, ambush, encirclement, and assault. Revolutionary guerrillas organize politically; they delegitimize and outadminister the enemy before starting to outfight it. To gain support for the revolutionary movement, they set up participatory and governing structures among people and provide needed services in health, education, and arbitration through institutions parallel and superior to those of the government. After isolating it politically and administratively, they begin to push the government out physically by guerrilla tactics. Eventually, they encircle the cities and the government's other strategic strongholds; then they assault and liberate them.

The West at first denied the universality of Mao's theoretical contribution. In 1948, the successes of the People's Liberation Army were ascribed to China's special circumstances: the unpopularity and corruption of the Kuomintang, the Japanese invasion of Manchuria, political fragmentation, warlords, and the country's unique size and population. From Algeria to Indochina, humanity paid a heavy price for that denial.

Now, in Afghanistan, the Islamic resistance leaders have, by and large, skipped the first and last stages of revolutionary development. There are said to be exceptions; the most frequently cited is Ahmed Shah Massoud, a commander in the Panjshir region who has organized politically and divided his forces into units under a coordinated command. However, Massoud belongs to the minority Tajik ethnic group and does not have a significant following among the majority Pashtuns. Abdul Haq, a Pashtun commander active in the Logar Kabul area, is also reported to have developed rudiments of the required structure of support. It is difficult, though, to estimate these commanders' capabilities. Both have a flair for public relations. Both have been promoted by their Western sympathizers: Massoud is a favorite of the European, especially French, connections of the Mujahideen; Abdul Haq is favored by the Americans. In any case, a few good commanders divided by personal ambition, geography, and ethnicity are not likely to ally strategically. Typically, neither of the two has participated in the siege of Jalalabad.

The costs of ignoring the political task of establishing organic links between the resistance movement and the institutions of civil society—tribes, villages, urban communities—have also been revealed in Jalalabad. The tribes that live around Jalalabad do not actively support the Mujahideen. In some instances, tribal groups that hitherto had participated in the jihad are now cooperating with Kabul. Firdows Khan Mohmand is a case in point. Formerly associated with the fundamentalist Hizb-e-Islami Party of Gulbuddin Hekmatyar, his militia has become friendly, since November 1988, with Kabul. "Like many others in Afghanistan," one Afghan friend remarked to me in Peshawar, "he has the common wisdom of his people." Several other chiefs, from the Mohmand, Shinwari, Khugiani, and Safi tribes, have also reached accommodation with the government.

More ominous for the Mujahideen organizations, the pattern of defection is duplicated elsewhere. For nine years, the Afghan people rallied around the call for jihad against the Soviet military intervention. But beyond generalized promises of an Islamic state, the resistance organizations offered no positive or consistent vision that could motivate the population. The "Islamic polity" did not materialize in the liberated areas even in its most basic forms. Rather, as victory approached, Mujahideen behavior became positively un-Islamic. More than seventy Afghans were murdered near Torkham last November after they had surrendered to the Hizb-e-Islami; a similar incident occurred in March soon after the battle for Jalalabad had begun. From the provincial capitals taken by the Mujahideen—Asadabad, Kunduz, and Maidan (the last two recaptured by the government)—one hears shocking stories of excess, indiscipline, and infighting. During July and August alone, more than three hundred persons were killed in a conflict between the Hizb-e-Islami and the Jamaat-i-Islami parties. My conversations with Afghans in Peshawar and in the refugee camps indicated that since March the number of rebel volunteers has steadily dropped. "The jihad," said Hasan Kakar, an Afghan academic who had spent years in the government's prisons, "has now lost its meaning."

It might be said that this development was inevitable so long as everyone involved in Afghanistan ignored the central assumption of Mao's theory: that the fulfillment of revolutionary tasks requires the sovereignty of the liberation movement, its independence from foreign powers. Washington's goals for Afghanistan—rebel seizure of power, dissolution of the present army and bureaucracy—appear revolutionary. "It is necessary," Ronald Reagan insisted at a news conference on November 4, 1988, "to start from scratch." Yet precisely because they are Washington's goals, they cannot also be revolutionary.

Meanwhile, the Mujahideen are often treated like mercenaries. Afghan observers and participants in the Jalalabad battle spoke of the assault on March 6 as being "ordered" precipitately, lending credence to Henry Kamm's April 23 story in the *New York Times*, which concluded that the decision to attack was taken in Islamabad by Pakistani and American officials without the participation of a single Afghan. A group of Afghan intellectuals complained bitterly that the story did not cause "a ripple" in Washington. Even the avowed friends of Afghanistan in Congress, such as Senator Gordon Humphrey and Representative Charles Wilson, remained silent. The Afghans find it incredible that foreign officials decided to send thousands of Afghans to die in battle. "And our so-called leaders obeyed!" they repeated in an angry and disbelieving tone. Radio Kabul broadcast the *Times* report for days.

In this story, and the harsh reaction to it, lies the fundamental difference between the resistance politics underlying the battle of Dien Bien Phu and that of Jalalabad. The Vietminh's supplies came from China; some were of Russian origin. But at no point did the Chinese or Russians tell the Vietnamese when and how to conduct their struggle. The achievements of national liberation movements are inextricably linked to the degree of legitimacy commanded by the resistance leaders and organizations. Political independence was essential in maintaining the legitimacy of the Vietminh as an authentic and sovereign national movement. Unfortunately for all sides to the conflict, the war in Afghanistan has been like *buzkashi*, the rough and costly Afghan game of horsemanship that invariably requires rich and powerful sponsors. One set of players has been managed by the Soviet Union; another by Pakistan and the United States. Since the Soviet troop withdrawal, the regime in Kabul has come to look relatively less like a foreign agent, and the Mujahideen have appeared to be increasingly dependent, divided, and directionless.

During two visits to Peshawar last spring I was impressed by the reversal of Afghan attitudes. In the camps and out, refugees speak of their Peshawar-based leaders, and of Washington and Islamabad, in terms previously reserved for the Najibullah regime and the Soviet Union. The talk is no more of the puppet government in Kabul or of the real and imagined progress of the resistance. There are complaints aplenty of disunity, corruption, excesses, and, above all, of the dependence of Mujahideen leaders on the United States, the Wahabis of Saudi Arabia and especially Pakistan. It is a raw experience which forces one to recall a well-worn cliché: the Mujahideen organizations and their sponsors have lost the struggle so crucial in wars of this sort for the hearts and minds of the Afghan people.

[1989]

# 44 / IN A LAND WITHOUT MUSIC

I have seen the future as envisioned by contemporary Islamists. It horrifies and does not work—anywhere. Today we look at two towns in Afghanistan.

Kandahar, an old city and monument in many ways to Afghan aesthetics, is a vast architectural ruin; its forbidden soul hides perhaps in the rubble. The town's physical destruction was caused largely during the war between the communist regime and its Russian patron and their Mujahideen opponents. After their "victory," the latter have robbed it, as they have most of Afghanistan, of hope and proscribed the pursuit of happiness. Music is banned in historic Kandahar, which had once been famous for its bards and storytellers. Play is forbidden.

Several among the Taliban who rule Kandahar marched a boy through the bazaar; a rope around his neck, hands on his shaven head. He had broken "Islamic law." He had been caught red-handed, I was told—playing ball. Football is forbidden under Taliban rule as are basketball, volleyball, and other games involving the movement of the body. I did not meet any of the Talib leaders. So I do not know what they claim as the reason for this prohibition. People, including those who should know, say that the Taliban's concern is morality, sexual morality to be exact, and its logic by analogy—*qiyas*—is the same that prohibits women from appearing unveiled in public: boys playing ball can constitute undue temptation to men.

In Islamabad and Lahore, friends told local stories to suggest that what I had encountered in Afghanistan is not the iceberg but only its tip. One of these had a well-known maulana object to Imran Khan polishing his cricket ball against the thigh on the ground that it was sexually provocative. The maulana's should have been entered into *Playboy*'s list of kinky kicks. In any case, the mention of cricket reminds me that in the matter of sexuality there may be a comparison of sorts between the English public schools and our religious *madaris*. In both, there is a deeply suppressed dimension of guilt and anxiety about sexuality; in both, an excess of fantasy and a culture of denial; in both, a presumption that suppression and secrecy can yield a moral community.

There are, of course, many differences between Harrow and the *deeni madarsah*. In context, one contrast is fundamental: in the English public school, the enforced prudishness is viewed as transitional, a necessary harnessing of adolescent drive although it does leave lasting scars on many grownup "boys," as John Le Carré's novels have brilliantly portrayed. In the *madarsah*, on the other hand, it aims at lasting socialization in an ideology, a way of life. I spoke to a couple of Taliban who sat in the bazaar, Kalashnikovs cradled in their laps. *Tihara* and *Ta'zeer*, purity and punishment, had constituted a core of their studies. They learned in Peshawar. The Taliban are products largely of our *madaris*, especially those run by the Jamiat-i-Ulema-i-Islami.

I counted a dozen persons clad head to foot in burka but in three days did not see a single woman in Kandahar. Women are forbidden from working in offices. The few who worked for foreign agencies were ordered to stay home. A similar order was enforced in Jalalabad. The day after I arrived there in June, heads of all the foreign agencies were called in by the Shura, given a long lecture in Pashto which they did not comprehend but which was summarized by an interpreter: you are not to employ an Afghan woman in your offices or in your projects if that entails any contact with a nonfamily male (*namahram*). A Pashtun lady doctor, who worked for a foreign agency, shook her head sadly, stoically.

Jalalabad's authorities are liberal compared with Kandahar's. The Shura is drawn from various parties among which the Hizb-e-Islami of Maulavi Yunus Khalis is dominant. Its governor, Haji Qadeer, is a brother of Abdul Haq, the Khalis group's most powerful commander. Together, the governor and the Shura have permitted schools to remain open; only a limited number are. The Taliban, on the other hand, have banned all schools for teaching corrupt knowledge. Fortunately or otherwise, they have not provided alternatives. Foreign women work in Jalalabad and can be seen moving in cars. More Afghan women in burka are seen shopping than in Kandahar.

It is an eerie experience to walk through the bazaars of Kandahar. Shops are shacks on the ruins of what had been a distinctive architecture of red clay over brick, reminiscent of Marrakech, where I had once spent restful, music-filled days. They are stacked with small electronic products, including transistor radios. Yet none is playing. These bazaars are devoid of music, which is banned in Kandahar, in homes no less than in public. Television is similarly banned. Homes are regularly raided, and people are harshly punished for listening to music. The chowkidar in the house next door to mine was caught in the act and badly mauled. He misses his recorder and the tapes of "sweet Afghan *naghma* [melody]." By contrast, Jalalabad's rulers frown upon music but do not enforce their antipathy with much zeal. Several times I heard the contraband played discreetly in Jalalabad, but never in Kandahar. "There are levels of hell," remarked an international expert from a Muslim country.

Smuggling is clearly not a sin. In both towns, its evidence is open and abounds. In Kandahar, you can see truckloads of tires, electronics, and glassware from Iran moving toward Quetta. From Jalalabad, the volume to Torkham is greater, and the trade is apparently mutual though by no means balanced or equitable. Nearly all food, wearable, and household items in Jalalabad are from Pakistan. Car smuggling is apparently brisker from Jalalabad than from the Kandahar side. I visited four "parks" in Jalalabad and found only one near Kandahar's Pakistan border. Each had hundreds of new cars; some bore Kuwait and Emirate license plates. Pricing suggested that one can get a Honda Civic delivered in Pakistan with a Pakistani license plate for about one and half lakhs, less than the standard Pakistan price. On larger cars, one saves more. "Traders support the Taliban," says an informed relief worker, "as they do the Jalalabad Shura. They respect commerce and protect property."

Drugs remain the largest single item of trade, but beyond hearsay and evidence of much unearned wealth concentrated in a few hands, it is not visible. In fact, Afghanistan offers a most bleak picture of a country denuded of all material, moral, and human resources. Nearly all of eastern and southern Afghanistan's intelligentsia has left the country. The few educated men I met in Jalalabad and Kandahar worked for a foreign agency, lived in hostels, and on weekends returned to their families in Peshawar or Quetta. Friends and families I knew had moved to Europe or North America.

Yet the two towns are viewed as havens of sorts by thousands of hapless victims of unholy warfare among the Mujahideen. They have moved from Kabul and its environs to the parched, sun-scorched inhospitality of the areas around Jalalabad and Kandahar. You see their dismal camps along the road to Pakistan. Leave your car; you stand upon a stark, burning earth, surrounded under the hot sun by very beautiful children. Grimy, ill-clad, obviously undernourished, yet with sparks of intelligence in their eyes and enough pride to refrain from begging. Some forlorn-looking men eye the scene from a distance without interfering, but there are no women in sight. They are obviously inside those small ovens made of tin and mud. *Salaam alaikum*, and the children light up. "Do you want water?" asks one boy.

Their positive disposition is an inheritance of a gentler past, an Islam not rigid like the one projected by contemporary Islamists and also less given to profit and consumerism. So what future awaits those children, who must grow in the harshest possible circumstances, without the "corrupting" influence of modern education, without play, and without music? I am haunted by what an old man in a mosque had said about the Taliban: "They have grown in darkness, amidst death. They are angry and ignorant and hate all things that bring joy and peace in life."

[1995]

Three aspects to the Taliban's unusual story are noteworthy: One, in the two years since they emerged as yet another group of "Islamic" warlords in Afghanistan, their victories have been unexpected and remarkably easy. Two, in power, they impose regimes of bestiality that have few parallels in history, including Muslim history. Three, the United States government welcomed the Taliban despite the fact that it casts itself as the global defender of human rights and declares Islamic fundamentalism as a menace to world peace. What "great games" underlie these ironies?

The Taliban emerged in the fall of 1994. The warlords who then controlled Kandahar, Afghanistan's southern province, blocked Pakistan's attempt to open a trade route to Central Asia. The Taliban challenged them. The blockade was lifted, and the young mullahs who were educated in Pakistan's religious schools won control of Kandahar rather handily. During a visit there in 1995, I reconstructed from interviews a pattern to the Taliban's victory: while they put on demonstrations of firepower, contacts were made with commanders on the other side, bribes were offered, and defections arranged. The rival warlords abandoned their positions when they sensed isolation and perceived Pakistan's Interservices Intelligence (ISI) as backing the Taliban, when battles promised to be costly and defections demoralized the warlords' remaining forces. (ISI had orchestrated for a decade the American- and Saudi-financed jihad against the Soviet Union; as such, it retains a certain hold on Afghan political imagination.) To date, the Taliban have not fought a sustained battle, preferring indiscriminate artillery and rocket attacks to encounters with the adversary. This pattern held right until September 20, when Jalalabad, near Pakistan's frontier, surrendered without a fight. This was a most strategic loss as it cut off Kabul's primary supply routes. A week later, the Taliban entered Afghanistan's battered capital after the forces of Ahmed Shah Massoud had abandoned it.

The logic behind this unusual pattern of warfare is worth noting. The Mujahideen's war against the Soviet Union was fueled by a mix of elements. Generous American and Saudi contributions provided the Mujahideen parties financial incentives; these multiplied vastly as a multibillion dollar trade also grew in guns and drugs. Afghan nationalism and the rhetoric of jihad against godless communism provided a framework of popular support for the war against Soviet occupation. Pakistan's military intelligence, the ISI, played a central role in balancing factional ambitions and maintaining a semblance of peace among rival Mujahideen leaders. International, especially American and Pakistani, backing of the Mujahideen held up their morale.

Soviet withdrawal from Afghanistan changed the relationship of forces on which the morale and motivation of the Mujahideen groups had rested. It ended the mobilizing role of nationalism and the ideal of jihad. People were tired of warfare and not inclined to take sides among warlords. The superpower withdrew its lucrative, reassuring patronage. With the termination of the West's covert operation, Pakistan's interest in keeping peace among Afghans diminished. What remained were the political ambitions and greed of leaders and commanders, trade in drugs, accentuated battles for turf, and a culture of dependency whereby real or imagined preferences of America, Pakistan, Russia, Iran, and India influenced the calculations of commanders and politicians. Warlords pursued their interests in isolation from the people. Alliances, shaped largely by mercenary considerations, shifted with dizzying frequency. Gulbuddin Hekmatyar became ally and adversary alternately of the Taliban, Uzbek warlord Dostum, and Tajik commander Massoud; so did all the others. Since the affiliations of leaders and followers were shaped by material calculations, there was a premium on deals and defections.

Taliban leaders are ignorant and rigid men. They have no aptitude for negotiations and compromises. It is obvious that they are being helped by professionals. But who? Afghanistan's ousted government has been accusing Pakistan. In September 1995, when Herat, an ancient town on Iran's border, fell to the Taliban, an officially sponsored mob burned down Pakistan's embassy in Kabul and mauled the ambassador. Rumors also attribute a role to the United States. Undersecretary of State Robin Rafel's visit to Kandahar last

April and meetings with Taliban leaders lent credence to those rumors. "What induces Washington to overcome its antipathy to the fundamentalist extreme," observers in Islamabad asked, "and what compels the Taliban to meet an unveiled foreign woman, a practice they denounce as un-Islamic?" Iran accuses Washington publicly and Islamabad privately. Pakistan denies these allegations. As in all covert operations, there is a lack of hard evidence.

Evidence abounds of the Taliban's oppressive ideology and style. They snatched former president Najibullah and his brother out of the UN's protection, tortured, then murdered them. Their corpses hung in a Kabul street for forty-eight hours, dollar bills stuffed in their mouths. What the Taliban inflicted on Kandahar, they are now inflicting on Jalalabad and Kabul. Girls of all ages are banned from school. Women are forbidden to work outside their homes and ordered to cover themselves from head to foot. Kabul's schools have lost 80 percent of their teachers, all female, government offices have 50 percent less employees, and hospitals have but few male nurses. An inch of exposed female body cause her to be beaten in public by gun-toting Talibs. During the three days following Kabul's "liberation," reporters witnessed four instances of female beatings. The Taliban's hospitality to Ms. Robin Rafel notwithstanding, they remain unreconstructed misogynists. Mullah Turabi, a member of their Supreme Council, stormed into a press meeting in Kabul on September 28. "Why are you talking to infidels?" he screamed at Officer Gul Mousa and slapped him. AP's Islamabad-based woman reporter was there, a lightning rod. "Quickly, tell this woman to get out," he ordered.

Men are better off, but only marginally. All have been ordered to grow beards. Schools are forbidden to teach corrupt—read modern, secular—subjects. Music is banned. So is play. I saw a twelve-year-old boy paraded along the bazaar in Kandahar, his head shaven, looking pained and bewildered. He had been caught red-handed, in an alley—playing ball. Last week, a foreign journalist's music cassettes were confiscated from his car in Kabul. Apparently the Taliban find boys playing ball to be sexually provocative, and music a carnal stimulation. I wish the American media would stop its "according to strict Islamic rules" qualifiers. The Taliban's strictures are products of pathology; they have nothing to do with Islam or Muslims. Thousands of Kabul's inhabitants are fleeing their homes. They are trapped in hell as Pakistan, refuge to some three million Afghans, has now closed its border.

The equanimity of official US reaction to the Taliban's capture of Kabul contradicts Washington's stance on human rights and extremism. The day

Kabul fell, Associated Press quoted a US official as saying that the Taliban "are unlikely to become the sort of Islamic fundamentalists like Iran because they follow a different brand of Islam." Reminded that Afghanistan's neighbors were concerned that the Taliban's victory may encourage fundamentalists elsewhere, the official said that "We are not persuaded that the concern is legitimate." The next day an unidentified State Department official told reporters that diplomatic relations with Afghanistan, in abeyance since 1979, shall be reestablished when the security situation improves. The State Department announced that a special envoy shall soon visit Kabul.

The Taliban are Sunni fanatics. As such, their hatred of Shia and neighboring Iran is theologically rooted, an opportunity the US government finds too tempting to miss. But this may not be the only incentive to forgo liberal commitments. Two American energy corporations—UNOCAL and Delta Oil—have been wanting to build gas pipelines from Turkmenistan to the Gulf coast of Pakistan. One pipeline from the Daulatabad field 890 miles to Pakistan is projected to cost $2 billion; another from Chardzhou to 1000 miles on the Indian Ocean may cost $2.5 billion. The pipelines must traverse Afghanistan. Both companies were said to be betting on the Taliban, who regard it a religious duty to support commercial interests. On October 1, Mr. Chris Taggart, executive vice president of UNOCAL, told Reuters that "We regard it [Taliban victory] as very positive." He urged the US to extend recognition to the new rulers in Kabul and thus "lead the way to international lending agencies coming in." Senator Hank Brown, one of a handful of legislators actively involved in that region, held that "the good part of what has happened is that one of the factions at last seems to be capable of developing a government in Afghanistan."

Senator Brown spoke too soon. The week after entering Kabul, the Taliban ran into trouble. Their advance to the north where Ahmed Shah Massoud's forces have retreated was stalled. They were ambushed and took heavy casualties. As minister for defense, Massoud was the mainstay of the government in Kabul. A talented tactician and able soldier, he was the most effective guerrilla commander against the Soviet forces in Afghanistan. But his government lacked viability because it was dominated by an ethnic minority, Tajiks like Massoud. It did not have credible representation of Pashtuns, the majority group which has long ruled Afghanistan. To offset this weakness, Gulbuddin Hekmatyar, the Pashtun extremist of the Hizb-e-Islami and longtime foe of Massoud, was brought in as prime minister last year. The move severely divided Massoud's supporters. It also alienated the moderate Pashtuns who had supported the government. Hekmatyar proved more a burden than asset. His whereabouts are not known.

A mere one hundred Taliban captured Jalalabad, the strategic Pashtun town near Pakistan's border, on September 20. In winter, Kabul cannot be supplied except from Jalalabad, Herat, and Kandahar, now all under Taliban control. Massoud's best option was to retreat to his stronghold in the north, regroup, realign, and counterattack. He made an orderly retreat, taking all his armor. In the last week, his forces have been mauling Taliban units around the Salang Pass which divides eastern Afghanistan from the north. He has also formed a coalition with Abdul Rashid Dostum, the powerful Uzbek warlord who was once a nationalist, then a communist, and always an intrepid opportunist. Abdul Karim Khalili, leader of the Shia of Hazarajat province, has also joined the new coalition. Thus the three largest ethnic minorities—Tajik, Uzbek, and Hazara, who make up a third of Afghans—have coalesced against the Taliban, who are Pashtuns with shallow roots and a dubious reputation among their own people. The stage is set for more warfare or the partition of Afghanistan along ethnic lines.

Britain is long gone. The Cold War is over. But the great game still casts its shadow on Afghanistan. Russia's consul general was present when the three anti-Taliban groups formally announced their alliance. The coalition is also supported by the former Soviet republics of Uzbekistan and Tajikistan, and, of course, Iran may be expected to lend a helping hand. Afghanistan is the calf in this *buzkashi*, the game of horsemen snatching at a hapless carcass. It is a loser's game. There is much bloodletting, and no one gets the beef.

[1996]

In his letter to *Zarb-i-Momin*, the Taliban publication, Mr. Azam Tariq, leader of Pakistan's violently sectarian Sipah-i-Sahaba party, is ecstatic over his ideological brothers' recent victories. His ecstasy is shared by Pakistan's national security managers, but for nonideological reasons. The attainment of "strategic depth" had been a prime object of Pakistan's Afghanistan policy since the days of General Zia ul-Haq.

In recent years, the Taliban replaced Gulbuddin Hekmatyar as the instrument of its attainment. Their latest victories, especially their capture of Mazar-i-Sharif, the nerve center of northern Afghanistan, brings the Pakistani quest close to fulfillment, if, that is, in addition to residing in some military minds, such a thing as "strategic depth" does exist in the real world.

In does not. In military thought, it is a nonconcept unless one is referring to a hard-to-reach place where a defeated army might cocoon. Far from improving it, the Taliban's victory is likely to augment Pakistan's political and strategic predicament. The reasons are numerous and compelling. Consider, for example, the following:

A fundamental requirement of national security is that a country enjoys good relations with its neighbors. If one is unfortunate enough to have a neighbor as an adversary, then its security interests are best served by maintaining excellent relations with the others around it. Pakistan has had the misfortune of being born in an adversarial relationship with India, a populous and resource-filled country. This enmity shows no sign of abating and is now augmented by the nuclear arms race and proxy warfare. The growth in provincial and ethnic discontents renders Pakistan especially vulnerable now to covert warfare. In this critical period, the country needs friends in the region. The regional environment has been favorable to consolidating old friendships and forging new ones. Instead, Islamabad is alienating both actual and potential friends.

Until recently, Pakistan has always had good relations with Iran and China. In this decade, new states emerged in Central Asia, augmenting the number of Pakistan's potential trading partners and strategic allies. Cold War's end also ended its hostility with Russia and held the promise of friendly regional alignment. Afghanistan was long an irritating but innocuous adversary with territorial claims on NWFP, Pakistan's largely Pashto-speaking province.

The Soviet intervention in Afghanistan and Pakistan's support of the anticommunist Mujahideen ended Islamabad's hostile relations with Kabul and rendered its influence dominant over Afghanistan. Pakistan has misused this gain to its detriment. Its Afghanistan policy—the quest of a mirage misnamed "strategic depth"—has deeply alienated trusty old allies while closing the door to new friendships. Its national security managers have in fact squandered historic opportunities and produced a new set of problems for Pakistan's security.

Tehran is openly hostile to Islamabad's support of the Taliban. "We had an agreement with Pakistan that the Afghan problem will not be resolved through war," said the judicious former president Hashemi Rafsanjani in his Friday *khutaba* [sermon] last week. "This has happened now and we simply cannot accept it." Thereafter, hundreds of Iranians protested in front of the Pakistan embassy in Tehran against the "fanatical, mediaeval Taliban" who held eleven Iranian diplomats hostage and mercilessly bombed civilian quarters of Bamiyan, a predominantly Shia town. Iran's foreign minister, Kamal Kharazi, called the Taliban's capture of Mazar-i-Sharif a "threat to the region." A resolution of the United Nations Security Council appeared to concur. Russia issued a warning. Tajikistan and Uzbekistan responded to Taliban advances by shoring up their defenses.

Pakistan's foreign office responded with strongly worded declarations of innocence and neutrality in Afghanistan. Not one diplomat at the UN headquarters in New York regarded these claims as credible. This worldwide loss of credibility is hardly a foreign policy achievement. Also, denials are not a substitute for policy. The fact is that Iran, an important and traditionally friendly neighbor, is deeply alienated by what it regards as Pakistan's sponsorship of the

Taliban. Russia, a major power, protests it. Recently independent states—Uzbekistan, Tajikistan, and Kirghizia—that had once looked up to Islamabad for help and guidance now regard it with apprehension. Pakistan appears today morally and politically isolated, a condition it shares with the Taliban, who present to the world a most distorted and uniquely repugnant visage of Islam. It is not possible yet to surmise the consequences of this isolation, but it is certain that it will greatly augment the sense of insecurity that for five decades has haunted Pakistan and contributed much to its misery and militarization.

The cost of Islamabad's Afghan policy have been augmenting since 1980, when Mohammad Zia ul-Haq proudly declared Pakistan a "frontline state" in the Cold War. Those costs—already unbearable in proliferation of guns, heroin, and armed fanatics—are likely now to multiply in myriad ways. The Taliban will certainly be assisted by Islamabad to consolidate their precarious conquests. Successful or not, this will be an expensive undertaking, an expense we are ill prepared to bear. Taliban victories have not put an end to their challengers; they are there and do not lack sponsors. The prospect is for protracted proxy warfare. It may cost some billions to keep the Taliban in the saddle, assuming that we avoid being sucked into a larger war with Iran or Russia or both.

Afghanistan's reconstruction cost is conservatively estimated at some $40 billion. We cannot muster such amounts even for ourselves, so who will keep the Taliban in business? The strategic dreamers of Islamabad dream of dollar-laden Saudi princes, Emirate sheikhs, and American oil tycoons laying transnational pipelines from Turkmenistan to Karachi. They are veterans of false and deadly dreams such as the great Kashmiri uprising in support of Operation Gibraltar in 1965 or the powerful reinforcements which the American Seventh Fleet was bringing to Pakistan's army in East Pakistan, now Bangladesh.

Pakistan is being trapped again in risky illusions, and again the people not the decision makers will pay the price. Without the resources of a great power, Pakistan has entered the game—both nuclear and nonnuclear—that great powers found difficult to sustain. So help us God!

The domestic costs of Pakistan's friendly proximity to the Taliban are incalculable and potentially catastrophic. Our embroilment, willy-nilly, in the bin Laden affair is a case in point. More importantly, the Taliban's is the most retrograde political movement in the history of Islam. The warlords who proscribe music and sports in Afghanistan, inflict harsh punishments upon men for trimming their beards, flog taxi drivers for carrying women passengers, prevent sick women from being treated by male physicians, banish girls from schools and women from the workplace are not returning Afghanistan to its traditional Islamic way of life, as the Western media reports sanctimoniously.

They are devoid of the ethics, aesthetics, humanism, and Sufi sensibilities of traditional Muslims, including Afghans of yesteryear. To call them "medieval" as did the protesters in Tehran is to insult the age of Hafiz and Saadi, of Rabi'a Basri and Mansur al-Hallaj, of Amir Khusrau and Hazrat Nizamuddin. The Taliban are the expression of a modern disease, symptoms of a social cancer which shall destroy Muslim societies if its growth is not arrested and the disease is not eliminated. It is prone to spreading, and the Taliban will be the most deadly communicators of this cancer if they remain so organically linked to Pakistan. The Sipah-i-Sahaba leader's greetings to his Afghan co-believers is but one signal of the menace ahead.

Policy makers in Islamabad assume that a Taliban-dominated government in Kabul will be permanently friendly toward Pakistan. The notion of "strategic depth" is founded on this presumption. This, too, is an illusion. The chances are that if they remain in power, the Taliban shall turn on Pakistan, linking their brand of "Islamism" with a revived movement for Pashtunistan. I have met some of them and found ethnic nationalism lurking just below their "Islamic" skin. It is silly to presume their debt to Pakistan as an impediment to their ambitions. Old loyalties rarely stand in the way of new temptations. Also, as the threat of local rivals recedes, their resentments against Pakistan's government shall rapidly augment, as Islamabad will not be in a position to meet their expectations of aid. The convergence of ethnic nationalism and religion can mobilize people decisively. However inadvertently, Islamabad is setting the stage for the emergence in the next decade of a powerful Pashtunistan movement.

There may still be time to help avert the disasters that are likely to accrue from the Taliban's domination of Afghanistan. Our interest lies in the establishment of a common peace there, one as welcome to Afghanistan's other neighbors as to us. Our future is best served if power in Afghanistan is pluralistically shared by its ethnic groups, for that alone can inhibit the pursuit of ethnically based territorial ambition. If we must live with a theocracy next door, it is better to live with an enlightened rather than a barbaric version of it. Also, if Afghanistan is to regain life, it needs a government hospitable to international aid; the Taliban are not.

It is unlikely that the architects of Islamabad's Afghanistan policy shall pay heed to arguments such as these. Dissenting points of view have always been ignored in Pakistan with tragic consequences. After hesitating for a while on the side of wisdom, Ayub Khan ignored them in 1965. We were relatively young and gullible then, so they lost a costly war and declared victory. In 1971, Yahya Khan, Z. A. Bhutto, and others dismissed the warnings of impending disaster as treachery and lost half the country. Z. A. Bhutto rejected friendly early criticism of the failings of his government, suppressed the magazine in which they were published, and ruled on to be overthrown and executed by a usurper of his choice. He alone paid for his blunders personally; for those of the others, only the land and the people continue to pay. Yet they do not hear and do not see even the obvious. No wonder they are looking for "strategic depth."

[1998]

# 47 / JIHAD INTERNATIONAL, INC.

The violence of Islamism has emerged as a subject of anxious concern throughout the world, especially the Muslim world. In the United States, the Islamic resistance to Israel's occupation of Lebanon, the West Bank, Gaza, and Golan and such incidents as the alleged plot to blow up the World Trade Center in New York City have aided the media and other propagandists' politically motivated campaign to demonize Muslims and Islam as a threat to Western interests and civilization itself. Their motivation is suspect as it condones Israel's US-aided violence on an enormously larger scale while condemning Arab resistance to it. It is suspect also because, as we shall presently discuss, the United States and Europe have played a historic part in spawning the violence of groups and individuals they now denounce, rather brazenly, as "Islamic fundamentalist." The US and European countries largely withdrew from the enterprise after their interests had been served, while the native peoples among whom they promoted the violent ideological enterprise are continuing to pay the heavy price for it.

Countries, such as Algeria and Egypt, are virtually in a state of civil war between the Islamists of differing hues and secular, regrettably authoritarian, governments. Among these countries, Pakistan is distinguished in several ways: One, it is the original staging ground of jihad as an international movement. Two, unlike Algeria and Egypt, it has had a parliamentary system of government, with four elections since 1988 in which the percentage of votes for Islamic parties has been declining. Three, unlike Algeria and Egypt, where Sunni majorities predominate, Pakistan is a multidenominational country where non-Sunni constitute an estimated quarter of the population. Furthermore, even the Sunni are divided by theological disputes—the one between the Barelvis and Deobandis is the primary example[1]—which have tended to turn violent. Hence there is a proliferation here of violence. So far we have witnessed the mutual terror of Sunni and Shia, the terror of Sunni groups against Christians and Ahmedis, and killings across the Barelvi-Deobandi divide. The potential is enormous. Four, Pakistan remains Islamism's "frontline state," so to speak. The war in Afghanistan continues and, in multiple ways which I discuss later on, impacts on the internal developments in this country. Finally, Pakistan's is an ideologically ambiguous polity; here, political paeans to Islam have served as the compensatory mechanism for the ruling elite's corruption, consumerism, and kowtowing to the West. As a consequence, the ideologically fervent Islamist minority keeps an ideological grip on the morally insecure and ill-formed power elite. It is this phenomenon that explains the continued political clout of the extremist religious minority even as it has been all but repudiated by the electorate. Yet horrors escalate by the day, and neither their original sponsors nor the victims are doing much about it.

Pakistan is a prime example of the mayhem and official failure to address it. From the bombing of the Egyptian embassy in Islamabad to the recent massacre in Lahore's Mominpura Cemetery, this country is strewn with innocent victims of Islamist extremism. Yet these tragedies have barely caused any reflection in this country and others whose policies sowed the seeds of the so-called Islamic terror. The bare truth is that as a worldwide movement Jihad International, Inc., is a recent phenomenon: a modern, multinational conglomerate whose founders include the governments of the USA, Pakistan, Saudi Arabia, Egypt, and Israel. It was the American-sponsored anticommunist crusade in Afghanistan that revitalized in the last quarter of the twentieth century the notion of jihad as the armed struggle of believers. Israel's invasions and occupation of Lebanon, the West Bank, Gaza, and Golan continue to invest it with moral meaning and give it added impetus.

Never before in this century had jihad as violence assumed so pronounced an "Islamic" and international character. The twentieth was a century of secular Muslim struggles. The Ottomans fought their last wars in essentially temporal terms—in defense of a tottering empire and, at least in the Middle East, against predominantly Muslim foes. From the rise of Saad Zaghlul [1857–1927] to the demise of Abdel Nasser [1918–1970], the Egyptian national movement remained secular and explicitly Arab and Egyptian. This was equally true of the Iraqi, Syrian, Palestinian, and Lebanese national struggles. The Turks attained their liberation under the banner of an intemperate secularism. Iranian nationalists fought and forged a Belgium-like constitution at the start of this century. In India, Muslim nationalism—opposed by an overwhelming majority of Indian ulema—defined the demand and achievement of Pakistan. All these movements had some resonance among other Muslim peoples who were similarly engaged in anticolonial struggles, but none had an explicit pan-Islamic content.

*Jihad* (noun) = struggle, from the Arabic root verb J.H.D. = to strive—was nevertheless a favored word among Muslims in their struggle of liberation from colonial rule. When my brother was expelled from school after raising the nationalist flag, he was welcomed in our village as a *mujahid* = one who struggles. In the Maghreb, Algerian nationalist cadres who engaged France in an armed struggle for seven grueling years were called mujahideen, and their news organ was named *El-Moudjahid.* This newspaper was edited for a time by Franz Fanon, a non-Muslim, and the struggle was led by a secular organization—Front de Libération Nationale (FLN). In Tunisia, the national struggle was led by Habib Bourguiba, a die-hard and Cartesian secularist who enjoyed nevertheless the title of Mujahidul-Akbar. The word "jihad" did occasionally appear as a mobilizing slogan of the 1978 Iranian Revolution, but *Enghelab* (*Inquilab*)—revolution—actually dominated as the symbol of the uprising against the shah. After seizing power, Iran's revolutionary government adopted *Jihad-i-Sazindazi*—jihad for reconstruction—as its mobilizing symbol. Without a significant exception, "jihad" was used during the twentieth century in a national, secular, and political context until, that is, the advent of the anti-Soviet war in Afghanistan.

For the first time in this century, the standard-bearers of a Muslim people's struggle for liberation were Islamic parties opposed to "godless communism," committed to its violent overthrow, and dedicated to the establishment of an "Islamic state" in Afghanistan. Theirs was a jihad in the classical, strictly theological sense of the word. Ironically, they had the support of Western powers as no liberation movement ever did. The United States and its allies supplied to the Mujahideen an estimated $10 billion worth of arms and aid. They also invested in this jihad the legitimacy of their enormous power and the luster of their media-made glory. On one especially memorable occasion, when Afghanistan's hard-line Islamists visited the White House, President Ronald Reagan described them as the Muslim world's "moral equivalent of our founding fathers." Similarly, the American and European media played up the war in Afghanistan as the greatest story of the eighties. Foreign correspondents combed the Hindu Kush for stories of Mooj heroism. Competition for jihad narrative was so great that in one instance a major network, CBS, paid handsomely to film a staged battle between Islam and communism. As the Western media carries great importance and authority in the Third World, its Afghanistan war coverage made an enormous impact, especially on Muslim youth.

Within a year of the Soviet intervention, Afghanistan's was on its way to becoming a pan-Islamic jihad. Hundreds, eventually thousands, of young Muslims from places as far apart as Algeria and the Philippines, Sudan and Sinkiang, traveled to Peshawar and Torkham, received training in the use of arms, and under the strict guidance of various Islamic parties became ideologically ripe and tasted more or less of the jihad-in-the-path-of-God. The United States government and its vaunted intelligence agency saw in this process a Cold War opportunity to pit militant Islam against communism. Had the Soviet Union not collapsed unexpectedly, it is likely that the United States would still be benefiting from this historic mobilization of jihad.

We knew of the violent pan-Islamic character which the Afghan war was assuming with American sponsorship. But no country—not Algeria, not Egypt—protested the participation of its nationals in a distant war. Pakistan was hospitable to a fault while all watched casually, then looked the other way, until, that is, the chickens of Afghan insurgency returned home to roost. I found in 1986, for example, that Egyptian intelligence had an effective presence in Peshawar and excellent information on the demography of jihad. They were merely keeping an eye. America after all was an ally and benefactor; they could not interfere with its agenda. The demands for extradition started to reach Pakistan from Algiers and Cairo only after the US had cashed in its investments in Afghanistan and the gates of all hell had broken loose in Algeria and Egypt. But whom can Pakistanis request to rid their country of the thousands of armed zealots their government has nurtured and continues to nurture?

The jihad's pan-Islamic dimension was a historic new phenomenon. Since the great crusades in the Middle Ages, jihad had not crossed cultural, ethnic, and territorial boundaries. Pan-Islamism did emerge briefly as a movement in the nineteenth century, its banner having been raised by such ideologues as Jamal al-Din Afghani and warriors such as Syed Ahmed Shahid. At the climax of this pan-Islamic drive, India's Muslims launched into the

Khilafat movement to save the Ottoman Caliphate. Khilafat's leaders, the Ali brothers, did often describe their movement as a jihad.[2] But this was a non-violent agitation supported by such non-Muslim pacifists as M. K. Gandhi and frowned upon by Mohammed Ali Jinnah, who later founded Pakistan. More to the point, it had negligible pan-Islamic resonance. Arabs, Iranians, and Turks alike viewed it as an eccentric, uniquely Indian phenomenon.

Pan-Islamism survived only as an abstract agenda of a microscopic minority of Muslim intellectuals. Its influence showed in the works of some modern writers and poets including Mohammed Iqbal. The generalized sentiment of Muslim affinity on which pan-Islamism relied was real nevertheless and from time to time manifested itself in peoples' expressions of solidarity with coreligionists in Palestine, Bosnia, etc. Yet the national struggles of Muslim peoples remained national, and pan-Islamism endured only as an inchoate sentiment of solidarity.

By contrast, with the Afghanistan war pan-Islamism grew on a significant scale as a financial, cultural, political, and military phenomenon with a worldwide network of exchange and collaboration. Myriads of institutions—*madaris*, Islamic universities, training camps, and conference centers—came into being in Pakistan and other places. Sensing its enormous opportunity, traders in guns and drugs became linked to the phenomenon, creating an informal but extraordinary cartel of vested interests in gun, gold, and god.

Transnational involvement in the jihad not only reinforced links among Islamic groupings, it also militarized the conventional religious parties. Pakistan's Jamaat-i-Islami is an example. Until their involvement in Afghanistan, it was a conventional party, cadre-based, intellectually oriented, and prone to debate and agitation rather than armed militancy. Today, it commands, outside Pakistan's army and rangers, perhaps the largest number of battle-hardened and armed veterans. In 1948–1949, its chief ideologue, Maulana Abul Ala Maududi, had rejected, on theological grounds, the notion of jihad in Kashmir. Today, his party openly boasts of its militant involvement there. In effect, while the US government and media blamed Iran as the source of organized Muslim rage, armed Islamic radicalism was actually nurtured in Zia ul-Haq's Pakistan with American funding and the CIA's help. In recent years, other conventional Islamic parties—the Jamiat-i-Ulema-i-Islam and Jamiat-i-Ulema-i-Pakistan—have also been militarizing, thanks to their linkages with the Taliban, thanks also to their involvement in Kashmir. In addition, other armed sectarian groupings—the Sipah-i-Sahaba, Lashkar-e

Jhangvi, Harkat-ul-Ansar, Sipah-i-Mohammed, Lashkar-e-Tayba, Anjumane Sarfaroshane Islam—have emerged to menace society no less than the state. They are all sectarian formations, apparently a far cry from Islamism as expounded by the older religious parties such as the Jamaat-i-Islami and Jamiat-i-Ulema-i-Islam. Yet the fact remains that their antecedents lie with these parties, and they draw sustenance from the neighboring wars which are cast in Islamic terms.

The birth of Jihad International coincided with another development which has had a particularly unwholesome effect on Pakistan. Following the prolonged hostage crisis during which Iranian radicals held American diplomats captive in Tehran, a contest began between two versions of political Islam, one conservative and the other radical. One was sponsored by Saudi Arabia and, until 1988, Iraq; the other was supported by Iran. While the United States was involved in this development, its logic was essentially regional. Iran's revolutionary Islamists were quite uncompromising in opposing the US as an imperial power and in their rejection of monarchy as an un-Islamic form of government. As a pro-US conservative kingdom, Saudi Arabia felt threatened by Iran. Riyadh was quick to counter Iran's proselytizing zeal and was supported in this mission by such Gulf sheikhdoms as Kuwait. With the start of the Iran-Iraq war in 1981, Saddam Hussein's secular government joined in the theocratically cast campaign against Iran. Islamic organizations all over the Muslim world became beholden to one or the other side of this divide. In countries with mixed Sunni-Shia population such as Lebanon, Pakistan, and Afghanistan, this development had the greatest impact as sectarian groups and individuals found new incentive to arouse old hatreds. Neither the Americans nor Saudis and Iraqis may have intended to arouse anti-Shia feelings. They were merely interested in promoting their brand of conservative Islam to counter Iran's growing appeal. But in local terms anti-Iran was easily translated into anti-Shia. The Sipah-i-Sahaba is one such product of this process in Pakistan. It was first funded by Saudis; later Iraq stepped in. The terror and counterterror which followed have involved murders of Iranian diplomats and trainees, American technicians, and ordinary folks in mosques, imambarahs, and, most recently a cemetery. Battles for soul often degenerate into a hankering after body counts.

Citizens, keep watch! The chickens of "jihads" once sponsored by imperialism and the state have been coming home to roost. Afghanistan threatens to become a metaphor for the future.

[1988]

# KASHMIR AND INDIA-PAKISTAN CONFLICT

## 48 / BEYOND MUTUAL DESTRUCTION

Diplomacy does occasionally wear a farcical look, but nowhere more often than in South Asia.[1] During bilateral talks in 1993, India and Pakistan exchanged carefully drafted position papers. These were called "nonpapers." An American academic, Stephen Cohen, has followed in this tradition. He is the author recently (1996) of a nonplan, labeled the Cohen Plan. It is the subject currently of much interest in Islamabad, which has, to the best of my knowledge, not given any thought to a plan of peace with India.

Cohen's is an outline not for a settlement of disputes between India and Pakistan but for US sponsorship of a "Camp David process." It offers no clue to American or even the author's thinking on the principles that may guide the agenda of this process. It merely argues that the climate for an American initiative is favorable, that peacemaking in South Asia will be less expensive for the United States than was Camp David, which entailed large aid to Egypt in addition to the hefty billions Israel receives from the US, and that it will require patience, bipartisan consensus, and a well-reputed American mediator.

The closest Cohen comes to revealing the substance of the initiative he recommends is his model of the Camp David Accord. He deems it, as most American policy analysts do, a great success. But was it? Surely, by removing Egypt from the rank of frontline Arab states, it rendered unthinkable an Arab war against Israel. By the same token, Arab states and people became the objects of Israel's ambition and aggression. It was after Camp David that Israel invaded Lebanon, killing thirty thousand civilians, maiming thousands more, destroying its ancient villages, towns, and the capital city Beirut, where Israeli forces oversaw the Phalangist massacre of Sabra and Shatila. A portion of Lebanon remains under Israeli occupation, the site of weekly killings and dying, a monument to Camp David.

The Palestinians—who are the core of the Arab-Israeli conflict as the Kashmiris are of the Indian-Pakistani conflict—fared even worse after Camp David. The United States pretended to an arbiter's and guarantor's role; in reality it was on Israel's side. When negotiations between Anwar Sadat and Menachem Begin deadlocked over the question of unlawful Zionist settlements in the West Bank and Gaza, Jimmy Carter staked his presidential prestige to assure Sadat that Israel would not establish more settlements. The ink had not dried on the Camp David Accord when Begin announced the establishment of new settlements. Jimmy Carter protested, verbally and in vain. While massive US aid continued to pour into Israel, it expropriated nearly 60 percent of Palestinian land and all of its water resources. The augmented harshness of the occupier rendered life well nigh impossible for the hapless people of the West Bank and Gaza. Dispossession on a large scale was one outcome; the outbreak of the Intifada was another.

The Camp David Accord is viewed, not incorrectly, as the foundation stone of the Oslo and Cairo agreements between Israel and the PLO. Officials no less than most journalists and scholars in the United States have been offering these as first steps toward Palestinian statehood. I, among others, have argued that Oslo is liable to yield not a Palestinian state but a state of apartheid in the Middle East. Its outlines had already emerged under Yitzhak Rabin and Shimon Peres, though both prime ministers were viewed in Washington as apostles of peace.

Two distinct humanities live in Israel and under its occupation—one Jewish, the other Arab. One enjoys full citizenship rights, the other does not. One claims sovereignty, the other is denied it. One controls the land and its resources, the other does not. They live in separated spaces, the one as a free people, the other as a besieged people. These realities become uglier and more complex as new roads, public facilities, and institutions are constructed with American aid. They create new facts of apartheid and inequality. It's an awesome tribute to the power of belief that perfectly normal scholars, like Professor Cohen, offer Camp David as a successful model.

As Washington shows interest in midwifing an India-Pakistan agreement, Pakistan's policy makers—where are you, oh, where?—ought to reflect on Camp David's example. No two histories are similar, yet analogies help analysis. Egypt and Israel went to war thrice in three decades; so did India and Pakistan. Palestine served as a major bone of contention in the Middle Eastern conflict as Kashmir does in South Asia. As Pakistan has over four decades, Egypt expended much energy posturing about resistance and liberation while ignoring Palestinian right to representation and paying scant attention to a changing world environment. As frustrations piled over failures, Egypt put all its eggs in the American basket. "Ninety percent of this problem can be solved by America," Anwar Sadat was fond of saying. Pakistan has been inviting third-party mediation for some time. As a ploy to engage the sympathies of others it has not worked. It is unlikely to serve as a mechanism to obtain even a modicum of justice for the Kashmiris or peaceable Indo-Pakistan relations. Rather, American mediation may harm Pakistan as it harmed the Arabs.

• • •

The United States' interests in South Asia are those of a great power, largely economic and partly strategic. Moral issues of human rights and self-determination play but a minor role in policy making. It is self-defeating to get distracted by Washington's professions of virtues and neutrality. Realistic analysis would suggest that in the role of mediator, the US shall be keen to bring about peace in South Asia while favoring India over Pakistan and the two states over the stateless Kashmiris. Consider, among other factors, the following:

India is a large market roughly eight times larger than Pakistan; this ratio is reflected in the current volume of American investments in the two countries. It is many times more endowed in natural resources than Pakistan. Also, India is better positioned for rapid economic growth by virtue of educated manpower, infrastructure, and standards of skill and literacy. Strategically, it is a large and populous country, in important respects a counterpoint to China. As a post–Cold War structure of international relations emerges, the United States seeks balancing mechanisms to strike a favorable equilibrium in its relations with China. India can serve this purpose better than any other country in Asia except Japan. For these reasons, Washington has to be more keen to ensure the goodwill and stability of India than of Pakistan.

Nations, realists are fond of reiterating, do not have permanent friends, or permanent enemies. They only have permanent interests. During most of the Cold War years, the United States government saw political Islam as its ally and an adversary of communism. Today the reverse is true; it views Islamic movements the world over with deep distrust and active hostility. Between 1989, when Kashmir's powerful nationalist insurrection began, and 1992, when it developed an Islamic character with Pakistan's help, America's intelligence services supplied their policy makers an alarming picture of militant Islam emerging in the strategic Kashmir valley with Pakistani, Afghan, and Iranian involvement. This impression of Kashmiri resistance has been reinforced by the proliferation of a score of armed Islamic groups in Kashmir.

Like all paramount powers, the United States is a status quo power. In areas of its interest and influence it favors stability over change. Kashmir's liberation movement has been increasingly perceived in Washington as a destabilizing force in South Asia, especially if it makes significant gains toward its goal of total separation from India. They see the Jamaat-i-Islami and Jamiat-i-Ulema-i-Islam gaining legitimacy, popularity, and armed strength from their role in Kashmir, thus changing the comfortable current balance in favor of temporal parties of Pakistan. In India, Kashmir's separation can only aid the militant Hindu parties, which have arrived perilously close to power. Above all, Kashmir's separation is likely to worsen India's tense communal environment; the BJP and its partners may ride the anti-Muslim wave. "We cannot afford," a Washington insider remarked some months ago, "Bosnia on a grand scale."

For these and more reasons, Pakistan will be wise to encourage US interest while declining its mediation in our relations with India. Thanks, but no thanks! Islamabad's challenge is to explore other, better options. Unfortunately, it does not appear poised to meet it.

A lasting peace between India and Pakistan remains, nevertheless, an urgent necessity. Hostility between the two will continue to distort the political and economic environment of both countries, inflict upon their inhabitants the augmenting costs of subversion and sabotage, inhibit regional cooperation, and force more than a billion people to live perpetually under the menace of nuclear holocaust.

Indian-Pakistani disputes over Siachin Glacier and Wullar Barrage are easily resolvable; in fact, the basics of agreement over these two issues have already been reached in bilateral talks. Kashmir is the primary source of conflict. It has outlasted most post–World War II conflicts—the Cold War, war in Indochina, the American-Chinese confrontation, South African apartheid, and the Israeli-Arab conflict. Three full-scale wars, frequent armed confrontations along the India-Pakistan border, years of Kashmiri uprising and Indian repression, and the beleaguered Kashmiris' enormous sorrows have not induced either India or Pakistan to shift from its position.

Delhi declares the matter settled, claims that Kashmir—under its occupation—is an integral part of India, regularly denounces and occasionally threatens Pakistan for its "interference in India's internal affairs," and has been trying for years to put down Kashmiri resistance—mercilessly, without pity, and in vain. Islamabad insists that Kashmir is an unresolved international dispute, and it must be settled by a plebiscite as originally envisaged by a UN Security Council resolution of over fifty years standing.

Neither position is sustainable. Pakistani and Indian decision makers will serve their countries well if they concede to the realities sooner rather than later. One, a military solution of the Kashmir dispute is not possible. Two, it is equally difficult to envisage, as India does, a unilateral political solution. Three, while the United States has a stake in peace between India and Pakistan, neither the great powers nor world opinion will make a decisive contribution toward resolving this conflict. Four, direct negotiations offer the only effective path to a peaceful solution. However, meaningful negotiations are not possible without Kashmiri participation. Hence the most sensible way to resolve the dispute is tripartite negotiations involving Pakistan, India, and a representative Kashmiri delegation. Direct negotiations do not preclude a facilitating role for the United Nation's or the United States. A discussion of these points follows.

Three models may be envisaged for a military solution: a conventional Indo-Pakistan war; a Kashmiri war of liberation ending like Cuba, Algeria, or Vietnam; and protracted guerrilla warfare followed, as India achieved in East Pakistan, by a decisive Pakistani military coup de grace. To a student of military strategy all three options would appear unrealistic. For differing reasons, neither Pakistan nor India is likely to win a conventional war. It shall, nevertheless, be unbearably costly to both countries. If perchance a decisive outcome appeared likely, nuclear weapons will surely enter the scene, resulting at best in an inconclusive cease-fire or, at worst, in a continental holocaust.

Military leaders in both countries share this estimation of the military balance and international environment. Barring the odd hawkish officer, they do not favor a full-scale military confrontation. That leaves the option of low-intensity warfare. In Kashmir, India is engaged as an incumbent; Pakistan supports the insurgency. It also happens in wars of incumbency and proxy that rivals hit each other with sabotage and subversion.

This Kashmiri uprising has lasted more than a decade, long enough for observers to discern its ramifications, possibilities, and limitations. India and Pakistan exchange accusations against each other on a regular basis. Since 1990, the two countries have engaged in a carefully calibrated war of proxy and subversion which has done both sides much harm. In the process, an estimated forty thousand Kashmiris are dead, and many more wounded. Kashmir's economy has been wrecked, and an entire generation of Kashmiris has already been deprived of normal upbringing and education. Yet armed struggle and Indian repression have not brought Kashmiris closer either to self-determination, which is Pakistan's demand, or to pacification, which India seeks. In fact, both countries are farther from attaining their goals in Kashmir than they were in 1989.

Kashmir's discontent is rooted in history, economics, politics, and psychology. The causes and dynamics of the Kashmiri movement lie in Kashmir and its experience with India. It is not a product of plotting and subversion by Pakistan. As such, it cannot be suppressed by force. Nor is it likely to be managed by electoral manipulations. Yet India has confronted the insurgency as incumbents normally do—with a combination of brute force, unlawful subversions, violations of Kashmiri humanity, and, above all, denial of reality.

In the last analysis, the successes and failures of counterinsurgency operations revolve around two questions: One, does the incumbent state enjoy at least residual legitimacy among the insurgent people? Two, is the incumbent power willing to accommodate those aspirations which converge to cause and sustain the insurgency? I have asked these questions twice before. Once, in 1965, in relation to America's war in Vietnam. Again, in 1971, concerning Pakistan's military operation in East Pakistan. For India, too, the answer to both questions is NO.

A rational approach to Kashmir shall elude India as long as its leaders are unable to confront this reality. The price of avoidance may not be for India the kind of military defeats which the United States experienced in Vietnam or Pakistan suffered in its eastern wing, now Bangladesh. Yet one can say with confidence that if India, Pakistan, and Kashmiris do not reach a mutually beneficial settlement, the protracted war among the three will continue, with lulls and heats. Its costs may be even greater in the future than the hapless peoples have already paid.

India's allegations notwithstanding, Pakistan had little to do with the insurgency which emerged full blown in 1989. In fact, Islamabad's military no less than civilian intelligence services were surprised by the intensity and scope of the uprising. It was united by and large behind a single organization, the Jammu Kashmir Liberation Front, which had most of the attributes of a winning young movement.

The great powers, especially the United States, have not evinced any interest in supporting Pakistan's position, which is legally and historically well founded. Islamabad has expended much effort and resources in trying to mobilize international opinion. In effect, lobbying for Kashmir has provided since 1989 the framework for hundreds of Pakistan's ministerial, parliamentary, and other international junkets. None of these has had any discernible impact. Even the United Nations and its Security Council, whose authority Pakistan invokes quite assiduously, have shown scant interest in the matter. An analysis of years of Pakistani effort to mobilize meaningful international support for its position on Kashmir suggests that neither the great powers nor international opinion are inclined to weigh in meaningfully on Pakistan's or the Kashmiri resistance's side.

• • •

India has lost Kashmir. Delhi's moral isolation from the Kashmiri people is total and, I think, irreversible in the sense that in order to reverse it India will have to envisage a qualitatively different relationship with Kashmir. But can India's loss translate into Pakistan's gain?

My answer is no! There is an inclination among policy makers to believe otherwise. This is not unusual. It is common in international relations for rival countries to view their contests as a zero-sum game whereby the losses of one side would translate into gains for the other. The American intervention in Iran (1953) and its costly involvement in Vietnam (1956–1975) were compelled in part by this outlook. The Soviet interventions in Hungary (1956) and Czechoslovakia (1968) were similarly motivated. History has repeatedly exposed this assumption to be false. The ratio of rival losses and gains is rarely proportional; it is determined by circumstances of history, politics, and policy. India's Kashmir record offers a chronicle of failures; yet none of these accrued to Pakistan's benefit. Rather, Pakistan's policy has suffered from its own defects.

Three characteristics made an early appearance in Pakistan's approach to Kashmir. One, although Pakistani decision makers know the problem to be fundamentally political, beginning in 1948 they have approached it primarily in military terms. Two, while the military outlook has dominated, there has been a healthy unwillingness to go to war over Kashmir. Three, while officially invoking the Kashmiri right to self-determination, Pakistan's governments and politicians have pursued policies which have all but disregarded the history, culture, and aspirations of Kashmir's people. One consequence of this is a string of grave Pakistani miscalculations regarding Kashmir. Another outcome has been to alienate Kashmiris from Pakistan at crucial times such as 1948–1949, 1965, and the 1990s.

The question asked at the beginning remains largely unanswered: has India's loss translated into Pakistan's gain? Another question needs to be asked: if both countries are failing in Kashmir, what next?

A reminder is useful: in the twentieth century, armed struggles have failed more often than they have succeeded. In the 1960s, no less than forty-five armed uprisings were in progress; six of these could claim success. A few, including the Kurdish, Irish, Timorese, and Filipino movements are still active. Their longevity suggests that while success may not be assured an armed uprising can endure or keep recurring if the aspirations on which it feeds are not addressed. A review of the Kashmiri movement suggests that it is falling in this latter category.

Popular support is an essential attribute of success. To win, consolidate, and maintain it is the greatest single challenge of an armed movement. To deny it popular following, drive wedges between it and the people, and reclaim the hearts and minds of the populace constitute the primary objectives of incumbents. This is one requirement the Kashmiri movement fully meets. As I argued earlier, India's federal government has lost all semblance of legitimacy and support among Kashmiri Muslims. Its moral isolation appears so total that it is unlikely to regain even a modicum of legitimacy without conceding in a large measure the Kashmiri aspirations which have converged around a single slogan—*Azaadi* [independence].

That slogan, Pakistan's policy makers and Pakistani partisans of Kashmiri struggle ought to acknowledge, translates as sovereignty for Kashmir. There exists among Kashmiri-speaking people but little enthusiasm for a plebiscite which would confine them to exchanging life under Indian sovereignty for life under Pakistan's sovereignty. It is only a rare Kashmiri—I found none among the dozens abroad or scores I have interviewed in Pakistan—who views Kashmir as an "unfinished agenda of partition." In the US, a Kashmiri academic from Srinagar asked: "East Pakistan has violently separated from the west. The Muslim nation of the Quaid-i-Azam is now divided into three sovereign states. So what unfinished agenda of partition are we Kashmiris required to complete?"

Unity is essential to success. But unity is rarely total. The Chinese, Algerian, Cuban, and Vietnamese movements confronted divisions, but in all four countries one party and leadership commanded hegemony over the others. At the start, the Kashmiri movement had the appearance of fulfilling this requirement. Soon after, the proliferation of parties began and became epidemic. There are no less than thirty-eight armed parties in the valley. Thirty of them are grouped in the All Party Hurriyat Conference, a welcome umbrella all but paralyzed by differing ambitions and styles.

Increasingly, the valley has become a free-for-all environment in which the distinction between crime and militancy has been blurred. The atrocities of the "reformed militants" are credited obviously to India's account. But it is also true that the excesses of other groups reflect on the standing of the movement as a whole. Pakistan is viewed as the purveyor of internal divisions as some parties and positions are known to be favored by Islamabad while others are not. In growing numbers, Kashmiris are beginning to regard themselves as dually oppressed.

Clarity and consistency of ideology and objectives are the third essential factor in keeping a movement strong and resilient. These are essential to maintaining the morale of cadres, solidarity of the people, and sympathy of neutrals at home and abroad. In an environment of armed struggle in which people invariably face great risks and cadres unusual hardships over long periods of time, morale, solidarity, and sympathy define success and failure in critical ways. Unfortunately, barely two years after it began, Kashmir's uprising started to suffer from split images.

At first, the movement led by the Jammu Kashmir Liberation Front appeared to be secular and nationalist. As such, it elicited support at home and a measure of sympathy both in India and abroad. When the Islamic parties, supported among others by the Jamaat-i-Islami of Pakistan, made a significant appearance on the scene, the effect was not only internal confusion and division but also the dissipation of actual and potential international support for Kashmiri struggle. To date, the governments of Pakistan and Azad Kashmir have spent millions of dollars to mobilize international support behind the question of Kashmir. Cumulatively, the score has been a pathetic zero. In effect, for each of these religious and secular, parliamentary and private carpetbaggers and patronage seekers, Kashmir's cause serves in Pakistan as one big pork barrel.

The creation and maintenance of "parallel hierarchies" of governance has been the distinguishing feature of liberation warfare in the twentieth century. Successful movements have tended to outadminister their enemy rather than outfight them. This is so because the gap between the military resources of states and the opposing guerrilla forces have widened greatly as a consequence of technological progress after World War I. An armed movement neither aims nor expects to defeat its adversary in conventional battlefields; events such as the battle of Dien Bien Phu are exceptions not the rule. Liberation organizations expect to exhaust the enemy—politically, economically, psychologically—through protracted struggle.

This is primarily political not military warfare. It demands systematic elimination of the incumbent's governing capability and its substitution by the movement's administrative and social infrastructure. Slowly and surely, the guerrilla organization assumes the functions of government—provides health facilities, schools, courts, arbitration, and collects (not extorts!) taxes. Thus the state's machinery becomes increasingly dysfunctional, delinked from the people. "Nous commençons légiférer dans le vide," the French had recognized first in Indochina, then in Algeria (We are legislating in a void!). And the liberation movement gets organically linked to the land and its people. It is this phenomenon that overcomes the vast discrepancy in the military power and material resources of the two sides. In 1989–1990, the Kashmiri movement showed signs of developing parallel hierarchies, an infrastructure of governance. Then, it lost interest no less than ability. It still has popular support but neither the will nor capacity to serve the people. In such a climate, a movement's support dissipates as people tire of hardships and suffering.

The location of the intelligentsia vis-à-vis a movement serves more as a signal than a decisive factor in wars of liberation. Individual exceptions notwithstanding, the intelligentsia is a cautious class, prone to opportunity seeking more than risk taking. In an environment of armed polarization, they wait and watch, and change positions as they sense the balance of forces shifting. The desertion of the intelligentsia from incumbency to the movement normally signals a decisive shift in favor of the latter. The opposite is also true.

In Kashmir, the intelligentsia inclined toward the JKLF in 1990, then began distancing from the movement as it recoiled from the excesses of Islamic militancy. Menaced also by Indian excesses, many middle- and upper-middle-class families moved to the safety of Jammu and Delhi. An estimated fifteen thousand Kashmiris are now enrolled at Indian universities. Although it is impossible to find an educated Kashmiri who does not disapprove of India's military presence in the valley, their class location vis-à-vis the struggle for Kashmir remains ambiguous.

Last, the material factors—the availability of arms, men, and logistical supplies—which significantly affect the course of a struggle. The best organized armed uprisings obtain much of their armaments from the enemy. "We must regard [French general] De Lattre as our quartermaster-general," was Vietnamese general Ngo Vuyen Giap's motto during the Indochina war. Algeria's guerrilla commander, Belkacem Krim, had his adversary, General Andre Beaufre, play roughly the same role. To my knowledge, Kashmiri militants are not capturing even 10 percent of their weapons from Indian forces. Their dependence on external sources of supply is total. I am not in a position to estimate the endurance and reliability of their external sources of weapons supply. One should expect it to be limited and sporadic.

Kashmir has a Muslim population of about 5.5 million. Of these, roughly half a million are estimated to be males of fighting age, between fifteen and thirty-five years. The state is their major employer, followed by agriculture and tourism, a trade wrecked by war. The pool of potential fighters is around a hundred thousand men. Of these, some forty thousand are dead, and an estimated sixty thousand have been disabled. Unbearable economic burdens on families are added to their enormous personal grief. There is a growing feeling among Kashmiris that the world, including their own world, has abandoned them.

The dispute over Kashmir is as old as independent India and Pakistan. This latest phase of violent strife has lasted over ten years. Yet while the human and material losses have mounted—beyond bearing for the Kashmiri people—neither India nor Pakistan has shown an inclination to end the bloodshed on any except its own terms. The three parties to this conflict have reached an impasse. It is now necessary for them to find a peaceful solution. I should first summarize the nature of the impasse.

If one views as crucial the distinction between governing a society and coercing a multitude, India has ceased to govern Kashmir. For reasons discussed earlier, its moral isolation there is total and irreversible if Delhi remains fixed on the terms which it currently offers. Its options then are threefold: One, to keep its coercive presence in Kashmir and hope that some day Kashmiris will tire and throw in the towel. Two, to negotiate with Kashmiri leaders on terms the latter could live with. Three, to negotiate a broader settlement with Pakistan and the Kashmiri insurgents who are grouped in the All Party Hurriyat Conference. We deemed a fourth, another India–Pakistan war, as an unrealistic option for settling the question of Kashmir.

India's current policy is to stick with option one while giving it a face-lift. This entails a focus on legislative elections and vague promises of greater autonomy. Although the US is encouraging it, the ploy is not likely to work because Kashmiri leaders distrust India's tenuous promise, and Pakistan encourages their rejection of it.

In comparison with the earlier period of their insurgency, the promises and options of the Kashmiris are circumscribed. The insurrection climaxed in 1993. That was an appropriate year for both Pakistan and Kashmiri insurgents to launch a vigorous political and diplomatic offensive. Since then the insurgency has not gained. Rather, its strength has been sapped. It faces internal divisions. The Kashmiri movement now confronts Indian-sponsored competitors and a more supple Indian counterinsurgency effort than was possible during Jagmohan's heavy-handed cruelties between 1990 and 1992.

· · ·

While Jagmohan cleared the ground of the more-or-less secular nationalists during 1990–1992, India's intelligence services connived, as Israel's had done earlier in Gaza, at the emergence of Islamic groupings in Kashmir. Pakistan's intelligence services appear to have missed the point. The emergence of multiple Islamic groupings has sectarianized the movement, dampened the enthusiasm of those Muslims who cherish their traditional, lived relationship to Islam, alienated a significant section of Kashmiri intelligentsia, and contributed greatly to militarizing what should have been primarily a political struggle.

US support for India's electoral initiatives has caused self-doubt and confusion among Kashmiri leaders. The lack of international support, civil war in Karachi, unrelenting reports of crisis and discontent in Pakistan and Azad Kashmir, and a drop in logistical supplies have also had a dampening impact on cadres and leaders. Above all, the people are showing signs of war weariness and economic hardship, and the movement has suffered from a decline in its manpower pool.

As a result, while Kashmiri insurgents are not about to surrender to India's coercion or manipulation, they are enfeebled politically, logistically, and psychologically. Itself in a severe economic crunch, Pakistan is unlikely to help in improving their fighting capability and morale with significantly larger logistical support. The outlook in Kashmir then is of low-intensity warfare continuing with ups and downs and costing its people heavily in blood, repression, and economic hardship.

All three sides are in a blind alley, back to back. India and Pakistan have the capacity, and apparently the inclination, to stay there indefinitely. Out of frustration and fatigue they might swing around one day and come to blows. The Kashmiris, being the weakest and most vulnerable party, have Hobson's choice: either give in to India and settle for what symbolic concessions they can get from the tormenting giant or continue with resistance, however sporadically. History is replete with examples of oppressed peoples who have done just that. Their sacrifices were always awesome. The shame and moral burden were always the oppressor's.

There is a third option of which the initiators can only be Pakistan and India. It requires those two armed adversaries to move toward the future, away from the fixed positions of half a century ago. For history moves by rendering fixed positions obsolete. Any good soldier, engineer, physician, philosopher, and historian knows the high costs of obsolescence. New realities are rapidly creeping over South Asia. Globalization is creating transnational assembly lines, breaking boundaries, forcing enemies to trade, creating transnational centers of power, and circumscribing sovereignties. South Asia governments are eager participants in the process. Prime ministers proudly claim MOUs [memoranda of understanding] as their achievement, cite figures of foreign investments, sign international trade agreements, and join regional cooperation treaties. India and Pakistan are signatories of the General Agreement on Trade and Tariffs (GATT), members in the World Trade Organization (WTO), Singapore-Australia Free Trade Agreement (SAFTA), and South Asian Association for Regional Cooperation (SAARC). Ironically, they cross swords in these councils of collaboration. New realities lead them to enter pacts of amity. Tired instincts and vested interests compel them to rake up the bile and bitterness of an earlier time.

One hand, stretched toward the future, is chopped off by another hand anchored in the past. This is but one, possibly the most harmful, manifestation of inorganic growth in the body politic of India and Pakistan. Such distortions will continue to grow as long as our governments do not restore to this region its natural millennial flow—of rivers and mountains, ecology and production, and commerce and culture. To become prosperous and normal peoples we must make peace where there is hostility, build bridges where there are chasms, heal where there are wounds, feed where there is hunger, prosper where there is poverty. Kashmir is the finest place to start, and not merely because it is the core of Indo-Pakistan conflict. Our histories, cultures, and religions have converged in Kashmir. Our rivers begin there, mountains meet there, and dreams rest there.

A framework of durable peace ought to provide incentives for each party to keep the peace and attach penalties for breaching it. The pertinent facts are the following: (i) Kashmir is divided. India holds Jammu, Ladakh, and the valley. Pakistan's sovereignty extends to Azad Kashmir, and the Northern Areas are virtually integrated into Pakistan as federal territories. (ii) With one major exception, the present division of Kashmir conforms to the principle on which the partition agreement was based in 1947. The exception is the valley, which is the center of opposition to Indian rule. (iii) While there exists no objective measure of nationalist sentiments, most observers believe that it runs deep, especially in the valley's Kashmiri-speaking population. (iv) The principle of free trade between India and Pakistan is now established. The actual resumption of normal trade is a question of time. To deprive divided Kashmir the right to exchange and trade will be to penalize the principal party and victim of the India–Pakistan conflict. (v) India–Pakistan relations, including trade, will not be stable until the question of Kashmir is settled by a tripartite peace process, and the arms race and war threat between the two neighbors will continue. (vi) In relation to Kashmir, India is the status quo power. Like all such powers, it is engaged in a "war of position." The Kashmiris are entering the second decade of an insurgency which aims at changing the status quo. As India's challenger, Pakistan should have engaged in a "war of movement," which in this instance translates into maintaining a politically and diplomatically dynamic and flexible posture. Instead, it matched India "position for position," thus creating for itself a crisis of policy and for the beleaguered Kashmiris an imbroglio of political fragmentation and diminishing resources.

Islamabad will continue to deny itself the advantages of a "revolutionary power" (i.e., one whose interest lies in changing the status quo) as long as it remains inexorably committed to the demand for a plebiscite, a demand for which there exists the backing neither of force, nor of the great powers, nor of international opinion. Rather, even the author of the plebiscite formula, the UN, is keen to repudiate it.

Hopefully, our policy makers realize that Pakistan's insistence on a plebiscite was a means to an end, not the end itself. That means is now out of date. A plebiscite is a noun without a verb, a car without an engine. Islamabad has to find other means to reach its goal of settling the question of Kashmir to the satisfaction of Kashmiri people and without compromising its own national interest.

The first step is to develop a policy, and a strategy to pursue it. It is unnecessary to spell out details. Details can change, and political maneuvers and diplomatic tactics alter to suit new developments and unforeseen events, while a broadly defined strategy continues to serve as a road map to the final destination. A key to developing a workable strategy is the concept of linkage.

In this instance, the question of Kashmir must be linked to the imminent liberalization of trade between India and Pakistan. Free trade may not survive and will not thrive if Kashmir is excluded from it, and the long miles of the India-Pakistan "line of control" remain closed to exchanges other than those of gunfire. The two issues ought to be presented as integral parts of a singular peace to be negotiated between India and Pakistan. The international community, which is keen to see the barriers of trade lifted between neighbors, should be urged to actively support a comprehensive settlement leading to normal trade and growing regional cooperation in South Asia.

It is difficult for nations not ravaged by war, as were Germany and Japan at the end of World War II, to shift suddenly from one state of mind to another. A period of transition, during which assumptions can be tested, trust is engaged, and new bonds are built across boundaries, is often preferable to precipitous peace of the kind that the Arabs of Egypt, Palestine, and Jordan have entered with Israel. In our case, it is important to proceed gradually, step by careful step, in a manner capable of absorbing shocks and building confidences. But peace, however gradual, must be based on common commitment to principles. These need spelling out.

One fundamental principle in this case is that the ultimate arbiters of the dispute over Kashmir are the people of Kashmir in all their diversity of past as well as recent history. Second, a settlement that does not restore the natural, millennial flow of Kashmiri history and geography is not likely to satisfy either Kashmiri aspirations or the requirements of durable peace between India and Pakistan. Third, the notion of sovereignty changed in the second half of the twentieth century; in the twenty-first century, it is in the process of changing drastically. Fourth, divided sovereignties are not synonymous with divided frontiers.

If these principles are followed, diplomacy might be directed at reaching an agreement which could be implemented in three stages, of autonomy, open borders, and shared sovereignty over historic Kashmir. If they fail to avail themselves of yet another opportunity, they shall remain holding unused and archaic cards in frozen hands. Such failures rarely harm the leaders. Only the people get hurt.

[1996]

# 49 / INDIA'S OBSESSION, OUR CHOICE

Young people to whom the future belongs are often right when powerful old men in khadis and suits are not. The Japanese youth who stood the other day holding a placard in Tokyo was absolutely right. "Nuclear test?" the placard asked after three tests by India, "Are you crazy?" Then there were five. "Gone berserk," was the Pakistan foreign minister's apt description.

It is well known that Indian leaders generally and the BJP-wallahs in particular are obsessed with projecting India as a big power. They view nuclear weapons as a permit to the club in which India does not belong and should not enter with a population of half a billion illiterate and four hundred million undernourished citizens. Furthermore, it is illusory to search for power through nuclear weapons. The nature of power changes in accordance with shifts in modes of production, knowledge, and communication. In our time, these shifts have been revolutionary. Power has changed in ways least understood by those who formally hold the reins of power.

Take the nuclear weapon. When first invented, it was viewed as a weapon of war and wantonly dropped on Hiroshima and Nagasaki. Its development and possession coincided with the rise of the US as a global power, a coincidence which confirmed it as a modern component of power. Its use also proved that it was a weapon of total annihilation, therefore not usable, notwithstanding the crackpot realists like Henry Kissinger and Herman Kahn.

After the USSR tested its hydrogen bomb, it became a weapon of terror and of deterrence against war between two giants in a bipolar world. It also served as an umbrella for covert, proxy warfare. Given these facts and its association with superpowers, in the 1950s, the identification of nuclear weapons with power was total. It was in the interest of the United States and the USSR to perpetuate this perception. But change has its own inexorable logic.

Three events helped devalue nuclear weapons as components of power. There were first the cases of Cuba and Vietnam. Together, the liberation movements of these two small nations reduced the most awesome nuclear power, in the words of Senator J. W. Fulbright, to "a crippled giant." Castro's revolution succeeded and survives to this day despite American nuclear power; in fact, the possession of nuclear weapons constricted American ability to destroy that revolution. The Vietnamese demonstrated that a nuclear giant can in fact be defeated, even militarily. France offered a negative example. It tested and inducted nuclear weapons as a means to challenge the paramountcy of the United States in Europe. It did not work.

A third, related reality dawned: the world was changing in a way that, for the first time in history, political economy took precedence over military might as a component of power. In Europe, the influence of France, now a nuclear power, does not surpass that of nonnuclear Germany. Similarly, Japan exercises much greater influence in the world than does China or France. South Africa and Israel offer contrasting examples. South Africa's prestige and influence in world politics increased after it had renounced and dismantled its nuclear arsenal, while Israel's considerable nuclear capability—so scandalously tolerated and augmented by the United States—has added not a bit to its influence or security in the Middle East or beyond. That, in 1998, India's leaders still view the possession of nuclear weapons as a necessary element to gain recognition as a world power speaks volumes about their intellectual poverty and mediocre, bureaucratic outlook.

In effect, these five tests may set back India's ambitions. As any politician and gang leader knows, power grows from the neighborhood. A country that does not command influence and authority in its own region cannot claim the status of a world power. India's standing with its neighbors, already low, will now sink further. It tested a fusion bomb, which demonstrated thermonuclear capability, then went on to test its ability to produce tactical weapons. This cannot but raise the anxiety of India's nonnuclear neighbors while contributing little to its military balance with China or Pakistan.

Similarly, while the tests may be psychologically satisfying or politically beneficial to the BJP's insecure leaders, the material losses to India may be greater than they surmise. India was expected in the coming years to achieve a growth rate of 7 percent. If the international sanctions, including technology transfers, are half as severe as Japan and the US are threatening, this may be in jeopardy. Lastly, with these tests Delhi may have put India in the fast lane of the arms race. A Third World country can crash more easily in such a race than the second world power did.

What then should Pakistan do? My advice is: do not panic and do not behave reactively. This translates as: do not listen to people like Qazi Hussain Ahmed and Benazir Bhutto who, either out of ignorance or more likely crass opportunism, are advocating nuclear tests, here and now. The arguments for steadying the jerking knee are compelling. Consider these: One, India is currently the focus of adverse world attention both governmental and popular and is likely to remain so for a while. A Pakistani test will immediately relieve the pressure on India and shift it to Pakistan with consequences surely worse for us than it would for India. Islamabad should not take Delhi's burden upon itself. Rather, this is time for it to mount diplomatic initiatives and international campaigns to put pressure on India both within the South Asian Association for Regional Cooperation [SAARC] and worldwide and reap some benefits for Pakistan's statesmanlike posture.

Two, Pakistan's objectives in developing nuclear weapons are different from India's. Delhi's nuclear program has been linked to the quest, however misguided, for power. Islamabad's is related to security. What Pakistan has sought is a shield against India's nuclear power. That requires the achievement of sufficient deterrence, which we possess by all appearances. India's five tests do not change that reality, at least not from what I know of strategic weaponry from a lifetime of studying it. Scientists and their managers like to test; that is what they do. The question we need to ask is: Are we less defense-capable today than a week ago? I don't think any honest person can answer in the affirmative.

Three, one major risk Pakistan runs is to get drawn into an arms race with India, a country with far superior resources than ours. There is evidence to suggest that India would like us to do just that. But we shall be getting into the wrong lane. The development of strategic armaments is an expensive business which carries little Keynesian logic. In other words, while it costs a lot, the economic multiplier is negligible. The reasons are that the development and production of strategic weaponry is a capital-intensive and largely secret activity, which means that it rarely yields either the economic multiplier or the technological spin-off. It is thus that the Soviet Union and its satellites such as Poland and Czechoslovakia became highly sophisticated arms producers but remained very underdeveloped economically. As a consequence, their states and societies grew disorganically and eventually collapsed. For Pakistan to avoid that fate, it must resist falling into the trap of seeking strategic equivalence with India. Our requirement is effective deterrence not equivalence. Deterrence demands fewer shifts in strategic planning and weaponry, providing a more stable environment for economic growth.

Finally, the most basic problems facing Pakistan today are economic and social. It is not an exaggeration to say that our future depends on how well we confront the challenges of economic slowdown and social fragmentation. Both are expressions of fundamental structural crises of our state and society, and neither is susceptible to simple crisis management. In an environment such as this, Pakistan is considerably more vulnerable to international sanctions than India, which, whatever its other weaknesses, has been and remains less dependent on foreign aid, loans, and technology transfers than we are. For these reasons and more, it is much better for Islamabad to stay cool and calculating and utilize the opportunities Delhi has presented. May reason prevail!

[1998]

I saw on television a picture more awesome than the familiar mushroom cloud of nuclear explosion. The mountain had turned white. I wondered how much pain had been felt by nature, God's most wondrous creation. The great mountain in Chagai will turn, in time, to solid ash! And we are so proud of our mountains. . . !

India's mindless right-wing leaders who started it all and then proceeded to goad Pakistan into baring its nuclear capabilities may never acknowledge that they have committed a crime against India and its neighbors and that not one good—strategic or tactical, political or economic—can accrue from their blunder. An Indian scientist, Dr. Vinod Mubayi, rightly says that the RSS has now killed Gandhi twice: his body in 1948 and his legacy fifty years later. India shall suffer for some time to come from the effects of these killings. It had enjoyed what the French call a *préjugé favorable* in world opinion, a mystique of being uniquely ancient and pluralistic, a land of Hindus and Muslims, Christians, Buddhists, and Zoroastrians, the spiritual home of Albert Luthuli, Desmond Tutu, Father Daniel Berrigan, and Martin Luther King. In a single blow, the BJP government has destroyed India's greatest asset. And more.

After decades of bitter squabble, India's relations with China, the world's most populous country and a fast-growing economic giant, had been improving for the last six years. Sino-Indian amity had reached a level significant enough for Chinese leaders to counsel Pakistan, their old ally, to resolve its disputes with India. In a conversation with me a few weeks ago, former prime minister I. K. Gujral cited Sino-Indian cordiality as a model for Indo-Pakistan relations. A high-level Chinese military delegation was in India when Prime Minister Atal Behari Vajpayee proudly announced his first three nuclear tests. These had preceded and followed anti-China rhetoric. India's greatest single foreign policy achievement of the last two decades was thus buried away like nuclear waste.

For nearly four decades, India's rate of growth had remained low at around 4 percent per annum. Economists the world over dubbed this mysterious consistency the "Hindu rate of growth." Then, a decade ago, the curve began to move upward, reaching a whopping 7.5 percent last year. Hope had never prevailed so widely in India since independence, and international capital had begun to view it as a grand investment prospect. Economists expected that in the next decade India would maintain a 7 percent rate of growth, just about wiping out the abject poverty that so assails its people. This expectation, too, has been interred in the Pokhran wasteland. International economists now estimate that in the current financial year (ending on March 31), India's growth will decline from the projected 7.5 percent to 5 percent; these estimates are based not on the effects of sanctions but on the adverse turn in the investment climate.

Excepting a few interregna, such as the short-lived government of I. K. Gujral, India's governments have not been very sensitive toward their neighbors. At regional and international conferences, a participant is often astonished at the antipathy delegates from Sri Lanka, Nepal, the Maldives, and Bangladesh express about India's policies. But I believe nothing has shocked and angered its neighbors more than India's unilateral and surprise decision to carry out its three-plus-two nuclear tests, thus starting a nuclear arms race and opening the way to a potential holocaust in South Asia. They have a right to anxiety and anger, as nature has so willed that they are no safer than Indians and Pakistanis from the nuclear fallout.

It is commonplace in Pakistan to hear that India seeks regional hegemony. A reminder is necessary, perhaps, that hegemony requires recognition of superiority by consent more than coercion. Delhi's latest actions deny rather than affirm the promise of hegemony. Pakistan does not have hegemonic ambition, yet I hope that Mr. Nawaz Sharif's government was gracious enough to at least inform our neighbors before the tests in Baluchistan.

Each historical time has had its own temper. But one factor has been common, throughout history, to the attainment of progress and greatness. Historians of culture describe this one factor variously as syncretism, openness, pluralism, and a spirit of tolerance. Where ideas do not clash, diverse influences, knowledge, viewpoints, and cultures do not converge, civilization does not thrive and greatness remains elusive. The rightist environment of religious chauvinism and intolerance that the BJP and its allies promote in India—it pervades Pakistan for other reasons—is deeply harmful to India's future. Nuclearization of nationalism has further degraded this environment. The tests have worsened the xenophobia of Hindutva supporters. Reaction, no less than a habit of emulation, among fundamentalist adversaries will undoubtedly reinforce right-wing sentiments and excesses in Pakistan.

In recent weeks, BJP supporters stormed a meeting of antinuclear scientists, attacked artist M. F. Hussain's home and destroyed his paintings, and, in retaliation against US sanctions, assaulted trucks carrying Pepsi and Coca Cola and disrupted a concert by Pakistani musician Ustad Ghulam Ali. "The atmosphere of intolerance has been gaining ground recently," says an editorial in the *Hindustan Times*. "Such actions will break up the very fabric of this country," warns Ambika Soni, a leader of the Indian National Congress. In Pakistan, government-owned television darkly and repeatedly suggested that opponents of a nuclear test were foreign agents.

India's leaders have long viewed nuclear weapons as a currency of power. They will soon realize that this is a counterfeit. I have pointed out previously that Hiroshima and Nagasaki had shown the bomb to be a nonusable weapon morally. Korea, Cuba, and Vietnam proved it to be unusable politically and militarily. By the mid-1960s, nuclear weapons had ceased to be a significant component of power. The rise of such nonnuclear giants as Germany and Japan and the collapse of the Soviet Union, a nuclear superpower, rendered the possession of nuclear weapons quite incidental to the equation of power in world politics. No advocate of nuclear tests has refuted me either in Pakistan or abroad. Then what in heaven's name were India's rulers seeking by detonating five nuclear devices? And why do we insist that Pakistan had no option but to follow India into the dumb pit?

I, and many others, have argued that Pakistan's best option was to let ambiguity serve the purposes it had served for a decade. There is no way to prove now whether we were right or wrong. The deed is done. A mountain is dead. But history demands that it be noted now that Prime Minister Nawaz Sharif's initially good instincts were overwhelmed by forces inside and outside Pakistan. Our knowledge of the factors that led to Pakistan's decision to carry out the tests is not complete, but enough is known to identify the main factors. The most important was the provocations of BJP leaders, but there were others, too numerous to recount here. These included a warning by L. K. Advani, India's home minister, that Pakistan should note a change in South Asia's "strategic environment," Prime Minister Vajpayee's statement that his government might forcibly take Kashmiri territory under Pakistan's control, the handing over of the Kashmir affairs portfolio to the hard-line home minister who had so enthusiastically overseen the destruction of the Babri Mosque, and the actual heating up of a limited but live conflict along the Line of Control. Pakistan's chief of army staff returned from the front line with an assessment that we may in fact be witnessing the slow beginning of a conventional war. To my knowledge, Delhi did little to reassure Islamabad.

These developments greatly reinforced a sense of foreboding among Pakistani officials. This was accentuated by what a decade of embargo under the Pressler amendment had done to the weapons sustainability of Pakistan's armed forces. During the decade of Mohammad Zia ul-Haq, Pakistan's defense forces reverted to heavy reliance on US arms. In the last decade, these have suffered not merely from obsolescence but also from a paucity of reliable spare parts. Pakistan could find itself unable to sustain a war with India without soon running into serious supply problems. In a military environment such as this, army leaders are likely to put a high premium on an assured deterrent capability. This much is known to interested military analysts the world over.

It is astounding that, under these circumstances, and after testing their nuclear device, India's leaders would engage in verbal and military provocations. Officials and legislators in Washington might also note that their antinuclear sanctions actually compelled a more rapid development and testing of nuclear arms.

In an environment so fraught, the government needed political support. Instead, Pakistan's opposition leaders—all except Ghinwa Bhutto, Air Marshal Asghar Khan, and Sardar Farooq Ahmed Khan Leghari—were in the streets taunting Mr. Sharif to "explode" a nuclear bomb. The pack was led first by Jamaat-i-Islami leaders, who were soon overtaken by Benazir Bhutto. She seems to have sensed in this national crisis an opportunity to restore her flagging fortunes. I know of few gestures in the ugly repertoire of Pakistani politics as revolting as her demagogic toss of bracelets at Mr. Nawaz Sharif.

The G-8 responded mildly and in a divided fashion to India's tests, signaling a soft response to the menace at hand and enhancing the Pakistani sense of isolation and risk. Finally, like the Indian tests, Pakistan's response was a tribute to the hegemony of the nuclear culture and notions of deterrence so assiduously promoted by the West during the Cold War.

The leaders of India and Pakistan have now appropriated to themselves, as others had done before, the power that was God's alone—to kill mountains, make the earth quake, bring the sea to boil, and destroy humanity. I hope that, when the muscle flexing and cheering are over, they will go on a retreat and reflect on how they should bear this awesome responsibility.

[1998]

The euphoria which had reportedly gripped India following the nuclear tests of May 11 and 13 has all but evaporated. The harsh realities of life in India are on the front burner again, and the BJP government appears no more stable that it did on May 10. Its precarious existence is back in the hands of Sonia Gandhi, the Congress president who can bring down Prime Minister Vajpayee's government almost at will. The eleven Indo-Pakistan tests have caused, however, a perceptibly greater public sentiment for peaceful relations with Pakistan.

Pakistan's high commissioner in Delhi is an unexpected beneficiary of this trend. During the week I was there, he was a featured speaker at two public events, arguing his terms for Indo-Pakistan peace. Both took place at the India International Centre, the hub of Delhi's intellectual life. I attended the second of the two meetings. Like the first, about which I read in the press, this, too, was distinguished more for the bonhomie that prevailed among the speakers than for the contours of peace they revealed. In both meetings, the Pakistani looked very good indeed but neither yielded nor obtained from his colleagues on the platform a shift from long-held positions. The dialogue was inconclusive.

Ashraf Qazi is a talented, very impressive man. He is soft-spoken, attractive, and wide-ranging. A well-read diplomat, he engages Delhi's intellectuals in smoke-filled rooms with the same ease with which he entertains guests at a formal dinner. He spoke first. The nuclear tests have inaugurated a "new era," he said, in Indo-Pakistan relations and invoked the necessity to jettison "obsolete concepts" such as balance of power, spheres of influence, even nuclear deterrence. The tests entailed a shift from an environment of ambiguity to openness, a playing out with nuclear weapons from a lower to a higher level, from implied to overt threats and preparations. In such an environment, the "probability of war" may be small, yet it entails "large consequences." Avoidance of war and quest for peace is a moral and political imperative, a responsibility we must not shirk. The governments of Pakistan and India, he said, have made exploratory proposals. Confidence-Building Measures (CBMs) are on the agenda. "But in the absence of trust these can be doomed. At the heart of the distrust between us," he came around to saying with a smile as charming as the suave Irish-Baluch-Pathan could muster, lies the "K-word"; "the K-word is the one thing that comes between us." During this part of doing his job—he did announce that he was not doing his job there and speaking only in his personal capacity—Ambassador Qazi threw a pregnant line. While arguing the necessity to put Kashmir seriously on the negotiating agenda, he said something to the effect that "delay in reaching a settlement notwithstanding, we need to find mutuality in dealing with the differences." The next speaker, a BJP official, failed to follow up on the opening Ashraf Qazi had offered. His failure appalled me as it did several Indians I talked to later.

Mr. N. N. Jha, a BJP expert on international affairs, is an adviser to Prime Minister Vajpayee. He started exactly the way Mr. Qazi had so fervently appealed against—with a polemical review of the past. The history of Indo-Pakistan relations shows, he argued, that we have made friendly and peaceable gestures not reciprocated by Pakistan, and [he] recalled the unrequited concessions India had made after the 1965 and 1971 wars. Then he proceeded to extol the virtues of bilateralism, which he insisted the international community favors as shown in the resolutions of the UN Security Council, the G-8, and the P-5.

In the end he, too, mellowed a bit. Displaying some pride in the scientific accomplishment of two South Asian countries—"the only Third World countries to become nuclear powers"—he argued that while India and Pakistan differ in respect of Kashmir and other matters, their positions on the Fissile Materials Control Treaty, Comprehensive Test Ban Treaty, and the sanctions are symmetrical. In these matters, the two should act jointly. "With joint effort we could both enter this most exclusive nuclear club." It was hard not to be amused and also feel a certain sympathy for his sweet dreams of club membership. I wondered though as to what Mr. Jha imagined to be the privileges of belonging to the "exclusive club." Since many Pakistanis nourish the same dream, our official ought to give serious consideration to Mr. Jha's low-cost, high-CBM-yield proposal.

Mr. Mani Shankar Iyer of the Indian National Congress began by announcing that he agreed much more with his "friend" Ashraf Qazi than with the BJP representative. He was forceful and very effective in criticizing the BJP government decision to test. "India's international standing today is the lowest since 1947. Even Russia failed to veto this time a Security Council resolution that refers to Kashmir, and Joseph Korbel's daughter is making statements about Kashmir no American official had dared make. An arms race with Pakistan may now be inevitable as the level of weaponization is likely to be a reciprocal process. It is not realistic to expect an agreement on the level of deterrence between the two countries. The BJP has now pitted India against China even though none of China's fourteen inter-continental ballistic missiles were aimed at India, and our relations were improving. The level of preparedness we now seek vis-à-vis China will compel Pakistan to catch up." It was a bitter broadside that made BJP supporters more uncomfortable than angry.

What then to hope for in the future? It is a question dozens of Indians, including influential citizens, senior ex-military officials, and opinion makers, are asking. Built into their questions are implied criticisms of the decision to go overtly nuclear. Most people I spoke to also acknowledged that BJP officials had pushed Pakistan toward carrying out its own tests, and nearly all were anxious for peace between the two countries.

"We think Nawaz Sharif wanted peace with India, and he enjoyed a large mandate. Chances of a settlement were never better than now," is a how a prominent columnist expressed a widely held belief in the centrist intelligentsia. Although some inquired into alternative solutions to the Kashmir dispute, I found no one who was willing to concede Pakistan's demand for a UN-supervised, two-way plebiscite in Jammu and Kashmir. Yet all hoped that Vajpayee and Nawaz Sharif will take a step forward toward peace when they meet in Colombo.

"It can't be," says Congress leader Mani Shankar Iyer and asks: "Does Sharif believe that Vajpayee will last?" He does not acknowledge that weakness can compel compromise and mistakes may induce reflection. Both leaders will arrive in Colombo next month carrying more burdens on their shoulders than feathers on their caps. Both need to show the world that they are statesmen, cognizant of the power they possess, and good at diplomacy. A first step obviously would be for them to order their foreign secretaries to start talking in accordance with the agreement already reached.

But other gestures and understandings may matter more: Pakistan's prime minister would do humanity and the Muslims of India a great favor if he were to openly denounce the recent massacre of a Hindu marriage party in Jammu. For whoever committed that ghastly crime were friends neither of Islam nor of Muslims, neither of Pakistan nor of Kashmir.

In turn, Mr. Vajpayee owes us a clear denunciation of the massacre which armed men committed in an Azad Kashmir village. Equally, he ought to be told that his government's connivance in building a temple over the ruin of Babri Mosque will be viewed in Pakistan as a repugnant act of bigotry which will create distrust and communal hatred. Finally, some means have to be found to end the exchange of savagery that takes place, invariably at the expense of innocent people, allegedly between the secret services of the two countries.

These do lasting damage to state and society and serve no national interests. They are the handiwork of men bred in an environment confused and violent. As Ashraf Qazi and Mr. Iyer said, a Kashmir settlement may be long in coming. Meanwhile, there is need to raise the threshold on nuclear warfare, and that requires an agreement on rules and some civility of exchange.

[1998]

# PAKISTAN: THE RETURN OF THE GENERALS

# 52 / NO, NOT AGAIN!

Rumors of the army's return to power are rife again. Those in high office—in and out of uniform—have issued denials. And those out of office are issuing coyly worded invitations to a "pol-mil" (politico-military) partnership. Political gossips, who may outnumber Kalashnikovs, smugglers, and dacoits in this country, have a field day; raconteurs tell tales of horses traded, plots identified, clearances obtained.

Instead of entering the unreal world of speculation, we would do well to reflect on our past and present. Half of our brief past as an independent country with an ironic name has been directly occupied by the warrior caste; the other half has been lived under its long and consuming shadow. The drawing-room conversations which mindlessly forecast the days of brass suggest either an affliction with amnesia or, more likely, an absence of operative concern.

We ought to remind ourselves of the fact that the military's involvement in politics has been an unmitigated disaster for this country, and all other countries I can think of. Mohammed Ayub Khan's much-vaunted "economic miracle" came to an unrequited end when he launched the ill-considered adventure in Kashmir and got into a war which his generals could not or would not win. Thereafter, he gave nepotism and corruption a new dimension in Pakistan. His policies, overall, sowed the seeds for the disaffection of East Pakistan—the earliest stronghold of the Pakistan movement and a good half of the country.

His successor, Mohammed Yahya Khan, had the reputation of a good and intelligent soldier. Assumption of power obviously dulled his military intelligence without investing him with political wisdom. His rule ended in the break up of Pakistan and a most abject, internationally televised surrender of the Pakistan army to the Indian army. Citizens rightfully hoped that this disaster would finally put the army's political interventions to an end. But this was not to be.

This unfortunate country was destined to live under the dark rule of Mohammad Zia ul-Haq for eleven years, each more harmful to its future than the preceding one. This last July 4, on the fifteenth anniversary of his putsch, I started to write an estimation of Zia's dictatorship. It became an exercise so unpleasant that I put off writing, hoping that time will bring me and future historians the gift of compassion in assessing his reign.

It is, nevertheless, necessary to underscore that the army has now been called out to clean up in Sindh not a mess created by civilian governments but the debris of Zia ul-Haq's rule. It is true that the civilian government which followed military rule did not undo in eighteen months what Zia ul-Haq had done in a decade. It was explicitly for this failure that the president dismissed, with the army's support, an elected government which had held its parliamentary majority.

For good reasons, we are discontented with the conduct of politics and government. Self-seeking and self-important politicians betray our hopes and make a mockery of representative government. In sheer frustration, we accept the military's intervention in politics. In doing so, we forgo the national experience no less than a sense of history.

We forget that there exists a dialectical opposition between rules of military organization and principles of governing a society. One relies on command; the other on consensus. One favors regimen; the other requires participation. One stresses discipline; the other values accountability. One rests on order; the other on participation. That is why, when they assume power, armies distort societies, repress politics, demoralize and corrupt themselves, and lose wars.

It is impossible in this country to hold a brief for politicians. With their lack of vision and integrity, their horse trading and plot chasing, their untrammeled and unprincipled opportunism, they have failed to fulfill a primary requisite of democratic politics: they have not tamed the warrior caste. In fact, it has been a nauseating experience to see them shifting around to stay on the good side of soldiers.

Yet there are three advantages to staying with politicians in a constitutional framework. The first concerns correction; the second liberty; and the third accountability. A parliamentary government is easier to change than a military dictatorship. Since democratic government is subject to periodic elections, the change is affected peacefully without large-scale agitation and rebellion and without the intercession of the Almighty.

Change of government by the ballot creates the mechanism for reform and correction. Out of office, leaders and parties can engage in self-examination and reform. In office, they can be challenged and called to account by a responsible opposition, an alert press, and a vigilant public. The corrective process is built into the democratic system, but for this mechanism to work efficiently, it requires an active and informed civil society.

Military rule is alien to notions of accountability and democratic succession. As a norm, it suppresses liberty and defies correction. Armies in power are notorious for their lack of accountability. In Pakistan, the army high command evinced an indifference to accountability not only to the people it unilaterally chose to rule but also to itself. The conduct of the 1965 war [with India] went largely unexamined; derelict commanders were not censured; tactical blunders were merely ignored. Mohammad Zia ul-Haq had laws passed by a rubber-stamp assembly to exempt his government and officials from trial and punishments for crimes committed in office.

Politicians have often paid for their mistakes; sometimes the punishment has been disproportionately greater than the sin. But not the army. Its high command failed to punish its own for committing crimes in East Pakistan, for cowardice no less than neglect of duty in war. This was an army proud of its soldiering traditions. No honest person denies that those traditions are in shambles today. But what is not generally recognized is that this has been a price primarily of military officers turning into politicians in uniform.

The last three and a half have been difficult and defective years of democracy in Pakistan. Yet these have been healthier, more promising years than any I can recall in the past four decades. Four years of relative freedom have yielded a lively press and valuable expository reporting. The conflict in Afghanistan has shifted away from Pakistan. Privatization and partial deregulation has stimulated growth to a healthy pace. Some local governments have shown surprising resiliency. Retrograde political parties have lost some of their stridency. Above all, civil society is beginning to take initiatives to solve problems which governmental neglect and mismanagement have compounded.

Those are small but important gains. We can do better. In this time of crisis and confusion, the greatest responsibility falls on our political class. In office and in opposition, they have been among the prime beneficiaries of democracy. Their enlightened interests lie in preserving it. Instead of working at cross-purposes, they should collaborate to save it. The first and immediate steps in this direction have to come from the prime minister: he must withdraw the "References," which are a travesty of justice;[1] and he should welcome a fair play of parliamentary procedures in Sindh even if it entails relinquishing his ill-earned monopoly of power in that province.

If we are to become a progress-oriented, democratic country, we must cease to entertain the option of military rule. We ought to internalize the truth that in our time there is no such thing as a benevolent dictatorship. A bad parliamentary government is better for our long-term future than a seemingly good dictatorship. In frustration, some citizens do crave for strong men. They forget that more often than not strong men produce weak nations.

[1992]

# 53 / THE SIGNALS SOLDIERS PICK

When and why do soldiers stage coups d'état? Ironically, in Pakistan, which has been the site of multiple attempts at both successful and bungled attempts at coups, this complex question has not been fully addressed. It is impossible to answer it in a newspaper column. So what follows are a few observations:

Military intervention in politics definitely ends only when the civilian polity has tamed the warrior class. That happens when the legitimacy of the civilian system of power is established over a period of time; when the principles of governance as embedded in the constitution, laws, and conventions of contemporary statehood are observed by governments and politicians; and when the civilian system of power is regarded by citizens normatively as just, appropriate, and authoritative.

It is precisely this process that has not taken its due course in Pakistan. We have been lacking both the political framework and leaders capable of investing the civilian system of government with authority and taming the warrior class. Our first decade after independence witnessed the early death of the founding father, disintegration of the founding party [the Muslim League], disputes and confusion over the constitutional framework, squabbling among politician, isolation of the majority province [East Pakistan], and the alignment of West Pakistan's landed elite with the military-bureaucratic oligarchy. Ayub Khan's coup was a product of this distorted environment. Hence, despite his initially moderate and modern instincts, his regime did not institute the reforms which this country had so badly needed. The relationship of land, labor, and capital remained what they were in the colonial times. The state continued to function without meaningful links or accountability to civil society. Typically, the oligarchy intervened in 1954, 1958, and 1971 to offset an actual or imminent affirmation of popular power. Each time, Pakistan's feudal elite applauded and collaborated with military rule. This state of affairs contributed decisively to the alienation of East Pakistan.

A new beginning was possible after East Pakistan's separation. The army's role in politics was discredited. Under Z. A. Bhutto, a popular and avowedly reformist leader, the country reached a rapid consensus on the 1973 constitution. The army yearned for and was provided rescue and rehabilitation under civilian rule. But then Mr. Bhutto proceeded to systematically squander his assets, turning the parliamentary into an autocratic government, enfeebling the constitution with harmful amendments, rendering the bureaucracy vulnerable to political and personal manipulation, hounding and alienating his parliamentary opposition, weakening the judiciary, making mockery of the rule of law, and using the army to suppress the resulting discontent. Tragically, he was executed by his creature, a disloyal putschist who inflicted lasting damages on this country. These included another "constitutional amendment" and wholesale sectarianization of government which infected also sections of the officers' corps.

Only once before, during 1972–1973, since its founding had the promise of Pakistan appeared greater than it did in 1988. Before the restoration of civilian government, there had been a sustained period of resistance to military rule led bravely by Begum Nusrat and Miss Benazir Bhutto. A significant number of citizens had demonstrated their commitment to democracy by taking risks, bearing harsh punishments and prison terms to resist military rule. When parliamentary government was finally restored, its legitimacy appeared finally secured. Hope had returned to this land, and it was linked to the promise of constitutional rule and reformist policies under a leadership which had paid its dues in a struggle for democracy.

The powers of Ms. Bhutto's first government were limited under a dyarchic arrangement, and her tenure was cut short by a dubious presidential intervention. Hence the public deemed her failings as forgivable. In 1993, she returned to office with enhanced powers, her term secured by the election of a party member as president. Yet at midterm her government drifts as the country drowns in violence and corruption and sinks deep in economic crisis. Rule of law has receded further as an increasingly pliable judiciary tolerates such extreme violations as torture and murders in government custody.

The window of hope is being shut on us again, and simple folks in villages and towns are starting to talk of authoritarian alternatives. What should worry us is that the men who were apprehended last month had merely picked up the signal which soldiers do when civilians fail.

Sense of failure in war or protracted frustration in achieving a strategic objective often induces military officers to blame the political system and leadership. Occasionally, resentment transforms into revolt. The officers who staged coups d'état in Egypt and Iraq in the 1950s had deeply resented Arab defeat in the 1948 war with Israel and blamed the corruption and mismanagement of their civilian governments for the loss of Palestine. The French generals who revolted in 1960 were frustrated by their inability to defeat the FLN in Algeria, deemed the government responsible for their failure, and envisioned a perfect conduct of war under their own government. The colonels who overthrew the government of Salazar in Portugal were similarly frustrated by their inconclusive engagement in Angola, Mozambique, and Guinea Bissao. But they had wanted to make peace, not more war, and did negotiate their way out of those colonies. The first officers' conspiracy in the Pakistan army, discovered in 1952, was caused by their frustrations in the 1948 Kashmir war. Humiliation in Bangladesh is said to have inspired the conspirators of Attock. And Kashmir is reported again to have contributed to this latest unrest. The prognosis for Kashmir—caught between Indian brutalities and Pakistani blunders—remains grim.

An environment of ideological confusion is hospitable to putschist tendencies. The characteristics of such an environment are fluidity of values, confusion over institutional norms, and opportunistic styles of politics. The mix can induce ideological zealotry no less than political adventurism. Pakistan has been a textbook example of ambivalent ideological environment. We have yet to resolve, in theory and practice, such fundamental questions as the relationship between state and religion, authority and accountability, the executive and the judiciary. The resulting instability is greatly augmented by the behavior in power of civilian leaders no less than military usurpers. Thus successive governments have tampered with the judiciary, by executive fiat changed rules and violated the conventions of the civil services, and manipulated promotions and transfers in the bureaucracy and the army. Cynicism and contempt of civilian order are also promoted when power is exercised not merely opportunistically but also without regard to rules, the national interest, and outside a moral framework. Similarly, a chief executive who publicly opposes sectarian politics and enters into partnership with sectarian groups does long-term harm to country and government.

Several politicians have remarked in recent weeks that a military putsch is a thing of the past. Invariably they have mentioned an "unfavorable international environment," meaning primarily American disapproval, as the decisive inhibition against coups d'état. This line of thinking reflects the deep sense of dependency which invests in the United States an omnipresent interest in shaping Pakistan's future and an omnipotent ability to do so. America is a great power. Where its interests require, Washington is still friendly with dictators; Suharto and Mubarak are but two prominent examples. Moreover, in the past, internal conditions not foreign preferences were the decisive stimulant to warrior ambitions in Pakistan. Worse yet, our politicians have had an uncanny ability to reproduce those conditions.

I do not wish to be misunderstood as arguing the imminence of another military adventure in Pakistani politics. To the contrary, an overwhelming majority of military officers are wary of getting into power again. They recognize that military governments have failed at least as badly as civilian ones and that the exercise of power damaged the army more than it benefited the country. Many of them know also that professionalism and politics do not mix and armies in power almost always lose wars. On the few occasions when I have met with military officers, a certain yearning has been noticeable for civilian leaders of integrity and stature, men and women a good soldier can salute with pride and honor. Only when these latter appear on the national scene shall the menace of men in uniform riding into power become a nightmare long past.

[1995]

The army is being called increasingly to rescue the country from its administrative failures. It went on a successful pursuit of ghost schools, whose very existence had been denied, not long ago, by a federal secretary of education. Until the Supreme Court ruled the antiterrorist courts unconstitutional, army officers presided over the special courts established to eradicate terrorism. Currently, the army is engaged in checking electric meters in private homes and cleaning up the Augean stables of the Water and Power Development Authority (WAPDA).

Citizens who have been troubled by the deterioration of public services and corruption in government departments have applauded the military's intervention. The press, too, has praised its evenhanded style of work. The relief and the applause are understandable. Some thought ought to be given, nevertheless, to the long-term costs of deploying the military to clear the mess created by bureaucrats and politicians.

It violates the principle of distancing the military from politics, quotidian life, and civil administration. Since millennia, this has been deemed essential to the health of the state and society no less than of military institutions and the morale of professional soldiers. When put in practice, this insight, which is almost as old as the state in human history, has been central to the consolidation and stability of states and empires. The violation of this principle has often been associated with the decline and failure of power. In the British Empire, the forerunner of the Pakistani state and armed forces, the spatial expression of this principle was the cantonment, a habitation reserved for the military. These were often adjacent with but normally separated from the civilian urban area.

This was by no means a British innovation. In his excellent account of early Muslim dominion in India, *The Rise of Islam and the Bengal Frontier, 1204–1760* (Delhi, 1994), Richard Eaton has noted that Muslim armies were "concentrated in garrison settlements located in or near pre-conquest urban centers. . . . The Turkish occupation of Bengal thus followed the settlement pattern found throughout the early Delhi Sultanate, anticipating in this respect the cantonment city employed by the British in their occupation of India in the nineteenth century."

The cantonment is still here of course, but the principle it symbolized has been violated, largely by Pakistan's military dictators but also by such elected governments as those of Z. A. Bhutto and Mr. Nawaz Sharif. Mr. Nawaz Sharif is a rare politician in Pakistan in that, like Bhutto, he has come close to subordinating the military to civilian authority. One can only hope that he does not lack the political wisdom to let this achievement slide away. He ought to be more mindful of history's lessons than Mr. Bhutto was.

It is easy to sympathize with Mian Nawaz Sharif's predicament. As prime minister, he confronts a deep, dual crisis of the state and the economy. Compared with the other institutions of the state, the armed forces retain their discipline and cohesion and appear capable of getting a difficult job done. It is tempting to call in the army where other state institutions fail to fulfill their public responsibility. The army delivers almost overnight. In the process, it inherits resentments and controversies and in unintended ways becomes enmeshed in local and national politics.

WAPDA is the latest case in point. Like the education ministries, which employ more men and women than the armed forces of Pakistan and whose swarm of "ghost schools" the army exorcised so effectively, WAPDA is a rotten outfit, up to the ears in corruption, a half-paralyzed white elephant. Called to clean up, the army has raked the muck, collected three billion rupees out of its more than seventy billion worth of unpaid bills, restored a thousand kilowatts of stolen electricity, and to great public applause charged more than a dozen Muslim League legislators of illegal tampering with electricity meters and power lines. Things look good, but they are not quite.

Steadily, the army becomes associated—however unfairly—with controversies, public complaints, and political maneuvering. Army personnel are checking out individual consumers and small enterprises, and into the third week of its operation people were starting to ask: why don't they go where the big thefts and defaults are, big industry, large institutions, government departments, the military itself, which is WAPDA's largest creditor? In our culture, complaints and stories escalate, enter the social scene, and erode the reputations of institutions no less than individuals.

When the army undertakes public administration, it inevitably becomes drawn into local conflicts, which abound in rural areas. Feudal and political families are particularly prone to feuds, which nearly always involve local officials. Among those alleged to have tampered with an electric meter is the outspoken, often controversial Syeda Abida Husain, the federal minister for population welfare and science and technology. She alleges that she has been framed by her antagonistic cousins. In her ancestral home and farm complex, there are nine electric meters. The lead of one of these was allegedly changed to slow it down. This was done by WAPDA technicians, she says, who arrived after the army had been called in. "No one on our premises has the technical ability to tamper with a sealed meter. Altogether, we pay an average of 700,000 rupees per year in WAPDA bills. Does it make sense to change one meter and save a few thousand rupees?"

I may be biased. Abida Husain is a friend. I found her explanation persuasive but did ask: "Do you pay taxes?" Yes, she says, "more than 3 million rupees per year in direct federal and provincial taxes." An independent inquiry, which she demands and deserves, should absolve her. The larger issue remains nevertheless: when the armed forces are pulled into this sort of work, they are inevitably implicated in societal conflicts and complaints, a phenomenon that is good neither for the army nor for society.

Typically, military interventions work temporary wonders, which is why martial law regimes in Pakistan have enjoyed short honeymoons. Soon enough, old realities begin to work their way in, institutional lethargy returns, corruption makes inroads even into the officers' corps, reputations are sullied, rumors spread, and public discontent revives. Rarely if ever have armies improved governance. Hence popular resistance to army rule always follows after the honeymoon ends. More importantly, engagement in civilian administration and politics nearly always has an adverse impact on army's leadership and morale. Hence militaries in power have rarely, if ever, won wars.

Pakistan has been a parliamentary democracy for a decade. No one expects military rule to return. Yet it is important to recall that the democratic system is still in its infancy, feeble and malfunctioning. Its limbs, the institutions of governance and public service, have to be rebuilt and reinforced internally. External inputs will serve at best as palliatives. If WAPDA, or our education ministries, or revenue collection agencies are not capable of reform by civilians, then soldiers will not be able to do it either, no matter how carefully the government phases them out.

The military is often called, and should be called, to aid civilian power in times of natural disasters—a great flood, a catastrophic earthquake, and so on. But to ask it to perform routine administrative tasks—collect bills, run a government department, dispense justice—admits to a failure of nerve and a failure of will to which no civilian government should be entitled.

Armies which intervene in politics are invariably those which, by design or force of circumstances, become engaged in the political process. Even the most professionalized military develops the putschist tendency when circumstances force it to engage in administrative and policing work. The French army started to become involved in administering civilians during its counterinsurgency engagement against the Vietminh in Indochina. During the Algerian war of liberation, it got so enmeshed in French politics that in 1958 it helped destroy the Fourth Republic and later its high command attempted a coup d'état, a putsch Charles de Gaulle alone proved capable of quelling. Similarly, protracted involvements in "internal wars" in Angola and Mozambique led the Portuguese army officers to overthrow in 1974 the regime of Marcello Caetano.

For the armed forces of Pakistan, this is, I believe, a time of great transition. New developments have occurred in the last few years to change Pakistan's threat perception. These changes await examination for their implications on the military outlook, strategy and tactic, training and force formation. The military high command has the awesome responsibility of preparing the armed forces to adapt to these. It is in the best interest of the country and the armed forces that they are not diverted from this essential task to perform duties which civilians ought to be doing.

[1999]

# NOTES

*Part I*

## INTRODUCTION

1. See in particular chap. 19, "At Cold War's End: A World of Pain," in part 3.

2. Eqbal Ahmad, "Revolutionary Warfare and Counterinsurgency," in Normal Miller and Roderick Aya, eds., *National Liberation: Revolution in the Third World* (New York: Free, 1971), p. 152. The article is also available in the Eqbal Ahmad Archives, Johnson Library, Hampshire College, Amherst Massachusetts. Ahmad's concept of legitimacy is Gramscian rather than Weberian. For Weber, politics remained a "profession" forever beyond the control of the masses. In Gramsci's conception, political legitimacy (or hegemony) was to be conquered rather than imposed. It referred to a strategy for gaining the active consent of the people through their self-organization, with the aim of creating a collective political will. As in Ahmad's conception, it involved the necessary and prior conquest of civil society and political and cultural leadership before state power could be won.

3. Ibid., p. 137.

4. Ahmad's critique of the *foco* theory anticipates the Zapatista analysis of the negative example of the Mexican guerrilla movements of the 1970s. See Subcomandante Marcos, "They began with a local military movement and expected that the base would slowly join in, or they would have been enlightened by the guerrilla *foco*." *La Jornada*, February 7, 1994.

5. The Tonkin Bay resolution passed ninety-eight to two in July 1965.

6. Ahmad, "Revolutionary Warfare and Counterinsurgency," p. 171 passim.

7. Throughout the war and even into the present, the United States maintained the fiction of two Vietnams and insisted that "North Vietnam" was violating the Geneva accords of 1954 rather than the United States.

8. Quoted in Ahmad, "Revolutionary Warfare and Counterinsurgency," p. 146.

9. Quoted in ibid., p. 198.

10. See, e.g., Susan Jeffords, *The Remasculinization of American: Gender and the Vietnam War* (Bloomington: University of Indiana Press, 1989); H. Bruce Franklin, *Vietnam and Other American Fantasies* (Amherst: University of Massachusetts, 2000).

11. Robert S. McNamara, *In Retrospect: The Tragedy and Lessons of Vietnam* (New York: Times Books, 1995).

12. "Yasser Arafat's Nightmare," interview in *MERIP Reports*, November/December 1983, pp. 18–23. Available in the Eqbal Ahmad Archives.

13. Ibid., p. 20.

14. Ibid.

15. Ibid., p. 21.

16. Ibid., p. 22.

17. See his "Comments on Skocpol," *Theory and Society* 11 (1982): 293–309, for an earlier version, written soon after the revolution, of the analysis he develops (and revises) here. See also "Special Issue on the Iranian Revolution," *Race and Class* 21, no. 1 (Summer 1979). Both are available in the Eqbal Ahmad Archives.

18. "Algeria's Unending Tragedy," *Dawn*, September 23, 1997, available in the Eqbal Ahmad Archives.


1. REVOLUTIONARY WARFARE

1. [See Eric Hobsbawm, "Goliath and the Guerrilla," *Nation*, July 19, 1965.—Eds.]

2. President Lyndon Johnson ordered a military invasion of the Dominican Republic on April 28, 1965, attributing a local revolt to reinstate ousted democratically elected president Juan Bosch to a Cuba-initiated Communist conspiracy.

3. Carlos Garcia, Magsaysay's vice president, assumed the presidency upon Magsaysay's death in 1957 and was thereafter elected to office, which he held until 1961.

4. Bao-Dai was the last emperor of Viet Nam; he served the French and the Japanese and, after abdicating in 1945, was recalled from the Riviera to serve the French again in 1949. Diem was installed by the United States in 1954 and overthrown in a US-supported coup in 1963 following brutal repression of Buddhists. The "musical-chair

generals" were a series of generals installed and overthrown in US-backed coups between 1963 and 1965 following Diem's ouster.

## 2. RADICAL BUT WRONG

1. Régis Debray, *Revolution in the Revolution?* (New York: Monthly Review Press, 1967), p. 21.

2. Régis Debray, "Le Castrisme: La Longue Marche de l'Amérique Latine," *Les Temps Modernes*, January 1965. The sentence quoted does not appear in the English version of the article: "Latin America: The Long March," *New Left Review*, September–October 1965. See also his second article, written in 1965: "Marxist Strategy in Latin America," *New Left Review*, September–October 1967.

3. Robin Blackburn and Perry Anderson, "The Marxism of Régis Debray," *Monthly Review* 20, no. 3 (July–August 1968): 64.

4. Note that Che Guevara pointed out at least five distinctive features of the Cuban setting: (1) Castro's personality; (2) the United States did not intervene, having failed to fathom the genuinely far-reaching aspects of the Cuban Revolution; (3) Batista's regime had lost legitimacy almost completely, so that even the bourgeoisie supported the revolution and many landlords were neutral; (4) the majority of the peasants were progressively proletarianized by the expansion of large, mechanized capitalist farms; (5) the emergence of a class of disaffected middle peasants in the Sierra Maestra. See Ernesto "Che" Guevara, "Cuba—Exception or Vanguard," in *Venceremos: The Speeches and Writings of Che Guevara,* ed. John Gerassi (New York, 1968), pp. 132–134.

5. This refers to the organizing and disciplinary principles of the Chinese Army of Liberation, which, with slight variations, were also adopted by the Algerian and Vietnamese liberation movements. They are: *The Three Tasks of the Army*—fighting, politics, and production. *The Three Main Rules of Discipline*—obey orders, do not take a single needle or piece of thread from the masses, turn in captured articles. *The Eight Points of Attention*—speak politely, pay fairly for your purchase, return borrowed things, compensate for damages, do not hit or swear at people, do not damage crops, do not take liberties with women, do not mistreat prisoners.

## 3. COUNTERINSURGENCY

1. *Webster's Collegiate Dictionary*, 5th ed. (Springfield, Mass.: G. and C. Merriam, 1939). *Webster's Third New International Dictionary* (1961) gives a similar definition: "a con-

dition of revolt against a recognized government that does not reach the proportion of an organized revolutionary government and is not recognized as belligerency."

2. Jonathan Schell, *The Village of Ben Suc* (New York: Knopf, 1967) and by the same author, *The Military Half* (New York: Vintage, 1968); and Yves Courrière, *Les Fils de la Toussaint* (Paris: Fayard, 1968), chap. 4.

3. Seymour Hersh, "My Lai 4," *Harper's*, May 1970, p. 72.

4. See Telford Taylor, *Nuremberg and Vietnam: An American Tragedy* (Chicago: Quadrangle, 1970). See a review of this important study by Richard A. Falk in the *New York Times Book Review*, December 27, 1970, pp. 4, 14. See also Clergy and Laymen Concerned About Vietnam, *In the Name of America* (Annandale, Virginia: Turnpike, 1968).

5. *New York Times*, February 8, 1970.

6. For an earlier, more impassioned, intelligent, but also more contradiction-ridden version of this strategy, see William R. Corson, *The Betrayal* (New York: Norton, 1968), chap. 12, pp. 262–290. Corson is an intellectual and politicized Marine Corps lieutenant colonel, now retired. His conversion to pacification and subsequent anger over the "sabotage" of the "other war" by the institutions and political processes at home resemble those of the French *officier-administrateur* of *La Guerre Revolutionnaire* (Paris: Payot, 1969), Gabriel Georges Marcel Bonnet, ed. He deserves special attention as the prototype of the military officers who become committed to the liberal-reformist view of counterinsurgency.

7. Sir Robert Thompson, *No Exit From Vietnam* (New York: McKay, 1970), pp. 61, 125, 163–164, 8, 169. See pp. 116 and 197 for his definition of victory. President Nixon quoted Thompson's evaluation in his televised speech of December 15, 1969. A year later (December 2, 1970), the *New York Times* reported Sir Robert as giving a "gloomy" report to President Nixon following his latest "secret mission" to evaluate the success of Vietnamization. There was a denial from the White House that the "over-all thrust of the story which leads to the impression that the pacification and Vietnamization programs are not doing well is an incorrect impression." But the White House press secretary refused to discuss the contents of the report "because it was secret" (*New York Times*, December 4, 1970). It is to be noted that the earlier but optimistic "secret" report was published as the concluding part of *No Exit From Vietnam* (pp. 208ff.).

8. Ibid., p. 199.

9. Ibid., p. 34.

10. Ibid., p. 198.

11. Typically, counterrevolutionary scholars and US government publications distort the history of Vietnam or suppress critical information. Very little biographical in-

formation is available in English on Thieu, Ky, and Khiem, all of whom fought on the side of France during Vietnam's War of Independence (1945–1954). Since these facts arc not generally known, it is worth mentioning a few: (1) *Thieu:* Graduated from Dalat Military Academy in 1948; participated in at least the following major French military operations against Vietnamese nationalists: Operation Occident—1949; Operation Hung Yen—1952 (this involved a notorious massacre); Operation Atlantic in Phou Yen. (2) *Khiem:* Enlisted with the French in 1947; staff officer of Secteur 2; commanded Operation Nettoyage ("clean-up") west of Hue; 1954–1955, Chief of Staff, V Military Corps area. (3) *Ky:* Born in Son Tay where US forces recently landed to "rescue" prisoners; enlisted with the French 1951; attended Reserve Officers School in Nam Dinh 1952 and Aviation School in Avord, France, 1954.

A reminder is necessary that the above operations and names, being more recent and more costly to the people at large, must be more poignantly remembered by the Vietnamese than are Bunker Hill or Valley Forge by the Americans. To expect any self-respecting Vietnamese to cooperate with or trust a government led by such men is like expecting George Washington and his colleagues to participate in a government led by Benedict Arnold and the commanders of the Hessian and British regiments.

12. "Innovation" is a favorite word with the second-ranking counterinsurgency experts whose works I have generally ignored lest I be accused of selecting the weaker examples of counterinsurgency theory. However, I should note that, with the exception of new machines and computers, bigger bombers, and a whole range of hitherto unknown killing and detection devices, there is nothing "innovative" about the American counterinsurgency effort. With the exception of the computerized HES (Hamlet Evaluation System), there is not one managerial innovation, one pacification gimmick in Vietnam—Agroville, New Life Hamlet, "Rev-Dev," Combined Campaign Plan, CORDS, Project Take-off, *Chieu Hoi, Phung Hong,* APC, the "New Model Pac," etc.—that was not previously conceived and applied by the French in Indochina and/or Algeria or by the British in Malaya. Of course, the French initials were different. A reminder is needed that the one "innovation"—the HES—informed us of pacification's dramatic success ("relatively secure" hamlets grew by more than 600, to 5,340) just before the Tet offensive. Anyone familiar with revolutionary warfare should know that even the most virtuoso revolutionary organization could not have pulled off the Tet offensive without massive, consistent, and covert support of the population in rural as well as urban areas. See Robert W. Komer, "Clear, Hold, and Rebuild," *Army*, May 1970, pp. 14–23, and "Pacification: A Look Back and Ahead," *Army*, June 1970, pp. 20–29.

13. United States Senate Committee on Judiciary, Subcommittee to Investigate Problems Connected with Refugees and Escapees, *Refugee and Civilian War Casualty Problems in Indo-China: A Staff Report,* 91st Cong., 2nd sess., September 28, 1970, pp. 4–5.

14. For an account of the Qui Nhon riot, see *New York Times,* December 4, 1970. For Luce's statement, see *Transcript WGBH/KECT The Advocates,* December 8, 1970. For an important statement by Ngo Cong Due, see *New York Review of Books,* November 5, 1970. For the revolutionaries' evaluation of the urban situation, see Jacques Decornoy's interview with Prime Minister Pham Van Dong, *Le Monde,* English weekly, December 9, 1970. For General Tri's statement, see *Africasia,* no. 27 (November 23, 1970): 37.

15. For a recent estimate of the extent and effects of chemical warfare in Indochina, see *New York Times,* March 15, 1970, and May 24, 1970; *Los Angeles Times,* December 31, 1970. Several scientific papers prepared by such eminent scientists as Meselson, Pfeiffer, Orians, Neilands, Mayers, and Galston and sponsored by the American Association for the Advancement of Science so far constitute the most reliable indicators of the effects of herbicides and other chemicals being used in Indochina.

16. See Herbert Mitgang, "The Air War in Asia and Its Cover-up in Washington," *New York Times,* August 31, 1970.

17. Roger Hilsman, *To Move a Nation* (New York: Dell, 1967), p. 415. Emphasis mine.

18. *New York Times,* serialized editorials on "Wars of National Liberation," June 30, July 2, July 3, 1970.

19. "Washington: The Larger Implications of Vietnam," *New York Times*, April 25, 1965.

20. W. W. Rostow, "The Great Transition: Tasks of the First and Second Post War Generations," February 23, 1967. Similar views have been expressed by Mr. Nixon on several occasions including his May 14, 1969, speech on Vietnam.

21. I. F. Stone, *In Time of Torment* (New York: Vintage, 1968), pp. 173–174.

22. US House of Representatives, Committee on Appropriations, Department of Defense Appropriations for 1963, Hearings, 87th Cong., 2nd sess., part 2, pp. 49–50.

23. Quoted in Committee of Concerned Asian Scholars, *The Indochina Story* (New York: Bantam, 1970), p. 93.

24. Congressional Record, October 16, 1969; *New York Times,* October 15, 1969. Westmoreland's address was given at the annual meeting of the Association of the United States Army.

25. Sir Robert Thompson, *Defeating Communist Insurgency* (London: Chatto and Windus, 1966), p. 14. Italics added.

26. E. L. Katzenbach, deputy undersecretary of defense in the Kennedy government, wrote: "We have fought wars of urban and industrial interdiction, while our own

Asiatic opponents *and the African opponents of our allies have patiently pursued a process of rural consolidation which has, in effect, given them an inviolable sanctuary from which they can attack and withdraw at will.*" Roger Hilsman presents a more sophisticated version: if armed revolutions result from international conspiracy, its nationalist expression must also have communist connections. The communists, says Mr. Hilsman, "*try especially hard to capture the extreme nationalists like Lumumba. They sponsor radical nationalism wherever they can find it.*" The message is clear: when a nationalist movement acquires radical content, it is to be regarded as a threat to the "free world." (Italics added.) See Lt. Col. T. N. Greene, editor, *The Guerrilla and How to Fight Him*, selections from *The Marine Corps Gazette* (New York: Praeger, 1962), pp. 21, 24.

27. Greene, *The Guerrilla and How to Fight Him*, p. 24.

28. His statement appeared to threaten a land invasion and foreshadowed the aerial invasion of North Vietnam: "It is important that the world become clear in mind that the operation run from Hanoi against Vietnam is as certain a form of aggression as the violation of the 38th parallel by the North Korean Army in June, 1950" (ibid., p. 59).

29. Put into practice, these plans have ended disastrously. Such was the case with US attempts to infiltrate guerrilla teams into North Vietnam, a practice that is believed to have begun in 1958 and continued at least until 1965. Bernard Fall, among others, has reported that these "[guerrillas] met with dismal failure . . . . Present losses are reported to run at 85 percent [of] the total personnel engaged in such operations" (*The Two Viet-Nams*, 2d rev. ed. [New York: Praeger, 1964], p. 402). *London Times*, April 20, 1968, reported that (a) the South Vietnamese agents were trained by the CIA in Special Forces camps, notably the 77th Special Forces group; (b) 95 percent casualties were admitted in 1963 ("a complete fiasco"); and (c) these operations became a conduit for opium trade. Marshal Ky, who was in charge of the parachute drops, was removed for his part in opium smuggling.

For additional information on the "offensive use of guerrillas," see Slavko N. Bjelajac, "Unconventional Warfare in the Nuclear Era," *Orbis* 4 (Fall 1960): 323–337; Robert Strausz-Hupe, William R. Kitner, and Stefan T. Possony, *A Forward Strategy for America* (New York: Harper, 1961); and Peter Paret and John W. Shy, *Guerrillas in the 1960's* (New York: Praeger, 1962), pp. 4, 63–69.

30. John Mecklin, *Mission in Torment* (New York: Doubleday, 1965), p. 303.

31. Greene, *The Guerrilla and How to Fight Him*, p. 60.

32. See Peter Paret, *French Revolutionary Warfare: From Indochina to Algeria* (New York: Praeger, 1964), chap. 7.

33. "International War: The New Communist Tactics," in Greene, *The Guerrilla and How to Fight Him*, p. 26.

34. Fall, *The Two Viet-Nams*, p. 464.

35. For an example, see Robert Komer, "Clear, Hold, and Rebuild" and "Pacification: A Look Back and Ahead."

36. *New York Times*, January 23, 1971.

37. Thompson, *Defeating Communist Insurgency*, p. 10.

38. Sheldon Wolin and John Schaar, "Berkeley: The Battle of People's Park," *New York Review of Books*, June 19, 1969, p. 29.

39. Quoted in Noam Chomsky, *American Power and the New Mandarins* (New York: Pantheon, 1967), p. 49.

40. See Douglas Pike, *Vietcong* (Cambridge, Mass.: MIT Press, 1966).

41. Richard M. Pfeffer, "Revolution and Rule: Where Do We Go From Here," *Bulletin of Concerned Asian Scholars* 2, no. 3 (April–July 1970): 89, reviewing Ezra Vogel's *Canton Under Communism* (Cambridge: Harvard University Press, 1969).

42. Pike, *Vietcong*, p. 276.

43. In Greene, *The Guerrilla and How to Fight Him*, pp. 31, 32.

44. The term "revisionist" in this context is credited to David Halberstam, although he used it to apply only to the question of land reform. See his "Voices of the Vietcong," *Harper's*, January 1968, p. 47.

45. Thompson, *Defeating Communist Insurgency*, pp. 24, 25.

46. For example, see E. L. Katzenbach Jr., "Time, Space, and Will: Politico-Military Views of Mao Tse-tung," in Greene, *The Guerrilla and How to Fight Him*, pp. 11–21. The writer goes so far as to ascribe the battle of Dien Bien Phu directly to Mao's "daring" (p. 21).

47. Paret, *French Revolutionary Warfare*, p. 20.

48. Thompson, *Defeating Communist Insurgency*, pp. 119–120.

49. Thompson, *No Exit From Vietnam*, p. 164.

50. Greene, *The Guerrilla and How to Fight Him*, p. 21. Italics added.

51. Richard M. Pfeffer, *No More Vietnams?* (New York: Harper and Row, 1968), p. 142.

52. Wolin and Schaar, "Berkeley," p. 25.

53. From Robert Sheer's eyewitness account of Santa Rita Jail, *Ramparts*, August 1969, pp. 50–51.


## 4. EPILOGUE: THE LESSONS OF VIETNAM

1. [Ahmad's comments were made in the context of a seminar held at the Adlai Stevenson Institute of International Affairs in June 1968. The other participants in the

seminar were former government officials, scholars with relevant expertise, and journalists. Included, among others, were Henry Kissinger Daniel Ellsberg, George Kahan, Sir Richard Thompson, Stanley Hoffman, Arthur Schlesinger Jr., and, of course, Samuel Huntington, professor of government at Harvard University, who served as a consultant to various administrations and wrote about Vietnam. Both Huntington's comments and Ahmad's response appear in Richard M. Pfeffer, ed., *No More Vietnams? The War and the Future of American Foreign Policy* (New York: Adlai Stevenson Institute of International Affairs, 1968). All the quotations from Huntington are drawn from this volume.—*Eds.*]

2. Professor Huntington has cited the case of Japan. One may also ask why the United States did not achieve comparable success in Cuba and the Philippines. While it is not central to the argument here, it may be noted that Bolivia is not the only noncommunist or nonoccupied country to achieve thoroughgoing land reform. Algeria, Tunisia, Tanzania, Egypt, and Syria are among the others.

3. For this reason, I believe in the "domino theory" in reverse. If the United States "wins" in Vietnam, it may have the effect of assuring the Thai rulers (whose propensity to promise elections has become proverbial) and the Filipino elite (who have the reputation of being the most corrupt in Asia) that the United States will save them from their people. The defeat of United States objectives in Vietnam, on the other hand, may have a salutary effect on their willingness to reform.

## 7. THE MAKING OF *THE BATTLE OF ALGIERS*

1. [The revolutionary strategy divided Algeria into six *wilayas* (military provinces or districts), each with sub-*wilayas* and village or town units. Each unit had a military commander and a political commissar.—*Eds.*]

2. The ALN got its arms from everywhere. The United States was very keen to have the Algerian Revolution on its side, so the Americans supplied arms. The Soviet Union was very keen to have the Algerian Revolution on its side, so the Soviets also supplied arms. Nasser of Egypt was keen to remain the big man of the Arab revolution, so he supplied arms. They were all arming the new Algeria.

## 8. ALGERIA BEGAN BADLY

1. [The official figure for the number dead in the civil war in Algeria in the 1990s is now set at around two hundred thousand.—*Eds.*]

# Part II

INTRODUCTION

1. We owe this note to Edward Said's analysis of Derrida in "Criticism Between Culture and System," in *The World, the Text, and the Critic* (Cambridge: Harvard University Press, 1983), p. 207.

2. Not included in this anthology because of space constraints but available in the Eqbal Ahmad Archives, Hampshire College, Amherst, Massachusetts.

3. Interestingly, "Christian fundamentalism" is now commonly used in the United States to refer to a religious politics that has entered the mainstream and wields considerable influence in the Republican Party, while Jewish fundamentalism is seldom invoked in the West to describe, for example, the settler movement in Israel.

4. Germaine Tillion, *Algeria: The Realities* (New York: Knopf, 1958).

5. Christina Buci-Glucksmann, "Hegemony and Consent," in Anne Showstack Sassoon, ed., *Approaches to Gramsci* (London: Writers and Readers, 1982), p. 119.

6. Eqbal Ahmad, "The Arms Habit," *New York Times,* April 15, 1979.

7. See "At Cold War's End: A World of Pain," in this volume.

8. Mary Louise Pratt in a recent essay continues such an analysis. She wonders what European modernity would have looked like if its peasantries had had nowhere to go. Would there, for example, have been agrarian revolutions in Ireland and Italy as well as Mexico and Russia? See Mary Louise Pratt, "Modernity and Periphery: Toward a Global and Relational Analysis," in *Beyond Dichotomies*, ed. Elizabeth Mudimbe Boyi (Albany: SUNY Press, 2002).

9. Samuel P. Huntington, for example, who reemerges in the 1990s as the author of the now standard paradigm for understanding the war on terror, "Clash of Civilizations," *Foreign Affairs* 72, no. 3 (Summer 1993): 22–49.

10. These articles are combined and presented in this volume as "Roots of the Religions Right."

9. FROM POTATO SACK TO POTATO MASH

1. [This is the first in a series of three essays on postcolonial societies that appeared consecutively in *Arab Societies Quarterly* in 1984. The second and third essays follow.— Eds.]

2. Barrington Moore Jr., *Social Origins of Dictatorship and Democracy* (Boston: Beacon, 1966), p. 452.

3. John Berger, "The Peasant Experience and the Modern World," *New Society*, May 17, 1979. See his *Pig Earth* (London: Writers and Readers Publishing Cooperative, 1979), the first of a projected three-part literary, analytical, historical work on the movement from peasant society to the modern city.

4. Berger, "The Peasant Experience."

5. Berger, *Pig Earth*, p. 201.

6. Karl Marx, *The Eighteenth Brumaire of Louis Bonaparte* (New York: International Publishers, 1963), p. 124.

7. Eric Wolf, *Peasant Wars of the Twentieth Century* (New York: Harper and Row, 1969), p. 279.

8. Germaine Tillion, *Algeria: The Realities* (New York: Knopf, 1958).

9. Franz Fanon, Les Damnées de la terre (Paris: Maspero, 1961), [available in translation as The Wretched of the Earth (New York: Grove, 1966), p. 166.—Eds.]

10. Ferhat Abbas, *La Nuit coloniale* (Paris: Julliard, 1962), p. 187.

## 10. POSTCOLONIAL SYSTEMS OF POWER

1. Franz Fanon, *Les Damnés de la terre* (Paris: François Maspero, 1961); Roger Murray, "Second Thoughts on Ghana," *New Left Review*, no. 42 (1967); Hamza Alavi, "The State in Post-Colonial Societies." *New Left Review*, no. 74 (1972).

2. See Quentin Hoare and Dennis Nowell Smith, eds., *Selections from the Prison Notebooks* (London and New York: Lawrence and Wishard International Publishers, 1971).

## 11. THE NEOFASCIST STATE

1. Martin Ennals, *Boston Globe*, November 26, 1978.

2. "Post-Colonial Systems of Power," *Arab Studies Quarterly* 2, no. 4 (Fall 1980): 351–352.

3. Jacques Langguth, "The Mind of a Torturer," *Nation*, June 24, 1978. See also A. J. Langguth, *Hidden Terrors* (New York: Pantheon, 1978).

4. On this point, see Frederick Nunn, "Military Professionalism and Professional Militarism in Brazil," *Journal of Latin American Studies* 4, no. 1 (1972); Jeffrey Stein, "Grad School for Juntas," *Nation*, May 21, 1977; Michael Klare, *Supplying Repression: US Support for Authoritarian Regimes Abroad* (Washington, D.C.: Institute for Policy Studies, 1977); and Noam Chomsky and Edward Herman, *The Washington Connection and Third World Fascism* (Boston: South End, 1979).

5. See Frances Moore Lappe and Joseph Collins, *Food First: Beyond the Myth of Scarcity* (Boston: Houghton Mifflin, 1977), especially chaps. 5, 6, 8.

6. *Business Week,* April 28, 1975, p. 8.

7. "I Have Heard the Cry of My People," May 6, 1973, unpublished.

8. Shelton H. Davis, *Victims of the Miracle: Development and Indians in Brazil* (New York: Cambridge University Press, 1977); and Chomsky and Herman, *Washington Connection*, pp. 109–118.

9. Chomsky and Herman, *Washington Connection*, p. 44. See especially tables 1, 11, pp. 43, 45.

10. Klare, *Supplying Repression*, p. 9.

11. Ahmad, "Post-Colonial Systems of Power."

12. A. Sivanandan, "Imperialism and Disorganic Development in the Silicon Age," *Race and Class* 21, no. 2 (Autumn 1979).

13. ISLAM AND POLITICS

1. See Norman Daniel, *Islam and the West: The Making of an Image* (Edinburgh: University of Edinburgh Press, 1958).

2. Edward Said, *Orientalism* (New York: Pantheon, 1978).

3. For a discussion on this question, see Stuart Schaar, "Orientalists in the Service of Imperialism," *Race and Class* 2 (Summer 1979).

4. Leonard Binder, *Iran: Political Development in a Changing Society* (Berkeley: University of California Press, 1962), pp. 61–62.

5. Marvin Zonis, "The Political Elite of Iran: A Second Stratum?" in *Political Elites and Political Development in the Middle East*, ed. Frank Tachau (New York: Halsted, 1975), pp. 212–213.

6. Syed Ameer Ali, *The Life and Teachings of Mohammed; or, The Spirit of Islam*, 3d ed. (London: W. H. Allen, 1899).

7. I owe this and the following point to Anwar H. Syed, *Islam and the Dialectic of National Solidarity in Pakistan* (New York: Praeger, 1983), chap. 2.

8. The literature on millenarian movements is quite extensive. A few basic works are: Vittorio Lanternari, *The Religions of the Oppressed* (New York: Knopf, 1963); N. Cohn, *The Pursuit of the Millennium* (London: Secker and Warburg, 1957); S. L. Thurpp, ed., *Millennial Dreams in Action: Comparative Studies in Society and History*, supp. 2 (The Hague: Mouton, 1962).

9. Syed, *Islam and the Dialectic of National Solidarity in Pakistan*, chap. 2.

10. See James Kritzeck and William H. Lewis, eds., *Islam in Africa* (New York: Van Nostrand-Reinhold, 1969). On the appeal of Islam among poor blacks in the United States, see the very powerful *Autobiography of Malcolm X* (New York: Grove, 1965); Archie Epps, ed., *Speeches of Malcolm X at Harvard* (New York: Morrow, 1968); B. U. Essien-Udom, *Black Nationalism: A Search for Identity* (Chicago: University of Chicago Press, 1962). Relatively little is known about the continuing conversion of Untouchables to Islam. For a brief description and references, see *World View: 1983* (New York: Pantheon, 1983), pp. 113–114.

11. For example, due to property expropriations and repression, in Jerusalem alone the Christian population had been reduced from twenty-five thousand in 1967 to seven thousand in 1980. Similarly, Palestinian Christians constitute a disproportionate number of political prisoners in Israel.

12. Germaine Tillion, *Algeria: The Realities* (New York: Knopf, 1958).

## 14. ROOTS OF THE RELIGIOUS RIGHT

1. Rajmohan Gandhi, *The Good Boatman: A Portrait of Gandhi* (New York: Viking, 1995), p. 35.

2. Amrita Basu, "Hindu Women's Activism in India and the Questions It Raises," in *Appropriating Gender: Women's Activism and Politicized Religion in South Asia*, ed. Patricia Jeffery and Amrita Basu (New York: Routledge, 1998), pp. 167–184 passim.

## Part III

### INTRODUCTION

1. This consensus was, in his famous analysis, one of the four "pillars" on which the American Century rested. See, in this section, "Cracks in the Western World (View)" and "Pioneering in the Nuclear Age," in part 4.

2. *New York Times*, October 29, 1965.

3. Interestingly, Ahmad points out, Gaddis's post–World War II "long peace" directly echoes the nineteenth-century "long peace" of Metternich and Bismarck. The dominant historiography of that period similarly neglects that it saw the most intense and brutal European colonization of the peoples of Africa, Asia, and the Middle East. Thus,

in its very naming, Gaddis's Cold War "long peace" illustrates its continuity with the centuries of Western colonization that preceded it and constitutes only the latest phase of what Ahmad names a "war system."

4. *boundary 2* 18, no. 3 (1991): 20–28

5. Quoted in Eqbal Ahmad, "Nightmare Victory," *Mother Jones*, March–April 1991.

6. For further elaboration, see "The Roots of the Gulf War," a talk he gave in November 1990 while the massive US mobilization for war in the Gulf was under way. Available from David Barsamian, *www.alternativeradio.org*; also available in the Eqbal Ahmad archives, Hampshire College, Amherst, Massachusetts.

7. Ahmad, "Nightmare Victory."

8. Ibid.

9. See "The Limits of 'Infinite Reach,'" *Al-Ahram,* September 10–16, 1998.

10. "A Time to Remember," *Dawn*, August 9, 1992; "West's Odious Role in Bosnia," *Dawn*, November 2, 1992; "Last Call for Bosnia," *Dawn*, May 23, 1993; "Welcome War in Bosnia," *Dawn*, 1994 (exact date unknown); "Why NATO Has Failed," *Al-Ahram*, April 8–14, 1999.

11. Ahmad, "Why NATO Has Failed."

12. Ibid.

13. "1992: A Requiem and a Prayer," *Dawn*, January 3, 1993.

14. As he was called by Amrita Basu, in a talk celebrating his legacies, given at Hampshire College in October 2000.


15. POLITICAL CULTURE AND FOREIGN POLICY

1. John Gittings, "The Origins of China's Foreign Policy," in *Containment and Revolution*, ed. David Horowitz (Boston: Beacon, 1967), p. 186, paraphrasing Woodrow Wilson's many speeches explaining the Open Door policy. In a 1907 lecture at Columbia University, for example, Wilson explained: "Since trade ignores national boundaries and the manufacturer insists on having the world as a market, the flag of his nation must follow him, and the doors of the nations which are closed must be battered down. . . . Concessions obtained by financiers must be safeguarded by ministers of state, even if the sovereignty of unwilling nations be outraged in the process. Colonies must be obtained or planted, in order that no useful corner of the world may be overlooked or left unused" (Woodrow Wilson, *Constitutional Government in the United States* [1908; reprint, New Brunswick: Transaction, 2002]).

2. Richard J. Barnet and Ronald E. Muller, *Global Reach: The Power of the Multinational Corporations* (New York: Simon and Schuster, 1975), pp. 16–17.

3. Cited in ibid., p. 19.

4. Ibid., p. 19.

5. Ibid., p. 13.

6. Ibid., p. 20.

7. Ibid., p. 20.

8. Henry Kissinger, *American Foreign Policy: Three Essays* (New York: Norton, 1969), p. 71. "Today the poorest Western country—Portugal—has the widest commitment outside Europe because its historic image of itself has become bound up with its overseas possessions. This condition is unlikely to be met by another European country—with the possible exception of Great Britain—no matter what its increase in power" (pp. 70–71).

9. Lyndon Johnson, "Why We Are in Vietnam" (speech, July 28, 1965).

10. I owe the quotations in this paragraph to Edward McNall Burns, *The American Idea of Mission* (New Brunswick: Rutgers University Press, 1957).

11. I owe the quotations and the argument in this paragraph to William Appelman Williams, *America Confronts a Revolutionary World: 1776–1976* (New York: Morrow, 1976), pp. 27, 30.

12. Henry Kissinger, "Defense of the 'Grey Areas,'" *Foreign Affairs* 33 (April 1955): 416–428.

13. Ibid., p. 423

14. Richard Hofstadter, *The Paranoid Style in American Politics* (New York: Knopf, 1965), p. 29.

15. Department of State Bulletin 24, May 28, 1951.

16. *New York Times*, October 29, 1965.

17. I. F. Stone, "The Threat to the Republic," *New York Review of Books*, May 27, 1976, p. 3.


16. THE COLD WAR FROM THE STANDPOINT OF ITS VICTIMS

1. John Lewis Gaddis, "The Long Peace: Elements of Stability in the Postwar International System," in *The Long Peace* (New York: Oxford, 1987), p. 216.

2. Ibid.

3. Ibid.

4. Ibid., pp. 232, 237.

5. Daniel Ellsberg, introduction to E. P. Thompson and Dan Smith, eds., *Protest and Survive* (New York: Monthly Review Press, 1981).

6. Henry Kissinger, *Nuclear Weapons and Foreign Policy*, abridged ed. (New York: Norton, 1969), p. 391.

7. Edward Said, *The Question of Palestine* (New York: Times Books, 1976).

## 18. CRACKS IN THE WESTERN WORLD (VIEW)

1. New York: Monthly Review Press, 1981.

2. *Force Without War* (Washington, D.C.: Brookings, 1978).

3. Kissinger argued for a nuclear option in these "grey areas." See Henry Kissinger, "Military Policy and the Defense of the 'Grey Areas,'" *Foreign Affairs*, April 1955.

4. Henry Kissinger, *Nuclear Weapons and Foreign Policy*, abridged ed. (New York: Norton, 1969), p. 391.

5. Ibid., p. 44.

6. William Beecher, "The Shift in Strategic War Plans," *Army*, November 1973.

7. James R. Schlesinger, "Remarks to Overseas Writers Association Luncheon," U.S. Department of Defense press release, Washington, D.C., January 10, 1974.

8. Noam Chomsky, "Israel's Invasion and the Disarmament Movement," *MERIP Reports*, September–October 1982, p. 40.

## Part IV

### INTRODUCTION

1. "Comments on the UN Seminar on the Inalienable Rights of the Palestinian People," paper delivered at the UN, March 15, 1982. Available in the Eqbal Ahmad Archives, Hampshire College, Amherst, Massachusetts.

2. For a discussion of the US as a settler colonial power, see chapter 15, "Political Culture and Foreign Policy: Notes on American Interventionism in the Third World," in part 3 of this volume

3. See Mahmood Mamdani, *Good Muslim, Bad Muslim: America, the Cold War, and the Roots of Terror* (New York: Pantheon, 2004).

4. Eqbal Ahmad, "Born Again Apartheid," *Dawn*, October 25, 1998. Available in the Eqbal Ahmad Archives.

5. Eqbal Ahmad, "Peace in the Middle East: A Lost Opportunity," *Agenda*, January 1995, pp. 4–5. Available in the Eqbal Ahmad Archives.

6. Eqbal Ahmad, introduction to Edward Said, *The Pen and the Sword: Conversations with David Barsamian* (Monroe, Maine: Common Courage, 1994).

7. Eqbal Ahmad, "An Accord on Apartheid," *Dawn,* October 1, 1995.

8. Handwritten original copy of the letter dated September 17, 1982, in the possession of Noubar Hovsepian.

9. Ibid.

10. Ibid.

11. Edward Said, *The Question of Palestine* (New York: Times Books, 1979), p. xxxvi.

## 27. PIONEERING IN THE NUCLEAR AGE

1. [E. P. Thompson and Dan Smith, *Protest and Survive* (New York and London, 1981). The introduction by Daniel Ellsberg leaves out two primary instances: Richard Nixon's explicit threat to employ nuclear weapons during the Jordanian-PLO conflict of 1970 and the US worldwide nuclear alert during the October 1973 war between Israel and the Arabs.—*Eds.*]

2. See Noam Chomsky, "Israel's Invasion and Disarmament," *MERIP* (Middle East Research and Information Project), September–October 1982, p. 40.

3. Samuel P. Huntington, *Political Order in Changing Societies* (New Haven, Conn., 1968), p. 4.

4. Edward Said, *The Question of Palestine* (New York, 1979), p. 95.

5. Theodor Herzl, *Complete Diary*, ed. Raphael Patai, trans. Harry Zohn (New York: Herzl Press and T. Yoseloff, 1960), 1:88, quoted in Said, *The Question of Palestine*, p. 13.

6. Joseph Weitz, *My Diary and Letters to the Children* (Tel Aviv, 1965), 2:181–182, quoted in Said, *The Question of Palestine*, p. 100.

7. [There is a paucity of information on these two crucial historical issues. There is, however, a recent emergence of interest, especially among Jewish scholars, in the role that Zionist leaders and organizations played in discouraging the rescue and resettlement of holocaust victims anywhere other than Palestine. There has been relatively less interest in a fuller inquiry into the extent of Zionist collaboration with the Nazis, although no serious scholars, including Zionist scholars, deny that such collaboration did occur.

On the role of Zionist organizations in the rescue of holocaust victims, see, for views from both sides, Aaron Berman, "American Zionism and the Rescue of European Jewry: An Ideological Perspective," *American Jewish History* 70, no. 3 (March 1981): 310–330; Sarah E. Peek, "The Campaign for an American Response to the Nazi Holocaust, 1943–45," *Journal of Contemporary History* 15 (April 1980): 367–400; Isaac Zaar, *Rescue and Liberation: America's Part in the Birth of Israel* (New York, 1954); Henry Feingold, *The Politics of Rescue: The Roosevelt Administration and the Holocaust, 1938–45* (New Brunswick, 1970); Arthur Morse, *While 6,000,000 Died: A Chronicle of American Apathy* (New York, 1968); Ben Hecht, *Perfidy* (New York, 1961); Walid Al-Khalidi, ed., *From Haven to Conquest* (Beirut, 1971), pp. 451–459 (excerpts of a 1939 statement to the US Congress by Rabbi Stephe Wise, cochairman of the American Zionist Emergency Council); Lucy Dawidowicz, *The Holocaust and the Historians* (Cambridge, Mass., 1981); and her article in the *New York Times Magazine* (April 18, 1982), pp. 47ff. (being a defense against "a stream of indictment against American Jews," actually an indictment of Zionist leadership by a few young Jewish scholars). Recently, a commission of study was formed by various Jewish organizations under the chairmanship of Arthur Goldberg, an active Zionist, former US ambassador to the United Nations, and a former judge of the US Supreme Count. The commission was, however, disbanded in controversy before it completed its work.

On Zionist collaboration with Nazis, see Hannah Arendt, *Eichmann in Jerusalem* (New York, 1963; since then, there have been several printings of this important book). See especially chapters 3 and 4, but evidence of Zionist collaboration with the Nazis in the first phase of the Fascist movement is interspersed throughout this brilliant report on the Eichmann trial. Professor Arendt, once a Zionist sympathizer, was widely reviled following the publication of this book. See also her "The Jew as Pariah," in *Jewish Identity and Politics in the Modern Age*, ed. Ron H. Feldman (New York, 1978), pp. 237–279; Jon Kimche and David Kimche, *The Secret Roads: The Illegal Migration of a People, 1938–1948* (London, 1954) (the authors approvingly describe "the full and generous cooperation" between Zionist emissaries and Nazi officials including Adolf Eichmann. One of the authors was the chief Israeli negotiator over the terms of Israeli withdrawal from Lebanon); Ben Hecht, *Perfidy* (Ben Hecht, a successful American Jewish author of, among other things, the film scripts of *Wuthering Heights* and *Scarface*, became a Zionist and supported the armed Irgun group. Following the publication of his polemical attack on Zionist collaboration, he was subjected to an organized campaign of vilification, and his book was generally condemned by pro-Zionist reviewers); Moshe Menuhin, *The Decadence of Judaism in Our Times* (Beirut, 1969); Faris Glubb, *Zionist Relations with Nazi Germany* (Beirut: Palestine Research Centre, 1978)(this monograph by a pro-Palestinian British author is based largely on secondary, mostly Jewish, including Zionist, sources).—*Eds.*]

8. [Figures supplied by the Greater New York Conference on the Soviet Jewry (8 West 40th Street, New York, NY 10018). *Jewish Week* (January 7, 1983) quotes Arych Dulzin, chairman of the Zionist Executive, as telling the Zionist Congress meeting in

Jerusalem that 180,000 went to Israel "where they have adjusted and integrated well. Only 3 % of them chose to leave Israel."—*Eds.*]

9. [Janet Abu-Lughod, "The Continuing Expulsion from Palestine: 1048–1982," in Justin McCarthy, ed., *Middle Eastern Refugees* (The Hague: Brill, forthcoming). According to Professor Abu-Lughod's well-researched estimates, "in addition to the 300,000–350,000 persons immediately displaced by the [June 1967] war, there have been displacements of an additional 400,000 persons (including offspring) since the occupation began."—*Eds.*]

10. See *Ma'ariv*, August 27, 1979.

11. Israel Shahak, *Translations of Hebrew Press and Report*, April 1981; *Ma'ariv*, March 19, 1978.

12. *Wall Street Journal*, January 10, 1983; *New York Times*, December 30, 1982; Jewish Telegraphic Agency, January 3, 1983.

13. Meron Benvenisti, *The West Bank and Gaza: Data Base Project Pilot Study Project* (1982 MS). [The final report was published as Meron Benvenisti, *The West Bank Data Project: A Survey of Israel's Policies* (Washington: American Enterprise Institute for Public Policy Research, 1984).—*Eds.*]

14. Ibid.

15. Ibid., p. 25 [no page reference available for 1984 published version—*Eds.*]; see also Uri Davis, Antonia E. I. Maks, and John Richardson, "Israel's Water Policies," *Journal of Palestine Studies* 9, no. 2 (Winter 1980): 3–31.

16. See Raja Shehadeh and Jonathan Kuttab, *The West Bank and the Rule of Law* (Ramallah, West Bank: International Commission of Jurists and Law in the Service of Man, 1982); Raja Shehadeh, "Legal System of Israeli Settlements," *Review* (International Commission of Jurists), no. 27 (December 1981): 59–74.

17. [In a lecture at Hebrew University in the spring of 1980, Yariv said "Some people talk of expelling 700,000 to 800,000 Arabs in the event of a new war, and instruments have been prepared [for the contingency]." This lecture was widely discussed and commented upon. See Ellen Cantarow and Peretz Kidron, "Israel Talks of a New Exodus," first published in *Inquiry* magazine (Washington, D.C.), December 8, 1980, and later included as an appendix to *The Zionist Plan for the Middle East*, ed. Oded Yinon and Israel Shahak, Special Document Number 1 (Belmont, Mass.: Association of Arab-American University Graduates, 1982).—*Eds.*]

18. Arnold J. Toynbee, foreword to *The Transformation of Palestine*, ed. Ibrahim Abu-Lughod (Evanston, Ill.: Northwestern University Press, 1971), pp. viii, ix.

19. Mark Selden, *The Yenan Way in Revolutionary China* (Cambridge, Mass, 1971), p. 177; for a good overview of the uses of crisis in the Chinese struggle, see chapter 5. For

a vivid account of the events leading up to and of the Long March itself, see Edgar Snow, *Red Star over China*, rev. ed. (New York, 1968). The best account available of the battle of Algiers is in Yves Roussière, vol. 2 of 4 (Paris, 1969); see also Alistair Horne. *A Savage War of Peace: Algeria 1954–1962* (London, 1977), chapters 9 and 10.

## 28. "A WORLD RESTORED" REVISITED

1. ["A World Restored" is the title of Kissinger's doctoral dissertation and his first book, initially published in 1957 as *A World Restored: Metternich, Castlereagh and the Problems of Peace, 1812–22* (Boston: Houghton Mifflin, 1957). The version Ahmad refers to in this article was published in 1964 as *A World Restored. Europe After Napoleon: The Politics of Conservatism in a Revolutionary Age* (New York: Grosset and Dunlap, 1964).—*Eds.*]

2. [There was one ceasefire and two "accords": November 1973 was the date of the ceasefire at kilometer 101. In January 1974, the first Israeli-Egyptian disengagement accord, an interim agreement, was signed at kilometer 101. The author calls it The Accord at Kilometer 101 in his subheading; the January disengagement in the text or the interim agreement (p. 325). (This is sometimes called Sinai 1, but the author doesn't refer to it as such.) The Sinai Accord of September 1975 as in the text is referred to by others as Sinai 2.—*Eds.*]

3. *Le Monde*, January 19, 1974.

4. *Time*, March 4, 1974.

5. *Foreign Affairs*, January 1974.

6. Background briefing, San Clemente, June 26, 1970.

7. Henry A. Kissinger, *A World Restored. Europe After Napoleon: The Politics of Conservatism in a Revolutionary Age* (New York, 1964), pp. 1, 3.

8. Henry A. Kissinger, *American Foreign Policy* (New York, 1969), p. 39.

9. Ibid., pp. 47–49, 39.

10. See, for example, ibid., pp. 80, 81, 84, 85.

11. Ibid., p. 80.

12. Ibid., p. 85.

13. Kissinger, *A World Restored*, p. 318.

14. Henry A. Kissinger, *Nuclear Weapons and Foreign Policy*, abridged ed. (New York: Norton, 1969), pp. 136–137.

15. Henry Kissinger, "Central Issues of American Foreign Policy," in *Agenda for a Nation* (Washington, D.C., 1969).

16. [Admiral Elmo Zumwalt, chief of naval operations, quoted in Michael Klare, "Defense Puts Out to Sea," *Nation*, July 2, 1973.—*Eds.*]

17. Henry Kissinger, "Defense of the 'Grey Areas,'" *Foreign Affairs*, April 1955, p. 423.

18. Marvin Kalb and Bernard Kalb, *Kissinger* (Boston: Little, Brown, 1974), p. 192.

19. Stanley Hoffman, "Choices," *Foreign Policy*, no. 12 (Autumn 1973): 11–12.

20. Kissinger, *American Foreign Policy*.

21. Alfred Grosser, "Europe: Community of Malaise," *Foreign Policy*, Summer 1974.

22. Hoffman, "Choices," p. 13.

23. [For examples of then Israeli ambassador Yitzhak Rabin's secret planning sessions with Kissinger, see Kalb and Kalb, *Kissinger*, pp. 186–209. The Kalbs write that Rabin would "joke rather proudly that he knew more secret ways in and out of the Executive Mansion [of the White House] than the secret service" (p. 204).—*Eds.*]

24. See *MERIP Reports*, no. 31 (October 1974); no. 30 (August 1974); and no. 8 (March–April 1972).

25. US Congress, *Persian Gulf Hearings* (1973), p. 6.

26. Ibid., p. 12.

27. Background briefing, San Clemente, June 26, 1970.


## 29. AN ESSAY ON RECONCILIATION

1. [Edward Said, *The Question of Palestine* (New York: Times Books, 1979), p. 235.—*Eds.*]

2. [Reinhold Niebuhr, letter to the editor, *New York Times*, November 21, 1947, p. 30.—*Eds.*]


## 31. THE PUBLIC RELATIONS OF ETHNOCIDE

1. [Within two weeks of the massacres at Sabra and Shatilla (16–18 September 1982) the Israeli government of Menachem Begin established a commission of inquiry into the atrocities, chaired by Yitzhak Kahan, president of the Supreme Court. The Kahan commission report was released in February 1983. It can be accessed on the Web at http://www.mideastweb.org/Kahan_report.htm. Excerpts of it appeared as a "special document" on p. 89 of the same issue of the *Journal of Palestine Studies* in which Ahmad's essay appeared (12, no. 3 [Spring 1983]: 31–40.—*Eds.*]

2. *New York Times*, April 14, 1983.

3. Hannah Arendt, *Eichmann in Jerusalem* (New York: Viking, 1963).

4. [Excerpts from "Israel in Lebanon: Report of the International Commission to Enquire into Reported Violations of International Law by Israel During Its Invasion of

the Lebanon, Cochaired by Sean MacBride," appeared as a "special document" on p. 117 of the *Journal of Palestine Studies* 12, no. 3 (Spring 1983).—*Eds.*]

## 33. BEYOND ARAFAT'S ANTICS

1. [Edward Said, "Rally and Resist for Palestinian Independence 1994," available on the Web at *http://www.labyrinth.net.au/~ajds/intifada/said6.htm.—Eds.*]

2. [Quoted in ibid.—*Eds.*]

3. [Ibid.—*Eds.*]

4. [Edward Said, *The Question of Palestine* (New York: Times Books, 1979), p. 95.— *Eds.*]

## 34. AN ADDRESS IN GAZA

1. [Theodor Herzl, *Complete Diaries,* ed. Raphael Patai, trans. Harry Zohn (New York: Herzl Press and T. Yoseloff, 1960), 1:88.—*Eds.*]

## 35. KING HUSSEIN'S DUAL LEGACY

1. [Reagan was alive though not exactly functional in 1999.—*Eds.*]

*Part V*

## INTRODUCTION

1. The lecture was delivered at the Centre for the Study of Developing Societies in Delhi, India, on December 26, 1998. A shorter version of this talk was published under the title "The Price of Freedom" in the *Index on Censorship* (London) 6 (1997): 52–58.

2. Jinnah's speech to the Constituent Assembly of Pakistan, August 11, 1947, quoted in Ian Talbot, *Inventing the Nation: India and Pakistan* (London: Arnold, 2000), p. 196.

3. *Pakistan Times,* July 7, 1977.

4. See "Jihad International, Inc.," chap. 47 in this volume.

5. Eqbal Ahmad, "In Afghanistan, Ceasefire Please," *Dawn,* April 7, 1991.

6. PBUH = Peace Be Upon Him.

7. Eqbal Ahmad, "As Afghanistan Goes," *Dawn,* September 24, 1995.

8. Eqbal Ahmad, "India's Obsession, Our Choice," Dawn, May 17, 1998.

9. MQM, or the Mohajir Quami Movement (since 1977, known as the Muttahida Quami Movement), is a political movement whose main constituency is the Muslim migrants and refugees who moved to Pakistan from India in 1947.

## 36. PARTITIONED LANDS, DIVIDED SENTIMENTS

1. Faiz Ahmed Faiz, *The True Subject: Selected Poems of Faiz Ahmed Faiz*, trans. Naomi Lazard (Princeton, N.J.: Princeton University Press, 1988).

## 38. THE BETRAYED PROMISE

1. [The Sharia bill and the Hudood ordinances were central to General Zia ul-Haq's Islamization campaign. The aim of the Sharia bill was to make the sharia the supreme law of Pakistan, a law that would stand above the constitution and the power of legislation. The bill prohibited appeals against judgments issued by the sharia courts from being heard by the supreme court of Pakistan. The Sharia bill was first introduced into the Pakistan parliament in 1985 by the Jamaat-i-Islami, which was closely allied with General Zia's regime. The bill failed to win parliamentary approval; however, General Zia enacted it by ordinance in 1988 after dissolving the national and provincial assemblies. An amended version of the Sharia bill was approved by the National Assembly during Prime Minister Nawaz Sharif's first term (1990–93) in office.

In 1979, General Zia ul-Haq introduced by decree a series of new laws broadly known as the Hudood ordinances aimed at bringing the criminal justice system of Pakistan in "conformity with the injunctions of Islam." The Hudood ordinances included laws regulating and criminalizing *Zina* (i.e., various forms of sexual relations and intercourse, including adultery); *Qazf* (false accusations of Zina crimes); and offenses against property and prohibition. In the Zina ordinance, rape is defined as "zina bil jabr" (i.e., forced adultery), and an offense of *zina* is said to have occurred whenever "a man and a woman . . . willfully have sexual intercourse without being validly married." Human rights activists in Pakistan have for long protested that the Zina ordinance has been used to discriminate against women in general and that these ordinance in effect have legitimized sexual violence against women.

The Qisas and Diyat laws of 1990 redefined acts of physical injury, manslaughter, and murder such that they are not seen as violations of the legal order of the state and thus prosecutable by the state but as acts affecting the individual victim, as private, negotiable matters to be resolved by victims or their heirs/survivors and perpetrators. These laws have been deemed by human rights activists as giving state sanction to the practice of honor killings.—*Eds.*]

2. [The Ahmadis (or Ahmadiyyas) emerged in the context of the rapid changes wrought by colonialism and nationalism in nineteenth-century North India. They are followers of a North Indian Muslim writer, Mirza Ghulam Ahmad, who declared himself the Mahdi (messiah). In 1974, Prime Minister Zulfiqar Bhutto amended the constitution and defined the Ahmadis as heretics, while they define themselves as Muslims. Since 1984, under General Zia's Islamization program, Ahmadis have been prosecuted under Pakistan's penal code for the crime of "pretending" to be Muslims.—*Eds.*]

## 40. PAKISTAN: SIGNPOSTS TO A POLICE STATE

1. I am not using the term "fascism" theoretically to indicate disapproval of the repressive policies of the PPP government, which, unlike Marshal Asghar Khan (leader of the liberal Tehrik-i-Istiqlal Party), I do not regard as being fascist. Rather, I discern a definite trend toward fascism in the structural and political sense of the word, a trend that, if permitted to mature, would make the present government's excesses only the first steps toward the kind of nightmare the people of Brazil, Iran, Chile, and Indonesia are undergoing.

2. An activist and leader of the National Awami Party, whose base was in Baluchistan and the Northwest Frontier Province.

3. For the percentage of votes polled by various political parties in (West) Pakistan in the election to the National Assembly of Pakistan, December 7, 1970, see table 1 in the appendix to this chapter. For seats captured by various political parties in the elections to the provincial assemblies of Punjab, Sind, NWFP, and Baluchistan, December 1970, see table 2 in the appendix to this chapter.

4. Excerpts from *The 1970 Election Manifesto* of the Pakistan Peoples Party:

*General Aims:*

The ultimate objective of the Party's policy is the attainment of a classless society, which is possible only through socialism in our time. This means true equality of the citizens, fraternity under the rule of democracy in an order based on economic and social justice. The aims follow from the political and social ethics of Islam. The Party thus strives to put in practice the noble ideals of the Muslim Faith.

The Party accepts the possibility of a mixed economy, the existence of a private alongside a nationalized sector. However, it is within the public sector that all the major

sources of the production of wealth will be placed. The private sector will offer opportunities for individual initiative in the areas of production, where small enterprises can
be efficient. Monopoly conditions will be abolished, so that private enterprise will function according to the rules of competition.

Nationalization of industries in the public sector will be all basic and key
industries.

All major industries will be nationalized. This will mean taking over into [the] public sector, textile and jute mills over a certain production capacity. In private ownership
these have been sources of excessive profits, inefficient production, wastage of resources,
and unhindered exploitation of workers. In the public sector will be not only the large-
scale production of electrical power, but also all other sources of energy supply, namely
nuclear material, gas, oil, and coal. All the exploitation of mineral wealth, both mining
and ore-processing, will be in the public sector.

As a necessary part of their employment in factories, the workers must be provided
with housing and adequate means of transportation to their place of work. They will be
entitled to paid holidays, and recreation camps will be opened where they can spend
their holidays in healthy surroundings. They will have the right to training facilities for
improving their skills. Hospitals and free medical attention will be incorporated in the
system of workers welfare.

A system of minimum wages, reckoned according to the cost of living, will be enforced both in the public and the private sector.

*Financial Measures*:

The possession of money institutions in the hands of private parties is the source
of exploitation, which uses national wealth and private deposits to create money for the
financing of monopoly capitalists. All big industries have been set up entirely on bank
loans, which means on the money of the depositors. Such loans can be said to have been
the misappropriation of public money by the bankers. To this sort of abuse, which is inherent in any system where banks are in private hands, there has been added the control of banks in cartels belonging to industrialist families.

Unless the State takes hold of all the banks by making them national property, it
will not be able to check inflation. The State's financial policy is at present a prisoner of
the bankers.

All banks and insurance companies will be forthwith nationalized.

*Reform of Taxation System*:

The establishment of a socialist order will, naturally, change the present form of taxation, which being designed for a capitalistic society favors the accretion of wealth with
the privileged classes.

*Agrarian Reform*:

The Party stands for elimination of feudalism and will take concrete steps in accordance with the established principles of socialism to protect and advance the interests of the peasantry.

The promotion of self-help groups and co-operatives is the best way to help the cultivators to improve their lot.

*Patterns of Proprietorship*:

The breaking up of the large estates to destroy the power of the feudal landowners is a national necessity that will have to be carried through by practical measures, of which a ceiling, the norm being the ownership of a maximum of 50 to 150 acres of irrigated land, the maximum varying from tract to tract and being determined on the basis of quality of soil, present productivity and the availability of irrigation facilities.

*Education*:

Primary and Secondary Education will be free up to matriculation, and primary education will be compulsory and free. A 5-year program will be formulated by the end of which all the necessary schools must be built and the primary school teachers trained. Free housing will be provided for such teachers, and their children will be exempted from secondary school boarding fees if they opt for the profession of teaching.

More secondary schools must also be established, with the aim that in due course education will become compulsory up to a prescribed age and level of secondary school education.

Among the compulsory subjects in schools, mathematics will be accorded the place of honor and taught by the most scientific modern methods.

5. Ten categories of industries were put under state control on January 2, 1972. The industries taken over were iron and steel; basic metals; heavy engineering; heavy electrical; motor vehicles; tractor plants; heavy and basic chemicals; petrochemicals; cement; electricity, gas, and oil refineries. A total of thirty-one industrial units which form a part of these ten categories were taken over on January 2, 1972, and January 16, 1972. See *Pakistan Times* (Lahore), January 3, 1973, and January 17, 1973.

6. Army: The Pakistan army consists of ten infantry and two armored divisions, one independent armored group, and one air defense brigade. Total strength, 359,000. General headquarters is at Rawalpindi. The entire officers' cadre receives its precommission training in the Military Academy at Kakul.

Navy: The fleet comprises three submarines (built in France in 1967–1971), one light cruiser (cadet training ship), four destroyers, two fast antisubmarine frigates, one survey ship, eight coastal minesweepers, one patrol craft, two seaward defense boats, two oilers, one water carrier, and four tugs. The principal naval base is Karachi. Naval personnel in

1972 comprised 950 officers and 9,550 ratings. The submarine *Ghazi* (ex-USS *Diablo*) transferred from the US Navy in 1964, was sunk during the India-Pakistan War on December 4, 1971. The destroyer *Khaibar* (ex-IINIS *Cadiz*), purchased from Britain in 1956, was also sunk in December 1971, as were three patrol craft built in Britain in 1965.

Air Force: The Pakistan air force came into being on August 14, 1947. It has its headquarters at Peshawar and is divided into flying (operations), administrative, and maintenance commands. Tactical units include one squadron of B-57B (Canberra) bombers, one squadron of Mirage III-EP supersonic fighters, about three squadrons of MIG 19(F-6) supersonic fighter-bombers acquired from China, one squadron of F-104-A Starfighter interceptors, five squadrons of F-86F Sabre and Canadian Sabre 6 fighters, Mirage III-RP jet reconnaissance aircraft, and two squadrons of C-130B Hercules turboprop transports. Flying training schools are equipped with T-37B/C jet trainers supplied by the USA, Mirage III-DPs, MIG-15Us, and other types. Albatross amphibians and HH-43 helicopters, plus a small number of Mil Mi-8 and Alouette III helicopters, perform maritime reconnaissance, search, and rescue duties. There is a flying college at Risalpur and an apprentices college at Korangi Creek. Total strength in early 1972 was about two hundred combat aircraft and fifteen thousand all ranks. An Aeronautical Engineering Academy had been opened. Source: *The Statesman's Year Book, 1973–74* (London: Macmillan Press Ltd., 1973, p. 1216).

7. For the percentage of government expenditure on defense vis-à-vis total revenue and gross national product, see table 3 in the appendix to this chapter.

8. Over thirteen hundred officers belonging to various administrative levels were prematurely retired on March 12, 1972. These included eleven CSP (Civil Service of Pakistan), five PFS (Pakistan Foreign Service), and six PSP (Police Service of Pakistan) officers. In addition, sixteen senior officers were retired, and two dismissed on August 19, 1973 (*Pakistan Times*, Lahore, March 13, 1972, and August 20, 1973). These officers were arbitrarily sacked under MLR No. II(4) without a "show cause" notice or a chance for putting forward a defense.

On August 20, 1973, Prime Minister Bhutto announced reforms in the administrative structure of the country. The two main advantages of the reforms are supposed to be (a) promotion on the basis of performance and not seniority and (b) induction of talent from outside the service through lateral entry. Both of these pave the way for packing the bureaucracy with PPP favorites from outside the bureaucracy and of promoting those within the bureaucracy. Moreover, the system of recruitment and training also ensures that probationers sympathetic to the government are retained. Unlike the old system where services were allocated on the basis of merit immediately after the competitive examinations, now the probationers undergo training and further exams and are retained or allocated services on the basis of their performance, which gives ample time to check their political attitudes.

9. The main opposition parties are: (1) The National Awami Party (NAP), (2) Jamaat-i-Islami; (3) Jamiat-e-Ulema-i-Islam (JUI) (Hazarvi); (4) Pakistan Muslim League (PML) (Council) (a section of this, however, now supports the government), and (5) the Tehrik-i-Istiqlal. The NAP is almost entirely concentrated in NWFP and Baluchistan. In the elections to the National Assembly in December 1970, NAP could not put up a single candidate from the Punjab; in Sind, it ran only six candidates, all of whom lost, securing only 0.3 percent of the votes. On the other hand, NAP ran sixteen candidates from the NWFP, three of whom were elected, securing 18.4 percent of the votes. Similarly, in Baluchistan, all three candidates put up by NAP were elected, securing 45.1 percent of the votes. In the provincial assemblies of Punjab and Sind, NAP did not get a single seat, while in the NWFP Assembly of forty seats, NAP got thirteen, and in the Baluchistan Assembly of twenty, it got eight seats. (See Mushtaq Ahmad, *Politics Without Social Change* [Karachi: Space Publishers, 1971.)

10. On assuming office as president, Bhutto sought the cooperation of the National Awami Party (NAP). He removed the ban on the party imposed by the Yahya regime and negotiated an agreement to form the PPP-NAP-JUI coalition in the provinces of NWFP and Baluchistan and also at the center. But differences arose when Bhutto appointed men of his choice as governors in these two provinces without consulting the NAP. The dispute was resolved when Bhutto agreed to replace these governors with NAP's nominees. The NAP-JUI coalition was allowed to form provincial governments in the NWFP and Baluchistan. But suspicions and misapprehensions continued, and the NAP did not join the central government. The final break came when the NAP leaders, after signing an accord on the permanent constitution, failed to get it ratified in their general council and had to go back on it. Bhutto retaliated by removing the NAP governors and dismissing the provincial government in Baluchistan.

11. No exact date can be given for the start of insurgency in Baluchistan; however, on February 29, 1973, it was officially announced that "federal forces" would be sent into Baluchistan to restore law and order at the request of the governor, which indicates the extent and intensity of the insurgency at that time. By early 1974, about 40,000 sq. miles (by some estimates, about 80,000 sq. miles) of the area was affected, an estimated twenty thousand insurgents were involved, and about five clashes were taking place in a week. (See *Outlook* (Karachi) 2, no. 4 [January 5, 1974]). The main areas of insurgency include Jhalawan, Sarawan, Marri Hills, and parts of Sibi, Kharan, Chagai, Mekran, and Lesbela. (Press release issued by the chairman and members of the Baluch Students Organisation

Camp at Marri Hill dated January 3, 1974.) Population 2.4 million according to *The Population Census of Pakistan 1972*.

12. The Jamaat-i-Islami, a fundamentalist right-wing party, draws its support largely from the petit bourgeois class in urban areas. The Tehrik-i-Istiqlal was formed in early 1970. It claims to be a movement rather than a party, therefore it does not have a rigid party discipline or attitudes. In the elections of 1970, its members contested elections as independents. The Tehrik believes that the single most real and important problem facing Pakistan is the unity of Pakistan and the restoration of democracy. It is an upholder of the "Ideology of Pakistan." Air Marshal (retd.) Asghar Khan is the convenor (see Asghar Khan, speech on radio and TV of December 1970, and also *Aims and Objectives of the Tehrik-i-Istiqlal* (Urdu), pamphlet published from the party office, Rawalpindi).

13. In 1974, Bhutto pushed through a constitutional amendment that categorized the Ahmadiyyas as heretics and therefore non-Muslims.

## 47. JIHAD INTERNATIONAL, INC.

1. [The term "Deoband" refers to the leading Muslim madarsah in South Asia, founded in 1867 by Muhammad Abid Hussain at the height of colonial rule. The Deobandi are a religious reform movement that emerged in colonial India and sought to grapple with the challenge of the Muslims' loss of temporal power to the colonial state. They were influenced by the eighteenth-century Muslim reformer Shah Wali Allah and by the Wahhabi movement. Like other nineteenth-century reform movements, the Deobandi looked to the past or to religious texts (in this case, the *hadiths* and the Quran) as a source for cultural and social revival. For the Deobandis, the *hadiths* became the basis for a critique of local customs and practices that they viewed as contrary to an authentic Muslim identity and practice. In the nineteenth and early twentieth centuries, the Deobandi were known for their emphasis on piety and their political quietism, and the majority of Indian ulema that came out of the Deoband madarsah opposed the Pakistan movement. The Deoband madarsah's influence has also extended to more recent movements such as the Taliban and other militant groups in Pakistan. For more on the Deobandis, see Barbra Daley Metcalf's *Islamic Revival in British India: Deoband, 1860-1900* (Princeton, N.J.: Princeton University Press, 1982).

The Barelvis were a competing reform movement that also emerged in North India in the nineteenth century. While historically the term referred to those from Barreilly, a city in North India, in more recent times the term refers to the followers of Ahmad Riaz Khan, a religious scholar and reformer from Bareilly. In contrast to the Deobandis, the Barelvi movement was more open to local customs and practices, including worship of sufi saints. Here, Ahmad is concerned about the fact that the terms "Deobandi" and "Barelvi" have to come to signify sectarian distinctions among South Asia's Sunni Muslims and that these distinctions have translated into political violence.—*Eds.*]

2. [The Khilafat Movement (1919–1924) was a pan-Islamic movement that sought to protest the dismemberment of the Ottoman Empire by the great powers after World War I. In addition, the movement sought to protect the status of the Ottoman sultan as the *khalifa*, or custodian, of the holy Muslim shrines in Mecca, Medina, and Jerusalem. Here, Ahmad is referring to the alliance between the Indian nationalist movement under the leadership of Gandhi and Mohammed Ali and Shawkat Ali, who were the main organizers of Central Khilafat Committee. Gandhi became a member of the Central Khilafat Committee in order to gain Muslim support for the Congress-organized noncooperation movement in the struggle for independence.—*Eds.*]

## 48. BEYOND MUTUAL DESTRUCTION

1. [This article is an edited version of a seven-part series on Kashmir that Ahmad wrote for *Dawn* in 1996. It is an index of his perspicacity that the passage of time—the Lahore bus ride, Kargil, and other developments—has not diluted the validity of his propositions for a situation as fluid and fluctuating as Kashmir's.—*Eds.*]

## 52. NO, NOT AGAIN!

1. [Here, Ahmad is writing specifically about the six "References" filed by then-president Ghulam Ishaq Khan in Special Courts to investigate charges of abuse of power and corruption by former prime minister Benazir Bhutto. Ahmad is concerned not with these specific references, however, but with the overall political context in Pakistan. In this context, the abuse of power and authority and corruption are the norm, where the army exercises undue control over the state and government and dictates terms to elected civilian leaders. In Ahmad's view, the law becomes not an instrument of justice and accountability but a means to rig the political system in favor of incumbents.—*Eds.*]

# PERMISSIONS

*Part I*

"Revolutionary Warfare: How to Tell When the Rebels Have Won" first appeared in *The Nation* (New York), August 30, 1965, pp. 95–100. Reprinted with permission of *The Nation*.

"Radical but Wrong" first appeared in the *Monthly Review* 20, no. 3 (July–August 1968): 70–83, as part of a collection of articles in response to Régis Debray's book *Revolution in the Revolution?* (New York: Monthly Review Press, 1967). Reprinted with permission of *Monthly Review*.

"Counterinsurgency" is excerpted from "Revolutionary War and Counter-insurgency," *Journal of International Affairs* 25, no. 1 (May 1971). Reprinted with permission of *Journal of International Affairs*.

"Epilogue: The Lessons of Vietnam," Eqbal Ahmad's comments on Samuel P. Huntington, first appeared in Richard M. Pfeffer, ed., *No More Vietnams? The War and the Future of American Foreign Policy* (New York: Adlai Stevenson Institute of International Affairs, 1965), 232–243. ©1968 by The Adlai Stevenson Institute of International Affairs. Reprinted by permission of HarperCollins Publishers

"PLO and ANC: Painful Contrasts" was first published as "PLO & ANC: Sad Comparisons" in *Dawn*, June 26, 1994.

"Iran's Landmark Revolution: Fifteen Years Later" first appeared in *Dawn*, February 13, 1994.

"The Making of The Battle of Algiers" is a hitherto-unpublished talk given at Hampshire College in 1998.

"Algeria Began Badly: Remembering Sidi Mohammed" is a combined version of two articles, "Remembering Sidi Mohammed," *Dawn*, July 3, 1992, and "Algeria Began Badly," *Dawn*, September 20, 1997.

*Part II*

"From Potato Sack to Potato Mash: The Contemporary Crisis of the Third World" first appeared in *Arab Studies Quarterly* 2, no. 3 (Summer 1980): 223–234. Reprinted with permission of *Arab Studies Quarterly*.

"Postcolonial Systems of Power" first appeared in *Arab Studies Quarterly* 2, no. 4 (Fall 1980): 350–363. Reprinted with permission of *Arab Studies Quarterly*.

"The Neo-Fascist State: Notes on the Pathology of Power in the Third World" first appeared in *Arab Studies Quarterly* 3, no. 2 (Spring 1981): 170–180. Reprinted with permission of *Arab Studies Quarterly*.

"War of the Rentier States" first appeared in *Khamsin: Journal of Revolutionary Socialists of the Middle East* 12 (1986): pp. 47–51. Reprinted with permission of Garnet Publishing incorporating Ithaca Press.

"Islam and Politics" first appeared in Yvonne Haddad, Byron Haines, and Ellison Findley, eds., *The Islamic Impact* (New York: Syracuse University Press, 1984), pp. 7–26. © 1984 by Syracuse University Press. Reprinted with Permission of Syracuse University Press

"Roots of the Religious Right" first appeared in *Dawn*, January 24, 1999.

*Part III*

"Political Culture and Foreign Policy: Notes on American Interventions in the Third World" first appeared in Allen F. Davis, ed., *For Better or Worse: The American Influence in the World* (Westport, CT: Greenwood, 1981), pp 119–131. © 1981 by American Studies Association. Reprinted with permission of Greenwood Publishing Group, Inc., Westport, CT.

"The Cold War from the Standpoint of Its Victims" is a hitherto unpublished paper in response to John Lewis Gaddis's "The Long Peace: Elements of Stability in the Postwar International System," *International Security* 10, no. 4 (Spring 1986): 99–142; delivered at "Rethinking Cold War History: A Conference in Honor of William

Appleman Williams," held at the University of Wisconsin, Madison, on October 18–20, 1991. The talk from which this article derived was called "Victims of the Long Peace."

"Yet Again a New Nixon" first appeared in *Dawn*, May 7, 1994.

"Cracks in the Western World (View): Questions for the US and Europe" first appeared in *Radical America* 19, no. 1 (1985): 37–46. Reprinted with permission of *Radical America*.

"At Cold War's End: A World of Pain" first appeared in *Boston Review*, June–August 1993, pp. 10–14. Reprinted with permission of *Boston Review*.

"Terrorism: Theirs and Ours" was a talk delivered at the University of Colorado, Boulder, on October 12, 1998, transcribed and edited by David Barsamian as an Open Media Series pamphlet, 2001. Reprinted with permission of David Barsamian www.alternativeradio.org.

"A Time to Remember" first appeared in *Dawn*, August 9, 1992.

"Welcome War in Bosnia" first appeared in *Dawn*, 1994 (exact date unknown).

"America's Gulf War: Neglected Perspectives" is edited from an article of the same name that appeared in the *Friday Times* (Pakistan), September 6–12, 1990, p. 6. "The Hundred-Hour War" first appeared in *Dawn*, March 17, 1991.

"Covering the Middle East" is edited from an article of the same name that first appeared in *Dawn*, May 5, 1991.

"After the Winter Bombs" first appeared in *Dawn*, December 20, 1998.


## Part IV

"Pioneering in the Nuclear Age: An Essay on Israel and the Palestinians" first appeared in *Race and Class* 25, no. 4 (Spring 1984): 1–20. Reprinted with permission of *Race and Class*.

"'A World Restored' Revisited: American Diplomacy in the Middle East" first appeared in *Race and Class* 17, no. 3 (Winter 1976): 223–252. Reprinted with permission of *Race and Class*.

"An Essay on Reconciliation" (review of "The Question of Palestine," by Edward Said) first appeared in *The Nation* (New York), March 22, 1980, pp. 341–343. Reprinted with permission of *The Nation*.

"On Arab Bankruptcy" first appeared in *The New York Times*, August 10, 1982. Reprinted by permission of the estate of Eqbal Ahmad.

"The Public Relations of Ethnocide" first appeared in *Journal of Palestine Studies* 12, no. 3: 31–40. © 1983 Reprinted with permission of the University of California Press.

"Peace of the Weak" first appeared in *Dawn*, September 12, 1993.

"Beyond Arafat's Antics" first appeared in *Dawn*, July 10, 1994.

"An Address in Gaza" was a lecture presented on September 9, 1994, at Gaza's first human rights conference.

"King Hussein's Dual Legacy" first appeared in *Dawn*, February 14, 1999.

*Part V*

"Partitioned Lands, Divided Sentiments" was a lecture delivered in 1997 at the Centre for the Study of Developing Societies in Delhi, India.

"Jinnah, in a Class of His Own" first appeared in *Dawn,* June 11, 1995.

"The Betrayed Promise" first appeared in *Dawn,* June 18, 1995.

"Letter to a Pakistani Diplomat" first appeared in the *New York Review of Books*, September 2, 1971.

"Pakistan: Signposts to a Police State" first appeared in *Journal of Contemporary Asia* 4, no. 4 (1974). Reprinted with permission of Journal of Contemporary Asia.

"General Zia Is Now the Law" first appeared in *The Nation* (New York), May 30, 1981, pp. 658–660. Reprinted with permission of *The Nation*.

"Bloody Games" (with Richard Barnet) first appeared in the *New Yorker*, April 11, 1988, pp. 44–86. Reprinted by written permission of Richard Barnet.

"Stalemate at Jalalabad" first appeared in *The Nation*, October 9, 1989, pp. 384–387. Reprinted with permission of *The Nation*.

"In a Land Without Music" first appeared in *Dawn*, July 23, 1995.

"Taliban's Unlikely Story" first appeared in *Dawn*, October 15, 1996.

"What After 'Strategic Depth'?" first appeared in *Dawn*, August 23, 1998.

"Jihad International, Inc.," first appeared in *Dawn*, February 14, 1988.

"Beyond Mutual Destruction" combines a series of seven articles on Kashmir that appeared in *Dawn* in 1996. The seven articles were "Camp David as Model" (July 21), "Confronting Reality in Kashmir" (July 28), "Where and When We Blundered" (August 4), "Kashmir: Elements of Impasse" (August 11), "Kashmir: Necessity of Choice" (August 18), "The Riddle of Crossing the River" (August 25), and "Kashmir: A Framework for Peace" (September 9).

"India's Obsession, Our Choice" first appeared in *Dawn*, May 17, 1998.

"When Mountains Die" first appeared in *Dawn*, June 4, 1998.

"No Alternative to Dialogue" first appeared in *Dawn*, June 28, 1998.

"No, Not Again!" first appeared in *Dawn*, July 19, 1992.

"The Signals Soldiers Pick" first appeared in *Dawn*, November 12, 1995.

"Shotgun Governance" first appeared in *Dawn*, March 21, 1999.

# SELECTED WRITINGS—SUBJECTS AND NAMES

Algerian Revolution (GPRA) 89, 90, 97, 98; wilaya districts, 95, 97, 98; UN debate on, 87–88

Aligarh University, 420

Ali Khan, Liaquat, 411

Allende, Salvador, 150, 208, 211

Almohad, 168

Almoravid dynasty, 168

Ambrose, Stephen, 229

Ameer Ali, Syed, 164, 174

American Century, 199, 239, 279

American exceptionalism, 194

American expansionism, 194

American Imperial Century, 193

American Jewish Committee, 366

American Pacification Program in Vietnam, 61

American Revolution, 212

American War of Independence, 206

Amin, Hafizullah, 463, 464, 465, 466, 467, 468, 469, 470, 471

Amin, Idi, 134

Ammar, Abu, 373

Amnesty International, 143, 144, 149, 247

*Among the Afghans* (Bonner), 479

Amstutz, J. Bruce, 475

Anarchists, 263

Anderson papers, 231

Anderson, Perry, 25

Andrews, C. F., 185

Andropov, Yuri, 474, 475, 476

Angola, 304

Anjumane Sarfaroshane Islam, 519

Annan, Kofi, 287

Anticolonialism, 126

Anticommunism, 214, 229

Anti-imperialism, 205, 290

Anti-Semitism, 145, 354

Antonius, George, 350

Anwar, Raja, 466, 467, 469

Apartheid, 79, 304, 309, 354

Aquinas, Thomas, 169

*Arab Awakening* (Antonius), 350

Arab: elite, postcolonial, 9, 293; nationalism, 289, 295, 326, 328, 347, 383; nationalist ideology, 300, 331; rejectionism, 358; revolt, 383; world, recolonization of, 198

Arabism, 300, 377

Arab-Israeli conflict, 114, 162, 275, 350; speculations on future (fifth) Arab-Israeli war, 329–331

Arab Socialist Union, 345

*Arab Studies Quarterly*, 108, 110, 112, 114

Arab-Israeli War of 1942, 384, 561

Arab-Israeli War of 1961, 309, 329, 353

Arab-Israeli War of 1973 (October War), 230, 237, 319–327, 329, 330, 331, 339, 345, 346, 347, 348; Abu-Rudeis oil fields, 320, 325, 326; Accord at Kilometer 101 (January 1974 disengagement), 319, 320–323, 325, 331; ceasefire (October 1973), 319, 321, 322, 323; DEFCON-3 nuclear alert, 237, 238, 319; Egyptian Third Army, 319, 320, 321, 322, 324, 331; Giddi and Mitla passes, 320, 323, 324, 325, 326; Israeli demobilization, 321, 324; Israel's options, 323–325; Sinai Accord (September 1975), 319, 320, 325–329; US-Israeli agreement, 327; US military support of Israel, 232, 319, 322

Arabists, Washington's, 346

Arafat, Yasser, 76, 77, 78, 79, 80, 257, 294, 369, 370, 371, 372, 373, 374, 375, 383

ARAMCO, 331

Architects for Social Responsibility, 233

Arendt, Hannah, 250, 367

Argentina, 143, 145

Armageddon, 299

Armaments industry, 157, 207, 311, 330

*Armed Forces Journal International*, 481

Armée de Libération Nationale (ALN), 10, 90, 97, 98, 581n2

Arms habit, 112, 113, 157

Arms market, world, 487

Arms race, 222, 223, 230, 231, 233, 235, 236, 237, 245, 255, 256, 298; and imperialism, 196, 234; India and Pakistan, 397, 403, 446, 509, 541, 544, 550; Middle East, 325, 329

Benvenisti, Meron, 312, 313
Berger, John, 117, 120
Berlin, 236
Berlin Wall, 196, 221, 245
Berque, Jacques, 162
Berrigan, Daniel, 165
Betancourt, Romulo, 35
Bharatiya Janata Party (BJP), 183, 187,
    188, 526, 539, 545, 549; government,
    543, 548, 550; leaders, 190, 540, 546
Bhutto, Benazir, 397, 541, 546, 560
Bhutto, Ghinwa, 546
Bhutto, Zulfiqar Ali, as Prime Minister of
    Pakistan, 82, 392, 425, 431, 432, 438,
    439, 440, 441, 442, 443, 448, 449, 484,
    513, 560, 564, 589–596n2, 599n8,
    600n10
Bigeard, General, 5, 20
Biharis, xv, 425
Bill of Rights, 206
bin Attar, Laila, 264
bin Ladin, Osama, x, 199, 258, 259, 261,
    264, 265, 266, 393, 511
Binder, Leonard, 163
Bir Zeit University, 314
Bismarck, 220
Bitat, Rabah, 95
Blackburn, Robin, 25
"Black Out" (Faiz), 410
Blacks, American, 215
Blair, Tony, 287
Blechman, Barry, 237
Bogomil, 267
Bolivar, 35
Bolivian Special Forces, 5
Bolsheviks, xi, xii
Bonaparte, Napoleon, 161
Bonner, Arthur, 475, 479, 480
Bosnia, 197, 248, 249–252, 256, 267–270;
    arms embargo on, 200, 251, 256, 271,
    273, 379; Bihac pocket, shelling of,
    272; Croatia, alliance with, 272; ethnic
    cleansing in, 183, 188, 250, 251, 267,
    271, 379; genocide in, 179, 200, 249,
    250, 267, 271, 272; Kupres, capture of,
    272; logistical isolation of, 272; mili-
tary gap with Serbia, 251; Muslims of,
    267; no-fly zone in, 251; Muslim
    world, responsibility of, 272–273; re-
    construction of, 270; Srebrenica, Serb
    assault on, 250; UN humanitarian aid
    to, 250; UN membership, application
    for, 252; UNRA peacekeeping forces
    in, 271; Vance-Owen plan, 251, 252;
    V-Corps, 272; Vancouver Summit
    Meeting, 250; war in, 271–273
Bosnia-Herzegovina, 183
*Boston Review*, 197
Boudiaf, Mohammed (Sidi Mohammed),
    94, 95, 97, 100
Boumedienne, Colonel Houari, 10, 90,
    95, 97, 98, 99, 100, 103
Boundary management, American, 75,
    216
Bourgeoisie: colonial, 433; comprador,
    216; Egyptian, 346; European, 112;
    expatriate, 189; haute, 433; indige-
    nous, 149, 208, 334; metropolitan,
    208; national, 138–140, 149–150; na-
    tional security, 151; nonstate, 151; pe-
    tite, 129, 140, 145, 150, 433, 434, 435;
    state, 139, 140, 149, 150, 151; Third
    World, 158; urban, 134
Bourguiba, Habib, 169, 175, 516
Bourguibism, 137
Boutros-Ghali, Boutros, UN Secretary
    General, 250
Brazil, 146, 148; coup of 1958, 148, 150
Brezhnev, Leonid, 461, 464, 468, 469, 473
Brezhnev Doctrine, 470
Britain, xi, xii, 162, 248, 251, 256, 273,
    288, 305, 306; India policy of divide
    and rule, 390, 405
British Guiana, 209
*British Plots Against Afghanistan* (Khalfin),
    457
Brookings Institution study, 237
Brown, Courtney, 210
Brown, Hank, 507
Brown, Harold, 233
Brydon, Dr., 458
Brzezinski, Zbigniew, 248, 461, 484

and, 114, 132, 152, 155, 156, 164, 168, 177, 308, 422; state and, 111, 112, 135, 142, 416

Class consciousness, 150

Class struggle, 129, 136

Clinton, Bill, x, 230, 246, 250, 252, 257, 268, 287, 288, 289, 381; impeachment of, 288

Clinton administration, 251

Clive, Robert, 360

Cognitive dissonance theory, 56

Cohen, Maier, 366

Cohen, Stephen, 523, 524

Cohen Plan, 523

Cold War, x, xii, 3, 46, 67, 113, 146, 162, 193, 194, 196, 200, 217, 219, 222, 223, 228, 229, 235, 254, 271, 288, 389, 511;bipolarity, 193, 196, 221, 229, 235; as bipolar rivalry, 245–246; consensus, 194, 239, 274; as imperial domination, 246; liberals, 65; as "long peace," 194, 196, 197, 219, 220, 221, 223, 224, 246, 579–586n3; orientalists, 114; nature, origins of, xi, 221, 245; neutralists, 17; and "reconnaissance revolution," 220; US policy in, 260; as war system, 223, 225;

Cold Warriors, 233

Collective memory, 410–411

Colonial ethos, 303

Colonialism, 54, 107, 108, 110, 111, 126, 139, 140, 146, 151, 205, 208, 303, 390, 404, 405; settler, 294, 295, 301, 302

Columbia, 27

Columbia University Business School, 210

Combined Action Platoons (CAPS), 49

*Commentary*, 366

Committee of Coordination and Execution (CCE), 94

Common Market, 268, 339

Communism, 22, 49, 50, 68, 146, 201, 212, 265, 270, 482, 485, 491, 516, 517, 525; conspiratorial, 211; global war against, 486; Vietnamese, xiii

Communist conspiracy, 50; Dominican, 14

Communists, 14, 17, 22, 34, 48, 78, 79, 143, 214, 217, 482, 492

Community Defense and Local Development Plan (CD and LDP), 54

Comprehensive Test Ban Treaty, 549

Con Son, tiger cages of, 43

Confidence-Building Measures (CBMs), 549, 550

Conscientism, 137

Conspiracy of silence, 16, 19

Conspiratorial theory, 47, 49, 50

Constitutions, secular, 182

Contras, 484–485

Convention on Genocide, 200

Convention Party [Ghana], 70

Cordovez, Diego, 475, 487, 488, 489

CORDS, 54

Corporate concentration, 148, 210

Corporations: and globalism, 210; ideology, 211; international, 334, 342, 346; metropolitan, 210; multinational, 145, 151, 158, 209, 210, 276, 357; multinational, influence over US foreign policy, 208, 209; multinational internationalism, as agent of, 210

Corson, William R., 576n6

Counterinsurgency, 3, 31, 52, 54, 528; academies and programs, 146; CIA experts on, 6; conspiratorial theory of, 47, 49, 50; conventional-establishment approaches, 37, 38; counterrevolution, as euphemism for, 36–37; and democratic institutions, 9, 62, 63; doctrine of, 53, 61; experts/specialists/theorists, xiii, 5, 7, 10, 47, 55, 58; French, 49, 56, 61, 63; Israeli strategy, 10; liberal-reformist approaches, 6, 37, 39, 54, 60, 61, 576n6; literature on, 47; logic of, 5, 6; in Malaya, 15, 16; mechanization of, 8; permanent, doctrine of, 40; punitive-militarist, 37, 39, 40; techniques of, 41, 48, 73; technocratic-military approaches, 38; technological-attritive, 37, 40, 45, 49, 61; theory and practice of, 37, 577n12; in Vietnam, 55; *see also* Insurgency, definition of; Pacification

Feudalism, 138
*Financial Times*, 428
Fissile Materials Control Treaty, 549
Fix and destroy, 37, 42; *see also* Search and destroy
Flexible Targeting, 230, 239, 240
*Foco, see* Revolutionary *foco*
Ford, Gerald, 210, 349, 381
Foreign Relations Subcommittee on United States Security Agreements and Commitments Abroad, 44
Fort Bragg, course books of, 13, 46
Fourteen Points, Wilson's, 205, 226
France, xi, 63, 101, 162, 248, 251, 256, 273; Algerian Revolution and, 16, 20, 52; Algerian workers in, 94; Fifth Republic, 39, 94; Fourth Republic, fall of, 21, 39, 62, 64, 94, 566; liberal-reformists in, 39; in Vietnam, 19, 61, 68, 87
Free bombing zones, 49
Freedom: procedural, 131, 144; of speech, 215, 444; substantive, 131, 132, 133, 137, 145
Free-fire zones, 38, 49
Free French Army, 39
French Foreign Legion, 62
French Resistance, 39, 494
French Revolution, 10, 81
Friedman, Thomas, 383
Front de Libération Nationale (FLN), 16, 17, 19, 49, 70, 87, 89, 94, 96, 101, 316, 516, 561; and ALN, 98; bureaucracy of, 99; Committee of Coordination and Execution (CCE), 94; FLN-France, 98; support, 94; *wilaya* commanders, 90; wilaya districts, 95, 97; wilaya districts, legitimacy of, 98
Front for Islamic Salvation (FIS), 100, 101–102
Fulbright, James W., 214, 540
Fundamentalism, fundamentalists 110, 114, 115, 179, 180, 186, 435, 491, 492; activist, 115; Christian, 179, 183, 582n3; Iran, 491; Islam and, 114, 167, 173, 179; Islamic, Muslim, 113, 275, 394, 442, 482, 504; Other, rejection of

the, 115, 181, 187, 188, 350, 407; religious, 183, 427, 441; restorationist, 114, 173; Sunni, 289

G-8, 546, 549
Gaddis, John Lewis, xi, 194, 219, 220, 221, 224
Gadhafi, Mu'ammar, 264, 358, 381
Gailani, Pir Sayed Ahmad, 480
Galiani, 54
Gandhi, Indira, 131
Gandhi, Mohandas, 165, 182, 186, 407, 408, 410, 417, 518, 543, 602n2
Gandhi, Rajmohan, 185
Gandhi, Sonia, 548
Garcia, Carlos, 574n3
Gaza, 156, 177, 276, 279, 288, 289, 296, 312, 348, 351, 357, 372; dispossession of Arabs, 353, 357, 368; Israeli withdrawal from, 369; Palestinian refugees in, 371, 380; Zionist settlements, 524
Geisel, 146
Gemayel, Amin, 363
Gemayel, Bashir, 362
Gemayel, Pierre, 363
General Agreement on Trade and Tariffs (GATT), 535
Geneva, 252
Geneva Conventions, 64, 288, 368
Genocide, 5, 8, 21, 45, 73, 108, 148, 179, 197, 309; in Bosnia, 179, 200, 249, 250, 267, 271, 272
Geopoliticians, 337
George, David Lloyd, xi
Germany, 145, 195, 222, 226, 262, 268, 279, 340; Croatian independence, support of, 256; West, 339, 342
Ghana, 135
Ghardimou, Tunisia, 33, 97
al-Ghazzali, 167
Ghosh, Aurobindo, 407
Ghulam, Ustad Ali, 545
Giap, Vo Nguyen, 18, 22, 29, 501 533
Gibb, H. A. R., 162
Giddi and Mitla passes, 320, 323, 324, 325, 326
Gladstone liberals, 458

Harvard University, 8
Hashemite dynasty, 382
Hastings, Warren, 360
Hauser, Rita, 366, 367
Hawatmeh, Niaf, 76, 78
Hekmatyar, Gulbuddin, 393, 394, 395,
    476–477, 481, 482, 490, 491, 497, 505,
    507, 508, 509
Helsinki Accords, 312
Herman, Edward, 149
Herzegovina, 249
Herzl, Theodor, 306, 352, 379
Hevroni, Colonel, 364
*Hidden History of the Korean War, The*
    (Stone), 281
Hijacking, 262, 297, 355
*al-Hilal* (magazine), 416
Hilsman, Roger, 45, 54, 57, 572–579n26
Hindu, Hinduism, 164, 913; ideologues,
    right-wing, 404; Mahasabha, 165, 188;
    militancy, militants, 185, 187; move-
    ment, 183, 405–406; Muslim relations,
    405; nationalists, 182; restorationism,
    181
Hinduism, 164, 185
*Hindustan Times*, 545
Hindutva, 545
Hiroshima, 236, 539, 545
Hiss, Alger, 229
Hista'drut, 322
Hitler, Adolf, 226, 277, 279
Hizb-e-Islami Party, 394, 476–477, 497,
    498, 501, 507
Ho Chi Minh, 18, 22, 68, 278–279
Hobeika, Elias, 363
Hoffman, Stanley, 340
Hofstadter, Richard, 194, 213, 229
Holmes, Oliver Wendell, 14
Holocaust, 187, 257, 262, 306
Holocaust Museum, 249
Holy See, 287
Hostage crisis, Iranian, 283, 469, 519
Hourani, Albert, 418
House of Wisdom, 168
House Un-American Activities Commit-
    tee, 229

al-Hout, Shafiq, 78, 369
Huckleberry Finn, 218
Hughes, Harold E., 40
Hull, Cordell, 218
Humanism, populist, 165
Human rights violations, 128, 131, 132,
    134, 136, 143, 144, 145, 148, 149
Humphrey, Gordon, 489, 490, 499
Humphrey, Hubert, 13, 45
Hunter, Allen, 219
Huntington, Samuel P., 8, 65–69, 71, 73,
    74, 294, 581n2
Hurd, Douglas, 250, 252
Husain, Syeda Abida, 565
Hussain, M. F., 545
Hussein, Amir, 383, 384
Hussein, King, 283, 307, 319, 328, 338,
    345, 371, 375, 381, 382, 383, 384
Hussein, Saddam, 154, 156, 159, 198,
    199, 248, 249, 255, 264, 266, 275, 277,
    278, 279, 280, 281, 282, 283, 285, 287,
    288, 289, 358, 381, 382, 384, 519
al-Husseini, 309

IBM World Trading Organization, 210
Ibn Jamaa, 167, 169
Ibn Khaldun, 399
Ibn Rushd, 168
Ibn Tumart, 168
Ideological illusion, problem of, 117
Ideology, 129, 137, 140; Arab nationalist,
    300, 331; corporate, 211; of difference,
    188, 379; ethnocentric, 312, 367; ex-
    clusionary, 175, 354, 380; fundamen-
    talist, 165, 174, 450, 482; legitimizing,
    290; nationalist, 271; revolutionary, 56,
    57, 201, 263, 348; sectarian, 391; Tal-
    iban, 506; Zionist, 366
Ijima, 172
Imambarahs, 188
Imperialism, 23, 83, 111, 129, 145, 154,
    155, 210, 211, 221, 229, 231, 246, 248,
    279, 280, 293, 303, 332, 351, 383; and
    arms race, 234; contradictions of, 226;
    dialectic of, 330; domestic support for,
    211; legitimacy of, 211, 334; United

States, 319; as war system, 225; welfare, 65; Western, 121, 172, 297, 281, 379; as world system, 224

*In Retrospect* (McNamara), 9

Incrementalism, 216

India, 110, 131, 139, 171, 179, 181, 183, 187, 188, 197, 396, 543–547; Bharatiya Janata Party (BJP), 183, 187, 188, 190, 526, 539, 540, 545, 546, 550; BJP government, 543, 548, 550; British rule, end of, 301; Cabinet mission Plan of 1940, 408; China, relations with, 543, 550; communal violence in, 405, 408; democracy, 406; Direct Action Day, 408; divide and rule, British policy of, 390, 405; elections of 1931, 404, 407, 417; elections of 1940, 422; growth rate, 544; Hindu militancy in, 185; Hindu-Muslim violence, 408; Hindu parties, militant, 526; Indian National Congress (Congress Party), 182, 404, 406, 407, 408, 416, 417, 418, 419, 545, 550; intelligentsia, 550; Jalian Wala Bagh, massacre of, 360; Janata Party, 190; job quotas, British policy of, 406; and Kashmir, moral isolation from, 529, 530; middle class, 405; Moghul, British dominion over, 161; Morley-Minto Reform Act of 1903, 406; Mughal, 415; Muslim aristocracy, 415; Muslim dominion in, 564; Muslim upper and middle classes, 406; Moslems, Muslims in, 415, 417, 427, 517, 551; national movement, 165; nuclear capability, program, 253, 285, 541; nuclear tests, 253, 397, 539, 540, 544, 546, 548; Pakistan, invasion of, 231; Pakistan, relations with, 403–411, 430, 509, 525, 535–537, 543–544, 548–551; Pakistan, trade with, 536, 537; partition of, 389–392, 396, 403, 404, 407, 408, 409, 419; politics, spiritualization of, 407; post partition uprisings, 404; Republic Day, 407; revolt in 1851, 405; "salariat," 405; secular constitution of, 182; self-rule, 406; Sikh dissidents in, 254; two nation theory, 390; ulema, 416, 417, 419, 516; United States, relations with, 446, 525; USSR, friendship pact with, 430

India International Centre, 548

Indian fighting, 54

Indian National Congress (Congress Party), 182, 404, 406, 407, 408, 416, 417, 418, 419, 545, 550

Indian Space Research Organization, 253

India-Pakistan nuclear rivalry and dialogue, 396–397

India-Pakistan war (1948), 396

India-Pakistan war (1965), 155, 396, 410, 462, 557

India-Pakistan war (1971), 410

Indian Parivar, 188

*India Today*, 404

Indochina, xv, 4, 16, 39; American policy in, 213; bombing of, 44, 45, 230, 288, 334; intervention in, US, 208; US defeat, withdrawal from, 233, 239, 332; US invasion of, 36; *see also* Vietnam war

Indonesia, 130, 135, 143, 146, 147, 148, 175, 209

Industrial revolution, 304; responses to, 181–183

Industrial Workers of the World, 215

Industrialization, 138, 145; state-sponsored, 135; turnkey concept of, 99, 135; uneven, 146

Institute for Policy Studies, 233, 393

Institute of Islamic Studies, 186

Institution-building, 69, 70

Insurgency, definition of, 36; *see also* Counterinsurgency

Insurgents, traditional, 118, 119, 126

Intellectuals, 20; revolutionary, 71, 72

Intelligentsia, 169, 174, 180–181, 379, 392, 418, 421, 422, 463, 502, 532, 534, 550

Inter-American Police Academy, 146

International Atomic Agency, 255

International Court of Justice, 255, 265

Islam, 110, 118, 162–172, 248; Apologist
school, 164; civilization, 167, 378;
community, 171; dictatorships, 269;
fundamentalism, 113, 394, 482, 504;
fundamentalists, ix, 179, 507, 514; idealism, ideals, 174, 420; imam, 166;
Christian discourse on, 161; ideological resurgence of, 178; interpretations
of, 290; law, Sunni schools of, 169;
militancy, militants, x, 188, 183, 394,
517, 526, 532; millennial traditions of,
167; movement, 100, 102, 110, 111,
168, 290, 372, 525–526; mystical tradition, 416; as Other, 114; philosophy,
186; political, as adversary of communism, 525; political, conservative and
radical, 519; political culture of, 170;
politics, relationship to, 111, 167; politics and religion, separation of, 160,
164, 165; polity, conditions of ideal,
166; radicalism, 518; as religion of the
oppressed, 171; religion and state
power in, 110, 165–166, 167; revisionist school of, 162; and revolt, legitimization of, 170; scholars of, 162;
Shia, sect of, 174, 289; spread of, 170–
171; state and civil society in, 416; and
state power, 182; studies, 160; theologians of, 167; theological legacy of,
186; ummah, 166, 167, 171, 172; in the
United States, 171; West, relationship
with the, 160–162; Western perspectives on, 162, 164; *see also* Muslim
*Islam and Resistance in Afghanistan* (Roy),
477
Islamicate, 110, 167, 171, 172, 279
Islamic Front, 10, 102
Islamism, Islamists, 101, 102, 114, 182,
183, 185, 186, 289, 290, 395, 500, 503,
512, 514, 519; Afghanistan's hard-line,
516; discourse, 186; extremism, 515;
fundamentalist, 289; Iran's revolutionary, 519; and segregation, veiling of
women, 189; violence of, 514; *see also*
Pan-Islamism
Islamic Welfare Party [Turkey], 102

Ismail, Hafez, 345
Isolationism, 212
Israel, 78, 145, 163, 165, 183, 188, 197,
198, 199, 256, 262, 275, 279, 294, 302,
306, 343, 345, 346, 348, 353, 354,
373–376, 384, 385, 523–524; aliyah
campaign, program, 306, 308, 309,
310, 311; apartheid state, similarities
to, 303, 524; Arabs in, 380; armaments
industry and Soviet immigrants, 311;
Arab labor, reliance on, 310; Arab-
Israeli war of 1967, 319–329; arms ex-
ports, 311; arms sales, arming of, US,
195, 230, 319, 329–330, 339, 342, 344,
347; ceasefire with PLO, 276, 282;
challenge of, 280; creation of, 351; demographic problem, balance, 316,
366; dispersion, policy of, 177; as
dominant power in Middle East, 372;
Egypt, relations with, 316; Eretz Israel,
181, 226, 309, 310, 312, 351, 352, 366;
establishment of, 301; ethnic cleansing, dream of, 270; expansionism, 301,
315, 329; expansionist dilemma, 314;
as *force de frappe* in the Middle East,
345, 348; Gaza, occupation of, 288;
Golan and Jerusalem, annexation of,
230, 288; isolation of, 348–349; *Jihad-
i-Sazindazi*, 516; Jews, immigration of,
294, 309; Jewish settlers in, 114; Judaization of, 308; *Jihad-i-Sazindazi*,
516; Kibbutzim, "socialist," 354;
Lebanon, invasion, occupation, 9,
196, 230, 235, 269, 274, 275, 282,
288, 295, 296, 297, 307, 316, 358, 359,
366, 523; Lebanon, policy of dispersion in, 177; as Mediterranean power,
328; military capability, 329–330; as
military power, 299; moral isolation
of, 297; nuclear capability, program in,
240, 253, 254, 285, 540; "Oriental
Jews," immigration of, 309; Palestine,
colonization of, 276, 370; Palestinians,
expulsion of, 308–312; Phalange,
relationship with, 175, 362; as proxy
for American power, 256, 268;

Macapagal, Diosdado, 16
MacArthur Foundation Genius Award, 233
MacBride commission, 368
MacDonald, Ian, 428
Macnaghten, Sir William Hay, 457
Madani, Abbasi, 102
Madani, Maulana Husain Ahmed, 417
*Madaris*, 100, 395, 396, 501, 518
*Madarsah*, 501
Madigan, Sheriff, 64
Magdoff, Harry, 209
Maghreb, 181, 516
Maghrebins, 170
Magsaysay, President Ramon, 16
Mahabharata, 186
Maisonrouge, Jacques, 210
Majrooh, Sayd Bahaouddin, 454, 455
Malaya, 41; British counterinsurgency in, 15, 16; Chinese squatters in, 15
Malayan Races Liberation Army, 50
al-Mamun (Abbasid caliph), 168
Malik, Abdullah, 427
Malkani, M. R., 188
Managerial elite, 140
al-Manar group, 181
Manchuria, Japanese policy in, 88
Mandela, Nelson, 9, 77, 80
Manifest Destiny, 162
Manto, Sadat Hasan, 409
Mao's dictum, 7, 10, 88
Mao Tse-tung, 7, 15, 24, 29, 59, 88, 317, 496, 497
Market system, international, 122
Marx, Karl (correspondent), 457
Marx, Karl, 122, 279
Marxists, Marxism, 83, 108, 109, 112, 118, 207, 234, 263; Left, 109; scholars, 140; theory, 25; writings, 128;
Massera, 146
Massignon, Louis, 162
Massoud, Ahmed Shah, 477, 478, 497, 505, 507, 508
Massu, General, 5, 40
Master Plan for the Development of Judea and Samaria, 313

Mathias, Charles, 485
Maudoodi (Maududi), Abul Ala, 190, 417, 518
al-Mawardi, 167, 169
McCarthy, 195, 229
McCormack, John, 342
McGhee, George C., 462
McGill University, 186
McGovern, George, 40
McMahon, John, 484, 486
McNamara, Robert, 9, 48, 233, 342
Mecklin, John, 51
Media, American, 274, 352, 381, 448, 517; bias of, 282–286; as propaganda, 281
Mediterranean and Indian oceans region: European participation in, 343; Nixon-Kissinger strategy in, 430; Russian influence, 338; superpower interests, 236, 237, 240, 341; US dominance, 338, 339
Meir, Golda, 262, 295, 318, 345
Menuhin, Moshe, 188
Menuhin, Yehudi, 188
Metropolis, 126, 128, 129, 134, 137, 138, 139, 140, 145, 148, 149, 151, 159, 162, 303, 315
Metternich, 220
Middle East, 10, 81, 155, 156, 165, 196, 222, 225, 226, 230, 236, 237, 239, 240, 253, 254, 255, 256, 268, 273, 274, 277, 279, 280, 284, 293, 296, 299, 301, 320, 331, 332, 338, 339, 345, 349, 357; colonialism and, 198; colonization of, 279; crisis of state and society, 383; experts, 162; hegemony in, US, 288; instability in, 289; interests in, US, 81, 237, 346; modernization of, 352; nuclear threat in, 234, 241; peace process, 195, 228, 230; political culture of, 290; recolonization of, 358; Soviet influence in, 340; strategic importance of, 333; U.S. led multilateral expedition to, 221
Middle East Research and Information Project (MERIP), 9, 10

Nationalism (*continued*)
ethnic, 512; ideological, 109, 145; Indian, 407, 415; Iranian, 158; Islamic, 469; Muslim, 407, 415, 418, 516; nuclearization of, 545; Palestinian, 371; radical, 50, 72, 112, 208, 217; reactive, 68; religious, 392, 435; secular, 290, 407; Serb, 183; Third World, 208

Nationalization, 136, 140, 150, 208, 290, 433

Nation-states, 111, 200, 210, 284, 290

NATO, 232, 240, 268, 337, 341, 494

Navarre, Henri Eugène, 495

Nazis, Nazism, 145, 208, 306

Necessity, doctrine of, 211

Nehru, Jawaharlal, 182, 390, 403, 408, 411, 416

Neocolonialism, 23, 151, 331

Neo-Destour party (Tunisia), 70

Neofascism, 112, 140, 143; as "developmental fascism," 147; roots of, 149–151

Neofascist government, 132

Neofascist regimes, 112, 133, 142

Neofascist states: characteristics of, 143–149; development, "disorganic," 152; denial of distributive justice, 148; development, model of, 147–148; development, contradictions of model of, 152–153; as "export-platform" countries, 148; extraction economy of, 145; and fascism, 145–146; ideological base of, 146–147; instability of, 151–153; leaders of, 146; legitimacy of, 145; and modernization, 147; multinational corporations, dependence on, 145; national security outlook, 147; and neofascism, roots of, 149–151; popular support, lack of, 145; ruling elites of, 153; secret police organizations, 146; social roots of, 151; terror, use of organized, 143–145; US economic and military aid to, 149; vulnerability of, 109

Neo-Islamists, 100

Netanyahu, Benjamin, 257, 383

Neto, Augustino, 79

New Democracy, 317

"New Dialectic of Tasks," 33

New Frontiersmen, 39

New Left radicals, 66

New World Order, 197

New York Park Avenue Synagogue, 258

*New Yorker*, 249, 257, 265

*New York Times*, 13, 19, 43, 45, 49, 214, 217, 257, 259, 282, 285, 295, 342, 360, 361, 366, 381, 382, 383, 425, 493, 498

*New York Tribune*, 457

Niazi, Maulana Kausar, 416

Nicaragua, 152; agrarian policy, 158; contras, 260, 484–485; literacy rate, 158

Nicaraguan Revolution, 152, 158

Niebuhr, Reinhold, 351

Nimeiri, Jaafer, 190

Nixon, Richard, 40, 41, 44, 45, 83, 194, 195, 196, 210, 211, 214, 228, 229, 230, 231, 238, 241, 255, 334, 341, 344, 345, 347, 441, 443, 464, 576n7

Nixon administration, 312, 339, 342

Nixon Doctrine, 199, 211, 213, 240, 284, 343, 382; "regional influentials" of, 83

Nixon-Kissinger doctrine, strategy, 148, 331–332, 430

Nizam-e-Mustafa, 181

Nkrumah, Kwame, 135, 443

*No Exit From Vietnam* (Thompson), 44

Nolting, Ambassador, 217

Nomani, Shibli, 174

North Africa, 156, 168, 170

North Korea, development of nuclear weapons in, 252

North-South conflict, xi, xiii

Nuclear: brinkmanship, 237, 338; crises, 236; deterrence, 220, 539, 541, 542, 547, 549, 550; diplomacy, 236, 240, 299; doctrine, American, 230; escalation, graduated increments of, 238; politics, 236, 253; tests, France, 540; tests, India, 253, 397, 539, 540, 544, 546, 548; tests, Pakistan, 544; tests, USSR, 539; threat in Near and Middle East, 234; war, 235, 239, 18

Nuclear arms, weapons: and American diplomacy, 238; antiproliferation laws,

US, 254; Brookings Institution study, 237; Comprehensive Test Ban Treaty, 549; control in South Asia, Pakistani proposal for, 254; Cruise missiles, 233, 235, 236, 239; Fissile Materials Control Treaty, 549; flexible targeting, 230, 239, 240; Foreign Assistance Act, Section 669 of, 487; India, 397, 539–542; Israeli, 285, 286, 288, 289, 329–330, 540; limited use of, 238; and limited wars, 337; missile systems in Sicily, 241; mutual assured destruction (MAD), 3, 230; MX missiles, 235, 236; NATO countries, deployment in, 239; nonproliferation policy, US, 252, 253, 254; North Korea, 252; Pakistan, objectives in developing, 541; Pershing missiles, 233, 235, 236, 239, 329, 330; and power, 539, 540, 545; proliferation, 197, 252–254, 255, 280, 285, 446, 487; sanctions against, international, 541, 542; sanctions against, US, 546; Sicily, missile systems in, 241; strategic, 541; tactical, 239, 240, 298, 540

"Nuclear War and the Second Coming" (Falwell), 18

Numeiry, Gaafar Mohamad, 344

Nuremberg, 7

Nuremberg Laws, 229, 270

Nusrat, Begum, 560

Nyerere, Julius, 134, 135

Obote, Milton, 134

Occupied Areas, fundamentalist Muslim groups in, 175–176

Occupied Territories, 10, 78, 79, 283, 288, 296, 321, 323, 353, 367, 370; Christian population in, 175; Jewish Zionist settlements in, 276, 313, 369, 374, 375, 380; Jews settling in, right-wing American, 310; Palestinian/Arab inhabitants, expulsion of, 309, 310, 312, 366; Palestinians in, 314, 316, 380

October Revolution, 279

O'Dwyer, Michael, 360

Oil: boycott, embargo, 232, 321, 323, 346, 347, 349; interests, 343; nationalization of Iranian, 290; prices, economics of oil, 283–284; politics of, 198; US control over, 199, 255, 277, 338, 349; world power, centrality to, 295

Oligarchies, right-wing, 208, 217

Oman, 284, 342

Omar, Mulla, 181

OPEC, 283

Open Door policy, 205, 586n1

Operation Desert Storm *see* Gulf war

Operation Gibraltar, 511

Operation Infinite Reach, 199

Organization of Islamic Countries (OIC), 269, 270

Organization of Nonaligned Nations (ONN), 134; charismatic leaders of, 135

Organization of the Secret Army (OAS), 39, 62

*Orientalism* (Said), 351

Orientalists, Orientalism 110, 160, 162, 164, 167

Oslo agreement, 295, 296, 524

Other, rejection of the, 115, 181, 187, 188, 350, 407

Ottoman Caliphate, 279, 407, 518

Ottoman Empire, 161, 182, 275, 383; conquest in 1463 A.D., 267; domination of the Balkans, 161

Ottomans, 515

Oujda, Morocco, 33, 97

Owen, Lord, 251

Oxfam (Oxford Committee for Famine Relief), 428

P-5, 549

Pacification, 39, 54, 73, 576n7; accelerated, 43; in Algeria, 39; campaigns, xiv; dialectic of, 57; partisans of, 37; principles of, 40; Program in Vietnam, American, 61; purists, 49; and reforms, 57; rhetoric of, 39; strategy and tactics of, 48; teams, 53, 54; techniques of, 61; theories, theorists of, 53, 64; in Vietnam, 42, 56, 326

Pacifism, militant, 165

Patriarchy, 180

Pax Americana, 268, 319, 341

Peace: activists, national symposium of, 234; associations, 226; definitions of, positive and negative, 221–22

Peasant, peasants, 117, 120, 122; French, 122; logic of caution, 119, 120, 123; millenarian movements, 120; nationalization of, 125–126; pauperization of, 123; rebellions, 16, 117, 119, 122; revolutions, 82, 117; in Third World, 117

Peccei, Aurelio, 210

People's Democratic Party of Afghanistan (PDPA), 463–464, 465, 466, 467, 478, 489; Khalq and Parcham factions in, 464, 466

People's Liberation Army, 497

People sniffers, 49

People's Party of Algeria (PPA), 96

Peoples' Park in Berkeley, demonstrators, 64

Peres, Shimon, 328, 524

Perle, Richard, 485

Peronism, 137

Persian Gulf, 277, 342, 343, 461

Personalism, 112, 155

Peter the Great, 461

Pfeffer, Richard, 56

Phalange, 316, 358, 362–365

*Philadelphia Inquirer*, 361

Philippine constabulary, 54

Philippines, 74; Central Luzon, 16; colonization of, US, 54, 208; coup of 1966, 150; Garcia administration, 16; Huk movement, 16

Phoenix (*Phung Hoang*) program, 44

Physicians for Social Responsibility, 233

Pike, Douglas, xii, 56, 58

Ping-Han Japanese railroad, 51

Pinochet, 146, 260

PLO-Israeli accord, 369–372

Poets, Muslim, of power and prophecy, 159

Political economy, 540

Political participation, 71

Political power, legitimacy and dispersion of, 120–121

Politics: Arab, 275, 307, 308, 355; autonomy of, 129; of boundary management, 75; of exclusion, 187; guerrilla, 486; Indian, spiritualization of, 407; international, 224, 232, 236, 241; of management, 215; mass, 138, 390, 404; Muslim, 114, 163, 167, 173; nuclear, 236, 253; of oil, 198; paradoxes of elite, 355; personalization of, 437; primacy of, 4, 9, 25, 26, 54, 78; and religion, 160, 164, 165, 183–187; resistance, 499; world, 3, 194, 196, 224, 225, 245, 246, 295, 299, 302, 337, 430, 540, 545

Polygamy, 182

Pontecorvo, Gillo, 4, 85, 91, 92

Popular Front for the Liberation of Palestine (PFLP), 371

Portugal, 144, 211, 341, 343

Postcolonial states, 110, 129, 149, 154, 301, 379, 392; Arab, crisis of, 293; condition, 410; balance of power, 224, 225, 238, 275, 299, 333, 335, 337, 342; centralization of, 99, 128, 437; configurations of power, 107; crisis, decline of US, 237, 239, 268; democracy and, 109; elites, 301, 379; expansion of, 139; Muslim, 110; decentralization of, 172, 408; hegemonic, 133; intelligentsia, 379; political, legitimacy of, 120–121; modes of, 131; oligarchic, 138; pathologies of, 107, 108; personalization of, 137; personalized system of, 134; precapitalist systems of, 120–121, 125; studies, 107; theorists, 113; traditional systems of, 123; *see also* Power, postcolonial systems of Power

Power, postcolonial systems of: ascriptive-palace, 129, 132, 133, 145; dynastic-oligarchic, 130, 133; elective-parliamentary, 129, 131, 132; Marxist-socialist, 130, 131, 144; neo-fascist, 130, 131, 136; pragmatic-authoritarian, 130, 133, 134, 145; radical nationalist, 109, 113, 130, 131, 134–138, 208

Power, state, 119, centralized and decentralized systems of, 121; and individual rights, 447; legitimate, 121; modes of, 109, 111; neofascist modes of, 113; pathologies of, 12, 107, 112

Power elites, 113, 140, 150; *see also* Ruling elites

Prasad, Rajendra, 407

Pratt, Mary Louise, 582n8

Pressler amendment, 254, 546

Production, capitalist relations of, 138

Proletariat, dictatorship of the, 121

Propaganda, "armed," 32

*Protest and Survive* (Thompson and Smith, eds.), 236

Provisional Revolutionary Government (PRG), 43

Provisional Revolutionary Government of the Algerian Revolution (Gouvernement provisoire de la République algérienne—GPRA), 89, 90, 97, 98

Public issues, transformation of private problems into, 125–126

Punjab, nationalist insurgency in, 404; unionist landlords in, 406

Al-Qaeda, x, 393

*Al-Qaeda* (Burke), x

Qadeer, Haji, 501

Qazi, Ashraf, 548, 549, 550, 551

Quaid-I-Azam, *see* Jinnah, Mohammad Ali

*Question of Palestine, The* (Said), 296, 350

Qui Nhon, anti-US demonstrations in, 43

Quran, 161, 170, 171, 172, 416, 478

Rabbani, Barnahudin, 393

Rabbani, Sayed Burhanuddin, 481

Rabin, Yitzhak, 328, 373, 383, 524

Racism, 72, 195, 196, 218, 351, 354

"Racism and the State: Coming Crisis of US-Japanese Relations" (Ahmad), 195

Radical-authoritarian regime/state, 112, 140, 142, 144, 149

Radical-authoritarianism, 109, 112

Radio Cairo, 96

Radio Kabul, 499

Rafel, Robin, 505, 506

Rafsanjani, Hashemi, 510

Rahman, Fazlur, 186

Rahman, Sheikh Abdul, 265, 266

Ram Janam Bhoomi campaign, 187

Ramadan, 289

Ramraj, 181

Rana, Mukhtar, 427

Rand Corporation study, 261

Rangers, 31

Rape camps, 179, 271

Rapid Deployment Force, 240, 281, 284, 461

al-Rashid, Harun, 168

Rashtriya Swayamsevak Sangh (RSS), 188, 543

*Reader's Digest*, 474

Reagan, Ronald, 241, 257, 258, 259, 265, 274, 361, 446, 461, 483, 485, 488, 490, 498, 516–517

Reagan administration, 393, 448, 484, 492

Reagan Doctrine, 486

Reagan Plan, 307, 313

Realpolitik, 200, 211, 238, 256, 332, 394

Recolonization, 302

"Reconstruction of Religious Thought in Islam" (Iqbal), 181

Red Sea, 325

Reeducation centers, 53

Reformism, reformists, 181, 182

"Regional influentials," 83, 240, 256, 284

Religion in politics, 183–187

Religio-political formations, 187, 188

Religio-political parties, 189, 190

Religious right, profile of, 187–190

Renaissance, 168

*Report on Torture* (Amnesty International), 144

Republican Guards, 287

Republican Party, 215, 341

"Resistance, pathology of," 113

Reston, James, 13, 46

Restorationism, 181

*Revolution and Betrayal in Afghanistan* (Anwar), 467

Revolutionaries: elite, 32; groups, non-Communist, 17; ideology, 56, 57, 201, 348; preparation, 26; process, 25; theory, 25, 34, 59, 263

*Revolution in the Revolution?* (Debray), 24, 25, 26, 28, 34, 35

Revolution, passive, 111

Revolutionary *foco*: Bolshevik model, 27; Cuban model, 27; guerrilla, 28, 33; isolation of, 30; in Marquetalia, Colombia, 27; military, 28, 29, 32, 33; mobile, 27; political, 33; self-defense zones, 27–28; and support of peasantry, 26; theory, 5, 25, 27, 30, 34, 573n4; *see also* Guerrilla war, warfare

Revolutionary Socialist Party (PSR), 95

Revolutionary warfare, 3, 10, 21, 46, 47, 53, 55, 57, 59, 86, 87, 88, 201, 214; American interpretation of, 14; American interest in, 13; conditions leading to, 17; and conventional warfare, 88; and conspiracy of silence, 16, 19; escalation, logic of, 6, 7, 20, 51; human factor in, 15; and intellectuals, 20, 22; moral isolation of government regimes, 4, 5, 9, 15, 17, 20, 22, 40, 52, 58; outadministering the enemy, xiii, 4, 5, 15, 16, 18, 29, 52, 78, 86, 87, 88, 307, 502 532; parallel hierarchies, counter-institutions, 4, 17, 47, 52, 532; political and organizational aspects of, 29; politics, political factors, primacy of, 4, 7, 14, 25, 26, 54, 78; process of, 29; and social change, 15, 17; techniques of, 45, 47; theorists and practitioners of, 5, 24; theory and practice of, 36, 300, 496; theory of, Washington's, 34; *see also* Guerrilla war, warfare

Rhodesian UDI (Unilateral Declaration of Independence), 308

Riaz Khan, Ahmad, 601n1

Richard the Lionhearted, 161

Richardson, Elliot, 344

Rifidim, Israeli air base in, 326

*Rise of Islam and the Bengal Frontier, 1204–1754, The* (Eaton), 564

Risorgimento, 111

Rockefeller, David, 211, 347

Rockefeller, Nelson, 146

Rodinson, Maxime, 162

Rogers, William, 238, 341, 344

Rogers Plan, 319, 341, 344, 345

Ronaldshay, Earl of, 455

Rosenthal, A.M., 248

Rosenthal, Abraham, 383

Rostow, W. W., 14, 34, 46, 50, 52

Roy, Oliver, 477

Roy, Raja Ram Mohan, 181, 406

Rubin, Trudy, 360

Ruling class, 137, 140, 168, 208, 215

Ruling elites, 10, 135, 136, 147, 153, 183; Arab, 331, 372; and modernization, 15, 17; Third World, 75, 109, 112–13; *see also* Power elites

Rumi, Mevlana Jalaluddin, 170

Rural sector, commercialization of, 123

Rusk, Dean, 14, 214

Russia, xiii, 251, 256, 273; *see also* Soviet Union

Rydbeck, Olof, 365

Sabra and Shatila massacres, 296, 360–368, 524; indirect responsibility, doctrine of, 362, 364, 365, 366; Israeli Commission of Inquiry, 360, 364; Kahan commission, 361, 364, 365, 366, 367, 368, 593n1; media reaction to, 360–361; Phalange militia, 362; Shatila refugee camp, 364

Sabri, Ali, 344

Sadat, Anwar, 163, 275, 295, 319, 321, 325, 327, 328, 331, 344, 345, 346, 347, 355, 371, 524, 525

Safavids, 160

Safire, William, 257

Safran, Nadav, 329

Safronchuk, Vasily, 467, 470

Said, Edward, 78, 162, 224, 225, 248, 294, 296, 300, 306, 350, 351, 352, 353, 354, 355, 369, 375, 377

Saigon regime, 42, 44, 55

Sakiet Sidi Youssef, bombing of, 21, 51

Sipah-i-Sahaba, 509, 512, 518, 519
Sisco, Joseph, 341, 343, 344
Sivanandan, A., 152
Slavery, 225, 309
Slavs, ethnic, 267
Smith, Dan, 236
Smith, Ian, 308
Smith, Wilfred Cantwell, 162
Social change, 15, 17, 66, 150, 215
Social engineering, technocratic, 118
Socialism, 34, 82, 99
Socialist regime, 140
Socialists, 136, 217
Social Scientists for Social Responsibility, 233
Society, societies: agrarian, transition to industrial, 108; precapitalist, 116–122; traditional, 108, 118, 123, 216; transitional, 116, 118; *see also* Civil society; Muslim societies
Solarz amendment, 254
Solarz, Stephen, 248, 280
Solidarity, communal, 119
Solinas, Franco, 91
Somalia, 135, 284
Somnath temple, 182
Somoza, 130, 158, 260
Sourani, Raja, 378
Soustelle, Jacques, 39
South Africa, 9, 76, 77, 79, 80, 304; apartheid, 309; divestment from, 79; nuclear capability of, 240, 540
South African Communist Party, 78
South America, 24, 27, 33, 208
South Asia, 187, 252–53, 273, 523, 526, 535, 537, 544; postcolonial, 182, 398; US interests in, 525
South Asian Association for Regional Cooperation (SAARC), 535, 541
Southeast Asia Treaty Organization, 462
Southeast Asia, 73, 165, 218, 332, 343
Southern Africa, 237, 299
Southwest Asia, 342, 446
Soviet Union, USSR, 3, 68, 144, 207, 213, 220, 228, 237, 238, 239, 253, 265, 270, 279, 332, 333, 337, 340, 499,

541; Afghanistan, war in, 461–478; breakup, collapse of, x, 193, 231, 245, 545; Constituent Assembly, dissolution of, xii; and Egypt, 344; as Evil Empire, 229, 258, 265, 267, 290, 483; India, friendship pact with, 430; and Iraq, 155, 247; Jewish emigration to Israel, 310, 311; and Middle East, 328, 333–334; Nixon's visit to, 196, 334; and wars of national liberation, 486; Western invasion of, 1912, xi, xii; *see also* Russia
Spain, 144, 168, 226, 341, 343; Muslim rule in, 161; expulsion of Arabs, 357
Spanish Civil War, 35
Special Warfare Units, US, 62, 63
State: apparatus, 137, 138, 139; colonial, 131, 138–139; formation, 138; metropolitan capitalist, 138, 139; national security, 113; neofascist, 142–153; police, 437, 438, 441; rentier, 112, 156–157; settler, 303, 309, 316; theocratic, 165; *see also* Neofascist states; Postcolonial states
Statism, 140, 234
Stern gang, 262
Stevenson, Adlai, xi
Stone, I. F., 47, 60, 281
*Stories My Country Told Me* (documentary), 390
Strategic Defense Initiative, 230
*Style para*, 40, 45
Sudan, 190, 266, 344; bombing of, x; Islamic government of, 183; missile strike on by, US, 199, 259, 264, 288
Suez Canal, 319, 321, 324, 325, 326, 327; cease-fire along, 341; nationalization of, 290
Suez, invasion of, 21, 51
Suffrage, universal, 132
Sufis, 185, 405, 478
Suharto, 147, 562
Suicide bombers, bombing, 10, 297
Sukarno, Ahmad, 130, 135, 175, 335, 443
*Sunday Times* (London), 361
Sunna, 172

Sunni, 416, 514, 515; terror against Christians and Ahmedis, 515
Syed, Anwar, 169
Symington, Stuart, 44
Syndicalists, 83
Syria, 135, 275, 277, 327, 328, 345, 348, 349, 371

Taalbi, Abdel Aziz, 181
Taggert, Chris, 507
Tagore, Rabindranath, 409, 410
Tajikistan, 508, 510, 511
Taleghani, Ayatollah Mahmud, 174, 176
Taliban, x, 181, 190, 395, 503, 504, 505, 518; Afghanistan, domination in, 512; coalition against, 508; ideology and style, 506; Jalalabad, capture of, 505, 508; Kabul, capture of, 395, 505, 506–507; leaders, 505–506; and *madaris*, 501; Mazar-I-Sharif, capture of, 509, 516 as misogynists, 506; sexual morality, 500–501; as Sunni fanatics, 507; Pakistan's support of, 510–518 United States and, 504, 506
Tanzania, 134, 135, 209
Taraki, Nur Muhammad, 463, 464, 465, 466, 467, 468, 469
Tariq, Azam, 509
Tashkent conference (1966), 430
Tass, 466
Taylor, General Maxwell, 4, 48
Technocratic evangelism, 8, 70
Technologic of extermination, 8
Tehran Radio, 467
Tehrik-i-Istiqlal, 442, 593–600n9, 594–601n12
Terror, terrorism, xiv, 7, 20, 22, 110, 114, 133, 191, 200–201, 257–266, 297, 355, 563; antiterrorist policies of US, 259; causes of, 259; counter, 58; criminal, 261; definition of, 258–259, 260; indiscriminate, 201; literature on, 259; and modern technology, 263; motives of, 260–261; organized, 143–145; Palestinian, 201, 259, 262, 355; pathological, 261; political, 261, 263, 443;

Rand Corporation study, 261; reign of, 64 religious, 261; revolutionary, 263; second-degree, 19; selective, 15, 18, 53, 58, 263; state, 260, 261, 262; systematization of, 142; "unofficial," 443; war on, 194
Terrorist organizations, 201
Terrorist regimes, 260
Thackeray, Bal, 181
Third World, 3, 10, 47, 66, 81, 82, 83, 84, 108, 109, 115, 116–118, 121, 122, 125, 132, 133, 195, 196, 197, 199, 208, 215, 234, 236, 237, 245, 280, 281, 298, 332; Americophilia in, 206; armaments, proliferation of, 157, 222; attributes of, 128; challenge of, 127; comparative research on, 128; crises of, 123, 127; and democracy, 109, 131, 255; democratic institutions in, 110; development in, disorganic, 301; development, endogenous alternative, 126–127; disarmament movement and, 234–236; dominance in, US, 113, 199; economic aid and arms supplies to, 245; effect of modern technology, 122; "export-platform" countries, 148, 210, 211; Latin Americanization of, 206; legitimacy, crisis, problem of, 125, 335–336; nationalism, US opposition to, 208; neofascist regimes, 142–143; perceptions, beliefs and expectations, 124–125; power, configurations of, 111; power, pathologies of, 107; radicalism, 109, 135; revolutionary challenge of, 122–126; ruling elites, 75, 109, 112–113; social change in, US response to, 215; societies, traditional, disappearance of, 123; societies, transitional, 178; states, 129, 130, 138; transition from rebellion to revolution, 216; US interventions, wars in, 74, 206, 207–209, 226, 239, 332, 336; US policy in, 65, 68, 74–75, 221, 334–337; weapons sales to, 235; *see also* Underdeveloped countries
Third Worldism, 236

211–212; national consensus, 215; national security establishment, 280; nationalism, response to, 67, 209; nonproliferation policy, US, 252–254; oil, control of Middle East, 199, 255, 277, 338, 349; Pakistan, military aid to, 284; Pakistan, mutual-security agreement, 491; policy makers, 237, 268; Power, crisis, decline of, 237, 239, 268; protofascist regimes, promotion of, 441; and ruling elites, Third World, 113; and Saudi Arabia, 343, 344; self-determination, support for right of, 205; South Asia, interests in, 525–526; Southern Africa, interest in, policy, 237, 340; Soviet relations, 230, 312, 332–334; Soviet Union, balance of power with, 333; Soviet Union as natural enemy of, 213, 332–333; Third World, policies toward, 65, 68, 74–75, 221, 334–337; Third World, response to social change in, 215; US-Israel strategic alliance, 342; and Vietnam, xiii, xiv, 22, 23, 27, 65–75

United States Congress, 36, 254, 268, 342, 485; and Afghanistan, 453, 478, 484, 486, 487, 489, 499; war with Iraq, 248, 274; and Pakistan, 253, 430, 446

United States Department of Defense, 299

United States Department of the Army, 64

United States House of Representatives, 288

United States Naval Intelligence, 210

United States Senate, 6; Foreign Relations Committee, 485; Judiciary Subcommittee on Refugees, 42

United States State Department, xii, 8, 37, 45, 210, 217, 229, 238, 341, 428, 462, 475, 482, 485, 507; International Narcotics Matters Bureau, 479

Universal Declaration of Human Rights, 200

University of Chicago, 163

University of Leeds, 46

UNOCAL, 507

Urbanization, 123; bomb-induced, 42

Urdu, 409, 415, 416

Uruguay, 28

"Usable troops," 62

USSR, *see* Soviet Union

Uthman, [ibn 'Affan], 166

Uzbekistan, 508, 510, 511

Vajpayee, Atal Behari, 181, 397, 544, 546, 548, 549, 550, 551

Vance, Cyrus, 251

Vancouver summit meeting, 250

Vanguard party, 33

Vatican, 287

Venezuela, 26, 27

Vietcong, 14, 18, 19, 20, 23, 44, 51, 56, 57, 59, 64, 214

Vietminh, 97, 494–495, 496, 499, 566; land reform under, 19; legitimacy of, 19, 499

Vietnam, North, 50, 206, 214; bombing of, 7, 22, 230; guerrilla teams in, US, 579n16

Vietnam, South, xiii, 8, 41, 49, 51, 56, 57; legitimacy of regime, 7, 22; refugees in, 42, 43

Vietnam war, xi, xiii, 7–9, 20, 29, 40–44, 48, 56, 61, 87, 194, 195, 215, 228, 229, 274, 336, 471; American military intervention, 65–75; American policy in, xv, 6, 8, 13, 14, 23; antiwar movement, 6, 8; Army of the Republic of Vietnam (ARVN), 40, 43; assassination of local officials in, 19; bombing of, 195, 196–197; Chieu Hoi (Open Arms) program, 44; civilian losses in, 74; Con Son, tiger cages of, 43; contested areas, 19; experts on, 7; as "forgotten war," 41, 336; generals, "musical-chair generals," 22, 68, 568–75n4; "gradual escalation," inefficacy of, 61; guerrilla warfare in, 13, 46; Haiphong harbor, mining of, 230, 334; Hamlet Evaluation System (HES), 8, 43, 577n12;